HALIFAX

Halifax

John A. Hargreaves

Halifax

Copyright © John A. Hargreaves, 1999, 2003, 2020

First published in hardback by
Edinburgh University Press and
Carnegie Publishing Ltd
Chatsworth Road,
Lancaster LA1 4SL
www.carnegiepublishing.com

British Library Cataloguing-in-Publication data
A catalogue record for this book is available from the British Library

ISBN 978-1-85936-237-2

Designed, typeset and originated by Carnegie Publishing
Printed and bound by Cambrian Printers

Commemoration of the Sunday School Centenary, Halifax Piece Hall, Whit Tuesday, 1880. Watercolour, 1890, by Henry Raphael Oddy (1851–1907). (Photograph: Calderdale Museums and Arts).

HALIFAX SUNDAY SCHOOL CENTENARY, SECOND COMMEMORATION, WHIT-TUESDAY, 1890

Dedication

To my wife Susan, our daughters Anne and Helen,
our sons Paul and Stephen, their spouses, Andy, Sarah and Felicity
and our grandchildren
Joshua, Adam, Naomi, Samuel, James, Thomas and Emily

Contents

List of Tables

Praise for *Halifax*

'A lively, clear and very well-illustrated account ... both academically sound and widely accessible ... the imaginative range of illustrations provides a strong visual sense of the character of the place at various points in time.'

David Hey in *Northern History*

'The author uses the voice of the people from all social circumstances to provide impressions of the town at every stage ... This carefully constructed book reflects his extensive knowledge and expertise.'

Susan Wrathmell in the *Yorkshire Archaeological Journal*

'This fine work of synthesis will be valued by many different species of historian, no less so because the standard of book production is exceptionally high.'

Richard Rodger in the *English Historical Review*

'Every local household that takes a serious interest in the town's rich past – so influential on our present – ought to own a copy of *Halifax*.'

William Marshall in the *Halifax Evening Courier*

'An exhaustively researched and superbly illustrated history of a town clearly dear to Hargreaves's heart ... for anyone who shares his love of Halifax, or is interested in the development of the West Riding, it is essential.'

Richard Hopwood in the *Yorkshire Post*

Preface and acknowledgements
to the first edition

'IN THE SAME PLACE where the wild boar made his repast on acorns, rich commerce smiles and industry and plenty make thousands happy!', reflected the anonymous author of a *History of the Town and Parish of Halifax*, published in 1789. How, when and why did such a transformation occur? Was Halifax's urban development entirely the product of the major economic and social changes which the town experienced from the late eighteenth century, as the anonymous author of the contemporary history appears to imply, or was it perhaps stimulated by an earlier phase of commercial expansion in the 300 years or so before the classic period of the Industrial Revolution? Indeed, what were the more distant origins of Halifax as a place of settlement and how did geography and environment shape its development as an urban centre? Moreover, how did the experience of industrial expansion and ultimately industrial decline affect the development of the town in the two centuries which followed the publication of this early anonymous history? Finally, how has the experience of history impacted upon the lives of those who live in Halifax and Calderdale today?

Although Halifax celebrated in 1998 the 150th anniversary of the granting of its municipal charter of incorporation, no full-length history has yet appeared attempting to explain the complex process by which 'a few straggling tenements built of wood, wattles and thatch' in the late medieval period developed into 'a town of a hundred trades' by the late Victorian period. Indeed, the last full-length history of Halifax for adult readers, John Crabtree's *Concise History of the Parish and Vicarage of Halifax*, appeared as long ago as 1836, a year before the accession to the throne of Queen Victoria in 1837 and twelve years before Halifax received its municipal charter in 1848. Moreover, Crabtree's history, like previous and subsequent histories, recognising that the fortunes of the town were inextricably linked with those of its hinterland, tended to focus more upon the history of the extensive parish of Halifax than on the history of the town itself. Even T. W. Hanson, the author of the most recent history of Halifax for children, *The Story of Old Halifax*, emphasised in 1920 that his narrative was 'not confined to the town of Halifax', but was 'also concerned with the tract of surrounding country' comprising the medieval parish of Halifax. Moreover, he concluded his story somewhat abruptly in the mid-Victorian period. His text therefore omits, for example, any reference to the origins and development of the institution which more than any other has been responsible for carrying the name of Halifax around the world and which remains today the largest private employer in the modern metropolitan district of Calderdale, namely the Halifax plc, formerly the Halifax Building Society.

This new history of Halifax, which takes account of research in the eighty years since Hanson wrote, attempts to distinguish the town from its periphery and to bring the account of the town's history up to the present, in the belief that history is essentially a continuing dialogue between present and past and that it is only possible to understand fully the present direction of our lives with a sense of historical perspective. The central aim of this new history of Halifax is, therefore, to enquire why Halifax exists today, in this place, with its distinctive built environment, with its prevailing economic, social, political and cultural charac-teristics, and with its current relationships with Calderdale, West Yorkshire, the United Kingdom and the world.

It might be considered presumptuous of a Lancastrian, a native of Burnley, some twenty miles to the west of Halifax, to attempt a history of a town in the heart of Pennine Yorkshire. However, the neighbouring towns and their modern metropolitan districts have much in common. Sharing a river with a common name and source, the Calder, and a prehistoric routeway, the Long Causeway, Burnley was a woollen town before it came to specialise in cotton weaving, while Halifax later diversified from woollen manufacture into worsted, cotton and silk production. Moreover, both towns have also had to discover new economic futures in the twentieth century as textiles have declined. Indeed, the extent of the post-industrial problems facing both towns was evident in their ranking in the bottom six of seventy-nine county boroughs according to rateable value per head of population in 1968. Coincidentally, Burnley was also considered for Business in the Community's pioneering partnership project in the 1980s before Halifax was finally selected.

My own association with Halifax arises from a family wartime connection during the period from 1940 to 1945. After the bombing of the Royal Engineers' barracks at Chatham by the Luftwaffe, my father's regiment moved to emergency bases in the West Riding, which included Ebenezer Sunday School, Halifax, where he was billeted before embarking for service in the Middle East. Later, at the end of the war, he returned to Shibden Hall, Halifax, prior to demobilisation in 1945. My mother became a regular visitor to Halifax during the war years and continuing friendships brought our family from Burnley to Halifax on a number of occasions in the 1950s. I also made an early educational visit to Shibden Hall with a party from Burnley Grammar School during this period. Following my marriage in 1972, I came to live in Halifax, where my wife was training as a midwife at Halifax General Hospital and where all four of our children were subsequently born. It is appropriate therefore that this book should be dedicated to members of my family who have helped to connect me with this place where I have now lived happily for nearly three decades.

My interest in the history of Halifax has also been fostered by membership of the Halifax Antiquarian Society, of which I have been secretary since 1986 and editor of its *Transactions* since 1992. It was always the ambition of the society's founding fathers in 1900 to produce a history of Halifax and I am delighted to have been able to contribute to the realisation of that ambition as the society approaches the celebration of the centenary of its foundation in the year 2000. I have found the numerous volumes of the society's *Transactions*, published annually since 1900, invaluable in researching this book and am indebted to the many authors, living and dead, for their exploration of so many aspects of local history. My understanding of the history of Halifax has also been developed through numerous discussions with individual members of the society and other local residents who have shared with me their knowledge of local history. I particularly wish to thank Donald Haigh and Alan Betteridge for their helpful comments on preliminary drafts of particular chapters of the book; A. J. Petford and P. M. Buckley for their careful drawing of the maps; Doreen Baxter, Emma Beaumont and Eureka, Ian Beesley, Stephen Gee, David Gilchrist and the Halifax plc, Sir Ernest Hall, David Hanson and the *Halifax Courier*, Nigel Herring and Calderdale Leisure Services, Andrew Lomax, Pat Sewell and the West Yorkshire Archive Service, Lord Somerleyton, Irene Spencer and Geoffrey Washington for assistance in supplying a variety of interesting illustrations and Colin Spencer for passing on to me his local history files. I am also grateful to a number of individuals from within the local community who gave me extended interviews which provided me with a range of invaluable twentieth-century perspectives on key themes. They included Sir James Birrell, Michael Ellison, Canon Robert Gibson, Sir Ernest Hall, Richard de Z. Hall, Chris Johnstone, Alan Machin, Alice Mahon MP, Gerard Norrie, Michael Scott and Wilfred Sharp.

I am also indebted to a number of other individuals for their advice and encouragement. My former tutors at the University of Southampton, Professor Colin Platt and Professor Paul Harvey commented perceptively upon Chapters two and three. Dr Steve Hindle of the University of Warwick, who provided me with valuable insights into current research on the sixteenth and seventeenth centuries at a revision course for teachers in Cambridge, also commented constructively on Chapter three. Professor Keith Laybourn of the University of Huddersfield, who with the late Dr David Wright supervised my Ph.D. thesis on 'Religion and society in the parish of Halifax, *c.* 1740–1914', shared with me his extensive knowledge of the inter-war years. My colleague, Mrs S. Riaz, kindly answered a number of enquiries about multi-cultural issues. My brother, Professor Ian Hargreaves, former editor of *The Independent* and *The New Statesman* made many stimulating observations particularly on twentieth-century themes. Dr Stephen Constantine, the series editor, provided challenging and helpful advice at every stage of this volume's evolution and Nicola Carr of Edinburgh University Press patiently guided the book towards publication. Finally, I wish to record my gratitude to my wife, Susan and family, Anne, Helen, Paul and Stephen for their constant support throughout the long period during which I have been engaged in researching and writing this book.

John A. Hargreaves, 1999

Preface and acknowledgements
to the second edition

THE SPEED WITH WHICH EVENTS UNFOLD in the rapidly changing world in which we live inevitably has implications for the currency of a history seeking to explore the distinctive characteristics of one particular place today and to explain how that place has been shaped by the impact of global, national, regional and local influences. Since the first edition of this book was published in 1999 we have moved from the twentieth century into the twenty-first century. A new census has provided us with up-to-date statistics not only about demographic, economic and social change but also, for the first time since 1852, about patterns of religious adherence. Some local firms such as Crosrol and Firth Carpets, which appeared to have a fairly secure future in Calderdale in 1999, have since closed. Other local businesses have experienced growth, notably the former Halifax plc, but through an entirely unexpected merger with the Bank of Scotland. Changing fortunes in the sporting arena have seen the relegation of Halifax Town AFC to the Nationwide Conference for a second time and the relegation of the Halifax Rugby League Club, no longer rejoicing in the name of Halifax Blue Sox, to the National One League for the first time. A general election in 2001 yielded few major surprises in the sphere of electoral politics, but a council by-election in 2003, which saw the election for the Mixenden ward of the first British National Party candidate east of the Pennines and further BNP successes in the subsequent council elections in May, changed dramatically the complexion of local politics. Finally, the local townscape itself has continued to evolve with, for example, the demolition of the former Smith Wire Works and the redevelopment of Charlestown Road and its hinterland as a major retail centre, breathing new life into a hitherto neglected sector of the town.

Moreover, the unremitting pace of historical research into every aspect of human activity in the past also has implications for the currency of a book whose scope extends effectively from prehistoric times to the present day. Even within the space of five years many new historical studies have appeared which have relevance to the history of Halifax including a host of recent articles in the *Transactions of the Halifax Antiquarian Society*. I was, therefore, immensely grateful when Alistair Hodge of Carnegie Publishing Ltd offered generous additional space for a full textual revision and the inclusion of many new illustrations to enhance the text of *Halifax*, whose first edition sold quickly and has been out of print for some time.

Consequently, every chapter of the book has been revised and expanded to take account of continuing research and the final chapter has been updated to take account of developments in the history of Halifax and Calderdale from 1999 to 2003. I am extremely grateful to all who have commented on the book in reviews and correspondence and facilitated the inclusion of additional illustrations for this new edition. They include Calderdale MBC, Anna Goddard, the *Halifax Courier*, Trevor Hughes, Alice Mahon MP, the Manchester Central Library, the National Portrait Gallery, Simon Ryder, Pat Sewell and the West Yorkshire Archive Service, Calderdale, Glyn Sutcliffe and Yorkshire Television. My debt to my wife, Susan and growing family, now augmented by our first grandson, Joshua, remains as ever undiminished. They have both supported my continuing research and writing and strengthened my conviction that each generation has a responsibility to share with future generations its understanding of the changes which have shaped and continue to influence the world in which we live.

John A. Hargreaves, October 2003

Preface and acknowledgements
to the third edition

IN THE SIXTEEN YEARS which have elapsed since 2003 the people of Halifax
and Calderdale have experienced major changes affecting many aspects of their
lives. Above all, the impact of the financial crisis of 2007–08 put the global spotlight
on Halifax on account of the failure of the amalgamated Halifax Bank of Scotland.
Although administered from lofty historic offices of the former Bank of Scotland
situated on The Mound in Edinburgh, the bank had nonetheless retained the trading
brand identities of its historic forebears including the former Halifax Building Society
and the administration of the Lloyds Banking Group's largest mortgage repository
remained in Trinity Road, Halifax. Politically, throughout the last sixteen years and
indeed without a break in continuity for over half a century since 1964 the Halifax
parliamentary constituency has continued to return female Labour MPs, whilst
council elections have returned a broader spectrum of party representatives, with
often no one party achieving overall control. The European referendum, however,
resulted in a clear majority of the Calderdale electorate for leaving the European
Union in 2016. Other changes following in the wake of the credit crunch included the
re-designation of Halifax's medieval parish church as a new urban minster in 2009,
a gesture of support from Stephen Platten, the last diocesan Bishop of Wakefield
for Halifax's recovery. However, the twin pillars of Halifax's nineteenth-century
phenomenal growth, textiles and engineering, both experienced dramatic decline in
the following two centuries, and their ultimate failure to recover was only partially
counterbalanced by the growth of services and the development of tourism.

Not only did Halifax and its neighbouring Calderdale communities experience
economic decline, they also had to adjust to profound religious, social and cultural
fragmentation. Many churches and chapels which had proliferated during the
Victorian and Edwardian eras and beyond experienced continuing numerical decline
after 1914, resulting in the closure of numerous once-thriving places of worship.
By contrast, new growth was also evident in the emergence of fresh expressions of
Christian mission through credit unions for those in debt; food banks for the hungry
at New Ebenezer; sanctuary for refugees at the St Augustine's Christian Community
Centre; Street Angels for casualties of the town's night time culture; together with
a continuing commitment to ecumenical understanding and inter-faith dialogue.
Enlargement also occurred in the reconstruction and expansion in the capacity of
Halifax's Central Jamia Mosque Madni from 2002, providing accommodation for

over 2,000 worshippers, and in the development of an increasingly multi-faith society throughout Calderdale. Another social hub, the public house, also ubiquitous in nineteenth-century Halifax, struggled to compete with changing attitudes to leisure, and the breweries which serviced them also disappeared. Even the traditional pie and peas and fish and chip shops became scarcer as a greater variety of fast-food options became available, including continental and global specialities, notably pizza and curry dishes, as society diversified and meals for many were frequently pre-packed rather than home-cooked. Meanwhile, growing numbers of people of all ages with dietary and fitness concerns became more conscious of the need to watch their waist-lines and weighing scales, hence the proliferation of joggers, cyclists and gym-goers.

The cultural scene exhibited both continuity and change. Whilst there was in many respects cultural efflorescence with the opening of the Victoria Hall in 1901, which gave Halifax the concert hall provision already enjoyed by some of its neighbours, notably Leeds and Huddersfield, within their town halls, it was in Halifax where the strong tradition of amateur choral singing first took root. The survival of the Halifax Choral Society, celebrating its bicentenary in 2018, achieved the coveted distinction of becoming the longest surviving United Kingdom amateur choral society with an unbroken continuity of performance, even during wartime. With the advent of television, theatres like the Palace and the Grand closed their doors, with cinemas following suit. Halifax was bereft of a single cinema until the opening of Vue on the Broad Street Plaza, across the road from the former Odeon, now a bingo hall. Dean Clough, developed by the vision of Sir Ernest Hall and his son Jeremy, has art galleries, a local radio studio, and a novel combination of businesses and the arts. These include the distinctive vernacular touring company Northern Broadsides at the Viaduct Theatre, directed with panache by Barrie Rutter until his departure in 2017, the formation of the Halifax Thespians in the 1920s, who acquired their own Playhouse, the former Hanover Street Methodist New Connexion Chapel, in 1949, and the Actors' Workshop Youth Theatre. Moreover, brass bands continued to exert a lively appeal, with the leading local exemplars, the Black Dyke Band, Queensbury, historically part of the ancient parish of Halifax, and the eponymous Brighouse and Rastrick Band. In addition there continued to be home-produced light opera, notably Gilbert and Sullivan, and a succession of new, talented musical and literary artists. Most prominent among these were the youthful Ed Sheeran, educated at Heathfield preparatory school, Rishworth, who dominated the pop music scene in the early twenty-first century, and the playwright Sally Wainwright, educated in Sowerby Bridge. Her television drama serials set in Calderdale and neighbouring Haworth were widely acclaimed for their compelling characterisation and enthralling story lines. These included the comedy drama *Last Tango in Halifax*, the police series *Happy Valley* and the historically inspired *Gentleman Jack*. The latter, produced by BBC/HBO based on Anne Lister's diaries and starring Suranne Jones, was aired in America in 2018, and in the UK in 2019. The success of the production resulted in a marked increase in Halifax tourism in general and visits to Shibden Hall in particular.

Sport, increasingly inclusive in all its variety of expressions, has also continued to provide a major focus of many people's sense of identity and leisure pursuits, rejoicing in the emergence of Halifax-born Hannah Cockcroft as an inspirational wheelchair racer, holding paralympic and world records for the 100 metres, 200 metres and 400 metres events in her classification. Hannah was the people's celebrity choice for tolling the bell announcing the re-opening of the refurbished Piece Hall on 1 August 2017, a venue destined to offer enhanced opportunities for economic and social community coherence. Thousands also lined the route to witness the passing of the inaugural Tour de France through Calderdale on 6 July 2014 and welcomed the decision to start the final day of the expanded race from Halifax Piece Hall in 2018. The successful development of the shared use of the Shay Stadium for both Association Football and Rugby League, together with the improved athletics facilities at Spring Hall, also stimulated both spectator and participatory sport in Halifax. There was also a greater evidence of inclusiveness in both amateur cricket and football throughout Calderdale and a growing participation across the age spectrum in regular athletic activities, as seen in the proliferation of gyms in Calderdale, some open round the clock. Moreover, the open countryside of Calderdale offers scenic challenges to people cycling, fell running, hiking and jogging along canal towpaths and on moorland paths in upland Calderdale along the Calderdale Way or exploring Calderdale's steep-sided valleys and cascading streams which have recurrently during the last sixteen years, as in the past, resulted in severe flooding in the valley bottoms.

Halifax's inner urban townscape has also developed new distinctive features with the completion of the Broad Street Plaza. The refurbishment of the Piece Hall, now widely recognised as Yorkshire's most significant secular building, has transformed the sole surviving cloth hall in Yorkshire into a major visitor attraction and equipped Halifax with a multi-purpose town square. The construction of a new central library and archives repository upon the site of the ruined Victorian Square Congregational Church, incorporating its iconic soaring crocheted spire and the extension and renovation of its predecessor, the red-bricked Georgian Square Chapel Centre for the Arts; the imaginative conversion of a former potato warehouse into the Orange Box as a resource for young people and the re-opening of the Calderdale Industrial Museum by a team of volunteers have further strengthened Halifax's cultural offer for both residents and visitors. Indeed, the opening of the transformed Piece Hall on 1 August 2017, Yorkshire Day, saw no fewer than 20,000 visitors to the new town square; national and regional media interest throughout the day and related social media enthusiasm from Halifax ex-patriates throughout the world. Dean Clough, on the northern perimeter of the town, continued to demonstrate its growing success as an internationally renowned centre for business and the arts, located on a landmark site that was once the world's largest carpet factory, with the last major mill buildings recently refurbished in what remains the most successful creative and commercially productive ravine anywhere in the world, whilst the popular Eureka children's learning and play centre continues to educate younger generations.

Local government has relocated to splendidly refurbished Victorian offices adjacent to Charles Barry's magnificent Town Hall, enabling redevelopment of the former Northgate civic centre, originally re-designated for retail, but now confirmed as a combined site of commercial and educational development as a tertiary college, designed to stem the exodus of sixth form students to colleges outside Calderdale. Plans were also implemented to provide new facilities for Ravenscliffe High School at Spring Hall for pupils aged 11 to 19 with severe and profound learning difficulties, closer to the redeveloped athletic facilities.

Priorities have also focused upon assisting Calder Valley communities experiencing serious disruption from torrential flooding especially in 2012 and in the Boxing Day Floods of 2015 which swept away historic bridges at Elland and Copley, leaving a bill for damage running into millions of pounds and opening a debate about the most effective strategies for future flood prevention and the consequences of global warming. Moreover, this debate was intensified when Storm Ciara brought strong winds, prolonged heavy rain and renewed flooding to the Calder Valley in February 2020. Other major challenges faced by Calderdale Council included health, housing and social care. Controversially, the Calderdale and Huddersfield NHS Foundation Trust, burdened with private finance initiative debts, resolved to retain accident and emergency facilities at the more recently constructed Calderdale Royal Hospital, though the move was vociferously opposed by Huddersfield residents who successfully obtained a review of the decision. Calderdale Council, for its part, sanctioned long postponed improved road access from Huddersfield, transforming the Elland by-pass and the ascent of Salterhebble Hill. Consideration was also given to re-opening Elland Station, which resulted in improved access to Halifax Railway Station and connectivity with bus transport networks, though electrification of the railway line to Manchester and Leeds remained elusive.

As in previous revised editions, this third revision has encompassed the whole of the volume from prehistory to the present, taking account of the unrelenting process of archaeological and historical research, which through the Halifax Antiquarian Society has been more thoroughly explored voluntarily than in many other places. All of which has enabled a comprehensive review of many millennia to be attempted to arouse interest in the rich panorama of Calderdale's fascinating history ranging from prehistoric occupation and passage through a review of the impact of successive invaders and settlers from the Romans via Saxons and Vikings to the Normans. Medieval and early modern Halifax are then re-assessed, together with the impact of industrialisation and the rapid urban development which it stimulated in the Victorian and Edwardian eras. The growth of interest in the continuing year-by-year commemoration of the centenary of the First World War (1914–18) was poignantly reflected in the creation of an award-winning new temporary gallery at Bankfield Museum in 2014, and a major permanent monument to the Duke of Wellington's Regiment's historic association with the town, which was unveiled by the 9th Duke of Wellington, a descendant of the 'Iron Duke', on 17 May 2019. Moreover, the experience of total war during the Second World War (1939–45) and of the holocaust during which the Kagan family established business interests in Calderdale continues to reveal how profoundly recent global history has shaped the lives of our contemporaries. Another decennial census in 2011 revealed that whilst Calderdale's population density remained the lowest of any local authority in West Yorkshire, nonetheless it continued as one of the largest in terms of area, with over four-fifths of Calderdale described as rural by the national census, whilst urban centres, particularly the west central district of Halifax, with a concentration of the descendants of British Pakistanis from Kashmir contributed to Calderdale's growing ethnic diversity.

This new fully revised edition would not have been possible without the encouragement and help of many people. I am grateful especially to members of the Halifax Civic Trust, which I have been privileged to chair for over a decade, who have supported this project because by providing a fully updated analytical narrative of Halifax's multi-faceted history, incorporating fresh research, it seeks to promote the growing interest in Halifax's unique and fascinating past. It thereby contributes to the central aims of the Halifax Civic Trust to celebrate, conserve and enhance the outstanding built and natural environment of Halifax and Calderdale. My own understanding of Halifax's history has been shaped by membership of the Halifax Antiquarian Society and by contributors to its annual *Transactions*, which I have now edited for over a quarter of a century, and by those who I have taught in secondary, higher and adult education in Calderdale and elsewhere who have stimulated my interest in local history and encouraged me to share my interest with others. In 2019 these included a party of thirteen students from Virginia, USA, led by my former student Professor David Hicks. They marvelled at Halifax Town Hall, Halifax Minster, Calderdale Industrial Museum and sampled pie and mushy peas in Halifax Borough Market. I also valued leading a guided tour of Halifax by a delegation from the city of Aachen visiting Halifax for Remembrance Sunday 2018 to share in the commemoration of the centenary of the end of the First World War. I am grateful to John Keneally, the former Editor of the *Halifax Courier* and David Hanson for help in locating and obtaining permission to reproduce images from this vital community resource, which provides week by week a record of Calderdale's unfolding history, and to Stephen Gee for supplying local photographic images from his vast personal collection.

I have valued the expert advice of Frank Jolley on prehistoric archaeology, Professor Paul D. A. Harvey on the medieval and early modern periods and Glyn Scott Sutcliffe of the Society of Indexers for compiling the index for this edition. I am also grateful to the University of Huddersfield, where I completed my further degrees which developed my understanding of Halifax history. Professor Keith Laybourn, in particular, has stimulated my research, and has been a constant source of encouragement in my role as a Visiting Research Fellow in History. I remain similarly grateful to Professor Rosemary Mitchell of the Leeds Centre for Victorian Studies at Leeds Trinity University for inviting me to become an associate of the outstanding international centre, developing my understanding of aspects of Victorian Halifax. A number of other individuals have shared their expertise with me in specific ways, broadening my understanding of particular aspects of Halifax's recent history including our neighbour, Mohammed Yousaf, who arranged for me to visit the Madni mosque on several occasions; guided me to its temporary precursors and introduced me to Muslims engaged in business around Queen's

Road and King Cross. I also remain grateful to staff, past and present, at the West Yorkshire Archives, Calderdale, Calderdale Libraries and Calderdale Museums Service for their invaluable help in facilitating my continuing research.

Finally, I remain grateful to my brother Professor Ian Hargreaves CBE, successively deputy editor of the *Financial Times*, editor of the *Independent*, the *New Statesman*, director of news and current affairs at the BBC and Professor of Journalism and Digital Economy at the University of Cardiff for his helpful encouragement and advice. I am also indebted to my wife, Susan, for her invaluable support, together with our daughters and sons, Anne, Helen, Paul and Stephen, all born in Halifax, their spouses Andy, Sarah, Felicity and our grandchildren, Joshua, Adam, Naomi, Samuel, James, Thomas and Emily, all regular visitors to Halifax, which has had such a formative influence on each of their lives. Finally, the fully revised third edition of this history would not have been possible without generous financial support from the Calderdale Community Foundation, through its officers, particularly Steve Duncan and Rob Billson; Calderdale Council through its Arts and Heritage manager, Claire Slattery, and her colleagues in Libraries and Museums, who, with the West Yorkshire Archive Service also facilitated my research and continuing access to relevant illustrations and the Halifax Civic Trust, and especially its indefatigable honorary secretary, June Paxton White. This has enabled Carnegie Publishing, under the expert leadership of Anna Goddard and Alistair Hodge, ably assisted by Rachel Clarke, Penny Hayashi and Lucy Frontani, to produce a fully revised and expanded illustrated text at a proportionately more affordable price for new generations of residents and visitors to explore the remarkable history of this extraordinary town, which has shaped its identity in so many discernible ways.

John A. Hargreaves, January 2020

1

Introduction:
geography and environment

'ALL HALIFAX HISTORY DEPENDS ON HALIFAX GEOGRAPHY', the novelist Phyllis Bentley (1894–1977) observed astutely in her introduction to a volume commemorating the centenary of Halifax's incorporation as a municipal borough in 1948.[1] Similarly, local geographer, John Ogden, introducing the newly-designated long-distance footpath, the Calderdale Way, concluded in 1978 that Halifax had 'by a complex interaction of geography and history' developed from a small medieval community 'on the banks of a minor Calder tributary, the Hebble Brook' into 'the major settlement' within the modern metropolitan borough of Calderdale.[2] A study of the urban development of Halifax reaffirms the aptness of these observations, for an awareness of the geographical constraints and environmental opportunities presented by the Calderdale landscape is a prerequisite to an understanding of the complex economic, social and political history of the town and its hinterland.

The modern metropolitan district of Calderdale, of which Halifax, situated towards its eastern perimeter on the mid-valley terrace of the Hebble Brook, is the administrative and urban centre, is located predominantly in the millstone grit area of the extreme south west of the county of West Yorkshire. It forms part of the rolling central Pennine plateau, which dips gently towards the east as it enters the lower coal measures. Geologically, the Pennine plateau in the west consists of alternate strata of coarse sandstones or gritstones and relatively narrow bands of shale or mudstone, generally covered by a raw peat soil. The lower coal measures in the east are made up of alternate strata of finer sandstone and shale. The plateau is drained by the rivers Calder and Ryburn and their tributary moorland becks, tumbling down narrow, steep-sided valleys. Descending eastwards, through ruggedly beautiful countryside, from its source at an altitude of 764 feet on the crest of the Pennines high above Todmorden, the Yorkshire Calder intersects the dale to which it gives its name, before continuing its 44-mile course eastwards to its confluence with the Aire at Castleford.

The impervious nature of the bedrock, the poor quality of the topsoil, the rough inhospitable terrain, and the cold and wet climate may have deterred invaders and settlers in the period up to 1500, when its geographical remoteness ensured that Halifax remained a relatively insignificant Pennine backwater. By creating conditions

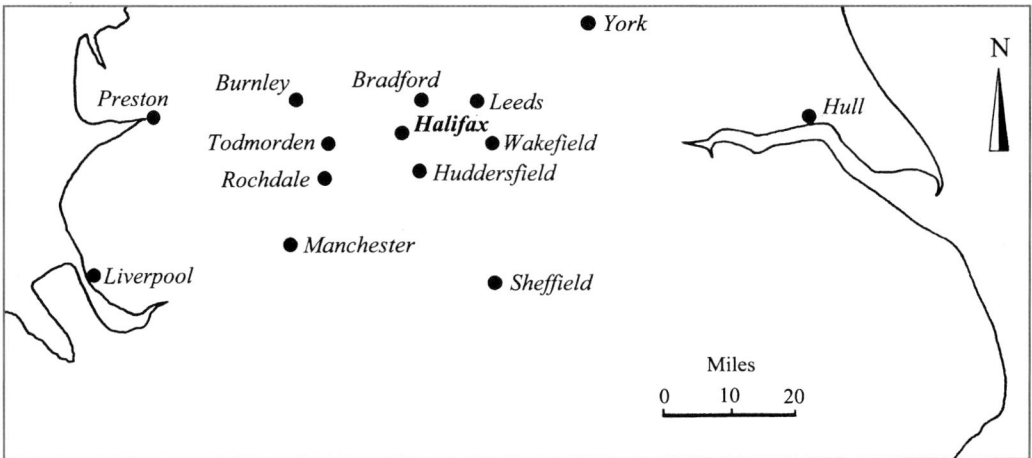

Halifax: location.

which militated against extensive arable farming, however, these geographical and environmental features also stimulated the development of the textile industry as a supplementary economic activity to subsistence agriculture in Calderdale towards the end of the medieval period. This transformation was assisted by another geographical advantage, a proliferation of swift-flowing moorland streams, which provided abundant supplies of soft water for the dyeing and finishing of woollen cloth, from streams which, Defoe later observed, 'were so parted and guided by gutters and pipes, and by turning and dividing the streams, that none of those houses were without a river … running into and through their work-houses'. Corn mills were easily adapted or converted for water-powered fulling, the process by which woollen cloth was pounded, scoured and textured by heavy wooden stocks. A distinctive dual economy of farming and textiles thereby emerged in the upland settlements of this remote Pennine valley. This stimulated the development of Halifax as the dominant commercial and urban centre for its periphery in the later medieval period and provided the basis for the town's remarkable rise to regional prominence in the early modern period as a manufacturing and marketing centre of woollen cloth, when Tudor contemporaries marvelled that so much wealth could be generated in such a bleak countryside.[3]

opposite: Halifax and the Hebble Valley viewed from the north. This late twentieth-century aerial photograph reveals the concentration of industrial development along the valley floor of the Hebble Brook. The former Crossley carpet manufacturing mill complex at Dean Clough occupies a vast site on the northern edge of the town centre extending for over half a mile along the line of the modern A629 Halifax–Keighley Road. The shield of hills skirting the eastern edge of the town centre which determined the direction of Halifax's urban expansion is clearly visible. The thickly wooded slopes now form a spectacular backdrop to the town centre, when viewed from ground level. The blackened structure of Halifax Parish Church stands in the distance, beyond the modern flyover which totally obscures the Victorian North Bridge over the Hebble Brook. (Photograph: *Halifax Courier*)

However, geographical factors also subsequently hindered the development of both internal and external transport and communications systems, from turnpike and waterway to railway, tramway and motorway. An impenetrable shield of hills encompassing Halifax from north-east to south-east presented a formidable barrier for eighteenth- and nineteenth-century turnpike, waterway and railway engineers. This allowed neighbouring Bradford, which established earlier connections to the expanding canal and railway network, to achieve pre-eminence as a regional textile marketing centre after 1800.[4] Moreover, Halifax derived relatively limited supplies of coal from its location on the western edge of the Yorkshire coalfield until the development of a waterway link between the town and the Calder and Hebble Navigation in 1828 enabled cheap supplies to be conveniently transported into the town from further afield. This encouraged the dependence of Halifax and its hinterland on water power and delayed the adoption by local entrepreneurs of coal-fired, steam-powered machinery. Halifax was therefore slower to develop as a centre of large-scale manufacturing industry than some other West Yorkshire towns, notably Bradford and Leeds. However, in consequence, Halifax developed a more diversified economic base than many similar sized towns, which enabled it to absorb some of the impact of economic recession in the late nineteenth and twentieth centuries. Meanwhile, the steep gradients and rugged physical terrain of an urban location which J. B. Priestley later described as the hilliest for any town of its size in England, ensured that Halifax remained a predominantly pedestrian town until the development of electric tramways and motorised transport after 1898.[5]

There were other disadvantages inherent in the town's location. The range of hills encompassing the north-eastern and south-eastern perimeter of Halifax imposed constraints on its economic and spatial development as an urban centre. This necessitated a predominantly westward direction of urban expansion in the eighteenth and nineteenth centuries and ultimately set limits on the town's urban growth in the early twentieth century, when all the potential development land

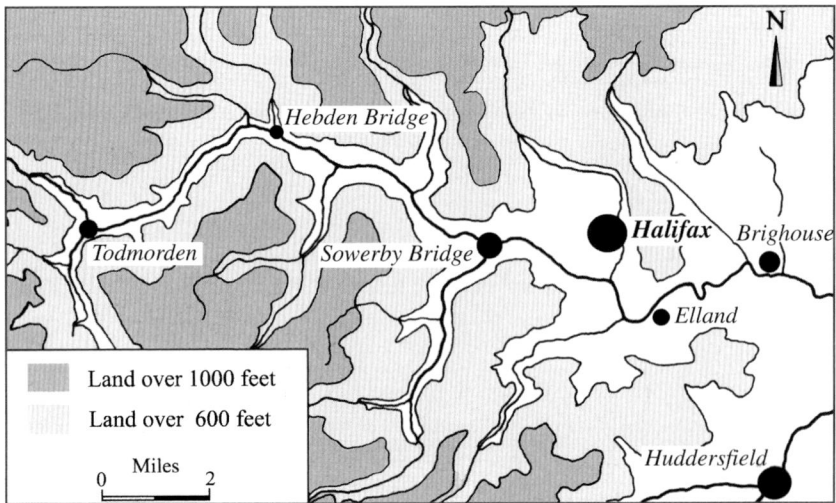

Halifax: relief.

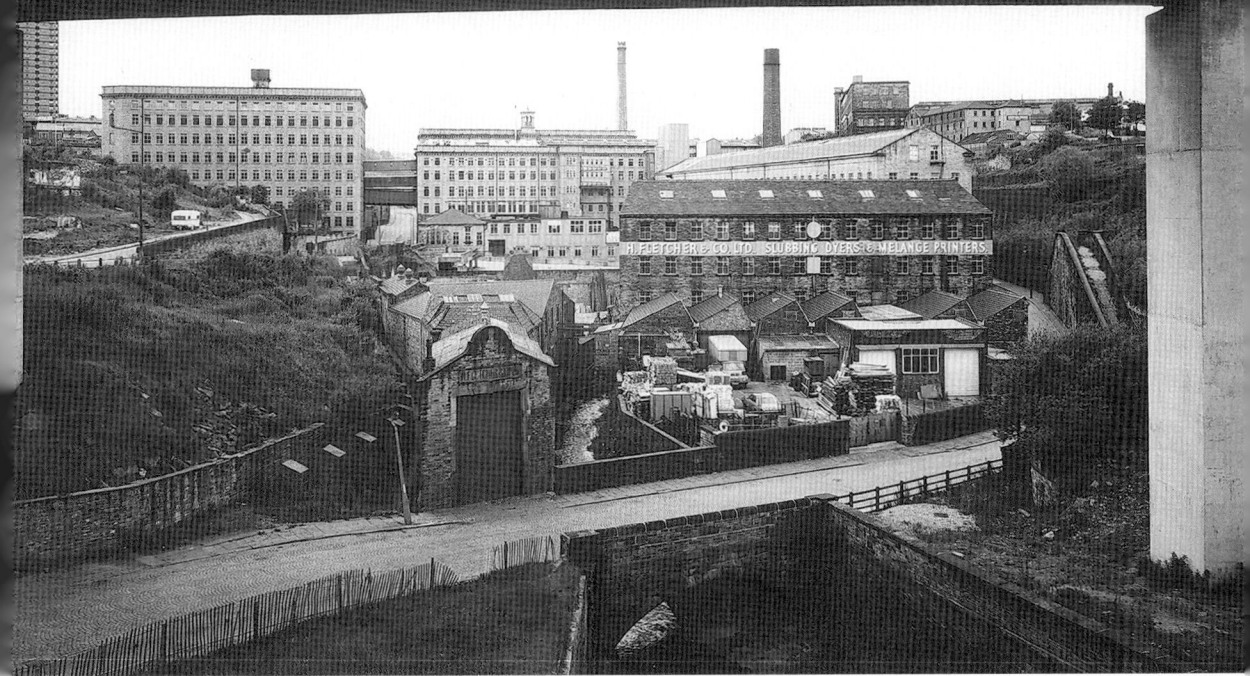

The Hebble Valley and Dean Clough viewed from the south. The Hebble Brook, which provided water power for the early mills situated along its course, is clearly visible in the foreground as it emerges from beneath the massive Dean Clough industrial complex. The mill in the foreground of this 1985 photograph still bears the evocative sign of H. Fletcher and Co. Ltd Slubbing Dyers and Melange Printers. Halifax began to develop from the late medieval period as a centre for the dyeing, finishing and marketing of woollen cloth. The Akroyds were the first to employ steam-powered machinery at their worsted mills on the Hebble from the 1820s. (Photograph: Ian Beesley)

within the orbit of the town centre had been acquired for industrial or residential purposes. Later industrial estates and business parks tended, therefore, to be located around the periphery of the town and at nearby Brighouse and Elland.[6] This changed from the 1980s, however, when the modern telecommunications revolution allowed greater flexibility of location for a burgeoning service sector, including the re-occupation of some previously abandoned multi-storeyed factories and warehouses close to the centre of the town. There were nevertheless some advantages of location which enhanced the physical appearance of the town. Plentiful supplies of a rich, honey-coloured, locally quarried sandstone enabled the development of a distinctive built environment in Halifax and its hinterland, although industrial pollution ultimately diminished its appeal until the implementation of clean air legislation and stone cleaning programmes in the late twentieth century. However, the dense fogs and steep descents into the town by road challenged the Halifax inventor, Percy Shaw, to pioneer the Catseye reflecting roadstud, which improved road safety not only locally but also globally, after securing such high-profile contracts as the Sydney Harbour Bridge.[7]

The picturesque, rugged natural beauty of the thickly wooded Calder Valley, its tributary valleys and its scenic rolling uplands encouraged commuters to both

Leeds and Manchester to settle in Calderdale, especially following the construction of the M62. The landscape, unchanged in many respects since time immemorial, is immortalised in the poetry of Ted Hughes (1930–98) who lived in Mytholmroyd as a child and with his brother Gerald developed a lifelong fascination with wildlife and the natural world. This surfaced in poems like 'Crow Hill' and 'Hawk Roosting', inspired by the moors and woodland around Mytholmroyd. He returned later to Heptonstall, where he founded a centre for creative writing and where his first wife, the American poet and writer, Sylvia Plath (1932–63), was buried after suffering severe depression and tragically taking her own life in London following their separation in 1962. Calderdale also provided appropriately dramatic film locations, not least for the popular twenty-first century serialised television romantic comedy, *Last Tango in Halifax* and the police drama, *Happy Valley*, penned by Huddersfield-born author Sally Wainwright, with its sardonic police moniker for a title, reflecting darker storylines such as the human cost of drug trafficking in the Calder Valley. The second of its two series, screened between 2014 and 2018, attracted an average of nearly ten million viewers. Starring Sarah Lancashire, who won a Bafta for her convincing lead role performance as police sergeant Catherine Cawood, and the realistic characterisation and compulsive dramatic themes, stimulated an already growing tourist interest in the stunning Calderdale landscape. Indeed, Wainwright, who was pronounced by Andrew Anthony, writing in *The Guardian*, as 'the titan of genuine reality television', earned the freedom of the Borough of Calderdale in 2019.[8]

Moreover, Halifax historically has produced a galaxy of extrovert non-fictional entertainers in real life. They ranged from Wilfred Pickles (1904–78), the first national BBC newsreader not only to speak with an uninhibited northern accent, but also to sign off his final bulletin with an impromptu flourish in the vernacular, wishing his northern listeners 'good neet'. Indeed, his ready repartee with ordinary people pioneered popular radio broadcasting, most notably in 'Have a Go', which ran for twenty-one years from 1946 to 1967, attracting its peak audience of 26 million listeners. In the late 1970s and early 1980s, the showmanship of Shirley Crabtree, the professional wrestler 'Big Daddy' (1930–97), became compulsive viewing for many, including prime minister Margaret Thatcher, on ITV's 'World of Sport'. Meanwhile John Noakes (1934–2017) established his immense reputation with audiences of children's television in the 1960s and 1970s, with his daring exploits on 'Blue Peter'. He finally arranged for his cremated remains to be rocketed skyward in November 2017 from his former school playing field at Rishworth as an ultimate explosive gesture in the valley which had first stimulated his irrepressible sense of adventure.[9]

A more serious dimension to Calderdale living was the recurring vulnerability to devastating flooding, deriving from the increasing concentration of communication routes, industrial, businesses and residential communities along the valley bottoms particularly during the nineteenth century. Indeed, even during the eighteenth century the canal engineer John Smeaton had been engaged to deal with consequential problems of flooding which nearly destroyed the Calder and Hebble Navigation, Calderdale's first engineered waterway. Flooding also created major problems, especially in 2012 and 2015, devastating homes and businesses from Todmorden to Brighouse, though not so much in Halifax itself, and destroying historic bridges most notably those at Elland and Copley. The scale of the damage necessitated costly restoration and raised issues ranging from upland land management, routine maintenance of waterways and support for the businesses and communities affected, where some 40 per cent of those suffering flood damage remained uninsured. But the floods stimulated a generous response both nationally and locally, within the closely-knit communities, shaped by such a challenging environment, which visitors to Calderdale had long recognised from Daniel Defoe to J. B. Priestley.

Indeed, Geoffrey Moorhouse touring England in the footsteps of J. B. Priestley in 1964 observed perceptively that 'the lie of the land in the West Riding has more than anything been responsible for a deep attachment to locality' particularly in 'the small communities lodged under the central Pennine spine' where 'the topography itself is most emphatic' and communities are 'segregated by the spurs and outcrops of the Pennines'.[10] And so these topographical constraints, which had sometimes impeded the economic and urban development of Halifax, helped to strengthen a remarkable sense of community cohesion existing in various local communities in different eras including popular radicalism, liberalism, conservatism and socialism. These all came to be represented in local politics, particularly after the turbulent years of economic and social dislocation in the mid-Victorian period, ultimately inclining more towards consensus than conflict in addressing potentially divisive issues. Cultural values were shaped by many influences, including a tradition of philanthropy, mutual improvement and voluntary service, which derived much of its impetus from the strong Puritan and Nonconformist presence in the town which had emerged during the Reformation and the Evangelical Revival, and which remained a vibrant force within the community into the twenty-first century.[11]

After the Second World War and continuing into the early twenty-first century, however, religious and cultural diversity was broadened by an influx of immigrants from the Indian sub-continent, seeking employment in the town's declining textile industries, and also by asylum seekers from northern and eastern Europe, the Middle East and parts of sub-Saharan Africa, including Latvia, Lithuania, Poland, Serbia, the Ukraine, Uganda and more recently Syria. During this period, Halifax became, in many respects, a model of a multi-ethnic, post-industrial society, pioneering new forms of partnership between the public, private and voluntary sectors, assisted by the innovative remodelled Calderdale Community Foundation, consolidating and co-ordinating grant aid to a wide range of projects, including the Calderdale Interfaith Council and various charitable and voluntary organisations for which Halifax had long excelled. It also turned some of the former disadvantages of its geographical location into new economic opportunities by exploiting the growing appeal of Calderdale's spectacular natural environment and unique built environment, initially with the striking renewal of Dean Clough and ultimately culminating in the transformation of the town's historic Piece Hall into a major attraction for both residents and visitors alike.[12]

A Pennine backwater:
Halifax before 1500

W HAT EVIDENCE is there for the occupation, settlement and function of the site on which the modern town of Halifax developed in the many centuries up to 1500? When did the settlement start to develop into an urban centre, with what economic purpose and with what social, political and cultural characteristics? How did its early development affect its later physical shape, built environment, urban character and its relationships with its surrounding settlements? From the outset, it has to be acknowledged that there is relatively little evidence of human habitation and settlement on the site of the modern town of Halifax and its hinterland before the Norman Conquest of 1066. This is perhaps not surprising as lowland sites before the tenth and eleventh centuries were generally densely wooded and poorly drained, and early settlers therefore tended to favour more elevated sites. Moreover, the footprint of prehistoric, pre-conquest or indeed later medieval settlement particularly on the site of the emerging urban centre of Halifax may well have been lost as a result of the encroaching built environment of the developing town.

Prehistory from the Stone Age to the Bronze Age

Archaeological investigation on hitherto relatively undeveloped sites was extended most notably by the Countryside Rights of Way Act of 2000, which introduced rights of access on mountains, moors, heaths and downs. This 'right to roam' legislation is now providing growing evidence of prehistoric occupation of the more sparsely populated, predominantly upland sites in the vicinity of Halifax and Calderdale. These sites, extending principally from the Mesolithic or Middle Stone Age (c. 8000 to c. 4500 BC), through the Neolithic or New Stone Age (c. 4000 to c. 2500 BC), which saw the emergence of farming, to the Bronze Age, (c. 2500 to c. 750 BC), include some extraordinary evidence of Mesolithic settlement on a lowland site within the later urban centre of Halifax, dating perhaps from the sixth millennium BC. Prehistorians have also emphasised continuities between the Bronze Age and the Iron Age which followed (c. 750 BC to AD 43), which was distinguished by extensive clearing of woodland using iron axes and iron plough-shares. However, re-use of stone tools found discarded at these locations may also suggest that particular sites were repeatedly visited over long periods of time, but only after the last glacial period finally ended *c.* 9500 BC does human activity become evident again from the remains of stone tools.[1]

By about 10,000 BC, during the Late Upper Palaeolithic or Old Stone Age (*c.* 12,700 to *c.* 9600 BC), the Yorkshire historian, David Hey, has noted that the receding ice that had covered much of northern Britain had resulted in the replacement of much of the open tundra by 'a wooded landscape of birch, hazel and pine trees' and the spread of 'oak, ash, elm and lime' on deep rich soils and 'alder and willow' in the wetlands. Consequently, 'reindeer and bison that had flourished in colder conditions became extinct locally' and were replaced by 'roe and red deer, elk, wild cattle, horses and pigs and a great variety of smaller mammals'. Hence 'armed with new tools and weapons made from flint, Stone Age people followed these animals over extensive hunting grounds in regular seasonal patterns'. Moreover, climatic and environmental research, relating to rising summer and milder winter temperatures, higher North Sea levels, consequent land erosion and ultimately the separation of Britain from the continent of Europe from around 6200 BC, has prompted archaeologists to postulate links between such changes and developing demographic and territorial pressures. These may be reflected in the archaeological record, for example, as changes in the raw material used to make stone tools. However, the observed variation, during the Mesolithic, of the use of flint and chert is not currently fully understood because these raw materials originated from different parts of the country and are not local to Calderdale. There is also a qualitative difference between the two materials. Indeed, the re-use of flint and other stone tools found discarded at these locations may also suggest that particular sites were repeatedly visited over long periods of time since flint and stone tools 'were used for half a million years'. However, there is no such evidence in Calderdale prior to the early Mesolithic, until about 500 BC, well into the Iron Age'.[2]

Between the publication of Geoffrey Watson's pioneering, if gender myopic, *Early Man in Halifax* by the Halifax Scientific Society in 1952 and the Yorkshire Archaeological and Historical Society's assessment of the archaeology of Yorkshire at the beginning of the twenty-first century in 2003, and the successive editions of David Hey's history of Yorkshire from prehistoric times to the present in 2005 and 2011, there has been a remarkable resurgence of localised interest in the prehistory of Calderdale. This has demonstrated that previous knowledge of the nature of human activity during the prehistoric era in the upland areas of Calderdale, centred upon Halifax, now requires considerable revision. The early stages of this fieldwork involved surveying the moorland extremities of Calderdale for standing stones and other prominent features such as ring works. Subsequent phases of investigation have sought to establish the nature of surviving rock art within the region, whilst other activities have included geophysical and measured surveys of archaeological features and a re-appraisal of both recently discovered and antiquarian collections of flint artefacts, many of which remain in private collections.[3]

The amateur hobby of flint hunting dating from the nineteenth century and still continuing unabated into the twenty-first century has provided one fairly accessible cumulative source of evidence for continuous human activity around Halifax from the Mesolithic to the Bronze Age. This has been recognised in the Yorkshire Archaeological and Historical Society assessment of archaeology in Yorkshire at the beginning of the twenty-first century, where T. G. Manby affirmed that 'the Pennine moorlands have continued to be a major area of collecting as well as some excavations of lithic debris patches, some with pits and hearths', but deriving almost exclusively in the Calderdale area from the Mesolithic era. Indeed, even the isolated attribution to the Upper Palaeolithic era of a flint blade reputedly found at the beginning of the twentieth century and identified at the time of discovery as a 'battered back blade' by no less an authority than the keeper of antiquities at the British Museum, but unfortunately subsequently lost, is no longer deemed by archaeologists to provide a challenge to the modern consensus now emphasising the significance of the Mesolithic era in the emergence of human activity in and around prehistoric Calderdale. For, as David Hey has concluded, it was in the more northerly carboniferous parts of the modern county of Yorkshire, extending from the Stainmore Pass in Teesdale as far south as Craven, where the earliest evidence of human activity in what is now Yorkshire has been discovered. Here in limestone caves or rock shelters, such as the Victoria Cave, two miles north of Settle, an antler point used as a harpoon by hunters during the Upper Palaeolithic or Old Stone Age, has been discovered together with animal bones, whereas there has been found 'little or no evidence' of human occupation in the more southerly millstone grit, foothills of the Yorkshire Pennines, which may have been 'among the last parts of England to be settled'.[4]

Consequently, Mesolithic microliths, obliquely-blunted flint implements from the Middle Stone Age, together with innumerable flint projectile points, blades, scrapers and tools of all types, including axes, borers and saws, are now considered to provide the earliest evidence of human activity not only of passage, but also, more significantly, of various types of occupation. However, they are principally, though not exclusively, confined to the rising moorland around the future site of Halifax.[5] Here, around 10,000 years ago, early hunters, operating from such temporary hunting camp locations as Ringstone Edge Moor to the south-west and Nab Water on Oxenhope Moor to the north-west, followed herds of red deer and other wild animals into the higher reaches of the Central Pennines. Archaeological evidence, supported by a series of radiocarbon determinations, suggests increasing numbers of hunters visited and exploited both the animal and vegetable resources of the Yorkshire Pennines by the later Mesolithic period.

Calderdale finds range from scatters of flints to more substantial upland gritstone sites on the Midgley, Ovenden, Saltonstall and Warley Moors. Untypically, and of particular interest in the exploration of Halifax's urban history, they also include an isolated lowland gravel site at Halifax, which was discovered by archaeologists in the early 1970s below the clay floor of an excavated thirteenth-century house in Gaol Lane, Halifax. The finds, comprising a microlith, quartzite hammerstone and nearly two dozen very rough, unretouched flakes and blades, dating perhaps from the sixth millennium BC, provide the very earliest evidence of human activity on

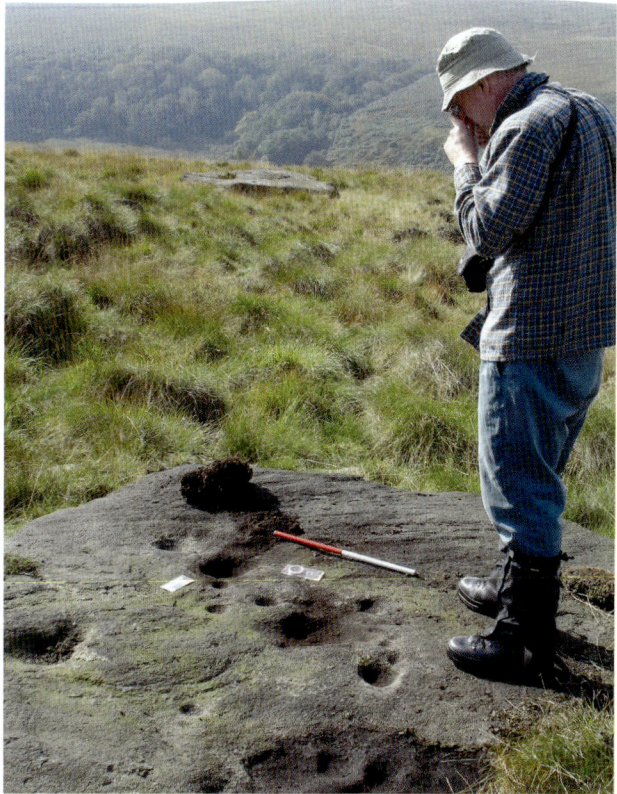

Surveying for rock art in the
Luddenden Valley.
(Photograph: David Shepherd)

the site of the town of Halifax itself.[6] Moreover, the outlying areas of Halifax to
the north and east are now considered to be of national importance for the study
of the Mesolithic because of the quantity of lithic material discovered there. So,
whilst models of temporary seasonal occupation and passage in the early Mesolithic
period remain valid, understanding of the nature of later Mesolithic activity is now
increasingly allowing for the possibility of more sustained patterns of occupation
as well as passage.

Traces of Neolithic occupation and passage have been discovered, but again at high
altitudes along the route of the ancient trans-Pennine trackway, later known as the
Long Causeway, linking the Halifax and Burnley areas. Neolithic, leaf-shaped flint
arrowheads, used in hunting and possibly also in warfare, have also been discovered
at former Mesolithic sites on the exposed uplands around Ringstone Reservoir,
Midgley Moor, Blackstone Edge, Great Manshead Hill, March Hill, Waystone
Edge and Windy Hill, suggesting possible re-use of previously occupied sites. The
discovery of a plano-convex flint knife, a polished-edge convex scraper and other
artefacts possibly provides evidence of a Neolithic occupation site at Holdsworth in
North Halifax, while the discovery of polished stone and flint axes over a wider area
suggests both the exploitation and management of woodland resources. Neolithic
people were no longer predominantly hunter-gatherers but were also beginning to

50
40
30
20
10
MM
10 20 30 40 50

Flint dagger from Upper Gorple: a fine example of Late Neolithic flintworking. (Photograph: Frank Jolley)

farm the land, keep domesticated animals and make distinctively grooved, patterned, coarse pottery, which they decorated with cord or bone, sherds of which from the Late Neolithic were discovered on Lindley Moor. Important artefact discoveries, like the polished flint axe found in Huddersfield in 2007, can equally be regarded as a votive deposit made by local occupants, rather than something lost by a traveller passing through the area.[7] Notwithstanding the absence in Calderdale of another salient feature of the New Stone Age, the construction of large communal monuments, such as long barrows, there is, nonetheless some evidence of a Neolithic presence in Calderdale, provided particularly by cereal pollen from Soyland together with a possible Neolithic site at Holmfield.

Prehistory from the Bronze Age to the Iron Age

More substantial evidence of settlement has been uncovered from the Bronze Age, a period characterised by the introduction of bronze, an alloy of copper with tin, particularly along the terraces of the valleys of the Calder and its tributaries, encompassing, for example, cinerary urns with cremations at Warley, Ovenden and Rastrick, circular earth structures, cairns, pottery and flint artefacts. Ever since the eighteenth century collared urns have been found, often during the course of clearing ground for stone quarrying and early forms of bronze axes also discovered revealing that even in those locations where settlement may not have been a permanent feature in the Neolithic era, it was developing very early in the Bronze Age.[8] A plain, thin-butted copper axe was found at Hipperholme as early as 1824; a small, thick-butted bronze flat axe was discovered at an upland site at Norland, to the south-west of Halifax, in 1984 and a well-preserved early Bronze Age flat axe recovered from Saltonstall in 2006. Indeed, the discovery, near Shelf, of a late Bronze Age metal hoard in 1856 while clearing for quarrying is a particularly significant hoard of late Bronze Age metalwork, whose importance was enhanced by its inclusion by Colin Burgess in his sequencing when he defined a typology of metalworking traditions for the British Bronze Age. It helped to define, what he termed, the Wallington/Wilburton Complex, dating between 1000 and 800 BC. The dating of this typology has only recently started to be refined but the Shelf hoard still forms a significant part of the definition for the chronological sequence.[9] Moreover, a re-interpretation of the Shelf hoard of bronze suggests that it was more likely to have been hidden by someone living locally rather than temporarily buried by a migrant trader.[10] Notwithstanding the emergence of farming, hunting appears to have remained important in the Bronze Age, with the discovery of barbed and tanged arrowheads at Mesolithic sites, for example Manshead, Ringstone Edge Moor, Inchfield and Langfield Moor, suggesting either continuity of occupation or Bronze Age re-use of sites. But evidence of sustained settlement from this period on the site of the town of Halifax itself is still absent.[11]

Extensive field walking has also led to the recording of numerous examples of rock art, predominantly cup marks. These are of simpler design than the well-known examples on Rombalds Moor to the north, raising the possibility that the Aire Valley was a boundary between two cultural groups. Alternatively, the Calder Valley examples may represent a stylistically earlier phase and consequently an earlier presence deriving from the very early Bronze or late Neolithic Ages since simple cup marks are considered to be typologically the first examples in the sequence. Given that rock art in Calderdale is, at present, almost totally represented by single cup marks, this implies either an earlier use of the form than along the Aire Valley or a representation in Calderdale of a different social group. Cist burials

Early Neolithic polished flint axe from Beaumont Park Huddersfield.

10cm

Early Bronze axe from Saltonstall. (Photographs: Frank Jolley)

probably dating from the early to middle Bronze Age have also been noted at Lower Gorple, Clough Head, Ringstone and Shaw Pasture and individual and grouped funerary cairns are distributed more widely.

Other features attributed to the early to middle Bronze Age include a series of enclosed urn cemeteries, extending across the area from Mount Tabor, Midgley Moor and Blackheath towards Thursden and Mosley Height just over the watershed to the west; a ring cairn at Blake Dean; the destroyed stone circles at Ringstone and Walshaw; and a number of features on Midgley Moor. The first evidence for prehistoric field boundaries in the region has also been recorded on Midgley Moor, consisting of simple demarcation boundaries set in stone that could have formed the base of hedge lines.

They are smaller scale examples of the type of structures observed on Dartmoor in the upland expansion of land-use in the Bronze Age and probably also date from that era. Although no dwelling structures generating the excitement of recent fenland discoveries have been discovered around Halifax (most notably the remains of two Bronze Age fire-damaged wooden roundhouses at Must Farm quarry in Cambridgeshire announced in December 2016, with their perfectly preserved Bronze Age textiles, cups, bowls, jars, jewellery, and a fragile 3,000-year-old wooden wheel complete with its hub), conceivably Mesolithic hearths have been located on Ovenden Moor. Cist burials have also been noted at Lower Gorple, Clough Head, Ringstone and Shaw Pasture, whilst individual and grouped burial cairns are distributed more widely.[12]

Ravines associated with post-glacial rejuvenation drain all valley basins such as Crimsworth, Greave, Widdop, Blackshaw and Green Withens. Above these narrow valleys a number of standing stones have been recorded, perhaps denoting liminal areas at the downstream terminations of areas of prehistoric occupation. The long axes of these standing stones are oriented to solar and lunar horizon events such as midwinter sunrise, the spring and autumn equinox and the major lunar standstill.[13]

Until relatively recently it was believed that there was only sporadic prehistoric activity in the area of Calderdale around Halifax, but this notion derived principally from the lack of any systematic archaeological fieldwork hitherto. Hence it was assumed that Calderdale was an area of passage through which people moved in prehistoric times rather than as a place where people lived. Moreover, even when perceived tentatively as a corridor for migration it was viewed as a secondary dispersal route for later trade and population expansion of lesser significance than the primary route through the Aire Gap.[14] In Calderdale evidence of prehistoric occupation and settlement remains elusive, compounded particularly by the acid soil, which destroys most forms of evidence except for flint and cereal pollen. Nevertheless, evidence which has survived confirming human activity in the vicinity of Halifax and Calderdale during the Bronze Age provides support for Francis Pryor's conclusion that during the Bronze Age 'a highly developed and sophisticated people' established 'regular links right across Britain and over to the Continent' although far less is known of their lifestyle in Pennine Yorkshire than the East Anglian fenlands.[15]

Burial cist near Ringstone Edge. (Photograph: David Shepherd)

From the Iron Age to the Roman Conquest

Archaeological evidence of Iron Age settlement in Calderdale is even less extensive, and there is still no evidence of any activity on the site of the town of Halifax itself during this era of over half a millennium. For several centuries before the arrival of the Romans the Iron Age is characterised by the introduction of iron weaponry and tools, including axe blades and ploughshares. This facilitated the clearance of woodland and the development of farming and, as Francis Pryor has observed, the era also saw 'the full development of the British landscape, including the construction of hundreds of hillforts'. Although Calderdale lacked the impressive hillforts of Almondbury in Yorkshire, overlooking the valley of the Holme, and Mam Tor in Derbyshire, both significantly occupying elevated former Bronze Age sites, several Iron Age enclosures have been identified in and around Halifax and Calderdale at Kirklees Park, Ovenden Moor, Norland and Meg Dyke, Barkisland. The latter, a rectangular enclosure with a double rampart, possibly formed one of a group of smaller defensive Iron Age earthworks in the South West Pennines, which may also have included the earthworks at Oldfield Hill and Royd Edge at Meltham. Further evidence of the Iron Age in the area later designated Yorkshire has come from pollen analysis, radio-carbon dating, the discovery of rotary beehive querns and burials, including the fine example of a chariot burial at Ferry Fryston dating from *c.* 300 BC, unearthed by road contractors during the upgrade of the A1 near Ferrybridge in 2003. A third-century BC log-boat preserved at Hasholme in the Humberside wetlands where it was discovered in 1984 providing evidence of early Iron age settlement in the lowland districts of Yorkshire as well as the Pennine uplands. However, pottery finds have continued to remain elusive.[16]

Celts first appear in classical historical sources and have been represented as occupying extensive swathes of central and western Europe, including the British Isles in the five centuries before the Roman Conquest. However, archaeologists have become increasingly more circumspect in claiming distinctive continental Celtic pedigrees for the various tribal groupings in Britain that faced the invading Roman armies from AD 43. There is also continuing debate about how far it is justifiable to regard the indigenous Iron Age communities of Britain as predominantly descendants of successive waves of Celtic invaders from across western and central Europe. Indeed, Patrick Ottaway has emphasised the importance of non-military factors such as 'the influence of trade and other forms of contact' in shaping the Iron Age tribal communities of Britain, now more generally designated Britons rather than Celts. Moreover, he has concluded that they are now also widely considered to have been 'very largely descendants of indigenous forebears going back to the Bronze Age and before', though he acknowledges that Celtic is still employed generically to describe the

above Base of prehistoric field boundary. (Photograph: David Shepherd)

Standing Stone on Heptonstall Moor. (Photograph: David Shepherd)

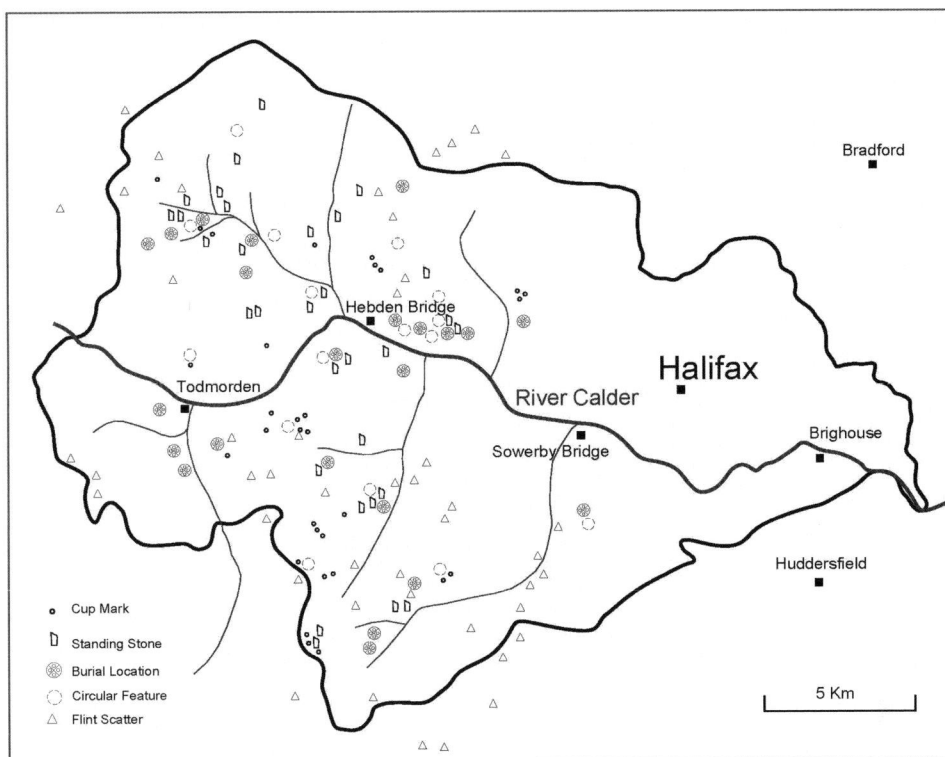

Distribution map of prehistoric features and sites identified by fieldwork 2002–15 reflecting discoveries made in areas that became accessible after the 'right to roam' legislation was implemented in 2004. (David Shepherd and Frank Jolley)

art styles and language of contemporary native Britons and their distinctive tribal societies.[17]

By the first century AD the iron-age communities in what later became Yorkshire formed part of the vast territory of Brigantia, which the second-century Greek geographer Ptolemy observed, stretched from sea to sea, apparently overlooking the adjacent Parisi communities occupying territory eastwards between Brigantia and the North Sea. Westwards Brigantian influence ultimately extended southwards from the line of the Hadrianic frontier to the Calder Valley and beyond. Its tribal capital appears to have been located initially on a relatively unimpressive, sprawling lowland site of perhaps 750 acres at Stanwick, north of Richmond from the last century BC until long after the Roman conquest of AD 43, when it appears to have moved southwards to Aldborough. Moreover, the Claudian invasion left Brigantia under its ruler Queen Cartimandua, the dominant military force in the north. The contemporary Roman writer, Tacitus (c. AD 54–120), considered the Brigantes to have been 'numerically the largest tribe in Britain', but the archaeologist of Iron Age Britain, Barry Cunliffe, has concluded that in the north 'the general impression given by the sparse material culture and the apparent lack of settlements is that the population was small compared with the south'.[18]

Indeed, Cunliffe characterised the Brigantian lifestyle as semi-nomadic and 'predominantly pastoral … tending flocks and herds in upland pastures', including an embryonic 'nucleated village' of huts at Grassington extending over 2 acres (0.8 hectares), intrinsically associated with *c.* 80 acres of rectangular fields. These remarkable surviving field patterns around Wharfedale, photographed memorably by O. G. S. Crawford in a pioneering application of the technique of aerial photography to archaeological investigation in 1932, together with adjacent valleys cultivating cereals reinforced by quern fragments discovered at Stanwick provide the most graphic illustrations of indigenous iron age settlement in the Yorkshire Dales. Moreover, Cunliffe concluded that the hillfort at Castle Hill 'must belong to the late first century BC or the first century AD' and that its destruction by fire cannot be precisely dated. However, he suggests that it may well have been linked to the advance of Petillius Cerialis, who was appointed governor of Britain in AD 71 and subjugated the Brigantes of northern England before his recall in AD 74.[19]

Classical literary sources have long been utilised to construct narratives of the establishment of Roman rule in Britain, extending from the exploratory expeditions of Julius Caesar in 55 and 54 BC. Caesar sought to prevent assistance from tribal communities in southern Britain to his continental enemies during his conquest of Gaul. Consequently, his expedition penetrated little further north than the Thames. However, the more sustained, if geographically limited, invasion of the Emperor Claudius of AD 43, encouraged by internal discord amongst the British tribes, led to the subsequent subjugation of the northern British tribes during the governorship of Agricola between AD 78 and 84. Thus, a period of Roman rule was inaugurated extending to AD 410 which for the greater part absorbed Britain 'into an empire based on the Mediterranean and subject to the direct impact of classical culture'. Stanwick, by far the most extensive Iron Age site in Britain, probably became the principal residence of Queen Cartimandua, the last ruler of the Brigantes, who accepted the role of client-ruler of the North, in return for Roman support against the forces of her estranged husband Venutius. Brigantia retained its semi-independence until AD 69 when Cartimandua finally divorced Venutius and co-habited with his armour-bearer, Vellocatus, which precipitated a major revolt by Venutius against the queen and her Roman supporters.[20]

Hey suggests that the revolt resulted in an increased Roman military presence in the north following the stationing of the Ninth Legion of the Roman Army under the command of Quintus Petillius Cerialis, hitherto based at Lincoln for a quarter of a century and with previous experience of the Boudiccan revolt. He established a new fortress at Eboracum, modern York, which quickly became the military capital and largest town of Northern Britain with military road links to Chester protected by forts on both sides of the Pennines at Slack and Castleshaw. After assisting Vespasian's forces in the capture of Rome in AD 69 and suppressing rebellions in the German provinces Cerialis was appointed governor of Britain in AD 71 and effectively subjugated the Brigantes in northern Britain before his recall to Rome in

AD 74. The Agricolan road system was developed to improve military movement during this period of consolidation of Roman rule, for if Agricola was to campaign even further north into Scotland it was vital that he should protect his rear, through firm military control of Brigantia. 'The cross-Pennine road, which linked the two major military bases at York and Chester,' as N. Redhead has remarked, played a vital role in maintaining 'the Agricolan stranglehold on Brigantia', with the forts at Castleshaw and Slack positioned at intervals that represented a day's march.

Such was the strategic importance of York in the extension of the northern frontier of the Roman Empire that Septimius Severus (AD 146–211), the Roman Emperor came to Britain with his two sons in AD 208, where he fought two campaigns in Scotland, intending to extend Roman rule to the whole island, but he died at York on 4 February 211. A later Roman emperor, Constantine (AD 274–337) was proclaimed Roman Emperor in York in AD 306. He succeeded in uniting the empire, establishing an eastern capital at Constantinople and issued his general edict of toleration for the Christian Church in AD 312. Ecclesiastical historians have concluded that it is probable that by AD 306 'there was then a small Christian congregation among the York citizens who acclaimed Constantine and by AD 314 the Christian community in York already had its own bishop who attended the Council of Arles in Provence in 314, so York was poised to became not only a major northern military base, but also an influential early Christian centre.[21]

The Revd John Watson (1725–83), the celebrated eighteenth-century historian of Halifax, who claimed the distinction of having first discovered the Roman forts at Slack, near Huddersfield, overlooking the Calder Valley and now partially submerged beneath the line of the M62 motorway, and Castleshaw, on a still accessible site in Saddleworth, failed to detect the remains of any Roman fort or settlement within the parish of Halifax itself. Meanwhile, another clerical antiquary, the Revd John Whitaker, in his history of Manchester, published in 1771, initiated an inconclusive enquiry into why the Latin name of the Roman fort at Slack had apparently been lost in antiquity and superseded by a topographical designation 'vulgarly denominated Slack in the township of Longwood' and speculating, as did others after him without success, whether the fort might have been either the Camulodunum in Ptolemy's *Geography* or Cambodunum of the Antonine *Itineraries*. Moreover, the traditional association of the paved trans-Pennine moorland road over Blackstone Edge with the Romans is now also discredited, and the presumed course of the Manchester to Ilkley Roman road through the parish of Halifax south of the Calder has also been questioned. However, it seems likely that a Roman road, constructed during the second century AD linking Ilkley with Manchester, did pass through Soyland, south-west of Halifax. In addition, in 1955 the claim of the topographer Roger Dodsworth (1585–1654) for the existence of a Roman site just within the Halifax parish boundary at Fixby was confirmed by the rediscovery of a Roman tile kiln in Grimescar Wood.[22] It has also been suggested that a hoard of Corieltauvi and early first-century Roman coins discovered at Lightcliffe between 1828 and 1831, may have been deposited by refugees from the Claudian invasion. Other coin finds dating from the third and fourth centuries are considered to represent activity related to contemporary altars, including an altar dedicated by Titus Aurelius Aurelianus to the Celtic goddess Victoria Brigantia and the deities of the two Roman Emperors, an interesting coalescence of indigenous and imperial religious observance, discovered at Greetland in 1597, and preserved at Cambridge University since 1750. This altar, one of three contemporary surviving altars (the others were from Longwood near Huddersfield and from Castleford) dedicated by people with family names honouring emperor Marcus Aurelius, has been dated precisely to AD 208, because the inscription refers to the Consulships of Antoninus III and Geta II.[23]

However, no comparable evidence has been discovered of either Roman military or civilian settlements in the immediate vicinity of Halifax, suggesting that this site may still have remained largely unpopulated, although it is not unreasonable to suppose that the fort, housing military units of up to 500, together with the vicus at Slack may well have generated a considerable hinterland of economic activity, which may have continued well into the later period of continuing Roman occupation. Pottery from the excavations of 2007–08 and re-assessment of the Roman material from the excavations of 1978–69 reveals that 'the civilian settlement developed almost immediately with the arrival of the military in the late first century AD' and that 'contrary to previous assumptions that the vicus was abandoned with the withdrawal of the military *c*. AD 120–140 there was continued civilian occupation at Slack' continuing 'to take advantage of its position alongside a strategically important route until at least the end of the second and early-third centuries AD'. Indeed, a large proportion of datable pottery was 'manufactured during the second-half of the second century AD, with a small number of North Yorkshire cream wares dating from the third and possibly early-fourth centuries AD', whilst black-burnished wares 'still arriving at Slack in quantity during the second-half of the second century AD' may suggest 'that the military utilised this site after the Roman frontier moved north to Hadrian's Wall'. This would confirm 'the continued importance of the Chester to York road, eventually changing from a strategic military frontier road to an economically important trade route across the harsh environment of the Pennines'.[24]

Patrick Ottaway, in the first full-length survey of Roman Yorkshire since 1936 published in 2013, has provided an assessment of the impact of approximately 340 years of Roman rule on the vast territory which long after the Roman armies were withdrawn in AD 410 became designated Yorkshire. Although Calderdale lacks the substantial evidence of the Roman occupation of York such as the Roman remains incorporated into the city's celebrated Multangular Tower, or Ilkley, with its fort, altar and tombstones or even neighbouring Huddersfield with its Roman fort and adjacent civilian settlement or vicus at Slack near Outlane and Roman tilery in the Grimescar Valley, discovered by charcoal burners as early as 1590, it, nevertheless, was strongly associated with the relatively early antiquarian interest in Roman antiquities in the county which sprang from the European Renaissance. The identification of the well-preserved Roman altar at Greetland, discovered by workmen in 1597 and first noted in the 1600 edition of William Camden's *Britannia*, established local interest in the discovery of evidence of Roman occupation and passage within Calderdale and its periphery. Moreover, the permanent display of this outstanding example of a Roman altar devoted to the goddess Victoria Brigantia in the Museum of Archaeology at the University of Cambridge, whilst emphasising its outstanding significance has inevitably resulted in this remarkable evidence of Roman religious observance being less well known within the locality of its construction today.

Ottaway also offers an explanation for the numerous coin hoards, including a deposit of fifty-seven coins at Lightcliffe, which he suggests were possibly the proceeds of trade beginning in the immediate pre-Roman period around AD 40 'kept as savings or for some other purpose' deposited around the same time as a larger hoard of over 200 coins at Castle Hill, Almondbury near Huddersfield. These contrast with a much smaller deposit of twenty-four coins at Honley, also near Huddersfield around AD 72–73, just after the northern advance of the Roman armies. All three hoards contained a predominance of Roman coins intermingled with issues of the Corieltauvi. He also commends recent work by the Huddersfield and District Archaeological Society which includes enthusiasts from Calderdale for 'accurately' plotting the line of the Roman road running south west from Slack to Castleshaw, a distance of about twelve kilometres, the base of which was composed of large slabs of sandstone'. He also plausibly suggests that Roman roads,

York tombstone of the Ninth Legion standard bearer Lucius Duccius Rufinus. (Photograph: York Museums Trust https:// yorkmuseumstrust.org.uk CC BY-SA 4.0)

initially built for the army, soon 'assumed an economic role in opening up the countryside, thereby linking farmland with consumers in the forts and associated settlements'.

The excavation of the fortlet at Castleshaw in 1984 by the Greater Manchester Archaeological Unit and the vicus adjoining the Roman fort at Slack between 2007 and 2010 by the Huddersfield and District Archaeological Society, whose membership extends into Calderdale, have led to speculation that both sites may have been occupied for much longer than previously allowed. At Slack the discovery of conduits and drainage systems remaining on the site of the vicus linked to natural springs and watercourses which are still discernible has illuminated further the reasons for the choice of this particular geographical location for the fort and

Roman altar from Thick Hollins, Bank Top, Greetland. This early third-century votive altar discovered in April 1597 at Greetland, some two miles south of Halifax, now forms part of the Cotton Collection in the Cambridge University Museum of Archaeology and Anthropology. It was dedicated by Titus Aurelius Aurelianus and his family to Victoria Brigantia and the Deities of the Two Roman Emperors and is one of a number of apparently isolated Roman finds from this vicinity of Halifax. (Photograph: Halifax Antiquarian Society)

its adjoining vicus, namely to access the extensive natural spring water supplies required for the sustenance of the large numbers of both human and equine users of the site. It has also led to a reconsideration of the extent of the Roman occupation of the military site taking it well into the third and possibly the fourth centuries AD and to speculation about the activity within the hitherto unknown vicus area adjacent to the fort and the Roman road linking the legionary fortresses in Chester and York.[25]

Britons, Angles, Saxons, Vikings and Normans

Relatively little is known about Halifax and its periphery even in the six centuries between the end of the Roman occupation and the Norman Conquest. Lacking archaeological evidence of 'mass invasions from across the North Sea' of pre-conquest Yorkshire, David Hey has emphasised continuities, with life in the rural northern communities continuing 'much as before', whilst also recognising the adverse economic consequences arising from 'the abandonment of Roman forts and the collapse of towns and markets' which he suggests may have languished 'until the late Anglo-Scandinavian period'. It is possible to identify from literary sources, most notably Bede's *Ecclesiastical History of the English People* of 731, but also from the lives of saints and the Anglo-Saxon Chronicle, a number of key changes in the political control of the area in which the future site of Halifax was situated before the Norman Conquest. After the Roman withdrawal from Britain, a number of independent kingdoms emerged in the fifth century, including the relatively populous British kingdom of Elmet, which stretched westwards from marshland at the head of the Humber into the vicinity of Leeds, where place-name suffixes such as Sherburn-in-Elmet and Barwick-in-Elmet, probably delineate its eastern borders and, by the early seventh century, it encompassed the modern county divisions of West and South Yorkshire. Literary sources reveal that Elmet reached its zenith in the second half of the sixth century, offering strong resistance to English expansion from the East Riding kingdom of Deira, a name whose meaning is unknown, which had been established by Angles from the Schleswig-Holstein peninsula entering the Humber and Derwent by sea and settling in territory formerly controlled by the Parisi during the Iron Age.

By the early seventh century Deira had expanded westwards 'over the whole of the territory that was to become Yorkshire and York had become its capital'. Moreover, following the formation of the kingdom of Northumbria, by the union of Deira and Bernicia, Elmet was also incorporated into the neighbouring kingdom in 617 by King Edwin. Both Welsh and English sources reveal that he had conducted vigorous warfare against the Welsh, following his expulsion of Ceretic, the last British king of Elmet. Indeed, the British never fully recovered from this subjugation even after Edwin himself was killed by the combined forces of Cadwallon of Gwynedd and Penda of Mercia at the battle of Hatfield Chase in Nottinghamshire in 633, followed by the death of Penda in battle near Doncaster in 655, after penetrating deep into Elmet. Nevertheless, despite these recurring clashes between Northumbria and Mercia, which resulted in Mercian domination of Northumbria from 633–34 and 641–54, Northumbria ultimately regained its independence until eventually overwhelmed by the Viking invasions of 867. It then remained under Danish control until the defeat of Eric Bloodaxe in 954. Thereafter, it was ruled by earls appointed by the kings of Wessex. Although some notion of England was already in existence by AD 900, as Pauline Stafford has observed 'the political reality was separate kingdoms, some of them by this date under Viking control', but the old kingdoms of Deira and Bernicia, she concludes, retained their identity under Viking rule. In general, Matthew Townend has concluded, 'there was likely to have been a good deal of give-and-take between the English and Scandinavian communities in Viking Age Yorkshire, as in the Danelaw more broadly'. The kingdom of Wessex which under the leadership of its king, Alfred the Great (849–99), had survived the Viking attacks, succeeded in asserting its dominance, but evidence of the impact of these political changes on settlement in Halifax and its environs is very sparse.[26]

However, Hey also offers tentative conclusions about the structure of Anglo-Saxon society from archaeological evidence from excavations at Wharram Percy. This suggests that 'the early Anglo-Saxons lived in scattered settlements and that villages were not created until the eighth or ninth centuries or later'. It also acknowledges the apparently exceptional contrary evidence of the excavation of West Heslerton

Excavations by the Huddersfield and District Archaeological Society to find route of Roman road between Slack and Castleshaw, August 2015. (Photograph: J. A. Hargreaves)

in the Vale of Pickering, the most extensively excavated site of early Anglo–Saxon settlement in England. This has yielded 'convincing evidence of a large village that was continually occupied from about 380 before the end of the Roman occupation to c. 850 when the site was abandoned'. Here, the post-holes of no fewer than 150 timber-framed rectangular buildings, together with granaries and outbuildings were very different from the structures of the earlier native round houses, whilst skeletons exhumed from a large contemporary neighbouring cemetery show no evidence of violent death in warfare thereby failing to provide support for the view that 'the early Anglian settlements were dominated by marauding warriors from across the sea'.[27]

Hey also suggests that culturally the development of language and the impact of religion were significant. Although it is not known when the native population of the kingdom of Northumbria started to speak Old English since most Yorkshire place-names were not recorded before the compilation of Domesday Book in 1086, more contemporary evidence is however available chronicling the establishment of Christianity in Northumbria and the building of the first church in York. An Italian monk, Paulinus, like Augustine, a papal missionary who had arrived in Kent in 601, had travelled north after Aethelburh, sister of Eadbald of Kent, had married Edwin of Northumbria in 625, to attempt the conversion of Northumbria. With royal support, Edwin, his nobles and 'a vast number of the common people' were baptised in 627, and Paulinus became bishop of Northumbria, with his see at York. The Venerable Bede, the monastic chronicler of Monkwearmouth and Jarrow, included a vivid description of Paulinus, by a man who had been baptised by him in the River Trent, as 'tall, with a slight stoop, black hair and a thin face', with 'a slender aquiline nose' who was simultaneously 'both venerable and awe-inspiring in appearance', which supplies the only surviving physical description of this key figure in the establishment of Christianity across an extensive area of northern England, including the West Riding. However, Paulinus's northern mission terminated abruptly with the death of Edwin in 633, when Paulinus returned to Kent with Queen Aethelburh to become Bishop of Rochester, an office he held until his own death on 10 October 644.

In the continuing absence of any archaeological investigation of the site of Halifax Minster, claims that Halifax may have been the site of a pre-conquest Anglo-Saxon church remain entirely conjectural, although Hey has suggested that 'few people living in the countryside in the western half of Yorkshire would have lived far from a church in the sixth and seventh centuries'. Indeed, the nearest tentative archaeological investigation has come to identifying a pre-conquest Christian site in Calderdale is the identification of crop marks in a field at Exley, one of at least nine sites in the former kingdom of Elmet with similar place names possibly incorporating the Latin term for church *ecclesia*, which may indicate the foundations of an early church deriving from late antiquity. Moreover, the identification of a late Anglian preaching cross or funerary monument from the tenth or eleventh centuries at Rastrick, which is currently located in the churchyard of St Matthew's at Rastrick, a fifteenth-century chapel-of-ease, within the parish of Halifax and a section of a sculptured pre-conquest cross-shaft stone of similar date discovered at Bean Hole Head farm, Stansfield, have been interpreted by J. A. Heginbottom as 'primary evidence for the former existence of an early church' in the upper Calder Valley. Indeed, the Exley place name evidence may signify one of the former places of Christian worship referred to in Eddius Stephanus's *Life of Wilfrid*, Bishop of York.[28]

William the Conqueror's pioneering Domesday survey reveals that a number of outliers or berewicks within the Calder Valley formed part of a pre-conquest royal manor of Wakefield, but remains tantalisingly silent about whether these encompassed Halifax itself. However, modern scholarship has tended to emphasise the deficiencies of the Yorkshire Domesday survey, which was apparently compiled hastily. Its shortcomings may reflect the ignorance of the new Norman lords and their officials about their possessions. By what has been most plausibly explained as a clerical error, Halifax appears to have been omitted from the recording of the nine constituent outliers of the royal manor of Wakefield in the Yorkshire Domesday survey. While nine outliers are enumerated within the royal manor of Wakefield, only eight are listed, namely: *Sandala* (Sandal Magna), *Sorebi* (Sowerby), *Werlafeslei* (Warley), *Micleie* (Midgley), *Wadesuurde* (Wadsworth), *Crubetonestun* (Cruttonstall in Erringden), *Langefelt* (Langfield) and *Stanesfelt* (Stansfield). Recognising the omission of Halifax from the list and reluctant to challenge the accuracy of the awesome Domesday survey, T. W. Hanson (1877–1967), and some other local historians of earlier generations mistakenly assumed that Halifax must have been represented by the suffix of *Werlafeslei*, an entry split between two lines of text in the original manuscript. However, close scrutiny of the original manuscript in 1935 by H. P. Kendall (d. 1937) revealed that the suffix *feslei*, although appearing on a separate line of text from its prefix, retained the lower case. Comparison of the entry with other early recorded forms of the name established conclusively that the combined prefix and suffix represent Warley, an extensive township which contained a large number of settlements in the Middle Ages. The absence also of references in particular to Heptonstall has led recent scholars, more aware of the deficiencies of the Yorkshire Domesday record than their predecessors, to account for the discrepancy between the specified number of berewicks and the list of recorded names by suggesting that the sub-manor of Halifax-cum-Heptonstall was omitted from the list in error.[29]

There is also some evidence to suggest that Halifax might have formed part of a pre-conquest ecclesiastical structure centred upon the ancient minster church of Dewsbury, since payments of tithes from Halifax to Dewsbury Parish Church are recorded in a fourteenth-century endowment deed. But archaeological evidence for an early Celtic Christian tradition in the area emanating from Lindisfarne is sparse. At Rastrick, a chapelry within the later parish of Halifax, a fragment of a tenth- or early eleventh-century Anglian carved stone cross has survived, but there is no such evidence from the site of Halifax itself. The Yorkshire Domesday survey records relatively few churches in the poorer western part of the county, but even the omission of a specific reference to a church does not necessarily imply that no such church existed, since Domesday does not provide a comprehensive record of ecclesiastical structures. However, whether the two unspecified churches and three priests referred to in the survey had any connection with Halifax or indeed with Heptonstall remains a matter for speculation.[30]

Place name evidence of early settlement, which must necessarily be used with caution since it also derives from post-conquest documentation, may nevertheless provide some tentative clues to pre-conquest patterns of occupation and settlement within Calderdale. Calder like many other Yorkshire river names and prominent topographical features is Celtic signifying 'rapid stream'; Exley, a hybrid name deriving from the Celtic *egles* and the Anglo-Saxon *leah*, possibly denotes the site of an Elmetian church; while, Walsden, deriving from Old English descriptions of the British, possibly indicates a valley settlement which retained a recognisable British character after the English occupation of Elmet. Other compound names with Old English suffixes such as: *land* (land), *worth* (enclosure), *feld* (unenclosed land), *denu* (valley), *shaw* (wood) and *leah* (forest clearing) may reflect an English ascendancy.

Local examples of these include: Elland (land by the river); Illingworth (Illa's enclosure), Holdsworth (Halda's enclosure); Langfield (long stretch of open country); Hebden (briar valley), Mixenden (dung-hill valley), Ovenden (the upper reaches of a valley), Shibden (sheep valley); Blackshaw (black wood); Midgley (midge-infested wood or clearing), Bentley (clearing overgrown with bent grass), Brearley (clearing overgrown with briar), Coley (cold, exposed clearing) and Wheatley (clearing used for growing wheat). Moreover, the sparsity of later Anglo-Scandinavian and Scandinavian names may confirm a continuing English ascendancy in Halifax. Erringden (Eric's valley) and Greetland (land strewn with boulders), exemplifying the former, and Sowerby (farmstead on sour ground) and Mankinholes (Mancan's hollow), exemplifying the latter, probably derive from Norse immigration in the tenth century and possibly denote later north-facing settlements on the south bank of the Calder.

A number of extraordinarily fanciful, highly influential, but entirely unsatisfactory explanations have been provided by William Camden (1551–1623), John Watson (1725–83), Dr T. D. Whitaker (1759–1821) and other antiquaries for the etymology of the name of Halifax, which has existed in its modern form only since the early twelfth century. The distinguished Calderdale place name expert, Professor A. H. Smith's derivation of the place name for Halifax as 'an area of coarse grass in a nook of land or amongst rocks' from the Old English *halh* (a nook of land) and *gefeaxe* (coarse grassland) is now preferred to such derivations as 'holy hair', 'holy face' and 'holy ways'. Smith dismissed these hallowed traditional explanations, based upon the Old English *halig* (holy), interwoven with legendary stories, some even suggesting that the holy face explanation possibly derived from an iconic representation of John the Baptist, which, if it ever existed, has not survived. Some of the responsibility for the enduring power of the myths surrounding the etymology of the place name of Halifax must be attributed to Francis A. Leyland F.S.A., a Victorian antiquary. Explaining to the assembled burgesses of Halifax, shortly after the incorporation of the municipal borough in 1848, his choice of a depiction of the grisly, bearded, disembodied head of John the Baptist as the centrepiece of his design for a new Halifax corporate seal, Leyland cited ancient tradition as the source of his artistic inspiration. He recounted that 'one of the companions of Paulinus, the first Christian missionary to the North, established a hermit's cell on the banks of the Hebble', where he became 'the first missionary to preach the gospel to the heathen inhabitants of Halifax'. He went on to explain that it was traditionally believed that the recluse may have possessed 'in his cell or oratory' as a devotional or didactic aid 'a wonderful resemblance of the baptist' and that the earliest Christian converts in Halifax were so impressed by this iconic representation 'that in the language of those days they called the spot 'Haley Fax' signifying the place of 'the Holy Face'. Moreover, Leyland's graphic design continues to be displayed most dramatically in the magnificent mosaic flooring of the Victoria Hall at Halifax Town Hall opened in 1863 and the elegant wrought iron gates of the Halifax Manufacturers' Piece Hall, installed after ownership of the former cloth market passed to Halifax Corporation in 1868. It was later also incorporated into the armorial bearings of the County Borough of Halifax in 1888, ensuring its continuing appeal. A *Halifax Guardian* editorial commending Leyland's design for the common seal expressed a sense of relief that 'it was not a botched-up job with a mill chimney in one corner, a wool sack in another and a power loom in the middle'.[31]

So, archaeological, documentary and place-name evidence for the pre-conquest development of Halifax remains skeletal and its interpretation problematic, making it difficult to assess the extent of settlement by 1066. It would appear, however, that pre-conquest settlement of the site of Halifax itself had not been very extensive, possibly constrained by the sort of geographical factors implicit in its place name derivation as 'an area of coarse grass in a nook of land or amongst rocks'.[32]

Medieval Halifax

The nature of the impact of the Norman Conquest and the extent of the devastation wreaked on the fragile pre-conquest settlement of Halifax by William the Conqueror's harrying of the rebellious north in 1069–70 are now difficult to assess, and historians have emerged sharply divided in their interpretation of the available evidence. The Halifax antiquary John Lister, analysing the lay subsidy returns of 1379, concluded in 1906 that 'the fact that this part of the country was desolated and laid waste by William the Norman would, to a large extent, account for its sparse population and poverty in the days of King Richard II', while more recently, the Domesday historian Michael Wood has maintained that the inhabitants of Yorkshire were 'marked for generations by fire and sword' after the harrying. David Carpenter observed that 'this was the crisis of William's reign and he knew it' following three Northumbrian revolts within two years. Hence, he hastened north on Christmas day, 1069, and 'wore his crown, especially dispatched from Winchester, in the ruins of York Minster' as a 'symbolic riposte to Edgar Atheling', who had raised his rebellion at York, supported by King Malcolm of Scotland. William viewed the Atheling's challenge as the biggest threat he had faced since his coronation and he acted with 'a combination of energy and conciliation' but it was the brutality which was so long remembered in Yorkshire.[33]

Despite the scepticism of some modern historians, as Carpenter has observed, 'the evidence is terribly powerful and consistent'. Indeed, the Anglo-Saxon chronicler unequivocally recorded that William 'went northwards with all his army he could collect and utterly ravaged and laid waste' to Yorkshire. Even the Anglo-Norman, Orderic Vitalis, who had admired many of William's achievements felt compelled to criticise 'this act which condemned the innocent and the guilty alike to die by slow starvation'. Refugees, young and old, women and children, fleeing the famine caused by 'the devastation' reached as far south as Evesham, where they died of weakness even as they ate the food provided by the abbot. Sixteen years later Domesday Book still recorded one third of Yorkshire lying waste and another sixteen per cent virtually without resources. Pauline Stafford also emphasised the devastating impact of the destruction of crops, cattle and farm implements with resulting dearth and famine in subjugating the potentially most serious challenge

The parish
of Halifax
before 1842.

to royal authority for a century and a half. Traditionally, the impact of the harrying was measured by the incidence in the Domesday survey of land classified as waste, comprising half the townships in Yorkshire, and the scale of the decline in the value of the land since 1066. In the manor of Wakefield, for example, the value of land was estimated to have declined by 75 per cent, from £60 to £15 since the reign of Edward the Confessor. However, W. E. Wightman has argued that since the manor of Wakefield, which contained large stretches of woodland, still had one third of its potential arable land under the plough in 1086, the decline in land value 'is not necessarily sufficiently severe in Yorkshire conditions to suggest any significant retreat in cultivation'. Moreover, since arable farming by manorial lords was mainly concentrated in the fertile lowland townships of Wakefield and the outlier Sandal

Magna, while much of the manorial woodland was situated in the upper Calder Valley, it seems reasonable to conclude that Calderdale's geographical remoteness enabled Halifax to escape relatively unscathed what has been described as 'the most fearful genocide in the history of England'.[34]

If Domesday reveals little or no arable farming by manorial lords in Calderdale in 1086, there is evidence of the subsequent exploitation of the area for pasture. The ancient Forest of Sowerbyshire, which extended westwards across Calderdale from Halifax to the Lancashire border, appears to have been used initially by the manorial lords primarily for hunting, but increasingly it was opened up for both cattle rearing and sheep pasture. Moreover, as cattle farms or vaccaries were leased to tenants, some were even converted from pasture into arable farmland. Until the end of the thirteenth century, peasant farmers principally cultivated oats, a cereal crop better suited to the cool, damp climatic conditions than other grains. They farmed in open fields on the hillside terraces, at heights of 700 to 1,000 feet, fertilising the land by pasturing their livestock in common on the open-field strips after the crops had been harvested. However, the Wakefield manorial records reveal an abandonment of this custom when the cultivated area was extended by the assarting or clearing of the valley slopes below the main terraces, particularly during the early fourteenth century. This process was stimulated either by the poor fertility of the cultivated soil or the pressure of population growth on the land. Moreover, Oliver Rackham has observed that the extent of woodland revealed in the Domesday survey for the West Riding excluding Craven in 1086, which amounted to sixteen per cent of the land area, was a considerably higher ratio than the figures for the North and East Ridings.[35]

There is also growing evidence of textile production as a supplementary economic activity throughout Calderdale from the twelfth century. The earliest evidence of textile manufacture in Halifax is a twelfth-century grave cover bearing a crude representation of cropper's shears discovered during the Victorian renovation of Halifax's medieval parish church. Land charters confirm that cloth making was developing in Halifax during the thirteenth century, and the Wakefield Court Rolls from 1274 record both a range of textile occupational names such as websters (weavers), listers (dyers) and walkers (fullers) and the existence of features in the landscape associated with the finishing processes of woollen cloth, notably fulling mills in Warley in 1286, Sowerby in 1296, Halifax in 1306, Hebden Bridge in 1347, Heptonstall in 1382 and a tentercroft in Halifax in 1414.[36]

Halifax, with relatively poor soil, may have been slower to develop both arable cultivation and textile manufacture than some of its neighbouring settlements. The lay subsidy returns of 1334 certainly reveal considerably lower property taxation assessments for Halifax than for the upland settlements of Calderdale, where more land had recently been brought into cultivation. Moreover, the total assessments for Halifax were also significantly lower in 1334 than the manorial vills in the fertile lowland around Wakefield, where arable farming had been more extensively practised since the eleventh century, and the older textile producing centres of the county such as Ripon. Halifax was also slow to develop as a commercial centre, unlike neighbouring Elland, which having acquired a market charter during the reign of Edward II (1307–27) paid almost as much in property taxation in 1334 as Halifax. However, incidental evidence in the manorial records of tolls and penalties imposed for the concealment of forestallers suggests that Halifax was beginning to emerge as an unlicensed marketing centre for its periphery during this period.[37]

Both Halifax and its neighbouring communities suffered a severe setback as a result of the Black Death, a catastrophic pandemic spread by fleas and rats, which reached England from Asia in June 1348. Conservative estimates suggest a mortality rate of 33 to 40 per cent in Sowerby and Warley from the deadly bubonic plague, which had engulfed virtually the whole of the British Isles by December 1349. It resulted in an estimated death rate nationally of 30 to 45 per cent and has been designated the worst disease in recorded history. It has been calculated that in the upper Calder Valley 40 to 50 per cent of land holdings were vacated by plague victims in 1349–50, when land clearance also came to an abrupt halt. In Halifax itself, plague claimed the lives of two successive vicars, Thomas Gaytington and Richard Ovenden, within the space of two months in 1349, whilst in Sussex the Black Death also claimed the lives of Lewes's prior, sub-prior and third prior, contributing to the economic problems of the priory during the fourteenth century, which would have also resonated in Halifax. Indeed, in Halifax as in England as a whole, during the Black Death up to half the people died and 'it took two centuries before the country reached the same number of inhabitants again'.[38]

Although lacking any explicit references to the plague, the Wakefield Court Rolls may nonetheless be interpreted as revealing implicitly the devastating impact of Black

Medieval grave cover, south porch, Halifax Parish Church, c. 1150. A pair of cropper's shears inscribed alongside the elongated calvary cross on the tombstone provides the earliest surviving evidence of the textile industry in the parish of Halifax. The shears were used for trimming the surface of the woollen cloth after the cloth had been fulled. During the later medieval period Halifax emerged as a finishing centre for the local woollen industry.
(Photograph: J. G. Washington)

Table 2.1 Lay Subsidy Returns, 1334 and 1379

	1334		1379	
Halifax and Heptonstall	11s.	0d.	12s.	8d.
Sowerby and Soyland	16s.	0d.	12s.	8d.
Warley	16s.	0d.	8s.	0d.
Midgley	13s.	0d.	7s.	4d.
Wadsworth	16s.	0d.	13s.	0d.
Stansfield	16s.	0d.	13s.	0d.
Langfield	14s.	0d.	7s.	4d.
Wakefield	120s.	0d.	95s.	8d.

Sources: B. Jennings, *Pennine Valley* (Smith Settle, Otley: 1992), p. 42; R. E. Glasscock, *The Lay Subsidy of 1334* (British Academy, Oxford University Press, Oxford: 1975), pp. 388–90, 394; J. Lister and J. H. Ogden, *Poll Tax (Lay Subsidy), 1379* (Halifax Antiquarian Society, Halifax: 1906), p. 39.

Death within the manor of Wakefield. Dr Helen Jewell has argued that the premature termination of the 1348–49 roll with the court of 14 July 1349 together with the devising of complicated arrangements for remainder and reversion possibly signified 'a very active apprehension of impending bereavements'. At Halifax, tourns, courts of record, were held in January, May and November 1349 and in May and October 1350, but there was only one in the following year on 25 July 1351, and in Brighouse none at all, before the normal twice-yearly cycle resumed in January and June in 1352. Indeed, Dr Jewell has explained the functional hiatus may have been a consequence of the Black Death paralysing 'the normal life of the Manor'. Moreover, insertions on the membranes of this court roll may also reflect an abnormally high mortality toll including John Brounson of Shelf, where at a tourn in January 1350 at Brighouse, it was presented direfully that the entire 'vill of Shelf is dead'. Jewell also speculated that it may well have been plague which carried off the first vicar of Wakefield, Thomas de Drayton, within a month of his institution on 21 June 1349. It may also have accounted for abandoned holdings such as those presented to the court held at Wakefield on 16 September 1350 by the tenants of Warley where it was complained that 'as much land lies waste and uncultivated there as used to render yearly 48s 2d', whilst the tenants of Hipperholme presented that 'as much land lies likewise as used to render 55s 10 3/4d'. Dr Constance Fraser, introducing the edition of the Wakefield Court Rolls for 1350–52, noted that the 'rhythm of the courts' was not resumed until June 1352 and attributed unequivocally the continuing disruption in the functioning of the manorial courts to the impact of the plague, which 'had paralysed the normal life of the manor', with courts not being held at their accustomed times, debts not being settled, holdings being abandoned and labourers seeking work away from home. In December 1351 the land of Thomas Robuck in Warley, having lain uncultivated for two years, was transferred to William Judson for life and to his heirs for a rent reduced from 4s. 5d. a year to 3s. 4d.[39]

There is also incontrovertible evidence in the manorial rolls of a migration of labour from the parish in 1352, in contravention of the Statute of Labourers of 1351, empowering justices to enforce wage levels customary before the plague and forbidding contract workers to leave their employment prematurely before their contract expired. At the tourn held at Halifax on 5 June 1352 the vill of Skircoat presented that Thomas, Margery and Cecilia Wassher 'are servants and will not serve in the vill or parish where they belong but have gone away against the ordinance'. Similarly, the vill of Ovenden presented that Thomas de Kent, a servant, would not serve in the neighbourhood and the vill of Sowerby presented five women and one man for seeking work outside the area. Moreover, Halifax, like the other Calderdale settlements, appears to have recovered slowly from the impact of plague in the second half of the fourteenth century, when a return of 'the great pestilence' in 1361–62 claimed the life of another vicar of Halifax, John Stamford, and further plague epidemics in 1369 and 1375 also took their toll. Estimates of population derived from the lay subsidy returns and an early rental suggest a mere 220 souls resident in Halifax by 1379, rising to perhaps 313 by 1439, though demographic data derived from the lay subsidy returns may not be totally reliable on account of evasion. However, the 1379 return does specify the comparative payments made by Halifax and its neighbouring vills, revealing that Halifax's total payment of 11s. was lower than Northowram (17s.), Stansfield and Wadsworth (each 16s.) Stainland (15s.), Midgley, Ovenden and Shelf (each 13s.) and, further afield, Wakefield (120s.), Leeds (73s.), Bradford (20s.), Almondbury (16s.) and Huddersfield (13s.4d.).[40]

Moreover, the village community appears to have contained few wealthy residents and manifested very little status differentiation within its social structure. Most Halifax women, for example, brewed their own ale at home, as the manorial records show many suffering penalties for doing so in contravention of statutory regulations. In 1379 none of the Halifax taxpayers was valued at more than a groat, the lowest levy in this graduated poll tax assessment, although only one beggar was granted exemption. Richard Robertson, lessee of the manorial fulling mill; John Milner, the tenant of the corn mill; and Robert Lister, the sole dyer within the town authorised by the lord of the manor, were all taxed at the same level as the rest of the non-mendicant inhabitants. Moreover, of the thirty-three tenants listed in a rental of 1439, no fewer than fifteen have been identified in the manorial rolls as serving terms of office as constable. The rental also reveals that one of the most substantial tenants in the village in 1439, Richard Peck, a silversmith, actually resided at Owram Hall in the neighbouring township of Southowram. The manorial tenant paying the highest rent in 1439 was Richard Lister, who held the property rented by Robert Lister in 1379, together with a number of other properties, including the pinfold, a compound for stray animals. His son and brother leased shares in the fulling mill at North Bridge, where the family dyed cloth.[41]

Archaeological excavation of late-medieval housing sites in Halifax reveals predominantly simple, low-walled, one-roomed, open-hearthed, single-storeyed accommodation, built with timber, stone, rubble and clay. These dwellings are in marked contrast to the spacious, late-medieval, timber-framed yeomen clothier aisled houses situated outside the urban township, but within the rural parish of Halifax, densely concentrated in the upper Calder Valley in Wadsworth, Warley, Sowerby and Ovenden, with their massive timber-and-plaster firehoods, king-post trusses and the housebody open from the ground to the roof. There are no finer surviving examples of such homes in England than these, apart from the Wealden houses of the prosperous yeomanry of Kent, confirming the view that living standards within Halifax itself were generally inferior to those of yeomen clothiers residing within its rural periphery. The predominance of northern gritty-wares among the pottery fragments recovered from the excavations of Halifax housing for this period further reinforces this impression of a lack of conspicuous consumption in Halifax itself.[42]

Since traces of the fabric of the Anglo-Norman Church at Halifax have survived, there has been a greater consensus about the post-conquest history of the largest stone building in Halifax throughout this period. However, there is no specific reference to a church at Halifax in William the Conqueror's otherwise seemingly exhaustive Domesday Survey of 1086, although there are references to priests and church buildings in unspecified locations in the Manor of Wakefield, which, it has been argued, may have included Halifax. By the early twelfth century the former royal manor of Wakefield had come into the possession of the Warenne Earls of Surrey, one of the most influential and wealthy Norman families who settled in England, possibly granted by Henry I for the second earl William's prowess in the Battle of Tenchebrae (1106), though Alfred Ellis insisted that it was granted to the first earl William de Warenne 'probably after the Conqueror's death, when he aided William Rufus and no doubt assisted him at the siege of Pevensey Castle, where he was also rewarded with his earldom'.[43]

Rising from small beginnings, the family had achieved recognition in Normandy in 1052–54 when William de Warenne had earned Duke William's gratitude and been rewarded with the confiscated castle of Mortemer together with extensive surrounding lands including possessions in the region of Bellencombre and Dieppe. William de Warenne had fought at the Battle of Hastings and subsequently played a key role in the defence of the Anglo-Norman kingdom. By the time of his death in 1088 he had been created first earl of Surrey and held land in no fewer than twelve English counties, making him one of the ten most wealthy landowners in Domesday Book. Between c. 1078 and 1080 William de Warenne endowed a new monastic foundation near his castle at Lewes in Sussex and this resulted in the eventual construction of a new Anglo-Norman Church in Halifax.[44] Denied safe access to Rome as a pilgrimage destination on account of the conflict then raging in northern Italy between empire and papacy in the late eleventh century, William and his wife Gundrada visited the Burgundian abbey of Cluny at Saône-et-Loire, near the Swiss border, which had originated in the Benedictine monastic reform movement of 909, and were impressed with the welcome they received.[45]

Gundrada, William de Warenne's wife, whose impressive, finely crafted black marble tombstone treated with black wax or resin, in a manner possibly copied from techniques used at Cluny, was discovered at Isfield Church in 1787, may well have played an instrumental role, since the inscription on her ornate tombstone refers to her bringing to the English church 'the balm of her goodness'.[46] Although she is no longer thought to have been the daughter of William the Conqueror, as the nineteenth-century Halifax historian John Crabtree suggested, but whose view was effectively challenged later by Sir Charles Clay and Professor D. C. Douglas, she may have had a Flemish brother who was a monk at Cluny.[47] Indeed, the motives of the Warennes have been variously interpreted as gratitude for hospitality received at Cluny where they found 'such great holiness and religion and charity' or as a thanksgiving for the earl's safe deliverance from a stormy channel crossing, as T. W. Hanson suggested, or possibly their desire to reward the Cluniac monks as part of their new-found prosperity, or simply as a result of the impact of the spirituality of the reformed Benedictine monastic community upon them.[48] Like William the Conqueror who founded the church of St Martin de Bello (Battle Abbey) after his victory at Hastings in 1066, his baronage may have sought both to extend the kingdom of God and, as Colin Platt has remarked, reinforce 'their self-esteem in the process'. Consequently, as the surviving foundation charter for the priory explains, William and Gundrada:

Memorial window to Gundrada, wife of William de Warenne, Church of St John the Baptist, Southover, Lewes. (Photograph: J. A. Hargreaves).

for the redemption of our souls, and with the advice and assent of our Lord, William, king of the English, gave to God and to the holy apostles Peter and Paul at the place called Cluny where the lord abbot Hugh presides, the church of St Pancras in the same land of the English with all the things which pertain to it. We asked the Abbot Hugh and all the holy body to give us two, or three, or four holy monks from their holy flock to whom we might give the church, which we had converted from wood to stone, below our castle at Lewes.[49]

The first and always the richest Cluniac house in England, this reformed Benedictine priory enjoyed a growing reputation for the purity of its religious observance and its fresh interpretation of the rule of St Benedict under its saintly abbots Odilo (d. 1049) and Hugh (d. 1109), setting a new standard of religious observance unmatched in the west. 'When men thought of religion', the distinguished medieval historian, Sir Richard Southern remarked, 'they thought of Cluny'.[50]

Tombstone of Gundrada, wife of William de Warenne, Church of St John the Baptist, Southover, Lewes. (Photograph: J. A. Hargreaves)

Indeed, the black-robed Cluniac monks were respected throughout Christendom for their daily sequential recitals from the Bible, their absorption with Christian history, their noble buildings and their standards of religious observance unmatched in the West. The contemporary chronicler William of Malmesbury maintained that 'none excelled it in the piety of its monks, in its hospitality to strangers, and in charity towards all'.[51] Moreover, Southern pronounced their religious piety 'incomparable perhaps in this respect to any form of Christian life developed before or since'.[52]

The successors of William and Gundrada founded other Cluniac priories and granted the sub-manor of Halifax-cum-Heptonstall in the manor of Wakefield, with the advowson for the church at Halifax to the Priory of Lewes some time between 1106 and the issuing of a confirmation charter by William de Warenne, third earl of Surrey, in 1147. There is a degree of uncertainty about the date. Sir Charles Clay has demonstrated that evidence from the charters should be treated with caution because of a tendency for evidence to be falsified by the monastic agents in order to secure the collection of dues to which they believed they were entitled, since monasteries were so frequently in debt. However, the grant has most recently been attributed to the enthusiastic and energetic young second earl William de Warenne. Indeed, Dr Graham Mayhew, historian of Lewes Priory, concluded that 'all the evidence from the Lewes Cartulary suggests that it was not until the 1080s and early 1090s that serious efforts were made to properly endow Lewes and push ahead with the building programme there'. With the first consecration of the Great Church at Lewes, following the completion of its eastern section including the crossing, the easternmost bay of the nave, the cloister and main domestic buildings towards the end of the 1090s, Lewes Priory was poised to assist in the expansion of the Cluniac Order in England.[53]

This was assisted by the restoration of peace to northern England during the reign of Henry I (1100–35), which Professor Judith Green has concluded created the conditions 'for that great flowering of monasticism of the early twelfth century' and for the better integration of the north with the south of his kingdom which Halifax's embryonic association with Lewes Priory demonstrably illustrates. Indeed, prior to 1100 Lewes had only one dependency at Castle Acre, founded by William the second earl of Warenne, c. 1089, but by 1291 there were no fewer than 35 English Cluniac houses, including Robert de Lacy's Pontefract Priory founded in 1090 whose 'grand building', Colin Platt has observed, was almost identical in plan to Lewes. Other Yorkshire churches and their dependencies were also given to Lewes Priory during this period, including those at Conisborough, Wakefield, Dewsbury and Burton. However, a thirteenth-century valuation reveals that the monks of Lewes derived more income from Halifax than they did from any other of their churches and manors. Of the £234 6s. 4d. received by the monks from their Yorkshire churches, £109 6s. 8d. was contributed by Halifax, by far the largest proportion.[54]

Between 1066 and 1154, in an age when the number of monastic houses rose six-fold from 48 to nearly 300 and the number of monks from about 850 to well over 5,000, as C. N. L. Brooke has observed, 'monasteries and monks played a very conspicuous part in the Norman Church' particularly 'among the people at large'.[55] Indeed, the acquisition of an interest in the remote sub-manor of Halifax-cum-Heptonstall provided both a missionary opportunity as well as an administrative challenge for the black-robed Cluniac monks who built a church at Halifax possibly around 1120, in the Romanesque style, which Dr Graham Mayhew has noted was the predominant style of the surviving masonry of Lewes Priory.[56] Moreover, at Halifax, fragments of Romanesque masonry were incorporated into later reconfigurations of the church, notably displaying the characteristic chevron or double chevron carved on ashlar, examples of which remain incorporated into the north wall of the nave and the Holdsworth chapel and elsewhere. Other traces of the Anglo-Norman church, which have survived because of their re-use in later re-building include fragments of string-coursing in the upper part of the north aisle wall; ashlaring in the lower part of the exterior north wall and pilaster buttresses, also in the north wall, with dimensions similar to those surviving at the Norman church at Adel near Leeds. It is possible that the dedication of the church at Halifax to St John the Baptist may have been influenced by practice at Lewes Priory, where monastic records for 1121 refer to a chapel of St John the Baptist within the cemetery of the priory. In 1263 there is a later reference to James de Divona as 'rector of the secular chapel of St John the Baptist, in the court of the Cluniac monastery of Lewes'. The chapel was later moved outside the priory gates and in the fourteenth century became the parish church of St John the Baptist, Southover.[57]

The monks who supervised the building of the church must have arranged for masons to travel to Halifax to work on their church, possibly from York, since the lack of stone building in Halifax during this period would have precluded the use of local masons. To what extent the monks themselves or their prior visited Halifax remains a matter of speculation, with John Lister suggesting that even if it seems unlikely that the prior visited the remote parish 'doubtless some of the monks of St Pancras priory came hither from time to time, and conducted the services in the

The Priory of St Pancras, Southover, near Lewes, East Sussex. (Photograph: J. A. Hargreaves)

church of Halifax and chapels of Elland and Heptonstall'.[58] Professor Frank Barlow, the historian of the Anglo-Norman Church, has observed that 'in mainstream Norman monasticism the influence of Cluny worked towards cultivated piety and devoted service in the choir rather than scholarship of any kind' and it is likely that Cluniac influence on liturgy and devotional singing helped shape worship at Halifax during this period.[59] The church at Halifax was certainly administered by largely absentee rectors appointed by the Warennes in the twelfth and thirteenth centuries. These included such distinguished figures as John Talvace, Hubert Walter and William Champvent. Talvace was appointed rector in 1150 and was the brother-in-law of the third earl, friend of Archbishop Thomas Becket and later Bishop of Poitiers and Archbishop of Lyons. Walter was appointed rector in 1180 and was a capable royal administrator to Richard I, accompanying the king on the Third Crusade in 1190 and on his return after the king's imprisonment raising the ransom for his release, then later serving as Bishop of Salisbury, Archbishop of Canterbury, and Justiciar of England, effectively ruling the country in the king's absence from 1194 to 1198. Champvent, the last rector, was appointed in 1250, and was later consecrated Bishop of Lausanne by Pope Gregory X in 1273.

Their attitude is encapsulated in a letter from Hubert Walter thanking the prior and monks for his appointment to 'the unknown church of Halifax', though John Lister found evidence in the Lewes charters that William Champvent occasionally visited Halifax.[60] The Earls of Warenne, much to the dismay of the monks, continued to appoint their ecclesiastical supporters to the rectory until the monks obtained a papal bull from Alexander IV approved by his predecessor enabling them to appoint a resident vicar for Halifax, and assigning the great tithes (corn, hay, wool and lamb) to the monks as rectors and the small tithes (calves, milk, pigs, geese, foals and bees) to the vicar.[61]

The first vicar of Halifax, Ingelard Turbard, who may have been a former monk at Lewes, was less well known than his eminent predecessors, but undertook to reside in the vicarage provided for him and commenced the rebuilding of the Anglo-Norman church. His installation was celebrated by the Vicar-General of the Archbishop of York and assisted by the rectors of Thornhill, Birstall and Heaton, and three of the black-robed monks of Lewes; a documented example of the continuing active involvement of monks from Lewes in the parish of Halifax. Under Turbard, the rebuilding of the church was begun in the late thirteenth century, and traces of this church are still visible on a section of exterior rough stone walling extending eastwards from the north porch, containing two small lancet windows in the Decorated style (a third window dating from this period was set into a later section of wall to the west of the porch). The economic problems for Lewes Priory resulting from the Black Death were exacerbated by anti-French hostility during the Hundred Years War of 1337 to 1453, due to the imposition of penal taxes on alien priories and the confiscation of their revenues. In 1351 Lewes Priory received a charter of denization making the priory, originally a French foundation, English. This was purchased by transferring the advowsons to the crown, thereby giving the crown the right to appoint clergymen to the churches in Yorkshire, Cambridgeshire and Norfolk that belonged 'to the prior and convent of Lewes on condition of being treated as denizens'. In 1480 a Papal Bull finally freed Lewes Priory from Cluny, the first English house to gain its independence. Consequently, from the late 1290s until the mid-fifteenth century, Lewes Priory was rarely free from debt. Financial difficulties led to a decline in the number of monks at Lewes from over 100 in 1240 to 40 in 1294, the same number in 1381, falling further to 29 in 1534. These changes, together with the loss of patronage following the demise of the de Warenne line in 1347, must have impacted on the degree of contact between Lewes Priory and Halifax, and also inhibited further redevelopment of the fabric of the church until the mid-fifteenth century. There is, however, evidence in the Wakefield Manorial Court Rolls revealing that an intriguingly precise quantity of 1,577 shingles (which possibly refers here, given the precise quantity specified, to rectangular wooden tiles rather than pebbles) being utilised for major repairs to the roof of Halifax Parish Church in 1352, a century before its major refurbishment.[62]

However, at both the churches of the manor of Halifax-cum-Heptonstall there were visual reminders of the association with Lewes Priory and its inaugural lay patrons the de Warenne earls of Surrey, as there were elsewhere in Yorkshire at Fishlake and Sandal Magna.[63] At Heptonstall the de Warenne arms were carved in a prominent position on the easternmost pier of the north aisle, from where the rood screen once extended across the church, whilst at Halifax a fall of plaster in 1874 revealed that the chancel had once depicted the distinctively chequered patterned de Warenne arms, even if their colours were identified as blue and silver-white rather than blue and gold by the Victorian antiquary F. A. Leyland, who recorded the discovery. The outline of a youthful saintly figure was also revealed, which Dr Graham Mayhew has suggested may have been a depiction of St Pancras, together with a mitred figure with a crozier, identified by Leyland as an archbishop and by Mayhew as possibly a prior of Lewes, who had been granted the use of pontificals in 1480.[64]

A 1439 rental for the township of Halifax, indicating the allotment of strips or selions in the arable fields, reveals that by the early fifteenth century open-field arable cultivation was practised in the town fields. By the late fifteenth century, however, Halifax was gaining a growing reputation for the making and marketing of textiles. The ulnager's accounts, that is the records of fees paid to crown officials for measuring and sealing finished cloth, reveal that by 1469 the parish of Halifax was second only to Ripon in cloth production, contributing almost one third of the West Riding's total output of cloth. By 1475, Halifax had even outstripped Ripon, producing more cloth than any other parish in the West Riding, five times the output of Leeds and eight times the output of Bradford. Moreover, the provision of spacious workshop and storage facilities in the aisled houses of yeomen clothiers in the Halifax area from the second half of the fifteenth century confirms the development of an organised system of textile production from the late fifteenth century.

The explanation of this success has been traditionally attributed to cheaper labour costs in the newer Pennine industrial centres, which were not subject to guild regulation; an abundance of fast-flowing, soft water for fulling; and the evolution of a highly cost-effective dual economy of textiles and farming in the Calder Valley in the late fifteenth century. The Wakefield Court Rolls of 1286 and 1296, and other contemporary sources refer respectively to fullers, namely Thomas Walker of Warley, Richard Walker of Sowerby Adam Walker of Hebden Bridge and Richard Nelleson of Heptonstall, granting the latter the fifteen-year lease of a site to build a fulling mill. These developments also coincided with a more favourable economic climate for cloth exports following the Treaty of Utrecht in 1474 and peace with France in 1475. By this period, it appears that Halifax had become a centre for cloth finishing for a dependent rural periphery: no fewer than eight out of seventeen Halifax cloth tradesmen indicted at Lancaster in 1467, following an affray in Burnley, were engaged in fulling. Indeed, Jeremy Goldberg has argued that at the same time York cloth 'may even have begun to lose ground' within the city's own markets, whilst Gerald Harriss has concluded that:

> York passed its zenith shortly after 1400 as immigration fell and its exports of medium-grade cloths to the Baltic suffered setbacks; but the end of its prosperity came after the mid-century with the Hanseatic crisis and the emergence of cloth-making centres in the West Riding, notably Bradford and Halifax.[65]

Indeed, the shears depicted on a medieval grave cover alongside an elongated calvary cross, dating from the mid-twelfth century and now displayed in the south porch of Halifax Minster, have been identified as cloth dressing shears, confirming the early emergence of Halifax as a cloth finishing centre and perhaps also the prosperity of the cloth dresser whose tomb it covered. Ultimately, York lost its 'pre-eminent position as a centre of textile production and distribution at some point in the middle to later fifteenth century' when West Riding clothiers were 'beginning to bypass York merchants and trade directly with the London merchants'.[66]

Besides cloth production, other forms of economic activity were in evidence within Halifax's rural periphery. Manorial records and slag deposits provide evidence of a number of medieval iron-working sites in the upper Calder Valley, and coal appears to have been mined for both domestic and industrial purposes from the thirteenth century. In 1274, Richard Nailer was granted permission to dig for coals at Hipperholme 'for forging'. Early fourteenth-century forges were located at Rastrick, Hipperholme and Erringden, and excavation and fieldwork has identified several medieval bloomery sites, including slag found beneath the floor of a late fifteenth-century timber-framed house at Boothtown, Northowram, and as surface deposits at Cinderhills, Siddal and Southowram. An innovative tilt or trip hammer, designated an 'oliver' in the manorial roll, was in operation in Warley in 1349. There is also evidence of a stone quarrying industry concentrated on the township of Northowram in the fourteenth and fifteenth centuries.[67]

This increasing economic activity stimulated the development of Halifax as a commercial centre in the late fifteenth century, albeit, as Bernard Jennings has remarked, remaining 'no more than a modest village, which had the mother church of a very large parish and a weekly market', if lacking, unlike neighbouring Elland, a market charter, but with a market developing during the first half of the fourteenth century. Hence the records of 'tolls of Halifax' and penalties imposed on the township for concealing forestallers, traders who bought privately goods which should have been bought in the market. Indeed, the reference in the Lancaster indictments of 1467 to four tailors, three butchers, two glovers, two smiths, a mercer, weaver and cobbler in addition to seventeen cloth tradesmen, provides a snapshot of the commercial life of Halifax by the second half of the fifteenth century. It reveals considerable commercial expansion since 1439 when a town rental specified one solitary shop, though both documents probably fail to reflect the full extent of commercial activity in Halifax in their respective periods. By 1475 ulnager accounts record that John Lister, recognising that the increased economic activity within the parish had implications for Halifax's commercial development, proclaimed the 'fortunes of the place were to all intents and purposes made'. Modern research has tended to confirm Lister's conclusion.[68]

The emergence of Halifax as a commercial centre during the medieval period also owed much to its development as a centre of manorial and ecclesiastical administration. This helped to establish a number of connections between Halifax and its surrounding periphery and indeed beyond. The combined manor of Halifax-cum-Heptonstall, a sub-manor of the royal manor of Wakefield, appears to have been granted by Henry I (1100–35) in 1106 to William de Warenne (d. 1138), second earl of Surrey, whose distinctive gold and blue chequered arms were later incorporated into the Halifax corporate seal. The sub-manor was later granted, with the advowson for the church, to Lewes Priory some time between 1106 and the issuing of a confirmation by William de Warenne, third earl of Surrey (d. 1148), in 1147. The principal seat of the earls of Warenne, who held the manor of Wakefield until the fourteenth century when it reverted to the crown, was located at Sandal Castle, and the nearby town and borough of Wakefield became the centre of manorial administration. However, the Wakefield manorial court travelled on circuit twice a year, usually in May and October. After 1274, the Wakefield court rolls record that it sat in Halifax at the Moot Hall, situated on Nelson Street on the northern perimeter of Halifax Parish Church and possibly part of a larger complex of buildings until its demolition in the 1950s, where it not only dealt with the administration of the demesne lands in the upper Calder Valley, but also held court leet or tourn sessions, examining cases of criminal infringement of statutory or manorial law. These latter sessions, presided over by the earl's bailiff, heard cases involving tenants, both servile and free, of both the manor and the sub-manor. Territorial administration within the sub-manor was dealt with in separate sessions at the Moot Hall, presided over by the proctor of the monastic lords of the rectorial manor. In addition, the earls of Warenne, as lords of the manor of Wakefield, enjoyed infangthief jurisdiction, that is the right to carry out summary trial and execution of thieves caught in the bailiwick of Sowerbyshire. The establishment

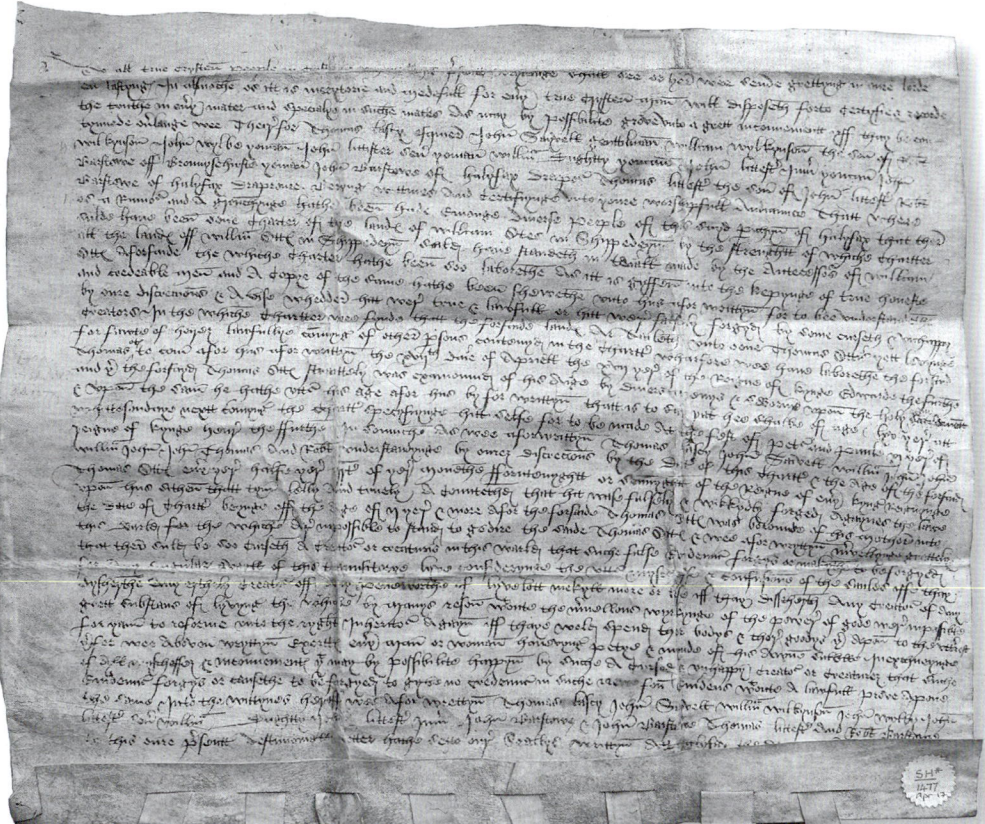

An early testimonial letter in English relating to the estate of William Otes of Shibden Hall, 1477. William Otes, the proprietor of Shibden Hall in 1477, was a grandson of William Otes, a prosperous Halifax cloth merchant, who built the house and farm in Southowram around 1420. Usually medieval legal documents were written in Latin and this is one of the earliest legal documents in English to have survived in Calderdale. Preserved among the title deeds of the Shibden Hall estate, it was written on 17 April 1477 and illustrates how questions affecting the title to real estate were settled in the late fifteenth century. The document has attached to it the seals of eight of the referees, all of whom were prominent residents in the Halifax area during this period. They included John Savile of Southowram, gentleman, Thomas Lacy and other substantial yeomen and tradesmen. (Photograph: West Yorkshire Archive Service, Calderdale)

of a prototype guillotine, or gibbet, as it was known locally, gained notoriety for the town, with some sixty-three recorded executions between 1286 and 1650. An apocryphal beggars' litany prayed: 'From Hull, Hell and Halifax, good Lord deliver us', linking the dreaded notoriety of Hull's harsh workhouse with the horrifying severity of Halifax's gibbet. The regular meetings of the manorial courts, the occasional executions, and the obligation for demesne tenants to pay suit at the manorial corn and fulling mills provided opportunities for manorial tenants and members of their families to visit Halifax, thereby developing connections between the town and its immediate periphery.[69]

Although Halifax remained an outpost of manorial administration throughout the medieval period, by the twelfth century the township had also become the religious centre of a vast parish extending westwards across the upper Calder Valley from Rastrick in the east as far as Stansfield and the Lancashire border in the west, containing 23 townships. Encompassing 118 square miles it was the largest parish in the historic county of Yorkshire, though slightly less extensive than the neighbouring parish of Whalley, which covered 170 square miles and considerably smaller than the parish of Simonburn in Northumberland, which extended over 249 square miles. The monks of Lewes had built the Norman church at Halifax around 1120. The church was administered largely by absentee rectors appointed by the Warennes in the twelfth and thirteenth centuries. The monks eventually obtained a papal bull permitting the appropriation of the rectory and the creation of a vicarage, which assigned the great tithes to the monks as rectors and the small tithes to the vicar, appointed in 1272, who undertook to reside in the vicarage provided for him, thereby enhancing and providing a more localised focus for ecclesiastical administration.[70]

Reviewing the evidence for both agricultural and industrial development in the upper Calder Valley, Nigel Smith has concluded that whilst evidence for partible inheritance remains elusive by the end of the thirteenth century, tenurial custom cannot be dismissed entirely as a subsequent economic driver of textile growth, since property provided abundant opportunities for rental income, which contributed to the augmentation of both farming and textile incomes. The historian of Lewes Priory, Dr Graham Mayhew, having examined contracts which survive for the period from 1286 to 1321 and isolated fourteenth-century accounts detailing annual income and expenditure from the important Cluniac estates centred on Halifax in Yorkshire and Melton Mowbray in Leicestershire, has recognised their economic value at least up to the late thirteenth century. His estimate is that taken together, the priory's Yorkshire lands represented approximately one eighth of the priory's revenues during a period when the priory's Sussex flocks numbered over 10,000 sheep and produced roughly 50 sacks of wool yearly. In the year 1360–61, according to the priory's procurator, £76 4s. 4d. of the £146 14s. 7d. revenue from the priory's Yorkshire estates, amounting to over half of the total, derived from Halifax and Heptonstall, where the prior of Lewes was both rector and lord of the manor. Rents of assize from the manors of Halifax and Heptonstall were worth a total of £10 13s. 0½d., whilst tithes of corn accounted for £48 2s. 4d. Tithes of sheep and wool were worth a further £15 8s. 0d. Moreover, Lewes Priory contracts included the largest single contract for the supply of wool entered into by any English monastery amounting to 863 sacks, roughly four times the quantity recorded for either of the two largest Cistercian wool producers, Fountains and Rievaulx.[71]

Indeed, at Halifax in 1366–67 more than three sacks of wool from the priory's

Halifax Moot Hall. The Wakefield Court Rolls confirm that meetings of the courts of the manor of Wakefield and sub-manor of Halifax-cum-Heptonstall were held in the Halifax Moot Hall from the late-thirteenth century. The building, which was originally timber-framed, was situated to the north-west of Halifax Parish Church in Nelson Street. During the medieval period, it was surrounded by a large common field called the Hallynge. From at least 1906, it was being used as a joiner's shop. It was demolished in 1956–7. (Photograph: S. Gee)

tithes were sold for £19 4s. 7½d. Such wealth enhanced both the churches at Heptonstall, where a carving of the de Warenne coat of arms, adopted also by the priory, still marks the position of the medieval rood screen on the easternmost pier of the north aisle in the now abandoned ruined church. Moreover, at Halifax a fall of plaster in 1874 revealed that the chancel had been decorated in the de Warenne colours and with the outline of a youthful saintly figure, possibly a depiction of St Pancras, together with a mitred figure with a crozier, possibly a prior of Lewes. Indeed, Roger Dodsworth, the Jacobean antiquary, also recorded surviving memorial windows to fifteenth-century priors of Lewes at Halifax Parish Church, including John Daniell (d. 1460), who is depicted in a window on the south side of the church. However, by the fifteenth century when the value of the estates was waning, the antiquary John Watson suggests that the central tower, begun in 1450, was paid for by several of the more powerful local landowners, including the Lacy and Savile families. Watson goes on to suggest that the great east window was financed by Thomas Wilkinson, vicar from 1439 to 1441. Mayhew, citing local tradition, also proposes that Wilkinson may have been the real driving force behind the initiative for the rebuilding of the church on a grand scale during a period when the priory's finances were faltering. But the priory's influence is also evident in other

Halifax Gibbet. During the period from 1286 to 1650 some 63 felons were beheaded on the Halifax Gibbet, a prototype guillotine, under the infangthief jurisdiction of the lords of the manor of Wakefield in the bailiwick of Sowerbyshire. By 1586, according to William Camden, Halifax had become famous 'by reason of a law there whereby they behead straight-ways whosoever are taken in stealing'. This engraving shows the blade about to be released by a horse tethered to the scaffold. The original blade preserved at Bankfield Museum is currently displayed at the Piece Hall. In 1974 a replica of the scaffold was erected on the original site of the executions in Gibbet Street, incorporating stones from the original platform. (Photograph: J. A. Hargreaves)

contemporary features, most notably a carving of a monk at prayer in the fifteenth-century sedilia and miserere stalls in the chancel which Mayhew suggests more likely accommodated senior visitors from Lewes rather than the more unlikely explanation that they were derived from the Cistercian Kirkstall Abbey after the Dissolution of the Monasteries in 1536–40.[72]

By the late thirteenth century at least two parochial chapelries existed within the parish at Heptonstall and Elland, where St Mary's Church still treasures surviving stained glass from the early fourteenth century, with chaplains appointed and paid by the vicar, and two other chapels-of-ease were created within the parish in the second half of the fifteenth century at Ripponden and Luddenden, with perpetual curates appointed by the vicar but paid by the chapelry. However, the requirement for attendance at the parish church for baptisms, marriages and burials and the celebration of Mass on all feast days, the payment of customary dues, alms and tithes to the mother church, and the development of fairs associated with the patronal festival of St John the Baptist, established further connections between Halifax and its periphery.[73] By the mid-fourteenth century, Halifax, Mayhew maintains, was the centre for the administration of Lewes Priory's Yorkshire properties, which comprised the manors and rectories of Halifax and Heptonstall, and the rectories of Braithwell and Conisbrough, together with various ecclesiastical pensions, rents

Left to right: Henry Raphael Oddy's 1906 sketch of the former meeting place of the medieval manorial court, west of Halifax Parish Church, with Briggs' Joiner's Shop in the foreground (Calderdale Libraries); housing in Church Street, Halifax, 1930s, south of the church (*Halifax Courier*); the Ring o' Bells Inn, 2011, on the south of the church (G. Sutcliffe).

and tithes. Moreover, Roger de Fryston's Halifax accounts show that he held courts in Halifax and Heptonstall in 1381–82, and collected the tithes of lambs and wool in Halifax, Heptonstall and Elland, forwarding the proceeds to Lewes.[74]

At Halifax, where the priory held both the manor and the rectory, a surviving deed from the time of the surrender of the priory in 1537 estimates the approximate extent of the manor of Halifax and its appurtenances. They encompass some 40 messuages, 20 cottages, 50 gardens, two dovecotes, 2,000 acres of land, 500 acres of meadow, 2,000 acres of pasture, 1,000 acres of woodland, 2,000 acres of moorland and heath and £130 of rent in Halifax, Heptonstall, Sowerby, Warley, Ovenden, Midgley, Wadsworth, Langfield, Erringden, Rishworth, Norland, Barkisland, Stainland, Elland, Greetland, Rastrick, Fixby, Toothill, Brighouse, Southowram, Northowram, Hipperholme, Shelf, Skircoat, Stansfeld and Clifton, together with land situated further afield. The surviving fourteenth-century accounts also mention a tithe barn at Elland, a mill at Heptonstall, a watermill called the Old Mill and a fulling mill at Halifax. Moreover, at Halifax the Moot Hall and its courthouse survived until the mid-twentieth century. There was also a grammar school adjoining the churchyard, suppressed at the Reformation, and probably also tithe barns.[75]

Manorial and ecclesiastical exigencies also contributed to the development of a route network centred upon Halifax, which further stimulated the commercial development of the town. The Wakefield Gate, sections of which have been preserved as a footpath, descended over the shoulder of Beacon Hill and crossed Clark Bridge into Halifax. It provided links for the major manorial holdings in the upper Calder Valley, which included the important hunting grounds and cattle farms in Erringden Park, with the commercial and administrative centre of the manor at Wakefield. The road also formed part of an important trans-Pennine

The Wakefield Gate at Dark Lane between Hipperholme and Halifax photographed by W. B. Crump in 1924. This surviving section of the medieval route from Wakefield to Halifax followed the line of the most gradual incline up the ridge from Hipperholme to Halifax, descending into Halifax over the shoulder of Beacon Hill down Old Bank via Bank Bottom and Clark Bridge. The route continued past the Parish Church and through Woolshops, the Shambles and Old Market, carrying traffic from the manorial estates in Wakefield to the upper Calder Valley, including hunting parties destined for the deer park in Erringden. As the textile trade developed supplies of raw wool and finished cloth were carried by pack-horses along the same route, which was also used by Sir Thomas Fairfax's troops after their disastrous defeat at the battle of Adwalton Moor in 1643. Condemned by Daniel Defoe in the early eighteenth century as 'so steep, so rugged, and sometimes too slippery' and 'exceedingly troublesome and dangerous' it was eventually replaced by new turnpike roads in 1741 and 1824. (Photograph: H. Armitage)

route, in particular for the transportation of salt from Cheshire to Yorkshire. There are also numerous references in the manorial rolls to kirkgates, early routes to the parish church, from such outlying townships as Hipperholme, Northowram, Southowram and Shelf, demonstrating the important influence of the church on the medieval road system. One route from Coley, still called Kirk Lane, joined the Wakefield Gate south of Hipperholme, and other routes from Hipperholme and Southowram crossed the Hebble by Clark Bridge, which derived its name from the constant traffic of clergy visiting the parish church during this period.[76]

Archaeologists now believe that the road and field layout of the medieval settlement of Halifax probably pre-dated the Norman Conquest, but how did the physical appearance of Halifax change in the period between 1066 and 1500? Settlement at Halifax followed an east-west axis, extending from the early focus of settlement around the church ascending the hillside to Cow Green, the likely site of Halifax Green. The open fields were laid out to the north and south of this axis. Tofts and rented tenements were built along the highway, each with a permanently allocated croft to the rear, and the open field beyond. Archaeological excavations between 1970 and 1975 revealed housing of late thirteenth-century construction on the south side of Northgate behind Woolshops. This was of high density and unplanned, and perhaps represents a period of late thirteenth-century expansion. However, this housing appears to have been demolished around 1300, perhaps following destruction by fire, when the precursors of Wade Street, Ann Street and Gaol Lane were laid out in typical grid plan development characteristic of growing settlements elsewhere during this period, such as Wakefield. After 1350, however, the village contracted dramatically, almost certainly as a consequence of the Black Death, and the new streets of tenements were abandoned. However, as Juliet Barker has shown, whilst York, Beverley and Scarborough were the northernmost manifestations of the Peasants' Revolt in the summer of 1381, its impact upon Halifax and other West Riding towns was less pronounced.[77]

Unfortunately, insufficient documentary evidence exists to corroborate the archaeological indicators of urban expansion in the late thirteenth century. However, taxation returns from the late fourteenth century, a rental of 1439 and a sixteenth-century manuscript recording the early reminiscences of John Waterhouse of Shibden (who died in 1540, aged 97) reveal a relatively small settlement. Waterhouse recalled 'a few straggling tenements built of wood, wattles and thatch', comprising some 32 houses, 45 rented dwellings including one cottage, nestling around the church, vicarage and market place, and extending westwards towards Cow Green. Robert Otes had a shop and some land at the west end of the churchyard, which had only recently been taken from the waste. The Moot Hall, a small timber-framed building, occupied a site to the north-west of the church, surrounded by the large common field called the Hallynge. The manorial fulling mill was situated further north, near North Bridge, and the manorial corn mill a short distance downstream, near Clark Bridge. The Mulcture Hall, where tolls were collected for corn ground at the mill, probably stood on a site to the north-east of the church, and the residence of the bailiff was situated east of the Hebble Brook at Bailey

Halifax Parish Church of St John the Baptist, photographed from the east in 1994. Halifax Parish Church has been described by the architectural historian Peter Ryder as 'without a doubt the largest and most impressive of the late medieval churches in the county'. A sizeable early medieval church of probable cruciform construction was remodelled in phases in the perpendicular style during the fifteenth century, commencing with the rebuilding of the nave in 1437 and culminating in the construction of the huge west tower between 1450 and 1480. Sir George Gilbert Scott and his son John Oldrid Scott undertook a major restoration of the building in 1879. (Photograph: J. G. Washington)

Hall. Two of the common fields, Blakelegynge and Southfeld, lay to the south of the church, the former in grass and the latter, accessed via Southgate, under the plough in 1439. The Neytherfeld, another large unenclosed common field, extended down to the 'miln-goit' and the Hebble Brook, while the Northfeld and Sydelynge lay on rising ground to the north-west.

Later in the fifteenth century, as cloth production began to expand within the parish, the market appears to have been moved westwards to a new site away from the church. The church itself, like contemporary East Anglian churches, for example Blythburgh in Suffolk, was considerably enlarged in a magnificent perpendicular rebuilding, presumably in order to offer more spacious accommodation for the growing population of the parish. One architectural historian has claimed that it is 'without a doubt the largest and most impressive of the late medieval churches in the county' and it was certainly the most prominent building in Halifax by the end of the fifteenth century. The late thirteenth- and early fourteenth-century construction had apparently re-utilised considerable amounts of stone from the earlier Anglo–Norman building, including some chevron-moulded voussoirs, which are scattered around the building, but the fifteenth-century rectangular remodelling left little evidence of the fourteenth-century cruciform church, apart from a three-bay length of masonry in the north wall of the north aisle. Rebuilding of the nave appears to have commenced in 1437 and the construction of the huge west tower was completed over a thirty-year period from mid-century: the elderly John Waterhouse, later recalled that he had 'with many more children stood upon the first stone of the steeple'.[78]

By 1500, then, Halifax, while little more than a village in size and population, was developing into an embryonic medieval town capable of supporting, with its rural periphery, a huge parish church. Moreover, it was beginning to display some of the characteristics of an urban centre in a period otherwise widely charac-terised by urban stagnation or decline. No more than two new urban formations of the fifteenth century, Bedale in the north east and Halifax in the south west, augmented the twenty-three urban settlements of varying size and status extending in a 'roughly crescent-shaped array' from 'the south and over to the west then northeast', which had emerged across Yorkshire between the tenth and the fourteenth centuries. George Sheeran, in a study of the emergence of urban culture in medieval Yorkshire, has argued that notwithstanding their apparent lack of borough status in 1500, both Bedale and Halifax 'seem to have changed from agricultural villages into towns' during the fifteenth century. Sheeran accounts for the emergence of Halifax as an urban centre as a 'response to increasing industrial activity, becoming a centre not only of wool-textile production, but also of wool and woollen cloth marketing' and maintains that 'although the town possessed the right to hold a market and fair, this was by prescription rather than charter, and there was no form of separate municipal government'.[79] Yet, he concludes, that within the context of Yorkshire's limited urban development in the Middle Ages 'by 1500 Halifax had become, along with Leeds and Wakefield', recognisably one of 'the principal towns' of medieval West Yorkshire.

Although documentary evidence for the settlement of Halifax only appears in the early twelfth century, archaeological and place-name evidence suggests intermittent occupation of the site and its hinterland from prehistoric times and continuity of settlement from before the Norman Conquest. During the twelfth and thirteenth centuries, Halifax emerged as a centre of ecclesiastical and manorial adminis-tration and increasingly during the later medieval period as a commercial and cloth finishing centre for the dispersed settlements of its rural periphery. However, for most of the period up to 1500 Halifax remained a Pennine backwater, due partly to the remoteness of its geographical location and partly to the devastating impact of the Black Death and other epidemics after 1349. Moreover, unlike Bradford and even neighbouring Elland, Halifax did not acquire a market charter during this

Pre-Reformation font canopy, Halifax Parish Church, 1981. The fifteenth century font, situated at the west end of the nave, is surmounted by an intricately carved wooden canopy, which originally would have been painted in different colours. Its design incorporates the carved York rose, suggesting that it originated before the accession of the Tudor dynasty in 1485. In 1645 the font was removed by Scottish soldiers, but the canopy was preserved and returned to the church in 1661.
(Photograph: J. G. Washington)

period. Nevertheless, during the second half of the fifteenth century there was evidence of commercial expansion and Halifax became poised to achieve its later regional prominence in the early modern period.

3

'The inhabitants do altogether live by cloth making': Halifax and its hinterland, 1500–1750

Halifax and the regional economy

THE POPULATION of the township of Halifax grew from about 313 in 1439 to an estimated 1050 in 1550; 2,600 by 1566; 4,350 in 1640 and 5,000 in 1743. Moreover, it is also evident that during this period the population of the parish of Halifax, covering a wider area, grew even faster, from about 1,000 in 1439 to an estimated 8,150 by 1550; 12,000 by the 1590s; 20,000 by the 1630s; 19,900 by 1640 and 31,000 by 1743. Indeed, the Halifax township's share of the parish population decreased from nearly one third in the mid-sixteenth century, to barely over one-fifth in the mid-seventeenth century, to around one-sixth in the mid-eighteenth century. This phenomenal population explosion within the parish of Halifax, peaking before it suffered the ravages of civil war and plague, was considerably higher than the national average, especially during the period from 1650 to 1750, but its growth was not uniformly steady. There were setbacks caused, for example, by epidemics of sweating sickness in 1551, typhus fever in 1587 to 1588 and bubonic plague in 1631 and 1645 together with the impact of the Civil Wars on mortality and migration from 1640. Indeed, a study of population trends in Halifax parish has concluded that it would seem that the impact of the Civil War was greater in the parish 'than it was on average for the country', with a decline of over one third from 19,900 to 13,350 in the most recent estimates.[1] But there were also spectacular surges of growth which attracted contemporary comment. The Elizabethan antiquary, William Camden, recalled that some inhabitants of the parish had boasted to him in the early 1580s that the parish population of some 12,000 people amounted to 'more men and women than other living creatures', presumably horses, cows and sheep, whilst the journalist and novelist, Daniel Defoe, recorded in 1725 that the parish population had 'increased one fourth, at least, within the last 40 years'.[2] In addition, analysis of birth and death rates from parish registers from 1539 and patterns of migration from poor law settlement certificates and removal orders suggests that migration into the area rather than natural increase was the principal cause of

Page from the eighteenth-century worsted pattern book of Samuel Hill (1678–1759), master clothier and woollen merchant of Making Place, Soyland, near Halifax, in the West Riding of Yorkshire. The brightly coloured cloth samples were referred to as Figured Amens. They were bound for Italy in 1750 and reflect the extent of Hill's business enterprise and the merchant's pride in his cloth, which he insisted was 'not to be outdone in England by any man'. (Photograph: West Yorkshire Archives, Calderdale)

population growth during the late seventeenth and early eighteenth centuries. Moreover, Nigel Smith's analysis of population estimates for upper Calder Valley townships from 1544 to 1831 and recorded settlements from 1300 to 1800 reveals a predictable decline in new recorded settlements around the time of the Black Death during the second half of the fourteenth century. This was followed by a gradual rise thereafter, climaxing during the seventeenth century, which also saw a surge of building activity as evidenced by large numbers of dated buildings, especially from the 1620s through to the 1720s, with the peak period being the 1630s and the lowest points occurring in the 1640s during the Civil War and in the 1680s. Moreover, fine examples of Pennine vernacular architecture ranging from Upper Cockroft in Rishworth (1607), Marsh Hall in Northowram (1626), Brearley Hall in Midgley (1626) High Sunderland in Northowram (1629). Holdsworth House in Ovenden (1633) and Norland Hall (1634) provide further indicators of rising prosperity at least for some sections of society, most notably those involved in textile production.[3]

This chapter will seek to explain why increasing numbers of migrant workers and their families were attracted to the parish of Halifax after 1500, identifying the key elements within the regional economy and analysing how they contributed to the growth of Halifax as an urban centre for its hinterland. As the parish recovered from the impact of plague and pestilence from the late fifteenth century, it did not return to a precarious medieval agrarian economy but developed a more sustainable dual economy of textiles and farming, while the township of Halifax developed as the commercial and service centre for its increasingly prosperous rural periphery. Both contemporaries and modern historians have professed amazement that a major cloth making industry developed in the bleak inhospitable countryside of the upper Calder Valley, with its relatively poor access to wool supplies and cloth markets. William Camden, writing in 1586, trumpeted the achievement as one of the wonders of the Tudor Age, while a modern historian of Yorkshire, Professor David Hey, writing in 1986, pronounced it 'the Halifax miracle'.[4]

Various environmental, social and economic explanations have long been adduced to account for the astonishingly rapid growth of cloth making from an initially low level in the rural hinterland of Halifax in the late fifteenth and early sixteenth centuries, in contrast to its decline in the older urban centres of the county such as Beverley, Ripon and York. Indeed, the first purpose-built Yorkshire cloth hall was erected at Heptonstall in 1545, trading textile products from distant centres of domestic production such as Saddleworth as well as the Calder Valley. Camden also observed that Halifax's cloth trade was so flourishing that its inhabitants 'greatly enrich their own estates and win praise from all their neighbours'. With its own conveniently located cloth hall modelled upon London's Blackwell Hall, it compared favourably with that of more populous towns by 1500, as evidenced in ulnage accounts recording compulsory payments for cloths made for sale. In 1561, a York corporation minute book recorded ruefully the exodus of the city's weavers to Halifax, Leeds and Wakefield, where they had conveniently-situated 'water mills', a plentiful supply of cheap labour and fuel 'which is in this city very dear and wanting'. The upper Calder Valley, with its higher than average rainfall and precipitous terrain, was particularly well-endowed with soft water for scouring and dyeing, and fast-flowing streams to power the fulling mills, as well as an abundance of peat and timber for fuel. Here, heavy wooden hammers pounded the woven cloth with fuller's earth to bond its fibres together and to clean it. This was the earliest application of mechanisation to the manufacture of woollen cloth, an industry which was otherwise slow to adopt technological innovation.[5]

Moreover, in the remote uplands of Calderdale, entry into the industry was not governed by the restrictive guild regulations which dominated the textile industries of the declining urban centres, and it required relatively little initial capital investment to rent land. It was possible for spinners and weavers with limited capital resources to purchase spinning wheels and looms for use in their own homes, since the cost of such basic equipment was considerably lower than local contemporary average prices for livestock. Labour costs were also cheap, because most of the Calderdale clothiers relied on the labour of their own families, supplemented occasionally by that of apprentices and journeymen. A kersey, the staple cloth of the Halifax area from the fourteenth century, could conveniently be woven in the interval of time between the weekly cloth markets, thus providing a regular income from a small investment in the raw wool, which was purchased in small quantities at the markets from 'broggers' or wool dealers, then spun and woven by the weavers and their families. However, by the seventeenth century, although Halifax was the fourth wealthiest parish in the North of England, Wakefield and Leeds had the considerable advantage of easier access to navigable rivers, whilst Leeds had become a chartered town in 1640.[6]

Historians have also emphasised the significance of demographic, tenurial and psychological factors, operating in conjunction with climate and topography, as explanations for the rapid growth of the textile industry in the upper Calder Valley. Professor Joan Thirsk and others have observed that a flexible system of partible or divisible inheritance developed as an alternative to primogeniture in the remote uplands of the manor of Wakefield. These equitable bequests of land between the surviving sons of customary manorial tenants meant that younger sons remained within the locality after marriage. However, this created a pressure of population on the means of subsistence in an agriculturally unproductive area and stimulated the early development of weaving to supplement family incomes. Moreover, it has also been suggested that the perennial struggle with an intractable environment fostered a spirit of 'unyielding industry', which was further reinforced by the work ethic intrinsic to Puritan preaching during the English Reformation.[7]

Perhaps the most reliable indicator of the timing and pace of the acceleration of industrial production is the steady expansion of fulling capacity in the upper Calder Valley from the early fifteenth century. The rate of expansion quickened from the early sixteenth century, so that by 1640 there were an estimated eighteen to twenty fulling mills in the parish of Halifax benefiting from fast-flowing streams down its steep-sided valleys. An examination of late fifteenth and early sixteenth century taxation returns, manorial records, chantry surveys and the distribution of aisled houses confirms the growing prosperity of parts of the parish and supports the

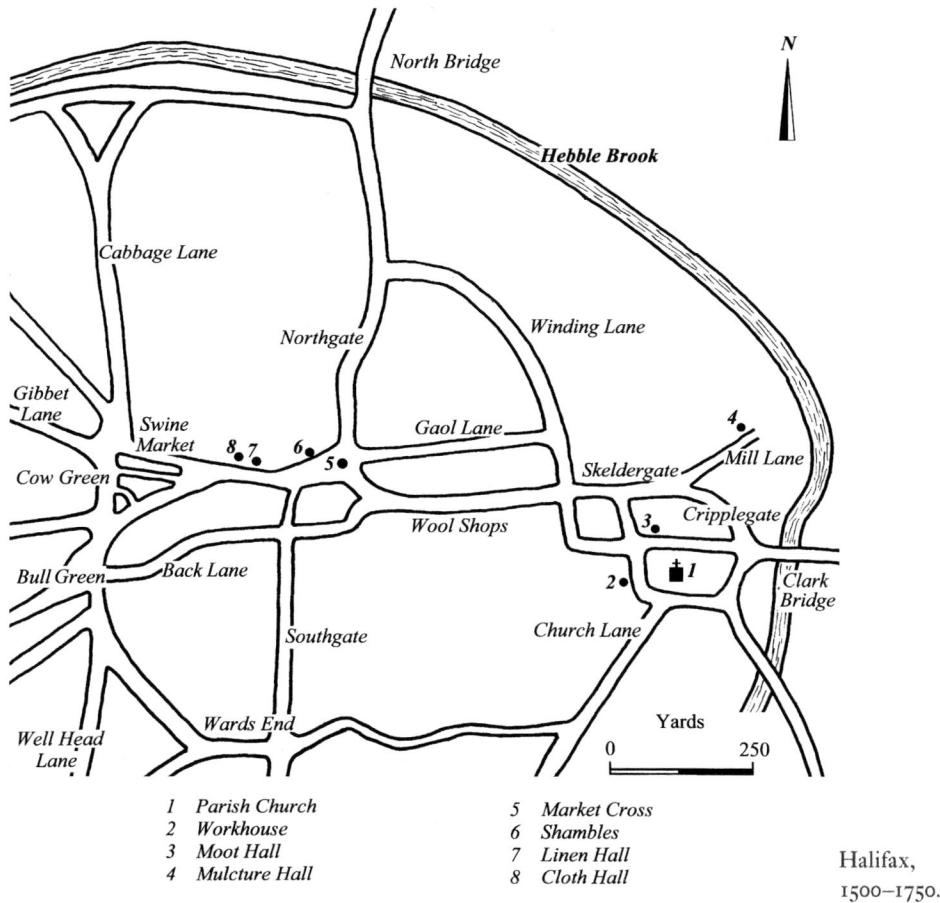

Halifax, 1500–1750.

1	Parish Church	5	Market Cross
2	Workhouse	6	Shambles
3	Moot Hall	7	Linen Hall
4	Mulcture Hall	8	Cloth Hall

proposition of Herbert Heaton, the historian of the Yorkshire woollen and worsted industries, that Halifax parish, rather than anywhere else in Yorkshire, was the stronghold of the textile industry from the fifteenth century onwards. Bequests for the improvement of highways; the rebuilding of bridges in stone; the construction of paved pack-horse causeways; the provision of additional 'free chapels'; the casing of existing timber-framed houses in stone and the building of impressive new stone residences provide further evidence of increasing trade, traffic and prosperity in the Calder Valley during the sixteenth and early seventeenth centuries.[8]

The primary textile products manufactured in the upper Calder Valley during this period were kerseys, cheap coarse narrow woollen cloths used particularly for hose, outer garments and, increasingly from the late seventeenth century, for military uniforms. Wills from the early sixteenth century contain numerous references to textile materials and equipment, by which time the market industry was well established. During the sixteenth century, as the woollen trade of Kersey in Suffolk decayed, the upper Calder Valley became the largest producer of kersey cloths in England, exporting them all over western Europe via the port of Hull.

Occasionally, however, there were complaints about the quality of local cloth, especially as a consequence of overstretching on tenters or mixing short fibre flocks with the longer-fibred wool normally used. For example, in 1533 a commission set up by Henry VIII to enquire into this malpractice led to the fining of 282 clothiers from the parish of Halifax.[9]

When the national economy entered a period of relative decline about half way through the reign of Henry VIII from which it did not recover until midway through the reign of Elizabeth, statutes of 1545 and 1552 tried to eliminate middlemen dealing in wool in order to minimise the cost of the product to the consumer. However, such middlemen occupied an essential role in the pattern of industrial organisation in Calderdale, and Halifax became one of the few districts to secure formal exemption from the effects of the legislation. The preamble to the 1555 Halifax Act proclaimed famously that the inhabitants of the parish 'altogether do live by cloth making' and explained that the majority of inhabitants being unable

> to keep a horse to carry wool, nor yet to buy much wool at once, had ever used only to repair to the town of Halifax ... and there to buy from the wool driver some a stone, some two, and some three or four, according to their ability, and to carry the same to their houses some three, four, five or six miles off, upon their heads and backs, and so to make and convert the same either into yarn or cloth, and to sell the same and so to buy more wool.[10]

The legislative protection enabled the woollen industry to prosper. In 1588 a correspondent informed the Vicar of Leeds that 'at Halifax there is no cloth made but yard broad kerseys', adding that they wove a fine wool, mostly from Lincolnshire, selling their coarse wool 'to the men of Rochdale'. Moreover, it also enabled Halifax to continue to grow as a marketing centre for both its hinterland and a wider region.[11]

During the second half of the seventeenth century local manufacturers diversified into worsteds, cloth woven from long wools, imported from Lincolnshire and Leicestershire along the Aire and Calder Navigation, for reasons which have never fully been explained. It is possible that the change was stimulated by stagnating markets for coarser woollen cloth or by Norfolk merchants around Worstead, which gave its name to worsted cloth, putting out work for spinning in the parish in the later seventeenth century, encouraging local clothiers to experiment with worsted weaving. Increasing amounts of worsted equipment and cloth certainly appear in local inventories after 1690. By 1706, Joseph Holroyd, a local clothier, was engaged in a large trade in bays, a coarse woollen cloth with a long nap used for coverings, curtains and warm clothing, and in 1715 an indenture of apprenticeship reveals that James Haggas was bound apprentice with John Jackson of Halifax to learn the art of weaving shalloons, light worsted fabrics. A decade later when Daniel Defoe, the foremost industrial commentator of the age, visited Halifax he estimated that the parish was producing 100,000 pieces of shalloons yearly. However, expansion of worsted production during this period remained sporadic. In 1738 Samuel Hill

(1678–1759), the Soyland clothier, wrote despondently that he was 'perfectly sick of the little or no hopes of the shalloon business', but by 1747 he had achieved a remarkable annual turnover of over £35,000, exporting cloth to Amsterdam, Rotterdam, Utrecht, Antwerp, Bremen and St Petersburg. By 1750, then, Halifax was not only an important centre for the manufacture of woollen kerseys, but also the most important worsted manufacturing centre in the West Riding and by 1770 worsted production in Halifax and its hinterland had reached the same level as that of Norwich.[12]

Dr Ronan Bennett's occupational analysis of male designations at marriage in the parish of Halifax between 1653 and 1658 identifies the percentage of clothiers and textile workers in the 24 rural out-townships of the parish of Halifax as 44.9 per cent and other textile workers as 22.3 per cent, totalling 67.2 per cent. This amounted to over two-thirds of workers engaged in textile-related occupations, whereas in the township of Halifax a mere 9.5 per cent were identified as clothiers and 6.3 per cent as other textile workers, totalling 15.8 per cent, but with more numerous additional categories in the urban centre, as might be expected, including 31.8 per cent artisans, 14.3 per cent labourers and 14.3 per cent food and leather traders.[13] The increasing preoccupation with textile manufacture especially in the rural out-townships meant that agriculture eventually came to be regarded as a mere supplement to income and that clothiers came to depend upon their sales of cloth to buy food, hence making the area less self-sufficient and more concerned with external trade. Commenting on the scale of farming in the parish of Halifax by the early eighteenth century, Daniel Defoe observed that 'they scarce sow corn enough for their cocks and hens'. Notwithstanding his observation that 'every manufacturer generally keeps a cow or two, or more, for his family', he concluded also that 'as to beef and mutton, they feed little or none', obtaining the bulk of their provisions 'from other parts of the country'.[14] Average landholdings in the parish remained small throughout the sixteenth and seventeenth centuries and the enclosure movement during this period did not result in a substantial increase in land under cultivation. Indeed, by the sixteenth and seventeenth centuries much of the corn consumed by the community was probably imported, although testamentary evidence reveals that oats and rye were grown locally. Many land deeds during this period also refer to a kitchen garden, supplying peas, beans and other vegetables for the family, and bequests were also often made of hives and swarms of bees. Sixteenth-century wills reveal that cattle were grazed in the township of Halifax and at least one chapman, Isaac Bates of Halifax, became interested in cattle farming as an investment, for in his will of 1608 he noted that he had spent £40 on cows and heifers. Some thirty other wills provide evidence of extensive sheep farming, and sheep and pigs are frequently referred to in presentments made at the manorial courts. Animals were pastured on the steeper hillsides and the common pastures around the developing town of Halifax, although by the mid-eighteenth century most of the township of Halifax was systematically enclosed, including Halifax Moor.[15]

Land within Halifax's rural periphery was also increasingly exploited, however,

Messrs Hendrick & Peter Kops.

Sirs, I have yor favor of ye prod. NS 10th yor remiss
Geo: Clifford & Sons on Richd Bloant wch shall send immediately for acceptance & when
pd shall Credd yor acco. & then the Ballance due to me will be £6:12:6 including
the Error wch I have given yo Credt (wch was in adding NS)

I cannt abate any thing of the prices of my Invoices, nor can
I deal wth any if they will not be pleased to allways to accept my goods at ye
market price when ready, as to yr paying the same price if goods had sat
is a mistake for I have all my time & shall very frequently as long as I follow
Buisiness send my friends my makeing — cheap as they expect just as it
happens, goods have declined betwixt the time of my promiseing them & the
time they became ready, but indeed most Gentlemen yt I serve have agreed
to take a certain quant. every year & they fix the mr wherein they desire
ym & then they are seldom or ever disapointed, but never any price fixed
but a market price when ready, & if it so happen yt yf I shall settle a correspondence, they very first time goods happens to fall yo will be fully concd
of my Hond as to the prices, I hope I shall never be such a fool as charg-
ing makeing higher than the same quality can be made by others I very
well know what all the makers can do, & when I cannt serve my friends
as well or better, I will leave of Buisiness —

I hoped you wod have been satisfied wth what I writ
yo of the 20 Decembr wherein I promised yo 2 Bales certain or 3 if the weather
proved good but we have had so much rain & snow that I cannt get yo more
than 2 in February mo on wch yo may rely & one or 2 in March if yo desire
them & will be content wth the prices I send to others and allow the Ballance
due to me when this Bill is pd £6:12:6 but if not I must study to serve such
as can find their acco. in the Managemt off   Gentm Yor most hum Serv

SH

P.S. If yo expect any Kerseys of mine in February please give me
a line in answer & yo allow my acco. and then I will immediately
forward two Bales wch shall be getting ready in the mean time

---

Messrs John & Peter Dorville &   Halifax 1 February 1737.8

Sirs I duly recd yor favor of ye Xber
wth yor remiss for £43:10 wch have noted to yor credt but according to my account when
pd will be 30s above the Ballance, as soon as we have Sun & the fine weather comes
on I shall have 20 Samuels I think the Best I ever made please write me what yo
will have packed wth them   I am

I cannt afford my Samuels at Less as 60s
I am very sorry yo cannt find yor acco. in dealing more wth me   Serv   Sam Hill
Yor most obed hum

Received 2d February 1737/   By order & for acco of Widow Benj Froxley
of Mr Christopher Bernard, by the Hands of Mr John Wilkinson the Sum
of Two Hundred Thirty Six pounds

for its coal and mineral deposits during the sixteenth and seventeenth centuri
There is evidence of coal mining at Hipperholme, Northowram, Ovenden, She
and Sowerby, where natural drainage assisted both open-cast and underground
mining operations. In 1582 Queen Elizabeth I granted all the coal held by the crown
in Northowram and a mine in Sowerby to Henry Farrer of Midgley. The manorial
court in October 1608 ordered that coalpits alongside the road in Wakefield Bank
be filled in by Christmas because 'man and horse cannot travel but in great danger',
and in the following year requested the inhabitants of Shelf 'to fill or fence about
their pits'. Occupational analysis of marriage records of the mid-seventeenth
century has also identified approximately three per cent of males in the parish
of Halifax as colliers. Moreover, the probate inventory of Charles Best, yeoman
clothier, of Woodend, Hipperholme, who died in 1723, reveals that he was in both
farming and working 'coal pits on Norwood Green'. Later, Defoe observed horses
carrying coal from hilltop seams, and in 1726 a horse gin was evidently in use at
Shibden to wind coal up to the surface.[16]

Conveniently located reserves of quality gritstone and sandstone sustained the
Great Rebuilding, which began earlier and was more prolonged in Calderdale than
in other parts of West Yorkshire and stimulated the development of skills in masonry
which local craftsmen utilised far beyond the parish of Halifax. In 1579 slate-stones
were being quarried at Northowram by Edward Carey, and references abound in
manorial records and churchwardens' accounts to stone delivery within the locality.
Further afield, Halifax builders, notably John Akroyd (1556–1613) and John Bentley
(1574–1615) were responsible for construction work for John Savile at Bradley
Hall and Methley Hall and, under the patronage of Sir Henry Savile, at Oxford,
including work on the Bodleian Library and on the fellows' quadrangle at Merton
College. Nearer home, prosperous clothiers such as James Murgatroyd of Warley
built a succession of impressive houses in the vernacular style, including Haigh
House, Warley (1631); Yew Tree (1643), Ovenden Wood (1643) and Kershaw House,
Luddenden Foot (1650).[17] Local clay and coal were also utilised in the seventeenth
century in the development of a regionally important earthenware industry and
a distinctive local pottery industry in Calderdale. Between 1640 and 1650 four
brothers, John, Richard, Abraham and George Halliday from Scotland settled at
Pule Hill on a bleak exposed Pennine hilltop near Ploughcroft, overlooking Halifax,
where they built a kiln and made slipware and black glazed articles. Around 1655,
the four brothers leased Bate Hayne from the Dearden family transferring their
operation there from Pule Hill, though later in the eighteenth century the business

opposite Extract from the letter book for 1736–38 of Samuel Hill (1677–1759) of Soyland. Samuel
Hill, who left an estate valued at £20,000, was the most outstandingly successful eighteenth-
century textile entrepreneur in the locality, putting out work to hundreds of domestic clothiers
in their Pennine homes. The extract details his trade with merchants in the Netherlands. By
1747 he had an annual turnover of over £35,000, exporting cloth to Amsterdam, Rotterdam,
Utrecht, Antwerp, Bremen and St Petersburg.
(Photograph: West Yorkshire Archive Service, Calderdale)

was moved by the succeeding Halliday generation to Howcans, near Ovenden. So, Halifax and its hinterland, although predominantly identified with cloth making after 1500, remained an area of diversified economic activity.[18]

There is, however, no evidence of the primary production of iron in Calderdale during the period 1500–1750, even though growing supplies of iron equipment such as cropping shears and tenterhooks were required by textile workers. Charcoal blast furnaces (which gradually replaced medieval bloomeries from the fifteenth century) at Holme in Cliviger and at Colnebridge, outside the parish, supplied Calderdale ironworkers. The forge at Colnebridge was of monastic origin, but later became part of the extensive Spencer syndicate, a partnership which dominated the iron industry of West Yorkshire and held the local monopoly of iron production during the seventeenth and eighteenth centuries. But there is some evidence of secondary iron production in Calderdale during this period. Grace Bolton of Skircoat, widow of Laurence Bolton, shearmaker, in her will of 1594 entrusted her brother Robert with the task of training her two sons in 'the craft and science of making and setting shears'. There is also evidence of nail-making at Halifax in the seventeenth century and wire drawing at Brighouse in the early eighteenth century.[19]

County rate assessments reveal the growing prosperity of Halifax over its parochial out-townships by the end of the sixteenth century as the town developed into the market centre for a range of goods produced regionally, especially textiles. In an attempt to gain revenue from the expanding local economy, the Waterhouse family of Shibden Hall had provided Cloth Halls for the town by the late sixteenth century, which were described in a lease of 1562 as 'Greater and Lesser Blackwell Halls' and pre-dated the Cloth Halls of Leeds, Bradford and Huddersfield. Indeed, the architectural historian George Sheeran has observed that by the sixteenth century Halifax had 'developed far more sophisticated markets and buildings for the sale of cloth than any other town in the county including York'. Before the opening of the new Cloth Halls, the merchants' shops or booths and warehouses of Woolshops had constituted the town's principal wool market. This market was supplemented from at least the beginning of the sixteenth century by a new, substantial, purpose-built Cloth Hall, which consisted of probably two parallel ranges, modelled upon the Blackwell Hall in London, the whole of which was estimated by an Elizabethan surveyor to measure ninety feet long by thirty-six feet wide. By the early seventeenth century Halifax, which was granted permission to hold a wool market in 1617, was the sole commercial centre in the parish. It was subsequently described as a market town in quarter sessions records and besides providing markets for cloth and wool, it already provided an extensive and growing market for provisions. Indeed, one contemporary, James Ryder, had written to Lord Burghley in 1589: 'it is incredible how far the town of Halifax excels York in uttering much and good meat'.[20]

By the early seventeenth century, Halifax was clearly becoming a commercial rival not only of older urban textile manufacturing centres such as York but also newer industrial centres such as Leeds and Wakefield. Indeed, when bills were introduced into Parliament in 1621 and 1626 to make the river Calder navigable to

Horse gin, West Riding Folk Museum, Shibden Hall. Daniel Defoe observed horses carrying coal from hilltop seams when he travelled through Halifax in the early eighteenth century and in 1726 a horse gin was evidently in use at Shibden to wind coal up to the surface. The twentieth-century museum reconstruction shows a shire horse from Stone Trough Brewery harnessed to a capstan so that as the horse moved round in a circle the winding machinery rotated, raising the coal from the mine. (Photograph: H. Armitage)

Halifax, they were blocked following intervention by the City of York, supported by the other two market towns. The failure to improve the Calder was a setback for the economic expansion of Halifax, since access to the town by road was often difficult. When Halifax clothiers sent in petitions of support for the improvement of the Aire and Calder Navigation in 1698, they stressed the poor condition of the pre-turnpiked roads, complaining that 'they are forced to stay two months sometimes until the roads are passable to market and many times the goods receive considerable damage through the badness of the roads by overturning'.[21] Celia Fiennes (1662–1741), an experienced traveller, was discouraged from visiting Halifax in 1698 because the roads to it were 'so stony and difficult', and Daniel Defoe later provided a graphic description of some of the problems he encountered on leaving the town:

> We quitted Halifax not without some astonishment at its situation, being so surrounded with hills and those so high, as … makes the coming in and going out of it exceedingly troublesome, and indeed for carriages hardly practicable … particularly the hill which they go up to come out of the town eastwards towards Leeds … which … is so steep, so rugged, and sometimes

so slippery, that, to a town of so much business as this, 'tis exceedingly troublesome and dangerous.[22]

Remarkably, however, the commercial development of Halifax continued apace, despite the problems of accessibility. The 1686 War Office returns of the number of guest beds and stabling in towns and villages throughout England reveal that Halifax with 130 beds and stabling for 306 horses had more accommodation for visitors than Ripon, Thirsk, Richmond and Pontefract.[23] Indeed, Defoe himself acknowledged that 'multitudes of people' crowded into the town on a market-day both 'to sell their manufactures' and 'to buy provisions'. He concluded that 'so great is the confluence of people hither, that except Leeds and Wakefield, nothing in all the north of England can come near it'.[24] The network of local and regional pack-horse routes continued to sustain the development of Halifax as a commercial and service centre for its hinterland, but the completion of the Aire and Calder Navigation in the first decade of the eighteenth century and the subsequent building of new turnpike links hastened that development. Indeed, in 1735 the Rochdale–Elland turnpike via Halifax became the first stretch of turnpiked road in West Yorkshire over seven decades since the establishment of the first turnpike trust in 1663 to repair and maintain a badly worn section of Great North Road in Hertfordshire. In 1741 Acts established trusts for turnpikes linking Doncaster, Wakefield and Halifax; Elland and Leeds and Selby, Leeds, Bradford and Halifax.[25]

Social structure, occupations and living standards

The development of Halifax during the period from 1500 to 1750 as a commercial and service centre for its rural hinterland shaped the social structure, occupations and living standards of the emerging urban community. There evolved within the market town a relatively undifferentiated social structure with a substantial nucleus of middling people, only a limited gentry presence, a declining proportion of labourers, and fluctuating numbers of poor.

The Saviles of Thornhill and Rufford Abbey, owners of almost half the townships of the parish of Halifax, had moved away to their estates on the eastern edge of Sherwood Forest in Nottinghamshire by the end of the sixteenth century. Moreover, since they owned very little land in the township of Halifax, they played a less significant role in the development of the town than they did in either Leeds or Wakefield. Other local gentry families who held land in the township of Halifax during this period, including the Farrers of Midgley, the Gledhills of Barkisland, the Lacys of Brearley, the Sunderlands of High Sunderland, and the Waterhouses and Listers of Shibden Hall, also preferred to reside around the town's rural periphery rather than in the town itself. Indeed, the wealthiest resident in the town by the mid-sixteenth century was Dr Robert Holdsworth, the last vicar of Halifax to be appointed by the Cluniac Priors of Lewes to the rich benefice of Halifax in 1526. He was brutally murdered by intruders at the vicarage, which had been broken into by robbers on no fewer than four previous occasions. He died possessed of fifteen

Shibden Hall, Halifax, 1996. The original timber-framed house was built by William Otes in the early fifteenth century in the popular H-plan design clearly recognisable in this photograph with the two half-timbered gables crossing with the hall. It remained in the Otes family for the remainder of the century. In 1505 it passed through marriage to the Saviles and in 1522 to the Waterhouses, in whose possession it remained until 1612. The Waterhouses collected tithes for the Priors of Lewes and their lay successors after the dissolution of the monasteries. They ultimately became lords of the sub-manor of Halifax-cum-Heptonstall and one of the wealthiest and most influential local families in the sixteenth century, when the house was modified and extended to the rear. Sections of the south front were later encased in stone in the seventeenth century. When Anne Lister came into sole ownership of the property in 1836, she commissioned the Lancashire born architect, John Harper (1809–42), who later practised in York, to produce new designs for the remodelling of the hall. A three-storey western gothic tower with a library was added, as was an east wing with new kitchen and servants' quarters and dressing rooms, and a gatehouse modelled on that of Kirkham Priory. 85 acres were turned into a landscaped park encircling the hall, including fish ponds, a high rock water cascade and a wilderness garden. However financial constraints and her untimely death in 1840 curtailed other developments. (Photograph: J. G. Washington)

houses, six cottages and a personal estate of 250 acres. However, his prosperous family background, his alleged misappropriation of charitable funds designed for the benefit of the parish, and his involvement in local gentry feuds made him very untypical of parochial clergy during the early modern period. Following the dissolution of the monasteries, the rectory sub-manor of Halifax–cum–Heptonstall passed eventually to the Waterhouses of Shibden Hall in 1545 and subsequently to the Ingrams of Temple Newsam in 1609. Both these families were far more conspicuous than the Saviles in the commercial exploitation of their land and properties in the town, particularly Sir Arthur Ingram (1565–1642), but generally, in the town of Halifax it was the absence rather than the social dominance of the landed gentry which was most evident in the early modern period.

Indeed, in the lay subsidy return for 1545, fewer individuals from the township of Halifax itself were taxed than from the parochial out-townships of Sowerby and Warley, and by 1588 Northowram had also more individuals liable for tax than Halifax. By the reign of Charles I, even townships like barren Langfield were ranking with Halifax in the amount of subsidy paid. A similar pattern also emerges from other sources, including fines for distraint of knighthood, hearth tax returns and parish assessments for the relief of the poor. In 1630, of 215 members of the West Riding gentry fined for distraint of knighthood by Charles I, no fewer than 37 per cent were from the parish of Halifax, an emerging Puritan stronghold.[26] However, none of the wealthiest landed proprietors within the parish resided in the township of Halifax, which furnished the crown with a mere £90 of the total fines for the parish, which amounted to £1,034 6s. 8d. Of the seven Halifax landowners incurring fines, Thomas Blackwood, who had built a house on Halifax Moor in 1617, was the wealthiest, contributing £20 to the royal coffers, followed by Robert Exley, Richard Barrowclough and Nathaniel Waterhouse, who each suffered fines of £13 6s. 8d., suggesting that the town was not dominated by a wealthy resident elite during the sixteenth and seventeenth centuries. Moreover, Dr Ronan Bennett's analysis of hearth tax returns for 1664 has revealed that no fewer than 1,319 individuals, more than one third of Halifax households, were exempt from payment on the grounds of poverty and that nearly as many, another 31.9 per cent were assessed for only one hearth and 'occupied a precarious economic position', perhaps because the majority of Halifax clothiers operated on a relatively small scale. However, he concludes that the proportionately heaviest concentration of pauperism in the parish of Halifax was not so much in Halifax itself, but in the five townships of Heptonstall chapelry where the destitute and labouring poor comprised three quarters of the population, with 28 per cent exempted from payment of the hearth tax and 49.5 per cent in one-hearthed houses. However, he suggests that many of Halifax's poor were 'part of a pauper class, locked into life-long destitution since one quarter of those exempted from the 1672 hearth tax had been in the same position in 1664', with some receiving outdoor poor relief for nearly a decade. Moreover, in the account book of Brian Crowther's charity in one note, the charity's feoffees recorded in 1658 'Samuel Pickles died starved'.[27]

Moreover, a study of local wills from the period 1558 to 1640 reveals a higher concentration of butchers, shoemakers, tanners and glovers in the social and occupational structure of the township of Halifax than in the parochial out-townships. However, most urban artisans were engaged in the cloth trade, outnumbering the yeomen, who were somewhat higher up the social scale. Moreover, between 1609 and 1663 the tenurial structure of the manor changed dramatically due to the enfranchisement of copyholders. Of around 200 copyholders in the manor in the late 1580s over 150 had been enfranchised by the late 1650s, indicating an enhancement of the legal and social standing of many of the town's inhabitants during the first half of the seventeenth century. Indeed, a rental of 1702 contains very few

Barkisland Hall. This magnificent three-storeyed prodigy house was completed in 1638 by John and Sarah Gledhill, whose initials are inscribed upon the porch. John Gledhill's father, Thomas, was one of the highest taxpayers in the township of Barkisland and had been granted a coat of arms in 1612. His wife, Sarah, was the daughter of William Horton of the Howroyd, Barkisland. The doorway is flanked by Doric and Ionic fluted columns and surmounted by a rose window, one of only four which have survived in Calderdale. The parlours in the wings and many of the upper chambers, with their multi-light mullions and transoms, were heated by fireplaces served by a large number of flues. Richard Gledhill was later knighted by the Earl of Newcastle and served in the royalist army in the Civil War, but was killed at Marston Moor in July 1644. (Photograph: Halifax Antiquarian Society)

references to copyhold property and Dr Alan Betteridge has concluded that 'the number of freeholders in relation to copyholders may have been greater in Halifax, at least during the early seventeenth century, than in many northern communities', suggesting that the town of Halifax was dominated more by independent artisans or freeholders than gentry families.[28]

Marriage records suggest that approximately half of those above the status of labourer in Halifax in the mid-seventeenth century were involved in the cloth

The Oak Room, Old Cock Hotel, Southgate, Halifax. A rare survival of an Elizabethan room from a northern town. Originally a town house built in the 1580s by William Savile of Copley following his marriage to Isabel Lacy in 1575, the Old Cock has been an inn since 1668. The central feature of the impressive oak-panelled chamber is an elaborately carved oak overmantel, dated 1581, with inlaid panels set inside arcades separated by grotesque caryatids. The Savile arms flanked by royal supporters in the plasterwork over the fireplace was probably added in the 1630s. The room is lit by a large transomed window of 20 lights infilled with colourful stained glass. David Hartley the notorious counterfeiter was arrested in this room in 1769 and the meeting which gave birth to the Halifax Permanent Benefit Building Society was held here in December 1852. (Photograph: Halifax plc)

trade, clothiers and tailors predominating. Indeed, by the 1690s a mere 9 per cent of those whose occupations are recorded in their wills worked outside the textile industry or the basic craft and provision trades such as carpentry, masonry and baking. These included a chapman, nailer, clockmaker, innkeepers, linen drapers, mercers, apothecaries, shoemakers and tailors. By the mid-eighteenth century, however, while over half the trades remained connected with textiles, there had been a dramatic fall in the number of clothiers in the town. A growing proportion of croppers, however, reflected the development of the town as a cloth finishing centre, while a rising number of woolcombers, provided an index of the growth of the worsted industry since the mid-seventeenth century. The decline of the small independent clothier may have been indicative of a trend towards increased specialisation within the textile industry under the control of a wealthier and economically more dominant entrepreneurial class, of whom Samuel Hill (1677–1759) of Soyland, who left an estate valued at £20,000, was the most outstandingly successful local example. The emergence of shoemakers, masons, joiners and carpenters as more significant occupational groups was undoubtedly a product of the growth of Halifax as a service centre in the early eighteenth century. Moreover, an increase in the number of non-traditional craft occupations recorded in local wills reflects a rising demand for a wider range of consumer goods from the residents of Halifax and its hinterland. Occupations such as innkeeper, cordwainer, linen draper, grocer and shopkeeper were relatively common by the mid-eighteenth century, but more unusual trades such as breeches maker, saddler and staymaker were also making an appearance.[29]

In addition, churchwardens' accounts together with literary and testamentary sources reveal a growing professional class, which included apothecaries, doctors, schoolmasters, ministers of religion, lawyers and a coroner, arising from the development of Halifax as a service centre for a wider community during this period. The main business of local lawyers, many of whom were primarily scriveners, quasi-legal practitioners and financial intermediaries, was conveyancing and wills. For example, John Hargreaves and his son of the same name, who practised in Halifax in the late seventeenth century, were very active in drawing up wills and deeds, but did not undertake more complicated legal work. During the eighteenth century, however, both the number of lawyers practising in the parish and the range of services that they offered increased dramatically. The number of schoolmasters and bookkeepers also increased, but it was not until the late 1730s that any of the surviving commercial account books show the influence of a bookkeeper's diligence. The growth of the professions and growing prosperity of the middling sort has led Dr John Smail to conclude that in Halifax 'by the mid-eighteenth century there was a self-conscious middle class demanding and receiving local political power and social prestige and transforming the social world in which they lived'.[30]

Marriage registers suggest that labourers constituted the town's largest single occupational group in the mid-seventeenth century, some of whom, no doubt, on occasions became dependent on charity or poor relief. Vagrants also created problems from time to time. Manorial officials in the 1530s and 1580s and parochial officials in the 1620s were concerned about the influx of vagrants into the town, and during the 1630s pauper children were being sent to Halifax from as far afield as Westmorland to serve apprenticeships. There were also periods when the number of paupers within the town reached alarming proportions. At the peak of an epidemic of bubonic plague in October 1645, the West Riding Justices of the Peace allotted the sum of £66 13s. 4d. for Halifax and Northowram, recognising that 'there are 1,632 poor people that live upon charity'. However, later the poor were less in evidence. When Defoe visited Halifax in the early eighteenth century, he observed that there was 'not a beggar, not an idle person to be seen, except here and there an almshouse, where people ancient, decrepit, and past labour might be found'. In the mid-eighteenth century labourers still formed the largest occupational group in the town, although their numbers in relation to the total population had apparently declined.[31]

Evidence from property deeds, hearth tax returns and wills suggest some differentiation in the quality of housing in Halifax in the early modern period. The townhouse of a more prosperous artisan of the sixteenth century normally consisted of a parlour, a shop, an entrance with rooms above and a basement, but from the late sixteenth century as the population grew an increasing number of property deeds included references to the division of houses into several apartments. Husbandmen would have leased small cottages, perhaps incorporating barns, or small houses with two or three rooms on the ground floor and upper chambers reached by a ladder. Labourers would have lived in single-storey cottages of one or two rooms. The hearth tax returns of 1664 reveal that the township of Halifax contained no fewer than 30 per cent of houses with three or more hearths, including 7 per cent with six or more, indicating fairly spacious living accommodation of at least seven to nine rooms. However, they also disclose that Halifax possessed the second largest number of poorer quality non-chargeable houses in the parish offering more limited accommodation.[32]

Nevertheless, Dr John Smail has argued that compared with other communities such as the Essex village of Terling, the hearth tax returns of 1664 suggest that Halifax's social structure was relatively undifferentiated and that the probate inventories confirm a relatively homogeneous material culture across a broad social spectrum. Basic household furnishings such as tables, chairs, stools, cooking utensils, show some slight variations in value amongst the deceased, but the inventories reveal a fairly widespread ownership of luxury goods in late seventeenth-century Halifax. Out of a total of 292 inventories from the period between 1690 and 1699, almost a third owned clocks and linen, a quarter owned glass cases and mirrors and a sixth owned white plate. Some items, however, appeared only in the inventories of the wealthier members of the community. Only three households, for example, owned chairs upholstered with 'russia leather', only nine had curtains on their windows, and only seven had maps decorating their walls. The earliest references to tea drinking found in Halifax probate records are in two inventories from the 1720s. George Mewson, a local attorney, had a tea table and a silver teapot worth over £12 and also a small amount of chinaware, whilst James Kitson, a stapler from Halifax owned 67 pieces of chinaware, a tea tray and a tea kettle when he died in 1725. Ann Smith left damask table linen, a silver coffee pot and stand, and six silver spoons to her daughter Elizabeth and table linen and a mirror to her daughter Jane. Nathaniel Priestley left his repeating clock, two silver sauce-boats and a silver coffee pot to his daughter, and books from his library to male family members.[33]

The pattern of births, marriages and deaths recorded in the parish registers suggests that Halifax and its hinterland suffered sharp rises in mortality as a result of epidemics in the sixteenth and early seventeenth centuries. An outbreak of typhus fever in Halifax during 1587–88 resulted in a dramatic rise in the number of burials, which remained at three or four times the monthly average for a period of four months and, in the space of five months, a bubonic plague epidemic in 1645 claimed no fewer than 529 victims in Halifax and Northowram. Although epidemics may have been less serious after the 1680s, the limited data obtained from tombstone inscriptions for the period 1701 to 1760, reveal that infant mortality was dramatically high even for the better off, with more than 25 per cent of deaths occurring in children under five. Within the age-group 25–45, mortality was slightly higher among women than men. However, women who survived beyond the child-bearing age tended to live longer than their male contemporaries, who often died in their early sixties. Very elderly members of the community were rare, although small numbers of both sexes survived into their seventies and eighties. However, the mean age at death in these records of 35.1 years probably accounts for the large proportion of orphans in local society during this period. Local residents who survived into adulthood, however, appeared healthy to contemporary observers. The Revd Thomas Wright, a curate at Halifax Parish Church, writing in 1738, remarked that 'the air is fresh and sharp, but good and wholesome, as may be seen by the clear and sound complexion of the natives'.[34]

Religion and politics

Reformation and Counter Reformation

William and Sarah Sheils have argued that 'in Halifax and its hinterland the Reformation years were disruptive ones' since the dissolution of the chantries and the disendowment of the extensive network of proprietary chapels-of-ease in the vast parish in 1548 'posed considerable problems for the inhabitants of Halifax', diminishing the pastoral provision which had been built up over the previous century. Changes in religious belief and practice affected the local community in many different ways during the period 1500–1750, when religion undoubtedly became the most keenly contested issue in the locality. Halifax as the centre of ecclesiastical administration for its hinterland inevitably became the focal point for much of this religious controversy, which spilled over into Civil War fighting in the 1640s. Moreover, the restoration of the monarchy in 1660 produced an uneasy settlement between the Established Church and Protestant Nonconformity, which ensured the continuation of religious divisions and social tensions in Halifax throughout the period up to 1750.[35]

One of the leading figures of the pre-Reformation Church, Yorkshire born and Cambridge educated William Rokeby, served as Vicar of Halifax (1502–21), Bishop of Meath (1507–11) and Archbishop of Dublin (1511–21), where he forbade clergymen to play football. He had celebrated Mass at Westminster Abbey when Thomas Wolsey received his cardinal's hat in 1515. He also assisted with other senior clergy at the baptism of Mary Tudor in 1516. He served as a member of the Irish Privy Council (1507–12) and lord chancellor of Ireland (1512–13 and 1516–21) but returned to Yorkshire to die in 1521. Moreover, in his will he left instructions that his body be interred in a new chapel at Kirk Sandal, but that his heart be entombed in a lead casket beneath the chancel of Halifax Parish Church and made a bequest for the building of a chantry chapel on the north side of the church. In 1535, Dr Robert Holdsworth, Vicar of Halifax 1525–56, who, in accordance with his father's wish, had built another chantry on the south side of Halifax Parish Church, allegedly declared in the year following Henry VIII's breach with Rome: 'if the king reign any space, he will take all that ever we have … and therefore I pray God send him a short reign'. He was the last Vicar of Halifax to be appointed by the Prior of Lewes. In 1537 the Cluniac priory was dissolved and its estates, including the rectory sub-manor of Halifax and Heptonstall, transferred to Thomas Cromwell.[36]

At the surrender of Lewes, as observed by Joyce Youings, provision was made for the payment of pensions to each member of the community. Thomas Cromwell's total grant, which included not only the site of Lewes Priory, but lands and 'spiritual' revenues 'as far afield Halifax in Yorkshire' was valued at over £527.[37] A surviving deed at the time of the surrender of the priory refers to the manor of Halifax and its appurtenances encompassing approximately 40 mesuages, 20 cottages, 50 gardens, 2 dovecotes, 2,000 acres of land, 500 acres of meadow, 2,000 acres of pasture, 1,000 acres of woodland, 2,000 acres of moorland and heath and £130 of rent in Halifax, Heptonstall, Townfleet, Wakefield, Conisbrough, Braithwell, Harthill, Kirk Sandal, Dinnington, Sowerby, Warley, Ovenden, Midgley, Wadsworth, Langfield, Erringden, Rishworth, Norland, Barkisland, Stainland, Elland, Greetland, Rastrick, Fixby, Toothill, Brighouse, Southowram, Northowram, Hipperholme, Shelf, Skircoat, Stansfield, Clifton, Warmsworth, Ranfield, Northing, Dalton and Greasbrough. Indeed, Mayhew reckons that with annual sales from the priory's Sussex flocks amounting to at least twenty sacks of wool, even in the sixteenth century Lewes Priory had received over £300 a year of its income from sheep farming, ranking it amongst the larger English monastic wool producers.[38] On Thomas Cromwell's disgrace and execution, they passed, with the advowson, to Anne of Cleves, and then to the crown, when Henry's marriage to Anne was dissolved.[39] If minor changes to the preambles of Halifax wills after 1526 reflect changing scribal practice, those of William Holmes and Robert Thomson, drafted in 1538, reveal a deliberate Protestant emphasis. Both rejected the intercession of the saints, commending their respective souls 'unto Christ Jesu, my maker and redeemer, in whom, and by the merits of whose blessed passion, is all my whole trust of clean remission of all my sins'. In 1538, Holdsworth, a theological conservative and worldly pluralist, submissively placed an English Bible in Halifax Parish Church and began the Halifax Parish Registers. But in the same year Robert Ferrar, prior of Nostell and a native of the parish of Halifax, writing to Thomas Cromwell, bemoaned the lack of Protestant preachers in Halifax and other West Riding towns, despite the fact that 'the people were hungrily desirous to hear and learn'. However, an erosion of belief in the importance of masses for the dead is revealed in the private dissolution of some chantry foundations and confiscation of their endowments before 1548. These included the endowment of the Frith chantry in Halifax Parish Church, which was lost to Sir Edmund Ackroyd, who took possession of the lands supplying it in 1539.[40]

After 1538 the proportion of Halifax wills omitting reference to the Virgin and saints rose sharply, confirming a growing Protestant commitment amongst the laity. The lengthy preamble to the will of Edward Hoppay of Skircoat, drafted in 1548, early in the reign of Edward VI (1547–53), included the affirmation that 'touching the wealth of my soul, the faith that I have taken is sufficient, as I believe, without any other man's work or works'. This provides one of the earliest provincial occurrences of a radical Protestant statement of belief and incontrovertible evidence of the impact of Protestant teaching and Bible-reading upon a middle-aged or elderly yeoman of modest means residing near Halifax. Traditionally, historians have attributed the emergence of Halifax as a radical Protestant centre to the survival of a strong Lollard tradition in the geographically remote parish. But the evidence for this has always been elusive. It now seems more likely that Protestantism travelled with merchants and tradespeople from cosmopolitan centres like London and Hull to market towns and manufacturing centres like Halifax and its hinterland, where it spread within local communities through kinship networks. Protestantism seems particularly to have rooted in Halifax families with textile connections such as the Maudes and the Bests, who were well established in the community, possessing lands and producing clerical sons.[41]

Holdsworth dutifully closed the chantries in the parish church and the proprietary chapelries throughout the parish following the enactment of the Chantries Act of 1548. The absence of churchwardens' accounts makes it impossible to measure the financial implications of the Act in Halifax, but William and Sarah Sheils have concluded that 'the principal inhabitants of Halifax were deprived of an important outlet for their individual and corporate social energies' which was not restored until the preaching ministry of John Favour and his Puritan protégés 'touched the charitable wellsprings' of the local community in different political circumstances after 1590. However, the switch to an English liturgy on Easter Day, 1549, little over a month after the publication of Archbishop Thomas Cranmer's first English prayer book, was considered sufficiently momentous to be recorded in the baptismal registers and probably helped to develop an increasing awareness of the Reformation changes among those sections of the community not versed in Latin.[42]

During the Catholic reaction of Mary Tudor's reign (1553–58), when Holdsworth readily restored the Latin Mass, the parish of Halifax began to display an increasingly militant Protestantism. The church courts at York heard of a succession of heretical offences ranging from 'looking down at the time of the elevation of the sacrament during the Mass and refusing holy water' to tearing down the crucifix and forcibly removing the reserved sacrament from the parish church. However, A. G. Dickens has expressed surprise at the relatively small number of cases of heresy from Halifax presented in the ecclesiastical courts under Mary, concluding that the clothiers of Halifax, like the closely-knit merchant community of Hull, 'avoided giving away much detailed evidence to contemporary persecutors and modern historians'. But Robert Ferrar, a former chaplain of both Cranmer and Protector Somerset, went to the stake at Carmarthen in 1555 for refusing to renounce his 'heresies, schisms and errors' and there were several local protests against the re-introduction of the Mass, for example in July 1554, when the host was stolen from Halifax Parish Church.[43]

In the decade following the death of Mary Tudor in 1558 local will formulations tended towards religious neutrality, since the Elizabethan church settlement, embodied in the acts of supremacy and uniformity of 1559, was accepted with minimal opposition in the parish. In 1559, shortly after the accession of Elizabeth I (1558–1603), when James Pilkington, Regius Professor of Divinity at Cambridge and an eminent Protestant reformer, preached at Halifax Parish Church, 'the congregation listened with joy'. Catholic recusancy and repeated absence from communion were rare within the parish, and in 1569–70 the parish remained famously loyal to the Queen during the Catholic rebellion of the northern earls, which sought to re-establish the Catholic religion and secure the succession of the Catholic Mary Queen of Scots. This allegiance was later attributed by Archbishop Grindal to the effect of sustained Puritan preaching in the local 'exercises' or 'prophesyings'.[44]

After a temporary lapse, monthly mid-week 'exercise-days' were revived by the celebrated Puritan Dr John Favour, Vicar of Halifax from 1593 to 1623, when 'multitudes of hearers' regularly flocked to listen to visiting preachers from near and far. Dr Favour, a former Oxford civil lawyer and fervent Calvinist preacher, published in 1619 his celebrated *Antiquity triumphing over Novelty*, a treatise critical of 'all new and late upstart heresies'. All four of Favour's lecturers at Halifax Parish Church were Puritans, as were most of the curates in the restored parochial chapelries. In all, thirteen Puritan ministers served as lecturers or curates at Halifax Parish Church during the period 1603–40. Favour's influential allies included Sir John Savile of Howley, Sir Arthur Ingram of Temple Newsam, and Archbishop Tobias Mathew (1606–28). When nationally the Marprelate tracts, satirising leading churchmen, provided the pretext for an anti-Presbyterian reaction, Favour succeeded in protecting the Puritan cause at Halifax.[45]

Favour's successors, Robert Clay (1624–28), Hugh Ramsden (1628–29) and Henry Ramsden (1629–38) all had local Protestant roots, and it was not until the appointment of Richard Marsh in 1638 that the vicarage was occupied by a Laudian. However, during the primary visitations of the Laudian Archbishop Richard Neile in 1632, 1633 and 1635 the churchwardens in the parochial chapelries were ordered 'to provide surplices and all the other necessary ornaments'. Puritanism was again proscribed and several local Puritans, including Matthew Mitchell, 'a pious and wealthy' Halifax layman, and Richard Denton, curate of Coley, emigrated to New England to escape the Laudian persecution during the period 1635–38. The strength of Protestant feeling within the parish was evidenced by the 1,127 signatures from Halifax appended to the 1641 Protestation oath 'to maintain and defend … the true Reformed Protestant Religion expressed in the doctrine of the Church of England, against all popery and popish innovations', and by the support for the parliamentarian cause during the English Civil War, despite the fact that Sir William Savile (1612–44), the largest landowner in the parish, was a commander in the royalist army.[46]

Civil War, Commonwealth and Protectorate

Edward Hyde, 1st Earl of Clarendon (1609–74), the royalist historian of the Great Rebellion, noted that Halifax, Leeds and Bradford, three 'very populous and rich' clothmaking towns, which 'naturally maligned the gentry', were wholly at

Dr John Favour (1556–1623). His ministry as Vicar of Halifax from 1593 to 1623 promoted the growth of Puritanism in the parish and an upsurge in charitable benefactions and bequests, including the endowment of Heath Grammar School. His celebrated *Antiquity triumphing over Novelty*, published in 1619, which condemned 'all new and late upstart heresies' was dedicated to his ally, Archbishop Tobias Matthew of York. His alabaster monument on the south wall of Halifax Parish Church, photographed in 1981, portrays the vicar in his pulpit, dressed in canonicals and ruffle, his left hand resting on a skull. (Photograph: J. G. Washington)

the disposition of the parliamentarian forces in the English Civil War. Indeed, a contemporary newsbook recorded that when Sir William Savile arrived at Halifax in July 1642 to raise some volunteers for His Majesty he was turned out of the town and not a man would obey him. Moreover, in September 1642, the royalist earl of Cumberland also failed to raise the trained bands of Halifax, being greeted with acclamations of 'A Fairfax, a Fairfax, they would live and die with a Fairfax!' by the inhabitants of the town which remained, with Bradford and Hull, a vital parliamentary recruiting ground throughout 1642. Captain John Hodgson of Coley Hall helped to repel the royalist attack on Bradford in December 1642, while Jonathan Scholefield, minister of Cross Stone, led the parliamentarian assault on Leeds in January 1643, with mainly 'inexperienced fresh water men taken up about Bradford and Halifax but upon the Saturday before'. The royalist Earl of Newcastle was intent on engaging Fairfax by moving his forces westwards in an attempt to drive the parliamentarian army out of the West Riding, capturing Howley Hall, the residence of Lord Savile, under the command of a cousin Sir John Savile, with casualties on both sides.

By the evening of 29 June 1643, the royalist army commanded by Newcastle had reached a high ridge to the east of Bradford on Adwalton Moor. His army of 10,000 men outnumbered the parliamentarian forces by two to one. The local topography, however, riddled by old coal-workings and rough hedges, as Trevor Royle has observed, rendered 'it difficult for Newcastle to gauge the strength of his opponents, led by Lord Fairfax and Sir Thomas Fairfax. However, after fierce fighting, Newcastle rallied and, in the account he gave to his wife Margaret attributed his change of fortune to the employment of his pikemen, including his shock troops, sardonically labelled 'the Lambs', under the command of Colonel Posthumous Kirton, 'a wild and dangerous man'. They 'fell so furiously upon the enemy, that the parliamentarian supporters forsook their hedges and took to their heels'. In the close-quarters fighting royalist casualties were high including the commander of the horse, George Heron, with Goring absent. However, these successes enabled the parliamentary army to garrison Leeds and Bradford and occupy Halifax. According to the official dispatch to the Speaker of the House of Commons, which was sent from Halifax on the day following the battle, no fewer than 500 men from the parish of Halifax fought with the parliamentarian armies under the Fairfaxes at the battle of Adwalton Moor on 30 June 1643. Their defeat by a greatly superior royalist army caused many casualties and forced many parliamentarian supporters, including the Halifax apothecary and antiquary, John Brearcliffe, to seek refuge across the Pennines.[47]

During 1643, it has been observed that 'there was a very large increase in burials in Halifax' and this huge rise in mortality can be attributed to the Civil War. The monthly pattern shows that the increase to above average levels started as early as March 1642. Subsequently the number of deaths steadily increased until July, while August saw another very marked rise. The partial returns for September and the lack of any returns for October probably, it has been surmised, conceal high figures of mortality at the height of the intense fighting much of it at close quarters. The November fatalities were also very high with 156 recorded burials, of which, unusually 135 were male. Many the burials which it has been suggested might underestimate the number who died from their wounds included those termed 'stranger', including people from outside Halifax parish such as Bradford, Burlington, Sheffield and Millom, Westmorland. Other references are to 'milat', 'solder' or poignantly and cryptically reflect individual local losses, such as the entry for 7 July: 'Jonas Crowther, Northowram, slain'. Following the failure of the Royalist attack on Heptonstall, with as many as one hundred Royalists killed and thirty-five wounded, the parish register of 4 January noted that two royalist soldiers were 'hanged on a gallows erected near our gibbet'.[48]

By 8 July 1643, a royalist army under Major General Sir Francis Mackworth had occupied the town of Halifax after a skirmish with the rearguard of Sir Thomas Fairfax's departing forces on Old Bank. It comprised four regiments of infantry and one regiment of cavalry, the latter stationed at King Cross, with an outpost

Lord Ferdinando Fairfax and Sir Thomas Fairfax. This Victorian print depicts Lord Ferdinando Fairfax (1584–1652), General of Parliament's northern army against Charles I, and his son, later Sir Thomas Fairfax, who became General of Horse for Parliament on the outbreak of the Civil War and Lord General of Parliament's New Model Army after the Battle of Marston Moor in 1644, where he had commanded the cavalry and his father the infantry. Both the Fairfaxes commanded strong allegiance in Halifax, where the royalist Earl of Cumberland had tried without success to raise the trained bands of Halifax in September 1642, being greeted with acclamations of 'A Fairfax, a Fairfax, they would live and die with a Fairfax'. (Photograph: J. A. Hargreaves)

at Sowerby Bridge to guard the strategically important route to the Lancashire border. A parliamentarian counter-offensive through Heptonstall in October 1643 harassed the royalist outposts and subsequently repelled a royalist assault on the craggy hilltop village on 1 November, inflicting heavy casualties. Another daring counter-offensive in December pursued the retreating royalists to within musket shot of Halifax. After securing reinforcements from Keighley, Mackworth marched upon Heptonstall on 9 January, but the parliamentarians had discreetly evacuated the village before he arrived. The raising of the siege of Nantwich by Sir Thomas Fairfax on 25 January 1644, and the threat from Parliament's Scottish allies, resulted in Mackworth finally withdrawing from Halifax on 28 January 1644, falling back on Bradford and Leeds en route to York. The subsequent royalist defeat at the battle of Marston Moor on 2 July 1644 secured the north for Cromwell for the rest of the war. Scottish troops were quartered in Halifax from April 1645 to June 1646.

On balance, more local residents probably died from the outbreak of bubonic plague in Halifax in 1645, which claimed 529 lives, than from the military conflict.

High Sunderland, drawn by John Horner, 1835. Situated on the hillside above Horley Green, this house with its striking frontage and distinctive embattled cornice, was a rebuilding of an earlier timber-framed gabled house. Langdale Sunderland of High Sunderland, the brother-in-law of Sir Marmaduke Langdale, one of the king's generals, commanded a troop of royalist horse during the Civil War. He subsequently suffered a heavy fine for taking up arms against Parliament and was obliged to sell the family estates at High Sunderland and Coley Hall.
Some of the features of High Sunderland are believed to have been incorporated into the novel *Wuthering Heights* by Emily Brontë, who taught at a neighbouring private school at Southowram in 1838–39. The house was finally demolished in 1951.
(Photograph: Calderdale Museums Service, Bankfield)

A large proportion of soldiers garrisoned in Halifax during the Civil War were from Scotland where the plague was rife, having wiped out half the population of Edinburgh. Although burials in the summer of 1645 were exceptionally high throughout the parish, they were exceedingly high in insanitary Halifax, where many of the troops from Scotland were quartered. Some dispersed residents of Halifax also died of natural causes as refugees in Lancashire. In July 1643, Phoebe Lister hurriedly buried the deeds of Shibden Hall, then fled for Manchester, dying there seven months later. Anne Tattersall of Warley was one of several local refugees buried in Burnley in the summer of 1643. The home of Joseph Priestley, a Puritan clothier of Goodgreave whose son Samuel had enlisted in Fairfax's army, was ransacked and plundered by royalist troops after other members of the family fled to Lancashire. Some local residents with royalist sympathies also suffered, including Richard Gledhill of Barkisland Hall, who was killed at Marston Moor, and Langdale Sunderland of High Sunderland, who, at the end of the war, was obliged to sell his family estates in Calderdale to pay the heavy fine of £878 imposed by Parliament. Tobias Law, who held land in Halifax, Northowram and Southowram, was also fined £350. Moreover, during the royalist occupation of Halifax, two royalist soldiers were hanged as deserters on gallows, erected near the gibbet. Nor were soldiers the only royalist casualties of the war. The wife of Richard Marsh, the royalist vicar of Halifax, went into premature labour and died in childbirth, when Parliamentarian soldiers arrived at the vicarage in 1643 to arrest her husband, who had already fled.[49]

During the parliamentarian occupation and the Commonwealth and Protectorate (1649–60) the royal arms were removed from the parish church, together with the baptismal font with its exquisitely carved decorative wooden cover, and geometrically patterned, clear-leaded glass windows were installed in 1652 by the widow of Nathaniel Waterhouse. Among the Presbyterian ministers appointed to the sequestered living at Halifax during this period was John Lake (1624–89), a native of Halifax. He subsequently became Dean of York and Bishop of Chichester and, as one of the seven bishops who opposed the extension of the royal prerogative, was imprisoned in the Tower by James II in 1688. The parish of Halifax, a Commonwealth fiscal area, was represented in Oliver Cromwell's Parliaments of 1654 and 1656 by Jeremy Bentley of Elland, but a bid to secure a municipal charter for Halifax in August 1654 failed. Halifax suffered considerably from the military occupation and the disruption of the woollen trade during the Civil War, but at least one local clothier continued to make regular journeys with pack-horse trains full of cloth pieces for sale in London throughout the period. Others, however, must have experienced severe deprivation, and for many the Restoration would have signalled a welcome return to normality. The churchwardens' accounts record payments to bell ringers to celebrate the end of the Commonwealth in 1659.[50] However, a discordant note was struck by Richard Smith of Northowram, who was tried in August 1660 for declaring 'The king is a bastard, and the son of a whore. I hope to see Lord Lambert King'.

Restoration, Glorious Revolution and Hanoverian succession

With the restoration of Charles II (1660–85) and the imposition of the Clarendon Code by the Cavalier Parliament, Puritanism was effectively outlawed. Dr Richard Marsh, the royalist Vicar of Halifax who had fled for his life in 1642, returned to Halifax in 1660 to 'administer the sacrament with surplice and red tippet', ousting the Puritan incumbent, Eli Bentley. Among several other local ministers ejected for their refusal to conform was Oliver Heywood, at Coley, whose inspired and determined leadership was crucial to the survival of Yorkshire Dissent during the period 1660–88. Following his ejection from Coley he went to reside at Northowram where he exercised both a powerful local and wider itinerant ministry, often travelling 1,400 miles in a year strengthening the morale of the many small congregations of artisans, craftsmen and farmers who continued to meet in cottage and barn in the small Pennine hamlets. Repeatedly excommunicated and fined, and imprisoned for a whole year at York in 1685, he wrote in his diary during the year 1683:

I am so fully satisfied in my conscience with my Nonconformity as a minister, that it is the way of God, and I have so much peace in my spirit, that what I do is for the main, according to the word, that if I knew of all the troubles beforehand, and were to begin again, I would persist in this course to my dying day.

Sir George Savile (1633–95), born at Thornhill, the son of Sir William Savile, royalist governor successively of Sheffield and York, served as MP for Pontefract in the Convention Parliament, which restored Charles II to the throne in 1660. He was created by Charles II Baron Savile of Elland and Viscount Halifax in 1668 and was involved in the high politics of the era. Admitted to the Privy Council in 1672, he opposed Charles II's covert pro-French and pro-Roman Catholic policies. However, he balanced this opposition by resisting the anti–Catholic Test Act of 1673, which proposed a relaxation of the restrictions on Catholics. In 1676 Halifax was dismissed from the Council for repeatedly opposing the king's chief minister Thomas Osborne, earl of Danby, but he regained his seat in 1679. He was created Earl of Halifax in 1679 and Marquess of Halifax in 1682. He served as Lord Privy Seal from October 1682 to February 1685. His exertions to maintain a balance between the Anglican fervour of the Houses of Parliament and the Catholic enthusiasm of James Duke of York earned him the soubriquet of 'The Trimmer', on account of his political neutrality and moderate position in the fierce party struggles of his day.[51]

James II's unconstitutional rule ultimately provoked seven statesmen to invite William of Orange to land an army in England, which together with the desertion of her father by James's younger daughter Anne, precipitated his flight to France. His elder daughter Mary and her husband William, on their acceptance of the Declaration of Rights in February 1789, which was embodied in the Bill of Rights of October 1689, became joint sovereigns as William III and Mary II. The dynastic revolution, Dr Edward Vallance averred, 'took place with remarkable rapidity and with little blood being spilt'. Indeed, given that the Interregnum between the reigns of James and William and Mary extended between 12 December 1688 and 12 February 1689, Dr Constance Fraser has observed that the three courts held in the Manor of Wakefield during that interregnum were erroneously ascribed by the manorial courts to James II on 14 December 1688, 4 and 25 January, accentuating the confusion at local level given the meteoric speed of events. However, there was no significant delay in Halifax where Protestant triumphs were used as the occasions for popular celebration in the late seventeenth and early eighteenth centuries, and the Halifax churchwardens' accounts reveal that the parish church bells rang out on the proclamation of William and Mary in February 1689; the Protestant victories of William III in Ireland 1690–91; on the 'day of rejoicing' for the Act of Union with Scotland in 1707 and following the 'glorious victory obtained over the rebels' at Culloden Moor on 16 April 1745. Moreover, John Tillotson (1630–94), son of the Puritan Robert Tillotson of Haugh End in Sowerby and subsequently Archbishop of Canterbury, preached the sermon at the national thanksgiving for 'the deliverance by the Prince of Orange' on 31 January 1688. Large sums of money were collected locally in 1689–90 for the relief of the Irish Protestants, reflecting the intensity of popular support for the Revolution Settlement. A degree of toleration had been granted to Nonconformists initially through Declarations of Indulgence in 1672 and 1687 and more permanently when Dissent became legalised under the Toleration Act of 1689. By 1689 there were seven Dissenting congregations in the parish of Halifax, including one at a newly licensed meeting house at Northowram, built by Oliver Heywood in 1688, which had a membership of fifty-one in 1703, the majority of whom were women. By the end of the century the first Nonconformist meeting house had been opened by Presbyterians at Northgate End in Halifax.[52]

By 1715, when the Hanoverian succession secured the Protestant ascendancy, the Northgate End meeting had no fewer than 600 adherents, and Dissenters in the parish, including Quakers and Baptists, as well as Presbyterians and Independents, numbered over 2,000. Daniel Defoe recorded no fewer than sixteen Dissenting meeting houses during his visit to the parish ten years later. But some congregations had evidently declined in numbers by 1743 when Dr George Legh, Vicar of Halifax, reported to Archbishop Thomas Herring a mere '300 Presbyterian families; scarce any Baptists or Independents; sixty Quaker families and very few Papists' resident in the parish. However, he also observed that there was 'one unlicensed meeting house where the people called Methodists assemble' at Lightcliffe, with 'several

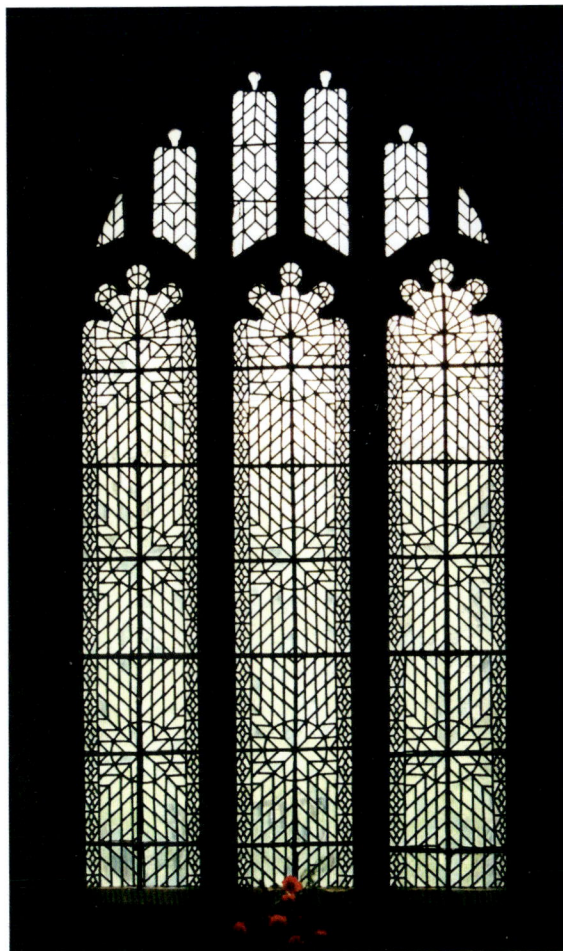

The Waterhouse windows, Halifax Parish Church. These distinctive, plain-glazed windows were donated to Halifax Parish Church in 1652 by Dorothy Waterhouse (1589–1652), widow of Nathaniel Waterhouse (1586–1645), in memory of her husband, a local merchant, salter and benefactor of the poor. They were considered more appropriate than stained-glass windows during the Puritan ascendancy in the Commonwealth period. Waterhouse had provided property in Halifax for use as a workhouse and house of correction. He had also endowed almshouses for the elderly poor and a Blue Coat School for the education of twenty orphans. (Photograph: J. G. Washington)

hundreds' attending the Sunday morning services which were conducted by teachers 'various and unsettled'. Two years later on 24 September 1745, Archbishop Herring urged his clergy 'to instruct and animate' their congregations 'to stand up against Popery and Arbitrary Power, under a French or Spanish Government'.[53]

In Halifax there was little evidence of sympathy for the Jacobite rebellion of 1745–46, though John Green, gentleman of Sunderland Hall, was arrested in Halifax and brought before magistrates on 'suspicion of being a papist and a person disaffected to His Majesty's Person and Government'. He was committed to York Castle, but released in December 1746 following the York Assizes. Indeed, the antiquary John Crabtree, a Halifax solicitor, insisted that there were 'unequivocal proofs of loyalty' to the house of Hanover in the town and parish. A voluntary association of the gentry and tradesmen was formed for 'the patriotic defence of the Altar and Throne, against the attacks of popery and arbitrary power'. Moreover, reports of the victories obtained over the Jacobites by the king's forces were joyfully greeted in Halifax, where the money expended by the churchwardens in distributing ale to the troops as they passed through the town en route to Culloden in April 1746 and the sums paid out to the bell ringers, formed 'no inconsiderable item in the parish accounts during that period'.[54] Arthur Jessop, the Holmfirth apothecary, who frequently visited Halifax, provided a graphic contemporary account of the rebellion in his diary, recording 'very good news' on

John Tillotson (1630–1694) was the son of Robert Tillotson, a Dissenting clothier of Haugh End in Sowerby. He was educated at local grammar schools and Clare Hall, Cambridge. He preached the thanksgiving sermon for 'the deliverance by the Prince of Orange' in January 1688 and became an influential ecclesiastical figure during the reign of William and Mary. He was appointed Archbishop of Canterbury in 1691. Despite his Puritan upbringing and early reputation as a Puritan preacher, his primacy was characterised by a liberal Latitudinarianism. (Photograph: Chetham's Library)

24 April 1745 that the duke of Cumberland 'hath killed and taken most of the Rebels' in a victory which was gained 'with very inconsiderable loss on our side'. He also observed that, as the news of the Jacobite defeat spread, bells were rung and bonfires lit.[55] Dr Jonathan Oates concluded that whilst Halifax 'did not play a decisive part in the dynastic struggle between the houses of Stuart and Hanover in 1745', collectively the town and parish subscribed £300 to the Yorkshire Association to help raise and maintain volunteer forces under the county lieutenancy. Of 252 Yorkshire towns and parishes which contributed, there were only three that contributed more than Halifax and Dr George Legh the Vicar of Halifax additionally subscribed £50 as an individual.[56]

During the 1740s Methodists were accused of being Jacobite emissaries and attempts were made to suppress itinerant preaching. In May 1744, John Nelson, the Birstall stonemason, who had preached the first Methodist sermon in the parochial out-township of Skircoat in 1741 was impressed for army service at Halifax. John Wesley, who had preached initially in out-townships at Lightcliffe and Skircoat during the period 1742–47, first preached in the centre of the town in the open air at the market cross on 22 August 1748. His preaching aroused an intensity of opposition reminiscent of Heywood's, when a 'most uproarious disturbance', initiated by a gentleman throwing money into the crowd, forced him to withdraw, mud-bespattered and bleeding, to a field at Salterhebble. Undeterred, however, he returned to the market place at dawn the following morning and shortly afterwards a Methodist society appears to have been formed, meeting in former Quaker premises in Cow Green.[57]

Religion therefore remained a contentious issue in Halifax and its hinterland throughout the early modern period, with Halifax remaining the focal point of religious controversy throughout the period from the English Reformation to the Evangelical Revival. But after the excitement and upheaval of the Civil War years, when political divisions had been largely fuelled by religion, parliamentary politics appeared humdrum by comparison in the period from 1660 to 1750. Halifax lost its short-lived status as a parliamentary borough at the end of the Interregnum, and freeholders had to travel to York to vote in the Yorkshire constituency elections, on one occasion in the middle of winter. Moreover, elections were rarely contested in Yorkshire, the largest English county constituency. Between 1708 and 1750 there were only three contests: in 1727, 1734 and 1741. The poll books for 1734 and 1741 show that a majority of Halifax freeholders supported the Tories, suggesting the emergence during the early eighteenth century of a Tory urban elite. In the 1741 contest, 109 Halifax township electors voted for the unsuccessful Tory candidate, George Fox, and 31 for the victorious Whig candidate, Cholmley Turner. Most of the leading Anglicans voted Tory, while most of the leading Dissenters supported the Whigs. Dr George Legh, the Vicar of Halifax, however, supported Walpole's Whig administration, perhaps because his appointment was in the gift of the crown. Indeed, Legh had been specially chosen by Walpole as the incumbent for what the Archbishop of York described as 'a most disaffected corner of my diocese'.[58] However, anticipating impending commercial upheaval during the Jacobite Rebellion of 1745, Arthur Jessop, the Huddersfield diarist, recorded that in November 1745 'The Clothiers are gone to fetch their cloth from Leeds and Halifax' though, as Dr Jonathan Oates concluded, 'Halifax did not play a decisive part in the dynastic struggle between the House of Stuart and Hanover in 1745'. He maintained, however, that 'church, gentry and people, both Whig and Tory, indicated their support for the status quo', displaying their loyalty to the Protestant King George II, whilst the Jacobite cause finally collapsed with the death of Charles Edward, the Young Pretender, in 1788.[59]

Local government

Dr Alan Betteridge has concluded that in 1585 Halifax was 'still firmly rooted in manorialism and many aspects of local social and economic life were regulated by manorial officialdom', whilst Dr Ronan Bennett, focusing upon the years 1640 to 1660, has affirmed that by 1660, Halifax 'may have been developing into an industrial urban centre' but administratively it was 'still rooted in manorialism'. During the seventeenth century, however, this situation was changing with the development of parochial and township government in Halifax and its hinterland and the growing responsibilities of the West Riding Justices of the Peace for the regulation of important aspects of the life of the local community. However, manorial administration played a key role in the development of the infrastructure of the emerging urban centre of Halifax in the sixteenth and seventeenth centuries. Moreover, although manorial control was weakening by the mid-seventeenth century as a result of the enfranchisement of large numbers of copyholders, the vestiges of manorialism survived beyond 1750.

The manor of Halifax-cum-Heptonstall, a sub-manor of the manor of Wakefield, had been a rectory manor owned by the Priory of Lewes until the dissolution of the monasteries, after which it passed first to the Waterhouse family of Halifax in 1545 and then to the Ingram family of Leeds in 1609, who sold Heptonstall in 1626. The parent manor of Wakefield had reverted to the crown in 1461 and was administered by the Duchy of Lancaster from 1554 until 1629, when it was given by Charles I to the Earl of Holland as part of a debt settlement. He had granted it to his son-in-law, who had promptly sold it to Sir Christopher Clapham, in whose family estates it remained until the beginning of the eighteenth century, when it passed to the Duke of Leeds. Both the parent manor and sub-manor had jurisdiction in Halifax. Although the Halifax court was legally subordinate to the manor of Wakefield, there was a history of conflicting jurisdiction and of encroachment of judicial powers from the Wakefield court. But in practice there was little differentiation at local level between the administrative and judicial business of the manor and sub-manor transacted at the manorial courthouse, the Halifax Moot Hall.[60]

The provision of an adequate water supply, the regulation of housing and the suppression of street nuisances were the most common administrative duties of the Halifax and Wakefield manorial courts, and in all these respects the business of the courts foreshadowed that of the town trustees in the 1760s. The source of the main town water supply was a spring at Well Head, and there were frequent presentments for pollution of the watercourse, particularly against butchers but also against others for allowing the water to be contaminated by geese and ducks, the disposal of garbage and the washing of wool and dirty clothes. In 1625 the Halifax court imposed a penalty on keepers of dyehouses for excessive use of water, and there were many presentments for the diversion of the watercourse for private use. In 1587 a local by-law, which anticipated national legislation of 1589, attempted to regulate the number of persons occupying property, since housing accommodation was clearly not keeping pace with population growth in the town. From the 1690s the court also attempted to check such nuisances as the riddling of ashes, the making of dunghills and the foraging of swine in the streets. In 1706 an order was issued prohibiting animal slaughter in the street, and fines were imposed on those who did not clean their market standings at the close of business on Saturdays.

Both manorial courts also heard and determined civil suits between tenants and dealt with problems of law and order which arose from manorial administration, but the Wakefield manorial court retained jurisdiction over criminal matters. Tenants had to be supervised to ensure that manorial property such as walls and stiles were kept in good repair. All manorial tenants, including freeholders and leaseholders, were obliged to do suit at the lord's corn and fulling mills, and attempts were also made from the late sixteenth century by the lord of the manor and his agents to gain revenue from local trade by control of the cloth halls. The custom of holding markets and fairs in the town may have been established during the fifteenth century, but rights cannot have been clearly defined, for the lord attempted to secure, and in 1607 was granted, a charter allowing him to hold markets at Halifax on Thursdays and Saturdays, fairs on the feast days of St John the Baptist and St Martin, and a court of piepowder to deal with disputes involving itinerants. There was opposition from the inhabitants, however, and, under the lordship of Henry Farrer and Dr Favour, the townspeople resisted the manorial control of the market and were eventually granted the right to hold markets in Halifax free of toll.

From the late sixteenth century until the 1630s the Halifax manorial court dealt with a wide range of local administrative matters, and its officials contributed greatly during this period to the maintenance of the social order and the regulation of economic life in the town. By the 1630s, however, it is apparent that the Halifax court was past its prime, and was falling into decay as an instrument of town government. The gradual disappearance of common rights and copyhold tenure, the emergence of the freeholder, and the tenants' constant opposition to obligatory suit at the manorial mills resulted in the decline of local manorialism. However, many of the functions of the court had not been superseded by 1750 and the court continued to play a vital role in regulating some aspects of the life of the urban community into the second half of the eighteenth century.

The evolution of parochial and civil township administration during the early modern period also profoundly influenced the future development of local government within the urban community and its hinterland. The Tudor

Sir Arthur Ingram (1565–1642).
A financier who amassed a
considerable fortune as Controller
of Customs for the port of London,
Ingram became one of the wealthiest
landowners in Yorkshire. Acquiring
the lordship of the sub-manor of
Halifax-cum-Heptonstall in 1609,
he sold Heptonstall in 1626. He also
encouraged the enfranchisement
of copyholders in Halifax, which
enhanced the legal and social status
of many of the town's inhabitants
during the early seventeenth century.
This portrait by George Geldorp,
the only surviving contemporary
image of Ingram, hangs at Temple
Newsam, which Ingram purchased
from the Duke of Lennox for
£12,000 in 1622.
(Photograph: Department of Leisure
Services, Leeds City Council)

governments gave new responsibilities, for example for poor relief and highway maintenance, to civil parishes, which, in large parishes like Halifax, eventually became devolved upon civil townships in both Halifax itself and the parochial out-townships. But the ecclesiastical parish authorities retained responsibility for the collection of the small tithes, the incumbent's main source of income which had been commuted into a complicated system of payments in kind and money in the 1530s, and the church rates for the maintenance of the fabric of the parish church. From the late seventeenth century there was a growing conflict between the historic centre of parochial power in Halifax, represented by the parochial vestry, and the parochial out-townships with their developing civil administration. For example, fixing the church rate, which appears to have been an annual assessment from 1620, was a frequent source of dispute, as in 1748 when the town and parish entered a costly litigation about moneys disbursed by the Halifax wardens on the church fabric without the consent of the out-township churchwardens or the vote of the parish vestry. Such tensions generally weakened the administrative cohesion of the area and resulted in a devolution and decentralisation of power which was not fully reversed until local government re-organisation in 1974.

The appointment of a parish clerk as the paid officer of the parish who served

Manor of Halifax-cum-Heptonstall, 1616. The copy surrender and admission, written in Latin and dated 16 August 1616, of a messuage in Dean Clough to the use of Humphry Drake of Halifax. The signature and paraph, a flourish around the signature designed as a precaution against forgery, are those of Nicholas Fenay, who was responsible for the record keeping of the manor. Born at Almondbury, where his ancestors had lived since the days of King John, Nicholas Fenay was also responsible for the re-building of Fenay Hall, Almondbury, in 1605, and was one of six residents who petitioned King James I for a charter to establish the free grammar school of King James in Almondbury in 1608.
(Photograph: West Yorkshire Archive Service, Calderdale)

under the churchwardens and the incumbent is recorded from the 1570s. From at least 1634 he occupied a special seat in the parish church near the pulpit, and during the eighteenth century he was provided with a gown and desk, outward symbols of his official status within the local hierarchy. Two churchwardens nominated annually met at monthly intervals with their colleagues from the parochial out-townships to deal with a wide range of ecclesiastical and secular business. Just as township business from the late seventeenth century was directed by the town vestry, the key questions of parochial administration were dealt with by substantial inhabitants from the whole parish. From 1677 parochial accounts had to be submitted annually to the vestry for inspection and approval, and from 1685 consent was required before more expensive repairs could be carried out on the church fabric. During the late seventeenth century, the vestry seems to have emerged as a parochial oligarchy with more official status and regular functions and to have assumed a greater measure of control over parochial business, probably at the expense of the incumbent and churchwardens who in the early seventeenth century had dominated parochial administration.

The gentry, yeomanry and professional classes were always well- represented in manorial, parochial and township administration during this period, but there is also evidence of participation in local government across the social spectrum. Between 1661 and 1692 the manorial office of steward was held by a Halifax scrivener and subsequently by members of the gentry. By the eighteenth century the jury of the manorial court was also composed exclusively of gentry, and members of the vestry were drawn predominantly from the upper ranks of the local community – merchants and professional men linked by ties of blood, marriage and administrative office. However, during the late sixteenth and early seventeenth centuries members of the gentry rarely held the office of overseer, which was occupied more frequently by tanners, woolmen, butchers, badgers, mercers, clothiers, chandlers and grocers, and in the 1730s the average value of property owned by overseers was approximately half that of the value of property belonging to churchwardens. So, the day-to-day administration of early modern Halifax was undertaken increasingly not so much by the neighbouring local gentry but by an urban professional elite and those even lower in the social hierarchy.[61]

Members of the neighbouring local gentry, however, maintained a regulatory role over important aspects of local government as Justices of the Peace, meeting at the quarter sessions, which rotated among the principal towns of the West Riding. Their responsibilities were extended under the Tudors to include not only the enforcement of law and order but the implementation of religious conformity, the regulation of commerce and employment, the operation of the Elizabethan Poor Laws of 1598 and 1601 and the maintenance of roads and bridges. Their role in the maintenance of public order included regulating the liquor trade, since alehouses were regarded with some suspicion possibly as agencies of social disorder. In 1635 a report by the West Riding Justices of the Peace revealed no fewer than fifty-one illegal alehouses in the town of Halifax and 134 in the parish, more than in any other township or parish in the West Riding. Occasionally, the responses of the county justices to local crises were regarded as inadequate by those most directly involved at local level. John Waite, the Vicar of Halifax, complained during the bubonic plague epidemic of 1645 that he 'was much wearied in labouring to rule the poor from rising to infect the town', but the county justices were 'backward to assist the town' to keep them in quarantine.[62]

A. G. Dickens has argued that the state of public order in mid-Tudor Yorkshire was lower than in most parts of England, citing the murder of Robert Holdsworth, Vicar of Halifax, 1526–56, during a robbery at the vicarage in May 1556, as one of the most shocking crimes of the era. Affrays were certainly commonplace in Halifax during the sixteenth century, involving both sexes and often also members of the local elite. In 1574, for example, John Waterhouse of Shibden, lord of the manor of Halifax, was fined ten shillings for his involvement in an affray on John Watmough, and in 1576 Sybil Wilson was fined five shillings after she 'made an affray and drew blood' from the wife of William Dickenson. Several assaults on the greave, the manorial officer responsible for the collection of rents, are also recorded in the manorial rolls between 1585 and 1600.[63]

Moreover, Dr John Addy's study of the consistory court records at York has led him to conclude that the parish of Halifax was 'uncontrollable and ungovernable' by the ecclesiastical authorities during the seventeenth century. Cases brought before the courts in 1635 and 1679 illustrate the problem. In 1635, during morning service at Halifax Parish Church, Richard Nicholson, churchwarden at Warley, and Abraham Parkinson, of Halifax, became involved in an unseemly brawl, during which Parkinson called Nicolson a lying rascal and 'bade a turd in his teeth'. In 1679, the parish clerk, John Wilson was presented to the archdeacon for 'defiling the church wall by pissing against it and very irreverently and contumaciously speaking of Richard Hook', the vicar.[64]

Between 1500 and 1750 the development of local government in Halifax involved the gradual reshaping of manorial and parochial responsibilities by an increasingly powerful local oligarchy and the evolution of the civil township in order to meet the growing demands of an expanding urban population for improved public services. In the process the urban community partially freed itself from manorial control while its links with its out-townships within the parish were weakened, though there is no evidence of any move to establish a new borough of Halifax during this period. By 1750, Halifax town had come to be run much more as an independent secular entity, managed by resident property owners, but the responsibilities of local government were largely confined to providing economic services, notably markets, basic amenities such as water and drainage, and maintaining law and order, within the wider framework of law enforcement in early modern Yorkshire. Other services which later devolved upon local government were largely provided initially by the voluntary sector, only supplemented later by ratepayer support.

Social welfare, education and culture

During the sixteenth and seventeenth centuries the yeomanry and gentry of Halifax and its hinterland assumed growing responsibility for social welfare, motivated by Puritan piety, humanitarian concern and a desire to maintain social stability. Their philanthropic activity, much of it inspired by the energetic incumbency of Dr John Favour as Vicar of Halifax between 1593 and 1623, supplemented the limited statutory provision for the poor and needy during this period. The Revd John Barlow, Favour's lecturer at Halifax Parish Church, calling on the local gentry to develop more of a social conscience, observed:

> Gentility consists not only in the cutting of a card, casting of a die, throwing of a bowl, watching of a cock, manning of a hawk, or in following after a deep-mouthed cry of hounds: but in good hospitality, virtuous actions and generous deeds.[65]

Such charitable deeds in Halifax were channelled mainly through perpetual trusts, established under isolated benefactions and bequests, and the cities of York and Hull excepted, Halifax gave more money for charitable purposes than any other place in Yorkshire between 1480 and 1640, most of it being donated in the years following Favour's arrival.[66]

The Brian Crowther Charity, which provided for the annual distribution of outdoor relief amongst the poor of the town under the terms of his will of 1606, was one of the town's earliest social welfare institutions. The account book of the charity, which was reconstituted following the Pious Uses Commission of 1651, provides fascinating insights into the condition of the poor. Much of the relief took the form of small money doles, ranging from one penny to eighteen pence, presumably to be spent on food, but emphasis was also placed on the provision of clothing. The specification in the accounts of such individual items of clothing as shoes, clogs, shirts, jumpcoats, smocks, stockings, hose, doublets, breeches, petticoats, gowns, waistcoats and vests, provides a vivid picture of the appearance of the poorer sort in late seventeenth-century Halifax. This complements the eloquent surviving testimony of Old Tristram, the wooden effigy of a licensed beggar who operated within the precincts of Halifax Parish Church during this period. It was carved by John Aked as a replacement for a previously damaged alms box of 1701 and depicts a bearded, gaunt, drably attired figure, clutching an alms box and bearing upon his chest a scroll with the legend; 'Pray Remember the Poor'. The principal reasons for destitution, as revealed in the charity account book, appear to have been old age, sickness, disability, confinement and dependent children, whose maintenance was also financed on occasions from charity funds.[67]

In 1610 Jane Crowther and Ellen Hopkinson, the widows of two Halifax clothiers, built almshouses for eighteen poor widows of the town, a particularly vulnerable sector within the local community. Each woman inmate was required to accommodate one pauper child to be taught by a specially appointed master in two adjoining rooms. In 1614, under Jane Crowther's will, the endowment was augmented by a small annuity which was to be paid towards the maintenance of the school and schoolmaster. In 1748 the almshouses and school were rebuilt at the expense of the town and allowances and clothing provided out of the rates. By the mid-eighteenth century, widows over sixty occupied the almshouses and children aged between three and ten years attended the school. In the 1640s further almshouses were established under the Waterhouse trust, the aims of which were to provide shelter, maintenance and clothing for twelve elderly poor. The provision seems to have been so carefully planned and generously endowed that, in spite of periods of mismanagement, the institution continues to provide sheltered accommodation for the elderly in the twenty-first century.

In response to the widespread poverty and escalating poor rates, a royal charter was granted to Nathaniel Waterhouse (1586–1645), a wealthy local merchant, for the establishment of a workhouse and house of correction. His frequent business visits to London had aroused his interest in the Bridewell, founded in 1552 to provide work for the poor within a disciplined environment. The workhouse was administered by a body of thirteen of the 'ablest and most discreet persons of the town and parish', headed by a master and prime governor, who were elected annually from within their ranks and who also served as Justices of the Peace within the town. During the period from 1635 to 1639, when the workhouse was apparently dissolved, the workhouse corporation was responsible both for the preservation of law and order in the town by the suppression of begging and vagrancy and for the provision of indoor relief and work for the poor. The inmates worked long hours from dawn till dusk with only short meal breaks, and discipline was severe, with some seventy workhouse inmates, men and women, whipped, several repeatedly, between 1635 and 1638. When the workhouse was reconstituted in 1682 during a period of acute economic hardship, a greater emphasis was placed on social welfare. In 1684 paupers capable of working were admitted into the workhouse, while those unable to work were badged and authorised to beg in the town. In 1687 a survey of the poor was conducted, following which cash allowances were provided for thirty-seven families suffering particular hardship. After the 1680s the workhouse appears to have declined and despite moving to new accommodation in 1700 was again inactive by 1710. In the 1740s it was again reconstituted largely at the town's expense, with accommodation for thirty residents.[68]

The growing concern for social welfare was also reflected in attempts to improve educational provision within the town. There are sporadic references in sixteenth-century manorial court rolls to schoolmasters and a grammar school in Halifax, but little evidence of institutional continuity before 1600, despite the granting of a royal charter for the establishment of Heath Grammar School in 1585. The fundraising activities of Dr John Favour ultimately ensured the financial viability of the school, which opened in 1600. Donations were secured from all the principal office-holders in the parish

Effigy of Old Tristram, Halifax Parish Church. Old Tristram was a licensed beggar, who operated within the precincts of Halifax Parish Church in the late seventeenth century. He is depicted wearing the typical apparel of a pauper during this period, clutching an alms box and bearing upon his chest a scroll with the legend 'Pray Remember the Poor'. The effigy, which stands at the west end of Halifax Parish Church was carved by John Aked, who also painted the royal arms of Queen Anne for the parish church in 1704. (Photograph: J. G. Washington)

and from Halifax men who had achieved success elsewhere, such as Sir Richard Saltonstall, Lord Mayor of London, Sir Henry Savile, provost of Eton and one of the scholars involved in translating parts of the New Testament from the Greek, and Joseph Lister, an alderman of Hull, and by the time of Favour's death over £800 had been raised as an endowment from gifts and bequests. Hipperholme Grammar School, which probably originated in the chantry chapel at nearby Coley, also secured a generous endowment from Matthew Broadley in 1648 and a permanent site by 1660. The curriculum of the grammar schools was classical and discipline severe. The novelist Laurence Sterne (1713–68), author of *Tristram Shandy*, who was educated at a local grammar school until his father's sudden death in Jamaica in 1731 left him penniless, recalled being 'severely whipped' by the master for inscribing his name on the newly whitewashed ceiling of the schoolroom. His uncle Richard, however, facilitated his progression to Jesus College, Cambridge, from where he matriculated in 1735, embarking initially upon a clerical ministry before emerging as a literary celebrity, following the publication of *Tristram Shandy* in 1760.

Although little is known about the early education of Henry Briggs (1561-1631), born at Daisy Bank in Warley, he did progress to St John's College, Cambridge in 1577, at the age of 16. He became the first Professor of Geometry at Gresham College, London, 1596-1620, and then proceeded to be the first Savilian Professor of Geometry at Oxford University from 1620 until his death. The latter chair had been founded in 1619 by Sir Henry Savile another native of Halifax. After John Napier (1550-1617) published his exposition of logarithms in 1614, Briggs met Napier and they agreed to pursue the furthering of logarithms to the base 10 to greatly facilitate calculation for all scientists. Following Napier's death in 1617 Briggs continued to produce the log tables necessary for convenient and speedy computation. These tables were used for more than three centuries thus demonstrating the importance of Briggs' collaboration based on Napier's vital innovation which was part of the rise of science in the Newtonian age and the concomitant work of other European mathematicians.

The grammar schools enabled the sons of the upper and middling ranks to proceed to the universities and into the growing professions of medicine and the law, as well as the church. By the Civil War more Halifax students were being sent to the universities than in the reign of Elizabeth, but the number was still relatively small.[69] Henry Power (1626–1668), the son of John Power, a wealthy manufacturer and trader in Halifax, known as the 'Spanish merchant', influenced perhaps by Thomas Browne (1605–82) with whom his father had had 'many serious discourses' on his foreign travels, proceeded to Christ's College, Cambridge, in 1641 on the eve of the Civil War to read medicine, subsequently qualifying as the first doctor in the Power family for five generations. He also began scientific experiments on barometric pressure in Cambridge, which he later continued in Elland, where he practised as a physician. On 6 May 1653 he conducted an historic experiment on Beacon Hill at Halifax demonstrating that the level of a mercury column operated as an altimeter. On 8 May 1661 he was admitted to the newly formed Royal Society through John Tillotson (1630–1694), a boyhood friend from Halifax and a future

Brian Crowther Charity, 1654–55. In September 1606 Brian Crowther devised by will to Dr John Favour and others a yearly rent of ten pounds out of land and property to be distributed annually amongst the poor of Halifax. After the death of Favour the charity appears to have been neglected and did not become fully operative again until 1654, as a result of the 1651 Pious Uses Commission. The dole account book, 1654–1692, records in minute detail the allocation of poor relief, providing valuable information about the structure of social welfare in the town, the nature of disease and disability and the condition of the poor.
(Photograph: West Yorkshire Archive Service, Calderdale)

Heath Grammar School. This unfinished early nineteenth-century sketch by an unknown artist shows groups of boys playing games in the foreground. A royal charter was obtained for the foundation of a grammar school in 1585, but the school did not open in Free School Lane until 1600. The fundraising activities of Dr John Favour after his appointment as Vicar of Halifax enabled the school to be built and provided an endowment fund to pay the schoolmaster. A public subscription provided £200 to enlarge and rebuild the school and house in 1777 and the school was further remodelled in 1879. (Photograph: Calderdale Museums Service, Bankfield)

Archbishop of Canterbury, who had also been educated at local grammar schools and Clare Hall, Cambridge. Power's book *Experimental Philosophy*, published in 1663 before that of his more famous contemporary Robert Hooke (1635–1703), was the first English work on microscopy.

The main function of the charity schools established under the Crowther-Hopkinson, Waterhouse and Smith trusts was to provide religious instruction, social conditioning and industrial training for those without private means. The Crowther-Hopkinson charity accounts indicate that children at the charity school linked with the almshouse foundation were taught to read, but there is no reference to their being taught to write. The Blue Coat Hospital established under the will of Nathaniel Waterhouse (1586–1645), was modelled on Christ's Hospital in London. It provided accommodation and education for twenty poor orphans of the parish, from six to fourteen years, in preparation for later apprenticeships. Dr Betteridge has concluded that notwithstanding the lack of emphasis on the teaching of writing, there is some evidence in local parish registers of improving standards of literacy by the 1750s, particularly amongst shoemakers, clothdressers, butchers and woolcombers, whose signatures demonstrate higher than average levels of literacy. However, husbandmen, labourers and clothiers displayed lower than average literacy levels.[70]

Laurence Sterne (1713–68). This portrait of Laurence Sterne in 1760 by Sir Joshua Reynolds, shows the Irish-born novelist in the year that his most influential semi-autobiographical comic novel commenced publication in London, transforming the hitherto unknown Yorkshire incumbent into a literary celebrity. He later wrote in his memoirs in 1767 that in the autumn of 1723 or the spring of the following year his father, whose brother owned property in Skircoat, placed him at a school near Halifax, 'with an able master' with whom he 'stayed some time'. Both the grammar schools at Heath and Hipperholme have laid claim to educating the future literary genius but the most recent assessment of the evidence by Dr J. T. Hughes has favoured the case for Hipperholme. (Photograph: National Portrait Gallery)

In 1626, the Vicar of Halifax, Robert Clay, converted the charnel house at the parish church into a parochial library. Records reveal how the collection grew by means of bequests and gifts, particularly from the Puritan clergy and laity, and indicate its careful maintenance during the Interregnum when many parochial libraries fell into decay. But its use was probably restricted to the local clergy and a narrow circle within the local laity for whom reading was a leisure activity. However, an early discussion of the implications of science for religious thought when Thomas Browne was engaged in writing his celebrated religious reflections, *Religio Medici*, in the mid-1630s probably at Upper Shibden Hall, Halifax, he lamented that 'it was penned in such a place, and with such disadvantage' that 'from the first setting of pen unto paper' he lacked 'the assistance of any good book' to stimulate his imagination or relieve his memory. The Yorkshire diarist Adam Eyre recorded purchasing in Halifax a recently published theological treatise, John Saltmarsh's *Divine Right of Presbyterie Asserted*, for a shilling in 1647, and a growing proportion of the parish inhabitants mentioned the possession of books in their wills during this period. Moreover, by 1708 the first history of Halifax, Samuel Midgley's *Halifax and its Gibbet-Law*, written while the author was imprisoned for debt in Halifax Gaol, had been published by William Bentley, parish clerk at Halifax Parish Church and member of the second generation of a family of Halifax booksellers. The

Sir Thomas Browne (1605–82).
An oil painting by Gerrard McIvor,
based on an engraving by David
Loggan, of the writer and physician who
wrote his earliest and most celebrated
work, *Religio Medici*, a confession
of faith, in the mid 1630s probably
while resident at Upper Shibden
Hall, Halifax, where he had a circle
of friends including John and Henry
Power, Anthony Foxcroft, Nathaniel
Waterhouse and Samuel Mitchell.
Educated at Winchester and Oxford,
he studied medicine at Montpellier and
Padua, settling in Norwich in 1637. His
Religio Medici was published without
his sanction in 1642 and reissued
with his approval in 1643. He has
been described as one of the greatest
and most neglected minds in history.
(Photograph: Dr J. T. Hughes)

book appeared in a second edition in 1712 and in 1738 the Revd Thomas Wright, a graduate of St John's College, Cambridge, and curate at Halifax Parish Church from 1732 until 1750, in his *The Antiquities of the Town of Halifax in Yorkshire*, printed by James Lister in Leeds for the Halifax bookseller James Hodgson, published a revised and more wide-ranging history which confirmed the growth of an elite of bibliophiles within the town.[71]

Some urban historians have detected considerable cultural polarisation during the Tudor and early Stuart period. Others, notably Dr Peter Borsay, have concluded that the English urban renaissance in the century after 1660 'opened up a cultural gap' between the higher echelons of society and 'the populace as a whole'.[72] The evidence from the developing urban centre of Halifax for the nature, timing and extent of such cultural differentiation is ambiguous. There is some evidence of an emerging cultural polarisation in Halifax from as early as the 1590s when Puritan moralists, led by Dr John Favour, condemned sexual immorality, drunkenness, sabbath breaking and the many excesses associated with popular recreation and leisure activities. William and Sarah Sheils have concluded that Dr John Favour 'seems to have won over the principal inhabitants of the parish to his reforming policy, and consistent and thorough presentments against sexual offenders, drunkards and profaners of the sabbath were made by churchwardens at successive visitations throughout the thirty years of his ministry'.[73] In 1596 two Halifax men were presented before the archdeacon at York by Dr Favour for playing shoolnige (shove-halfpenny) during evening prayers. In his meticulous annotation of the moral lapses of his parishioners in the parish registers, Dr Favour recorded that Widow Foster of Halifax had been 'an infamous prostitute'; William King of Skircoat Moor 'a common swearer, drinker and most filthy adulterer'; Richard Theaker of Sowerby 'a drunkard drowned in his own drunkenness'; and that Richard Bridge of Southowram had 'lived an incestuous life and died excommunicate'. He also established that bastardy had recurred in some Halifax families across four generations.[74]

The extent and the effectiveness of Favour's moral crusade is difficult to assess. Dr Betteridge has concluded that the Halifax illegitimacy ratio, ranging from approximately two per cent to approximately six per cent in the 1590s, although extremely high by national standards, was probably no higher than that of many other northern parishes. Indeed, the illegitimacy ratio in Halifax was considerably lower than the ratio of ten per cent recorded for the same decade in the neighbouring parish of Rochdale. However, Dr Addy has calculated from visitation returns that some 226 Halifax couples were presented to the archdeacon for ante-nuptial fornication during the seventeenth century. One woman, Sara Fielden, was recorded as having 'committed fornication on a dark night in the open field with whom she knows not', and a young man, John Hardcastle, was reputed to have 'slept so long and so often with Ann Mitchell that she had made him so weak he could scarce eat fried eggs'. When Oliver Heywood commenced his ministry at Coley Chapel, he remarked: 'Oh what rioting, rebelling, gluttony, drunkenness, abominable beastly luxury, lechery scarce heard of among the heathen'. He later recorded instances of incest and adultery and reckoned that illegitimacy had been commoner in Halifax parish in the years following the Restoration than at any time in living memory. He reported that the vicar had prepared a list of over thirty cases currently under consideration. He wrote in his diary in 1691: 'I have seldom heard of so many young women with child by fornication as lately and some of them to cover their shame do marry – great wickedness'.[75]

Oliver Heywood also recorded in his diary a recurrence of sabbath breaking in Halifax on Easter Sunday in 1681, when 'there were hundreds of people … in the churchyard and on the green, and all along the town playing stool-ball and other recreations, without any control'. He also condemned midsummer and May Day revelling in Halifax. On 24 June 1679 Heywood found 'a great tumult in the town', during the midsummer fair week, with 'young men all in a heap striking and laying about each other'. He recorded that when the constables were sent for 'one was sorely wounded in the struggle'. On Saturday, 1 May, in the following year, he observed:

a great number of persons of the poor and baser sort began early in the morning, even while it was yet dark, to bring in May. There were men, women and big youths, and all had white waistcoats or sheets about them; they carried garlands, flowers or branches of trees. They were accompanied by pipers and fiddlers; some had drums, and some carried white banners with red crosses. They rambled about most of the day. Towards night many of them were drunk and mad.[76]

Puritan preachers from Favour to Heywood also endeavoured to discourage popular beliefs in magic and superstition. Dr John Favour recorded cases of heretical practices involving the alleged use of magical powers. Oliver Heywood later recorded in his diary that he was called to Wakefield in October 1665 to see a young man judged to be possessed or bewitched, and in February 1672 he attended the funeral of another young man who had apparently been taken away by strange diseases attributed to witchcraft. His own scepticism, however, is evident in an entry in his diary in May 1683, where he criticised a local physician, Dr Thornton, for his treatment of 'a strange illness that had fallen upon one of his flock' at Northowram. The doctor had evidently taken the view that his patient 'hath some hurt by an evil tongue' and had refused to prescribe any medicine for him until a mixture of his urine, hair, wheatmeal and horse-shoe stumps had been baked in a fire. Heywood ultimately convinced the patient that spiritual healing through prayer and fasting was preferable.[77]

Cockfighting and horse racing also attracted Heywood's censure, though his denunciations evidently failed to suppress these popular recreational activities. Moreover, their continuing appeal to participants from both the gentry and 'the poorer sort of Halifax', emphasises the very limited development of cultural differentiation in the town by the late seventeenth century. Nevertheless, Heywood's denunciation of the unseemly brawl which developed at a cock fight in a purpose built cocking house at the rear of the Cross Inn in May 1680 – where 'they all fought desperately a long while', 'an abundance of money was lost and won', and 'they drank all night and were so high in swearing and ranting that they were heard far in the town' – constitutes a vigorous assertion of alternative cultural values. When horse racing was held in Halifax in 1678, Heywood observed that the sporting event was a pretext 'to gather the country to drink their ale, for it was hoped it would be as profitable to the town as a fair'. A similar occasion at Northowram in 1681, hosted by John Mitchell of Scout Hall, attracted crowds of between 400 and 500, including 'many idle persons' from Halifax, Boothtown, Ovenden and Holdsworth.

Horse racing appears to have been resumed in Halifax in 1736, when the principal innkeepers of Halifax, joined by the vicar, a couple of gentlemen, and several prominent manufacturers, entered into an agreement to finance a regular race meeting on Skircoat Moor in an effort to improve the tone of such events. An advertisement in the *Leeds Mercury* for a three-day race meeting on Skircoat Moor in June 1738 revealed that spectators were expected from a wide area. Moreover, additional attractions included 'in the forenoons, cock fightings betwixt the gentlemen of Yorkshire and the gentlemen of Lancashire', and in the evenings 'for the amusement of the ladies there were assemblies, for social intercourse and dancing at the Assembly Rooms', suggesting that the appeal of these events crossed social barriers.[78]

Puritan values made a considerable impact on Halifax and its hinterland from the late sixteenth century, particularly in the sphere of social welfare and educational provision, where considerable charitable activity was stimulated. However, Puritan moralists appear to have been less successful in promoting sexual propriety and sabbath observance, in discouraging beliefs in magic and superstition, and in suppressing a range of popular recreational activities. Dr John Smail has characterised the Puritanism of seventeenth-century Halifax as basically egalitarian, concerned more with orthodoxy of belief than with social status, arguing that this was typical of upland or urban communities which lacked 'a strong local gentleman and where economic and social conditions allowed immigration and economic independence'. Consequently, Smail has argued, the society which emerged in Halifax after the demise of Puritan ideology 'was dominated by a large and relatively undifferentiated social middle'. It found expression, for example, in the installation of a new Snetzler organ in Halifax Parish Church on the recommendation of no less a figure than William Herschel (1738–1822), a Hanoverian-born musician, more universally known as an astronomer. In 1789, Herschel produced a telescope with a mirror diameter of 48 inches and a focal length of 40 feet, recognised as one of the marvels of eighteenth-century technology, and in 1781 he discovered the planet Uranus, which he had proposed to name Georgius Sidus (Georgian Planet) in honour of his sovereign patron George III of England, from whom he received a knighthood in 1816. He also developed a hypothesis that nebulae were composed of stars, and the theory of stellar evolution. Thus, it is also apparent that as Halifax developed as a leisure centre for its hinterland during the early modern period, some activities, such as the installation of an organ at the parish church would have appealed more to a cultured elite, whilst other attractions such as cockfighting and horseracing brought together people from different social classes, thereby generating sociability amongst the participants but also arousing criticism of the resultant drunkenness, gambling and boisterous behaviour associated with these activities.[79]

'A pretty well-built town of stone'

Population growth, economic development, changes in social structure, alterations in local government and the work of the voluntary sector affected the size of the town and the number, distribution and appearance of its buildings and streets during the early modern period. Although Halifax was emerging as a busy market town by the late sixteenth century, a contemporary visitor described it baldly as a town 'of no great account'. In contrast, the diarist John Aston commended it in 1639 more enthusiastically as 'a pretty well-built town of stone', populated mainly by clothiers. By the early seventeenth century, Halifax was beginning to display many of the characteristics of an urban centre, with its cloth halls, many markets, shops and inns, its wide range of trades and services, its occupational structure all pointing, as Ronan Bennett has observed, 'to an increasingly urban environment'. Contemporary quarter sessions records refer to Halifax as a market town, and its cloth halls served as commercial centres for the buying of wool and cloth. Moreover, its open market, corn and cattle markets and proliferating shops supplied a growing range of provisions for the voracious population of its rural hinterland, which the late sixteenth-century visitor who had been singularly unimpressed by

John Mitchell (1659–96) and Scout Hall, Northowram. A naive painting by an unknown artist of this local nouveau riche gentleman, with his home at Scout Hall in the distance. The grandson of Samuel Mitchell (1597–1645), a Halifax cloth merchant, John Mitchell was frequently castigated by Oliver Heywood, the Northowram Nonconformist preacher for dissipating his energies and inherited wealth on horse racing, gambling and drinking and went to an early grave at the age of thirty-seven in 1696. (Photograph: Calderdale Museums Service, Bankfield)

the town had described as 'wonderful populous and strong'. Moreover, there are no signs of it having suffered depopulation as the town expanded during the early modern period. The township also abounded in alehouses and inns, including the Turk's Head, the Swan, the Talbot, the Crown, the Star and the Cross, where John Aston found accommodation for the night and which he described as 'one of the fairest inns in England'.[80]

No early maps of the town have survived, but a reconstructed town plan for the mid-seventeenth century based upon documentary evidence, and the later survey of the town by the energetic and enterprising excise officer John Warburton in 1719, identifies the medieval route from Wakefield across Clark Bridge leading to a street of Woolshops connecting the old and new markets. Continuing westwards, the High Street merged with Gibbet Lane, ascending to Halifax Green and over Halifax Moor to Highroad Well and Lancashire. From the market place, Northgate and Southgate branched north and south and not far from the market place were Cow and Bull Greens and Swine Market. The most prominent local public building remained the medieval parish church, extended in the sixteenth century with the addition of the Rokeby and Holdsworth chapels in 1533 and 1554 financed by clerical bequests.[81] There was also a grammar school adjoining the churchyard, which was suppressed at the Reformation, and as Mayhew also suggests, there may also have been tithe barns within the vicinity of the parish church before the dissolution of Lewes Priory. The *Valor Ecclesiasticus* of 1535 confirmed the value of the tithes in a single entry, revealing that 'Halifax profits ... the rectory' with all its profits and commodities amounting annually to £133 6s. 8d.[82]

Buildings constructed after 1500 included the woollen Cloth Hall at Hall End, one of the earliest cloth halls to be built in Yorkshire and perhaps the largest cloth hall in the west of the county, the Linen Hall, erected nearby in 1629 and the Mulcture Hall, with its handsome plaster ceiling, built by John Power, a prosperous merchant who had leased from the Lord of the Manor the mills and cloth halls of the town. The market cross, referred to by John Aston, and the Maypole, were both located in the market place in the seventeenth century notwithstanding Puritan opposition to the latter. Nathaniel Waterhouse's workhouse of 1635 was situated to the west of the parish church near to the medieval Moot Hall which was located to the north-west of the church. Moreover, unlike Bradford and Leeds, Halifax did not suffer heavy bombardment in the English Civil Wars, emerging relatively intact, and subsequently developing into a commercial centre. Indeed, a Dutch merchant living in Halifax in 1665 regularly despatched 300 to 400 kerseys to Holland via Hull and Newcastle-upon-Tyne. The substantial timber-framed 'house at the top of Woolshops', dated 1670 on a stone corbel, appears to be the latest dated timber-framed building in West Yorkshire and is one of only three dozen buildings with exposed external timber-framed walls that have survived in the county. Built on a corner site with two original stone walls separating it from adjacent buildings its construction was influenced by new legislation introduced in the wake of the Great Fire of London of 1666, which required new timber-framed buildings to have stone fire-break walls built between adjacent properties. Its distinctive red-lead coloured timbers, herringbone patterned panels and jettied upper storeys have been authenticated and enhanced by modern restoration. Later engravings illustrate other buildings in the town with this characteristic feature revealing that timber-framed buildings continued to be constructed in towns like Halifax until the late seventeenth century in contrast to the countryside where stone

Scout Hall, Northowram. A conjectural drawing by John Horner published in 1835. The imposing three-storeyed rectangular Caroline mansion built in 1681 for John Mitchell exhibits tall cross-mullioned windows combined with asymmetrically placed oval windows and a stylish hipped roof, which the artist has modified in this representation. It is one of the earliest examples in the county of a formally designed double-pile, lesser gentry residence with a near-symmetrical facade. The hall was flanked by heated parlours, with a kitchen and cellars to the rear. (Photograph: Calderdale Museums Service, Bankfield)

buildings were more usual after 1600. These included fine examples of Pennine vernacular architecture ranging from Upper Cockroft in Rishworth (1607), Marsh Hall in Northowram (1626), Brearley Hall in Midgley (1626), High Sunderland in Northowram (1629), Holdsworth House in Ovenden (1633) and Norland Hall (1634) in Norland. In 1696–97, a Presbyterian meeting house, the town's first Nonconformist chapel, was erected at Northgate End on the northern perimeter of the town and remained the only purpose-built chapel in the town until the construction of a new Quaker meeting house in Clare Road in the 1740s.[83]

In 1708, Lord Ingram, lord of the manor of Halifax let to John Fourness of Ovenden 'all those buildings commonly called by the names of Woollen Hall and Linen Hall, heretofore commonly used for the selling of cloth', principally white dressed kerseys following which they were reconstructed and continued as a market for cloth held on Saturday mornings. Leeds merchants in particular

The house at the Maypole during demolition in the summer of 1890. The house formerly stood at the junction of Crown Street and Corn Market in Halifax and was one of the finest examples of a wealthy northern merchant's house outside York. Dated between 1480 and 1510, the house frontage was adorned with lavish wood carvings, including the arms of the Merchant Adventurers of York. (Photograph: Halifax Antiquarian Society)

bought large quantities of white dressed kerseys in the remodelled Halifax Cloth Hall which they transported to Hamburg and Holland, whilst foreign merchants and other 'wealthy traffickers' bought great quantities of cloth to sell in London. Unable to cope adequately with the surge in trade M. W. Garside has suggested that rows of stalls were probably set up in the streets, between the Cloth Hall and the Butchers' Shambles, where another market for coloured cloth was held, until these arrangements were eventually superseded by the new Halifax Manufacturers Hall in 1779.[84] Indeed, Halifax, although emerging as a busy market town, with its unpaved streets and largely uncovered water supply, still displayed some features of an overgrown village and was less well-developed as an urban centre than Leeds. Moreover, although by the early seventeenth century much of Halifax's common wasteland had been enclosed, unenclosed moorland west of the town was still considered 'so barren and unfruitful' that it was 'not worth 2d. the acre by the year'.[85]

However, by the mid-eighteenth century most of the township had been enclosed and the land parcellation of the town during the early modern period through piecemeal enclosure is now regarded as an important factor in the patterning of the spatial structure of the nineteenth-century industrial town. But despite widespread enclosure beyond the urban perimeter, there is no evidence of extensive dispersed settlement within the township. The expanding town, which doubled in size between 1500 and 1750, remained quite firmly nucleated and its focal centre did not experience a major locational shift. Halifax was also served by a network of packhorse causeways.[86]

Stone-cladding, however, had radically altered the external appearance of many of its older timber-framed buildings, and brick was beginning to appear in the construction of town houses from about 1700. The appropriately named Red Hall in Old Market, a three-storeyed house with stone surrounds, string courses and quoins, referred to in a deed of 1714, built around 1700 and demolished in 1866, was probably the first brick building to be built in the town. Nevertheless, a 1735 valuation records a score of barns within a stone's throw of the market cross, and

The house at the Maypole after its re-erection at Shibden. Recognising the importance of this former merchant's residence, the antiquary, John Lister of Shibden Hall arranged for its reconstruction on the Shibden estate, where it was re-named Daisybank. The elevation of the building consists of three bays indicated by the projecting chamber windows, supported by richly carved corbels. The heraldic carving of a Tudor rose and a portcullis suggest embellishment during the reign of Henry VII (1485–1509), but the construction of the house, which also provides an example of the use of chevron framing with additional offset studs, may well have begun earlier. The building originally had a through passage with access to a courtyard at the rear of the property. (Photograph: Halifax Antiquarian Society)

the Revd Thomas Wright's bird's-eye description of the town from Beacon Hill accentuates its compact development and rural character:

> So compact is now the town and so contrived by art, that from the hill which leads to and from Wakefield, it represents a cross, or rather two large beams laid cross one upon another with the left arm rather declining; the whole consisting chiefly of four streets in the midst whereof stands the market cross and a large, and plentiful, shambles for the sale of meat. To the town thus described are annexed many regular and well-walled closes variously chequered with the different beauties of corn and grass, that from the aforesaid heights the most curious traveller hath not seen a more delightful landscape, if such prospects are viewed in their proper seasons.[87]

Over the next century the appearance of the town, and much else about its people, would be transformed.

Half-timbered house at the top of Woolshops, dated 1670, photographed in 1971. The sole surviving timber-framed building in the modern town centre, and the latest dated timber-framed building in the modern metropolitan county of West Yorkshire. Subsequently restored and incorporated into the redeveloped shopping precinct, which was completed in 1984. (Photograph: J. A. Hargreaves)

4

'An astonishing trading town': Halifax in the age of industrial expansion, 1750–1850

Commercial and industrial expansion

ALTHOUGH BY 1750 THE TOWN OF HALIFAX was already a place of significance within its parish, it hardly as yet rated as a substantial town nationally or even, in truth, regionally. Indeed in 1781, when William Bailey's *Northern Directory* became the first commercial directory to include Halifax, it was evident that the town's commercial and industrial expansion, although clearly burgeoning, remained at a relatively modest level, with, for example, no more than one dozen grocers, seven drapers, four druggists, four ironmongers, two iron founders, a brass founder, a hat maker, a silk merchant and a watchmaker amongst the listed traders. However, economic development was to draw into the urban centre considerable numbers of people, and changes of production were to alter dramatically over the next century the social structure, living standards, politics and appearance of the town.

During the age of industrial expansion from 1750 to 1850 the population of the town of Halifax quintupled, rising from around 5,000 in 1743 to 25,159 in 1851, while the population of the parish as a whole rose at almost the same rate from around 31,000 to 149,257. As Table 4.1 shows, the town's share of the parish population, averaging around fifteen per cent during this period, therefore remained remarkably stable, arresting the downward trend of the period 1550–1750, though failing to reverse the trend until after 1851. It is readily apparent how this demographic growth occurred. High mortality rates, particularly of infants, were offset by a growing migration into Halifax from the outlying townships as former domestic workers were absorbed into the new urban factory workforce, and by large numbers of extra-parochial immigrants, many of them Irish. During this period Halifax not only remained the commercial hub of the parish but also emerged as a major manufacturing centre, acquiring spacious new factory and warehouse accommodation, progressive banking and insurance facilities and increasing access to turnpike, waterway and railway networks.[1]

Economic growth was evident particularly within the established woollen and worsted industries. Dr Richard Pococke, the well-travelled Irish bishop, visiting

Halifax in 1750, commented on its 'very plentiful market' and observed that the residents of the town were 'all people of business' engaged in 'a great manufacture in serges and cloths'.[2] In 1758 the Revd John Watson recorded no fewer than thirty-nine fulling mills in operation in the parish, over a fifth of them in the immediate vicinity of Halifax. He commented that by 1775 there was 'scarcely a single instance in the whole parish of a man's living entirely by farming'.[3] Besides supplying a growing domestic market and clothing British armies in the colonial conflicts of the late eighteenth century, export markets developed with Spain, Portugal, the Levant and Guinea where, Thomas Pennant observed in 1770, the cloths were 'wrapped in an oilcloth painted with negroes and elephants to captivate the natives'.[4] The Revd Thomas Twining, a Colchester cleric, visiting Halifax in 1781 remarked that 'the appearance of trade, population and advancement of every kind there is striking', with 'a perpetual stream … of men carrying bundles of cloth' to and from the magnificent new Manufacturers' Piece Hall opened in 1779, in the year which also saw the opening in Shropshire of Thomas Telford's new suspension bridge inaugurating a new phase of more intensive industrial expansion.[5] In 1788, Charles Dibdin, the popular composer, pronounced Halifax 'an astonishing trading town for its size' and compared the cloth hall with its 'prodigious number of cells' to a bee-hive humming with activity on market day.[6]

However, by the second decade of the nineteenth century, if not earlier, Halifax had lost its ascendancy in West Riding worsted production, which it had enjoyed since 1750, to neighbouring Bradford. Bradford's population was increasing at an even faster rate than that of Halifax after 1801 and receiving substantially higher rebates on the tax on soap used in the processing of wool for worsted manufacture during the period 1810–30, suggesting higher levels of worsted production. Paradoxically, because Halifax had a superior supply of water power, Bradford was compelled to make the transition to steam power earlier, exploiting its richer coal supplies. Halifax, on the periphery of the West Yorkshire coalfield, had fewer local reserves, and it proved costly to transport coal into the town until the opening of a direct canal link from the Calder and Hebble Navigation in 1828. Indeed, Dr John Simpson of Bradford, comparing the fortunes of the two towns in 1825, pronounced that Halifax 'can scarce be called a manufacturing town, yet it is a place of considerable trade, but that trade is considerably on the decline and has been ever since Bradford began to rise into notice'. However, Pigot's *National Commercial Directory* of 1834 identified the town's 'chief articles of manufacture' as 'shalloons, calimancoes, taminets, moreens, shags, serges, baizes, coatings and carpets; with narrow and broad cloths and kerseymeres, both for domestic use and the army'.[7]

In truth, worsted manufacture continued to grow in Halifax and its neighbouring townships. No fewer than 50 per cent of the textile labour force was engaged in worsted production by 1835. Moreover, new textile industries were also successfully established in the parish, notably cotton and silk. Cotton manufacture had grown to predominance in the western townships of the parish bordering on Lancashire after 1780, and by the 1790s no fewer than one-third of the 140 cotton mills in the county of Yorkshire were located in the parish of Halifax. As shown in Table 4.2,

Table 4.1 Population of the township and parish of Halifax 1743–1851

Date	Halifax township population [% change]		Halifax parish population [% change]		township % share of parish population
1743	5,000		31,000		16.1
1764	6,360	[+27.2]	41,220	[33.0]	15.4
1801	8,886	[+16.1]	63,434	[53.9]	14.0
1811	9,159	[+ 3.1]	73,415	[15.7]	12.5
1821	12,628	[+37.9]	93,050	[26.7]	13.6
1831	15,382	[+21.8]	109,899	[18.1]	14.0
1841	19,881	[+29.2]	130,743	[19.07]	15.2
1851	25,159	[+26.5]	149,257	[14.2]	16.9

Sources: Herring and Drummond Visitation Returns, 1743 and 1764; Census Returns, 1801–51.

by 1835 the number of cotton mills in the parish had risen to fifty-seven, though only two of these were situated in the township of Halifax. There were also four silk factories in the parish, where it was considered that local conditions were 'peculiarly adapted for the preservation of its colour', including two in the township of Halifax. By 1835, 16 per cent of textile workers in the parish were employed in textile mills in the township of Halifax. In 1837, the diarist Anne Lister, who only six years earlier had contrasted 'the fine clean air of Halifax' with the smoky atmosphere of Bradford and Leeds, observed that 'Halifax is now brightening into the polish of a large smoke-canopied commercial town'.[8]

Table 4.2 Textile mills and workers in the township and parish of Halifax, 1835

	township		parish	
	mills	*workers*	*mills*	*workers*
Woollen	4	160	35	2,104
Worsted	14	769	45	2,551
Cotton	2	351	57	4,267
Silk	2	272	4	777
Unoccupied	0		12	
Total	22	1,552	153	9,699

Source: Returns to Factory inspectors, 1835.

The transition to factory-based production was a gradual process in the parish of Halifax. Technological breakthroughs before 1780 in carding and spinning had stimulated the move towards factory production of cotton yarn during the last two decades of the eighteenth century and cotton power-loom weaving had become widespread by the late 1820s. But the mechanisation of the woollen and

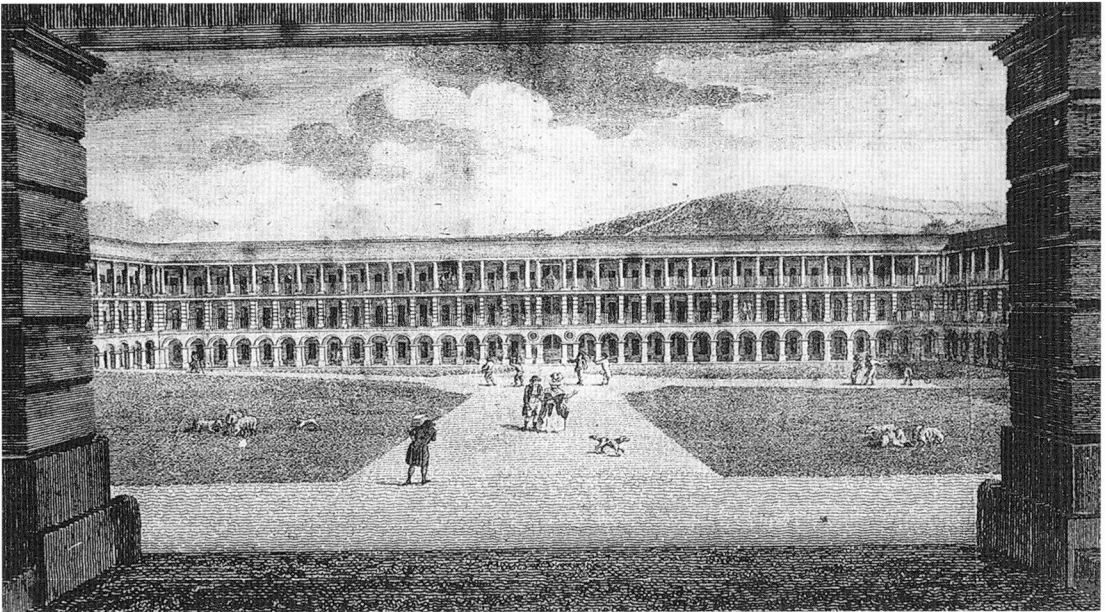

Contemporary engraving of Halifax Piece Hall by William Burgess, 1788. This massive rectangular structure, enclosing a spacious courtyard, was built at a cost of over £12,000 as a market for woollen cloth between 1775 and 1778. It was opened on New Year's Day 1779 and was unusual because the clothiers made their sales from individual rooms accessed from the galleries. Although the hall flourished for three-and-a-half decades, buyers subsequently made their purchases directly from factory warehouses and by the early 1830s fewer than 200 of its 315 rooms were occupied. (Photograph: J. A. Hargreaves)

worsted industries was more gradual, extending over a period of at least sixty years. While woollen scribbling and worsted spinning had been mechanised by 1800, woollen spinning and worsted weaving were not mechanised until the 1820s. Woollen weaving and worsted combing remained predominantly cottage-based hand processes until the late 1840s and 1850s respectively. Indeed, until the 1840s there were no fewer than eleven gig mills engaged in the finishing process of woollen cloth, and these were still dependent on human or horse power. Water power was extensively used within the parish until the 1870s. Steam power was used initially only to supplement water power, and by 1806 only twelve steam engines can be identified in use in mills around Halifax. At least 47 were installed between 1807 and 1833 and a further 73 between 1834 and 1851, the majority in cotton and worsted mills.[9]

By 1851 the number of textile mills in the parish had risen to 254, including eighteen new spinning mills in the municipal borough of Halifax. During this period there were shifts in industrial location as new mills sprang up along the lines of the new railways into Halifax and other growing urban centres in the valley bottoms outside the town. By the time of the 1851 census 22 per cent of adult males in the Halifax registration district were employed in worsted manufacture, compared with 9 per cent in woollen and nearly 4 per cent in cotton manufacture. A sample study of 10 per cent of the working population of the Halifax and Skircoat Green registration districts shows that almost half of the total textile workforce was employed in the worsted industry.[10]

Although the economy of the town therefore depended primarily on textiles, it was the diversity of its manufactures by the second quarter of the nineteenth century that particularly impressed contemporary observers. Comparing Halifax and Bradford as centres of worsted manufacture in 1849, the journalist Angus Bethune Reach of the *Morning Chronicle* concluded that Halifax possessed a greater industrial diversity:

> The mayor, Mr Crossley, for instance, is the chief partner in an immense carpet manufacturing establishment, employing about 1,500 hands, principally adult males, and paying about £1,000 weekly in wages. Besides this and other establishments of different kinds, the worsted manufacturers of Halifax prepare so great a variety of the staple production that periods of distress fall in general lighter upon them than on their Bradford neighbours.[11]

When Ralph Waldo Emerson (1803–82), philosopher and founding father of the modern American intellectual tradition, visited Halifax in the previous year as the guest of James Stansfeld, a Unitarian local solicitor and judge, he toured Crossley and Sons' carpet mills. The firm was sending patterns for carpets and textiles for Queen Victoria, and Emerson thought that the 'vista made by the looms' in the Crossleys' mill 'resembled a church aisle'. He also visited Edward Akroyd's stuff mills which 'employ 5,000–6,000 operatives' where in one hall he saw '800 looms'. 'In many,' he continued, 'they were making ponchos'. He also visited the factory school, 'spaciously built and well furnished for the children'.[12]

Besides textiles, carpet manufacture, trades allied to textiles such as dyeing, an embryonic machine-tool industry, and card-making (all businesses located principally in Halifax itself), there was also substantial pottery manufacture in the adjoining townships of Northowram and Southowram and fairly extensive coal mining and stone quarrying in the south east of the parish, employing at least 1,200 men by 1831. In the upper Calder Valley, at the time of the 1851 census, about one in eight families had some involvement with farming, many households still practising a dual economy, although by 1851 this often took the form of one or more members of the household working in textile factories. The topographer William White declared that Halifax by the middle of the nineteenth century ranked 'next to Leeds, Bradford, and Huddersfield as one of the principal seats and emporiums of the woollen and worsted manufactures' and that:

> the scenery, viewed from the surrounding heights, exhibits a tract of country, which perhaps more than any other in the kingdom, serves to show how completely the wealth and industry of man can triumph over the most stubborn indispositions of nature.[13]

Dean Clough Mills, Halifax, *c.* 1803. In 1802, John Crossley (*c.* 1772–1837) and his business partners Thomas Crossley and James Travis took out a twenty-year lease of the premises at Dean Clough illustrated in this contemporary sketch. When the lease expired in 1822, the partnership was dissolved. John Crossley then renewed the lease for £340 and set up his own business. In 1824 he moved with his wife, Martha, and family to the house alongside the mill. By the time of his death in 1837, the firm, with 150 looms and some 300 employers, ranked as the fourth largest in the country. He left a personal estate of around £18,000 and was 'deeply lamented by his family and numerous circle of friends'. Three of his sons, John, Joseph and Francis, continued their father's business after his death, trading under the name of John Crossley and Sons. (Photograph: West Yorkshire Archive Service, Calderdale)

However, 'stubborn indispositions of nature' continued to hinder the development of transport systems. The rough, hilly terrain of the parish presented early road builders and later waterway and railway engineers with formidable problems. Some remoter parts of the parish continued to depend on the pack-horse until at least 1850. Elsewhere, increasing use was made of horse-drawn waggons. Details of regular services offered by carriers, no fewer than fifty of whom were operating in the town by 1845, were advertised in local newspapers and directories. Further turnpike roads were constructed, including routes to Keighley in 1753, Burnley and Littleborough in 1760, Huddersfield in 1777, and Leeds in 1814 and 1826, but some of the major difficulties of approach to Halifax were only overcome by major feats of civil engineering during the nineteenth century. The Godley cutting and the Shibden embankment were constructed under a Turnpike Act of 1824, amended in 1827 and completed in 1830. Hailed by the diarist Anne Lister as 'a stupendous feat', the project involved cutting through 731 metres of rocky hillside and building a high embankment to take the road across the Shibden valley to Stump Cross. On the Halifax side of the cutting, Old Bank gave way to New Bank in 1837, leading towards the high-level six-arched North Bridge, which had been re-constructed in stone and opened for traffic in 1774, and which later became associated with

Martha Crossley (1775–1854).
Following her marriage to the carpet manufacturer John Crossley in 1801, Martha Crossley became 'the backbone of the family', taking 'a full share in the labours and responsibilities of her husband', in the view of the Victorian prophet of honest toil, Samuel Smiles. She later recalled that 'in addition to carpet making we carried on the manufacture of shalloons and plainbacks, the whole of which I managed myself'. She also 'made and stitched, with assistance, all the carpets that we sold retail', rising regularly before dawn. The oil portrait commissioned by her youngest son, Sir Francis Crossley, shows her plainly attired in silk bonnet, white shawl and dark dress, with an open Bible on her lap. Her earnest evangelical Nonconformity and celebrated vow that, 'if the Lord does bless us at this place, the poor shall taste of it', inspired a lavish philanthropy in her sons.
(Photograph: Lord Somerleyton)

disorder during the Plug Plot disturbances of 1842, along with the steep incline at Salterhebble which defined access to Halifax from the south.[14]

An Act of Parliament had been passed in 1700 for the construction of the Aire and Calder Navigation, the first project of its kind in England. However, its extension, the Calder and Hebble Navigation, surveyed by John Smeaton in 1757–65, and designed to bring the navigation into the parish of Halifax, was beset with problems, and the whole length of the navigation to Sowerby Bridge did not open until September 1770. Moreover, the critical trans-Pennine link with the Rochdale Canal was not made until 1802, and the Halifax Branch Canal from Salterhebble to Bailey Hall, linking Halifax directly with the new trans-Pennine route and the Calder and Hebble Navigation system, was not opened until 1828. The ascending gradient, rising thirty and a half metres in one-and-a-quarter miles, required the construction of no fewer than fourteen locks between Salterhebble and Bailey Hall and a pumping station at Siddal to augment the supply of water at Bailey Hall. The extension of the canal facilities to Halifax in 1828 enabled coal to be transported more easily into the heart of the town for use in manufacturing. Indeed, Anne Lister, who was keen to exploit the coal reserves on her own estates at Shibden, recorded ruefully in 1828 that local coal carted

Pack-horses, 1814. West Riding clothiers transporting their cloth to market on Galloway ponies as illustrated by the Leeds artist George Walker. The rough, hilly terrain of the parish of Halifax presented road builders with considerable problems and some remoter parts of the parish relied on the pack-horse until at least 1850. (Photograph: J. A. Hargreaves)

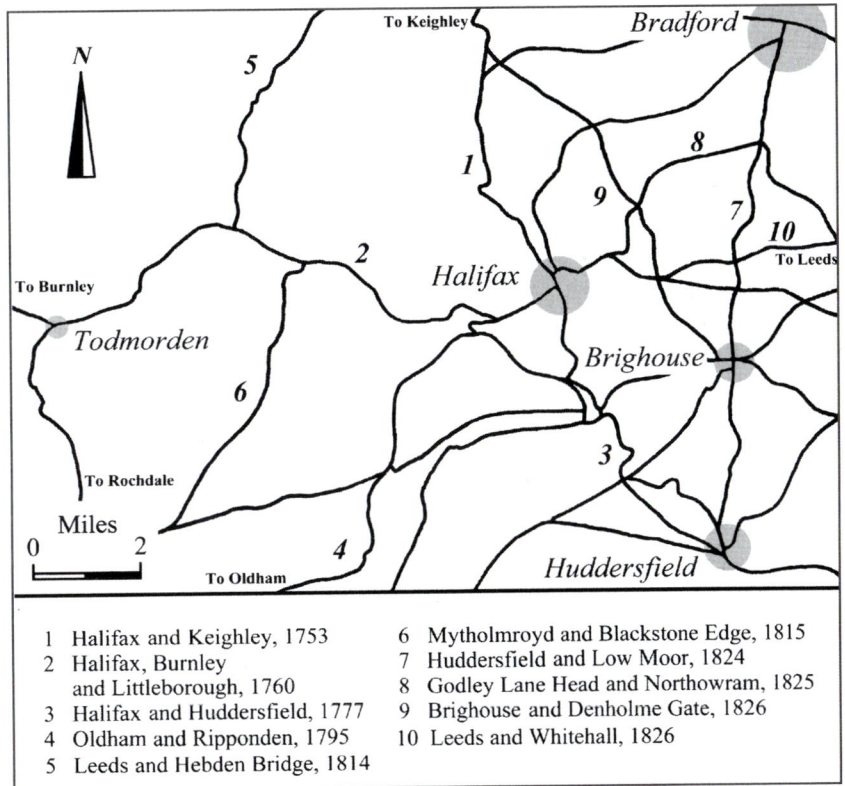

1 Halifax and Keighley, 1753
2 Halifax, Burnley
  and Littleborough, 1760
3 Halifax and Huddersfield, 1777
4 Oldham and Ripponden, 1795
5 Leeds and Hebden Bridge, 1814

6 Mytholmroyd and Blackstone Edge, 1815
7 Huddersfield and Low Moor, 1824
8 Godley Lane Head and Northowram, 1825
9 Brighouse and Denholme Gate, 1826
10 Leeds and Whitehall, 1826

Turnpike roads, 1750–1850.

Share certificate of Japhet Lister, a Halifax merchant, in the Calder and Hebble Navigation, 1760. A meeting at the Talbot Inn, Halifax, on 2 September 1756 had decided to seek an Act of Parliament to make navigable the Calder from Wakefield 'to Elland, and so on to Halifax' with the purpose of improving raw wool and corn supplies to the town. An Act of 1758 authorised the extension of the navigation and the whole works were surveyed and superintended by the builder of the Eddystone lighthouse, John Smeaton. In October 1767, however, a torrential storm so severely damaged the navigation that a further Act of Parliament was necessary before the ruined locks and sluices could be restored.

(Photograph: West Yorkshire Archive Service, Calderdale)

HALIFAX
Union Contract.
IN ONE BOTTOM.
Now Laying on,
THREE CRANES WHARF,
QUEEN-STREET, CHEAPSIDE, LONDON,
The Fast-Sailing Sloop
ALTISIDORA,
S. STANSFIELD, Master.
SHE IS INTENDED TO SAIL ON 24 Sep.
Direct to SALTERHEBBLE.
WILL TAKE IN GOODS FOR
WAKEFIELD,   BRIGHOUSE,   TODMORDEN,
HORBURY,   ELLAND,   ROCHDALE,
DEWSBURY,   HALIFAX,   MANCHESTER,
MIRFIELD,   SOWERBY-BRIDGE, STOCKPORT,
HUDDERSFIELD, HEBDEN-BRIDGE, And Places adjacent.
Agents:
Mr. JAMES BOYNE, Halifax,
Mr. RICHARDSON, Wakefield,
SILLS, RAMSAY and SILLS, London.
The THREE CRANES WHARF is situate in the very Heart of the City, and of the Shipping
Houses, which renders it of great Advantage to Shippers in general.
Printed by T. WALKER, Silver-Street, Halifax.

Advertisement for the fast-sailing sloop, Altisidora, for the transhipment of cargo from the Three Cranes Wharf at Cheapside 'in the very heart of the City' of London to Salterhebble. The advertisement was printed in Halifax in the 1820s by T. Walker of Silver Street for James Boyne, the Halifax agent of the Union Contract Vessels. The handwritten note on the poster suggests that the cargo included flax destined for local mills. Goods would be transported from the Navigation Yard at Salterhebble by wagon into the town until the opening of the Halifax Branch Canal in 1828. (Photograph: West Yorkshire Archive Service, Calderdale)

from Swales Moor to Halifax was considerably more expensive than coal fetched by canal from Kirklees to Salterhebble.[15]

There were similar delays in bringing the railway to Halifax; both Bradford and Huddersfield had the commercial advantage of earlier direct rail links. While the Calder Valley was along the route of the first trans-Pennine railway route, the Manchester and Leeds Railway, completed in 1841, a branch line to Halifax was not completed until 1844. Moreover, owing to a combination of difficult terrain and financial stringency, only a single line to Shaw Syke was constructed initially. Before 1844, passengers for Halifax had to alight at Sowerby Bridge and finish their journey by road. By 1850, the line had progressed as far as Low Moor but Halifax was only served by a temporary wooden station at the bottom of Horton Street, and this was not replaced by a more permanent stone structure until June 1855.[16]

It is evident, therefore, that the location of the town of Halifax gave rise to problems, but that its demographic and economic growth had not been thwarted by them. Halifax had become and remained by 1850 a principal manufacturing as well as retailing centre, one among several such new industrial towns in the West Riding of Yorkshire. But this transformation was more than economic. It carried implications for social structure and living standards.

Social structure, occupations and living standards

Few landowning gentry families continued to reside in the parish of Halifax during the period of its industrial transformation in the late eighteenth and early

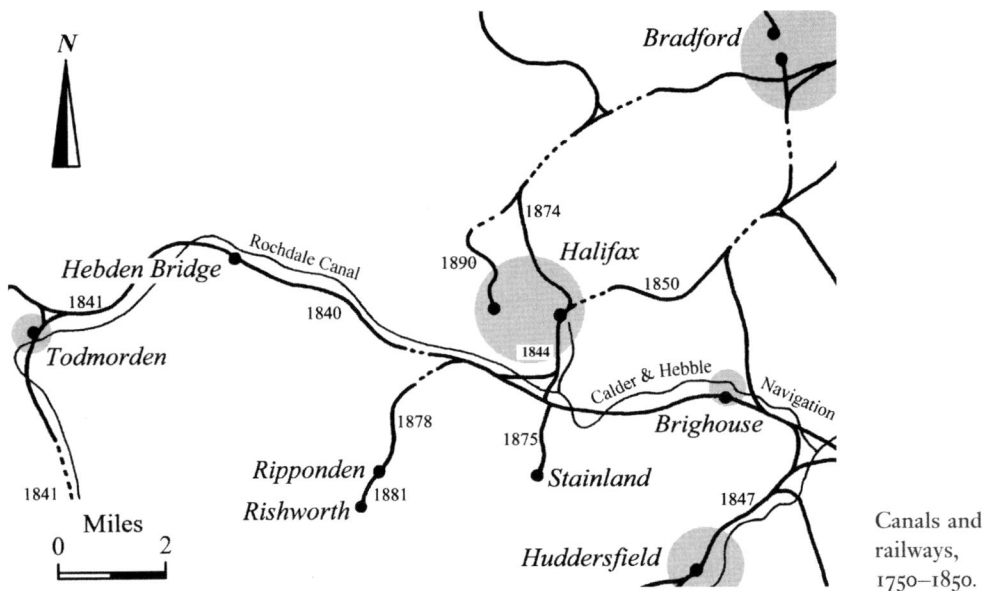

N

Bradford

1874

Hebden Bridge

Rochdale Canal

1890

Halifax

1850

1841

1840

Todmorden

1844

Calder & Hebble

Navigation

Brighouse

1878

1875

Ripponden

1881

Stainland

1847

1841

Rishworth

Miles

0   2

Huddersfield

Canals and railways, 1750–1850.

nineteenth centuries following the departure of the largest landowning family, the Saviles, in the early modern period. An assessment list of thirty-eight gentry from the parish who paid the male servants' tax in 1780 revealed only seven property owners with more than one male servant. Only two, John Rhodes and Samuel Smith, each with two servants, resided in the urban township of Halifax. Joshua Horton (1720–93) of Howroyd, Barkisland, who headed the list with five servants, was exceptional, serving as a county magistrate and initiating hare hunting in the parish in 1754. The only other property owner assessed for more than two servants in 1780 was John Caygill, one of the wealthiest merchants in Halifax, most noted for providing the extensive site for the Halifax Manufacturers' Piece Hall, which opened in 1779. The Caygills inherited the Shay following the marriage of Martha Stead to John Caygill in 1705 and it was their son John who commissioned the distinguished architect John Carr (1723–1807) to build the Shay mansion *c.* 1770. Caygill also developed Halifax's only Georgian Square, remarkable for its idiosyncratic design, which has survived only in the name of the red-brick chapel modelled on George Whitefield's Tabernacle in London which was restored successively in the twentieth and twenty-first centuries. He married Jane Selwin and they had one child, a daughter named Jane, but usually referred to as Jenny, on whose marriage to Sir James Ibbetson, the ownership of the Shay passed into the Ibbetson family. In an advertisement of 1807 the extensive landscaped grounds were described as:

> beautifully situated on the south side of Halifax with a convenient terrace on the south and east fronts; reclining grass banks, shrubbery, serpentine and other walks … adorned with plantations and a pleasure garden; well stocked

with wall and standard fruit trees ... a hothouse and greenhouse, with vines, exotic and other plants.

The mansion itself comprised on the ground floor a large dining hall, breakfast room, butler's pantry, servant's hall, large kitchen and gallery 'fitted with every modern improvement for cooking on the steam principle', an elegant staircase with a double flight of stone steps leading to a spacious gallery and rooms on the second floor, while the drawing room and five lodging rooms with dressing rooms boasted doors of solid mahogany'.[17]

Increasingly, by the early nineteenth century, socially aspiring families such as the Rawsons, the Edwards, and the Listers without such connections with the landed gentry combined land or property ownership with manufacturing or trade, and their newly acquired wealth was reflected in their lifestyles. Elizabeth Threlkeld (1745–1837), a second cousin of the mother of Dorothy and William Wordsworth, and a prominent Unitarian, who had married William Rawson, a prosperous Halifax millowner and banker, in 1791, moved from the rather remotely situated Mill House at Triangle to the more fashionable and conveniently located Savile Green at Skircoat in 1806.[18] Dorothy Wordsworth (1771–1855), on her return to Westmorland in 1817, recalled the hospitality and domestic comforts of the Rawsons in their 'large house' at Savile Green in Halifax with 'servants to perform the work as by magic'.[19] Sir Henry Edwards (1812–86), a prominent Sowerby Bridge woollen manufacturer also commissioned John Carr to build his large palladian mansion at Pye Nest. Anne Lister (1791–1840), who inherited the Shibden estate from her uncle, James Lister (1748–1826), was perhaps the most remarkable. Astutely managing her rental incomes and exploiting the limited mineral resources on her estate sufficiently to sustain extensive European travel, she bequeathed to posterity, when she finally succumbed to a fatal fever-carrying tick in the Caucasus in 1840, a candid four-million-word diary. It revealed her business acumen, clandestine lesbian lifestyle and disdain for *nouveaux riches* worsted manufacturers, whose Liberal politics and Nonconformist roots she despised.[20]

The opulence of many other local merchants and manufacturers is evident from the fine Georgian mansions they commissioned in the late eighteenth century on the southern edge of the town. They impressed contemporary visitors to the town such as Thomas Twining, who in 1781 commented on 'the many magnificent houses lately built, and now daily building', in and about the town 'by the manufacturers chiefly'.[21] They included Stoney Royd, Hope Hall, Clare Hall, Well Head, Savile Hall, Pye Nest and, close to the centre of the town, Somerset House. This last was built in 1766 by the celebrated York architect, John Carr, for John Royds, a prosperous woollen merchant and financier, who provided overnight accommodation in his new mansion for King Christian VII of Denmark on his northern tour in 1768 and lived in the house until 1781.[22] Dr John Simpson of Bradford remarked, in an entry in his journal for 1825, that 'the neighbourhood of Halifax is

Howroyd, Barkisland, drawn by John Horner in 1835, was the seat of the Horton family, the most prominent local landed gentry family in the late eighteenth and early nineteenth centuries. The hall-and-cross-wings house with hearth-passage was constructed in 1642. A 1655 inventory reveals a dining parlour, little parlour and maids' parlour in the east wing, a lower parlour and timber store in the west wing, a kitchen and buttery to the rear. The hall, open through two storeys, served as an impressive reception area with its decorated fireplace, plaster overmantel and ceiling, gallery and painted glass windows. (Photographed courtesy of Calderdale Museums Service, Bankfield)

much better filled with families of respectability than most provincial towns'. He concluded that 'Halifax is a much genteeler place than Bradford'.[23]

Indeed, Halifax even gained some recognition as a fashionable Regency spa following the opening of a suite of hot and cold baths and extensive pleasure gardens by Thomas Rawlinson, an enterprising Halifax plumber, on a site adjoining Lilly Lane, which he acquired in 1784. Early patrons included Charles Howard (1746–1815), eleventh Duke of Norfolk, who in July 1806 pronounced the buildings 'elegant and commodious' and 'highly creditable to the town of Halifax'. An advertisement in the *Halifax Journal* in 1803 maintained that the baths at Lilly Lane were as 'completely fitted up' as those of Bath, Buxton and Matlock, while Walker's *Directory* of 1846 boasted that Halifax possessed 'one of the most extensive suites of baths to be found in Yorkshire, consisting of hot, cold, tepid, swimming, shower, vapour and sulphur baths, with suitable and convenient dressing rooms'.[24]

During the first half of the nineteenth century yet more manufacturers who had risen from obscure beginnings established their town houses and mansions in Halifax. In 1818 Jonathan Akroyd (1782–1847) moved from the remote hilltop

Anne Lister (1791–1840), portrayed here by the Halifax artist Joshua Horner. Although born in Halifax on 3 April 1791, Anne Lister spent her childhood years in the East Riding and was educated at Ripon and York. She moved to Halifax in 1806 and to Shibden Hall in 1815 to live with her uncle and aunt, inheriting the 400-acre Shibden estate in 1826, on the death of her uncle. She subsequently embarked on a lesbian affair with Ann Walker of Crow Nest, a neighbouring heiress. They ultimately contracted a clandestine 'marriage', developing the coal deposits on their estates with entrepreneurial flair and energy. Her journal, partly written in a secret code, commenced in 1806 and runs to almost four million words. (Photograph: Calderdale Museums Service, Shibden Hall)

The Russian passport of Anne Lister of Shibden Hall, Halifax, 1839. Anne Lister was already an accomplished European traveller when she left Shibden in June 1839 to embark on her final journey to Russia, the Caucasus and the Middle East, where she hoped to ascend Mount Ararat. She had been the first amateur mountaineer to reach the summit of Vignemale in the French Pyrenees in August 1838, beating the Prince of Moscow by several days. Her travels, described vividly in her journals, were brought abruptly to an end when she was bitten by a fever-carrying tick on 8 August and died in Georgia on 22 September 1840. Her body was brought back to England for burial in Halifax Parish Church and her obituary in the *Halifax Guardian* in October 1840 compared her exploits to those of such distinguished contemporaries as Lady Mary Wortley Montagu and Lady Hester Stanhope. (Photograph: West Yorkshire Archive Service, Calderdale)

farmstead where his father James Akroyd (1753–1830), a small yeoman clothier specialising in the production of 'little Joans' and figured 'Amens', had founded the family worsted manufacturing enterprise, to a town house in North Parade, Halifax, conveniently situated near the firm's Bowling Dyke Mills, and later to a mansion at Woodside. His son, Edward (1810–87), who inherited an estate valued at £300,000 and one of the most successful textile firms in the country on his father's sudden death in 1847, set about transforming the small house at Bankfield, which he had purchased on his marriage in 1838, into a more substantial Regency style mansion. John (1772–1837) and Martha (1775–1854) Crossley, founders of the carpet-weaving dynasty at Dean Clough remained close to their Dean Clough mills, but their sons, John, Joseph and Francis, who inherited the family business in 1837, lived in town houses in Halifax until, following their marriages, they moved to more commodious mansions on the outskirts of the town.[25]

Walker's *Halifax Directory of 1846*, the first comprehensive directory listing Halifax businesses, trades and professions, reveals a strong presence in the town of accountants, architects, attorneys, auctioneers, bankers, chemists, land surveyors,

A view of Stoney Royd from the grounds of Hope Hall by John Horner in 1835. Stoney Royd, built for Christopher Rawson 'a little before 1764' was an early example of fashionable brick construction in Halifax. Christopher Rawson (1712–80), the third son of John Rawson of Bolton, who married Grace, the daughter of John Rawson of Beckfoot, was succeeded in the possession of the house by his elder son, John (1744–1815), who married Nelly, the daughter of David Stansfeld of Hope Hall. Stoney Royd as depicted here was of square design with slightly projecting pedimented central bays on two visible sides and a hipped roof. The house was demolished after the grounds were purchased by the borough for a public cemetery and hospital in 1860. (Photograph: Calderdale Museums Service, Bankfield)

A view of Hope Hall by John Horner from the grounds of Stoney Royd in 1835. Hope House, as it was then known, was erected in 1765 for David Stansfeld, a cloth merchant from Leeds, by James Green. It replaced an earlier building on the site and is one of the few remaining examples of find Georgian mansions built for local merchants and manufacturers on the southern edge of the town in the late eighteenth century. However, the unusual winged two-way stone stairway at its east front entrance and its extensive landscaped grounds have not survived. The house became the home of Christopher Rawson (1777–1849), the eldest son of John and Nelly Rawson, a leading Halifax banker, after his marriage to Mary Anne Brooks of Westminster in 1808. It was acquired by the Albany Club in 1906.
(Photograph: Calderdale Museums Service, Bankfield)

merchants, physicians, surgeons and veterinary surgeons; together with a great variety of manufacturers, retailers and traders. These encompassed bakers and flour dealers, basket makers, beer retailers, blacksmiths, boot and shoe makers, butchers, cabinet makers and upholsterers, china, glass and earthenware dealers, clock makers, confectioners, dress makers, fish and fruit dealers, grocers and tea dealers, hair dressers and perfumers, hatters, hoteliers, joiners and builders, linen drapers, milliners, pawnbrokers, saddlers, shopkeepers, straw hat makers and tobacconists. The *Directory* also specifies no fewer than three artists, some fifteen booksellers, stationers and bookbinders and eight music dealers and preceptors. The music dealers included Henry William Pohlmann of 22 Waterhouse Street, the only piano manufacturer outside London, whose grandfather, Johannes Christoph David Pohlmann had manufactured one of the first pianos in London in 1765. The Halifax firm exported pianos all over the world, especially to South America, New Zealand

Britannia, Somerset House, George Street, Halifax. The York architect John Carr built a magnificent town house for the prosperous Halifax woollen merchant John Royds in 1766, with ornate rococo plasterwork by Giuseppe Cortese. In the saloon, the coved ceiling represented Royds as Neptune surrounded by his four daughters, while above the fireplace his wife was depicted as Britannia. The couple provided overnight accommodation for the young King Christian VII of Denmark on his tour of northern England in 1768 and for the Marquess of Rockingham's enquiry into counterfeiting in 1769. (Photograph: Ian Beesley)

and Australia and produced innovative designs of pianos with overstrung iron frames. The company also introduced hire purchase terms for customers, advertising a rosewood 'Piano d'Artiste' at 70 guineas, or hire purchase at two guineas a month.[26]

The leading property owners, merchants, industrialists and representatives of the professional classes of the town and its environs formed an urban elite which dominated the social and cultural life of the town for most of this period. Indeed, they have been characterised by the historian John Smail as 'a self-conscious middle class' who, 'demanding and receiving local power and social prestige', transformed 'the social world in which they lived'. As a result of the burgeoning woollen industry it has been calculated that some 60 to 70 textile manufacturers had established substantial fortunes and 50 to 150 medium-sized fortunes by 1750. However, the Southampton-born entertainer and song writer, Charles Dibdin (1745–1814), found Halifax a 'black, dismal town' in 1788 with 'very few people of any consequence', while the doctor and author, Augustus Bozzi Granville, a well-travelled native of Italy who had served as physician to the British Embassy in Constantinople, remained singularly unimpressed by the social ambience of Halifax in 1839:

> Society affords, perhaps, fewer resources in Halifax than one would be led to expect, considering the large number of opulent families, resident in or about the place. There is not much intercourse among the various sections of the community: and although six great public balls are given in the very handsome Musical Hall, few families of distinction are known to attend them.[27]

Nevertheless, socially and culturally, the town was bursting with activity and as Dr Rachel Cowgill has argued, it was 'the gradual enrichment of the textile merchant-manufacturers' which enabled them to set the cultural agenda in the town in the late Georgian era, providing 'the chief catalyst' in the absence of a powerful local gentry for the development of a profusion of cultural initiatives and 'a musical life of such remarkable richness and vitality'. There were two public circulating subscription libraries, one founded as early as 1769, the other in 1823; a music club formed in 1767 by the musician hired to play the parish church's new organ; a harmonic society established in 1792 specifically to promote 'the discussion of and appreciation of music and musical performance'; a choral society, founded in 1818, by William Priestley, for which Mendelssohn in 1842 composed a setting of the 114th Psalm; a conversational society launched in 1822; an orchestral society, founded in 1833; a madrigal society, founded in 1844; a Mechanics' Institute, founded in 1825; a literary and philosophical society, founded in 1830, and a host of other clubs and societies. One of the first purpose-built provincial theatres was opened at Halifax in 1790, superseding earlier open-air venues in the inn yards of the Old Cock and White Lion and the Assembly Rooms at the Talbot. Adaptations of Shakespeare's plays were regularly performed, together with much of the drama of the Restoration era and numerous Harlequinades at the theatre which was financed by local business and professional men. New Assembly Rooms were opened in Harrison Road in 1825, and the Oddfellows' Hall, described by one contemporary visitor as 'by far the handsomest edifice in the town', was opened in St James Road in 1840, both buildings providing extensive accommodation for a wide range of social and cultural activities.[28]

Moreover, the Edwards of Halifax bookbindery in Old Market had gained a national reputation, as Thomas Twining observed in 1781, as 'one of the best and most elegant binders in England', supplying and binding books for the most discriminating collectors throughout the land.

William Priestley (1779–1860), founder of the Halifax Choral Society. (Photograph: J. A. Hargreaves)

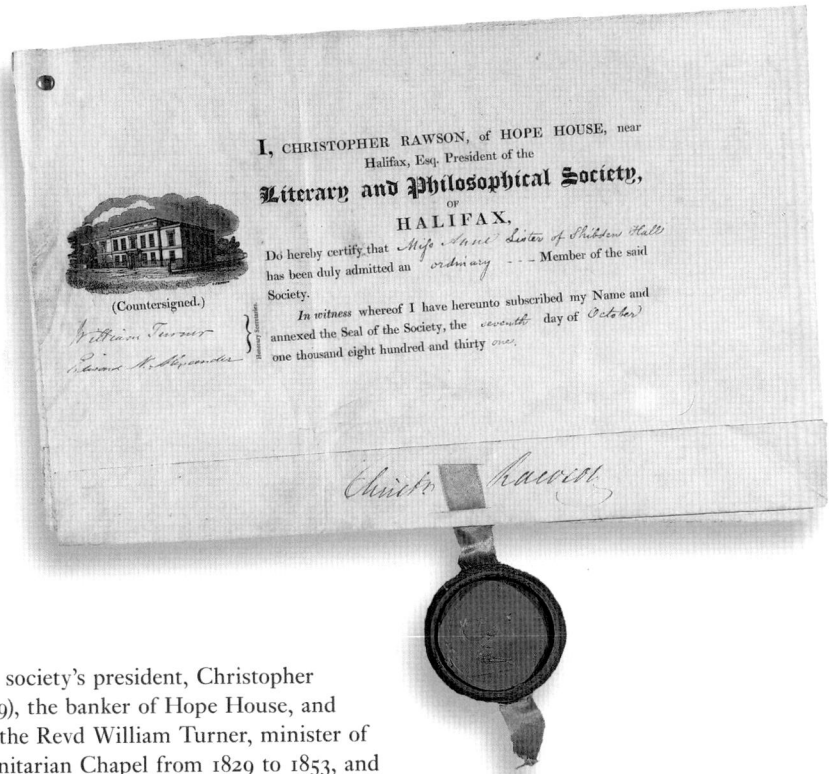

Certificate of membership of Miss Anne Lister of Shibden Hall in the Halifax Literary and Philosophical Society, 1831. It was signed by the society's president, Christopher Rawson (1777-1849), the banker of Hope House, and countersigned by the Revd William Turner, minister of Northgate End Unitarian Chapel from 1829 to 1853, and Edward N. Alexander, partner in the firm of solicitors, Alexander and Hammerton. The illustration is of the New Assembly Rooms, Harrison Road, built in 1828 and the home of the society from 1830 to 1836, when its own lecture hall and museum was opened in Harrison Road. In 1897 the museum's archaeological and ethnographical collections were transferred to the new Bankfield Museum, while its natural history specimens formed the nucleus of a new museum at Belle Vue. The society was finally dissolved in 1964. (Photograph: West Yorkshire Archive Service, Calderdale)

opposite above: Lilly Lane Baths, Halifax. Extensive bathing and recreational facilities were developed by Thomas Rawlinson, an enterprising Halifax plumber, on a site at Coldwell Ing leased from the trustees of the Waterhouse Charities in 1784. Of fashionable brick construction, the baths ultimately comprised the long oval-shaped open-air pool, illustrated in this contemporary lithograph by N. Whittock, an entire suite of indoor baths, dining and dressing rooms, extensive pleasure gardens, a quoits ground and bowling green. An early patron, Charles Howard, eleventh Duke of Norfolk, pronounced the buildings 'elegant and commodious' and 'highly creditable to the town of Halifax'. (Photograph: Calderdale Museums Service, Bankfield)

opposite below: Bankfield. Edward Akroyd, the Halifax worsted manufacturer, purchased Bankfield following his marriage in 1838 and defended it against an attack by a Chartist mob in 1842. It was extended and redesigned in the Regency style in 1857. In 1867 the Atkinson brothers of York transformed it into a grand Italianate mansion with 100 rooms, at a cost of £80,000. Shortly before it was sold in 1886, the *Halifax Courier* compared the house with the residences of Sir Titus Salt at Crow Nest and John Crossley at Manor Heath: 'They were not just so many spacious buildings: they were the homes of men who were dear to their fellows by reason of the love they bore to them and the good they did, true living philanthropists with souls far above the huge businesses which each had to conduct'. Appropriately, it soon re-opened as a museum and public library. (Photograph: J. A. Hargreaves)

For the BENEFIT of Mr. GODSALL, and Mr. BUTLER.
At the THEATRE in HALIFAX.
FRIDAY Evening, being the 4th of January 1760, will be presented a celebrated TRAGI-COMEDY, call'd, THE

SPANISH FRYAR.
O R
The Double Discovery.
Written by Mr. DRYDEN.
The Part of TORRISMOND, by Mr. WHITLEY,
Bertran, by Mr. MITCHELL,
Raymond, by Mr. BARRET,
Lorenzo, by Mr. OWEN
The Part of the FRYAR, by Mr. PARKER,
Alphonso, by Mr. WHEELER,
Pedro, by Mr. LISTER,
The Part of GOMEZ, by Mr. GODSALL
The Part of the QUEEN, by Mrs. WHEELER,
Teresa, by Mrs. BREEZE
And the Part of ELVIRA, by Mrs. FARREL,
With several Entertainments of SINGING and DANCING,
1st A Comic Dance by Mr. FARREL
2d. The Comic Song of the Satire on all Trades.
3d. A Diverting Epilogue on Every Body, spoke by Somebody in the Character of Nobody
To which will be added a Diverting Entertainment call'd,
The DEVIL to PAY,
O R,
The WIVES METAMORPHOS'D.
The Part of Sir JOHN LOVERULE, by Mr. WHITLEY, with the Songs in Character
JOBSON, the Cobler, by Mr. FARREL,
Conjurer, by Mr. BARRET,—Butler, by Mr. WHEELER,
NELL, by Mrs. OWEN—And Lady LOVERULE by Mrs. WHEELER
Tickets to be had at Mr. Mellin's, at the Talbot,
To begin exactly at SIX.
Printed Copies of the Satire on all Trades, to be had at the Printing office.

Theatre bill for 1760. Before the opening of the first purpose-built Halifax theatre in 1789, plays were performed in the inn yards of the Old Cock and the White Lion and the Assembly Rooms at the Talbot. Indeed, surviving play-bills exist from as early as 1758 announcing performances at 'The New Theatre at the Talbot' in Woolshops, where the tragi-comedy 'The Spanish Fryar' was to be presented in January 1760. A regular London theatre-goer, writing to the Halifax *Union Journal* in 1759, recalled the pleasure enjoyed 'this night at the performance at the little theatre in the town' and concluded that 'there are performers now here worthy of the attention and applause of the judicious'. (Photograph: West Yorkshire Archive Service, Calderdale)

On the other hand, William Milner (1803–50) of Swine Market and later Cheapside, was one of the pioneer publishers of popular cheap editions of literary classics. The *Union Journal*, one of the earliest Yorkshire newspapers, published from 1759 to 1761, was printed by Pressic Darby, a pioneering Halifax printer. A successor, the *Halifax Journal*, published between 1801 and 1811, was also relatively short-lived. However, the *Halifax Guardian*, established in 1832, survived until its amalgamation in 1921 with the *Halifax Courier*, founded in 1853, providing evidence of a growing urban readership and reflecting the increasing interest in local politics following the borough's enfranchisement in 1832.[29]

Rateable values of property in the township of Halifax climbed steadily in the second half of the eighteenth century from £3,117 in 1750 to £5,960 in 1800. However, in 1832, of the 20,000 inhabitants of the townships of Halifax, Northowram and Southowram included within the boundaries of the new parliamentary constituency of Halifax created by the 1832 Reform Act, only 531 adult men qualified for the new £10 householder franchise. Indeed, the proportion of relatively poor households

New Halifax Assembly and Concert Rooms. Built by public subscription in the 1820s, the New Assembly Rooms provided commodious rooms for many purposes which the Old Assembly Rooms at the Talbot Inn in Woolshops could no longer accommodate. The circulating library there in 1836 contained 7,000 volumes and in 1881 the first municipal library was housed there. The rooms became the venue for dinners and balls held by the West Yorkshire Yeomanry. The rooms were demolished by 1898, when the site was used for the erection of the Halifax Borough Police Court, which was opened in October 1900. (Photograph: Calderdale Museums Service, Bankfield)

in the township of Halifax appears to have increased in the late eighteenth and early nineteenth centuries as Halifax developed into a manufacturing as well as a commercial centre. In 1760 it was reckoned that over half of the population of the township of Halifax could not be expected to contribute towards water rents, some because they resided outside the supply area but the vast majority because they simply could not afford it. Moreover, Dr John Smail's analysis of the land tax returns of 1782 has revealed that no fewer than 83 per cent of the 1,514 households in the township of Halifax were exempted from payment. This was twice the number exempt from the hearth tax in 1664, suggesting that there were double the number of households in late-eighteenth century Halifax living at or below the poverty line than there had been a century earlier. He has therefore concluded that the impact of the development of large-scale manufacturing on Halifax's society was 'an increasingly polarised social structure that no longer corresponded to the social world of the middling sort' of the early modern period.[30]

Technological and structural innovation in the primary textile industries of the parish in the last two decades of the eighteenth century and the first half of the nineteenth century, when Halifax masters strove vainly to halt the area's relative decline as a centre of textile production in the face of growing competition from Leeds, Bradford and Huddersfield, had a devastating effect on some sections of the

Old Market, 1800. A prospect taken from the window of Thomas Edward's famous bookshop by John Horner in 1835. Edwards' eldest son Walter Fawkes Edwards and his son-in-law Thomas Adam were subscribers to Horner's collection of prints of buildings in the town and parish of Halifax 'drawn from nature and on stone' and the view of Old Market completed the series. Several open-air stalls are visible displaying a variety of wares and the soldiers in the foreground are wearing the uniform of the Halifax Volunteers. (Photograph: Calderdale Museums Service, Bankfield)

community and in particular on the domestic outworkers. The transition from an extensive web of relatively small-scale domestic manufacture to an all-embracing system of factory production was a slow, painful and inexorable process for the individuals, families and communities most directly affected. Large numbers of male handloom weavers and woolcombers, for example, experienced not only a marked decline in their material prosperity and an erosion of their independent artisan status, but also a diminution of their authority within their own families as the demand for female and juvenile factory labour increased.[31]

Returns to the factory inspectorate in 1835 reveal that textile factory workers then represented 10 per cent of the population of the township of Halifax: of these 46 per cent were male, 54 per cent female and 71 per cent under twenty-one. A sample study of the Halifax and Skircoat census returns for 1851 has shown that, sixteen years later, one-third of the total work force of the two townships was under twenty years of age, with a higher ratio of females to males, and one in eight of the workers were under fourteen. Most of the younger children in full employment were employed as spinners, doffers and menders in textile factories, though examples could still be found of very young children working for their fathers at home.[32]

Controversy erupted in October 1830 over the treatment of young factory workers when, following Richard Oastler's famous 'Yorkshire Slavery' letter to the *Leeds Mercury* denouncing the worsted mills in the town and neighbourhood of Bradford as 'magazines of infantile slavery', another correspondent, Richard Webster of Halifax, promptly alleged that conditions in the mills around Halifax were even more miserable. The controversy was fuelled by the issue of a pamphlet at the height of the campaign for a Ten Hours Bill in 1833 which made more specific allegations about long hours, harsh regulations, severe punishments, low wages and inequitable truck systems in local mills. These allegations were strongly repudiated at the time by the Halifax masters, but over the next two decades, as a response to the unremitting efforts of the factory reformers, factories became subject to increasing statutory regulation and inspection. Indeed, in 1849, Angus Bethune Reach was most favourably impressed by the congenial working environment at Holdsworth's Shaw Lodge Mills and Akroyd's Bowling Dyke Mills, the two largest worsted factories in Halifax. They contrasted markedly, he judged, with the rapidly deteriorating conditions of the local domestic outworkers he also visited.[33]

The poorer sections of Halifax society were also, of course, more susceptible to sickness and disease, which could have devastating effects. Cornelius Ashworth (1752–1821), who combined handloom weaving with the management of a smallholding at Waltroyd, Wheatley, abandoned his weaving in 1785, following an illness. Three years earlier in his diary he had recorded observing ten open graves in Halifax parish churchyard, 'nine of them for children, and was informed that 110 children had been interred in the above yard in four weeks who had died of smallpox'.[34] In 1807, on the initiative of the Vicar of Halifax, the Revd Dr H. W. Coulthurst (1753–1817), the Halifax General Dispensary was founded, particularly to meet the needs of poor patients residing within the township of Halifax. It opened in 1808 in Hatters Close, moving subsequently to premises in Dispensary Walk owned by the trustees of the Waterhouse Charities. In 1825 a surgical ward was opened in nearby cottage property and by 1830 some 213 patients had been admitted for treatment, of whom 178 were casualties, many of them admitted as a result of industrial accidents caused by 'the general and extensive introduction of machinery'. However, demand continued to grow and in 1838 the magnificent new Halifax Infirmary and Dispensary with its imposing portico, designed by George Townshend Andrews and financed largely by public subscription, was opened on a site in Blackwall adjacent to the New Assembly Rooms.[35]

However, death rates in general and infant mortality in particular remained high, and in 1845 the Health of Towns Commission reported that the average life expectancy at birth within the Halifax Poor Law Union was 26 years 10 months and of those surviving into adulthood 53 years 9 months. The commissioners' report identified the lack of an adequate sewerage system and the industrial pollution from the steam-powered factories along the Hebble as major problems, but reserved its most severe strictures for the poor-quality housing. It condemned the 'damp wretched looking dwellings' in the east end of the town and the folds or enclosed spaces in other localities in which 'the lowest grade of working people' were confined in 'very damp and filthy' conditions as 'seats of poverty and disease'. It commented that 'with a low state of finances and morals' they were 'kept in a depressed condition by the outward filth and effluvium which assails them at every step'.[36] One informed observer commented particularly upon the courts and cul-de-sacs inhabited by the very poor – including many Irish families:

> I inspected several very closely and found them reeking with stench and the worse source of abomination. The ash-pits and appurtenances were disgustingly choked ... and among all this muck, uncared-for children sprawled by the score, and idle slatternly women lounged by the halfdozen. One old woman who had been more than thirty years in England talked dolefully of the decline in the hawking trade. Poor people now seldom earned more than a shilling or eightpence at the very most for a hard day's work.

Many lived in cellar dwellings 'sleeping upon greasy mattresses, partially covered with foul rags and rolled up in corners'. In another cellar, which was almost totally dark. In one such dwelling:

> A grey-headed negro – an old man-of-war's man – had lived for seventeen years, vegetating there in a world of dirt and darkness. The corporation of Halifax have a perfect Augean stable to clean requiring urgent attention.[37]

During the period from 1750 to 1850 there was growing concern for the cultural deprivation and moral depravity of the lower classes not only in Halifax itself, but also in its hinterland. John Styles has argued that the rise of the yellow trade, a novel combination of counterfeiting and clipping gold currency, in Cragg Vale and other parts of the Calder Valley in the late 1760s, was 'facilitated by the isolation of the locality from those sources of formal and informal authority which sustained eighteenth-century law enforcement'. The activities of the coiners, which by 1769 were believed to be 'so firmly established in the neighbourhood of Halifax' as almost 'to bid defiance to the civil power', sent shock waves through the urban community when William Dighton (or Deighton), supervisor of the excise at Halifax, was assassinated at Savile Close, near to the centre of the town, in 1769. His death prompted a government enquiry conducted by the Marquess of Rockingham and a series of trials which resulted in the executions of David Hartley and James Oldfield in 1770; Robert Thomas in 1774 and Matthew Normanton in 1775. The bodies of Thomas and Normanton were hung in chains on Beacon Hill, Halifax, at the request of magistrates in the hope that 'such a notorious and public example may happily deter any future crimes of so shocking a nature being perpetrated in a neighbourhood that has long been infested with a most dangerous set of villains'.[38] However, there were further prosecutions for counterfeiting in 1779 and 1782,

Waltroyd, Wheatley, photographed from the south in 1938. The handloom weaver, Cornelius Ashworth farmed at Waltroyd from *c.* 1780 to 1816 with the assistance of two or three men, possibly relatives. The property consisted of three bays each with low mullioned windows at ground floor and first floor levels and a simple doorway. (Photograph: Halifax Antiquarian Society)

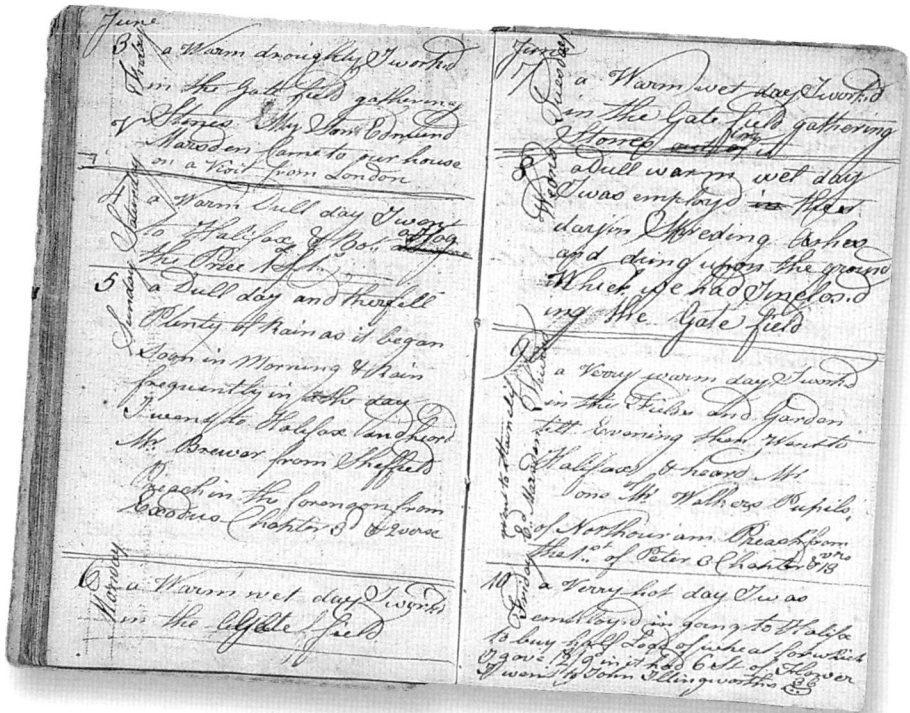

Extract from the diary of Cornelius Ashworth of Waltroyd, Wheatley, 1785. Ashworth appears to have been exceptionally literate and served in 1780 as overseer of the poor for the township of Ovenden. His four diaries covering the period from 1782 to 1816 provide invaluable information about the domestic system of cloth production, farming, the climate and social conditions. In 1785, following an illness, he abandoned his weaving and concentrated on farming his smallholding. The extract records visits to Halifax to attend Sunday worship. (Photograph: West Yorkshire Archive Service, Calderdale)

Halifax General
Dispensary.
A meeting at the Talbot
Inn called by the Revd
Dr H. W. Coulthurst, the
Vicar of Halifax in 1807,
resolved to establish the
first general dispensary
in Halifax, where medical
treatment, medicine
and advice could be
received by the poor 'free
from all expenses'. The
total number of patients
admitted to the dispensary
from its opening in Hatters
Close in February 1808 to
1831 was 80,346. In 1825 a
surgical ward was opened in
a nearby cottage property.
(Photograph: Calderdale
Museums Service,
Bankfield)

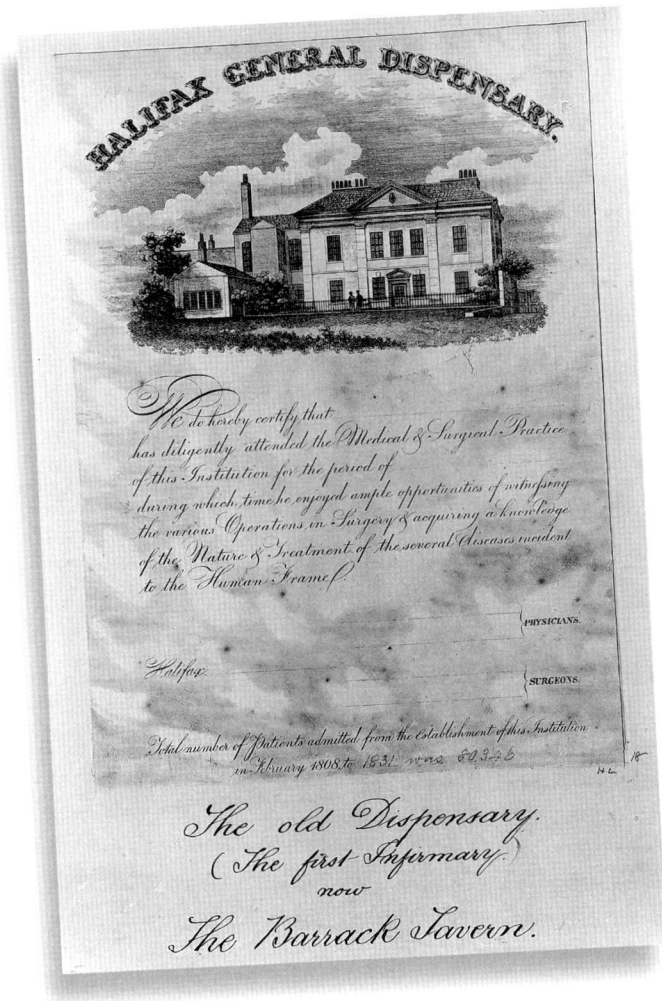

when three Halifax coiners originally sentenced to death were later reprieved and transported for life. In 1783 another former coiner, Thomas Spencer, was arrested with a recently discharged young soldier, Mark Sattonstall, for inciting a starving mob to seize supplies of corn from carts and wagons in the centre of the town. The two ringleaders were tried at York 'for being concerned in the late riots in the town and neighbourhood of Halifax', sentenced to death and executed on Beacon Hill, the last public executions to take place in Halifax. Moreover, quarter sessions records reveal a social world built around the workshop and the alehouse, often issuing in petty theft and sexual slander. In 1783, Isaac Schofield, a weaver, and some of his mates, who were woolcombers, perpetrated a series of thefts over several months. They stole rabbits, ducks, fleeces, bags of shot and coal, generally selling what they took and spending the money on beer. An earlier defamation case in 1769 depicted the same kind of workshop and alehouse culture. Elizabeth

Halifax Infirmary. This drawing by John Horner shows the new infirmary, which replaced the old dispensary. Designed by George Townshend Andrews and financed largely by public subscriptions it opened on a site in Blackwall adjacent to the New Assembly Rooms in 1838. In 1845 a member of the commission inquiring into the sanitary conditions of large towns described the new infirmary and dispensary as 'an elegant and commodious house, where good attention is paid to patients', though the housekeeper and her assistants 'much complained' of deficiencies in the sanitation. (Photograph: Calderdale Museums Service, Bankfield)

Hitcheon claimed that Absalom Wilkinson, who had been drinking ale with his shopmates, called her a 'whore and a brimstone whore'.[39] Later, G. S. Philipps, secretary of the Huddersfield Mechanics' Institute, visiting Cragg Vale in 1848 where counterfeiting had formerly thrived, formed an impression of continuing cultural and moral deprivation:

> there is an aspect of ... barbarism about the people which is very melancholy. The children are ragged and dirty, running about the roadside, as if they belonged to nobody. The men are uncouth, brutal, and cast in the most animal moulds. Their leisure hours are spent in playing at pitch-halfpenny, in eating, drinking, and all manner of debaucheries ... The women, likewise, are unwomanly in their appearance, reminding one of the sexless witches in

P.P.P.Previes.

Standidge & Co Litho Old Jewry

VIEW OF OPEN SEWER
ABOVE CORN MARKET, HALIFAX.

Open sewer, Corn Market, Halifax. The report of the Health of Towns Commission in 1845 identified the lack of an adequate sewerage system as a major problem in Halifax. The town was only partially sewered and there was a great need for under-sewerage. In April 1845 a branch of the Health of Towns Association chaired by the Vicar of Halifax, Archdeacon Musgrave, was formed, but William Ranger, surveying the sanitary provision in the township of Northowram in 1850 commented on the lack of privies and discovered that in Middle Street, Haley Hill, there was only one privy for the use of 221 persons. (Photograph: Halifax Antiquarian Society)

Government proclamation issued by the Solicitor to the Royal Mint from the White Lion, Silver Street, Halifax 14 December 1769. The government despatched William Chamberlayne, Solicitor to the Royal Mint, to Halifax in December 1769 following the assassination of William Dighton, supervisor of the excise at Halifax by local coiners. His first action was to issue a proclamation in the form of a handbill and as a newspaper advertisement offering rewards for information leading to the conviction of those engaged in clipping or counterfeiting coin of the realm. (Photograph: J. A. Hargreaves)

WHEREAS the Practice of Clipping the Gold Coin of this Kingdom hath for a confiderable Time laft paft been carried on in the Parifh of Halifax, and Towns adjacent, and in divers other Places within the Weft-Riding of the County of York,

AND WHEREAS there is great Reafon to believe, that numbers of Perfons have been drawn in to the Commiffion of the faid Offence, not knowing at the Time, that by the Laws of this Realm, the fame is declared to be HIGH TREASON, and afterwards having come to the Knowledge of the Confequence of their Offence, have neverthelefs continued in the Practice thereof, from an Apprehenfion that they could not make a Difcovery without convicting themfelves;

It is therefore thought proper to give this Public NOTICE,

That by an Act of Parliament paft in the Seventh Year of the Reign of his late Majefty King William the Third, any Perfon guilty of Coining, Clipping, or Diminifhing the Current Coin of this Realm, who fhall afterwards Difcover two or more Perfons who have committed either of the faid Crimes, and give Information thereof to any One of his Majefty's Juftices of the Peace, fo as Two or more be convicted of the fame, is thereby declared intitled to his MAJESTY's PARDON for all his faid Crimes which he may have committed before fuch Difcovery, and if fuch Perfon be an Apprentice, he is thereby declared to be a Freeman, and hath thereby Liberty to Exercife any lawful Trade, Profeffion, or Myftery, with all Liberties and Priviledges, and in as full and ample Manner as if he had ferved the full Time of his Apprenticefhip, and is moreover by the faid Act intitled to the Reward of FORTY POUNDS for every Perfon convicted.

WM. CHAMBERLAYNE,
Sollicitor to his Majefty's Mint.

WHITE LION, HALIFAX,
14th DECEMBER, 1769.

N. B. The Towns of *Halifax*, *Leeds*, and *Bradford*. have offered a Reward of TEN GUINEAS for every Perfon convicted, over and above the Reward allowed by Act of Parliament.

Plug Plot rioters at North Bridge, 15 August 1842. Disturbances erupted in Halifax in August 1842, following the rejection of the second Chartist national petition. Rioters converged on the town from both Todmorden and Bradford, determined to halt factory production by removing the plugs from the mill boilers. Large numbers of special constables were sworn in to supplement the two companies of infantry and two troops of cavalry already stationed in the town. The *Halifax Guardian* estimated that at the height of the trouble there was a mob of around 25,000 people on the streets of Halifax, which succeeded in bringing most of the mills in the town to a standstill. On the following day a crowd threatened the Akroyd mills at Haley Hill. Shots were fired, the cavalry made a number of charges, three men were wounded and over thirty prisoners taken. However, by 19 August the riots had subsided and the mills had re-opened. (Photograph: The *Illustrated London News*)

Macbeth … I think *missionaries* were never more wanted, not even in the floating islands of Polynesia, than amongst this sad, degraded people.[40]

In 1849 Edward Akroyd, shocked by the rural and urban rioting which accompanied the Plug Plot disturbances in the summer of 1842, commenced his first model industrial community at Copley, near Halifax, where he had purchased mills in 1844. This attempt to raise the living standards of the labouring classes and develop an industrious and loyal factory workforce, was an early manifestation of 'a general movement in the West Riding which saw the introduction of a whole range of paternalistic measures to heal class divisions and indoctrinate working men and women with the middle-class values of respectability, earnestness and self-help'. However, the movement only came to maturity after 1851.[41]

Religion and politics

The cultural deprivation and moral depravation evident within the new industrial society of Halifax and its hinterland in the late eighteenth and early nineteenth centuries also presented a challenge to both the Established Church and Nonconformity during this period. Nowhere did the Church of England's parochial and diocesan structure appear less well-equipped to respond to the impact of social and economic change than in the vast, sprawling upland parish of Halifax, situated on the remote south-western periphery of the huge diocese of York. Covering an area larger than that of the county of Rutland, the parish of Halifax was the largest parish in Yorkshire, and twice as large as the neighbouring parish of Bradford. While the establishment of two medieval parochial chapelries at Elland and Heptonstall had effectively subdivided the parish into three more manageable administrative units, the parochial district of Halifax, the largest of the three units, encompassed no fewer than ten civil townships. The inadequacies of the parochial system were mirrored by the inadequacies of the diocesan structure. Until the creation of the diocese of Ripon in 1836, Halifax occupied a far-flung corner of the huge diocese of York, with its 903 parishes and chapelries.[42]

Where Anglican provision was weak or non-existent, Evangelical Nonconformity tended to be strong. John Crabtree, the first local historian to take account of the industrial transformation of the parish, attributed the 'rapid increase of dissenting meeting houses' within the parish by 1836 to 'the want of church accommodation'. By 1843 Edward Baines's denominational survey identified 110 Nonconformist chapels in the parish with accommodation for almost a third of the parish population, more than double that provided by the 22 Anglican churches. Moreover, Nonconformist Sunday school enrolment of 22,713 scholars had completely outpaced that of the Church of England with its 5,633 scholars. When the Census of Religious Worship was taken in 1851, only 31 of the 126 places of worship included in returns from the Halifax Poor Law Union were Anglican. Total Methodist attendances alone in the incomplete returns for the Halifax Municipal Borough amounted to 73.28 per cent of total Anglican attendances.[43]

Despite a series of damaging secessions in which the Halifax Wesleyans lost nearly half of their membership to the Independents in 1762, over a quarter of their membership to the Methodist New Connexion in 1797, and over a third of their remaining membership to the Wesleyan Reformers in 1851, the Halifax Wesleyans still recorded the largest number of Nonconformist attendances at worship in Halifax on Census Sunday in 1851. Membership growth was steady rather than spectacular in the middle years of the eighteenth century, reaching 1,000 in 1786, but accelerated dramatically during the Great Yorkshire Revival of 1793–94. John Wesley himself visited the town for the opening of the new South Parade Wesleyan Chapel in 1777, and when news of the death of the founder of Methodism on 3 March 1791 reached Halifax the chapel was immediately shrouded in 'the habiliments of mourning' with 'obsequies befitting the death of a king' and no expense spared. It remained draped in black for a whole year. A second, more ornate chapel, named Wesley Chapel, in honour of the founder of Methodism, displaying in its architectural style, John Crabtree acclaimed, 'a degree of taste' unsurpassed 'by any chapels belonging to this denomination of Christians in the West Riding', was opened at Broad Street in 1829. As Halifax had become the centre of ecclesiastical organisation for its hinterland, it also became the focal point for Methodist organisation. Halifax became the head of a new Wesleyan circuit in 1785 and a new Wesleyan district in 1791, when the Halifax superintendent minister, the Revd William Thompson, a conciliatory Ulsterman, succeeded John Wesley as President of Conference.[44]

Wesley Chapel, drawn by John Horner, 1836. The years 1827 to 1829 were years of sustained growth in membership for Halifax Wesleyanism. The growing confidence was signalled by the opening of a second Wesleyan chapel for the town in November 1829 in Broad Street to relieve overcrowding at the South Parade Chapel, which had been opened in 1777 and extended in 1812. The new chapel which was praised for its 'general symmetry', 'handsome palisadoes' and 'chaste, comely and pleasing' interior was completed at a cost of £4,000, a quarter of which was raised in collections at the opening services conducted by leading Wesleyans, including Jabez Bunting, a former circuit superintendent minister. The chapel closed in August 1949 and was demolished in September 1968. (Photograph: Calderdale Museums Service, Bankfield)

A Halifax superintendent minister also became first President of the Methodist New Connexion in 1797, when the Revd William Thom, a cultured Aberdonian, amazed his Wesleyan associates by defecting to the Kilhamites in Leeds. By 1801 Halifax was also the head of a large Methodist New Connexion Circuit extending as far as Bingley, Keighley and Burnley by 1819. The first purpose-built Salem Chapel, erected on North Parade in 1798, was reconstructed 'in a plain, robust style' in 1815 and enlarged in 1845, and a second Hanover Chapel, serving the expanding western sector of the town, was opened in 1836. The Primitive Methodists opened their first Ebenezer Chapel on Cabbage Lane in 1822, when the new Halifax Primitive Methodist Circuit became the nucleus of revivalistic preaching in no fewer than twenty-three surrounding localities. The Wesleyan Reformers, whose attendances on Census Sunday in 1851 at their one place of worship in Halifax narrowly exceeded those of the Primitive Methodists, formed their first society in Halifax in 1849.[45]

The Independents or Congregationalists had also established a strong presence in the town by 1851, although this is not apparent from the published returns for the municipal borough of Halifax for the Census on Religious Worship of 1851: this inexplicably not only lacks data for the Independent congregations, but also for the Particular Baptist, Unitarian and Roman Catholic congregations. The Wesleyan secessionists of 1762 under the leadership of Titus Knight, a self-educated collier

Hanover Street Methodist New Connexion Chapel. The Methodist New Connexion chose a location in the expanding western sector of the town for their second chapel at Hanover Street. Laying the foundation stone for the new chapel, the Revd William Ford proclaimed confidently that the New Connexion Methodists now 'were advancing in a cheering degree, as might be proved by comparing their followers, as to wealth, numbers and station with any other species of seceders'. The new chapel, which opened in 1836, was both 'commodious' and 'entirely free from ornamentation'. After the closure of the chapel, it was acquired by the Halifax Thespians for conversion into the Halifax Playhouse. (Photograph: Calderdale Museums Service, Bankfield)

converted by the preaching of John Wesley, built the new Square Independent Chapel – a magnificent red-brick Palladian building – in 1772, with financial assistance from the Countess of Huntingdon. In 1819 a second, finely proportioned, Sion Chapel was opened in Wade Street, and in 1837 a third, classically styled, chapel opened in Harrison Road.[46]

Both the General and Particular Baptists had places of worship in Halifax by 1851, the former reporting attendances of 298 on Census Sunday. The Presbyterian congregation at Northgate End espoused Unitarianism in 1775, and the chapel, which had been modified in 1762 and 1817, was further enhanced by the addition of an impressive new west front in a bold classical style in 1847. The foundation stone of St Mary's, the first Catholic church to be built in Halifax since the Reformation, was laid in 1836 and the church opened three years later. Almost a century elapsed, however, before the church was completely free from debt and ready for formal consecration in 1934, an indication of the poverty of the Roman Catholic community in Halifax, many of whom were Irish immigrants.[47]

Nonconformity appealed particularly to artisans, shopkeepers and women during this period. The diaries of Cornelius Ashworth, handloom weaver and smallholder, record his frequent attendance at Baptist and Congregational preaching services, and domestic outworkers figure prominently in the non-parochial registers and trust deeds of Halifax Nonconformist chapels from the late eighteenth century. Some early industrialist entrepreneurs also had Nonconformist backgrounds, for example the carpet manufacturers John and Martha Crossley and the worsted manufacturers J. and J. Baldwin, who were Congregationalists, and the worsted spinners James and Jonathan Akroyd, who were New Connexion Methodists. Nonconformists were also prominent in the public life of the town during the early nineteenth century. For example, Rawdon Briggs, one of the first Members of Parliament for Halifax, was a Unitarian banker; John Baldwin, the first Mayor of Halifax, was a Congregationalist manufacturer and George Buxton Browne, the first Chairman of the Halifax Poor Law Union Board of Guardians, was a Wesleyan civil engineer. Many others served as township trustees and later as town councillors and aldermen. Ralph Waldo Emerson was impressed by the younger John Crossley, who before the end of 1848 would begin his four-term period as mayor of Halifax and who 'was one of the most energetic philanthropists in Britain, contributing thousands of pounds for urban revitalisation projects, including the construction of an almshouse, an orphanage, a chapel, a school building, and a hospital in Halifax, and many other charitable enterprises'.[48]

Although the demographic, economic and social changes in the parish during the period 1750–1850 imposed an increasing strain on already overstretched Anglican structures and resources, the Church of England was far from moribund in the parish of Halifax during this period. Episcopal visitation returns reveal an impressive level of pastoral concern and devotion to clerical duty at parochial level. Recognising the need for a second church to serve the growing population of Halifax township, the Revd Dr Henry William Coulthurst, Vicar of Halifax from 1790 to 1817, obtained a special act of Parliament to build the new Holy Trinity Church,

Square Independent Chapel, drawn by Thomas Bradley, 1772. The design of both the chapel, which opened in 1772, and the adjacent Halifax Piece Hall, which opened in 1779, have been attributed to Thomas Bradley (1753–1833), but this has not yet been demonstrated conclusively and there has been speculation that his father of the same name may have played a greater role in the construction of Square Chapel than has been hitherto supposed. The classical red-brick chapel, which was situated in the south-east corner of a field known as Talbot Croft in the Square, was adapted for use as a Sunday School when the adjacent Victorian Gothic Square Congregational Church was opened in 1857. When both buildings closed, after years of neglect, the Square Chapel Trust acquired the chapel building, which was noted for its remarkable cubic design and its unusual red-brick construction with the largest self-supporting roof structure of Norwegian pitch pine and English oak in Georgian Britain, in 1988 for restoration as an arts centre. (Photograph: Calderdale Museums Service, Bankfield)

Sion Independent Chapel, drawn by John Horner, 1836. Occupying a building in Wade Street formerly used by Wesleyan Secessionists and Southcottians, Sion Chapel was an offshoot of Square Chapel in 1816. In 1819 a ashlar-fronted building of classical design was opened with seating for 1,020 and a schoolroom in the basement. Among the first trustees of the chapel was John Baldwin, who became first Mayor of Halifax in 1848. The chapel and school were enlarged and extended between 1846 and 1866, but the church finally closed in 1959. In 1989 the facades of both the church and school buildings were incorporated into the design of the new bus station. (Photograph: Calderdale Museums Service, Bankfield)

which opened in 1798. The Revd Dr Charles Musgrave, Vicar of Halifax from 1827 to 1875 and first Archdeacon of Craven, who held the incumbency for almost half a century, initiated an ambitious programme of church building, supported by Charles Longley, Bishop of Ripon, and assisted by Robert Peel's ecclesiastical reforms. Two more churches, St James's and St Paul's, were opened in expanding western sectors of Halifax in 1832 and 1847. By the end of his incumbency no fewer than thirty-eight churches throughout the ancient parish had been constructed or completely restored.[49]

The churches and chapels also made an invaluable contribution to the educational and cultural development of the town and parish during this period, through their Sunday schools, day schools and mutual improvement societies. The 1833 Education Enquiry reported that there were some 5,567 children under instruction in fifty-seven schools in the township of Halifax, 68 per cent of whom attended Sunday schools and 14 per cent of whom attended charity schools. The Sunday schools, moreover, made a particular contribution to the provision of education for girls, for whom there was a paucity of other educational provision. The 1833 Education Enquiry revealed that while only 42 per cent of the children receiving elementary education at the day schools in the Halifax township were girls, 50 per cent of the Sunday school scholars in the township were girls. However, educational

General Baptist Chapel, Haley Hill, by William Burgess, 1788. The chapel sprang from the evangelistic outreach of a General Baptist society at Queensbury during the pastorate of the Revd John Taylor (1742–1818), supported by his brother, the Revd Dan Taylor (1738–1816). After cottage meetings in 1773 the fledgling society met initially in a rented room in Gaol Lane in 1775, moving to a new chapel on Haley Hill opened in September 1777. In 1782 when the society formally separated from the Queensbury society it had a membership of 30 and in October 1783 Dan Taylor became its pastor for almost two years before reluctantly responding to pressure for him to move to London in the wider interests of the connexion. In 1854 the congregation moved to a more central site on North Parade.
(Photograph: Calderdale Museums Service, Bankfield)

provision failed to keep pace with the rapid rise in population. Literacy rates, measured by the number of bridegrooms able to sign their names in the parish registers, appear to have plummeted in Halifax during the early nineteenth century. In 1845 a Young Men's Society was commenced at Square Chapel, together with a Saturday evening class 'to promote a taste for reading' in the older boys. In 1850 a Young Men's Christian Society was formed at Sion Chapel 'for mutual improvement by means of lectures and discussions'.[50]

Churches and chapels also helped to foster a strong musical tradition. When Charles Dibdin, the popular composer, visited Halifax in 1788, he pronounced the town 'the most musical spot, for its size, in the kingdom', marvelling at 'the facility with which the common people join together ... in every species of choral music'. Handel's *Messiah*, composed in 1741, was first performed in Halifax in 1766 to celebrate the opening of the new Snetzler organ at Halifax Parish Church, and such was its popularity by 1788 that Dibdin observed graphically that 'cloth makers as they sweat under their loads in the cloth hall roar out "For his yoke is easy and his burden is light"'. Indeed, Joah Bates (1741-1799), whose father Henry Bates was Halifax parish clerk and a Halifax innkeeper, attended

Manchester Grammar School and gained scholarships to Eton College and King's College, Cambridge, becoming a Fellow of King's in 1763. He is credited with the introduction of the Messiah to a choral club at his father's house near Halifax Parish Church in about 1766 and later in his career achieved musical celebrity status in London as the director of the Handel Commemoration of 1784. However, there was entrenched Nonconformist opposition to the theatre in the town. Thomas Wilson Manly, travelling theatrical impresario, faced such opposition in 1835 that he had to plead that 'the religious and virtuous life is not impaired by an occasional engagement with rational amusements'.[51]

Another club, the Halifax Union Club, was founded in 1756 following the outbreak of the Seven Years' War (1756–63), from which Britain emerged as the leading world power, albeit at the cost of nearly doubling the national debt and fostering a distinctly bellicose nationalism. The Halifax Union Club was so called because it was perceived as 'a congress of parties, in order to sacrifice all their differences to the good of the state'. Under the nominal leadership of Sir George Savile (1726–84), a politician, who had served as a captain against the Jacobite rebels in 1745, it was an intensely patriotic attempt to unite Whigs and Tories in common cause against the French and in support of local commercial interests. Both the Calder Navigation and the association that was formed to build the Halifax Piece Hall emerged from the deliberations of this socially exclusive, convivial club. Religious divisions, and their associated social distinctions, inevitably impacted also upon electoral politics, especially with the emergence of sensitive moral and religious issues such as the abolition of the slave trade and Roman Catholic emancipation in the late eighteenth and early nineteenth centuries. The poll books of 1734 and 1741 reveal that on the whole Halifax freeholders supported the Tories. However,

Jonathan Akroyd (1782–1847). The reclining effigy of this prominent Methodist New Connexion worsted manufacturer surmounted his tomb in the Akroyd mausoleum at the All Souls' Burial Ground, Haley Hill, Halifax. Akroyd had originally been buried in the graveyard of Salem Methodist New Connexion Chapel, North Parade, Halifax, following his sudden death at a stormy election meeting in 1847. Part of the £300,000 legacy that he bequeathed to his sons Edward and Henry was used by Edward to finance the construction of All Souls' Church, Haley Hill and his body was later exhumed and reinterred in the nearby All Souls' Burial Ground. The photograph shows the vandalised Akroyd mausoleum in the All Souls' graveyard in 1967. Further extensive damage to the mausoleum resulted in the decision by the All Souls' Parochial Church Council to demolish the structure.
(Photograph: *Halifax Courier*)

St James's Church, drawn by John Horner. The second new Anglican church to be built to serve the growing population of the town during this period, it was financed partly by public subscription and partly 'out of the fund at the disposal of the commissioners appointed by parliament for the erection of new churches'. Michael Stocks gave the stone for its construction from his quarries at Shibden Dale. The church was designed in a 'pseudo-Gothic' style and was opened in St James Road, formerly Cabbage Lane, on 2 January 1832. It was described in a contemporary directory as 'a very handsome edifice of stone'. The church was demolished in 1955 and its district, which had been declared a Consolidated Chapelry in 1842, was combined with that of St Mary's, Rhodes Street, until St Mary's closed for worship in 1986 and was itself demolished in 2001. (Photograph: Calderdale Museums Service, Bankfield)

contested elections in England's largest county remained relatively rare on account of the prohibitive costs involved in providing refreshment for voters attending local election meetings and transport to the poll at York. Dr E. A. Smith has calculated, for example, that the 1807 Yorkshire election left the three candidates with a total bill in excess of £200,000. But when contests were anticipated or held between 1750 and 1832, they generated greater interest from electors than had early eighteenth-century elections. This was partly on account of the growing importance of commercial issues after 1750. For example, in December 1758 Sir George Savile, an independent Whig and major landowner in the parish of Halifax, gained almost universal support from Halifax's freeholders, many of whom had voted Tory in 1741, when he canvassed their support for his anticipated candidacy, which helped to secure his election as MP for Yorkshire in 1759, because the passage of the Calder Navigation Bill through Parliament had forged a commercial consensus in Halifax which transcended party divisions.[52]

The growing political awareness of the Halifax electorate was also a consequence of the development of a provincial parliamentary reform movement against a

British School Rules. The non-denominational British and Foreign Schools Society opened the Halifax British School in rented premises in April 1813. The school, which aimed 'to enable the scholars to read the Scriptures', acquired 'large and commodious', purpose-built premises in Albion Street in 1818 and received support from members 'of almost every Christian denomination, including the Church of England'. In 1833 there were some 508 scholars enrolled at the school, vastly more than at any other school in the township. Parents of scholars were requested to display these printed regulations 'in some conspicuous part of the house'. They included the injunctions to children 'to come to school orderly and quietly, and leave in the same manner'; 'to avoid the company of bad children' and 'to be regular in attendance at their Sunday schools and the place of worship to which they belong'. (Photograph: West Yorkshire Archive Service, Calderdale)

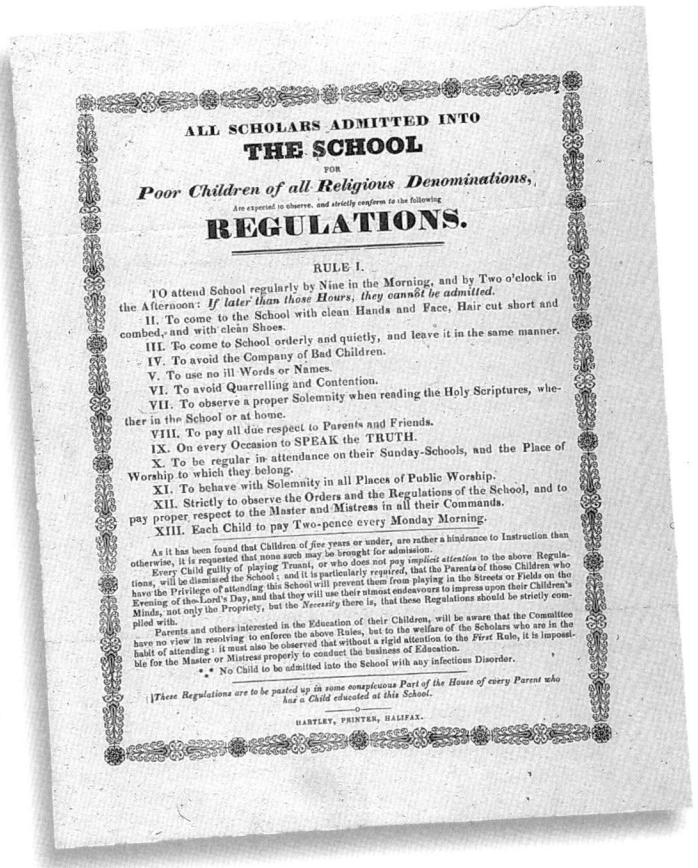

ALL SCHOLARS ADMITTED INTO
THE SCHOOL
FOR
Poor Children of all Religious Denominations,
Are expected to observe, and strictly conform to the following
REGULATIONS.

RULE I.

TO attend School regularly by Nine in the Morning, and by Two o'clock in the Afternoon: *If later than those Hours, they cannot be admitted.*
II. To come to the School with clean Hands and Face, Hair cut short and combed, and with clean Shoes.
III. To come to School orderly and quietly, and leave it in the same manner.
IV. To avoid the Company of Bad Children.
V. To use no ill Words or Names.
VI. To avoid Quarrelling and Contention.
VII. To observe a proper Solemnity when reading the Holy Scriptures, whether in the School or at home.
VIII. To pay all due respect to Parents and Friends.
IX. On every Occasion to SPEAK the TRUTH.
X. To be regular in attendance on their Sunday-Schools, and the Place of Worship to which they belong.
XI. To behave with Solemnity in all Places of Public Worship.
XII. Strictly to observe the Orders and the Regulations of the School, and to pay proper respect to the Master and Mistress in all their Commands.
XIII. Each Child to pay Two-pence every Monday Morning.

As it has been found that Children of *five* years or under, are rather a hindrance to Instruction than otherwise, it is requested that none such may be brought for admission.
Every Child guilty of playing Truant, or who does not pay *implicit attention* to the above Regulations, will be dismissed the School; and it is particularly required, that the Parents of those Children who have the Privilege of attending this School will prevent them from playing in the Streets or Fields on the Evening of the Lord's Day, and that they will use their utmost endeavours to impress upon their Children's Minds, not only the Propriety, but the *Necessity* there is, that these Regulations should be strictly complied with.
Parents and others interested in the Education of their Children, will be aware that the Committee have no view in resolving to enforce the above Rules, but to the welfare of the Scholars who are in the habit of attending: it must also be observed that without a rigid attention to the *First Rule*, it is impossible for the Master or Mistress properly to conduct the business of Education.
* * No Child to be admitted into the School with any infectious Disorder.

|*These Regulations are to be pasted up in some conspicuous Part of the House of every Parent who has a Child educated at this School.*

HARTLEY, PRINTER, HALIFAX.

background of dearth and distress when harvests were poor as in 1783. Although the release from imprisonment of John Wilkes, 'the popular champion of the people's rights', in April 1770 was greeted in Halifax with the 'ringing of bells, fireworks and other demonstrations of joy', it was the political crisis generated by the War of American Independence between 1775 and 1783 that gave birth to the agitation for parliamentary reform in Yorkshire in the late eighteenth century. Moreover, despite the collapse of the Revd Christopher Wyvill's Yorkshire Association movement for parliamentary reform shortly before the general election of 1784, and the loyalty to the government interest of the Vicar of Halifax and other leading parishioners, the Associationist candidates William Wilberforce and Henry Duncombe were supported by some influential merchants and manufacturers in Halifax and most of the leading Dissenters. Moreover, the reform movement was sustained during the 1780s by Major John Cartwright's radical constitutional societies and Protestant Dissenters in their unsuccessful campaigns for civil and religious liberty. However, it was not until 1791–92 that an organised popular radical movement developed in the West Riding, stimulated by the outbreak of the French Revolution, the publication of Tom Paine's avowedly republican *Rights of Man*, the foundation of the Sheffield

Halifax Parish Church Choir. This oil painting by Thomas Farrar (*fl.* 1796–1811) shows members of the Halifax Parish Church Choir accompanied by musicians practising at the Ring o'Bells Inn on Church Street close to the parish church. It has been suggested by Dr Rachel Cowgill that the central figure is probably Henry Bates, parish clerk, but that the painting may be a nostalgic depiction of the Bates family and their musical acquaintances. The clerical figure on Henry Bates's immediate right may have been the Revd Mr Charlesworth and the two figures on his right Grace and Henry Bates junior, the children of Henry Bates senior. Their brother Joah Bates (1741–99), who achieved scholarships to Eton and King's College Cambridge, achieved musical celebrity in London as director of the Concerts of Antient Music and the Handel Commemoration of 1784 and probably introduced Handel's celebrated oratorio, the *Messiah*, to his musical acquaintances in Halifax. (Photograph: Calderdale Museums Service, Bankfield)

Society for Constitutional Information and the London Corresponding Society. By November 1792, when magistrates at Bingley obliged a Halifax bookseller who had sold copies of a penny paper, *The French Constitution*, to acknowledge the error of his ways, a Jacobin society had been established at Halifax, and at a huge open-air meeting in the town on Easter Monday 1794, plans were approved for a National Convention. Such activity stirred Pitt's government into a policy of repression which continued throughout the wars with Revolutionary and Napoleonic France.

A growing popular political awareness resulted in an increasing involvement of non-electors at election meetings. During the elections of 1806–07, a detachment of Inniskillen dragoons had to be dispatched to the town to quell disturbances erupting at the poll. In 1806, both William Wilberforce and Henry Lascelles addressed well-attended election meetings at the Halifax Piece Hall, but Lascelles, weakened by his family's reputation as slave-owners and his own controversial role in the woollen-trade committee of 1806 which had alienated many West Riding clothiers, subsequently withdrew from the contest, allowing Wilberforce and Walter Fawkes to be returned unopposed. When, in the following April, George III dissolved Parliament to prevent the passage of a Roman Catholic Emancipation Bill through Parliament, a public meeting in Halifax supported by the Vicar, the Revd Dr Henry Coulthurst, and other leading local landowners and manufacturers, presented a loyal address to the king, expressing gratitude for his 'support and protection of the Protestant religion and his constitutional exercise of the royal prerogative'. During the ensuing election campaign, the three candidates, Wilberforce, Lascelles and Viscount Milton, the son of the Whig lord lieutenant, Earl Fitzwilliam, all visited Halifax. However, despite Milton's provision of nine free barrels of beer for the crowds attending his election meeting at the Piece Hall and the subsequent spectacle of two supporters impersonating Lord and Lady Milton being carried around the town by men with blackened faces caricaturing the slaves on the Lascelles' West Indian plantations, 95 votes of Halifax freeholders went to both Wilberforce and Lascelles and only 74 votes to Milton. Moreover,

Halifax Choral Society Rule Book, 1825. The initiative for forming a choral society in Halifax sprang from a 'musical evening' held at the home of William Priestley in Lightcliffe. Its first meeting was held at the Ovenden Cross Inn, but meetings soon moved into inns in the centre of the town and the Court House, where the society's début concert, a rendition of Haydn's *Creation*, was performed on 9 February 1819. Henceforward, four concerts were given each year, reflected in the original name of the society, the Halifax Quarterly Choral Society. By 1825, however, the name had changed to the Halifax Monthly Choral Society and a new set of rules had been agreed. (Photograph: West Yorkshire Archive Service, Calderdale)

THE SUBSTANCE OF
THE SPEECH
OF
WILLIAM WILBERFORCE, Esq.
ADDRESSED
To the Gentlemen, Clergy, and Freeholders,
OF
HALIFAX AND ITS VICINITY,
Assembled in the PIECE-HALL, on the 2d of May, 1807.

GENTLEMEN,

It cannot now be necessary to detain you by an appeal to the principles by which I have been actuated in a long line of conduct. With these principles I began, and on a review of their influence, I have the satisfaction to say, that whatever may have been the vicissitudes of the empire, or the changes of administration, from them I have never deviated.

I trust there is not a man living more loyal in principle, or more sincerely attached to the religion, and to the liberties of my country. I must say, and it is natural for me to remind you, that by these principles I commenced the high duties of representing you in Parliament in 1784. And I am the same man to this day.

At that period, when the great question was agitated, on which an appeal is now made to the sense of the nation, whether the Crown had a right to choose its own officers, to watch over its interests, and over the interests, the happiness, and the liberties of the Subject with equal care, my principles were formed.——Loyalty and Liberty are naturally combined; they must subsist or fall together: and it is solely by their union, that this Country has enjoyed so vast a period of internal repose, and of exterior wealth, grandeur, and prosperity. We owe the whole to a constitution which comprises in itself the aggregate good of every other form of government, which posterity has admired and approved.

GENTLEMEN, these are the principles on which I commenced my career with the great Statesman, just named, *(alluding to the speech of the Honourable Henry Lascelles, in which honourable mention was made of the late Mr. Pitt.)* He entered on the duties of his high office, at a crisis like the present. He began by asserting the rights of the crown; that His Majesty had an uncontrouled authority to choose ministers in whom he could confide. He recalled the country to the principles of her constitution; and his comprehensive mind grasping the immense interests of the whole empire, he preserved her independance and happiness amid dangers the most serious to which she had ever been exposed.—— It was at this period, that my principles were formed, and my mind fixed in its views and attachments. And it gives me pleasure, *(turning towards his friends)* to see myself surrounded by Gentlemen, who have uniformly acted on the same principles. They have been long tried; and they will carry you safely through the vicissitudes of life, and the commotions of the world.

If you shall do me the honour of again electing me to represent you in Parliament, I shall esteem the choice of this great and free county as the highest approbation of my conduct. And I shall continue, as have ever been the warmest sentiments of my heart, to pay the most unremitting attention to all your civil and commercial interests.

Again, Gentlemen, I thank you for this fresh instance of kindness and attachment to me; and it shall be more and more the object of my future life, to merit your confidence and approbation.

N. B. Mr. WILBERFORCE was so modest that he did not so much as hint at the Abolition of the Slave Trade, a subject which has peculiarly endeared him to the hearts of the Freeholders of Yorkshire.

Holden and Dowson, Printers, Halifax.

Speech by William Wilberforce, anti-slavery campaigner, at Halifax Piece Hall during the Yorkshire election of 1807. Wilberforce, who had represented the Yorkshire county constituency since 1784, appealed to the freeholder electorate for their support on the basis of his 'unremitting attention' to their 'civil and commercial interests', without making explicit reference to the campaign for the abolition of the slave trade. An appended note confirms that his campaign had 'peculiarly endeared him to the hearts of the freeholders of the county'. Indeed, Wilberforce headed the county poll with 11,806 votes, 95 of which were cast by Halifax freeholders. (Photograph: West Yorkshire Archive Service, Calderdale)

Poster advertising John Hodgson's offer to grind corn at no charge to help the poor of Halifax, 6 May 1812. Corn prices reached their peak for the whole of the nineteenth century in 1812, a year of acute distress throughout Halifax and West Yorkshire. During the first half of the year Luddite disturbances erupted across the textile belt. The death of Samuel Hartley, a Halifax cropper in a Luddite raid on William Cartwright's Rawfolds Mill in the Spen Valley in April had prompted a large display of radical sympathy at his funeral at the South Parade Wesleyan Chapel. (Photograph: West Yorkshire Archive Service, Calderdale)

TO THE
Gentlemen
and principal
Inhabitants
of the
TOWN OF HALIFAX.

In the Present distressing Times, when the Poor from want of Work and dearness of Provisions, are unable to get the Necessaries of Life; Mr. JOHN HODGSON takes this Opportunity of acquainting the Gentlemen and principal Inhabitants of the Town of Halifax, who feel for and wish to alleviate the Distresses of the Poor, that if they will come forwards with a Subscription and Purchase Corn, he will Grind and Dress the same, free of any Expence, so that the Poor in this Time of dearness, may have Bread at the bare Price of the Corn.

Halifax,
Four-Mills, May 6th, 1812.

Printed at Jacobs Office, Halifax.

during the poll, the *Halifax Journal* reported intense excitement in Halifax, with the town being disturbed each evening by 'a riotous and desperate mob' carrying effigies of Lascelles, and concluded that 'nothing since the days of the Revolution has ever presented such a scene as has happened during this fortnight'. Wilberforce headed the constituency poll with 11,806 votes, followed by Viscount Milton with 11,177 and Henry Lascelles with 10,989. Milton, elected with Wilberforce, served until the eve of the Great Reform Act and Wilberforce until 1812, when ill health forced him to give it up in favour of the less demanding small borough of Bramber.[53]

The death of Samuel Hartley, a local cropper, in a Luddite raid in the Spen Valley in 1812 prompted a large display of radical sympathy at his funeral at the South Parade Wesleyan Chapel, and when Major Cartwright renewed his campaign for parliamentary reform, some 17,000 signatures were collected in under two months in 1813 for a petition for parliamentary reform. Reform meetings near Halifax in December 1816 and January 1817, stimulated by post-war distress, were also well-attended, and reaction to the 'Peterloo Massacre' at St Peter's Field in Manchester in 1819 was vociferous and indignant. As the Tory diarist, Anne Lister, commented, Halifax was full of talk 'of the sad work at Manchester', and on Monday, 4 October, an estimated 50,000 'male and female reformers' attended a large open-air meeting in the town. Attired in black and led by sixteen bands through pouring rain 'with the same solemnity as at a funeral'. This was followed by a patriotic dinner, during which toasts were proposed to 'The People, the source of all legitimate power', 'The Saviour of our country, Major Cartwright', and 'Henry Hunt, the Champion of Liberty'. Moreover, in 1820, the ladies of Halifax expressed their radical sympathies by presenting a loyal address to Queen Caroline, the estranged wife of the unpopular George IV. Later, when the Whig lawyer, Henry Brougham, visited Halifax during the general election campaign of 1830, he was given a rapturous reception when he proclaimed:

> We don't live now in the days of barons. We live in the days of Leeds, of Bradford, of Halifax and Huddersfield. We live in the days when men are industrious and desire to be free.[54]

However, others remained determined to resist support for parliamentary reform. A meeting of Halifax loyalists, with Thomas Halton Esquire in the chair, declared:

> We being inhabitants of the town of Halifax observe with indignation the attempts ... by disaffected and deluded persons to overthrow the glorious Constitution of the British Empire, and to eradicate from the hearts of the people every feeling of loyalty and religion. We view with horror, the widely extended circulation of blasphemous and seditious publications, calculated to poison the mind of man; to deprive him of his greatest consolation, the grounds of his hopes hereafter; and to inspire him with hatred and contempt for the necessary restraints of an equitable government and mild laws. We are convinced that the objects of ... those who call themselves Reformers, are not Reform, but Revolution, Anarchy and Plunder.[55]

The parliamentary reform movement reached its climax during the struggle for the Reform Bill in 1831–32, particularly following the rejection of the bill by the House of Lords in October 1831 and the resignation of Earl Grey in May 1832. On 17 May, after the Duke of Wellington had failed to form an administration, his effigy was carried through the streets of Halifax and then burned. Anne Lister recorded in her diary that 'the town was like a fair. The people had a bonfire of three carts of coal for rejoicing at the speedy return of Lord Grey'. However, the size of the ten-pound householder electorate of the new two-member borough of Halifax created under the terms of the Great Reform Act of 1832 was scarcely larger than the electorate which had qualified for the county franchise as 40-shilling freeholders before 1832. In 1807 Halifax electors had constituted 6 per cent of the adult male population; in 1832 the proportion had risen to 7.5 per cent and even by 1847, when the size of the borough electorate had almost doubled to 1,022, the electorate still only represented 11.7 per cent of the adult male population.[56]

J. A. Jowitt has characterised the electoral politics of the new two-member parliamentary borough of Halifax during the period 1832–47 as a 'conflict between the Tory oligarchy whose strength lay in the upper crust and professional electors and the Whig-Liberal oligarchy whose power lay in textiles'. He has also emphasised the 'potent and powerful force of religion' in determining election outcomes. Although serious divisions had arisen within the local Tory Anglican elite during an acrimonious dispute over the levying of tithes between 1827 and 1829, Anglican and some Wesleyan voters provided a nucleus of support for the Tories in the electoral politics of the period 1832–47, while other Nonconformist voters tended to support candidates of the Whig-Radical alliance. Religious issues often dominated election campaigns. For example, the Tories fought the 1835 election under the slogan 'the Established Church in danger', and the Radicals fought the 1847 election on the issues of disestablishment and educational voluntaryism. Indeed, the Radical-Voluntaryist challenge of the Chartist Ernest Jones and the Political Dissenter Edward Miall in 1847 forced the upper crust to close ranks, and only a high incidence of cross-party voting secured the election of the Whig candidate, Charles Wood, and the Tory candidate, Henry Edwards, a prominent Anglican textile manufacturer. Edwards topped the poll and became the first Tory Member of Parliament to be returned for the borough.[57]

All the other candidates returned in the five Halifax borough elections between 1832 and 1847 were either Whigs or Radicals, including Halifax's longest serving Member of Parliament, Sir Charles Wood (1800–85), who represented the borough from 1832 to 1865. Curiously, he was drawn not from the local urban industrial elite, but from the county landed aristocracy. Wood, the son of Sir Francis Lindley Wood, a former Deputy Lord Lieutenant of the West Riding and son-in-law of the Whig prime minister Earl Grey, was the only leading Whig politician of his generation to enjoy such a long relationship with an urban-industrial constituency. He served in every Whig-Liberal government from 1832 until his retirement in 1874, including a term as Chancellor of the Exchequer from 1846–52. He was created first Viscount Halifax in 1866.[58]

UNION

OF

Whiteley & Stocks

Electors of Halifax!

Will you suffer yourselves to be bound, Hand and Foot, by the Two noisy Factions, who aspire to be the *Tyrants* of this Great and Opulent Borough? The *Fellows*, who would surrender you to a *Place-man* and a *Place-man's Lacquey:*—The *Blues,* who have called in the Son of the *Waverer* to turn you round with the *Weather-Cock of Wortley?*

Independent & unfettered Voters!

Now or never is the Time for Action! Arouse yourselves, and secure your Rights and Liberties, by supporting the only Men worthy of your Votes—two independent and high-minded Men—*no interloping Strangers,* but Men of your own Parish, who *know* both you and your Wants—Men, untrammeled by Party-ties, and free to think and act for your Interests—Men, whose *ear-alled Characters,* whose good *Deeds,* are familiar to you as household Words.

WHITELEY & STOCKS for ever!!!

Vote for WHITELEY!—the great Corrector of Abuses! the Terror of Evil-doers! the *Deliverer of Sowerby!* the *Hercules* who has purged that Augean Stable of Thieves and Coiners! and who will, in like manner, purge the Treasury Bench, the Exchequer, the Bank of England, and the India House! The disinterested *Patriot* who for your sake, and the sake of your Wives and Children, has *forsaken* the *Tap,* the *Auction-hammer,* the *Hat-stick,* and the *Gold-stick*—and, to qualify himself as *your Representative,* is making himself into a *Statesman* and a *Legislator* by studying Night and Day Goldsmith's History of England!!!

Vote for STOCKS!—the tried *Friend of the People!* the upright Magistrate who gave the Poor Man *Law* and *Justice!* whose *exalted Character* his enemies sought in vain to asperse, and saw it come *unchanged* like *fine* Gold from the Furnace at York!!!

Free and Independent Voters! Up and be doing!

Friends of WHITELEY and STOCKS!—Form an instant Coalition! Let a Central Committee sit daily at the Hare-and-Hounds, in Halifax, with Branch Committees at the Star, in Sowerby, and the Black Bull, in Beggarington.

Three Cheers for WHITELEY & STOCKS!!

P. S. Mr. Whiteley and Mr. Stocks will have the Honor to address the Electors at the Piece Hall, on Saturday next, at 12 o'Clock.

Halifax, June 28, 1832.

WHITLEY AND BOOTH, PRINTERS, HALIFAX.

Halifax Borough election poster, 1832. The poster for the first parliamentary election for the new two-member borough constituency was issued only weeks after the Reform Bill reached the statute book in June 1832. By the time the election took place in December, John Whiteley, constable of Sowerby, had been discredited and had withdrawn from the contest. Michael Stocks, a local radical businessman and magistrate, polled 186 votes. Rawdon Briggs, a local Whig Unitarian banker, topped the poll with 242 votes. The other two candidates, the Whig Charles Wood and the Tory James Stuart Wortley, who polled 235 and 174 votes respectively, were denounced as 'interloping strangers' from outside the immediate locality. (Photograph: West Yorkshire Archive Service, Calderdale)

Although the electorate remained relatively small throughout the period up to 1850, the turnout was high, averaging 91 per cent for the five borough elections held between 1832 and 1847. There was a wider public interest at the hustings and campaign meetings, reflecting a strong tradition of extra-parliamentary protest in the town. Indeed, there was intense excitement throughout the 1835 general election campaign in Halifax, with booing, hissing, cheering and scuffles in the vast crowd of some 6,000 non-electors punctuating the nomination procedures at the Piece Hall hustings and serious rioting erupting at the close of polling, when it became clear that the Tory candidate James Stuart Wortley had secured his election for one of the two seats by a single vote over the Radical candidate Edward Protheroe. Anne Lister commented that 'the town was in sad turmoil', with 'the windows, glass and frames of many of the principal houses, inns and shops' of prominent Tory supporters 'smashed to atoms', the two front doors of the vicarage broken down and the carriage of Christopher Rawson (1777–1849), the Tory banker, broken up in the election which lived on in people's memories as 'the window breaking election'. J. A. Jowitt's analysis of the social composition of the Halifax borough electorate from 1832 to 1847, reproduced in Table 4.3, reveals a predominance of craftsmen, textile manufacturers, and other businessmen and tradesmen, averaging 72.48 per cent of the electorate with smaller strata of upper crust and professional voters, averaging 17.26 per cent, and a dearth of working-class voters averaging 2.35 per cent.[59]

Sir Charles Wood (1800–85), MP for Halifax from 1832 to 1865. Wood was not a member of the urban industrial elite, but a scion of the county landed aristocracy. The son of Sir Francis Lindley Wood, a former Deputy Lieutenant of the West Riding and son-in-law of the Whig Prime Minister Earl Grey, he was the only leading Whig politician of his generation to enjoy such a long relationship with an urban-industrial constituency. He served in every Whig-Liberal government from 1832 until his retirement in 1874, including a term as Chancellor of the Exchequer from 1846–52. He was created first Viscount Halifax of Monk Bretton in 1866 and was patron of the Halifax Permanent Building Society from its formation until his death in 1885. (Photograph: Halifax plc)

Sir Henry Edwards of Pye Nest (1812–86).
A prominent local woollen manufacturer and later Captain of the 2nd West York Yeomanry cavalry, which he was instrumental in raising during the Plug Plot disturbances of 1842. At the extraordinary Halifax Borough election of 1847 he topped the poll with 511 votes as a result of tactical voting by upper crust voters determined to prevent the election of both the Chartist, Ernest Jones, and the Political Dissenter, Edward Miall, thereby becoming the first Tory MP for Halifax. Despite his vigorous association with the movement for factory reform, however, he lost his seat at the 1852 election when the Liberal candidates Charles Wood and Francis Crossley headed the poll. (Photograph: J. A. Hargreaves)

Table 4.3 Social composition of the Halifax borough electorate, 1832–47

Occupation	1832	1835	1837	1841	1847
craft	16.06	19.97	23.97	20.17	20.48
shopkeeper	14.43	16.64	15.38	15.20	18.74
textile	16.26	19.97	21.19	17.33	15.06
upper class/professional	16.67	20.63	15.38	16.19	17.45
drink	9.35	8.99	6.68	6.82	7.91
business	10.98	11.31	10.09	9.94	9.53
other	1.42	2.16	3.91	2.56	1.73
unclassified	14.83	0.33	3.40	11.79	9.10

Source: J. A. Jowitt, 'Parliamentary Politics in Halifax, 1832–47', *Northern History* XII (1976), p. 174.

Anne Lister's account in her diary for Wednesday 7 January 1835 of disturbances following the 1835 general election in Halifax. Anne Lister had campaigned for the Tory candidate, the Hon. James Stuart Wortley, mainly by ensuring that her own enfranchised tenants voted in the Tory interest. After two days of polling, the Whig candidate Charles Wood headed the poll with 336 votes, but Wortley only secured election for the two-member constituency by the skin of his teeth, with 308 votes, just one vote more than Edward Protheroe, the Radical candidate. The result, in what Benjamin Wilson later recalled became known as 'the window breaking election', produced serious rioting in the town. Anne Lister observed that 'the town was in sad turmoil – the windows, glass and frames of many of the principal houses, inns and shops' of Tory supporters 'smashed to atoms'. (Photograph: West Yorkshire Archive Service, Calderdale)

The lack of working-class representation in Parliament gave birth to the Chartist movement seeking support for the People's Charter, published in 1838, and the establishment of Feargus O'Connor's Great Northern Union in Halifax in July 1838. In October, a contingent from Halifax marched behind two bands to the first of many open-air West Riding Chartist demonstrations in the Spen Valley at Peep Green. The People's Charter contained six points demanding universal manhood suffrage; equal electoral districts so that one man's vote would be as valuable as another's; the removal of the property qualification for Members of Parliament and the introduction of payment for them to enable working men to be elected to Parliament; a secret ballot so that voters would not be intimidated and annually elected parliaments in order to ensure the accountability to their constituents of those elected and to reduce the scope for bribery and corruption. Peter Bussey of Bradford, the West Riding delegate to the Chartist National Convention, which opened in London in February 1839, presented 52,800 signatures from his 'constituents' for the National Petition, including 13,036 from Halifax, where £40 was also collected to support the delegates. Whit Monday, 1839, witnessed another massive West Riding Chartist demonstration, opened in prayer by William Thornton from Halifax, who was complimented by Feargus O'Connor. Clapping him on the shoulders, he promised that 'when we get the People's Charter' he would see that he was made Archbishop of York. A Halifax branch of the National Charter Association was formed in 1840 which within a year had established twelve branches in the out-districts forming a district. The Chartists attended the hustings at the general election of 1841 in force and the Liberal candidates Protheroe and Wood were questioned intensively by Ben Rushton and John Crossland, a member of the handloom weavers' central committee, demanding why no action had been taken to relieve their plight. Wood's response was to urge recognition of the need for the abolition of the Corn Laws. The Chartists in this poll advised support for the Tory candidate, Sir George Sinclair, a strong advocate of factory reform and an opponent of the New Poor Law but both Protheroe and Wood were returned. The displacement of large numbers of domestic outworkers in the woollen and worsted industries, especially handloom weavers and woolcombers, provided the basis for considerable working-class organisation and agitation during the successive social crises between the Reform Bill struggle and the last major Chartist demonstration at Kennington Common in 1848, although Halifax Chartists suffered the embarrassment of failing to ensure that their signatures reached London in time to be appended to the third national petition presented in that year.

Moreover, there was growing concern about the increasing militancy of domestic outworkers during the 1840s. The normally cautious *Halifax Guardian* reported at the end of March 1842 that 700 outworkers in the upland hamlets around Halifax were armed with muskets and in April, a Halifax magistrate reported that there were handloom weavers practising drilling. Moreover, some of the most serious Plug Plot disturbances in the country occurred at Halifax on 12 August 1842, when thousands of rioters converged on the town from Bradford and Lancashire, turning out mills along the way and seeking to halt production by withdrawing the plugs from mill

Allegation of physical force Chartist activities around Halifax in 1839. This undated note was probably written in November 1839 when there was evidence of armed preparations by some Chartists at Queens Head, near Halifax, timed to coincide with the Newport rising led by John Frost in South Wales in early November 1839. The letter, signed by James Rawson and Thomas Aked, alleges the 'casting bullets from Saturday night until Sunday night' and that one of the Chartists has 'a spike and a gun in his possession'. It concludes that had not Peter Bussey of Bradford 'been taken badly' the West Yorkshire Chartists would have commenced a rising on 'the same day that Frost did'. (Photograph: West Yorkshire Archive Service, Calderdale)

boilers or by releasing water from mill lodges. At Halifax 1,302 special constables were sworn in and during the disturbances there were at least three fatalities, including one soldier, whilst, in addition 'many a tale of wounded men lying out in barns and under hedges was told'. Following an abortive attempt to rescue seventeen prisoners being escorted to Elland station by a detachment of the 11th Hussars for their part in the disturbances, the soldiers were ambushed at Salterhebble on 16 August on their return journey to Halifax by a mob of several thousand, many of them youths, who hurled boulders from nearby railway construction spoil heaps down on the cavalrymen. 'At no time during the Chartist period', the pioneering historian of public order in the Chartist era, F. C. Mather concluded, 'had regular troops come nearer to being overwhelmed by rioters', whilst Major General Sir Charles Napier described Halifax as 'wickedly Chartist'. Napier was particularly alarmed at the scattered disposition of the cavalry in the town and by rumours of plans to cut off the soldiers in their billets. He rebuked the Halifax magistrates for quartering the cavalry 'in the very worst, most dangerous way' warning that 'fifty

Attack on the military at Salterhebble, 16 August 1842. Following the Plug Plot disturbances on 15–16 August, rioters attacked a military escort taking seventeen of those arrested in Halifax by horse omnibus to Elland station en route to Wakefield for examination by the magistrates. They failed to rescue the prisoners, but later ambushed the returning troop of cavalrymen of the 11th Hussars at Salterhebble. The soldiers were pelted with stones by the rioters. When three cavalrymen were hurled from their horses they were kicked and beaten by the angry mob. Order was only restored after the troops opened fire on the crowd. 'At no time during the Chartist period', concluded the historian F. C. Mather, 'had regular troops come nearer to being overwhelmed by rioters' (Photograph: The *Illustrated London News*)

resolute Chartists might disarm and destroy the whole in ten minutes!' As late as 1848, when the Halifax borough police force was in process of formation, concern about the ability of the magistrates to maintain public order prompted one Halifax magistrate to advise the Home Office of the impracticability of removing the military force from Halifax 'for a very long time, if ever'.

Halifax, unlike some other West Riding localities, continued to maintain a Chartist organisation in the years following the unrest of 1842, and from 1844 the West Riding organisation was also based in Halifax, from where the regional secretaries, John Crossland and Christopher Shackleton, 'the finest speaker in the district' and the indefatigable treasurer, Ben Rushton, a handloom weaver, were drawn. Other stalwarts in the local leadership included Isaac Clissett, John Culpan, John Snowden, a self-educated woolcomber, George Webber, a weaver, and Ben Wilson, who also advocated co-operation, and whose memoir *Struggles of an Old Chartist* remains an invaluable contemporary account of Halifax Chartism. O'Connor's Land Plan attracted some enthusiastic local support, though others like Thomas Cliffe lost faith in O'Connor and left the movement. Indeed, in March 1847, Halifax was one of only two localities in the country whose nominations for the Chartist executive did not include O'Connor's name. When the ten hours agitation resumed from 1846, Chartists took a leading role, including handloom weavers who hoped that a limitation in factory hours would increase demand for their labour. However, some local manufacturers, including Edward Akroyd, incurred unpopularity by resisting the legislation before it reached the statute book in 1847. In 1848, stimulated by declining trade and the outbreak of the French Revolution of February 1848, Halifax Chartists, with younger recruits among their number, marched through the streets in military order proclaiming 'France has the Republic, England shall have the Charter'. Ernest Jones, representing Halifax at the Chartist National Convention, reported that 'to a man they were ready to fight'. Following an open-air meeting attended by thousands of Chartists on Skircoat Moor on 10 April, they formed a procession more than 10,000 strong, accompanied by twelve bands and displaying such menacing banners proclaiming 'Tyrants, prepare to meet your God'. Women marched prominently in the procession, bearing such slogans as 'Mothers, claim the rights of your children'. Unfortunately, however, the Halifax Chartists suffered the humiliation of failing to ensure that their signatures reached London in time to be appended to the third national petition of 1848. Moreover, tension rose throughout April, fuelled by further outdoor meetings, open drilling and widespread arming, prompting Halifax magistrates to swear in 500 special constables on one day alone. However, undeterred by their defeat in the parliamentary election of 1847 the Halifax Chartists, in alliance with radical dissent, succeeded in returning Chartist candidates in the first municipal elections in the town and the first town meeting, soon after the elections, passed resolutions incorporating Chartist demands.[60]

Local government

During the period 1750–1850, the functions of local government within the ancient parish of Halifax were exercised by a diverse and bewildering array of authorities. They included firstly the county magistracy, secondly the lords of the manor of Wakefield and the honor of Pontefract and their sub-manors, thirdly the parochial and township vestries and finally, in Halifax itself, a body of improvement commissioners or town trustees, brought into being by a series of local Acts of Parliament between 1762 and 1823 in response to the needs of a rapidly expanding urban community. Superimposed upon this unwieldy structure of local government in 1837 were the Poor Law Unions of Todmorden and Halifax, and then, at last, in 1848, the municipal borough of Halifax was created.[61]

Before this reorganisation of responsibilities, the county had been concerned with the administration of justice through the West Riding quarter sessions, presided over by a group of Justices of the Peace, and had maintained the county gaol at Wakefield. The county justices also played a key role in local government, for example, monitoring the appointment of township officers such as the overseer of the poor and surveyor of highways, approving local assessments and rates, and resolving thorny poor relief questions relating to migration and settlement. They were also responsible for the maintenance of the majority of the bridges in the county and were empowered to levy a charge for this purpose as part of the county rate. For most people, however, the county authorities were remote, and as a social unit they mattered only to the gentry.[62]

The vestiges of manorialism continued to impinge upon many people's lives throughout the eighteenth century. The manorial court with its quaint medieval nomenclature, though divested of much of its former authority, was still an institution of some importance in the local community. Constables were formally sworn in at the court leet by the steward, who after 1750 was usually an attorney. By the eighteenth century, the manorial court, which continued to meet at the Moot Hall in Halifax, had come to be selected exclusively from the local gentry who controlled parochial and township administration. The provision of an adequate water supply, the suppression of street nuisances and the control of sanitation remained the most common administrative duties of the court until they became the responsibility of the town trustees in the 1760s.

The parochial chapelries remained under the ecclesiastical authority of the Vicar of Halifax, who approved the appointment of their chaplains and paid them an annual stipend, until the sub-division of the parish was authorised under Peel's legislation in 1842 and commenced in 1843. They were allowed to exercise the right of baptism, marriage and burial, free from the jurisdiction of the vicar. Within the parish there were a number of chapels-of-ease, each with its own perpetual curate who was appointed by the vicar but paid by the inhabitants of the local chapelry. The vicar, assisted by a curate, a lecturer and various parochial officers, was thus a key figure in the local administrative hierarchy, providing a link between town, chapelry and parochial district, vicarage and diocese. His main income continued to be derived from the small tithes and vicarial dues until 1829, when they were finally commuted into a vicar's rate, levied on each township. The main sources of parochial revenue were the church rates, burial fees and revenue derived from sales of parish property.[63]

Until 1837 the basic unit for the management of community affairs throughout the parish remained the civil township. The administration of the township was the responsibility of four sets of officers acting under the direction and control of the vestry, a select group of the township's most influential inhabitants, who met annually to examine the previous year's accounts and appoint the township officers: the constables, surveyors of the highways, overseers of the poor and the church-wardens. By the end of the century poor relief was by far the largest branch of township government and the responsibility of the townships for the administration of poor relief continued until Poor Law Unions were established under the terms of the Poor Law Amendment Act of 1834, which replaced the overseers of the poor by elected Boards of Guardians. Eighteen townships from the parish of Halifax were joined with Hartshead and Clifton to form the Halifax Union. The Halifax Guardians were elected in February 1837, and the Halifax Union Workhouse was opened in 1841.[64]

The rapidly expanding population of the urban township of Halifax during the second half of the eighteenth century and the first half of the nineteenth century imposed a tremendous strain on the machinery of local government. In 1762 statutory powers were obtained from Parliament to establish a body of commissioners or trustees charged with the responsibility of supplying the town with water and empowering them to levy rates on all who made use of the water supply. A further local Act was obtained in 1768 to make the 1762 Act more effective and to extend the range of functions of the town trustees to include 'better paving, cleansing, lighting' and the removal of 'all nuisances, encroachments and obstructions' within the town. A subsequent Act in 1823 included provision for the employment of watchmen. Other local acts provided for the establishment of a new market in 1810 under a separate body of trustees and for the creation of the Halifax Gas, Light and Coke Company in 1822, which later became associated with the trustees in the public lighting of the town.

The trustees appointed under the Act of 1762 were a non-elective body of 224 male property owners, with power to fill any vacancy which arose among their number. The act of 1768 appointed a further 80 trustees, and the act of 1823 allowed tenants as well as owners of property valued annually at £40 to hold office, enabling craftsmen, shopkeepers and tradesmen to take their places as trustees, alongside more wealthy manufacturers, merchants and professional men. An analysis by G. R. Dalby of serving trustees has identified at least 80 manufacturers and merchants; 33 professional men, including doctors, lawyers, bankers and a civil engineer and 105 tradesmen and shopkeepers, including joiners, grocers, drapers, chemists, painters, plasterers, ironmongers, plumbers and plasterers. The trustees' financial resources consisted of property and water rates, which yielded an average annual income of £3,507 during the years 1840–49, loans up to a permitted maximum of £3,000, and public subscriptions. However, by 1839 the trustees had accumulated a debt of £12,000 and outstanding rate arrears of £5,000.

A more rigorous financial policy was initiated under the leadership of Joseph Thorp, a Quaker woolstapler, but financial retrenchment meant that many improvement schemes had to be postponed. In his evidence to William Ranger's enquiry into the sanitary condition of Halifax in 1851, Thorp concluded that 'slovenly methods in the execution of their enacted duties' by the trustees 'had resulted in affairs being carried out in an irregular and unbusinesslike manner'. At a meeting convened by the constable on 7 May 1847, Thorp had seconded a motion proposed by another trustee, John Abbott, a retired carpet manufacturer, calling for a petition to be sent to Queen Victoria for a charter of incorporation for the town. This was granted in 1848. Halifax at last became a municipal borough with the same boundaries as the parliamentary constituency created in 1832 under the terms of the Great Reform Act. The borough council was to consist of a mayor, ten aldermen and thirty councillors, elected by six electoral wards. All those who paid the poor rate were entitled to vote. The final electoral roll contained 1,609 names, almost one-third more electors than had qualified to vote at the 1847 parliamentary election.[65]

The outcome of the first Halifax municipal election held on 20 May 1848, a year after the defeat of the Radical-Voluntaryist alliance of Ernest Jones and Edward Miall at the general election of 1847 and only a month after the rejection of the third national Chartist petition by Parliament, was sensational. The veteran Chartist Benjamin Wilson hailed it as a triumph for the 'friends of Jones and Miall', who had 'carried all before them'. Henry Martin, editor of the *Halifax Reformer*, declared that the 'Whig Tory victory' at the 1847 election had been 'fully and fairly avenged' with only a handful of Whigs and Tories elected, the remainder being 'all of the movement party – friends of progress, of retrenchment and of reform'. It was also acclaimed as a triumph for Nonconformity, since 'only three or four' councillors 'are churchmen'; while there are:

> three members of the Society of Friends, three Baptists, nine or ten Independents, one Wesleyan, four or five of the Methodist New Connexion; and, altogether at least five-sixths of the body are Nonconformists.[66]

Halifax from the south east, 1775. This view reveals the limited urban expansion and predominant rural character of the townscape at this date. Indeed, a terrier compiled by John Moore of Hipperholme in 1797 reveals almost 600 small closes or enclosed fields within the township. However, Dean Tucker observed in 1774 that 'the towns of Birmingham, Leeds, Halifax and Manchester ... being inhabited by tradesmen and manufacturers are some of the richest and most flourishing in the kingdom'. Evidence of the finishing of woollen cloth in the town is provided by rows of tenterframes in the fields.
(Photograph: J. A. Hargreaves)

'A large smoke-canopied commercial town'

The continuing economic transformation of Halifax from a market town into a manufacturing town during the century from 1750 to 1850, the activities of interest groups like churches and chapels and the efforts of those responsible for local government had significantly transformed the physical appearance of the town by 1850. In 1774 Dean Josiah Tucker (1713–99), economist and divine, observed that 'the towns of Birmingham, Leeds, Halifax and Manchester ... being inhabited by tradesmen and manufacturers are some of the richest and most flourishing in the kingdom'. However, a terrier compiled by John Moore of Hipperholme in 1797 reveals almost 600 small closes or enclosed fields within the township, and contemporary prints of the town in the late eighteenth and early nineteenth centuries confirm its strikingly rural setting and appearance. A commercial directory for 1819–20, published in Manchester, pronounced Halifax 'a populous and flourishing town' with a 'stately and venerable' old church, 'with many extraordinary monuments of great antiquity' and 'houses generally built of stone' with 'some more modern ones ... large and handsome'. But it commented less enthusiastically on the town's location on a tributary of the Calder 'in barren and mountainous country' and on Halifax's streets which it considered 'mostly narrow and irregular'.[67] The *Yorkshire*

New Street, 1788, by William Burgess. The view of most of the west side of New Street may have included the home of the artist. A handbill published by E. Jacob, the Halifax printer, advertising the publication in weekly parts of Jacob's *History of the town and Parish of Halifax* in 1789 announced that William Burgess, an engraver from London, who had taken a house in New Street, Halifax, had been engaged to engrave the plates for the new publication. The houses appear light and spacious with cellar, ground and first floor accommodation and land to the rear. The street also appears to have been neatly paved and setted. (Photograph: Calderdale Museums Service, Bankfield)

Directory of 1822–23 described Halifax as a 'large and handsome, but irregularly built town' with houses principally of stone standing 'on a gentle slope enclosed by a chain of hills' concluding that it is 'a manufacturing place of great celebrity, both for the quality and extent of its different articles in the woollen trade'. These consisted of 'woollen stuffs, shalloons, tammies, duroys, calimancoes, moreens, shags, serges, and baize'. Moreover it also noted that the cotton trade had emerged in Halifax and its neighbourhood.[68] However, as late as 1825 the Bradford doctor, John Simpson, was reluctant to designate Halifax 'a manufacturing town', whilst Pigot's *National Commercial Directory* of 1834 insisted on denoting Halifax 'a large and handsome market-town', albeit with considerable quantities of shalloons exported to Turkey and the Levant, and growing cotton, woollen card and paper making industries.[69] But by 1837, the year in which Victoria ascended the throne, astute observers, such as Anne Lister of Shibden Hall, were pronouncing the birth of the new 'smoke-canopied commercial town' of Halifax. For the remaining years of Queen Victoria's long reign observers found themselves hard-pressed to find a kind word to say about the town's appearance.[70]

Contemporary plans reveal that by the mid-eighteenth century the built environment of the town had expanded westwards beyond Cow Green and Bull Green. In 1750, the township of Halifax contained some 1,200 houses, which had increased to 1,912 by 1801. Robert Brown, conducting a Board of Agriculture survey in 1793, noted that 'the houses, in general, are built of brick though free stone is also used'. An early example was Halifax's solitary Georgian Square built by 1759 by one of the wealthiest men in Halifax, the merchant and property dealer, John Caygill (1708–87) of the Shay, an elegant Georgian mansion house with its terraces, serpentine walks, pleasure garden and greenhouse displaying vines and exotic plants. Caygill, a native of Halifax had London connections and married Jane, daughter of William Selwin of Down Hall in Essex. She had outlived her husband by nineteen years by the time of her death in 1806. John Caygill's Georgian Square, whose elegant red-brick terraced townhouses with stone quoins and double gates for carriages, like the Shay reputedly designed by John Carr of York, possessed handsome interior fireplaces, decorated ceilings and cornices. Houses were grouped, in the style of an elongated London square with an enclosed communal garden accessed from New Road, later re-named Square Road. They were later extensively sub-divided and finally demolished by Halifax Corporation in 1959.[71] Other predominantly red-brick buildings erected in the town in the late eighteenth and early nineteenth centuries included a new market building operated by a company under a local Act of Parliament of 1810; shops in the High Street; the new Georgian Square Chapel with its vivid red-brick façade, named either on account of its adjacent square or geometric design; the baths and pleasure gardens in Lilly Lane. The most outstanding building – contrastingly constructed entirely from stone during this period – was the magnificent Georgian Halifax Manufacturers' Hall of 1779, soon being referred to by those who traded their woollen pieces of cloth there rather more pithily as the Piece Hall. It replaced the former Cloth Hall at Hall End established in 1572,

Northgate, 1824, by John Horner. This drawing, published in 1835, shows old houses in Northgate which were demolished in 1824. The view looks south towards Crown Street and Woolshops. The building in the foreground on the left was the Malt Shovel Inn and the inn sign is clearly visible. The street is paved and setted, but four sheep can be seen straggling the street. (Photograph: Calderdale Museum Service, Bankfield)

Lower Kirkgate, 1825, by John Horner. This drawing, published in 1835, also shows old houses prior to their demolition in 1825, heralding a period of urban expansion in the second quarter of the nineteenth century. One of the half-timbered buildings in the foreground bears the sign: 'Bradley, Gingerbread Maker, Wholesale and Retail'. (Photograph: Calderdale Museum Service, Bankfield)

Woolshops, 1833, by John Horner. This drawing, published in 1835, also records old houses scheduled for demolition in the second quarter of the nineteenth century. The columns supporting the building on the right are identical in style to those still visible at the Halifax Piece Hall. The alignment of the buildings on both sides of the relatively narrow street is quite irregular and a cooper is working on the street in the foreground on the left. (Photograph: Calderdale Museums Service, Bankfield)

but renovated as recently as 1708. This 'massive neo-classical market of Roman quality with a giant central courtyard was surrounded by two and three tiers of arcades' has been enthusiastically hailed by the architectural historian Dan Cruickshank as 'the most extraordinary example' of a market building design in the Georgian era.[72]

Astonishingly, however, conclusive evidence of the identity of its architect remains elusive, even with the recent recovery of the minutes of the Piece Hall Management Committee, which cover the operation of the building, though not the period of its construction. They do, however, confirm the involvement of the young local architect and later canal engineer, Thomas Bradley (1752–1833), assisted by his father William Bradley, in the design and construction of a porter's lodge, since demolished, on the eastern side of the northern entrance of the Piece Hall.[73] Moreover, he is explicitly recognised in William White's *Historical Gazetteer and Directory of the West Riding* as early as 1837 as the originator of the design for the building in a publication whose commercial credibility depended on its reputation for factual accuracy.[74] Bradley's claim was also supported by his credentials as architect of the residence of wool merchant William Walker at Crow Nest, Lightcliffe in 1788, whose plans were published in George Richardson's *New Vitruvius Britannicus* in 1802, where the author acknowledges that this building, which later became the home of the industrialist Sir Titus Salt is 'very much admired both for the beauty of the stone and the excellency of the workmanship'.[75] As a protégé of John Caygill (1708–87), the Halifax merchant who provided the site for the building of the Piece Hall on Price's Field, and as engineer to the Calder and Hebble Navigation Company from 1792, Bradley, like Caygill, was himself a strong supporter of locating the cloth hall for commercial reasons within proximity of the anticipated terminus of the Calder and Hebble navigation at Bailey Hall. He recognised the economic potential of such a convenient link with the waterway network, despite the vociferous opposition of a minority of merchants who appear to have preferred the convenience of the former cloth hall's location at Hall End, close to the accustomed amenities of Halifax Market Place and who canvassed unsuccessfully for a nearby site on Cross Close. Bradley also rejected suggestions for a circular, street-modelled, design as adopted by Sir John Ramsden for the Huddersfield Cloth Hall, which he judged would have not been feasible on a descending gradient. Moreover, Maurice Garside, an informed researcher in 1921 who obtained access to the minutes of the Piece Hall Committee through the auspices of the Rt Hon. J. H. Whitley M.P., also supported Bradley's claims to be regarded as the architect of the Piece Hall. He concluded, citing F. A. Leyland, that Thomas Bradley, 'the local architect entrusted with the fashioning of the plans of the Hall, advised that the edifice should not only be of colossal proportions so as to be well adapted for the primary use to which it was devoted but also that it should conform in design with the principles of Roman Classical Architecture as adapted to more modern circumstances by the greatest artists of the Italian Renaissance.'[76]

However, the extant fragmentary evidence also suggests the potential involvement of other experts, notably Samuel and John Hope of Manchester, who provided a

The Lewins, Bull Green, Halifax, acquired by the Lewins family in 1881 but trading under other names during its history, and only allowing entry to women customers from 1969. (Photograph: J. A. Hargreaves)

detailed, dated and costed estimate of £8,460 18s. 8½d. for the construction in 1775, but more dubiously appeared in a satirical songsheet of doubtful provenance allegedly produced for the opening of the Piece Hall in 1779 designating just one of the brothers as architect. However, Professor James Stevens Curl, with an international reputation for 'thorough investigation in little-known fields of research', has suggested that Bradley remains the most likely originator of the complex design concept of this classically influenced, symmetrically styled building on a problematical sloping site, countered by an ingenious tapered-tier structure, possibly with the assistance of the Manchester Hopes as quantity surveyors or executant architects. Moreover, such a *via media* has also been preferred by Colum Giles in his architectural guide to Halifax buildings, who acknowledges the difficulty of assessing unproven rival claims and by Ruth Harman, in her revised Pevsner guide, who suggests that the youthful Bradley, whom she acknowledges was in his early twenties, may have been the 'author of the overall design while the more experienced Hope brothers acted as executant architect and surveyor respectively'.[77] Despite his relative youth, however, Bradley appears to have been apprenticed to his father William Bradley, an experienced joiner, as early as 1758, allowing him considerable opportunity over nearly two decades to acquire relevant experience for the challenge. Moreover, his signed drawing of the frontal elevation of the neighbouring Square Chapel has resulted in the attribution to Bradley of the design of this other acclaimed Georgian building, in whose graveyard he was buried close to the site of the Manufacturers' Hall.[78]

Moreover Bradley, with his engineering instincts, also perceived the practical difficulties of constructing a circular building on a site with a pronounced gradient which ruled out, in his view, modelling the building on Sir John Ramsden's Cloth Hall at Huddersfield. There is also continuing confusion about whether the estimate

Crown Street, 1836, by N. Whittock. This busy commercial thoroughfare, formerly called the High Street, carried the pack-horse traffic from Wakefield to Lancashire. The street contained two inns, the Upper George and White Swan, serving the needs of stagecoaches arriving in the town. A commercial directory reveals a variety of commercial premises in Crown Street in 1834 including a booksellers and stationers, a grocers and tea-dealers, two confectioners, a hat dealer, four drapers, a saddler, two braziers and tin plate workers, three ironmongers, two chemists and druggists, a clog and pattern maker and several boot and shoe makers. (Photograph: Calderdale Museum Service, Bankfield)

submitted by the Hopes was from the branch of the family based at Liverpool, or another branch based near Manchester, who appeared stronger candidates on account of a family connection with George Legh (1693–1775) the former Vicar of Halifax and their later participation as monumental masons in the memorialisation of Mary Sayer at Halifax Parish Church in 1781 and Samuel Hope's monument of 1787 to John Caygill at Halifax Parish Church, which is surmounted with an urn very similar in design to an original stone ornamental urn at Halifax Piece Hall.[79] The claims of another contender John Carr (1723–1807), who is known to have worked on a gentry residence for John Caygill at the Shay, also have their supporters, but the leading authority on Carr, Dr Ivan Hall, does not include the Piece Hall amongst Carr's commissions.[80] Moreover, another putative contender is John Aked, a joiner, raff merchant and speculative house builder, whose surviving house buildings in Aked's Road and West Parade lack comparability in terms of either design or scale of construction to that of the Piece Hall. However, local historian Stephen Gee has claimed that a cryptic contemporary newspaper report in the *Leeds Intelligencer* is indicative of support for the acceptance of Aked's design, but the provenance of the report and indeed the status of the meeting which allegedly adopted his plan remains uncorroborated and another recent researcher has concluded that 'the

A more modern view of Halifax: Commercial Street shop fronts in the 1960s. (Photograph: J. A. Hargreaves)

weight of circumstantial evidence points to Aked's design having not been put into execution' since the aggregation of votes cast at the meeting falls short of the total number of subscribers eligible to vote.[81] Indeed, Thomas Bradley, who is officially minuted as having been entrusted with his father to construct the later addition of a porter's lodge to the Piece Hall's high profile north facing side, and who was later recognised as a highly accomplished navigational engineer (the Calder and Hebble Navigation Company ultimately rewarded him by substantially increasing his salary by £100, plus a lump sum of £500), given his exceptional engineering credentials and his architectural experience in the design of Crow Nest at Lightcliffe, and his recognition explicitly in a directory of 1837 as architect of the Piece Hall, therefore remains the most likely, albeit unproven, contender for designation as architect.[82]

A host of other impressive churches and chapels appeared in the town during this period, including the new church of Holy Trinity, Harrison Road, 1795, by Thomas Johnson – in a classical design with a domed tower – and the commissioners' church of St James, by John Oates, demolished in 1955, remembered now only by the name of the road on which it once stood. There was also a profusion of new chapels, ranging from the acclaimed Square Chapel of 1772, also attributed to Thomas Bradley, largely on the basis of a surviving drawing of the frontal elevation which he signed. Christopher Wakeling has suggested plausibly that the symmetrical square shape of this chapel was modelled on George Whitefield's London Tabernacle which Titus Knight, the first minister of Square Chapel had previously visited, and whose preaching both he and the Countess of Huntingdon, who may have helped finance the building's construction, emulated in order to disseminate Whitefield's Calvinistic doctrinal tenets. John Wesley pronounced it larger than Dr Taylors's Octagon at Norwich but equally superb and 'finished with the utmost elegance', though Wesley preferred to preach in the cow-market in the open air in order that his Arminian doctrinal standpoint might not be compromised. Nevertheless, with its cubic design and red-brick construction, enhanced by the application of ox blood, it boasted the largest self-supporting roof structure of the era and has been described as 'one of Yorkshire's greatest Georgian chapels'. The façade of its daughter church, the Sion Congregational Chapel, Wade Street, of 1819, with its imposing classical Greek Doric style, was incorporated into the Halifax Bus Station after its demolition, together with features of the Sion Schools building of 1846, in 1989. It has been attributed to R. Dennis Chantrell (1793–1872), a pupil of Sir John Sloane, and constitutes one of two churches he designed in Halifax. The other, St Paul's King Cross, 1845–47 is survived only by its steeple. In 1837, the new classically-styled Carlton Congregational Church and School was erected in Harrison Road. Methodist Chapels included the South Parade Wesleyan Church, the classically styled Georgian Wesley Broad Street, 1829; Salem Methodist New Connexion Chapel of 1815 and its daughter chapel, Hanover Street of 1834, later converted into the Playhouse, and the original Ebenezer Primitive Methodist Church of 1822, whose centennial successor still occupies its prominent site in St James Road. A General Cemetery was opened in Lister Lane in 1841 with a small Grecian mortuary chapel, where many Nonconformists are buried.[83]

New secular buildings in Halifax included a succession of law courts from 1775, culminating in the opening of a capacious new court room and debtors' prison in Harrison Road in 1828; a purpose-built theatre at Ward's End in 1790; prestigious new assembly rooms in 1823–25; a Mechanics' Institute in 1825; a Literary and Philosophical Hall in Harrison Road in 1834; the Halifax Union Workhouse of 1837–38, one of the town's largest public buildings, and the Oddfellows Hall of 1840. In addition, there were handsome mansions such as Hope Hall, designed by James Green, for David Stansfield, a Leeds cloth merchant in 1765; Somerset House, erected in 1766 and attributed to John Carr, and more modest town houses such as Holly House, erected in 1755, with a columned porch flanked by a pair of wings added around 1765. By 1822, according to Baines's *Directory*, the town was 'generally well built, partly of brick but principally of stone, which latter material is very abundant'.[84]

Fine new buildings there may have been, but, as Robert Brown noted in 1793, 'little care appears to have been paid to laying out the town at first'. In 1822 the streets remained narrow 'and very irregular' in their layout. An explosion of new building in the second quarter of the nineteenth century merely exacerbated the problem. T. J. Maslen, who offered advice on improvement to a number of northern towns, described Halifax in 1843 as a 'mass of little, miserable, narrow,

Halifax from the south east, 1847. The expansion of Halifax by the mid-nineteenth century is evident in this distant view of the town. Edward Akroyd compared the town in 1848 to a 'growing lad, thrusting his arms beyond his sleeves and his legs out of his trousers, putting out an arm at Haley Hill and a leg at Caddy Field'. (Photograph: J. A. Hargreaves)

ill-looking streets, jumbled together in a chaotic confusion, as if they had all been in a sack, and emptied out together upon the ground'. Using a different metaphor, Edward Akroyd likened Halifax at the time of the incorporation of the borough in 1848 to a 'growing lad, thrusting his arms beyond his sleeves and his legs out of his trousers, putting out an arm at Haley Hill and a leg at Caddy Field'. The northern and southern expansion of the town had begun, alongside a continuing expansion, westwards.[85]

So, in sum, although Halifax had by 1850 achieved through economic development some regional and indeed national eminence as a manufacturing and commercial centre, and although it now contained both a substantial population and a thriving elite culture, a century of unplanned development had left a legacy of problems for future generations. These included extremes of poverty, extensive educational and cultural deprivation and an ill-shaped, heavily polluted and in places distinctly unsavoury built environment.

5

'Town of a hundred trades': Victorian and Edwardian Halifax, 1851–1914

D URING THE MID-VICTORIAN ERA, the population of the municipal borough of Halifax more than doubled from 25,159 to 65,510. This increased Halifax's share of the total population of its ancient ecclesiastical parish from 16.9 per cent in 1851 to 37.8 per cent in 1871, reversing sharply the trend of the previous 350 years. The scale of the demographic expansion of Halifax during this period becomes most apparent when the age structure of the population of the municipal borough is analysed. By 1871, as a consequence of an exceptionally high birth rate, almost one-third of the borough's population was under fifteen years of age. The relatively high degree of fecundity appears to have resulted from a high marriage rate, which was entirely compatible with the economic organisation of the local textile industry during its period of most rapid expansion up to 1871. This positively encouraged early marriage and extensive family formation amongst adolescent and young adult workers by providing expanding employment opportunities for men, women and children. Thereafter, as the population began to age, the rate of population growth in the borough was less dramatic, and between 1879 and 1901 the birth rate declined from 31.6 per 1,000 to 22.8 per 1,000. Nevertheless, by 1881, the population of the municipal borough had increased to 73,630 and, by 1891, following Halifax's redesignation as a county borough in 1889, to 89,832. The population of the new county borough continued to rise, peaking at 104,936 in 1901, but subsequently declining to 101,594 by 1911.[1]

However, boundary extensions to the municipal and county boroughs between 1865 and 1901 may have masked a levelling off in the growth of Halifax's urban population in the last quarter of the nineteenth century. Moreover, by 1901 there were also other substantial urban centres in the former ecclesiastical parish. Todmorden and Brighouse, with populations of 25,418 and 21,735, acquired borough status respectively in 1896 and 1893, and there were rapidly expanding urban centres at Sowerby Bridge and Elland, with populations of 11,477 and 10,412 at the turn of the century. In general, industrial development had mushroomed around the waterway and railway networks in the valley bottoms of the Calder and its tributaries in the second half of the nineteenth century, while the remoter upland handcombing and handweaving settlements had steadily declined.[2]

Halifax's population growth was sustained by increasing industrial diversification in the second half of the nineteenth century, when the new municipal borough earned a reputation as 'a town of 100 trades'. At least one local contemporary writer believed the town to be a city in all but name by 1877. However, Halifax failed to achieve the coveted city status acquired by Wakefield in 1888, Leeds in 1893 and Bradford in 1897. Halifax was considered too geographically remote to become the centre of ecclesiastical administration for the new diocese of Wakefield in 1888, and geographical constraints inhibited Halifax's industrial and urban expansion, denying the town the late nineteenth-century industrial and commercial pre-eminence of Leeds or Bradford. Indeed, Halifax reached the peak of its demographic and economic expansion around the turn of the century and both the cotton and worsted industries had begun to contract before the outbreak of the First World War.[3]

This chapter will seek to explain how the economic expansion which sustained Halifax's demographic growth for most of this period developed; what the consequences were for social structure and living standards; how it might have affected and been affected by political life and how social and economic changes were reflected in the cultural activities of the community and the physical appearance of the town.

The economy: industrial diversification and the service sector

Although industrial diversification became a characteristic of Halifax's economy between 1851 and 1914, nevertheless textiles, which accounted for over half of the exhibits from Halifax at the Great Exhibition of 1851, remained vital to the local economy throughout the period up to the outbreak of the First World War. This was notwithstanding the difficulties experienced by the various branches of the local textile industry as a consequence of the Cotton Famine in the 1860s, changes in ladies' fashions, increasing foreign competition from France and Germany from the 1870s, and the imposition of protective tariffs by the United States of America in the 1890s. In 1871, 8,431 adults were employed in textile manufacture in the municipal borough of Halifax, compared with 1,552 in the extractive and metallurgical industries. Almost half of these textile workers were women, who outnumbered men in worsted manufacturing by 2,416 to 1,280, but remained in a minority of 339 to 809 in the heavier woollen manufacturing sector. Increasing numbers of women were employed during the period up to 1891, and also children from as young as ten or eleven years of age, who were allowed to start work early as half-timers after demonstrating relatively modest levels of educational attainment under a Halifax School Board by-law. By 1901, 19,342 adults and children were employed in the various branches of textile manufacture in the county borough of Halifax compared with 7,622 in the extractive and metallurgical industries, and women and girls outnumbered male textile workers by 11,668 to 7,674. The Secretary of the Halifax Chamber of Commerce listed no fewer than eighteen varieties of textile trades being pursued in Halifax in 1915, the largest single category of commercial activity.[4]

Crossley carpet design for the Great Exhibition of 1851 in Hyde Park, London. Masterminded by Albert, consort to Queen Victoria, on a site spanning nineteen acres, the Great Exhibition was the largest trade exhibition the world had ever known and was visited by some six million people between May and October 1851. Such was the impact of the Prince Consort's untimely death in December 1861 that a bronze memorial equestrian statue, funded by public subscription, sculptured by Thomas Thornycroft and unveiled by Sir Francis Crossley was originally erected in 1864 at Ward's End and subsequently relocated to Albert Park in 1901.

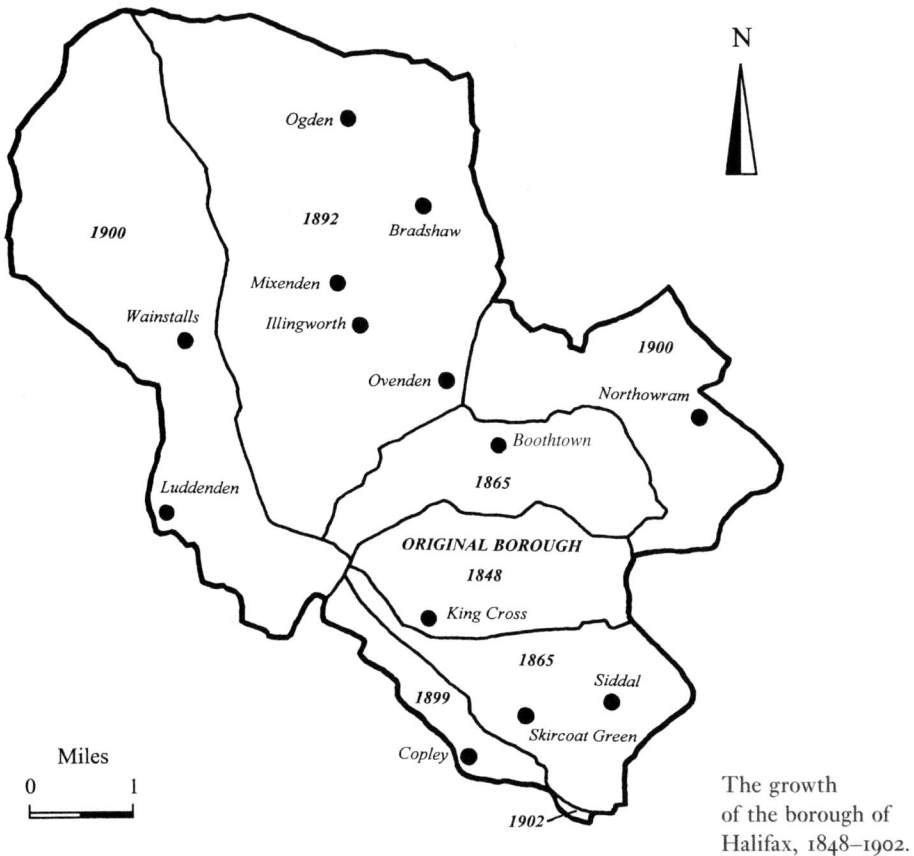

Ogden ●

1892

●
Bradshaw

1900

Mixenden ●

Wainstalls
●

Illingworth ●

1900

Ovenden ●

Northowram
●

● Boothtown

1865

Luddenden
●

ORIGINAL BOROUGH
1848

King Cross
●

1865

Siddal
●

1899

Skircoat Green
●

Copley ●

1902

Miles

0   1

The growth
of the borough of
Halifax, 1848–1902.

After 1851, there was an enormous expansion in both the number and size of textile factories in the town, exposing the myth that Britain was already a country dominated by huge factories by 1851. Indeed, between 1851 and 1865 the number of factories in Halifax more than doubled from 24 to 56. Moreover, in 1851 fewer than ten local firms employed more than 100 workers; by 1861 the number had trebled. By 1871, following a period of sustained expansion in the West Riding textile trade, over one-third of the local textile labour force was employed in factory units of more than 100 hands and nearly a half in workshops of 50 or more. At the turn of the century, a dozen leading firms accounted for around 40 per cent of textile employees in the town. The Crossleys had employed only 350 workers in 1837 but had increased their labour force to 5,000 by 1871, and this figure was maintained until 1914.

From mid-century, the use of steam power technology expanded, although water power continued to be used by some local firms until the late nineteenth century. In 1851, for example, the patent rights of George Collier, who had first applied the power loom to linen manufacture in Barnsley, and the American inventor Erasmus Bigelow were vested in trust to John Crossley and Co., harnessing the techniques of power loom weaving and mass production to carpet manufacture, which placed the firm in the forefront of the carpet industry. However, it was not until 1856 that woolcombing machinery was in regular use in the Halifax worsted industry and, during this period of transition, many Halifax woolcombers 'had to endure much privation and had no prospect of employment in future', and some emigrated to the United States.[5]

The role of textiles within the local economy had begun to decline, however, before 1914. In 1897 the *Halifax Guardian* reported that while Halifax

> has largely multiplied the number of its industries, its production of textile fabrics has for some years been on the decrease and the fear is entertained that ... its looms will gradually cease to run.[6]

The most spectacular casualty was the former Akroyd worsted manufacturing empire, which was gradually dismantled during the period from 1893 to 1918, passing into the ownership of smaller textile concerns. The causes of decline were increasing foreign competition and restrictive tariffs imposed by the United

Weaving shed, John Whiteley and Sons Ltd, card makers, Brunswick Mills, Halifax, 1894. All the looms have female operators. By the 1890s female textile workers in Halifax outnumbered males by nearly two to one. (Photograph: West Yorkshire Archive Service, Calderdale)

Memorial card to victims of an explosion and fire at Wellington Mills, Halifax, 4 December 1873. The victims, all young girls aged between eight and eighteen, were among 120 employees on the premises of Lister's silk mill when an explosion occurred. Gas escaping from a pipe during the repair of a meter ignited on the lower floor of the mill causing the devastating explosion and disastrous fire. Many other workers suffered severe burns and the mill was totally destroyed. (Photograph: S. Gee)

States of America in 1890, 1895 and 1897 and by France in 1892, which seriously affected British textile exports. As the *Times* remarked in 1897 within a week of the inauspicious *Halifax Guardian* report:

> Time was when many important continental countries looked to Halifax for clothing their men-of-war but, one after the other, have developed industries of their own.[7]

The decline of Halifax's textile industry was partially offset by the town's growing industrial diversity. It was Halifax's developing cable, confectionery, construction, extractive, engineering and machine tool industries which earned it a reputation as 'the town of 100 trades' during the period between the Great Exhibition and the outbreak of the First World War. In 1915, in addition to its highly variegated textile industries, Halifax boasted sixteen varieties of iron trades including Hargreaves Iron

Mechanics' shop, John Whiteley and Sons Ltd, card makers, Brunswick Mills, 1894. John Whiteley and Sons, founded in July 1791, was one of the earliest local manufacturers of wire for card making. The firm moved from Winding Road to Brunswick Mills in the 1840s and by 1891 it employed a total of 300 workpeople. (Photograph: West Yorkshire Archive Service, Calderdale)

Founders, who began in 1896 and continue to operate world-wide from Halifax, with offices as far afield as Shanghai; ten varieties of building trades; a total of 899 registered workshops; a large and flourishing firm of manufacturing jewellers (Charles Horner Ltd); the largest carpet and toffee manufacturing firms in the world; and the leading producer of drilling and boring machinery. Indeed, by the early twentieth century, engineering had become the second most important industry in Halifax and, like the textile industry from which it developed, it was inherently diverse.

Most local engineering firms started from very small beginnings, expanding rapidly during the mid-Victorian period while potential competitors in America and Europe were distracted by the American Civil War of 1861–65 and the Franco-German War of 1870–71. It is striking that many began by manufacturing accessories for the textile industry and maintaining and repairing mill machinery. James Ryder Butler (1842–1917), a former apprentice engineer and carpet mill foreman for John Crossley and Sons Ltd, started his own loom making business in a small factory in Weymouth Street in 1868. He subsequently acquired premises in Adelaide Street, diversifying into the manufacture of machine tools in 1873. After a succession of business partnerships, his two sons entered the firm in 1892, and by 1910 Butler had become leading specialist manufacturers of planing machines. William A. Asquith (1840–1901), returning to his native Halifax in the wake of the American Civil War after working in the gold fields of Canada and the American West, founded his firm in 1865 in a converted weaving shed in Raglan Street. Initially undertaking general engineering work, the firm expanded rapidly, particularly during the Franco-German War, moving to larger premises in Highroad Well in 1871. In 1902 Asquiths became the first local machine tool firm to supply machinery bearing the firm's own distinctive trade plate to merchant distributors for export. In January 1903, the business became a limited company and the firm began to specialise in the world-famous Asquith radial drilling machine, which superseded the practice of punching in constructional engineering. This specialisation was the basis of the firm's rapid expansion in the period up to 1914.

Other engineering firms that also expanded through increasing specialisation during this period included John Stirk and Sons Ltd, founded in 1866, which initially produced a wide range of machines to order before specialising on the manufacture of the single belt planer, and Frederick Town and Sons Ltd, founded in 1903, which opened a new purpose-built factory for the specialist production of radial drills at Mile Cross in 1914. Gas construction engineering began in Halifax as early as 1847; boiler-making and heating-apparatus engineering after 1858; the manufacture of woodworking machinery from 1875; and the development of automated cash registers in 1886. Wire manufacture, which had been utilised primarily for carding in the first half of the nineteenth century, became more technically advanced after 1851, producing wire in a wide variety of gauges and metals. James Royston's wire drawing firm, founded in 1797, produced hundreds of tonnes of 'charcoal wire' for the first Atlantic telegraph cable in 1856. In 1859, a former employee, Frederick Smith, established his Caledonia Works in Charlestown Road, specialising in the production of high quality steel wires for

William Asquith Ltd, Highroad Well. In 1902, William Asquith Ltd became the first local machine tool firm to design and fix their own trade plate on machinery supplied to merchant distributors for export. Founded in 1865 by William A. Asquith in premises in Raglan Street, the firm moved to larger premises in Highroad Well in 1871, which were gradually extended as the firm expanded and equipped with new offices, fitting and pattern shops in 1899. In January 1903, following William Asquith's death in 1901, the business became a limited company and the firm began to specialise in the manufacture of the world-famous Asquith radial drilling machine, which superseded the practice of punching in constructional engineering. This specialisation was the basis of the firm's rapid expansion in the period up to 1914, when the firm became wholly engaged in war work. (Photograph: J. A. Hargreaves)

marine and colliery applications, and the firm patented several types of continuous wire-drawing machines. With the rapid growth of the electrical industry, Frederick Smith and Co. produced high-conductivity copper wire, but later moved to Salford, where proximity to the Manchester Ship Canal eased the supply of raw materials and eliminated the heavy overland freight costs to Halifax.[8]

There were other very different industrial developments by the later nineteenth century, reflecting a sensitivity to market demand. Rising real wages, growing consumerism among the masses, increasing opportunities for leisure and cheaper supplies of raw materials from overseas, such as sugar, stimulated the development of the confectionery industry, which like engineering grew rapidly from very small beginnings. In 1890 John Mackintosh left his employment at Bowmans' cotton mill to open a pastrycook's business with his new wife, Violet, in King Cross Street. Their most popular line was a novel blend of traditional English butter scotch toffee and American caramel, and by 1892 the couple had moved into wholesale marketing of their new product. In 1894 they secured their first warehouse in Bond Street and in 1895 a second larger one in Hope Street, where John set up his 'Steam Confectionery Works'. To finance further expansion, he set up a joint-stock limited liability company, John Mackintosh Ltd, and built a new factory in Queen's Road at a cost of £15,000. After a devastating fire at the premises in October 1909, he used his insurance compensation to resume production in the empty Albion Mills, which had the advantage of proximity to both the canal and the railway. By 1912, the works comprised a general office staffed by at least twenty clerks and typists; a huge manufacturing plant where toffee was boiled and produced; a five-storey mill where hundreds of girls wrapped toffee; and a four-storey mill where tinned toffees were packed for transport by rail. His flair for publicity earned Mackintosh the soubriquet of 'toffee king' and Halifax that of 'toffee town'. Other confectionery firms established in the town during this period included Riley Bros, toffee manufacturers, and John Whittaker, the first large-scale biscuit manufacturers in the town, established c. 1900.[9]

Halifax's extensive and diversified manufacturing economy and expanding population also stimulated a highly sophisticated local retail trade. Halifax was

Robinson Brothers Cork Growers and Manufacturers of Halifax. William White's Directory of the Clothing Districts of Yorkshire in 1853 listed George and William Henry Robinson, cork manufacturers, at 10, Broad Street, Halifax. They later moved to premises in Horton Street nearer to the railway station, when the firm had become the headquarters for an operation extending to Portugal. Their specialist business in the manufacturing and trading of cork, which was in heavy demand for sealing bottles, jars and earthenware pots in which a wide variety of products were stored, reflects the diversity of industry and commerce which had developed in Halifax by the second half of the nineteenth century, earning Halifax the reputation as the 'town of a hundred trades'.
(Photograph: West Yorkshire Archive Service, Calderdale)

to become, indeed, the region's principal service centre, linked to its periphery by an extensive network of corporation tramway and motor omnibus routes by 1914. A commercial handbook boasted that in 1915 Halifax offered 'handsome and well-equipped business establishments superior to those of many towns of considerably greater population', gaining 'a reputation throughout Yorkshire as a shopping centre hard to beat'. In 1884, for example, Messrs Simpson and Sons Ltd, upholsterers, carpet warehousemen, decorators, painters, complete house furnishers, removal and storage contractors, opened an impressive new store in Silver Street. By 1895 the firm, which had been founded in 1815 in Woolshops, was the largest furnishing establishment in the north of England. Its five-storey showrooms, all linked by elevator, held, it was claimed, one of the largest selections of furniture outside London, embracing 'almost every requisite for the complete furnishing of a mansion or cottage'. They advertised in 1895 that 'a dining room might be furnished from stock at any price from £20 to £250; a dainty drawing room from £25 to £300, and even the cheapest articles may be in good taste, style and quality'. Bedroom suite prices ranged from five guineas to £150, and the firm emphasised that they 'guaranteed the absolute purity as well as the undeniable comfort of their bedding' which was made on the premises. They also carried comprehensive stocks of office furniture and a vast range of carpets, linoleum, drapery, curtains, decorating materials and timber. 'Prices', the firm maintained, 'were fixed on the basis of the barest working margin of profit and adhered to'.[10]

Alongside the private retail establishments were the new borough markets and central co-operative stores. Developed on the site of the Georgian red-brick market in Market Street, the magnificent, turreted, Victorian Borough Markets, designed in a French Renaissance style by the Halifax architects Joseph and John Leeming, were completed at a cost of £130,000 and officially opened by the Duke and Duchess of York in 1896. The market complex, hailed by contemporaries as 'amongst the very finest in the country', accommodated nineteen shops and one public house on its outer perimeter and forty-three shops and over 100 stalls under its domed interior of glass and iron construction. In addition, the fish market, originally a separate enclosure under the same roof, contained sixteen lock-up shops inside the building and six outside. The vast central co-operative stores in Northgate were opened at a cost of £23,400 in October 1861, ten years after the foundation of the Halifax Industrial Society. They included drapery, boot and shoe, jewellery, ironmongery, crockery, furniture, grocery, and hosiery departments, plus a large butcher's shop, fruit and fish store, coal office, clogger's shop, confectioner's shop and cafe. The society also boasted the 'most modern and convenient stables in town' in Culver Street, tenanted by 'some of the finest draught horses in the country'; a slaughterhouse at North Dean; and a bakery in Queen's Road. By January 1901, when the Halifax Industrial Society celebrated its jubilee, it had no fewer than thirty-four branches and a turnover in the last year of the century approaching half-a-million pounds and profits in excess of £50,000. All these developments within the retail sector reflected an increase in consumer spending in the late-Victorian era which helped to establish Halifax as a regional service centre.[11]

John and Violet Mackintosh on their wedding day, 29 September 1890. A few days after their marriage the young couple opened a pastry-cook's shop in King Cross Lane, Halifax, postponing their honeymoon and investing all their modest joint savings in the new business venture. 'From the opening day', John Mackintosh later recalled, 'this shop attracted customers, the aim of the owner being to offer only articles specially good in an establishment that was spotlessly clean'. Their most popular line was a novel blend of traditional English butterscotch toffee and American caramel, and by 1892 the couple had moved into wholesale marketing of their new product. From these small beginnings the business developed into the largest toffee manufacturing company in the world. (Photograph: J. A. Hargreaves)

This was reflected also in the remarkable development of financial services in Halifax, which was sustained by industrial and retail expansion during the period between 1851 and 1914. The Halifax Joint Stock Bank, which had moved to new premises in Crossley Street in 1858, was registered as a limited liability company in 1880, and acquired the Midland Banking Co. of Huddersfield in 1881. In 1898 it amalgamated with the Halifax and Huddersfield Union Banking Co., which had opened imposing new premises in Commercial Street that year, and became the West Yorkshire Bank Ltd in 1910, with a capital of one million pounds. In 1852 Edward Akroyd, seeking to encourage thrift by his employers, had started the Woodside Penny Savings Bank at Boothtown, and this became the Yorkshire Penny Savings Bank in 1856 and the Yorkshire Penny Bank in 1871. It acquired new branch premises in Halifax in 1876, and by 1892 there were no fewer than seventy-one district branches in the parish of Halifax. Other banks in Halifax in 1914 included the Halifax and District Permanent Banking Co. in Princess Street, the London City and Midland Bank Ltd in Waterhouse Street, and the Halifax Equitable Bank Ltd in Silver Street, founded by the Halifax Equitable Building Society in 1899.[12]

However, in the financial sector, Halifax became in this period principally associated with the growth of the building society movement. The earliest known building society had been established in Birmingham in 1775 and in the following

The opening of the Halifax Borough Market, 1896. The new Halifax Borough Market, constructed on the site of the former red-brick market, was opened by the Duke and Duchess of York, later King George V and Queen Mary, on their return to Halifax station, after they had performed the opening ceremony for the Royal Halifax Infirmary on Saturday 25 July 1896. From 1810 the market had been run by a private company until 1853, when Halifax corporation took control by compulsory purchase. The decision to redevelop the market was taken in 1890 and plans exhibited in the Mechanics' Institute. The design contract went to two Halifax brothers, Joseph and John Leeming, currently working as architects in London. (Photograph: J. A. Hargreaves)

half-century some 250 societies were formed in the North and Midlands. In Halifax the movement grew out of the friendly societies. For example, the Loyal Georgean Society, which was founded in 1779 and which met at the Old Cock Inn, soon developed the practice of lending money to its members for building houses, including a terrace in St James Road. During the nineteenth century, so-called terminating building societies, which wound up once the properties whose construction they had financed had been completed, mushroomed throughout the town. They included the Halifax Union or 'Go-Ahead' Building Society, established in 1845, with Edward Akroyd and Francis Crossley among its trustees. This had the ulterior motive of seeking to increase the number of forty-shilling freehold voters at a crucial stage in the campaign for the repeal of the Corn Laws. There was also the West Mount Building Society, which erected fourteen back-to-back houses in Lincoln Street and Penn Street in 1870, and the idealistically named Halifax and District Perfect Thrift Building Society with offices in Ferguson Street in 1894. Indeed, until the last quarter of the nineteenth century the majority of building societies nationwide were terminating societies. Moreover, until 1914 the private mortgage market remained the major source of funding for the finance of house purchase.

More significant for the future development of the building society movement, however, were the permanent benefit building societies which were established in the period 1846–51 at Wakefield, Leeds, Otley, Bingley and Bradford. Then, in 1853, several members of the Loyal Georgean Society took the initiative in founding the Halifax Permanent Building Society. It therefore formed part of a wider Yorkshire movement, with a broader social appeal than the traditional banking institutions. John Fisher, manager of the Halifax Joint Stock Banking Co. and the first president of the Halifax Permanent, maintained that working men believed that banks were only for the rich and that building societies were the bankers of the poor. Jonas D. Taylor assumed the role of secretary from the initial meeting in the Old Cock, holding the office for almost half a century until his death in 1902. Indeed, his personal commitment, integrity, organisational ability, and long tenure of office was a major contributory factor to the success of the newly formed society. The society opened for business in February 1853 in a room over a shop in Old Market, rented for £10 p.a., and by the end of the year had assets totalling £12,074. During the first three years of its operation it advanced more than £40,000 mainly for multi-house purchase by rentiers, with only about one-fifth of advances for individual owner-occupation purchasers. Branch offices were opened at Sowerby Bridge, Thornton and Queenshead in 1853; Brighouse in 1854; Hebden Bridge and Stainland in 1855; Luddenden in 1859; Cornholme in 1860; and even in Huddersfield in 1862, two years before the establishment of the Huddersfield Building Society. In 1854 the head office of the Halifax Permanent moved to Waterhouse Street 'over the offices of the County Fire and Life Assurance Company', where a single room housed J. D. Taylor and his staff of just six clerks and an office boy until the society opened its first purpose-built head office in Princess Street in 1873.

The society grew steadily during the 1860s and 1870s. The first 34 balance sheets of the society record an annual increase in aggregate assets, with the single exception of 1865, and by 1885, the Halifax Permanent had the largest reserves of all the Yorkshire building societies. Progress in the 1880s and 1890s, however, was slow and the society's assets which had reached £1 million in 1881 were still only just over a million in 1896. When Jonas D. Taylor died in September 1902, the Halifax Permanent Building Society had some fifty branches, mostly in the villages and small towns around Halifax, but also including major branches further afield at Hull, Leeds and Bradford, a tribute to Taylor's insistence on the need for a policy of expanding branch and agency provision. Nevertheless, all the branches except one at Darlington were in Yorkshire and nearly all were in the West Riding. The society remained in 1902, in the view of O. R. Hobson, who wrote the centenary history of the society in 1953, 'a local building society and no more', still with a relatively small head office staff often working overtime. By 1905, however, the society had more accounts than any other building society and by 1913 had assets exceeding £3 million, more than any other society.

Moreover, in 1913, the second largest building society was also situated in

Jonas Dearnley Taylor (1829–1902). A Halifax solicitor's clerk, Taylor became a founder and the secretary of the Halifax Permanent Building Society from its formation in 1853 until his death in September 1902 and senior partner in the firm of J. D. Taylor and Co. Chartered Accountants. A prominent Nonconformist associated with both the Sion and Park Congregational Churches, his integrity and organisational ability contributed to the success of the society, which he served for almost half a century. During his lifetime the number of head office staff never rose above ten. Staff salaries and office running costs were kept to a minimum by drafting letters on re-used envelopes and Taylor himself 'picking his way through the crowds' escorted by a junior clerk laden with heavy bags of cash to bank the receipts from the society's branches at the Halifax Joint Stock Bank. He declared at the society's 49th annual meeting in March 1902 that 'the success of the society had always been the great aim of his life and that his foremost thought had been that everyone who brought money to the society should receive it back again'. (Photograph: Halifax plc)

Halifax, namely the Halifax Equitable Building Society, started in 1871, by Walter Common, Registrar of Marriages in Halifax, who became its first secretary and a group of bankers and businessmen, including Henry Haley, James Bowman, Thomas Turlay, Edward Ingham, Josiah Aked and John Waterhouse, who became its first trustees. The success of the building society movement in Halifax before 1914 owed much to the development of a culture of nonconformity and thrift in the town. Joseph Harger Mitchell, secretary of the Halifax Equitable Building Society from 1897 until 1927 and a prominent Wesleyan Methodist in Greetland, claimed in a paper presented to the Building Societies' Association, meeting in Halifax in 1908, that the amount invested in building societies in the Halifax district was forty times as great in proportion to population as the average for the whole country. The success of the movement was also related to rises in living standards, the increase in savings to be invested, and the increase in incomes for the purchase or especially renting of houses. Analysis of rate books has revealed that a mere 13.8 per cent of property in the County Borough of Halifax was owner occupied in 1901. Despite their early concern to appeal to the working classes, both societies tended to favour the upper end of the property market before 1900. The average house price in Halifax in the second half of the nineteenth century was £109.20. However, during the 1850s the Halifax Permanent had an average mortgage of about £430, with only 4 per cent of mortgages granted for sums below £100 and a further 25 per cent for sums below £200. In 1896, a quarter of all advances from the Halifax Equitable were above £500 and 17 per cent above £1,000. Nevertheless, in his 1901 report the chairman stated that the society had 248 mortgages where the debt did not exceed £500 'showing that they did a very large business with small borrowers, and this was the business they decidedly wished to cultivate'.[13]

As Halifax centred upon itself increasingly diverse manufacturing and service sector operations, the development of improved internal and external communication helped the town to overcome some of the constraints of its geographical location. In the early 1850s railway links were constructed between Halifax, Bradford, Leeds and Wakefield, and the distinguished engineer, John Hawkshaw (1811–91), who was responsible for tunnelling through Beacon Hill, designed a splendid Gothic portal, providing rail travellers from Leeds and Bradford with a sudden dramatic vista of Halifax's industrial townscape on emerging from the tunnel.[14] Moreover, in 1855 a magnificent new Palladian styled station with baroque embellishments, designed by Thomas Butterworth of Manchester, was opened for the Lancashire and Yorkshire and Great Northern railway companies, both of whose Grade II listed warehouses survive, the Lancashire and Yorkshire Railway's of 1849 and the Great Northern Railway's of 1885.[15] An extension to Holmfield for goods traffic was completed in 1874, with provision for passengers from 1879. In 1874 a rare surviving range of coal drops was constructed near to Halifax station, comprising fifteen wooden bunkers each supported by rock-faced ashlar stone piers and with metal doors, which were raised on an iron ratchet geared pulley system indicative of the scale of the goods operation at Halifax. A new station at North Bridge was opened in 1880 and more direct high-level access to Halifax Station from Horton Street was provided in 1886, by which time there were seven platforms for passengers. Although a high-level railway linking King Cross and Pellon with the Halifax–Bradford line of the Great Northern Railway was constructed in 1890, repeated efforts to extend the main line of the Midland Railway from Huddersfield to Halifax in 1864, 1874, 1897, 1899 and 1902 all proved abortive and as late as 1918 a commercial directory concluded, ruefully, that Halifax might have been 'more advantageously placed from a railway point of view'. Nevertheless, by 1910 there were some 163 train departures every day, and Halifax even had its own boat train which connected with the night steamer to Belfast.[16]

The Halifax Chamber of Commerce, formed in 1862 with 155 subscribing members drawn from the banking, manufacturing and business communities, was very much aware of the problem and strongly supported schemes to improve transport and communications, including rail, water, telegraph and postal links with the town. The Halifax Exchange was founded in 1863 for local businessmen and the Halifax Chamber of Trade in 1903. A new General Post Office, designed by Henry Tanner, was opened in Commercial Street in 1887. It was the first purpose-built accommodation in the town for the post office, which had changed premises three times in the preceding half century. Its scale of business is evident from White's *Directory* of 1887, which listed its opening hours from 7.30 a. m. until 10.00 p. m. on weekdays and 7.30 a. m. until 10.00 a. m. Sundays. The Halifax Chamber of Commerce also established with Halifax Corporation a joint advisory committee on telegraphs and telephones. It secured concessions to telephone users

Halifax Permanent Building Society Head Office, Princess Street, 1873. In 1869 the Halifax Permanent Building Society acquired a site for a head office opposite the new Town Hall with frontages on Princess Street and Crossley Street, adjoining the Mechanics' Hall and the White Swan Hotel. Competitive designs for the building were received from numerous architects and the design of Samuel Jackson, architect and surveyor of Bradford, was ultimately accepted. The foundation stone was laid on 5 April 1871. The new office, which cost £8,579, opened on 30 May 1873 and reflected the society's growing prosperity. In 1874 the society became incorporated under the Building Societies Act of 1874 and from 1874 to 1880 the profit divided among investing members was 1½ per cent per annum. (Photograph: J. A. Hargreaves)

in the town and urged the government to constitute the woollen districts of the West Riding into a single telephone area with regional charge rates, recognising the importance to the development of the local economy of telecommunications: these were ultimately to be the saviour of regional businesses in the future.[17]

There was also a growing recognition of the need to improve local internal lines of communication. One witness told the Ranger inquiry in 1850 that the roads within the town were 'steep and not yet paved, and in a wretched condition', lying in large pools of foul water in which 'carts sink up to the nave', while another witness complained about 'the badly constructed and hilly suburban roads'. Some improvements were undertaken by the new municipal council, but, because of the nature of its terrain, Halifax remained largely a pedestrian town for the majority of its inhabitants until the turn of the century. Early proposals to develop steam or cable tramways in 1882 appeared likely to prove costly given the nature of the local terrain, and consequently failed to secure council backing. A horse omnibus service operated by John Marsh and Co. offered some relief from 1886 until 1898, when an electric tramway system, operated by Halifax Corporation, commenced operation, forcing Marsh and Co. into liquidation in 1900. Only Blackpool, Dover and Leeds had corporation electric tramways before Halifax, and the Halifax system, which was completed by 1905, had a number of distinctive features. A narrow gauge track and small, light tramcars proved necessary to cope with the town's steep gradients and narrow streets. Even so, there were serious accidents in 1906 and 1907 when tramcars were derailed on North Bridge and at Pye Nest. However, travelling by the new 'gondolas of the people' became increasingly popular. In 1914 some 20,276,000 passengers were carried safely on the Halifax tramway system, plus additional passengers by motorised omnibuses, also operated by the corporation from Halifax to the remote upland village of Mount Tabor from 1912.[18]

During the Victorian and Edwardian eras Halifax absorbed more of the population of its periphery and centred upon itself increasingly diverse manufacturing and service sector operations, reaching the limits of its demographic and urban expansion around 1900, when geographical constraints placed limits on the town's spatial development. Moreover, there were also signs of decline by 1900 in some branches of textiles as a result of external factors, especially increasing foreign competition during the 1890s. After 1851 both the local business community and the Halifax Corporation became increasingly aware of the need to improve

General Post Office, Commercial Street. Opened on 23 June 1887 during the celebrations for Queen Victoria's Golden Jubilee, the new General Post Office building on Commercial Street was designed by Henry Tanner, architect to the local board of works and constructed in Yorkshire stone at a cost of around £13,000. It was the first purpose-built accommodation for the Post Office, which had changed premises three times in the preceding half century. Its scale of business by 1887 is evident from White's *Directory* of that year, which listed its opening hours from 7.30 a.m. until 10.00 p.m. weekdays and from 7.30 a.m. until 10.00 a.m. on Sundays. A popular innovation in 1902 was the provision of tramcar letter boxes. The new premises were enlarged in 1926–27 to provide accommodation for the first local automatic telephone exchange. (Photograph: J. A. Hargreaves Collection)

internal and external communication links if Halifax were to counteract some of the constraints which its geographical location placed upon its economic and urban expansion. However, although improvements in transport and communications were evident by 1914, Halifax's hilly terrain continued to present problems for its pioneering electric tramway system and the town remained relatively inaccessible by rail in comparison with other neighbouring West Riding towns and cities, notably Bradford and Leeds, which continued to grow after 1900.

Social geography

The economic changes of the period 1851–1914 had a profound effect upon the social structure of the locality. The late-Victorian period witnessed a further decline in the influence of the older absentee aristocratic landed elite and the rise of a new entrepreneurial elite, whose wealth was derived from the Industrial Revolution. This new *haute bourgeoisie* colonised the exclusive residential suburb of Skircoat on the southern perimeter of the town, and the fashionable area around People's Park, with a profusion of spacious, though predominantly unostentatious, villa mansions. Beneath them in the social hierarchy was a more modest business and professional middle class residing on the manor house estates in and around Skircoat and parts of Northowram and in the superior terraced housing in the vicinity of People's Park. Then there were the struggling lower middle classes, occupying more basic terraced housing at King Cross, along Queen's Road, on Lee Bank, Lee Mount and Claremount. Finally came the manual workers, inhabiting the numerous back-to-back houses, often situated close to the factories where they worked, or the slum ghettos, which by the end of the nineteenth century were concentrated around the parish church, at Cross Fields, Chapeltown, on Foundry Street and at the junction of West Parade and King Street.[19]

As in the earlier Victorian era, the most appalling housing conditions were inhabited by the very poor, 'including the Irish'. Inspecting several of the properties very closely they were found 'reeking with stench and among all this muck, uncared-for children sprawled by the score and idle slatternly women lounged by the halfdozen'. One old Irish woman who had been more than thirty years in England 'talked dolefully of the decline of the hawking trade' confirming that the poor people were reduced to inhabiting inferior, dark and dismal cellar dwellings since they 'now seldom earned more than a shilling or eightpence at the very most for a hard day's work', posing a continuing challenge to Halifax Corporation.[20]

At the other end of the social spectrum, during the late-Victorian period a number of symbolic vestigial links with Halifax's long-departed rentier landed aristocracy were loosened when Skircoat Moor, Shroggs Park and Highroad Well Moor were acquired from the Savile family by the Halifax Corporation, now dominated by the new business elite. Skircoat Moor, a vast estate on the south-eastern perimeter of the town, valued at £40,000, was re-named Savile Park and sold to the corporation for a nominal fee of £100 in 1866 by Captain Henry Savile, who also surrendered all his manorial rights on condition that the corporation undertook to abate the pervasive smoke nuisance. Shroggs Park, an area of 24 acres of woodland to the north of the town, was leased to the corporation by Henry Savile for 999 years at an annual rent of one pound in 1881, after Edward Akroyd had realised its potential as an amenity for the residents of his model housing development at Akroydon. Finally, Highroad Well Moor was given by Lord Savile in 1899 for development by two local manufacturers, Henry McCrea (1810–1901) and Enoch Robinson (1835–1926), into West View Park.[21]

The Revd Francis Pigou, Vicar of Halifax from 1875 to 1889, maintained that few English parishes could compare with Halifax for its concentration of wealthy manufacturers and merchant princes by the late-Victorian era, including

> Akroyd, Crossley, Baldwin, Foster, Edwards, Watkinson, Hall, Huntriss, Rawson, Appleyard and many more who … living quietly and unostentatiously, are men of large fortunes … and by intermarriages fortunes are kept in families … there are several handsome family mansions … and a recent noble effort to build a new Infirmary at a cost of some £100,000 amongst the evidences of wealth.[22]

George Sheeran's study of the wealth of the West Yorkshire industrial elite during this period as revealed in their domestic architecture, business investments, philanthropic benefactions and probate records confirms the validity of Pigou's impressions. The Crossley family of carpet manufacturers, whose mansions, almshouses, orphanage, hotels and offices featured prominently in the local townscape 'made two or three fortunes in magnitude of half a million to one million pounds'. H. C. McCrea, an Irish entrepreneur who had settled in Halifax in 1834, not only channelled his surplus profits from damask production into the landscaping of West View Park and Albert Promenade in Halifax, but also into the development of the seaside resort of Blackpool, leaving an estate valued at £294,000 at his death in 1901.

Others who had acquired vast fortunes from industrial expansion, however, had dissipated most of their wealth by the time of their deaths. Edward Akroyd, joint heir of an estate valued at £300,000 in 1847, promptly spent £100,000 of it on the building of All Souls' Church and subsequently donated substantial sums for its upkeep, including nearly £400,000 between 1869 and 1872. In addition, he spent large sums of money on charities, political campaigns, his two model housing developments at Copley and Akroydon and his Italianate villa at Bankfield, leaving an estate valued at £1,234 when he died in straitened circumstances at St Leonard's-on-Sea in Sussex in 1887. Similarly, the second-generation John Crossley's immense fortune was whittled away through a combination of lavish philanthropy and ill-judged investments, leaving an estate valued at under £8,000 when he died in 1879, in marked contrast to the legacies of £800,000 and £900,000 of his brothers Francis and Joseph.[23]

Moreover, long before the period had ended some local industrial magnates had made the transition from entrepreneur to leisured gentleman, and like the landed

People's Park. Following a visit to the United States of America in 1855, where he had marvelled at the natural beauty of the White Mountains, Francis Crossley resolved 'to arrange art and nature that they shall be within the walk of every working man in Halifax; that he shall go to take his stroll there after he has done his hard day's toil, and be able to get home without being tired'. Sir Joseph Paxton of Crystal Palace fame was engaged to design and landscape a park from 'five flat fields, bounded on three sides by public roads, containing an area of twelve acres and a half, destitute alike of prospect, of water, of wood'. The site was excavated, large quantities of topsoil introduced, trees and shrubs planted, and flower beds, rockeries and ornamental lakes constructed at a cost of £50,000. The park was officially opened on 14 August 1857, amidst scenes of popular rejoicing. (Photograph: J. A. Hargreaves)

gentry of an earlier age had withdrawn to country retreats some distance from the town. Following the death of Sir Francis Crossley at Belle Vue in 1872, his widow had closed up the family mansion and moved permanently to the family's large country estate at Somerleyton in Suffolk, which Crossley had purchased in 1861. His son, Sir Savile Brinton Crossley, became a member of the Tory landed elite. Other members of the third generation of the Crossley family, however, continued to live locally until the last decade of the nineteenth century, in elegant mansions designed to accommodate their developing scientific interests. Edward Crossley (1840–1905), the eldest son of Joseph Crossley, lived at Bermerside, in Skircoat, where he constructed a well-equipped observatory in the grounds, only to find that the smoke-filled atmosphere impaired the use of his giant reflecting telescope. He therefore withdrew to his summer residence on the Isle of Wight in the 1890s, returning to Halifax only to chair the annual meeting of shareholders at Dean Clough. His cousin, Louis John Crossley (1842–91), the only son of John Crossley, remained a director of the firm until his death at the age of forty-nine, but made frequent visits to his property in Windermere, where he enjoyed sailing on the lake. At Moorside, his home in Skircoat, he had installed a fully equipped electrical laboratory and workshop in the house and an electric tramway system in the grounds. The drawing room was furnished in ebonised wood and gold and contained a huge electric organ in a carved case set in a carved alabaster screen 'somewhat similar to the great organ in the Royal Albert Hall'. His final years were

Crossley and Porter Orphanage. John, Joseph and Francis Crossley jointly contributed over £56,000 towards the erection and endowment of the orphan home and school, which was designed by John Hogg of Halifax and built in 1864. In 1887, Thomas Porter, a Manchester yarn merchant, augmented the endowment fund by a donation of £50,000. By 1895, according to a contemporary directory, 'the orphanage and school liberally feeds, clothes and educates from 200 to 300 children'. Children of both sexes were admitted from the age of seven years from all parts of Britain, boys remaining until the age of fifteen, girls until the age of seventeen. In 1919 the governors were granted the royal assent to change the orphanage into a secondary school, which merged in 1985 with Heath School. (Photograph: J. A. Hargreaves)

dogged with ill-health and he died after undertaking a round-the-world voyage in search of recovery.[24]

Manufacturers who remained economically active continued to reside close to their workplaces. Harold Mackintosh, the future first Viscount Mackintosh, son of John Mackintosh, 'the toffee king', recalled that he had spent the first twenty-five years of his life at 8 Park Terrace, one of eight houses sharing a communal garden 'within a square mile' of which were 'to be found the first shop, the first warehouse, the first factory, our home, our chapel and our day schools'. His father later moved to Greystones, a very comfortable but unostentatious house, which was not even detached, on the edge of Savile Park. However, while the first and second generations of the Holdsworth family had all lived virtually within a stone's throw of Shaw Lodge Mills, Clement Holdsworth, who succeeded to the sole ownership of Shaw Lodge Mills in 1887, purchased the Scargill estate at Kettlewell in 1900.

He finally moved from Shaw Lodge to Netherside Hall, a country mansion near Grassington, in 1912, drawing an average of £4,500 a year from the business between 1885 and 1913 and an annual salary of between £1,000 and £1,750 until 1913 to sustain a lifestyle of fishing and shooting in Wharfedale.[25]

Beneath these wealthy entrepreneurs in the social hierarchy were the professional classes and upwardly mobile shopkeepers, merchants and small businessmen. Contemporary directories suggest that the numbers within some professional groups remained remarkably stable throughout the period. For example, the number of auctioneers remained at 10 between 1853 and 1874 and the number of chemists and lawyers rose only slightly from 19 to 21 and 21 to 25 respectively during the same period. Moreover, the number of architects and surveyors and physicians and surgeons actually declined slightly from 18 to 12 and 27 to 22 between 1853 and 1874. However, the number of accountants and agents more than doubled from 17 to 38 between 1853 and 1874. Moreover, the number of professionals enumerated in the censuses more than quadrupled from 368 to 1,525 between 1881 and 1901. The directories and censuses also reveal a sharp rise in the number of shopkeepers and specialist wholesalers and retailers. The number of jewellers and watchmakers, for example, rose from 16 in 1853 to 20 in 1874 and by 1901 there were no fewer than 423 men and 86 women employed in these establishments. Managers, designers and commercial travellers at John Crossley and Sons Ltd earned salaries ranging from £300 and £600 between 1875 and 1882. Many professionals and retailers were therefore able to afford properties on the new manor house estates around Savile Park with their superior terraced housing and imposing villas. Restrictive covenants were incorporated into their sales agreements to ensure the preservation of the exclusive character of this Victorian residential suburb. The *Halifax Courier* of June 1877 revealed that the land adjacent to Savile Park was rapidly being covered:

> a large villa for Mr Shoesmith the auctioneer; lower down a terrace of ten houses for Councillor Denham; the Manor Royd for Mr Patchett, who has also commissioned four large semi-detached villas. Below Heath Villas a new mansion for Councillor Longbottom and one adjacent to it for Mr George Webster, the grocer.[26]

Next in the social hierarchy came the struggling lower middle classes, comprising the multitude of small masters, agents, brokers and dealers who were particularly numerous in Halifax, and the growing army of 'white-collar' clerks and shop assistants staffing the profusion of banks, offices, commercial establishments and more specialist retail outlets in and around the town. In 1881, there were no fewer than 776 small masters, 60 agents, 52 brokers, 273 dealers, 747 clerks and 507 shop assistants. However, the number of skilled craftsmen and artisans, such as smiths, masons, tailors, coopers and other independent, *petit-bourgeois* producers and distributors, was declining during this period. Alderman J. H. Waddington, surveying the changes which had taken place in Halifax during the Victorian and Edwardian eras, observed that:

some trades have become smaller and smaller, while some have entirely gone out. We think of … cloggers, button makers, cloth cap makers, straw hat makers, coopers, curriers, saddlers, stay makers, carvers and guilders, blacksmiths, oat cake makers, and makers of clay pipes for smokers.[27]

But new wealth and increasing sophistication had generated a new range of small businesses. For example, a newer breed of restaurant owners, eating-house keepers and beer sellers was undermining the earlier predominance of innkeepers, lodging-house keepers and general publicans.[28]

Finally, near the base of the social pyramid came the manual workers and domestic servants, varying in their status and incomes according to their gender, occupation and the fluctuating demands for their labour. In 1901, by far the largest

All Souls' Church, Haley Hill and statue of Colonel Edward Akroyd (1810–87). Completed in 1859, All Souls' Church was commissioned by Colonel Akroyd as the crowning feature of his model housing development at Akroydon. The spire, almost 73 metres in height, was the second tallest church spire in Yorkshire. Designed by Sir George Gilbert Scott, the new church won immediate acclaim. The *Building News* concluded that it was 'one of the most elegant specimens he has produced', while the architect himself pronounced it 'on the whole, my best church'. The statue of Colonel Akroyd by J. Birnie Philip, originally located at the southern end of North Bridge, was moved to Haley Hill in 1901 to allow the development of the tramway network. (Photograph: Ian Beesley)

proportion of manual workers of both sexes, some 8,811 men and 13,624 women, were employed in textile and clothing manufacture. A further 6,281 men were employed in engineering, 3,333 in the building and construction industry and 2,746 in the transport and haulage industry. The largest form of employment for women outside the textile and clothing industries was domestic service, which accounted for 2,771 women and 458 men in 1901. Within domestic service there was some status differentiation related to the type of tasks performed and the status of the employer. Butlers and housekeepers were considered of superior status to general servants, who regarded themselves as superior to washerwomen and charwomen. Within industry, a 'labour aristocracy' of exclusively male mechanics and engineers enjoyed higher wages than the bulk of semi-skilled and unskilled labourers. For example, mechanics in the machine tool trade in Halifax were paid around 31s. (£1.55) a week in 1870.[29]

The vast majority of textile workers earned considerably less. A wage census of 1886 confirmed that worsteds was one of the poorest paying of the major textile industries and that wage rates in neighbouring Bradford were as much as five shillings a week higher than in Halifax for the same jobs. Moreover, women, who performed the lighter, intermediate textile processes of spinning, doubling, hanking and warping, were paid between one-third and one-half the wages of men, who dominated the heavier preparatory and finishing processes of sorting, winnowing, felting, scouring, milling, shearing, pressing and packing. In 1870, before the West Riding textile industry suffered a depression as it struggled to compete with increasing foreign competition, Halifax male wool sorters could earn up to 28s. (£1.40), engine tenters and mechanics around 30s. (£1.50) for a 72-hour week, but for females employed in spinning, twisting and reeling the rates were from 8s. (40p) to 14s. (70p). Piece work weavers might earn up to 18s. (90p), but were generally hired by the piece and in periods of depression were often kept waiting for the next piece to arrive, losing income through broken time. Woolcombers similarly were rarely paid a full week's wages and juvenile textile workers working part-time were paid an average of 3s. 8d. (18p) in the late 1880s. Their meagre earnings nevertheless provided a welcome supplement to working-class family incomes.[30]

Most working-class housing, located predominantly around the industrial complexes of western and central Halifax, remained relatively poor in quality. The building of cellar dwellings continued to be permitted until 1869, but national legislation and local by-laws increasingly inhibited the building of sub-standard housing and made provision for better drainage and ventilation in the second half of the nineteenth century. However, most building was speculative and cheap and confined to back-to-back construction of two and three rooms, which was estimated to make up 65 per cent of all housing provision in Halifax in 1888. Wilfred Pickles, the son of a building construction worker, remembered Conway Street, where he was born in 1904, as 'a drab thoroughfare, paved with stone setts, its tiny back-to-back houses sheltering so many people that I now wonder how they could find space to move'. The *Halifax Guardian* ran a series of articles on the slums of Halifax in 1889 which focused on houses near the Halifax Parish Church which were 'squalid beyond description', many of which were demolished following a local government enquiry in 1893, and no more back-to-back houses were built in Halifax after 1900. By contrast, the emergence of 'improving' lower-middle and working-class residential districts on the western and north-western fringes of the town, especially between 1860 and 1890, were expressions of lower-middle and working-class respectability, physically removed from the vice and depravity of the slum ghettos.[31]

The economic changes in Halifax between 1851 and 1914 therefore supported a shifting social hierarchy. The influence of the old landed elite continued to decline and the town became dominated socially and economically by industrial wealth. The growing importance of Halifax as a service centre stimulated the development of the town's professional and business classes, but the vast majority of the town's adult workforce supported themselves and their families through relatively low paid manual labour or domestic service. The widening income gap between those at the top and those at the bottom of the social pyramid, the increasing social segregation of housing and the conspicuous inequalities of living standards contained the potential for social conflict within Halifax which found expression in the growth of class politics in the late nineteenth century.

Politics: Chartists, Liberals, Labour and the Suffragettes

Although four Chartists were elected to the new municipal council in Halifax in 1848 and Chartist organisation was maintained in the town until 1858, Kate Tiller has concluded that after 1848 Halifax Chartism as elsewhere 'undoubtedly lost its

Household servant, Shibden Hall c. 1860. The wages bill for household servants at Shibden amounted to £59 15s. 0d. for the first half of the year up to June 1859, but records reveal neither the names nor the number of servants employed at the hall at this time. The largest form of employment for women outside the textile and clothing industries in Halifax during the period from 1851 to 1914 was domestic service, which accounted for 2,771 women and 458 men in 1901. Within domestic service there was some status differentiation related to the type of tasks performed and the status of the employer. Butlers and housekeepers were considered of superior status to general servants, who regarded themselves as superior to washer- and char-women. (Photograph: West Yorkshire Archive Service, Calderdale)

Cottage in Back Foundry Street, Halifax, 1901. In 1851 the small, two-storeyed, stone-built cottage was the home of Richard Horsfall, a Scottish weaver, and in September 1850 it became the original store of Halifax Working Men's Co-operative and Provident Society. Its small size, however, restricted the development of the business and in January 1851 the society moved to larger premises in Cow Green. (Photograph: J. A. Hargreaves)

momentum'. Despite collections for the imprisoned Chartist leader, Ernest Jones, the Chartists had to abandon their meeting hall and increasingly channelled their energies into co-operation, mutual improvement and temperance. John Snowden (1822–84), for example, a woolcomber and Chartist since 1838, who had 'worked for the Charter with might and main while Chartism was a possible force to be reckoned with', after 1848, 'sensibly espoused the cause of gradual reform, working steadfastly at the task nearest hand, training his brain the while with home study of history and of political principles'.[32]

The triumphant return of Ernest Jones in a carriage drawn by four greys to an enthusiastic reception in Halifax, following his release from prison in July 1850, stimulated a short-lived Chartist revival, particularly amongst local woolcombers, who were suffering wage reductions and unemployment. The main focus of Chartist energies was Jones's second parliamentary candidature in Halifax in 1852, although the very limited franchise did not offer them much prospect of electoral success. Moreover, middle-class radicals had found themselves a strong candidate in the carpet manufacturer, Francis Crossley, who promised his support for a household, ratepaying suffrage and secret ballot. By 1852 Sir Charles Wood had severed his electoral pact with the Tory, Henry Edwards, and now stood with his fellow Liberal, Crossley. This partnership could attract almost every shade of elector in the Whig–Liberal spectrum, but left the Tories and the Chartists electorally vulnerable.

At the poll, Wood and Crossley were returned with 596 and 573 votes, while Edwards and Jones were defeated, polling 521 and 38 votes respectively. Moreover, the pattern of Liberal voting displayed in 1852 was not significantly disturbed again until after the Reform Act of 1867, and neither the Tories nor the Chartists seriously challenged the dominance of the Liberal–Radical alliance in Halifax during this period. In June 1853 the ostensibly secular funeral of the Ovenden handloom weaver and veteran Chartist Ben Rushton, witnessed by an estimated crowd of 15,000, proved to be 'the last great Chartist occasion in Halifax'. While the absence of trade union organisation deprived Halifax Chartism of a whole dimension of potential growth, Halifax Chartists maintained their organisation longer than in most other provincial centres. The leaders of working-class politics in the town continued to be drawn from the Chartists for almost twenty years after the demise of the movement. However, Eric Evans has concluded that the ten pound householder qualification remained a rough-and-ready means of borough enfranchisement for those with sufficient property to be trusted with the vote, even taking compounding into account where rates were paid as part of tenants' rent. Indeed, as late as 1866, even with the modest effects of inflation increasing the number of qualified voters year by year, the proportion of the electorate that could be described as working class in Halifax as in Leeds was no more than 10 per cent.[33]

At the general election in 1857 Wood and Crossley were again re-elected but, on this occasion, Crossley topped the poll with 830 votes, with Wood and Edwards polling 714 and 651 votes respectively. When Crossley opted to seek election for the West Riding constituency in 1859, Wood and James Stansfeld, another Liberal, the barrister son of a local county court judge, were returned unopposed. However, in 1865, Wood reluctantly resigned, anticipating a strong challenge from the Halifax worsted manufacturer, Edward Akroyd, who had lost his seat as Whig Member of Parliament for Huddersfield, and Stansfeld and Akroyd were returned unopposed. Akroyd held the seat until his retirement in 1874, by which time he was regularly entering the division lobbies with the Conservatives. The 1867 Reform Act extended the borough franchise to householders and lodgers who had occupied lodgings worth ten pounds a year for at least one year. This increased the local electorate from 1,900 to 9,328 in 1871 and 11,998 in 1884, thereby enfranchising about 70 per cent of all adult males within the constituency, a higher proportion of voters than in other West Riding urban industrial constituencies.[34]

Nevertheless, most of these male householders were evidently content to vote for Liberals and Whigs and therefore for candidates from higher social classes. In 1868 Liberalism again split into two wings represented by Edward Akroyd, Whig, Anglican and National Reform Unionist, and the radical James Stansfeld, Unitarian and Reform Leaguer. A working man's candidate, E. O. Greening, co-operator, Dissenter, temperance campaigner and Reform Leaguer was adopted in opposition to Stansfeld and Akroyd, with no Tory standing. After a lively campaign Stansfeld and Akroyd were returned with 6,278 and 5,141 votes respectively, while Greening, whose supporters had included five of the ten leading Chartists of the 1850s, came bottom of the poll with 2,802 votes. After the election the radicals set up the Liberal Electoral Association as a rival to the official Liberal Registration Association, but an uneasy *rapprochement* was achieved, following a shock Tory victory in a by-election in the neighbouring West Riding constituency in 1872. However, only the first School Board elections of January 1874 finally reunited the various strands of Halifax Liberalism, when the former Chartist lecturer, John Snowden, headed the poll.

In the ensuing general election of 1874 John Crossley, elder brother of the late Francis, and James Stansfeld were returned with 5,563 and 5,473 votes respectively, with McCrea, the Conservative candidate, in third place with 3,927 votes. Crossley's sudden retirement in February 1877 as a result of ill-health and financial

Ernest Jones (1819–69). This photograph of Ernest Jones as a Reform League lecturer was taken in 1866, three years before his death. As a Chartist in the 1840s and 1850s, Jones contested two parliamentary elections in Halifax. In 1847 he joined forces with the Political Dissenter, Edward Miall, the proprietor of the *Nonconformist* newspaper and one of the leading critics of the Whig government's proposals to bring in a system of national education, to challenge the Whig candidate Sir Charles Wood, who had represented Halifax since it was created a parliamentary constituency in 1832. In the event, neither Jones nor Miall was successful and Wood was elected together with the Tory candidate, Sir Henry Edwards. Following a period of two years imprisonment for sedition in London, Jones returned to Halifax and contested the 1852 election, again without success, polling a mere 38 votes (Photograph: Manchester Archives and Local Studies, Manchester Central Library)

embarrassment, arising from imprudent speculative investment, evinced much popular sympathy, and at the ensuing by-election J. D. Hutchinson, the Liberal candidate, achieved a comfortable victory over the Conservative, Gamble, by 5,750 votes to 3,624. At the 1880 general election Stansfeld and Hutchinson again defeated the Conservative candidate, Barber, the three candidates polling 6,392, 6,364 and 3,452 votes respectively. When ill-health forced Hutchinson to resign in 1882, his Liberal successor, Thomas Shaw, was elected without opposition. Thereafter, Shaw and Stansfeld were returned with comfortable majorities over the Tory candidate, Morris, in both the general election of 1885 and the by-election of 1886, which followed Stansfeld's appointment for a further term as President of the Local Government Board. In 1885, Ben Wilson organised a social evening for twenty-two former Chartists, all now enthusiastic Gladstonian Liberals, at Maude's Temperance Hotel, Broad Street, Halifax to celebrate 'the incorporation in the law of the land of the principal portion of the charter' with the passing of the Third Reform Bill in 1885. The *Halifax Courier* commented:

> at the time of the Chartist agitation they were all poor working men [now] the majority … have become men of business and in some cases employers of labour, and a few by economy, industry and temperance have secured a competency for their old age.[35]

The increasing segregation of middle- and working-class housing, which became more pronounced after the revision of ward boundaries in 1892, together with the polarisation of middle- and working-class interests over education, were underlying

Halifax Borough Election, 1857. Political sketch by Humphrey Thwackem, the younger, showing the three 'horses' running in the 1857 general election, namely Sir Charles Wood and Mr Francis Crossley, the successful Liberal candidates, and Major Henry Edwards, the unsuccessful Conservative candidate. Francis Crossley topped the poll with 830 votes, followed by Sir Charles Wood with 714 votes. The veteran Charles Wood, who had been re-elected without opposition on 3 March 1855 on becoming First Lord of the Admiralty, congratulated Crossley on heading the poll. Major Henry Edwards, who obtained 651 votes, had now suffered defeat in three successive Halifax contests and subsequently secured election for Beverley. (Photograph: West Yorkshire Archive Service, Calderdale)

factors in the emergence of class politics in Halifax in the late nineteenth century. However, the immediate stimulus was provided by the deterioration of industrial relations in the late 1880s and early 1890s, the rise of 'new unionism' and the foundation of the Halifax Trades and Labour Council in 1889 by delegates from eighteen craft unions, including iron moulders, carpenters and joiners, wiredrawers and silk dressers. Trade union organisation in Halifax, pronounced 'hopeless' by Ben Turner in his autobiography, had been traditionally weak in the West Riding textile industry, where the majority of workers were women and young people. However, it was the much stronger craft unions within the expanding, male-dominated, engineering industry that provided the initiative for the founding of the Halifax Trades Council, whose membership fluctuated between around 3,000 and 4,000 members in the 1890s.

Though it drew its support from across the whole spectrum of trade union political opinion, the Halifax Trades Council very quickly gravitated towards Labour politics after Socialism arrived in Halifax in 1891, infused through a middle-class Fabian ideology and organisation. In July 1892 the Halifax Fabian Society joined with the Halifax Trades Council to form the Halifax Labour Union, the forerunner of the Halifax Independent Labour Party, established in the following year. Membership of the Halifax Independent Labour Party fluctuated between 500 and 700 members between 1893 and 1899, and during the 1890s Halifax had the second largest ILP organisation in the country after Bradford. The growing electoral support for the ILP in Halifax in the period up to the outbreak of the First World War is evidenced by its increasing success in municipal elections, rising from 10 electoral successes in the period up to 1900 to 34 in the period from 1900 to 1906 and 63 in the period from 1906 to 1914. Moreover, John Lister obtained 3,024 votes as ILP candidate in the parliamentary by-election of 1893, and 3,818 votes in the general election of 1895, notwithstanding a bitter division within the local party which had erupted in 1894.

Liberalism had remained the dominant political creed of the textile Nonconformist millocracy until the late 1890s, when some prominent local Liberals, including members of the Crossley family, espoused Liberal Unionism. Liberalism had also found widespread support amongst the working-class voters of Halifax until the rise of a trade-union dominated Labour movement in 1892 'whose emergence', Dr P. Dawson has concluded, 'shook the foundations of the political system in Halifax'. It eroded Liberal support and enabled 'a strengthened, business-directed Conservative Party' to benefit from the split-vote system, most notably in the general elections of 1895 and 1900, when they made electoral gains at Liberal expense. Conservative support was drawn predominantly from professionals, gentlemen, land and property owners and their tenants, some manufacturers and their working-class employees, and the drink interest, which felt threatened by the temperance element within municipal Liberalism. In June 1895, James Stansfeld's distinguished 36-year representation of Halifax as Liberal Member of Parliament concluded when he retired with a knighthood from Queen Victoria and the honorary freedom of the county borough. In the general election of 1895, the Liberal vote was split between W. Rawson-Shaw and James Booth, who polled 5,085 and 4,283 votes respectively, allowing the Conservative wire manufacturer Alfred Arnold to top the poll with 5,475 votes.

Sir Savile Brinton Crossley (1857–1935), the only son of Sir Francis Crossley, who had been defeated as a Liberal Unionist candidate in the 1897 Halifax by-election by the Liberal Alfred Billson, stood for election as Conservative candidate for Halifax in the khaki election of 1900, while on active service in South Africa. He topped the poll with 5,931 votes, losing the seat as decisively in the Liberal landslide of 1906, when he came bottom of the poll with 5,041 votes. John Henry Whitley (1866–1935), a partner in the family cotton spinning firm of S. Whitley and Co. and a Halifax Liberal councillor from 1892 to 1900, came second in the poll at the general election of 1900 to Crossley with 5,543 votes and was returned as Liberal member for Halifax. Keith Laybourn has attributed the success of J. H. Whitley's political career to his emergence as 'an unusual unifying political figure in Halifax politics', combining his commitment to social reform with a range of Old Liberal and New Liberal values'. Hailing from a well-established industrial family, 'he supported Home Rule and the taxation of land values, but combined with this a fervent commitment to social welfare and a recognition of the rights of trade unions and workers'. Such varied policies 'allowed him to draw support from a deeply divided Halifax Liberal Party and to also gain support from the emergent trade unions and Independent Labour Party', which contributed to his electoral success in 1900.[36] At Westminster, he campaigned vigorously against the Education Act of 1902 and the Licensing Act of 1904 and at the general election of 1906 topped the poll with 9,354 votes, sharing parliamentary representation with James Parker, the Labour MP from 1906, in a constituency which was one of the centres of the emergent political Labour movement. In 1907, when he was appointed a junior treasury minister, he was returned unopposed, and in the two general elections of 1910 again topped the poll in Halifax with 9,504 and 8,779 votes respectively.

No less remarkable than this Liberal revival, which benefited from the growing unpopularity of Tory domestic and foreign policies, was the advance of Labour. James Parker (1863–1948) was elected as the first Labour MP for Halifax in 1906, on a progressive alliance with the Liberals to defend free trade. Parker, who had

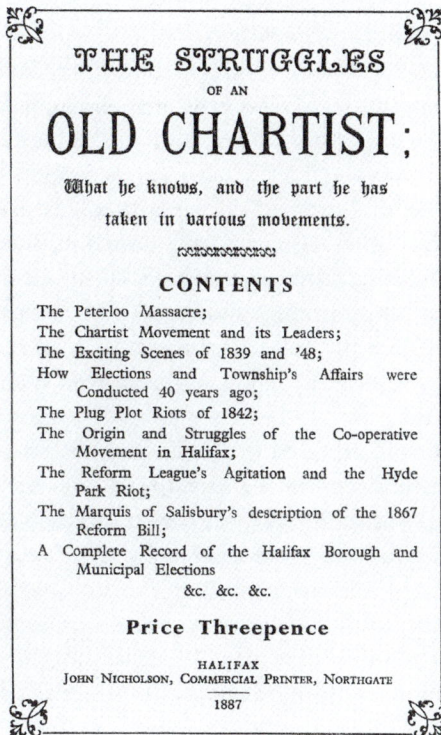

THE STRUGGLES
OF AN
OLD CHARTIST;
What he knows, and the part he has taken in various movements.

CONTENTS

The Peterloo Massacre;
The Chartist Movement and its Leaders;
The Exciting Scenes of 1839 and '48;
How Elections and Township's Affairs were Conducted 40 years ago;
The Plug Plot Riots of 1842;
The Origin and Struggles of the Co-operative Movement in Halifax;
The Reform League's Agitation and the Hyde Park Riot;
The Marquis of Salisbury's description of the 1867 Reform Bill;
A Complete Record of the Halifax Borough and Municipal Elections
&c. &c. &c.

Price Threepence

HALIFAX
JOHN NICHOLSON, COMMERCIAL PRINTER, NORTHGATE
1887

Title page of Benjamin Wilson's *The Struggles of an Old Chartist*, published in Halifax in 1887. Wilson was born of humble parentage in 1824 at Skircoat Green, which Wilson noted in his autobiography 'had long been noted for its Radicalism'. Wilson was put to work at an early age as a farm labourer and domestic textile worker. He joined the Chartist movement in 1839 and in the Halifax parliamentary elections of 1847 and 1852 supported the Chartist candidate Ernest Jones, with whom he developed a close personal friendship, representing the Halifax Branch of the Reform League at his funeral in Manchester in 1869. After 1868 Wilson identified increasingly with Gladstonian Liberalism, organising a reunion of twenty-two former Chartists to commemorate the passing of the Third Reform Act. He spent his declining years denouncing the formation of the Independent Labour Party, which he feared would sap the strength of Liberalism, and died suddenly during Queen Victoria's Diamond Jubilee Celebrations in 1897. (Photograph: J. A. Hargreaves) worked for a local electrical engineering company until becoming full-time secretary of Halifax ILP, had come to Halifax as a navvy at age of nineteen from Louth, where his parents were farm labourers. He was re-elected in the two Halifax general elections of 1910, obtaining 9,093 and 8,511 votes respectively. Moreover, although the Liberals did well in parliamentary elections between 1906 and 1910, municipal elections show the erosion of their local power base, as allegiances shifted to the Conservatives and to Labour. During the period from 1903 to 1913, the number of Liberal councillors and aldermen serving on Halifax Corporation declined from 44 to 25, whereas the number of Conservative and Labour councillors and aldermen rose from 10 to 24 and 6 to 9 respectively. The Labour movement was also making a cultural as well as a political impact in Halifax in the period up to 1914. By 1898 the Halifax Labour Church was meeting regularly twice on Sundays with its primary objective 'the emancipation of Labour and the re-construction of society upon the basis of justice and brotherhood', and by 1900 the Halifax Socialist Sunday School had attracted 159 members. The Clarion Movement, founded by Robert Blatchford in the early 1890s, with its numerous cycling, field, scout, glee and vocal unions, also became well-established in Halifax during this period.[37]

Electoral politics, however, were still dominated by men, but the campaign for the extension of the franchise to women gathered momentum in Halifax following an open-air meeting on Savile Park addressed by the militant suffragette Annie Kenney, soon after her release from prison in August 1906. A Halifax branch of the Women's Social and Political Union was formed in January 1907, and Emmeline Pankhurst visited the town shortly afterwards to address a meeting at the Halifax Trades and Friendly Club. On 14 February, Halifax women travelled to London to join the 700-strong crowd which marched on the House of Commons, and Mary Alice Taylor, wife of Councillor Arthur Taylor, a Skircoat Green blacksmith, was arrested following clashes with the police. The 63-year-old grandmother was charged with disorderly behaviour and detained at Holloway Prison until 27 February. On her return to Halifax Station she was greeted as a heroine by hundreds of supporters. Other Halifax women also suffered imprisonment, including Mrs Dinah Connelly, mother of Mrs Laura Mitchell, a later Mayor of Halifax, who spent her twenty-eighth birthday in Holloway, and Mrs Laura Willson, aged thirty-three of 117 Beechwood Road, Ovenden, the secretary of the Halifax WSPU branch and wife of the Halifax engineer, George Willson, who spent two weeks at Armley Prison in February 1907. It has been suggested, however, that she may have lapsed in her membership of the WSPU since she is listed as compliant in the 1911 Census. Similarly categorised was Elizabeth Berkley, aged twenty-seven, a button-hole machinist living with her two sisters, also machinists, five of her surviving seven children, and her widowed mother, aged fifty-two years in a four-roomed household at 21, Bankside, Hebden Bridge.The *Halifax Courier* sympathised with the suffragette cause but condemned the aggressive tactics adopted by some of the women, arguing that since women in Australia and New Zealand already had the vote 'there is nothing to cause alarm in the prospect of the franchise being extended to women' in Britain.

John Lister (1847–1933). Lister inherited Shibden Hall and estate in 1867 at the age of twenty and was the last member of his family to reside at the hall, which after his death was opened to the public as a museum by Halifax Corporation in June 1934, eight years after the opening of Shibden Park. Notwithstanding his gentry connections, Lister became a founder member of the Independent Labour Party and stood as the first Labour candidate for Halifax in the parliamentary by-election of 1893, polling 3,024 votes as ILP candidate and 3,818 votes in the general election of 1894. He founded the Shibden Industrial School and was a strong supporter of St Joseph's Roman Catholic School and Hipperholme Grammar School, where he was a governor for forty-seven years. He was a founder member of the Halifax Antiquarian Society and with a classicist from Bradford Grammar School cracked the code used by his ancestor, Anne Lister, for secret sections of her diary. (Photograph: West Yorkshire Archive Service, Calderdale)

Membership certificate for Nimrod Howarth of the National Independent Labour Party, 1895. Among the national officials of the new party listed on the certificate were two Halifax activists, James Tattersall, a member of the National Administrative Council and John Lister, who served as treasurer, but both drifted out of the local and national organisation after a series of acrimonious disputes in 1894–95. The Halifax branch of the ILP was established in 1893 and membership fluctuated between 500 and 700 members between 1893 and 1899, when Halifax had the second largest ILP organisation in the country after Bradford. The growing electoral support for the ILP in Halifax is evidenced by its increasing success in municipal elections, rising from 10 electoral successes in the period from 1893 to 1900 to 34 in the period from 1900 to 1906 and 63 in the period from 1906 to 1914. (Photograph: West Yorkshire Archive Service, Calderdale)

James Stansfeld (1820–98). The son of a county court judge, James Stansfeld was born in Halifax and educated at London University before being called to the bar. He served as Liberal Member of Parliament for Halifax for thirty-five years from 1859 to 1895 and in a succession of ministerial appointments. These included lord of the admiralty, 1863–64; under secretary of state for India, 1866; lord of the treasury, 1868–69; financial secretary to the treasury, 1869–71; president of the poor law board, 1871 and president of the local government board, 1871–74. He was also a prominent Unitarian, a leading opponent of the contagious diseases acts and a supporter of women's suffrage. He was knighted by Queen Victoria and granted the freedom of the borough of Halifax. (Photograph: J.A. Hargreaves)

A distinctly non-violent form of protest was the campaign to persuade women to resist the official attempt to count them for the 1911 census since their unfranchised status reflected that they were not considered 'full' citizens. Halifax evaders included Laura Willson, aged 33, of 117 Beechwood Road, Illingworth, who lived in a seven-roomed property with her husband, a machine toolmaker, her son, daughter and mother-in-law, Dr Helena Jones. Indeed, suffrage historian Jill Liddington has identified Dr Jones as 'an impressive local suffragette', who lived at 3 Rhodesia Avenue, a property with seven rooms, employing one servant. The Census Enumerator noted that 'Dr Helena Jones (Suffragette) did not pass the night of Sunday 2 April in this dwelling and did not arrive in this dwelling on the morning of Monday 3 April'. She had chaired a meeting of the local Women's Social and Political Union on Thursday 30 March 1911 at the Halifax Mechanics' Hall at which Emmeline Pankhurst declared 'until women rank as people, in the full sense of the word, we refuse to be numbered among the people, and we advise other women to join us in this protest'. Whilst her inspiring speech won enthusiastic support it also prompted a local Unitarian minister to challenge her ethically for undermining census accuracy and thereby future welfare legislation. The other two Halifax suffragettes categorised as evaders were Lavena Saltonstall, aged twenty-nine, who had moved from Hebden Bridge to 13 Park Place, Halifax to work as a cotton weaver, where she made friends with a group of confident women who shared her commitment to women's suffrage. At the time of the 1911 Census, it is suggested that she normally boarded with a slipper-making household at a property comprising four rooms, like Mary Taylor, aged about forty-seven, who normally resided at 32, Skircoat Green with her husband a forty-six-year-old blacksmith, in a property comprising six rooms. Neighbouring Huddersfield appears to have had no evaders, with all five entries signifying compliance. Bradford, in contrast, notes one suffragette as having hosted a mass evasion of nine other females and another eight, whilst one other suffragette is also listed as evading.[38]

For most of the period from 1851 to 1914, politics in Halifax therefore remained largely hierarchical, reflecting the local social structure, and was dominated by the business elite because of the restricted franchise following the defeat of Chartism. It also remained predominantly patriarchal, with the implementation of women's franchise delayed until after the First World War. A mid-Victorian Liberal consensus emerged, absorbing radicalism and binding together middle-class entrepreneurs like Crossley and Stansfeld, many of whom were Nonconformists, and working-class ex-Chartists like Snowden. They shared broadly similar radical-liberal individualist values, and in spite of some friction maintained a coalition which excluded the Tories from success in parliamentary elections until the late nineteenth century, when greater class conflict developed. This was consequent upon a widening franchise, increasing urban segregation and economic stresses which stimulated the development of trade unionism and the rise of Labour. From 1897, Labour began to make gains first in municipal elections and then, from 1906, in parliamentary elections, thereby presenting a challenge to the Liberal hegemony and creating opportunities for a revival of Conservative fortunes as the defenders of property.

The provision of local services

Economic change and the emergence of social and political elites stimulated the provision of a growing range of local services by the Halifax Municipal and County Borough Councils, the Halifax Board of Guardians and the Halifax School Board during its 33-year existence from 1870 to 1903. Moreover, this plurality of provision was supplemented by a remarkable variety of philanthropic activity which provided almshouses, business loans, model housing, a new infirmary, an orphanage, parks and promenades for the expanding town. But the nature and scale of some of the problems created by the rapid industrial and urban expansion of Halifax during the nineteenth century and the constraints of the town's geographical location meant that Halifax lagged behind many other towns in the provision of some services, for example, public transport networks and systems for the water carriage of sewage.

Edmund Minson Wavell, town clerk of Halifax from 1849 to 1864, later recalled that the new municipal corporation, which included seventeen radicals, four Chartists, six Whigs and three Tories, had been 'cradled in strife'. It had failed to set a borough rate in its first year of office on account of a legal technicality and consequently was distracted by acrimonious litigation until June 1851. The by-elections which took place following the election of aldermen had strengthened the representation of the Whigs, the Nonconformists and the manufacturing and commercial interests. The final composition of the council thus included nine retailers, seven merchants, seven manufacturers, six gentlemen, three corn and fodder dealers, two farmers, two agents, two dyers, an inn keeper, a plumber and a joiner. Having resolved its initial difficulties, the council proclaimed its intention 'to confer upon Halifax all the advantages possessed by any other municipal borough, and to keep the local rates low, so as to afford inducement for manufacturing and commercial enterprise and to offer residential advantages'.[39]

The publication of William Ranger's highly critical reports on the sanitary condition of the new borough in 1850 and 1851 ensured that municipal endeavour after 1851 would be focused primarily upon environmental improvement, and, in particular, the urgent need to provide a better water supply for both industrial and domestic consumers. The town clerk told the Ranger enquiry that 'the entire district' lacked an adequate water supply. Ranger commented particularly on the acute lack of provision for the labouring classes who were 'subjected to privations, not only of water for the purpose of ablution and house cleaning, but of wholesome water for drinking and culinary purposes'. The council was advised by a leading civil engineer who had been responsible for the construction of the Manchester and Glasgow waterworks to establish an extensive gathering-shed for water, and a series of new reservoirs were constructed, including the new Victoria, Albert and Ogden reservoirs between 1851 and 1864; Fly Flatts, Dean Head, Castle Carr, Mixenden and Widdop between 1864 and 1878; Roils Head in 1884; Ogden Kirk in 1894–95 and Walshaw Dean in 1915. By 1892, the corporation was able to supply water for the county borough 'unsurpassed in purity' at the rate of 5.5 million gallons per day, realising a clear annual profit of over £9,500.[40]

The provision of a comprehensive sewerage system, however, took longer to develop in Halifax than in most other towns. In 1853 William Ranger planned a network of drains and sewers for the borough divided into five districts with the main outlet emptying into the Hebble Brook below Water Lane bridge. Yet despite expenditure of some £145,924, nearly half a century elapsed before a sewage treatment works was opened at the confluence of the Hebble and Calder at Salterhebble, and most houses within the county borough remained without water closets until the inter-war years. Indeed, a survey by the Local Government Board revealed that Halifax was one of only 15 out of 95 English towns with populations exceeding 50,000 where the conservancy system, rather than the water carriage of sewage, prevailed in 1911. Only Rochdale, Gateshead, South Shields and Warrington had a higher proportion of houses without water closets in 1911 than Halifax, where barely a quarter of houses had them.[41]

The 1853 Halifax Improvement Act empowered the council to construct the new Victoria cattle market in order to remove cattle sales from the streets and to undertake much needed drainage and street-widening schemes, some of which were undertaken in conjunction with manufacturers such as the Crossleys anxious to improve access to their factories. The Act also transferred to council management the new markets, which had been operated by a private company since 1811. Subsequently the Halifax Corporation also became responsible for supplying the town with gas from 1855; maintaining parks from 1857; providing public baths from 1859; cemeteries from 1861; isolation hospitals from 1872; libraries from 1881; electricity from 1894; an electric tramway service from 1898; and a limited bus service from 1912. The corporation gained valuable revenue from the ownership of many of these public utilities during this period. For example, revenue from the markets between 1853 and 1863 amounted to £5,571. In 1914 profits from gas yielded £83,200; electricity, £10,637; and tramways and omnibuses, £13,643.

However, the council's main source of revenue throughout the period was derived from the rates. Indeed, the rateable value of the Halifax township alone quadrupled from £50,884 in 1848 to £201,133 in 1893, while the rateable value of the county borough increased from £358,189 in 1893 to £503,571 in 1914. The boundaries of the municipal borough were extended in 1865, and in 1889 Halifax was redesignated a county borough. Its boundaries were further extended in 1889, 1892, 1899, 1900 and 1902, absorbing less successful communities around its periphery, increasing the number of contributing ratepayers but also requiring an extension of service provision to a larger population over a wider geographical area. Hence, Halifax, like other expanding Pennine towns such as Bradford, appeared below the national average in 1914 in the provision of some services, for example the supply of consumers with gas slot meters and gas cookers.[42]

Table 5.1 Municipal seats in Halifax, 1891–1913

Year	Conservative	Labour	Liberal	Others	Year	Conservative	Labour	Liberal	Others
1891	8		22		1902	14	5	40	1
1892	12	3	20		1903	10	6	44	
1893	10	2	23	1	1904	10	6	43	
1894	13		13	2	1905	15	4	40	1
1895	16		16	4	1906	15	4	40	1
1896	21		24	3	1907	17	6	36	1
1897	20	1	26	1	1908	16	7	36	1
1898	15	1	32		1909	16	8	35	1
1899	18	2	32		1910	17	7	35	1
1900	19	2	37	2	1911	17	8	34	1
1901	17	4	38	1	1912	19	8	31	2
					1913	24	9	25	2

Source: P. A. Dawson, 'The Halifax Independent Labour Movement' in K. Laybourn and D. James, eds, *The Rising Sun of Socialism* (West Yorkshire Archive Service, Wakefield: 1991), p. 52; P. A. Dawson, 'Halifax Politics 1890–1914', Ph.D. Thesis (CNAA, Huddersfield: July 1987), p. 129, cf also Dawson on the social composition of the electorate in the late-Victorian era.

E.M. Wavell, J.P., 1898. Edmund Minson Wavell was appointed town clerk of Halifax in April 1849, following the resignation of Jonathan Crowther, who had for many years been clerk under the Halifax Improvement Act of 1823 to the Town Trustees. Wavell continued in office for fifteen years until 1864. He later recalled that the new municipal corporation of Halifax, which included seventeen radicals, four Chartists, six Whigs and three Tories, had been 'cradled in strife'. It had failed to set a borough rate in its first year of office on account of a legal technicality and consequently was distracted by acrimonious litigation until June 1851. During the period from 1848 to 1893, Wavell recounted in a survey of the growth of the borough of Halifax, the rateable value of Halifax had increased from £50,884 to £358,189. (Photograph: J.A. Hargreaves)

In 1863, after considerable political controversy and growing ratepayer concern about the cost of the project, Halifax acquired a magnificent new town hall to replace the converted warehouse building in Union Street which had previously been used for council meetings. Designed in a free North Italian cinquecento style by the architect of the Houses of Parliament, Sir Charles Barry, it was completed by his son Edward Middleton Barry, who added the mansard roof with its decorative ironwork cresting and soaring tower and spire. Alternative designs and sites had been canvassed by rival manufacturers Edward Akroyd and John Crossley. Akroyd had commissioned Sir George Gilbert Scott to design a Gothic town hall at Ward's End on the southern edge of the town, while Crossley had produced a classical design by the Bradford firm of Lockwood and Mawson for a site which he was engaged in clearing and developing near the northern perimeter of the town. Following an acrimonious press campaign, in the event neither design was adopted, but Crossley who was currently both a town councillor and member of the building committee succeeded in securing his preferred site. In a memorandum, Barry argued that the town hall should be 'the exponent of the life and soul of the city and should therefore be as much as possible in the heart of it' but that it should be entirely devoted to the serious business of municipal politics and should not include 'lavish expenditure' on a concert hall. Accordingly, it was designed specifically as a municipal hub, housing municipal offices, court house and police station.

The final cost of the building, however, which the borough surveyor had

Halifax Town Hall, 1863. The magnificent new town hall was opened by the Prince of Wales during the mayoralty of John Crossley, on whose initiative the project was conceived. It was one of the last buildings designed by Sir Charles Barry, architect of the Houses of Parliament. After his death in 1860, his son Edward Middleton Barry saw the work through to completion, adding the mansard roof with its ironwork cresting. The exquisite stone carving and sculpture was the work of John Thomas, who had worked with Barry on the Houses of Parliament. Colonel Akroyd and his supporters had favoured an alternative site at Ward's End for a building designed by Sir George Gilbert Scott. (Photograph: J. A. Hargreaves)

originally estimated at £17,000, ran to around £50,000. This sum included £2,592 for the prestigious opening ceremony by the Prince of Wales in August 1863, the first visit to Halifax by a member of the British Royal Family and the first official visit by the heir to the throne to a provincial urban centre following his marriage in March. A triumphal arch was erected in Princess Street, new civic robes ordered and the town hall illuminated with thousands of batswing gas burners. The only disappointments were the sudden withdrawal from the visit at the last moment by the Princess of Wales, who appears to have been suffering from morning sickness, and the torrential downpour which dampened the spirits of the vast crowds, many of whom had travelled to Halifax on 164 special trains to witness the spectacle. Moreover, the heavy downpour resulted in muddy streets which prompted the *Illustrated London News* to complain about the muddy streets around the Piece Hall and *The Times* reporter to opine that Halifax might be considered to have been 'deficient, as a general rule, in what Londoners would call streets'. The mayor,

The arrival of the Prince of Wales at Halifax Railway Station, 1863. The arrival of the royal train at Halifax Station was signalled by the firing of a royal salute from two 32-pounders of the Heckmondwike Volunteer Artillery Corps on Beacon Hill and the raising of the Royal Standard above the station. The Prince, the first member of the British royal family to visit the town, was met by the mayor, John Crossley, and the councillors in their new corporate robes. A guard of honour was mounted by 300 Halifax Volunteer Riflemen under Colonel Edward Akroyd. The royal party travelled to Manor Heath for lunch and then toured the factories of John Crossley and Sons, James Akroyd and Sons and John Whiteley and Sons. Further visits were made to People's Park, All Souls' Church and the Piece Hall on the following day before the climax of the visit, the official opening of the new town hall. Some 85,000 people travelled to Halifax by rail to witness the royal visit. (Photograph: The *Illustrated London News*)

John Crossley, for whom the royal visit represented a huge personal triumph, emphasised in his speech at the opening ceremony that the cost and furnishing of the building 'will not entail any serious burden on the inhabitants of the borough, being met mainly by funds accruing by judicious management of the local revenues and resources'. This proved to be an over-optimistic appraisal of the situation. While £13,000 was raised from profits from gas and markets, the remaining debt of £37,000 was not paid off until 1933–34.[43]

A survey of educational provision in Halifax undertaken, for practical reasons, by the borough police force on behalf of the newly formed Halifax School Board in 1871 revealed a deficiency of elementary school accommodation within the borough for 9,942 children. Moreover, only twenty schools were regarded as efficient, the majority of which were administered by the Church of England. This presented

Poster commemorating the visit of HRH The Prince of Wales to Halifax to open the Town Hall, 4 August 1863, the first official visit of a member of the British Royal Family to the town. (Photograph: S. Gee)

a formidable challenge to the eleven members of the first Halifax School Board, elected without a contest in 1871. The new board embraced a cross-section of representatives from both the Established Church and Nonconformity, including three industrialists, two tradesmen, two gentlemen, a solicitor, an architect, a banker's clerk and a Roman Catholic priest. From the outset it pursued a series of controversial and boldly innovative policies, erecting an ornately designed new board school, with a lofty portico and belfry, at Queen's Road, which exceeded official space and staffing ratio regulations; opening a Higher Board School in

Prescott Street in 1882; inaugurating school medical inspections in 1898 before they became a statutory requirement; and installing a swimming bath at Warley Road School in 1897. When the Halifax Education Committee took over from the School Board under the terms of the Balfour Education Act of 1902 there were twenty-three schools administered by the board with over 12,875 scholars and nine voluntary schools. Four years earlier the Halifax Corporation had also assumed full responsibility for the technical school erected in Hopwood Lane in 1895 from the proceeds of a 'whisky money' windfall grant provided by the Inland Revenue. From 1904 the Halifax Education Committee offered ten annual scholarships to boys whose parents earned under £200 per year to attend Heath Grammar School, one of several struggling local endowed schools, which had 125 pupils on roll in 1907, but was criticised for failing to make similar provision for girls. In 1914 the

below: The reading of the loyal address at the opening of Halifax Town Hall, 4 August 1863. The town clerk of Halifax, E. M. Wavell, in the centre of the picture, prepares to read the loyal address to the Prince of Wales, watched by the Bishop of Ripon, the Mayor of Halifax and other invited guests. The address thanked the Prince for honouring the borough with his first 'special visit' to a 'provincial municipality' and declared that 'the consideration which the town of Halifax enjoys, alike from its antiquity, from the fact that it is the commercial centre of an important manufacturing district, and from other causes, will henceforth be greatly enhanced by the distinction which it receives this day, in the dedication to public service of the edifice in which we are now assembled'. In his reply, the Prince alluded to 'the general prosperity' of the industries of the town which he had witnessed during his visit 'aided by the most ingenious machinery'. (Photograph: The *Illustrated London News*)

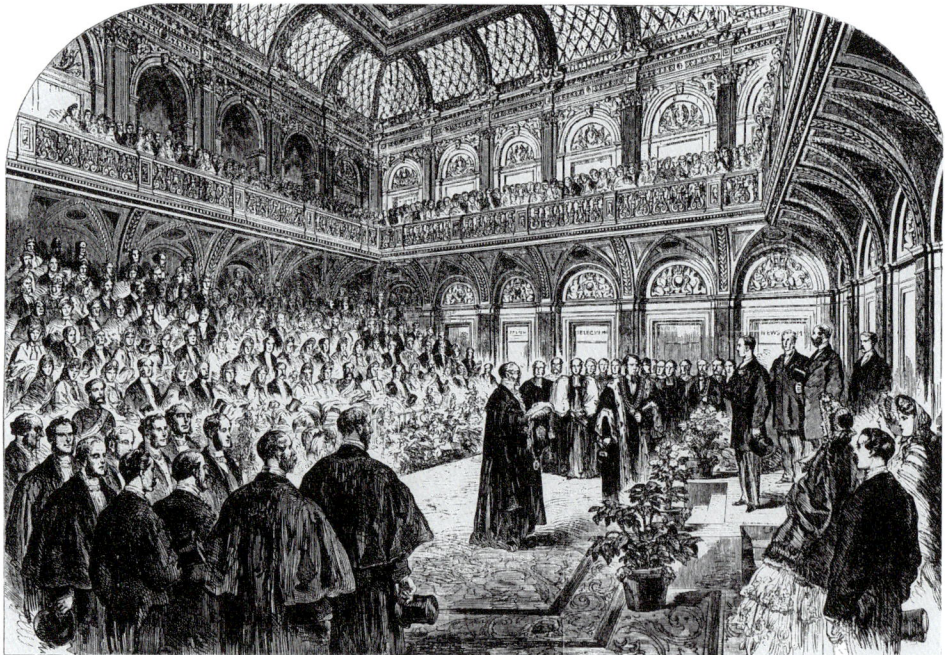

Woodwork class, Queen's Road Board School, 1906. Queen's Road Board School was one of the first purpose-built board schools to be established in Halifax following the 1870 Education Act. When it opened in July 1874, there were 1,074 children on roll, including half-timers. The ornate architecture of the building, with its lofty portico and belfry, aroused criticism from those who had favoured a more functional and less expensive style of construction. (Photograph: J. A. Hargreaves)

Misses Whitley, descendants of Nathan Whitley, a member of the first Halifax School Board, donated their refurbished West House mansion to the Corporation for use as Education Offices.[44]

Edward Akroyd's former Bankfield Mansion was acquired for £6,000 in order to accommodate a town museum and local branch library, which opened in 1888 after over £10,000 had been expended on necessary repairs and alterations. However, unlike neighbouring Keighley, Halifax had failed to secure a purpose-built central library to complement its Victorian and Edwardian townscape. The problem of providing a free public library had first been solved by renting the former Assembly Rooms in Harrison Road, however by 1886 the lease was due to expire. The Library Committee dismissed the offer of another Halifax entrepreneur, H. C. McCrea, to secure the site, on the grounds that the estimated cost of building at £5,000 exceeded the affordability of the penny rate available for this purpose. Instead, negotiations were completed for the purchase of Sir Francis Crossley's former Belle Vue mansion at a cost of £8,000, and Estcott, the borough surveyor, was instructed to draw up plans for the conversion into

St Luke's Hospital, Salterhebble. The new purpose-built Poor Law hospital at Salterhebble was erected in 1901 at a cost of £98,000 by the Halifax Board of Guardians, who had previously cared for the sick in the union workhouse premises in Gibbet Street. Designed by W. Clement Williams, the hospital was opened by the chairman of the building committee, J. W. Tillotson, on 9 April 1901. Its 400 beds were acquired for military use in December 1915 and additional accommodation for 302 provided in marquees in the grounds. Altogether no fewer than 1,300 beds were provided for military use in central Halifax during the wartime emergency. (Photograph: J. A. Hargreaves)

a free public library of the elegant but inconveniently situated building 'a tram ride from the centre' of the town.[45]

The Halifax Board of Guardians, elected by ballot after 1894, remained responsible for the relief of poverty in the Halifax Poor Law Union throughout the period up to 1914, under the central direction of the Local Government Board from 1871, whose first president, the Liberal Member of Parliament for Halifax, James Stansfeld (1820–98), sought to curb the extent of outdoor relief. The Halifax Union Workhouse had 291 inmates in 1851, including 60 sick patients. In 1871 it provided for 510, of whom 298 were accommodated in adjacent new three-storey infirmary buildings. By 1901, because the Halifax Union Workhouse was constantly full, the Halifax Union was spending £11,820 on outdoor relief, more than any other union in the West Riding except Leeds. After Leeds and Bradford, Halifax also had the largest number of lunatics in asylums in West Yorkshire at an annual cost to the union of over £10,000. In 1901 a new hospital designed by W. Clement Williams, was erected by the Halifax Board of Guardians at Salterhebble at a cost of £98,000. The largest public building in the town, it relieved pressure on the workhouse premises in Gibbet Street, which, with 656 inmates in accommodation designed for 466 in 1900, were extended in 1905.[46]

Philanthropy, inspired by a combination of altruism, evangelicalism and industrial paternalism, also made a significant contribution to health, housing and social welfare provision in Halifax in the period up to 1914. During the 1850s and 1860s model industrial communities were developed by Edward Akroyd at Copley and

Akroydon and by John Crossley at West Hill Park. They provided superior housing, gardens and allotments and a range of other self-help institutions such as savings banks, cultural, educational and religious institutions. Collectively they served as 'powerful agencies for ushering in a period of much closer social harmony between millowners and employers'. A succession of generous benefactions commencing with Francis Crossley's trail-blazing People's Park, designed by Sir Joseph Paxton and opened in 1857, provided the town with an abundance of public parks and promenades, including Savile (1866), Shroggs (1881), Akroyd (1887) and West View (1904–05) Parks and Albert Promenade (1861). Almshouses, an orphanage and temporary business loans for men and single women or widows of good character

Joseph, Sir Francis and John Crossley. The three youngest sons of John and Martha Crossley, photographed in the 1860s, continued the family carpet manufacturing business after their father's death in 1837, trading under the name of John Crossley and Sons. By the time of John's death in 1879 it had become the largest carpet manufacturing firm in the world. Joseph, who unlike his brothers played no prominent role in public life, is often characterised as the partner most closely involved in the day-to-day management of the firm, while Francis has been portrayed as the most enterprising and innovative, taking the initiative in the development of steam-powered tapestry carpet production, which provided the springboard for the firm's mid-century expansion. However, John's association with the firm, extending over half a century, was the longest and on his retirement he expressed particular satisfaction that for nearly forty years 'no dispute or misunderstanding has occurred but such as was there and then, by mutual compromise, adjusted'. All three brothers contributed munificently to a variety of philanthropic schemes within the town. (Photograph: West Yorkshire Archive Service, Calderdale)

were also provided by the Crossley brothers during the period 1855–68, honouring their mother Martha's vow that 'if the Lord does bless us in this place, the poor shall taste of it'. Francis Crossley, writing to his brother Joseph in May 1857 about their plans to open an orphanage, concluded: 'every loom and every wheel will work all the more merrily and joyfully when their profits are consecrated to such worthy objects'.[47]

However, perhaps the most remarkable local example of community provision through philanthropy, self-help and mutual co-operation in the history of the locality was the voluntary hospital movement which financed the building of the Royal Halifax Infirmary in Free School Lane, opened by the Duke and Duchess of York in 1896. Some £60,000 was raised through numerous voluntary contributions from ordinary men, women and children as well as more substantial donations from wealthy local families such as the Appleyards, Baldwins, Crossleys, McCreas, Porters and Whitworths, whose names designated the wards which they helped to finance.[48]

By the early twentieth century, a new middle-class philanthropy had emerged in the Guild of Help movement, which had originated in Bradford in 1904 in response to the rising unemployment of the Edwardian era. It offered a more community-based solution to the problem of poverty, emphasising the moral responsibility of the middle classes to help the poor and the moral discipline required by the recipient, in an attempt to ward off the threat of state socialism. A Halifax Citizens Guild was formed in 1905, which participated in arrangements to provide free school meals to children during the severe economic depressions which occurred in the winters of 1905 and 1908; supported attempts to find work for the unemployed through 'distress committees'; encouraged the local authority to appoint health visitors; and worked closely with the probation service. Responding to the high infant mortality rate in Halifax in his annual report, Dr Neech, the Halifax Medical Officer of Health, highlighted the need to encourage breastfeeding, which prompted the Mayor of Halifax, Alderman William Wallace to announce on 1 January 1908 in the Council Chamber that he would give a gold sovereign to each of the first hundred infants born in the borough that year, provided that they attained the age of one year, a scheme officially entitled 'The Mayor's Infantile Mortality Fund', but more popularly dubbed the 'Bounty Baby' Scheme. Each registered participant in the scheme met the Mayor at Akroyd Park for a progress check and to be photographed and it was reported that fifty-nine of the eighty-one infants present were now being breastfed.

The Halifax guild expressed its concern at the hunger marches 'in this well-to-do borough' in 1909 and hoped that the new Labour Exchange opened in 1910 would resolve the problem. However, as Professor Keith Laybourn has demonstrated, the revival of trade and Liberal social legislation immediately before the First World War also had a positive impact on infant welfare by reducing the problem of unemployment and offering longer term strategies for dealing with the problem of infant mortality.[49]

Culture: religion and recreation

Institutional Christianity, reflecting to some extent the local social hierarchy, shaped cultural forms as well as religious expression in Victorian and Edwardian Halifax, but during this period there was also a shift from organised religion to more commercialised recreation. Although the Census of Religious Worship revealed that over half of the population of the municipal borough apparently failed to attend worship on Census Sunday in 1851, many inhabitants of the town during the period up to the First World War lived their lives from the cradle to the grave in close association with church, chapel and Sunday school. In 1851, it has been calculated that Halifax ranked fourth out of fifty-five urban centres in the strength of its Sunday school enrolment, but forty-third in church attendance. However, indices of church attendance derived from the 1851 Census of Religious Worship have to be treated with caution, since the published returns omit statistics for the Congregationalists, Particular Baptists, Roman Catholics, Quakers and Unitarians, all of whom had congregations in the municipal borough by 1851. Nevertheless, the revelations of the Census, the rapid increase in the urban population after 1851, a

Mothers and babies photographed with the Mayor of Halifax, Alderman William Wallace outside the conservatory at Akroyd Park on 2 July 1908. His initiative with Dr Neech, the Medical Officer of Health for the Borough, was designed to encourage breast feeding and curtail the borough's high infant mortality rate of 101 for all wards. (Photograph: G. Sutcliffe)

growing rivalry between religious denominations and a shared concern for social cohesion stimulated both the churches and chapels into renewed efforts to reach the unchurched masses, resulting in an upsurge of church building. Dr S. J. D. Green has calculated that probably two-thirds of all those churches, chapels and mission churches ever built in Halifax were constructed between the passing of the second Reform Bill in 1867 and the death of Queen Victoria in 1901. Whereas in 1851 there were some twenty-five churches and chapels serving the recently incorporated municipal borough, by 1900 there were probably around ninety-nine churches and chapels scattered about the new county borough.[50]

An attempt in 1875 to make Halifax the nucleus of a new diocese for the industrial West Riding, however, proved abortive and Halifax remained a remote outpost of the diocese of Ripon until the creation of the new diocese of Wakefield in 1888. Although Halifax became one of two new archdeaconries within the new diocese, the new diocesan structures lacked the resources to make a significant impact on parish life for most of the period up to 1914. Many of the urgent recommendations of the first bishop's diocesan commission of 1889, for example, had still not been implemented when the second bishop's diocesan commission reported in 1909, and it was not until 1914 that the large Rural Deanery of Halifax was sub-divided. It is not therefore surprising that the Revd Francis Pigou, one of the most dynamic vicars of Halifax during this period, should have acknowledged in 1898 that his parish remained a Nonconformist stronghold 'supported by the influence and purses of wealthy capitalists' and that 'the Church of England does not do much more than hold her own'. Indeed, during this period Halifax produced one of its most distinguished Nonconformist preachers, J. H. Jowett (1864–1923), who achieved both national and global recognition. Jowett delivered his first sermon at the age of seventeen to a 'congregation of homely people' at the schoolroom at Range Bank, a preaching station opened in 1852 of Square Road Congregational Church, and his first evangelistic address shortly before this to the 'inmates of a common lodging house in Halifax'. Jowett went on to become one of the most famous preachers of the age.[51]

Although there was no late-Victorian census of attendance at religious worship in Halifax, an indication of the continuing vitality of the religious institutions within the parish can be gauged from the number of participants at the last Sunday School Jubilee Sing to be held in the Halifax Piece Hall in 1890. The *Halifax Courier* reported that there were no fewer than 30,985 participants from 93 Nonconformist Sunday schools within the ancient parish. Collectively the Methodists accounted for 15,212 scholars, comprising 5,923 Wesleyan, 3,678 United Methodist Free Church, 3,366 Methodist New Connexion, and 2,245 Primitive Methodist scholars. The Congregationalists and Baptists accounted for 6,472 and 2,593 scholars respectively and other Sunday schools 1,010, including 320 from Northgate End Unitarian Sunday school. No Anglicans were present, but diocesan records reveal that there were a further 17,498 scholars enrolled at Anglican Sunday schools within the Halifax Deanery in 1889. When both figures are aggregated it becomes apparent that there were at least 48,483 children within the boundaries of the ancient parish associated with Sunday schools in 1890. Given that the population of the County Borough of Halifax in 1891 was 89,832, this figure must have included an exceptionally high proportion of children from within the local community.

This evidence also confirms the impression that religious institutions within the parish, which collectively represented the largest form of voluntary association within the life of the local community during this period, displayed a continuing vitality in the late-Victorian period. Indeed, their success was remarkable when compared with the success of other voluntary associations. For example, membership of the Halifax Trade Societies fluctuated between 3,000 and 4,000 and that of the Halifax ILP between 500 and 600 during the 1890s, while membership of registered Liberal, Conservative and Working Men's Clubs in the borough of Halifax in 1903 amounted to 1,122, 1,067 and 1,072 respectively. Even the maximum attendances of over 15,000 at the Halifax Rugby Club's newly opened Thrum Hall stadium barely exceeded half the number of participants in the Halifax Piece Hall Sings.

However, by the outbreak of the First World War the number of confirmation candidates was declining at Halifax Parish Church, and the tractarian Vicar of Illingworth, the Revd G. R. Oakley, discerned an ebb in church attendance and

Royal Halifax Infirmary. In 1896 a new infirmary in Free School Lane was formally opened by the Duke and Duchess of York. During the opening ceremony the Duke announced that the infirmary was to be named the Royal Halifax Infirmary, by command of Queen Victoria. An 1895 directory described the building of the new infirmary as 'one of the most important and public spirited enterprises ever undertaken by the Halifax public'. Designed by Messrs Worthington and Son of Manchester, the hospital was built upon 'the very latest principle approved by the leading hygienic scientists of the day' with 'the wards built separate from the main administration building', each named after an individual or family benefactor – Crossley, Porter, McCrea, Baldwin, Appleyard and Rawson. (Photograph: J. A. Hargreaves)

religious observance in the period before the First World War which he attributed to 'the materialism of the prosperity of the pre-war years'. Moreover, by the end of the first decade of the twentieth century, virtually all the available indicators reveal that Nonconformity had already reached its peak and was experiencing a declining rate of growth before the outbreak of the First World War. Roman Catholic baptisms and Easter Mass attendances at Halifax also show a pronounced downward trend after 1901. Baptist and Congregational membership in Halifax peaked in 1905 and 1907 respectively. Even the underlying trend in Wesleyan membership recruitment was downward after 1890, and United Methodist recruitment after 1907.

The reasons for this pattern of decline experienced by all the major religious denominations in Halifax before 1914 are complex, but declining membership appears to have followed declining population trends and evidence of contraction within some sections of the local economy. Other reasons included the growth of religious pluralism and the emergence of new denominations such as the Salvation Army in the late nineteenth century; declining levels of Sunday school recruitment; the suburbanisation of middle- and lower middle-class housing; the advance of the

Park Congregational Church. Designed by Roger Ives in the early geometric Gothic style, it was erected in 1869 at a cost of £11,200, including the purchase of the site from Sir Francis Crossley, who laid the foundation stone. It was constructed from Northowram stone and lay close to the West Hill Park model housing estate built by John Crossley between 1863 and 1868. The principal entrance was in the south front, beneath a large five-light traceried window. The tower at the south-west corner was surmounted by a spirelet rising over 36 metres in height. The building provided accommodation for a congregation of 932. In 1875, new Sunday School buildings were erected behind the church, which, since the closure of the church in 1980, are now also used for worship. (Photograph: J. A. Hargreaves)

Labour movement and a growth in religious scepticism; the rise of state educational and welfare provision; the growth in company size and the decline of the family firm; improving living standards and the growth of organised leisure.[52]

Better communications, wider education, rising real incomes and shorter working hours for those in employment, following the institution of the Saturday half holiday in 1873 and half day closing for shops in 1912, brought increased opportunities for leisure in late Victorian and Edwardian Halifax. Where social life was not centred upon the church or chapel, it was likely, at least for working men, to revolve around the ubiquitous public houses or working men's clubs, facilitated by the fish and chip shops which proliferated from the 1860s, with Halifax attaining a coveted position in the top ten Pennine towns for fish and chip provision by 1914. The piano manufacturer Henry William Pohlmann (1853–91) recorded in his diary for Saturday 6 June 1874 that he had seen 'a great many drunken men' on his way to the station to meet the 10.42 p.m. train, commenting that 'Saturday being market

When Halifax Piece Hall became a wholesale fish, fruit and vegetable market after its acquisition by Halifax County Borough it became increasingly difficult for it be used as a venue for the Sunday School Jubilee Piece Hall Sings, the last of which was held there in 1890. (Photograph: S. Gee)

day there are always many who stay and get drunk and go home by the last trains'. There were some 543 outlets of the liquor trade in Halifax Poor Law Union in 1895 and 179 in Halifax itself. The last quarter of the nineteenth century was a period of considerable prosperity for the six main Halifax brewing companies. However, by 1900, with the growing diversification of consumer spending into expanding alternative outlets, the demand for beer had begun to fall and the breweries found themselves in a situation where there was not enough trade to support the large number of houses, profit margins were reduced, and many of the smaller local breweries did not survive.[53]

Outside the public houses, music ranging from choral singing to brass bands; amateur and professional theatre; organised sport and commercialised popular entertainment, came to play an increasing part in many people's lives before 1914. Charles Hallé established the first provincial orchestra, accessible by rail or bus in Manchester, or at frequent performances in Halifax and other West Riding venues. For its part, Halifax lays undisputed claim to the foundation of the earliest amateur choral society in Britain, formally constituted in 1818 and maintaining an uninterrupted series of annual performances of Handel's *Messiah* for the ensuing

Theatre Royal. The Theatre Royal, opened on 7 August 1905 with a performance by the Halifax Amateur Operatic Society of Gilbert and Sullivan's 'The Mikado'. The new theatre occupied the site of an earlier theatre established in 1790 and demolished in March 1904 and land in Ward's End previously occupied by the old Shakespeare Tavern, a shop that adjoined and four cottages in Shakespeare Street. The Theatre Royal was one of two recently opened theatres in Ward's End. The Palace Theatre had opened on 30 July 1903. Moreover, there was also the Grand Theatre and Opera House, situated at North Bridge, which had opened in 1889. A contemporary directory boasted that 'there are few towns in which a clearer appreciation of real histrionic talent find expression than in the town of Halifax'. (Photograph: H. Armitage)

two centuries. Indeed, it draws inspiration from a well-established musical tradition originating in the Georgian era, when the town also held one of the earliest performances of Handel's *Messiah* north of the Trent in 1766. By 1914, Halifax had a new concert hall, the Victoria Hall, opened shortly after the death of Queen Victoria in 1901. The town also boasted three theatres, the Grand Theatre at North Bridge, opened in 1889, the Palace Theatre, opened in 1903, and the Theatre Royal, rebuilt in 1904. There was also a growing number of cinemas, following the opening in 1910 of the Electric Theatre in the former Riding School building in Ward's End, the first theatre to be opened in Halifax solely for showing the new silent pictures. There were also pleasure gardens, a museum, a zoo, and spectacular surrounding countryside for the rambler, cyclist and motorist to explore.

Local league matches in both cricket and football were legion, and large crowds of spectators regularly converged on Thrum Hall from 1886; Sandhall Lane from 1911 to 1916 and Exley from 1919 to 1921 to watch rugby league and association football in Halifax. Formed in 1873, Halifax Rugby League Club achieved the double in 1902–03, winning both the Rugby League Challenge Cup and the first division title. Moreover, the Challenge Cup was won again in 1903–04.[54] Although Association Football had been played in Halifax towards the end of the nineteenth century, it was not until 1911 that Halifax Town AFC was formed, following a meeting at the Saddle Hotel on 23 May 1911. Indeed, a letter in the *Halifax Courier* in the previous month had queried why 'the local enthusiasts of the dribbling code are so backward in establishing a town club in Halifax', since the West Riding of Yorkshire was already home to five Football League Clubs. They included the first at Leeds, elected in 1905; two clubs in neighbouring Bradford, which had attracted many supporters from Halifax, and one in Huddersfield, elected to the League in 1910, two years after they had been formed.[55]

Older surviving pastimes such as knur and spell attracted considerable popular interest at Skircoat Moor and West Hill Park in the mid-Victorian period, and when golf courses were opened at Lightcliffe in 1895, Ogden in 1901, West End in 1906 and Bradley Hall in 1907. Early golfers were referred to as 'knur and spell players in knickerbockers and spats' and the nine-hole course laid out at Bradley Hall on land 'unsuitable for agricultural development' was described by the *Halifax Guardian* as being of 'undulating character and requiring judicious treatment'. By 1910 a temporary small hut was replaced by 'a more commodious clubhouse' built from members' donations and by 1912 club membership had risen to nearly one hundred. Public baths were opened at Park Road in 1859 and Woodside in 1893, and the Halifax Swimming Club was founded 1864. The Halifax and Calder Vale Hunt probably initiated the Halifax and Calder Vale Steeplechase in 1877, which had acquired a race course and grandstand at West End by 1878. However, the racing seasons lasted only until 1884, and by the 1890s the former race course was being used for shooting matches before its development as a golf course in 1906.[56]

A profusion of cultural and debating societies mushroomed in the town in the late-Victorian era including the Halifax Geologists' Field Club and Scientific Association (1874), the Halifax Art Society (1879), the Halifax Photographic Society

(1885), and the Halifax Antiquarian Society (1900). Rather belatedly for a medium-sized provincial town, Halifax also acquired its first evening newspaper when the weekly liberal *Halifax Courier*, founded in 1853, was published daily from 1892. However, its circulation of around 13,000 in 1892 was dwarfed by that of the *Halifax Original Clock Almanack*, founded in 1865 and edited for fifty years by the celebrated Halifax dialect poet and raconteur, John Hartley (1839–1915), which achieved an average annual circulation of 120,000, sponsored by advertisements for such popular remedies as Williams' Worm Lozenges and Page Woodcock's Wind Pills.[57]

Both religion and recreation, though clearly reflecting the local social hierarchy in some respects, also demonstrated a capacity to transcend social barriers in other respects and during this period there is evidence of an emerging, more inclusive culture. An outstanding example of racial inclusiveness was Andrew Watson, who became the first black player for a senior football team in the UK and the world's first black international football captain. Born in 1857, his early life was spent in British Guiana (Guyana). He was later admitted to Heath Grammar School in August 1866 and he may have lived at the Crossley Orphan Home, both Halifax institutions. He attended Glasgow University from 1895 to 1896 and played for

Halifax Zoo and Amusement Park. Advertised as 'the most up to date amusement park in the country', Halifax Zoo opened at Chevinedge, Exley, for the Whit weekend in 1909, when it attracted no fewer than 41,000 visitors. The zoo was well-stocked. Its aviaries were filled with gaily plumaged birds from South America and Australia, an eagle and a vulture. There were two African lions, two bears, hyenas, jackals, wolves, zebras, an Arabian camel, an Indian elephant, a yak and a monkey house. There was also a refreshment conservatory, an ornamental bandstand and a lake under construction, soon to be graced by black and white swans, ducks from China and India and a fountain. (Photograph: J. A. Hargreaves)

Queen's Park, Scotland's oldest football club from 1880 to 1897, captaining the side the side in 1881. More generally, the period also saw the abandonment of some older forms of leisure activity and the emergence of more ordered, rule-bound, often commercialised or municipalised leisure activities, and a shift from religion to more commercialised recreation.[58]

'Restless Renaissance city'

Following the incorporation of Halifax as a municipal borough in 1848 and the publication of the highly critical Ranger Report on its sanitary condition in 1851, the physical appearance of the town was considerably enhanced by two major phases of redevelopment in the second half of the nineteenth century. The first phase in the 1850s and 1860s saw the development of Crossley and Princess Streets, improvements to Crown Street and Old Market and continuous westward and northward urban expansion. The construction of Barry's magnificent neoclassical town hall, opened by the Prince of Wales in 1863, modelled on Sansovino's library of St Mark's, Venice, was the preferred design of the carpet manufacturer, John Crossley (1812–79), triumphing over Edward Akroyd's advocacy of a Gothic design by Sir George Gilbert Scott and an alternative location at Ward's End. The new Town Hall, incorporating the Borough Court, the offices of the overseers of the poor, the poor rate officers, the market inspector, police offices and basement cells, 'symbolised authority', as Colum Giles has observed, and in the view of Clyde Binfield, enhanced Halifax's civic identity, giving Halifax the character of a Florentine 'restless Renaissance city'. A directory of 1866 opined that the 'site was too irregular to permit the adoption of a perfectly classical style, whilst a pure Gothic edifice would have presented too strong a contrast to the lofty and handsome palladian buildings' which surrounded the town hall. It also noted that 'many handsome villa residences have also been erected principally in the western suburbs and numbers of new streets have been formed in the outskirts since 1850. The second phase of urban development in the 1880s and the 1890s as the town's population after 1881 surpassed 73,000 included the major Commercial Street development and the reconstruction of the borough markets under the direction of Joseph and John Leeming, which were opened by the Duke and Duchess of York in 1896.[59]

In addition, during the second half of the nineteenth century, there was a profusion of church, chapel, commercial, public and residential building in the town and its suburbs. The most striking examples included Sir George Gilbert Scott's magnificent All Souls' Church, Haley Hill (1859), whose steeple, the historian Tristram Hunt has observed, remains the town's 'chief architectural glory'. Indeed, the architect himself considered it 'on the whole, my best church' and the *Building News* averred that it was 'one of the most elegant specimens he has produced'.[60] It complemented Edward Akroyd's adjacent model housing development of Akroydon, and rivalled the Crossley's Dissenting Gothic Square Congregational Church (1857) and inspired outstanding later Gothic examples such as St John's Wesleyan Church (1880); the ornate Crossley and Porter Orphanage (1864), a multitude of technical and board schools; imposing almshouses, hospitals, banks, building societies, shops, markets and theatres; a plethora of mansions, villas, terraces, mills and warehouses and extravagantly designed buildings which defy easy categorisation such as Wainhouse's tower, an ambitious Victorian folly, completed in 1875. The town also acquired an imposing new railway station in 1855, replacing the original vernacular styled terminus building at Shaw Syke, after the completion of the Lancashire and Yorkshire Railway line to Bradford. Designed by Thomas Butterworth of Manchester as a 'long Italian villa, baroque in character' with a two-storeyed, pedimented centre section, connected to the pavilions by ranges delineated by 'a magnificent decorative cornice running the entire length of the frontage', the new station was built in a style 'more in keeping with the growing prosperity of the town'. It changed to the more recent higher-level access when it was extended in 1884. Halifax also acquired its only equestrian statue during this

Built between 1871 and 1875, Wainhouse Tower was originally designed as a chimney for the Washer Lane Dye Works, situated in the valley below on the estate of John Edward Wainhouse. Wainhouse's primary motive appears to have been to relieve the valley of the smoke pollution from his dyeworks. His architect, Isaac Booth, designed a conventional brick mill chimney with an outer octagonal stone casing containing a spiral staircase leading to four pedimented balcony features. Towards the end of 1873, following a bitter feud with his neighbour, Sir Henry Edwards of Pye Nest, Wainhouse disposed of the dye works, but was unable to sell the unfinished chimney. When the original architect who had also worked for Edwards felt obliged to relinquish his commission, his successor, R. S. Dugdale, brilliantly re-designed the top of the tower as an observatory. (Photograph: J. A. Hargreaves)

Photograph of Commercial Street, Halifax in 1912, with its fine Victorian and Edwardian architecture, looking south from the ornate Victorian Post Office, before it was enlarged to accommodate the telephone exchange in 1926, towards Ward's End before the Halifax Permanent Benefit Building Society established its offices further along the street on the left. A stationary opened-topped tram, advertising Lipton's Tea, appears close to the Post Office.
(Photograph: S. Gee)

period, a splendid bronze memorial erected to Prince Albert in Ward's End in 1864, but later removed to Albert Park in 1902 to make way for the trams.[61]

The density of the built environment in central Halifax, the inadequate sanitation and the pervasive industrial pollution which had prompted the sanitary inspector and artist J. R. Smith to describe Halifax at the beginning of the period as 'a veritable muck-midden' and the novelist Charles Dickens to pronounce the town 'as horrible a place as I ever saw' in 1858, highlighted the town's exacerbating environmental problems. Henry William Pohlmann, the Halifax piano manufacturer, wrote in his diary that he had observed from Southowram Old Bank on a walk in the evening of 4 June 1874 'that some parts of the town were practically hid by a dim vapour of smoke'.[62] Similarly the author J. S. Fletcher, writing in 1912, recalled the 'great canopy of dun-coloured smoke which seemed to hang night and day above the grey old town from Beacon Hill to the edge of Skircoat Moor' during his childhood, while the abiding impression created by the town on Holroyd Jackson in 1910 was of a bleak urban landscape where:

lines and lines of streets and mills stretched and turned away in every direction ... before falling away ... like walls of rugged chasms into the greyness of the world.[63]

However, J. S. Fletcher, on balance, considered Halifax by 1900 as 'a revivified place – a town of new buildings, new houses and mansions, new streets' observing that there were few towns in England with 'such steep streets and winding ways as there are in Halifax' whilst Montague Blatchford, if conceding that no one could have seriously described Halifax in 1901 as pretty, maintained that:

> there are times – as on a sunny day, when the atmosphere has been washed by heavy rain, or on a clear dark night, when a thousand lamps are twinkling on the hillsides – when Halifax has a picturesque charm, compared with

North Bridge and Bowling Dyke. This sketch of Halifax from the Mount, Haley Hill, was drawn by the architect J. R. Smith in the 1860s and printed by Stott Brothers in 1893. It depicts the modified stone bridge of 1774, prior to its replacement by the modern cast-iron structure in 1868, and the concentration of industrial development in the Hebble Valley. There is an extensive view of Northgate as far as Northgate End Chapel and the tower of Halifax Parish Church and the spire of Square Congregational Church are visible in the distance. James Akroyd and Sons' warehouse is also conspicuous at Cross Hills. (Photograph: J. A. Hargreaves)

Charlestown, Halifax from the south, 1909, taken on a relatively clear day, reveals a profusion of mill chimneys. The viaduct, left of centre, since demolished, was part of the Great Northern Line between Halifax Town Station and North Bridge Station. The author J. S. Fletcher, writing in 1912, recalled the 'the great canopy of dun-coloured smoke which seemed to hang night and day above the grey old town from Beacon Hill to the edge of Skircoat Moor' during his childhood. (Photograph: H. Armitage)

which, most of the manufacturing towns of Lancashire, and even Yorkshire, look dismal beyond description.[64]

Indeed, despite the dramatic expansion of the urban built environment during the late Victorian and Edwardian eras, there remained vast stretches of uninhabited or sparsely populated countryside within easy reach of the town centre. When Samson Clark, a London businessman visited the town in 1915 'with the aid of a swift car driven by one who was familiar with every inch of the town and country for miles around' it was the rural aspect of Halifax's setting which particularly impressed him:

As we sped through and around the town, up steep hills and down through the dales, along the crests of the high country and out across the moors, the impression obtained was that of a delightful variety within the reach of all. The unavoidable discomforts of factory life are here minimised by the close proximity of God's own country, where the sun and the breeze, the hills and moorland delight the eye and fill one with the joy of life.[65]

6

Halifax at War and Peace, 1914–45

THE PERIOD FROM 1914 TO 1945 opened with one world war and closed with another. Both wars resulted in larger numbers of local casualties than had been sustained in any previous international conflict. They also witnessed greater involvement by civilians on the home front in supporting the war effort. Consequently, both wars made a greater impact on the lives of local communities than previous wars. Between the wars it is also easy to identify signs of difficulties and decay in a period often characterised as one of economic depression, mass unemployment, dole queues and hunger marches. But there may be paradoxical components in times of war and recession: evidence of economic restructuring, of new roles for local government, of new political alignments, of new cultural practices, and even of tentative urban redevelopment also need to be assessed.[1]

Wars

There are few memorials in Halifax and its surrounding communities to the local soldiers who died in international conflict before 1914. The Stoodley Pike obelisk commemorates the conclusion of the Napoleonic and Crimean Wars, but provides no record of local casualties, only ten of whom are commemorated elsewhere in Calderdale. Two casualties of the Second Afghan War (1878–81) lie in the Halifax General Cemetery and the Soldier's Memorial in West View Park commemorates 73 of the 91 local casualties of the South African War (1899–1902), most of whom died of disease. By contrast, no fewer than 243 war memorials in the modern metropolitan district of Calderdale testify to the appalling slaughter of the two global conflicts between 1914 and 1945. They record the names of some 5,174 dead from the First World War, of whom 2,226 were from Halifax, and 1,317 from the Second World War of whom 588 were from Halifax.

The vast majority of the casualties from the First World War, some 93 per cent of the Calderdale total, were from the army. Out of Halifax's 1,610 dead infantrymen, no fewer than 46 per cent belonged to the Duke of Wellington's Regiment, whose regimental headquarters and barracks were situated at Highroad Well, Halifax. Based at the Drill Hall, Prescott Street, the 1/4th battalion was the battalion more closely associated with Halifax. The 1/4th battalion had been formed in 1908, under the army reforms of R.B. Haldane, Secretary of State for War from 1905 until 1912. These created the volunteer Territorial Army, part-time reserve.

The battalion endured the first major gas attack of the war in trench warfare, in the Ypres Salient, in December 1915. The battalion was subsequently decimated in the abortive attack on Thiepval on 3 September 1916 during the Somme offensive, when a mere 80 survived the attack upon the barbed-wire entanglements and machine-gun emplacements of the Schwaben Redoubt. Another battalion, experiencing its first action in the trenches around Beaumont Hamel early in 1917, later suffered numerous fatalities in the unsuccessful attack on Bullecourt. Huge losses were also sustained in the German Spring offensive of 1918. At sea, local servicemen were involved in most of the major naval actions of the war from Coronel in 1914 to Zeebrugge in 1918, and Calderdale seamen perished with virtually every ship that went down at Jutland. Apart from continuing deaths from war wounds, many of the casualties of 1918–19 were victims of the Spanish flu pandemic, which swept across Europe at the end of the war.

Table 6.1 Halifax casualties in the First World War

1914:	66
1915:	237
1916:	437
1917:	665
1918:	654
1919:	167
Total:	2,226

Source: T. R. Hornshaw, 'Calderdale and the wars of the twentieth century', *Transactions of the Halifax Antiquarian Society* 6 (1998), p. 124.

The Great War, as it was known to contemporaries, resulted in many personal tragedies as well as some remarkable stories of survival for Halifax families. The following selection of examples provides a poignant demonstration of this, some from the centennial commemoration of the war in an award-winning exhibition at Bankfield Museum from 2014 to 2018.

Samuel Walker, the second son of Arthur and Jane Walker of Arden House, Halifax, may have been one of the earliest casualties of the war. Enlisting on the morning on which war was declared, Samuel began his training as a despatch rider with the Royal Engineers within a week. He died instantly from the fumes of a high explosive shell on 25 April 1915, aged 23, before crashing into a ditch.[2] Three brothers from Boothtown, Arthur, Fred and Ernest Smith, all served in the war. Despite suffering injuries, all survived. The eldest, Fred, a pre-war territorial in the 4th Battalion Duke of Wellington's Regiment, went to France in April 1915, but suffered 'trench foot' and was sent home in December 1915. He spent the rest of the war in England in a reserve battalion. His younger brother, Arthur, joined up at the end of December 1915 in the Royal Horse Artillery and later served in the Army of Occupation in Germany until October 1919. The youngest, Ernest,

Soldiers' Memorial, West View Park. In the reconstruction of the British army in 1881 the 33rd and 76th Regiments of Foot were joined to form the Duke of Wellington's Regiment with their headquarters at Halifax. There was no great enthusiasm in the town for the new regiment until the formation of the 1st Volunteer Battalion of the regiment in the town prior to the second South African War. During the war a strong detachment of the battalion formed part of the force under Lord Roberts which compensated for the disasters of the early part of the campaign. The memorial to 73 men who lost their lives in the war, many of them local volunteers, was unveiled by Major Sir Leslie Rundle, K.C.B. on 7 November 1904. (Photograph: J. A. Hargreaves)

Halifax territorials, 5 August 1914. On the day following the British declaration of war on Germany on 4 August 1914, Halifax volunteers enlist for service in the armed forces. Watched by large crowds, some 500 territorials marched from the Drill Hall at Prescott Street to board a special train at Halifax Station bound for a secret destination. During the first week, nearly 2,000 men left the Halifax district for some form of war service. In November, a Red Cross corridor train arrived in Halifax with 100 wounded soldiers from Ypres 'all showing the unmistakeable signs of having been among the shrapnel'. They were taken for treatment to the Royal Halifax Infirmary and St Luke's Hospital, Salterhebble. (Photograph: S. Gee)

was conscripted into the Leinster Regiment late in 1916 and was wounded on three occasions. May Elizabeth Pugh from Gerrard Street, Halifax, volunteered to join the Women's Army Auxiliary Corps and served in France, and when her eldest son, at the age of eighteen, graduated from the cadets and enlisted, she and her son managed to meet up in Calais. Edith Wormald, a nurse at St Luke's War Hospital, Halifax, met her future husband while he was recovering from injuries sustained in the war there; her elder sister Ethel was a Queen Alexandra's Imperial Nursing Reserve who served in Salonika. Saville Walker from Northowram served with the Royal Army Medical Corps. He was awarded the Military Medal for bravery, but was killed 1 October 1918, aged 21. Stanley Gilbert Dyson, born in Halifax to Julia and John Dyson, trained as a teacher serving at Halifax Parish Church (Senior Mixed) School before moving to Cambridge, where he enlisted in the Royal Army Medical Corps, before transferring to the Royal Flying Corps, which later became the RAF. He was severely wounded in action and died 1 June 1918, aged 26. Reginald Peel Pohlmann of the Halifax piano making firm was a pilot with the 25th Royal Flying Corps Squadron and lost his life during aerial combat with German Jasta 36 Squadron in 1917. Maynard Percy Andrews, headmaster at Hipperholme Grammar school, was aged 44 with three children when war broke out so would not have been conscripted. Nonetheless, he volunteered and was deployed to France in April 1915 along with former and current members of the school, but was killed in Flanders on 14 August 1915 whilst coming to the aid of wounded men. A young Halifax boy who sold postcards of himself to raise money for the Halifax Courier Comforts Fund to send supplies to men serving overseas became well-known locally as 'Little Khaki George'.[3]

There was evidence of strong minority pacifist attitudes within Halifax and its vicinity, such as that of Joseph Edgar Spencer, a plumber and glazier and a Christadelphian, who faced a military tribunal in Elland on 13 June 1916, and was assigned work of national importance at His Majesty's Factory at Gretna, making cordite, an explosive. David Millichope, however, has argued that 'once war had been declared local communities were broadly speaking staunchly supportive of the war effort'. Halifax was surprised by the outbreak of the war in August 1914, but soon offered sanctuary to Belgian refugees, with voluntary fundraising organisations bearing witness 'to an incredible self-help ethic that supported the troops at the front, their dependent families on the home front and returning wounded'. However, 'struggling local industry was revitalised by government orders for khaki cloth, machine tools and munitions', with Halifax contributing bomb release mechanisms and flame thrower projectors to the war effort. Millichope effectively dismissed claims for a Halifax provenance for the Tommy's iconic bowl-shaped steel helmet, which was indisputably patented in London by J. L. Brodie, although its manufacturing process may, he suggests, have derived inspiration from the metal-stamping expertise of the Halifax firm of Willis and Bates.

He later discussed the controversies surrounding alternative proposals for the official commemoration of the dead, including plans suggested by leading Halifax architects Joseph Walsh in 1917 and Charles Edward Fox in 1918, creating a

Halifax Cenotaph following its unveiling at Belle View 1922. (Photograph: S. Gee)

memorial garden and promenade with Wainhouse Tower as the focal point. The suggestion was rejected by the Halifax War Memorial Committee which met in April 1919, perhaps because 'its association with the status of a folly would detract from its dignity'. Ultimately Halifax Corporation opted for a replica of E. L. Lutyens' Whitehall Cenotaph located initially in Belle Vue Park before it was later moved to Cripplegate in 1988. Many businesses, villages, schools and sports clubs created Rolls of Honour, listing those who had volunteered to serve in the war. One example from Standeven & Co. Ltd, a worsted manufacturer based at Ladyship Mills, Halifax, lists the names and regiments of 66 employees who served during the war, thirteen of whom were killed in action. Frank Haigh has suggested that it was the shortage of young men which made a women's football match very popular on 11 November 1918, before peace rejoicings took place in the following year when the ex-servicemen were given a civic welcome and 120 Sunday Schools assembled to sing music of praise for peace and in a gesture of friendship Metz-en-Coutre in France was officially linked with Halifax.[4]

There were some 75 per cent fewer Halifax fatalities in the Second World War. As in the First World War, the majority of local casualties were men serving in the army (61 per cent), including Hanson Victor Turner, a 33-year-old Halifax Corporation bus conductor, the sole local recipient of a posthumous Victoria Cross, killed in action with the West Yorkshire Regiment in Burma on 6 June 1944. Others served with the 4th battalion of the Duke of Wellington's Regiment (redesignated the 58th Anti-Tank Regiment in 1938) in Norway, France and North Africa, landing at Salerno in September 1943 and continuing in action until the end of the war in Europe, or with the 68th Anti-Tank Regiment in the war in Singapore, many of whom suffered prolonged imprisonment by the Japanese. Losses were also sustained at sea in both the royal and merchant navies (13 per cent), and in the air (23 per cent), and women were amongst the Auxiliary Territorial Service and civilian casualties. Although Halifax escaped relatively unscathed from the German bombing offensive, eleven civilians were killed and ten injured when a 100kg bomb fell on Hanson Lane on 22 November 1940. The ten other local bombing incidents between June 1940 and December 1944 mostly involved the haphazard discarding of bombs and incendiaries after raids on Manchester and claimed no further casualties. Indeed, Halifax was considered sufficiently safe for King George VI and Queen Elizabeth to rest overnight in the royal train at Copley en route to inspect bomb damage in Liverpool in 1943 and for evacuees from Bradford, the Channel Islands, London and the South of England to be billeted in the town.

Peter Thomas, born in 1941, the author of a book on the Home Front in Halifax and the Calder Valley during the Second World War, relates the experiences of people from the locality living through the war facing the challenges of the blackout, rationing, bombing, an influx of soldiers and evacuees, issues for women and the experiences of the Home Guard. He contrasts living in Halifax, where Halifax 'never had to suffer the ordeal of a prolonged bombing "blitz" as did the nearby cities of Manchester and Sheffield', and concludes that 'the Second World War was fought on such an immense scale that it involved everyone'. For example, many local factories were pressed directly into the war effort, and with so many men conscripted into the armed forces, the pressure was on women to replace

Halifax suffered less than many larger towns and cities from bombing in the Second World War. However, on 22 November 1940 a single bomb dropped by a solitary German aircraft devastated Hanson Lane killing eleven, injuring ten and damaging over 500 houses, 37 of which were left uninhabitable. (Photograph: *Halifax Courier*)

them on the factory floor or by joining the Land Army to support the drive to produce more food. Civilians were also expected and sometimes compelled to engage in fire-watching or joining such organisations as the Auxiliary Fire and Ambulance Services, Air Raid Precaution or the Home Guard and contribute into successive war savings drives. Halifax and its neighbourhood became filled with incomers new to the area billeted in factories and church halls, or children arriving as evacuees in waves in 1939, 1940 and 1944, returning home when it was deemed safe to do so. Enduring friendships were formed in these circumstances. My own father, Ronald Hargreaves, serving in the Royal Engineers before serving mainly in the Middle East, was moved to Halifax after the bombing of the Royal Engineers barracks at Chatham by the Luftwaffe, and at the end of the war was demobbed from Shibden. My mother, Edna, visited him in Halifax in those early war years and they both formed friendships with a Halifax couple named Jack and Peggy Mottram and visits were exchanged long after the end of the war.[5]

Halifax auction during the Second World War. Alderman George Barker, Mayor of Halifax 1939–40, presides at an auction of a variety of plants, china, freehold property and livestock in aid of the allied war effort. The slogan reminds his audience that others have already given their lives for their country. The two world wars of the twentieth century resulted in larger numbers of local casualties than had been sustained in any previous international conflict. They also witnessed greater involvement by civilians on the home front in supporting the war effort. Shortly after this photograph was taken, Alderman Barker, a Siddal grocer, collapsed and died at the Crossley and Porter School speech day in July 1940. (Photograph: S. Gee)

Table 6.2 Halifax casualties in the Second World War

Year	Casualties
1939:	1
1940:	54
1941:	64
1942:	79
1943:	113
1944:	189
1945:	70
1946:	18
Total:	588

Source: T. R. Hornshaw, 'Calderdale and the wars of the twentieth century', *Transactions of the Halifax Antiquarian Society* 6 (1998), p. 130.

Population

The average age of death of the local casualties of both wars was almost identical at around twenty-six years of age. It is not surprising therefore that the carnage of international conflict accentuated the downward demographic trend in Halifax during the period 1914–45.[6] The population of the County Borough of Halifax declined by 2.4 per cent from 101,594 in 1911 to 99,183 in 1921 and by a further 1.1 per cent to 98,115 by 1931. At the first post-war census in 1921, it was evident that the population of the county borough was ageing, with more than one-third of the population aged 45 or over. This was in marked contrast to the mid-Victorian period, when only one fifth of the population came into this age group in the census of 1871. This changing age profile was a consequence of a decline in both birth and death rates and a net loss by migration from the region of a younger generation in search of more favourable economic opportunities elsewhere as the staple textile industries of the West Riding contracted, leaving Halifax and neighbouring Bradford among those towns with the highest proportion of native-born inhabitants in the 1920s and 1930s.[7] Moreover, a determination to improve family living standards in an uncertain economic climate, coupled with growing employment opportunities for married women and increasing educational opportunities for children, tended to foster smaller sized families with no more than three or four children, particularly amongst textile workers in the inter-war years. Alderman J. H. Waddington, an informed contemporary observer, commented in 1937 that whereas 'in former days', families had been generally large, 'in latter days they are generally small'. He had also been told that:

> young married people today say 'they are not having many children because they cannot afford them'. You never heard married people of 50 years ago talking that language.[8]

There were also continuing risks associated with childbirth three decades after the philanthropic mayoral bounty baby scheme. Indeed, maternal mortality figures remained high in Halifax until 1938, when the figures reached their lowest for twenty years.[9] The infant mortality rate in Halifax also remained higher than the national average throughout the period 1920–38, peaking at 98 deaths per 1,000 live births in 1921, then declining to 62 by 1930, only to rise again to 86 in 1933 before declining sharply during the rest of the decade to 57 in 1938.[10]

The economy: boom, bust and restructuring

The outbreak of the First World War resulted in an immediate shortage of raw materials, which brought the Halifax textile industry to an abrupt standstill. Moreover, since Germany had been one of the industry's most important overseas customers for tops and yarn, many exporters found themselves owed substantial debts by German customers. However, government orders for khaki and navy cloth for the armed forces soon created boom conditions for both larger firms like John Holdsworth's of Shaw Lodge Mills and smaller firms like J. E. Bentley and Co. of Dunkirk Mills. At Holdsworth's Shaw Lodge Mills, for example, from December 1914 until November 1915 overtime was being worked throughout the mill. Overtime hours were reduced in 1917–18 because of a government order restricting the consumption of wool, and in October 1917 the army ordnance depot requisitioned four floors of warehouse space for a boot repair depot. Nevertheless, during the period 1914–18 sales had soared from £189,000 to nearly £447,000 and profits from £3,900 to more than £40,000. As 'the largest firm of British moquette manufacturers', Holdsworths congratulated itself in a wartime advertising leaflet on having built up an industry at home 'which for many years was in the hands of the Germans'. Meanwhile, the largest British carpet manufacturing firm, Crossleys of Dean Clough, also utilised their spinning and weaving equipment for the production of millions of yards of webbing, blankets and khaki yarn for government contracts, while the firm's machine shops were turned over to shell production.[11]

But the stimulus of war was temporary. The inflationary wartime and post-war boom was followed by 'the great commercial depression' of 1920–21, when the Halifax Chamber of Commerce reported that 'the trade of the town and district came

John Holdsworth's Shaw Lodge Mills, by local artist Monica Lewin. Holdsworth's by 1914 was 'the largest firm of British moquette manufacturers'. (Photograph: G. Sutcliffe).

practically to a standstill and the textile and engineering trades practically received the death blow'. Adverse exchange rates, unsettled overseas markets, volatile wool prices and rocketing fuel prices brought trouble for many local businesses. Smaller firms such as J. E. Bentley and Co. struggled for survival, while larger firms such as Holdsworths faced intermittent short-time working throughout 1920 and 1921 and again in 1924, when a further local recession ensured a fall in Holdsworths' annual profits from an average of £43,000 between 1918 and 1920 to an average of £26,500 during the period 1921–24.[12] A return to the gold standard in 1925 at the pre-war parity, cuts in government expenditure, and the tight monetary restriction of a high bank rate created an unfavourable climate for industry. Consequently, when the Northern Joint Industrial Council, which had already imposed wage reductions of 5 per cent on woollen and worsted workers in 1921, attempted to secure further reductions in 1925 it provoked the largest strike and lockout in the industry's history. It was supported by nearly 12,000 workers in Halifax and paralysed all but nine local firms from the end of July to mid-August until a court of inquiry settled the dispute, ruling against the proposed reduction.[13] In 1925–26 local cotton firms also faced 'exceptional difficulties' following turmoil in overseas markets in China, Egypt and the Near East.[14]

Women in the burling and mending department, Standeven and Co. Ltd, Ladyship Mills, 1926. The company which had originated in Mixenden in the 1880s, subsequently moved to Ladyship Mills, Old Lane, Ovenden. Some 700 employees were engaged in designing, making and marketing worsted cloth in October 1926, when the factory was visited by the Prince of Wales. During the Second World War Standevens produced some 2,500,000 yards of khaki for battledress. However, the firm experienced increasing difficulties in the 1960s and finally closed in 1969. (Photograph: *Halifax Courier*)

The General Strike, which followed a dispute in the coal industry, was greeted with 'unparalleled enthusiasm' by the Halifax Branch of the National Union of Railwaymen', whose position was reported as 'unchanged' and 'solid' on 11 May. Although the General Strike was only a nine-day stoppage in May it was called out by the Trades Union Congress in support of the miners who remained on strike until November. However, Halifax's MP, J. H. Whitley, as Speaker of the House of Commons, declared resolutely that parliamentary business would continue by candlelight, if necessary.[15] It caused further disruption to the local textile industry, resulting in short-time working at Holdsworth's Shaw Lodge Mills for most of May 1926, and was blamed by Phyllis Bentley for the stroke which caused the death of her father, who 'saw ruin for the mill ahead'. However, the strike proved less devastating in its effects on Halifax than on some other industrial towns. Indeed, the editor of the *Halifax Chamber of Commerce Journal* concluded that Halifax had secured its 'fair share of business' during the year of the strike, which was 'reflected in unemployment figures showing a bare 2,000 in May totally unemployed, the lowest for many years' in Halifax. In October, when the Prince of Wales visited the town, he was impressed by the multi-coloured designs at Standeven's Ladyship Mills, where he observed all the processes of manufacture from raw wool to finished cloth. At Crossley's Dean Clough Mills he toured a factory which had succeeded in installing electric power and lighting despite the difficulties of the early 1920s.[16]

But this easing of economic difficulties was temporary. The complete collapse of world markets between 1929 and 1932, following the Wall Street Crash, produced distressing conditions throughout West Yorkshire. In 1930 the Northern Joint Industrial Council failed to secure agreement with the unions for further wage reductions to prevent 'the bleeding to death of the industry', and in June 1930, following a ten-week strike, a court of inquiry found in favour of wage reductions and the workers were obliged to accept the employers' terms. The employers proceeded to impose reductions of about 9.5 per cent in 1930 and 11.7 per cent in 1931, although a few employers only imposed a proportion of the reduction. Indeed, a handful of local family firms, where union influence remained weak, including Holdsworths, were again unaffected by the strike, 'the operatives turning up in full strength'.[17] However, intermittent short-time working continued at Holdsworths until November 1931, while at Crossley Carpets some workers were laid off and others obliged to work a three-day week during the slump.[18] The suspension of the gold standard in 1931 and the implementation of a cheap money policy with lower interest rates stimulated investment in the 1930s, but orthodox budgetary policy remained a restraint and other government measures had only a marginal impact on stimulating economic growth until rearmament began in the late 1930s.[19]

Following a revival in the railway trade and a return of confidence in the depressed motor coach industry, production at Holdsworth's Shaw Lodge Mills alternated between full-time and overtime working between 1932 and 1936, apart from one month in the autumn of 1934. As the firm developed a wider range of products, Holdsworths' net profits, which had averaged only £4,000 between 1925 and 1931, rose to more than £36,000 between 1932 and 1936.[20] The introduction of the Duravell process at Crossley Carpets under licence from Leas Fabrics of America, formally inaugurated by the Princess Royal in March 1933, enabled the company to manufacture a blend of nylon and viscose rayon and resulted in a sharp increase of trade with the motor industry. Local woolcombers and topmakers also increased their share of world trade during these years by a vigorous exploitation of new markets for semi-manufactured goods in Canada, Finland and China, and the artificial silk trade, which had been established in Halifax by 1928, also continued to thrive despite the recession.[21] By 1937, encouraged by tariffs on cheap foreign imports, there was also a growth in the domestic market. However, towards the end of 1937 the high levels of production in the Halifax textile trade began to slow down, when wool prices suffered from the deteriorating international political climate, bringing intermittent short-time working back to Shaw Lodge between September 1937 and 1939. Indeed, the shortage of work was so acute that the mills worked as little as twenty-five hours a week in July 1938 and profits fell from £33,000 in 1936 to £2,000 in 1938.[22]

After the outbreak of the Second World War, Crossleys continued to make carpets for the American market, but became increasingly involved in the production of webbing for military accoutrements such as respirator cases. Meanwhile the firm's machine shops were extended to produce ground equipment for the RAF and torpedo motors for the Royal Navy.[23] After some short-time working during the first year of the Second World War, Holdsworths' looms were kept busy weaving cotton canvas for khaki webbing and fabrics for hammocks, camouflaging and blackouts. The company also produced electrically heated linings for flying suits to keep flyers warm at high altitudes. Between 1940 and 1945 average annual sales rose from £268,000 to £378,000, but tightly controlled prices restricted average annual profits to around £30,000. The Ministry of Supply was the firm's most important single customer during the war, followed by the railway companies, furnishing and motoring firms. But by 1944 the firm was becoming increasingly concerned about the restrictive wartime regulations, the loss of normal markets and the future of the industry.[24]

The local economy experienced more than boom and slumps during this period: there was also a chequered history of restructuring, involving losers and winners. In manufacturing, events in the inter-war years ensured that there would be no long-term recovery of the textile industry in West Yorkshire. Overseas markets in the USA and the Far East were contracting, and local firms were operating within a shrinking world market.[25] Unemployment levels in the Yorkshire textile industry peaked at 25 per cent in 1931 and averaged 17 per cent between 1929 and 1936.[26] The inter-war censuses revealed a decline of 18 per cent in the number of textile workers employed in the county borough of Halifax from 15,612 in 1921 to 12,812 in 1931, though there was an increase of 3 per cent in those employed in clothing manufacture. The number of insured textile workers in Halifax also declined during the period 1935 to 1939, when Halifax had fewer textile workers than most of the historic centres of the textile industry in West Yorkshire with just over one-third of the number of textile workers as neighbouring Bradford and under two-thirds the number of Huddersfield.[27]

On the other hand, as early as 1918 the Halifax Chamber of Commerce, while recognising that textiles were still of 'first importance' to the local economy, also emphasised the growing importance of engineering, machine tool construction, boiler making, card-clothing manufacture and building supplies. Such industrial diversity ensured that Halifax never felt 'the pinch of industrial crises' as severely as single industry towns and protected the town from the worst effects of the economic recessions of the inter-war years.[28] A contributor to a publicity brochure published by the Halifax Chamber of Trade in October 1931 commented that while Halifax 'scarcely ever experienced a boom', it never suffered 'from those terrible slumps which affect such towns as are dependent on a single industry'. In 1936 Percy Saunders, the town clerk of Halifax, observed that 'distress has for a considerable time' been less prevalent in Halifax 'than in any other industrial town in the country'. Halifax's buoyant machine tool trade, for example, kept unemployment down to 6 per cent in 1937. However, W. H. (Billy) Hughes (1894–1981), a skilled wood-working joiner with F. and H. Sutcliffe in Hebden Bridge, and father of the poet laureate Ted Hughes and his brother, Gerald, went on short-time working in mid-1937 when most local factories were reduced to working only two or three

First World War munitions workers photographed in West View Park, Halifax. Most local engineering firms became engaged in intensive munitions manufacture during the war, often doubling shifts and employing auxiliary workers, many of them women. Asquiths specialised in the manufacture of shells; Butlers produced gun boring lathes and shell cases; Stirks contributed numerous gun and shell lathes; Sagars designed a propeller-shaping machine and Gledhills developed a bomb release mechanism. (Photograph: S. Gee)

days a week, and even applied in desperation for work with the government in Glamorgan in South Wales.[29]

Many local engineering firms had become engaged in intensive munitions manufacture during the First World War, often doubling shifts and employing auxiliary workers. Asquiths specialised in the manufacture of 9.2 mm shells; Butlers produced gun boring lathes and shell cases; Stirks contributed 'thousands of gun and shell-lathes'; Sagars designed a propeller-shaping machine to cut the blades for the Flying Corps aircraft; and Gledhills developed a bomb release mechanism. The war stimulated improvements in research and industrial organisation in the machine tool industry. Indeed, Butlers were the prime movers in the formation of the Association of British Machine Tool Manufacturers in 1917, a marketing organisation which promoted specialisation within the industry, with Butlers, for example, concentrating thereafter almost exclusively on the production of planing, shaping and slotting machines.[30]

The local engineering industry, however, also suffered severe disruption during the recessions of 1920–21 and 1924 and was 'the last to show any material recovery from the slump'.[31] Some local firms such as the United Brass Founders and Engineers Ltd, founded in 1910, which had invested heavily in new premises and plant in Spring Hall Lane 1916, were unable to sustain wartime levels of production

Asquith munition girls posing with heavy artillery in West View Park, close to W. H. Asquith Ltd's Halifax factory during the First World War. (Photograph: S. Gee)

during the post-war recession and the company sought voluntary liquidation in March 1920. Developments at Butlers' Mile Thorn site were also severely restricted by the slump when orders dwindled. Machines were built mainly for stock, and diversifications included toffee-making machines and presses for stuffing church hassocks.[32] As the heavy industries recovered from the coal dispute, however, the 'Halifax machine tool trade began to benefit'. But the total number of workers employed in metal manufacture in the county borough declined by 27 per cent between 1921 and 1931 and several local engineering firms, for example Oldfield and Schofield, were only rescued from impending bankruptcy by rearmament orders filtering through from the mid-1930s.[33]

Some firms secured major orders even during the most depressed years of the 1920s and 1930s. Asquiths obtained a contract from Dorman Long of Middlesbrough in 1924 for 40 drilling machines for the construction of the Sydney Harbour Bridge; Kitchen and Wade secured a very substantial order for drilling and boring machines from New Zealand Railways in 1926; J. and J. Mallinson supplied large numbers of lathes to assist the development of the nascent Indian cotton industry; while Butlers clinched a contract for some 200 planers, shapers and slotters from Stalinist Russia between 1931 and 1934. Cornelius Redman and Sons Ltd, following a management reorganisation and the redesign of their lathes and planers, also prospered despite the generally depressed state of trade, increasing their workforce from around 30 in 1927 to 115 by 1930. As Churchill Redman from 1935, the firm developed a new range of precision lathes and shapers, and in 1937 secured an agreement with Jones and Lamson of Springfield, USA, to build Fay automatic lathes under licence. This enabled the firm to extend their factory and increase their workforce to 200 by 1939.[34]

The Second World War provided another boost to the engineering sector. The machine tool factories worked round-the-clock on their standard lines, with some variations. Churchill Redman adapted their general purpose lathes for the manufacture of bomb cases; Greenwood Standard Gear Cutting Co. Ltd produced turret rings for tanks; Gledhills produced field service levels, scientific sun compasses, booby traps, aircraft components, tanks and torpedoes; while the newly established Ajax Machine Tool Co., taking the name of the cruiser adopted by Halifax during the war, manufactured many small drilling machines for government orders.[35] HMS *Ajax* is remembered in particular for involvement in the Battle of the River Plate in December 1939. As a result of aerial bombardment in the Midlands and South East, some firms were relocated in Halifax. Coventry Machine Tools moved into Stirks' premises at Ovenden, and Alfred Grahams, an offshoot of Siemens manufacturing marine electrical and communication equipment, came to Box Trees, Wheatley, after suffering bomb damage at Woolwich.[36]

On the other hand, both world wars adversely affected the process of restructuring. Sugar, butter and milk rationing in the First World War and the added burden of sweet rationing in the Second World War created problems for Halifax's developing confectionery industry. Supplies of confectionery for domestic consumption were severely restricted and the export business entirely lost. However,

Newspaper advertisement for Mackintosh's toffee, 1914. Enormous quantities of Mackintosh's toffee were despatched to the armed forces during the First World War and wartime newspaper advertisements, many of them based on suggestions from serving soldiers, depicted how Mackintosh's toffee helped along 'the weary hours' in the muddy trenches. For example, in the autumn of 1914 when the Allied troops were resisting the German invasion of Belgium and France, a full-page newspaper advertisement depicted the Kaiser standing astride Belgium and France glaring at a monster tin of Mackintosh's toffee resting on a map of the British Isles under the caption: 'Ah! that's what makes them fight so well'. (Photograph: J. A. Hargreaves)

during the First World War the food value of Mackintosh's toffee for those serving in the armed forces was recognised by the military authorities. Indeed, government orders accounted for a high proportion of the firm's wartime output. Moreover, one Halifax soldier serving on the western front later recalled that when he first went over the top: 'All he could remember was that he was eating "Mackintosh's toffee"'. Wartime advertisements for the firm, many of them based on suggestions received from serving soldiers, depicted how Mackintosh's toffee helped along 'the weary hours' in the muddy trenches. Nevertheless, during the First World War, there were difficulties since many male employees of the firm left for military service, while hundreds of the girls who had been accustomed only to wrapping toffee learned to handle deadly explosives or heavy shells in munitions factories. Indeed, John Mackintosh wrote: 'It becomes more and more difficult to steer our "toffee de luxe" ship through the troubled seas. We had over 1,000 workpeople before the War, and now we have not quite 250'.[37]

After a period of lean years in the mid-1920s, the firm began to expand. It established production plants overseas and acquired A. J. Caley's chocolate manufacturing business in Norwich, which enabled the development of the celebrated 'Quality Street' chocolate and toffee assortment, one of its most popular products in Halifax from 1936. During the Second World War, the firm's workforce was again depleted by conscription, and Harold Mackintosh, the son of the founder and managing director of the firm, became increasingly involved in the war savings movement. Production was also severely restricted through the rationing not only of the raw materials used in manufacture but also of the confectionery itself, and domestic consumption was halved. However, the destruction of the firm's new £700,000 manufacturing plant in Norwich by the Luftwaffe on 29 April 1942 resulted in the transfer of production and key personnel to Halifax, where the factories remained intact with plenty of spare capacity.[38]

The building industry too, in spite of ups and downs, managed to grow in this period. Although building work was curtailed during both world wars, the inter-war years witnessed a major expansion in the construction industry, which helped to mitigate the effects of the recession and may well have played a crucial role in the 1930s recovery. Indeed, the numbers employed in the local building industry rose by 25 per cent between 1921 and 1931, more rapidly than in any other local industry.[39] The expansion also stimulated the growth of the building supply industry. By 1930 Joseph Brooke and Sons of Lightcliffe had become the largest suppliers of roadway and building materials in the world, while other local firms patented Fulcherite reinforced concrete and Marshalite prefabricated stone.[40]

Meanwhile, the growth of the motor trade in the 1930s brought prosperity to another local firm which had pioneered the remarkable Catseye reflecting roadstud. The unique qualities of these roadstuds were their positioning in the road surface itself and the later development of a low maintenance self-wiping mechanism which helped to reduce accidents, in darkness and fog. Patented in 1935 by Percy Shaw, his invention was hailed in the House of Commons following his death as 'the most brilliant invention ever produced in the interests of road safety'. Reflecting Roadstuds Ltd at Boothtown achieved peak sales during the early wartime blackout, before the Japanese invasion of Malaya later restricted the availability of rubber; despite experiments with synthetic rubber the firm's output dropped dramatically. However, with Ministry of Transport approval, the Catseye was poised by the end of the war to resume production, which continues in its original premises in the twenty-first century.[41]

The most significant area of expansion for the future of Halifax, however, was the growth in financial services during the inter-war years. It is true that both the Halifax Permanent and the Halifax Equitable Building Societies disposed of the banks which they had sponsored since 1900 and 1910 in 1917 and 1927 respectively, and the demise of Halifax's own independent banking system occurred in 1919 when the town's oldest banks, the West Yorkshire Bank and the Halifax Commercial Bank were swallowed up in mergers (the former with Lloyds and the latter with the Bank of Liverpool and Martins). Nevertheless, the inter-war years also saw a remarkable expansion of the building society movement.[42] This growth was in part inspired by Keynesian economics involving Government intervention leading to the building boom of the inter-war years. This was allied to the vision and commitment of Enoch Hill, Managing Director of the Halifax Permanent, 1917–38 and chairman of the Building Societies Association, 1921–33, and Joseph Harger Mitchell, Managing Director of the Halifax Equitable, 1920–27.[43]

Although by 1918 the Halifax Permanent was the largest building society in the country, its branches were mainly based in Yorkshire and Lancashire, with a few agencies in Durham, Lincolnshire, Nottinghamshire and North Wales. Between

1918 and 1928, around 100 new branches and agencies were opened, including the first office in southern England in Shaftesbury, Dorset in 1919. It was followed in the early 1920s by agencies in Bournemouth, Plymouth and Worthing. In 1924, the first London office was opened at 124 Charing Cross Road by the Rt Hon. J. H. Whitley, MP for Halifax and Speaker of the House of Commons. A patron of the Halifax Permanent, Whitley represented a family of Halifax industrialists, Liberal in politics and Nonconformist in religion, who had been closely associated

Percy Shaw (1890–1976) Percy Shaw was born into a large family in Halifax in 1890 and left school at the age of thirteen to commence work as a labourer in a blanket factory, later developing a range of practical skills through a succession of jobs in welding, boiler making and machine tool construction. Having been a keen cyclist, he became one of the earliest motorists in Halifax and his concern to improve road safety derived from his experience of negotiating the hazardous, steep descent to Halifax from Queensbury. His invention of the Catseye reflecting roadstud was hailed in the House of Commons as 'the most brilliant invention ever produced in the interests of road safety'. *The Times* obituarist observed that his Catseye studs now marked 'traffic lanes on highways all over the world'. Not since the death, 200 years earlier, of John Harrison (1693–1776), whose marine chronometer enabled navigators to compute their longitude at sea within an accuracy of half a degree, had an invention by a Yorkshireman had such a universal impact on travel safety worldwide. This photograph shows Percy Shaw with the broadcaster Alan Whicker in Halifax in 1968. (Photograph: Yorkshire Television/Granada Visual)

VOTE FOR
SIR ENOCH HILL,
THE ANTI-SOCIALIST CANDIDATE & SAFEGUARD YOUR HOME.

LILYWHITE LTD   PHOTO PRINTERS, TRIANGLE R LONDON

Sir Enoch Hill (1865–1942). Born in Leek, Staffordshire, the eldest of seven children, he was selected from 300 applicants to succeed J. D. Taylor as secretary of the Halifax Permanent Building Society in 1903. He became Managing Director in 1917 and President from 1928 to 1938 and directed the remarkable expansion of the Halifax Building Society which resulted in it becoming the largest society in the world. He also served as chairman of the Building Societies Association from 1921 to 1933 and became a freeman of the City of London in 1924 and was knighted in 1928. He served as chairman of the Halifax Conservative Association and between 1922 and 1929 unsuccessfully contested four parliamentary elections at Leek and Huddersfield. (Photograph: H. Armitage)

with the development of the building society movement in Halifax almost from its inception. His father, Nathan Whitley, and uncle, John Whitley, business partners in a firm of card-clothing manufacturers, were trustees of the Halifax Equitable, and his brother, Brigadier-General Sir Edward Nathan Whitley, became a director of the Halifax Permanent in 1919 and later served as President of the amalgamated Halifax Equitable and Halifax Permanent Building Societies from 1938 to 1945. In his address, Whitley reflected that twenty-four years ago Halifax had 'got rid of him to London', but that now 'Halifax came to London itself ... offering to the less fortunate Londoners great benefits built on Yorkshire thrift'.[44]

The younger Halifax Equitable expanded rapidly in the decade after the First World War, advancing from the eleventh largest society in 1911 to second in 1924. In 1928 its assets of £14,044,972 were just under half the £32,936,510 assets of the Halifax Permanent. Both societies had common roots in the culture of nonconformity and thrift of the Pennine town and were led by a cross-section of representatives of the local banking, industrial and municipal communities. In a number of cases different members of the same families, most notably the Crossleys and the Whitleys, served both societies as directors or trustees, and so the announcement of the merger of the two societies on 22 September 1927, although it took the building society movement by surprise, quickly found strong backing from the membership of both societies. Following the merger, the Halifax directors proclaimed: 'the society is no longer a parochial institution; it is becoming nation-wide in its scope.' By 1934 the assets of the society had doubled to £92,600,000. Between 1935 and 1939 the rate of increase slowed down, but by 1939 the society's assets had almost trebled since the merger to £128,200,000, and during that period nearly 100 new branches and agencies had been opened.[45]

During the First World War, both Halifax societies made a major contribution to the war effort, facilitating withdrawals by subscribers for investment in war loans, the Halifax Equitable declaring that its main object was 'to turn as much money as possible into government channels'. Moreover, by the end of the war the Halifax Permanent had £1,300,000 and the Halifax Equitable £642,000 invested in government securities. In the Second World War, the society not only encouraged the public to maximise its savings but by 1945 had also invested £30,000,000 of its liquid assets in British government loans. Moreover, the appointment of a Halifax Building Society director, the toffee manufacturer Harold Vincent Mackintosh, as chairman of the National Savings Committee during the Second World War, conferred further national recognition upon the society. Mackintosh readily acknowledged that his early association with the building society movement in Halifax had provided the essential training for his later leadership of the national savings movement, which underpinned Britain's contribution to the Allied victory over Nazi Germany in the Second World War. Some 39,000 properties mortgaged to the Halifax suffered damage involving claims during the war, and Halifax House itself sustained heavy damage during the London Blitz in April 1941, when one employee of the society was killed and another injured.[46]

Halifax also remained an important retail centre during the inter-war years. Walter Brenard, the Mayor of Halifax, opening the fourth Halifax Chamber of Trade Shopping Festival and Exhibition in October 1936, declared that Halifax had 'steadily progressed' into a major West Riding shopping centre.[47] There had, however, been a number of recent changes in retail provision in the town. Alderman Harold Waddington, reviewing retail developments in the fifty years since he had started his apprenticeship in a large town centre store in 1886, observed that the major innovation was 'the change from the one-man shopkeeper to the multiple stores'. In his youth there were:

no cash furnishing companies, no hire purchasing shops, no Boots Cash Chemists, no Fifty Shilling Tailors, no Maypole Dairy Companies, no Woolworth's Stores, no Marks and Spencer's branches.[48]

Many smaller family businesses, such as Mitchell's ladies' and gents' outfitters, where Wilfred Pickles worked as a young shop assistant, benefited from the growing range of retail outlets. Pickles recalled that on Saturdays, in particular, 'the town had all the atmosphere of a big city, with its packed shops, people coming from smaller towns and nearby villages to shop, to watch a football match and go to the pictures at night'.[49]

The economy of Halifax during the inter-war years exhibited elements of both continuity and change. Notwithstanding the difficulties experienced by

Halifax gas and electricity stations in the 1960s, prior to closure. (Photograph: J. A. Hargreaves)

Halifax viewed from the east, in the late 1960s, with John Mackintosh and Sons Limited newly constructed premises in the foreground, Halifax Parish Church on the extreme right of the photograph and Halifax Town Hall in the distance, partially obscured by the tower of Square Church. (Photograph: J. A. Hargreaves)

the textile and engineering industries during the inter-war years, these staple industries remained the two largest employers of labour in the county borough of Halifax in the censuses of 1921 and 1931. Although the numbers employed in both industries declined between 1921 and 1931 by 18 per cent and 27 per cent respectively, textiles still employed 12,812 workers in 1931 and engineering 5,747 workers. Moreover, despite the growing pre-eminence of Mackintosh's in the confectionery industry during the period, the numbers employed in the food and drink industry in Halifax also declined by 6 per cent from 953 to 896, along with the numbers employed in mining and quarrying, woodworking and furniture manufacture and public administration. By contrast, however, the numbers employed in building and construction increased by 25 per cent from 1,221 to 1,530; personal services by 23 per cent from 3,424 to 4,199; commercial and financial services by 22 per cent from 4,203 to 5,127; the professions by 9 per cent from 1,322 to 1,441 and transport by 4 per cent from 2,857 to 2,953, indicating an expanding service sector.[50]

The census figures also reveal that textiles remained the largest employer of female labour during the inter-war years, though the actual number of women employed declined from 9,863 in 1921 to 3,677 in 1931. By contrast, there was a rise in the number of women employed in the commercial, financial, professional and service sectors, some in occupations which had been strongly male preserves before the First World War. The 1918 annual report of the Halifax Permanent Building Society, commenting upon the changes necessitated by the war, assured shareholders that every effort 'will be made to carry on the work of the society efficiently, with the help of the patriotic and capable female workers'. By 1921, no fewer than a third of the Head Office staff of the Halifax Equitable Building Society were women, four of whom had worked for the society since 1915.[51] In 1915, the first woman gas inspector was appointed in Halifax and in the same year the first local female telegraph messengers and tram conductors were employed. This trend was to accelerate in the period after 1945.[52]

Local government

During the first half of the twentieth century, which has been described by Dr John Stevenson as 'the heyday of local government', the functions of municipal government became more extensive in Halifax than at any time previously in the history of the town, although they became increasingly subject to central government direction. In 1903, following the Education Act of 1902, the local authority had taken over responsibility for state education from the school board. In 1930 it became responsible for the relief of poverty following the abolition of the Poor Law Unions. Moreover, despite the recommendation of the Desborough Committee that police forces in boroughs with populations of under 100,000 should be merged with their county forces, Halifax County Borough Council continued to be responsible for policing until 1968. The enforcement of public order within the county borough was facilitated from 1924 by the inauguration of the Halifax quarter sessions, which were replaced by the Crown Courts in 1972. Besides responsibility for education, social welfare and public order, the county borough council also remained responsible during this period for public health; the fire service; highways and transport; housing and planning; markets, baths, parks, libraries and art galleries; and the supply of electricity, gas and water.[53]

However, the rising cost of services brought increasing tensions during the inter-war years between the county boroughs of the West Riding and the West Riding County Council. Halifax and the other four original West Riding county boroughs had extended their boundaries between 1889 and 1912, divesting the West Riding County Council of some 33,000 acres of suburban land with a rateable value of £550,000. Moreover, between 1913 and 1915 the county's ratepaying land had been further reduced by the creation of three new county boroughs. So, when in 1919 and 1920 Halifax and six other county boroughs applied for boundary extensions which would have deprived the county of a further £2.23m in rates amounting to nearly one-quarter of the county's assessable rateable value, there was strong resistance from the county authority. In consequence, following an official enquiry, the Halifax proposal for an extension to its county borough boundaries by 11,264 acres, which would have augmented its population by 52,535 and its assessable rateable value by £242,811, was dropped. A further proposal in the Halifax Extension Bill of 1934 would have extended the boundaries of the county borough to include the urban districts of Sowerby, Luddenden Foot, Midgley and Hipperholme and the parishes of Norwood Green, Coley, Wadsworth and Heptonstall and parts of other adjoining urban districts, an extension of 24,826 acres with a population of 32,232 and rateable value of £148,226. However, this was rejected by a House of Commons Select Committee on 17 July 1935 after fierce opposition from the county.[54]

Denied the increase in rate revenue which would have accrued from an extension of its boundaries, the Halifax County Borough Council sought to exploit to the full its revenue from the management of municipally owned services such as gas, water, electricity and public transport. By 1939 the Halifax Corporation gas manufacturing plant was producing 900 million cubic feet of gas per annum for domestic and industrial consumption and 100 gallons of benzine. A policy of prudent investment and plant modernisation had reduced the debt on capital expenditure from £700,000 to £333,000 by 1935, and profits had also contributed some £409,000 to the relief of the rates. Halifax Corporation also supplied water to a population of 220,000, more than double that of the resident population of the county borough, in neighbouring authorities as far afield as Batley, Dewsbury and Morley in the east and Todmorden in the west via a mains network of more than 200 miles. Electricity was also supplied in bulk to the neighbouring Hebden Royd Urban District Council. In 1935 an additional plant was brought into commission, so that by 1939 the municipal electricity undertaking was declared to be 'in a particularly healthy financial position, affording supplies at the cheapest and most reasonable charges' and offering consumers hire purchase terms for the wiring of their homes and the purchase of electrical appliances such as cookers, wash boilers, vacuum cleaners and refrigerators. Until

Public Library, Belle Vue, Halifax, 1937. The first Halifax public library had been opened in rented accommodation in the Assembly Rooms in 1882, but in 1889 the Halifax Corporation purchased Belle Vue, the former residence of Sir Francis Crossley for £8,000, where it re-opened in September 1890. The extension of state education after 1870 provided the main impetus for the development of the service and sub-branches were established in several local board schools during the 1890s. During the 1920s pioneer purpose-built branch libraries were opened at Skircoat and Ovenden and other service points developed throughout the county borough. In 1930 a separate children's department opened at Belle Vue. In the photograph adult readers can be seen selecting books in the lending library on the northern side of the building. (Photograph: West Yorkshire Archive Service, Calderdale)

the late 1920s the Halifax Corporation Tramways earned substantial profits, some of which were used for the relief of the rates. However, during the period 1926 to 1930 increasing competition from motor buses resulted in huge losses and by 1929 the debt on passenger transport, including road reinstatement, amounted to £403,394. Alderman Arthur Gledhill, Chairman of the Tramways Committee, instituted an immediate policy of debt reduction, which almost halved the debt within ten years. Nevertheless, the committee ultimately decided to abandon its tramway routes in 1939, as it had its less extensive trolley bus routes in 1926, in favour of the more efficient motor bus services which it had operated in conjunction with the London, Midland and Scottish Railway Company since 1929.[55]

The town council faced constant pressure from the local business community for retrenchment in public expenditure throughout the inter-war years. The Halifax Chamber of Commerce, in the wake of the recessions of 1920–21 and 1924, expressed the hope that the 'prominent business men' in municipal politics would secure a reduction in local government expenditure in the interests of both 'industry and ... the whole community' so that local taxation should match 'the capacity of the ratepayer to pay'. Alderman Harold Waddington observed ruefully in 1936 that the proportion of shopkeepers on the Halifax Town Council had declined during the half century from 1886 to 1936 from nine out of a total of forty to eight out of a total of sixty, though half of the eight remaining shopkeeper councillors in 1936 served on the Finance Committee. An article published in the *Local Government Journal* in April 1935, however, confidently entitled 'Halifax: the outcome of civic initiative', emphasised the integral relationship which had been forged between civic administration and local industry, since the Corporation provided the 'essential framework of the industrial structure' with its facilities for 'the education, training, housing and health requirements of the workers'. It averred unequivocally that public services in the county borough were 'highly developed', 'well organised and maintained at a high pitch of efficiency' and concluded enthusiastically that 'thanks

The Institution, Gibbet Street, Halifax, formerly the Halifax Union Workhouse. The Board of Guardians of the Halifax Poor Law Union, which consisted of 22 townships, first met in 1837 and the workhouse, one of the first to be opened in the mid-Pennines under the New Poor Law of 1834, received its first inmates in March 1840. The workhouse was extended in 1856, 1864 and in 1870–71, when new infirmaries, fever wards, lunacy and reception wards, a dining hall and chapel were added at a total cost of over £30,000, providing accommodation for between 400 and 500 inmates, including children. In 1929, Poor Law Unions were abolished and the responsibilities of the Board of Guardians transferred to local authority public assistance committees. The workhouse subsequently became St John's Hospital and was demolished in 1972. (Photograph: J. A. Hargreaves)

MAIN BLOCK EAST, THE INSTITUTE, GIBBET ST, HALIFAX.

LILYWHITE LTD.
TRIANGLE HALIFAX

to the steadily pursued and skilfully administered policy of its Corporation' Halifax was rapidly solving 'the problem of combining intense and successful modern industrialism with a taste for civic beauty and amenities and a cultivated pursuit of science and the arts'.[56]

In reality, however, the development of secondary education in Halifax during the period 1914–45 in response to the Fisher and Butler Acts of 1918 and 1944 and the Hadow Reports of 1926–33 proceeded slowly and unspectacularly, suffering from the severe constraints on public expenditure during the inter-war years. The Fisher Act of 1918 raised the school leaving age to fourteen and abolished the half-time system, which had been extensively adopted in Halifax, where no fewer than 1,057 children were employed as half-timers as late as 1917. The influential Hadow Report on the education of the adolescent, commissioned by the Labour government of 1924 and commended to local authorities by Stanley Baldwin's Conservative government in 1926, paved the way for free compulsory secondary education for all. However, the Halifax Education Committee was much slower

Tram Smash, Lee Bridge, Halifax, 22 May 1915. On Saturday 22 May 1915, a Halifax Corporation tramcar ran out of control and overturned below Lee Mount on the Nursery Lane route. No lives were lost in this accident, but twenty passengers were injured. The shortness of the wheelbase and the narrowness of the gauge of the Halifax tramcars can be clearly seen on the upturned vehicle in this photograph. The steep gradients and narrow streets in the Halifax area necessitated a small, light tramcar, so the tracks were laid to a gauge of 3ft 6in, which imposed limitations on the technical development of the system and contributed to the cause of a number of serious accidents over the years. Halifax Corporation ultimately decided to abandon its tramway routes in 1939 in favour of more efficient motor bus services. (Photograph: J. A. Hargreaves)

than Labour-dominated Bradford to reorganise along Hadow lines. Although its proposals for reorganisation were accepted by the Board of Education in April 1929, it was March 1931 before the first changes were implemented. Full implementation was not completed until after the Butler Act of 1944.[57]

The Halifax Secondary School, absorbing the Junior Commercial School for girls, had operated at the Halifax Technical College since the war, and it became the Halifax Modern School in August 1931, providing 'an education of a practical character' for boys and girls aged from eleven to fifteen, while the Junior Technical School was to provide preparatory training for boys from thirteen to fifteen proceeding to apprenticeships in local trades. The voluntary schools and some smaller outlying schools continued to offer both elementary and secondary education on the same premises for some time, but pupils at the larger council schools were transferred at the age of eleven to senior schools at Siddal, Haugh Shaw, Battinson Road, Akroyd Place, Sunnyside, Lee Mount and Moorside. However, the reorganisation was not completed until 1949, and only one new purpose-built non-selective secondary school was constructed in Halifax in the whole of the period from 1902 to 1945, namely Ovenden School. Opened in 1937 by Kenneth Lindsay, parliamentary secretary at the Board of Education, it was built to serve an extensive neighbouring council estate development, and its impressive facilities, including a gymnasium, swimming pool and playing field, prompted James Parker, the town's first Labour MP, to declare that 'children attending Ovenden are better provided for than those attending Eton or Harrow'.

The Crossley orphanage received the Royal Assent to change into a secondary school in 1919, but it was only after 1944 that it was incorporated within the local authority. Meanwhile, in 1925 Heath Grammar School for Boys and in 1931 the Princess Mary High School for Girls had been brought under the control of the Halifax Education Committee. The former provided 'a good general education, fitting boys for a business career', higher education and the professions, while the latter, occupying new purpose-built accommodation at Craven Lodge, provided 'a sound, liberal education, leading up to the universities and preparing girls for home life'. However, it was most unusual for even better off Halifax girls to proceed to university in the inter-war years. Phyllis Bentley was the first girl among her family's acquaintance to take a university degree and as such was regarded as 'quite a rarity'. However, Dorothy H. Farrar (1899–1987), the daughter of a Halifax machine maker, after attending a boarding school at Arnside, proceeded to Bedford College at the University of London where she obtained a BA in English Literature and a Ph.D. in Psychology in 1931. A lifelong Methodist, she became a lecturer at the Wesley Deaconess College at Ilkley and only the second woman to serve as Vice-President of the Methodist Conference in 1952–53. But her educational experience was exceptional. Betty Hoyle, a local millowner's daughter, who married in 1939 Paul Bryan, a Cambridge graduate who later became MP for Sowerby, attended a boarding school at Bexhill and a finishing school in Switzerland. Her husband later recalled that the daughters of the Halifax manufacturing elite 'were not burdened with a serious education', while their brothers went to middle rank

Sunnyside Infants' School, Range Lane, Halifax. When Sunnyside Board School opened on 7 October 1901 it provided accommodation at a cost of £22,500 for 350 boys, 305 girls and 308 infants, although initially there were only 266 boys and girls and 99 infants on roll. The school's name derived from Sunnyside Street, one of the streets bordering the new school, and in 1931 the school attempted to live up to its name by adding a solarium to its buildings. This photograph of a nursery class in the 'Sun Room' taken in 1939 shows the early development of a purpose-built nursery unit. This self-contained, light and airy wooden structure in the school playground was equipped with a large sand pit, paddling pool, indoor and outdoor play areas, and camp beds, which folded out each afternoon to enable the children to have an hour's sleep. (Photograph: D. Baxter)

public schools, such as Sedbergh and Giggleswick in the north and Shrewsbury and Marlborough in the south, though rarely onwards to Oxford or Cambridge.

By 1939 there were 6,103 children attending council elementary schools, but only 479 secondary school children registered at the Halifax Modern School. A further 320 boys attended Heath Grammar School; 305 girls Princess Mary High School and 340 boys and girls Crossley and Porter School. In addition, some 1,787 children were enrolled at Church of England schools, including the Holy Trinity Senior School established at Savile Hall in 1933, and 1,146 at Roman Catholic schools. There was provision for children with special needs at Quarry House and Bermerside. School attendance continued without interruption during the Second World War, augmented at some schools by evacuees, after some initial precautions had been taken including the filling of thousands of sandbags for protection against air-raids. The war years saw a considerable expansion in the school meals service, because of food rationing and the employment of mothers in factories, and the inauguration of the youth service, which had 50 per cent of its expenses funded by the Board of Education from 1940.[58]

During the period 1914–45 increasing concern was expressed about the standard of living of working-class families. Addressing the Halifax Rotary Club in 1929, W. H. Ostler, clerk to the Halifax Education Committee from 1902 to 1933, had sharply criticised the 'foul conditions' in which so many Halifax children lived, emphasising the need for improved facilities in public health and housing. Phyllis Bentley, a volunteer helper in the 1930s at the Halifax Child Welfare Clinic, held in a Sunday school up Range Bank, 'a poor part of the town' consisting of 'rows of small old smoke-blackened houses, with bad ventilation and no modern conveniences', was profoundly affected by the 'extremely poor circumstances' of the mothers attending the clinic. She recalled that 'incipient anaemia showed in their pale gums; their hands were dirty and work-worn, their hair greasy, unwashed, often in curlers beneath their shawls' while their children were 'sometimes thin, sallow, fretful' and 'the orange juice, proprietary children's foods and remedies to counteract the effect of limeless water on growing bones' sold at wholesale prices were 'often beyond the pockets of the mothers'. Halifax Corporation attempted to cope, and by 1939 it provided a maternity and child welfare service, a school medical service, a general hospital with maternity and children's wards, an infectious diseases hospital, a tuberculosis sanatorium and dispensary, an orthopaedic service and a service 'for dealing with mental deficiency'.[59]

However, the question of birth control remained a more sensitive issue during the inter-war years. When a local committee of ladies assembled by Lady Hattie Fisher-Smith (the American born wife of the Halifax wire manufacturer Alderman Sir George Henry Fisher-Smith), following an initiative from the National Birth Control Association, applied to the local Medical Officer of Health for premises to start a family planning clinic, their request was declined. Undaunted, on 10 October 1934 in the Toc H rooms at 32 Clare Road, they opened the Halifax Women's Welfare Clinic, funded entirely by public subscriptions with the first medical officer, Dr Heynemann, and the first nurse, Miss Williamson, acting as unpaid volunteers.[60]

Other voluntary provision, financed by legacies and public donations, included extensions to the Royal Halifax Infirmary, two of which were opened by HRH The Princess Mary, Countess of Harewood, the most frequent royal visitor to the town, who was created the Princess Royal in 1932. Between 1921 and 1929 new maternity, open-air and X-ray wards, an orthopaedic outpatients' department, new operating theatres, a pathological laboratory, and a nurses' home were constructed. Other new buildings included the Sir Enoch Hill ante-natal clinic opened in 1940, financed partly from a testimonial fund set up to mark Hill's retirement from the Halifax Building Society. In 1937 a new purpose-built Halifax Children's Holiday Home, funded by voluntary donations, was opened on Norland Moor to provide 'a place of joy, where the foundations of true happiness, health and character will be laid'.[61]

Other environmental health improvements by the local authority included limited smoke abatement measures; slum clearance and road widening schemes in central

Halifax; the designation of residential, industrial and shopping zones in Ovenden, Bradshaw, Warley and Skircoat; the recycling or incineration of household and domestic refuse at a mechanical refuse disposal plant; new methods of street cleansing utilising mechanical appliances such as sweepers, gulley emptiers and sprinklers; the extension of the water carriage of sewage between 1924 and 1930; and the opening in 1929 of one of the most up-to-date abattoirs in the country by the Rt Hon. Arthur Greenwood, MP, Minister of Health. Further parks, recreation grounds and open spaces were also acquired. The extensive Shibden Hall estate, including the hall and grounds, was purchased in 1923 for the Halifax Corporation by Arthur Selby McCrea, son of the Victorian philanthropist Henry Charles McCrea. The park was officially opened for public use by the Prince of Wales on 15 October 1926 and the hall opened to the public as a period museum in 1934, following the death of its last resident, the antiquarian John Lister in 1933. Finally, Manor Heath, the former residence of the carpet manufacturer, John Crossley, was purchased by

Visit of the Princess Royal to Halifax, 1940. The Princess, in her capacity as Commander-in-Chief of the British Red Cross Society, presented first aid, nursing proficiency and service awards to nurses of the Halifax detachment of the British Red Cross Society at the Princess Mary High School on 13 July 1940. She also inspected the headquarters of the Halifax YMCA in Union Street where she met officers and members of the armed forces. This was her second visit to the town in 1940. She was the most frequent royal visitor to the town during this period. (Photograph: S. Gee)

Halifax Corporation for £18,500 in 1929, so that by 1936 there were no fewer than twenty-nine parks, open spaces and recreation grounds within the county borough.[62]

However, the evolution of municipal housing policies, within the framework of new government legislation during the inter-war years, had ultimately the greatest impact on working-class living standards. In 1921 there was a higher percentage of families living in overcrowded conditions, that is with more than two persons per room, in Halifax (13.2 per cent) and Huddersfield (13.6 per cent) than in Bradford (10.7 per cent) and Leeds (12.0 per cent). By 1931, the percentage had fallen in Huddersfield to 7.8 per cent, Bradford to 6.9 per cent and Leeds to 8.2 per cent, leaving Halifax with the highest percentage of overcrowding at 10.0 per cent. The Halifax figure had been more than halved to 5.2 per cent by 1935, though this was still a higher percentage than neighbouring Bradford (2.4 per cent) and Huddersfield (4.6 per cent). The first schemes projected under post-war Housing Acts in Halifax were for 36 houses at Spring Hall Lane and 26 houses at Heathy Lane. However, the Ministry of Health declared the tenders too high for acceptance, and the Council proceeded to erect 36 houses at Pellon by direct labour between October 1919 and December 1921 at an average cost per house of £1,183, exclusive of land, streets and sewers, during a period when building costs were exceptionally high. By 1929, when a total of 1,029 houses had been erected, the average cost of construction had fallen to £345. By 1939, 3,061 council houses had been constructed, with two to five bedrooms, but also including some

The proposed site for the Halifax Children's Welfare League Children's Holiday Home at Norland. A building appeal fund was launched in September 1935 by Halifax's first woman mayor Alderman Miriam Lightowler. In less than two years almost £4,000 had been donated and the home opened in June 1937. It aimed to provide 'a place of joy, where the foundations of true happiness, health and character will be laid' and enabled poor children from Halifax to take a fortnight's holiday in the open countryside above Sowerby Bridge. (Photograph: Irene Spencer)

pioneering old people's bungalows, flats and maisonettes, all vastly superior to previous working-class housing. Moreover, Halifax council rents in the 1930s were considered some of the lowest in the country.[63]

There were also a number of important private housing initiatives inspired by both the philanthropic tradition of Victorian Liberalism and the concern for social welfare issuing from the rise of Labour. Violet Mackintosh, the widow of the founder of the toffee manufacturing firm, built and endowed the John Mackintosh Memorial Homes adjoining the Albert Promenade for couples of at least sixty years of age with low incomes, preferably employees of the firm or members of the Queens Road United Methodist Church, which her husband had attended. Opened in 1925 by J. H. Whitley, accompanied by the Minister of Health, Neville Chamberlain, they consisted of twelve cottages, a matron's cottage and an assembly hall designed by W. B. Walton of Blackpool. Later, in 1929, Laura Willson and her husband George, one of the founders of Willson Lathes Ltd, who had been actively involved in house building schemes since 1922, helped trade union and Labour activists to purchase new houses in Atalanta Terrace, Pye Nest. These had toilets, bathrooms with hot running water, electricity in every room, and a gas fire in the kitchen.[64]

Local politics

In Halifax, as in many other West Yorkshire towns and cities, an anti-socialist alliance operated in municipal politics during the inter-war years, when it was common for a Labour candidate to be opposed by only one of the other party candidates. There was a three-year cycle of elections for the forty-five council seats, one councillor being elected each year for each of the fifteen wards. Fifteen aldermen were also elected for six-year terms of office by the councillors from within their own ranks, bringing the total membership of the council to sixty. In 1921, for example, in the seven seats where there were Labour candidates the contests were all between a socialist and an anti-socialist and in all the other seats except one, where there was a contest between a Liberal and a Conservative, anti-socialist candidates were elected unopposed. Moreover, the anti-socialist alliance was maintained in Halifax throughout the 1920s and 1930s, unlike in Leeds where the decline of Liberalism made it inoperative after 1925.

Remarkably, as in neighbouring Huddersfield, the Liberals remained the largest group on Halifax Council throughout the inter-war years. However, Labour was also doing as well as the Conservatives. The Labour Party's continuing interest in housing, family allowances, unemployment and education enabled the Halifax Labour Party to expand its membership from under 1,000 in 1935 to 1,200 in 1937. Liberal strength was concentrated in both the inner urban and suburban wards, including the Central, Copley, East, Northowram, Ovenden, Skircoat and Warley wards, and also in Kingston, where they vied with the Conservatives for the control of the ward. The Conservatives held sway in the Illingworth and South wards, while Labour dominated the Akroydon, North, Pellon, West and Southowram wards.[65]

Table 6.3 Municipal seats in Halifax, 1921–38

Year	Conservative	Labour	Liberal	Others
1921	16	15	27	2
1922	17	14	27	2
1923	15	15	24	2
1924	18	17	25	
1925	19	17	23	1
1926	18	17	24	1
1927	19	15	25	1
1928	17	17	25	1
1929	17	17	26	
1930	17	17	26	
1931	17	16	27	
1932	16	18	26	
1933	17	19	24	
1934	16	20	23	1
1935	18	18	23	1
1936	21	15	24	
1937	19	18	23	
1938	21	17	22	

Source: J. Reynolds and K. Laybourn, *Labour Heartland* (Bradford University Press, Bradford: 1987), pp. 59, 159.

Although women ratepayers had been allowed to vote in municipal elections since 1869 and stand for election as councillors since 1907, the councillors elected in Halifax during the inter-war years were almost exclusively men. Phyllis Bentley recalled campaigning unsuccessfully for the return of a woman councillor, commenting that it was 'typical of the period' that the attempt failed, and no woman councillor was elected in Halifax until 1924. Indeed, during the inter-war years Halifax had only two women councillors, the Conservative Miriam Lightowler and the Liberal Jennie Latham. Miriam Lightowler, the first woman to be elected to Halifax Town Council, had by common consent discharged her duties as the last chairman of the Halifax Board of Guardians 'zealously under difficult political conditions': when the Board ceased its operations in 1929 the pauperism rate in the Halifax Poor Law Union of 118 per 10,000 of the population was lower than both the West Riding and national averages. She subsequently became the first woman chairman of the Halifax Council Finance Committee and the first and only woman mayor of Halifax in the inter-war years. Moreover, Brighouse and Todmorden had to wait until after the war for their first women mayors and a quarter of a century elapsed before Halifax had another woman mayor. However, women had been admitted to the Halifax bench in 1920, and the number of women magistrates had more than doubled if only to eight by 1945.[66]

In parliamentary contests the Liberals worked with the Conservatives to secure the election of the Rt Hon. J. H. Whitley for the Coalition Liberals in 1918 with a majority of 18,100 over the Socialist Labour Party candidate Arthur McManus. McManus, a Clydeside trade unionist, attracted the support of Halifax trade unionists, especially engineers, but lacked the support of other Labour groups and polled only 4,036 votes. The electoral pact and divisions within the local Labour Party ensured that the outcome of the election was never in serious doubt and produced a turnout of only 53 per cent, the lowest for a parliamentary election during the period 1914–45, despite the widening of the franchise in 1918 to include all adult males and women aged thirty and over.

Labour Party divisions in Halifax had arisen during the First World War. James Parker, Halifax's Labour MP from 1906 to 1918, and Alderman Arthur Taylor, a leading local trade unionist, had upset many ILP members by their pro-war stance and active participation in the recruiting campaigns of 1914. Parker had declared that 'if Britain were defeated in the war, the working class would have everything to lose and nothing to gain', while Taylor, though professing his hatred of wars, had concluded that 'there were times when it was absolutely necessary that people should recognise war as inevitable'.[67] This created bitter dissension within the Halifax ILP and Trades Council, which had increasingly adopted an anti-war stance after 1916. For almost a decade between 1918 and 1928 this erstwhile Labour stronghold was unable to find a candidate to contest the single Halifax seat left after the introduction of the Representation of the People Act of 1918. The formation of the Halifax Labour Party in 1918 with its new constitution and local organisations also cut across the established links between the ILP and trades councils.

Moreover, the Halifax MP, J. H. Whitley, who became the first northern Nonconformist manufacturer to serve as Speaker of the House of Commons in 1921, had gained a national reputation as the initiator of the consultative councils between employers and employees which bore his name in 1917–18 and was held in high esteem locally for his commitment to education and his work with socially disadvantaged youths. Following his election as Speaker, an office he held with distinction, displaying 'a quiet tact, confident yet tolerant firmness and utter impartiality', J. H. Whitley was unopposed in each of the three elections between 1922 and 1924.[68] Whitley's election as Speaker was significant in a number of respects. He was the first Nonconformist Speaker and the only Speaker representative of religious dissent since the Restoration, thereby setting a precedent for other Nonconformist Speakers to follow. He was the first Speaker to be engaged in manufacturing, since speakers before him were drawn chiefly from the landed gentry and the law. Indeed, northerners have been relatively rare among those holding the office of Speaker, and Yorkshire incumbents even rarer. Before Whitley was called to the Speaker's chair over a century had elapsed since the previous Yorkshire Speaker, Charles Manners Sutton, had occupied it from 1817 to 1835. Both he and his Tudor predecessor Sir Thomas Gargrave (1495–1579) represented north Yorkshire constituencies as Members for Scarborough and York respectively. J. H. Whitley was the first Speaker of the House of Commons to represent a north of England industrial urban constituency and his only Yorkshire

Miriam Lightowler (1875–1958), photographed with the fire engine named in her honour, was the first woman to be elected to Halifax Town Council, the first woman chairman of the Finance Committee and the first and only woman mayor of Halifax in the inter-war years in 1934–45. (Photograph: *Halifax Courier*)

successor has been Betty Boothroyd who was born in Dewsbury, but was MP for West Bromwich, 1973–2000, becoming the first woman Speaker in 1992. Whitley was also the first Speaker since the Municipal Corporations Act of 1835 with extensive experience in municipal politics. Uniquely, he was the very first Speaker who engaged in innovatory philanthropy among the poor through the Halifax Guild of Help and with underprivileged young people in Halifax through his Recreative Evening School Gymnasium and annual Poor Boys' Camps. Also unusually, but like his immediate predecessor, the Conservative Speaker James Lowther, later Viscount Ullswater, he was elected Speaker after serving previously as Chairman of the Committee of Ways and Means and Deputy Speaker. Whilst his Speakership, curtailed by ill health, was relatively short, his effective chairmanship of committees of the House since 1910, even continuing sitting through the General Strike in 1926 and capably dealing with such complex and contentious issues as Irish Home Rule, significantly expanded his impact and service in these roles. If his progression to the chair was somewhat unusual, his lack of progression to the House of Lords in retirement was astonishing to many of his contemporaries in that he declined, for personal reasons linked with his own and his son Percival's involvement in social work in Halifax, the accustomed offer by George V of the hereditary viscountcy which had become the expected reward for service as Speaker since 1789. Whitley's determination and impartiality led him to his subsequent role as chairman of the governors of the BBC. In this role

HALIFAX R.E.S. GYMNASTIC TEAM.
Winners of the International Competition (Adams Shield), 1905.

G.P.Smith, C.Eastwood, W.Greenwood, J.H.Whitley,Esq.,M.P., J.C.Collins, J.R.Granger, A.Lumb, A.W.Haddon, R.Hirst
(Assistant Hon. Sec.) *(Instructor.)* *(PRESIDENT.)* *(Captain.)* *(Hon. Sec. & Treas.)* *(Trainer.)*
E. Dyson, W. Hirst, G. Marsland, H. Cooke,
I. J. Lumb, L. Chapman.

J. H. Whitley and the Halifax Recreative Evening School championship–winning Gymnastic Team, 1905. (Photograph: B. Mellor)

J. H. Whitley's voice was the first to be heard on air in introducing King George V in the historic first Royal radio broadcast to Britain and the Empire on Christmas Day of 1932. He had earlier achieved distinction as Chairman of the Royal Commission on Labour in India from 1929 to 1931.[69]

When he resigned in 1928, however, the Labour Party had recovered sufficiently to secure the election of Alderman Arthur W. Longbottom, a former Mayor of Halifax, as his successor as MP for Halifax. In a three-way contest, he was returned for Labour at the by-election with 17,536 votes, a majority of 4,951 over the Liberal and Conservative candidates, who polled 12,585 and 10,804 votes respectively. Although Labour remained a minority group within the Halifax Town Council because of the operation of anti-socialist coalitions at municipal elections, it was able to achieve success at parliamentary elections in an open contest, winning on a minority of votes. In the general election of the following year Longbottom retained the seat for Labour with an increased majority of 7,063 over his Conservative and Liberal opponents, Gilbert Gledhill and Elliot Dodds, who polled 16,713 and 15,823 votes respectively, in the highest turnout of electors during the period 1914–45. The Conservatives had increased their share of the vote to come second, leaving the Liberals in third place. Longbottom's share of the vote dropped slightly and was below the Labour average for West Yorkshire, but in his victory speech in Bull Green, he declared that the result proved 'conclusively that Longbottom for Halifax is as safe as the rock of Gibraltar'.[70]

His confidence, however, proved misplaced when national events resulted in a change of political climate. Following the collapse of Ramsay MacDonald's second

Labour government in August 1931 after it attempted to reduce unemployment benefit by 10 per cent, MacDonald further alienated many Labour supporters by his agreement to lead a National Government in coalition with the Conservatives and National Liberals. Consequently, in the general election of October 1931, the Conservative Gilbert Gledhill, youngest son of George H. Gledhill, founder of the local cash register manufacturing firm, topped the poll with 36,731 votes, taking 65.7 per cent of the vote. The National Government won a landslide victory, and the election proved disastrous nationally for the Labour Party, which had been damaged by MacDonald's attempt to reduce unemployment. In Halifax, Longbottom was clearly ousted by Liberal voters supporting the National Government. However, in view of Labour's performance nationally, he did well to poll 16,601 votes and maintain the same percentage share of the vote which he had obtained in 1929 (29.7 per cent), even though this again fell below the West Yorkshire average. F. Sykes, standing as an anti-National Government candidate after the local Liberal Association had decided not to put forward a candidate, polled 2,578 votes. Gledhill retained the seat for the Conservatives in 1935, but

Halifax Boys' Camp, Filey during the inter-war years. This undated photograph shows poor boys from Halifax on a summer camping holiday on the east coast. This annual Halifax Boys' Camp was initiated as a charitable venture in the 1880s by J.H. Whitley. In 1892, Whitley became a borough magistrate and in the following year was elected a town councillor. He remained a member of the town council until 1900, when he entered Parliament as Liberal member for Halifax. After a distinguished parliamentary career, he served as Speaker of the House of Commons from 1921 to 1928 and subsequently as chairman of the Royal Commission on Labour in India from 1929 to 1931. (Photograph: West Yorkshire Archive Service, Calderdale)

with a considerably reduced majority of 2,632 votes, indicating, perhaps, that at least some Liberals who had voted National in 1931 were now willing to support Labour in order to challenge the Conservative-National candidate. Longbottom, who came second with 21,471 votes to Gledhill's 24,103, increased his share of the vote to 39.5 per cent, a figure above the West Yorkshire average, indicating the strength of Labour's recovery, while A. Mitchell for the Liberals came third with 8,736 votes.[71]

In 1945, Winston Churchill was given a 'rousing reception' when he addressed an estimated 20,000 strong crowd in Bull Green in June, a tribute to his wartime national leadership. He urged his audience to let 'philosophical discussions about

Visit of Winston Churchill to Halifax, 27 June 1945. Winston Churchill was given 'a rousing reception' when he addressed an estimated 20,000-strong crowd in George Square during his post-war election campaign tour of the industrial north. His speech in support of the Halifax Conservative candidate, Gilbert Gledhill, the sitting MP, appealed to the patriotic sentiment which had enabled Britain to achieve victory over Nazi Germany. He declared: 'By our firmness of character, by our moderation of behaviour in every way, by our good and settled state of law, we have raised ourselves in the storm of war to the very van of the conquering nations and by preserving those characteristic qualities of the British, and I may say of the Yorkshire character, we shall continue to march forward at the head of nations'. Nevertheless, Labour was swept to power in the ensuing general election, including Dryden Brook for Halifax.
(Photograph: S. Gee)

the future system of society stand aside until the main practical jobs we have on hand are carried through', such as the provision of housing which would be treated 'as if it were a military operation'. Nevertheless, Clement Atlee with his vision of a welfare state, swept Labour to power in the ensuing general election, winning 21 of the 23 West Yorkshire seats, including Halifax, Sowerby and Elland. Dryden Brook, a wool merchant and Halifax Labour Councillor came top of the Halifax poll with 25,605 votes, securing a majority of 10,781. Gilbert Gledhill, the Conservative came in second place with 14,824 and the Liberal candidate Arnold Gelder a close third with 14,631 votes. Labour had secured its highest share of the vote (46.5 per cent) in any parliamentary contest, and the Liberals their highest number of votes and highest share of the vote since 1929 on a turnout of 77.4 per cent. The former Conservative vote appears to have defected to Labour and the Liberals in somewhat equal measure, giving Labour its majority. It remained to be seen whether this Labour triumph would survive the post-war experience.[72]

Table 6.4 Parliamentary election results in the Halifax constituency, 1918–45

Election	Turnout (%)	Candidate	Party	Votes	share (%)
1918	53.4	*J. H. Whitley*	Lib	22,136	84.6
		A. McManus	SLP	4,036	15.4
1922		*J. H. Whitley*	Lib	Unopposed	
1923		*J. H. Whitley*	Lib	Unopposed	
1924		*J. H. Whitley*	Lib	Unopposed	
1928	78.7	*A. Longbottom*	Lab	17,536	42.8
		H. Barnes	Lib	12,585	30.8
		F. S. Crossley	Cons	10,804	26.4
1929	81.3	*A. Longbottom*	Lab	23,776	42.2
		G. Gledhill	Cons	16,713	29.7
		G. E. Dodds	Lib	15,823	28.1
1931	80.5	*G. Gledhill*	Cons	36,731	65.7
		A. Longbottom	Lab	16,601	29.7
		F. Sykes	Ind Lib	2,578	4.6
1935	76.9	*G. Gledhill*	Cons	24,103	44.4
		A. Longbottom	Lab	21,471	39.5
		A. Mitchell	Lib	8,736	16.1
1945	77.4	*D. Brook*	Lab	25,605	46.5
		G. Gledhill	Cons	14,824	26.9
		A. Gelder	Lib	14,631	26.6

Source: F. W. S. Craig (ed.), *British Parliamentary Election Results, 1918–1949* (Glasgow 1969), p. 140.

What the contests for 1918 to 1945 also indicate is that all parties were largely competing for the middle ground. This is confirmed by the limited appeal in Halifax of parties of the extreme right and left such as the British Union of Fascists and the Communist Party of Great Britain, neither of which fielded candidates in parliamentary elections in Halifax during the inter-war years. Moreover, Edward Kennedy, a Communist candidate, who had suffered four months' imprisonment for his part in a demonstration in Todmorden in 1932, polled only 74 votes in a municipal election in Halifax North Ward in 1933, against Labour's 1,034. However, there was some enduring sympathy locally for Ralph Fox, a talented local author killed in action in the Spanish Civil War in 1937. Born into a middle-class Halifax family in 1900, he was educated at the Heath and Bradford Grammar Schools and Oxford University, where he gained a first-class degree in modern languages. A prolific writer and lecturer, he became a founder member of the British Communist Party in 1920. On the outbreak of the Spanish Civil War, he was one of the first volunteers for service with the International Brigade and within six weeks of enlisting he was killed in heroic circumstances in heavy fighting around the town of Lopera near Cordoba in southern Spain.[73]

During the growing international crisis of the later 1930s, the novelist Phyllis Bentley, who had become a crypto-socialist during the 1920s, sensed a growing opposition to European Fascism and the National Government's policy of appeasement both within her own staunchly Conservative, middle-class family and amongst the wider Halifax public. Indeed, in February 1938, she appeared on a public platform in opposition to the government's recognition of the Italian occupation of Abyssinia, and in November 1938 she wrote to the *Yorkshire Post* repudiating Chamberlain's appeasement of Hitler, following which, she later recalled, 'some Halifax shopkeepers … murmured in my ear their thanks'. She subsequently joined the ARP organisation, attended anti-gas classes and qualified to drive an ambulance. On 26 May 1940, following the Nazi occupation of Holland, Belgium and northern France, she recalled that, although an agnostic, she 'was proud to march in ARP uniform in the mayoral procession' to Halifax Parish Church to observe a national day of prayer for the desperate international situation. By 1940 political divisions in Halifax as elsewhere had been subsumed in united opposition to the tyranny of European Fascism.[74]

Culture: religion and recreation

The economy and the politics of Halifax from 1914 to 1945 had experienced discontinuities while retaining strong links with the past. Could that also be said of the cultural life of Halifax during the inter-war years? One indication is that the churches and chapels which had largely blessed the First World War, as they were later to accept the grim necessity of the Second World War, took a prominent role in celebrating the peace. After the armistice in November 1918, a local Congregational minister, the Revd Henry Iremonger, proclaimed in Halifax: 'The men who fought for freedom have commenced a task which is left for us to fulfil. Peace is the end of destruction and the beginning of construction.'

Moreover, a Sunday school celebration at the Thrum Hall Rugby Ground became the focus of the town's peace thanksgiving following Germany's signature of the Treaty of Versailles on 28 June 1919, indicating the continuing influence of religious life in the town, notwithstanding the trauma of the recent conflict. It was a remarkable occasion and 'one of those great scenes which those who saw it will never forget', commented the *Halifax Courier*. The gathering concluded with expressions of jubilation as 'people leapt to their feet, shouted until they were hoarse and waved handkerchiefs and hats', before 'joining in the singing of the National Anthem and the Doxology'.[75]

No fewer than 120 local Sunday schools had taken part in the Thrum Hall celebrations, and one local commentator, the toffee manufacturer John Mackintosh, writing to the *Halifax Courier* in 1919, repudiated any suggestion that the churches were in decline following the experience of war:

> It is not true to say that the churches are empty in England, and whoever says so is wrong ... My own church (Queen's Road United Methodist Church) has 250 members and more adherents. We have 400 scholars and about 50 teachers. There is something taking place nearly every night in connection with one department or another.[76]

Phyllis Bentley as an ambulance driver, 1939. Phyllis Bentley confided in her autobiography that as the approach of war became imminent 'with many thousands of other anxious citizens I joined the A.R.P. (air raid precautions) organisation, attended anti-gas classes and qualified myself to drive an ambulance', which was not without its lighter moments. 'The huge ramshackle old vans on which we were given tuition', she continued, 'were most exhausting and difficult to handle – after a prolonged wrestle with one on an afternoon amid the West Riding hills, or worse still on a blackout practice at dead of night, my own car felt like a perambulator'. In the event, however, there were relatively few air attacks on Halifax during the war and she was never required to drive an ambulance in an air raid. (Photograph: J. A. Hargreaves)

While Primitive Methodism and Wesleyanism in Halifax experienced a further spurt of growth in the 1920s, the United Methodist Church, despite Mackintosh's conviction of its continuing vitality, displayed a declining rate of membership recruitment in Halifax virtually throughout the whole of the period from 1908 to Methodist re-union in 1932. Indeed, the Revd D. B. Proudlove, a local United Methodist Church minister, acknowledged in 1929 that while the town was noted for 'its chimney stacks and church steeples', Halifax with its four Wesleyan Circuits, two Primitive Methodist Circuits and four United Methodist Circuits served by eighteen ministers was 'somewhat overchurched'. Indeed, he questioned the need for so many spacious Methodist churches within such close proximity of each other near the centre of the town.[77]

His concerns about a superabundance of chapel accommodation were echoed later in 1937 by Alderman J. H. Waddington, surveying the changes which had occurred during the previous fifty years:

The number of churches and places of worship in Halifax today is the same as it was 50 years ago, but what a difference there is in the attendance on the Sabbath Day, while week-night preaching has practically gone out … Today with a 25 per cent larger population, the attendance at church is not half what it was when I was young. Then, too, the great Sunday School festivals which were held in the Piece Hall are merely items of history today … In those days what big enjoyable Sunday School treats were held on Whit-Monday and Whit-Tuesday in gardens and fields, sponsored by officers of the Church of England and Nonconformist churches and chapels.[78]

United Sunday Schools Peace Commemoration, Thrum Hall, 28 June 1919. Children and teachers from some 120 local Sunday schools gather in an act of thanksgiving for the signing of the Treaty of Versailles, which formally concluded the peace settlement at the end of the First World War. The event, attended by thousands, provides evidence of the continuing influence of religious life in the town, notwithstanding the trauma of the recent conflict. It was a remarkable occasion and 'one of those great scenes which those who saw it will never forget', commented the *Halifax Courier*. (Photograph: *Halifax Courier*)

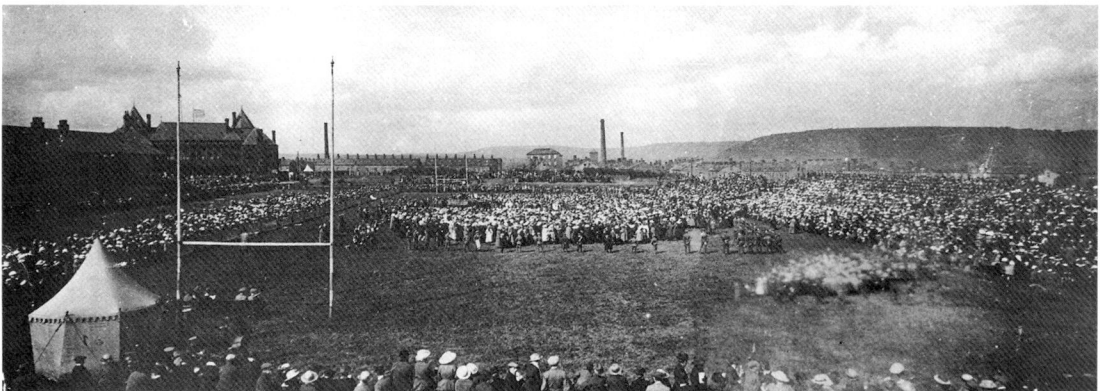

Similarly, the poet, Ted Hughes, also discerned similar changes between the wars in his native Calder Valley: 'throughout my lifetime, since 1930, I have watched the mills of the region and their attendant chapels die'.[79]

Even the achievement of Methodist reunion by 1932 and increased co-operation between Anglicans and Nonconformists in the town during the vicariate of Bishop George Frodsham from 1920 to 1937 failed to revive spiritual confidence and halt the decline of institutional Christianity as it struggled to compete with the increasing range of alternative secular leisure activities during the inter-war years. For example, at the AGM of the Bradley Hall Golf Club in March 1921, Frank Cookson, the secretary reported that a card ballot in 1920, indicating 50 votes in favour and 35 votes against playing golf on Sundays had determined that 'golf on the Sabbath was played for the first time in the history of the club' on 2 May 1920. As Dr Simon Green concluded in his study of religious organisations in Halifax, Denholme and Keighley, 'some time during the 1920s the local religious classes lost heart. They ceased to believe in their mission to evangelise the nation', which was now capable of making 'increasingly effective decisions about which organisations to devote its loyalty (and its time and money) to'. The 'much-heralded "threat" of the Labour Party, or the Sunday Lecture Society, or even of various bicycle clubs' became a real distraction from religious association for an increasing number of men and women after 1920.[80]

Alternative leisure activities beckoned. There was a further shortening of working hours in the woollen and worsted industries from 55.5 hours to 48 hours in 1919, and by 1945 a standard working week of 45 hours had been secured by national agreement. Employers appeared increasingly sympathetic to the leisure interests of their employees. In March 1937, for example, Shaw Lodge Mills closed half an hour early so that workers could attend the third round Rugby League cup tie between Halifax and Castleford, while in 1939, the engineering firm F. Pratt and Co. Ltd gave their workforce Saturday morning off and paid the return fares for 200 employees to travel to Wembley to watch Halifax play in the Rugby League Challenge Cup Final. Moreover, during the inter-war years, before annual holidays with pay became compulsory, the Halifax Building Society developed a programme of 'co-operative organised holidays' for their staff, granting one-third of the scheduled cost to employees who took part in them. Starting with motor tours of Devon, more exotic destinations were later chosen, with cruises to Norway, the Baltic and the Canary Islands. Indeed, the travel writer, William Holt, encountered holiday makers from Brighouse and Halifax, 'the sort of people who might otherwise have gone to Blackpool', singing music-hall songs in the Hotel Fontaine at Ostend in August 1934, but destined for a sightseeing coach tour taking in quaint places like Middelburg as well as the Great War battlefields. Meanwhile, the annual wakes week holiday established before 1914 continued a more informal tradition of communal holidays at seaside locations during the inter-war years when factories closed and large sections of the local population travelled to such popular resorts as Blackpool, Cleethorpes, Great Yarmouth, Morecambe, Scarborough, Skegness and Southport.[81]

For those who stayed at home, local beauty spots, parks and pleasure gardens enjoyed continuing popularity during the 1920s and 1930s. At Sunny Vale, Hipperholme, managed by the Bunce family until 1945, up to 100,000 visitors each year arrived by tramcar or train to sample the delights on offer. These included trips on the lake by steamer, lakeside rides on the miniature railway, and dancing in the open air. Indeed, the craze for dancing was evident across Halifax society during the inter-war years. Phyllis Bentley recalled attending weekly dancing classes in order to participate in the proliferation of tea dances and private evening dances at local hotels, as well as engaging in other recreational activities including table-tennis and badminton. Elsie Driver became a keen amateur gymnast after enrolling at a night school class aged 23 and performed pyramids at a church gala in 1921. Two Fives courts were constructed at Crossley and Porter School in 1928, whilst pupils were photographed playing croquet on the lawn in the 1930s. There were also good attendances at local hospital charity events and at the Great Yorkshire Show, which attracted record attendances when it was held in Halifax in 1928.[82]

There was a phenomenal growth in spectator sport in Halifax during the inter-war years. The Halifax Rugby Union Club, founded in 1919 and placed on a firm footing with the backing of Sir William Bulmer, moved to Ovenden Park

Office staff excursion, John Holdsworth and Co., Shaw Lodge Mills. This photograph, taken in the 1920s, shows the office staff of John Holdsworth and Co., worsted spinners and manufacturers of Shaw Lodge Mills, about to set off on a staff outing by charabanc, a popular form of transport during the inter-war years. The majority of the staff are women, well wrapped up for a ride in the open air. In the background can be seen part of the vast industrial complex which, by the end of the nineteenth century, as a late-Victorian directory observed, had 'assumed gigantic proportions' affording 'an example of organised technical industry not surpassed anywhere in the Yorkshire textile trade'. (Photograph: J. A. Hargreaves)

Sunny Vale Pleasure Gardens, Hipperholme, were opened by Joseph Bunce in 1883 and remained in the ownership of the Bunce family until 1945, when they were sold to Fred Thompson of Cleveleys. In their Victorian and Edwardian heyday they annually attracted 100,000 visitors. In the 1920s and 1930s, 'Sunny Bunce's', as they were affectionately known, enjoyed continuing popularity, with regular open-air dancing to local bands. Local author, Eve Chapman, recalled: 'I suppose what both we and the band lacked in elegance we made up for by enthusiasm, as we clumped around in our ordinary shoes, the boys probably in heavy boots, to the steady beat of brass band instruments, showing off our waltzing, our valeta, the newest foxtrot, the military two step or even the intricacies of the lancers'. (Photograph: J. A. Hargreaves)

in 1925 and won the Yorkshire Cup three years in succession from 1926 to 1928. The Halifax Rugby League Football Club, making a number of shrewd signings in the 1920s of both former rugby union players and players from more severely depressed areas than Halifax, such as Dai Rees from Wales and Andrew Murdison from Scotland, won the Rugby League Challenge Cup for the first time since 1904 in 1931, with a 22–8 victory over York at Wembley. To mark the victory, twenty-two fog detonators were set off as the train carrying the returning team arrived at Halifax Station to a rapturous reception from a crowd estimated at 100,000. The scenes were repeated in 1939, when Halifax beat Salford 20–3. In 1914, Halifax Town AFC secured its first trophy when it won the Bradford Charity Cup, only three years after the club's foundation. In 1919 the club moved from Sandhall Lane to a rather less accessible ground at Exley and in 1921 to a new stadium at the Shay, where over 10,000 spectators at their first league match on 3 September saw Halifax Town achieve a 5–0 victory over Darlington. Halifax Town also reached the fifth round of the FA Cup in 1932–33 and became Division 3 North Runners-up in 1934–35. However, finance remained a recurring problem.[83]

Amongst various expedients to achieve financial solvency was a Speedway, in action from 1928 to 1951, initially until 1929 at Thrum Hall Cricket Ground, using

The Halifax Rugby League team returns home with the Rugby League Challenge Cup, 1939. The team had beaten Salford by 20 points to 3 against all predictions at Wembley in the Rugby League Challenge Cup Final. Led by the Lee Mount Brass Band, the victorious team's open-topped bus passes through crowds of supporters in Bull Green en route to a civic reception at Halifax Town Hall. Within four months, local sporting fixtures would be disrupted by the outbreak of the Second World War. (Photograph: S. Gee)

a cinder track which had been previously used for pedal cycle races. Attendance at the opening event was estimated at 11,000, though it subsequently averaged at around 5,000, 'with spectators clinging to telegraph poles and perched precariously on walls and other vantage points'. Indeed, notwithstanding rising unemployment and 'a great deal of short time working in the textile industries', dirt track racing proved more successful in Halifax than in neighbouring Bradford or Huddersfield, however the amount received by the cricket club had dropped from £517 1s. 2d. to £144 by 1930, even though Halifax came third out of the eleven towns competing in the Northern Dirt Track League in 1929. Greyhound racing, which replaced speedway bikes at Thrum Hall in 1931, failed to attract any more than 5,000 spectators after 1931, however. The track remained independent of any governing body for 44 years before it affiliated with the National Greyhound Racing Club in 1975, ceasing to run under National Greyhound Racing Club rules in 1979.[84]

Another new attraction which achieved a popular following was wrestling, in Halifax particularly associated with the larger than life character Shirley Crabtree (1930–97), whose televised shows ran for nearly twenty years, skilfully promoted by his brother Max. From 1974 he adopted the name and persona of 'Big Daddy' and opened a night club in Halifax with the same name. A John Bull-like character,

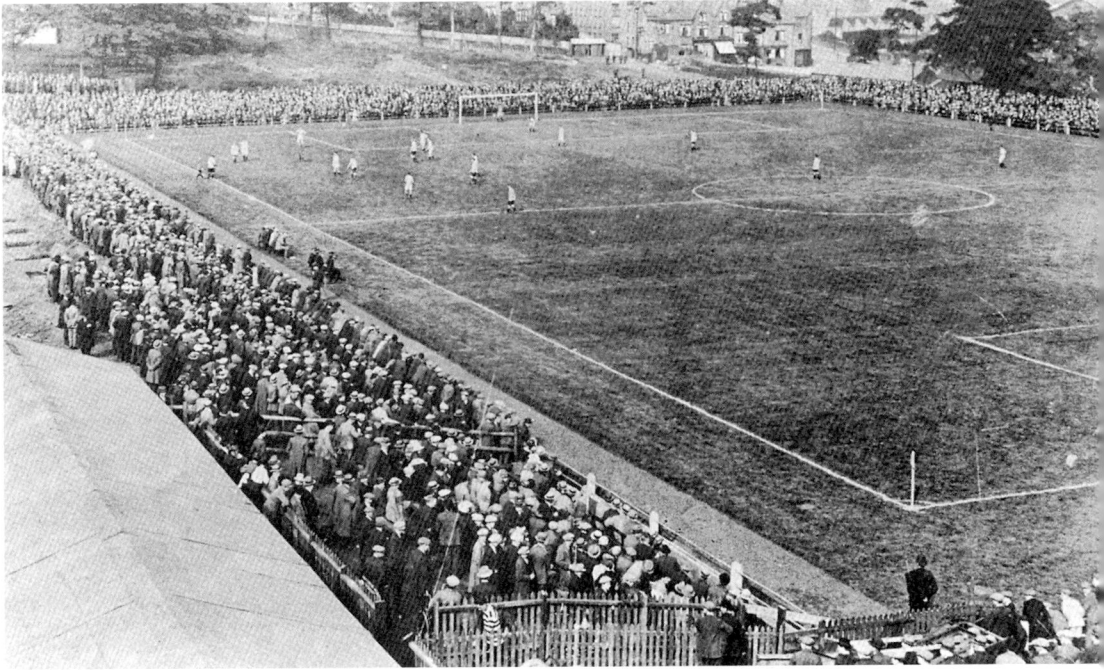

Halifax Town AFC first league match at the Shay, 1921. Halifax Town A.F.C. was founded in the summer of 1911 after a crowded meeting at the Saddle Hotel on 24 May under the chairmanship of Mr E. H. Braginton, who had agreed to the formation of a limited company to fund the club. Braginton later became one of the club's first directors. The first ground was at Sandhall Lane and the opening match against Bradford City Reserves at Valley Parade in the Yorkshire Combination. The first home game the following Saturday, 16 September 1911, against Scarborough attracted a crowd of 2,000. In 1913 the club was defeated in the first round of the F.A. Cup by Queen's Park Rangers. In 1919 the club moved to Exley and on 3 September 1921, ten years after the formation of the club, the first league match was played at the Shay, when more than 10,000 spectators watched Halifax achieve a famous victory of five goals to nil over Darlington. (Photograph: J. A. Hargreaves)

'with a mop of blonde hair under a silver or gold sequined top hat', Shirley would enter the ring 'in his shimmering cape' accompanied by the Seekers' hit 'We Shall Not be Moved' and his audience chanting 'Easy! Easy! Easy!'. At the time he appeared on 'This is Your Life', he weighed twenty-six stone and was six feet two inches in height and his fans were as much attracted by his show business antics as his wrestling. Raised with his two younger brothers in poverty, his father (b. 1906), a drayman, professional rugby league player and wrestler, walked out on the family in 1937, leaving his wife, a mill worker, to bring up the three children.

The Theatre Royal and the newer Palace Theatre also continued to attract large audiences during the inter-war years. Wilfred Pickles recalled seeing the Theatre Royal packed 'from floor to ceiling' for Shakespeare productions by Henry Baynton's company, and he made his own professional stage début there as an extra in a crowd scene from *Julius Caesar*. Phyllis Bentley recalled that attending the theatre in large parties became 'an accepted way of entertaining one's friends'. Even Halifax rugby players visited the theatre as part of their preparation for the Rugby League Challenge Cup final in 1931. Wilfred Pickles and Eric Portman, both later to become stars of stage and screen, developed their early interest in drama through the King Cross Amateur Dramatic Society, one of a host of local societies active during the inter-war years. In 1927 the Halifax Thespians was founded, and after the Second World War they acquired a redundant Methodist chapel for use as a playhouse.

Wilfred Pickles (1904–78) became a pioneering popular radio broadcaster in 1946 when he was invited to compere a trailblazing new radio quiz show, 'Have a Go', which became the first broadcast quiz show to give away prizes, including a jackpot of £3. It ran for 21 years until 1967 and made Pickles one of the most popular broadcasters in the history of the medium: at its peak the show attracted an audience of 26 million. The basis of the show's appeal was Pickles's genius in presenting people to people and the show's celebration and affirmation of the values and enjoyments of northern working-class life. Wilfred Pickles's unique talent was his ability to create a homely and relaxed atmosphere for contestants with catch-phrases which soon entered everyday parlance such as 'Ow do, 'ow are yer?', 'Are yer coortin?' and 'Give him the money, Barney', which was even cited in Hansard.[85]

The career of Halifax-born Eric Portman (1901–69), educated at Rishworth School, who had been an enthusiastic member of the Halifax Light Opera Society before auditioning for Henry Baynton and joining successively Robert Courtneidge's Shakespeare Company and the Old Vic Company at the Lyric, Hammersmith, where he played *Romeo*, led to his rapid rise to stardom in British motion pictures on both sides of the Atlantic. His lead role as a ruthless Nazi U-boat commander in Michael Powell and Emeric Pressburger's *49th Parallel* (1941) made him a star overnight in the 1940s and in 1941 he made a personal appearance at a showing of the film to a packed house in Halifax, receiving a standing ovation. In 1942 he appeared in *One of Our Aircraft is Missing*, a film about Allied pilots in occupied Holland and in 1954, he interrupted filming to back a local campaign at the Grand Theatre to help bring repertory back to Halifax, after the theatre had closed through lack of support. Indeed, he brought the entire London production of Terence Rattigan's *Separate Tables* to Halifax for a charity performance, but without successfully reviving the theatre. After further film and television roles in the 1950s, he retired to Cornwall, suffering from exhaustion, but was remembered in Halifax in a pub which traded for a while under the name of the Portman and Pickles. His oft-repeated claims that he had dined in London in 1937, with Joachim Von Ribbentrop, Germany's Ambassador to Britain in London and later Hitler's foreign minister, who had purportedly assured him that 'when Germany wins the war Portman would be installed as the greatest English star in the New Europe, at a purpose-built studio in Berlin', although viewed by some as apocryphal, it nonetheless fuelled perceptions of Portman as a controversial, anti-Semite, who died in relative obscurity.[86]

There was also a growing local cinema-going public, especially after the first 'talking' picture, 'The Singing Fool' starring Al Jolson, was shown in Halifax in September 1929. By 1936 there were no fewer than ten cinemas in Halifax, including the Alhambra, occupying the former Oddfellows Hall, the Cosy Corner Picture Palace in Queen's Road, and the Pioneer Picture House at Ovenden, while films were also now shown regularly at the Grand Theatre and the Victoria Hall. Then, in 1938, the new spacious purpose-built Odeon and Regal Cinemas were opened in Broad Street and at Ward's End. However, not everyone welcomed the growing popularity of the cinema in the inter-war years. James Parker bemoaned the fact that 'the cinema has displaced the singing rooms in public houses and little groups of village glee singers'. He claimed that it stifled the 'gaiety that was obvious when, in a less ambitious way, we provided our own amusement to a much greater extent; in school concerts, basket suppers, and bazaar entertainments'.[87]

Parker acknowledged, however, that Halifax remained very much 'a musical town', citing as evidence the popularity of the Halifax Light Opera Society. Similarly, J. B. Priestley remembered Halifax folk delighting 'in singing Handel and Gilbert-and-Sullivan operas'. The town's musical tradition owed much to its Nonconformist heritage. Halifax's most famous musical son, George Dyson (1883–1964), was the son of the organist and choirmaster of North Parade Baptist Church and a pupil of Arthur Collingwood, organist at Rhodes Street Wesleyan Chapel. A Fellow of the

The Picture House, Commercial Street, Halifax. One of the first purpose-built cinemas in Halifax, it opened on 20 October 1913, showing silent pictures. 'Talkies' were first shown in the town in September 1929. The Picture House was subsequently renamed the Gaumont and later the Astra. It was one of a dozen cinemas which opened in Halifax before 1939. It finally closed as a cinema in May 1982. In the 1990s, under another new name, the Coliseum, with discotheque dancing and four themed bars, it became one of the most popular nightclub venues in the region. (Photograph: S. Gee)

Royal College of Organists by the age of seventeen, he served as Director of the Royal College of Music between 1908 and 1937. He was most active as a composer between 1928 and 1949, with ten major compositions to his name, including the cantatas *In Honour of the City* (1928), which he conducted in Halifax in 1935, and *Canterbury Pilgrims* (1931), his best-known work. Knighted in 1941, he composed the *Confortare* motet sung at the coronation of Queen Elizabeth II in 1953 and at her Golden Jubilee Thanksgiving Service in 2002. Dyson was a leading campaigner for the development of music in the provinces and became President of the Halifax Chamber Music Society in 1943. The Halifax Choral Society, proud of its tradition as the oldest choral society in the world with an uninterrupted musical programme, continued its concerts throughout the two world wars. However, in 1930 the society's president reluctantly acknowledged that the Huddersfield Choral Society was the only really strong choral society outside London because of its greater success in attracting recording and broadcasting contracts.[88]

In 1930, when the quintessential local history society, the Halifax Literary and Philosophical Society, held its centenary exhibition at Bankfield Museum, there were some 500 local societies, including the fledgling Halifax Authors' Circle, founded in 1926. Its most prolific member was Phyllis Bentley, whose novel *Inheritance*, inspired by her own family's experience of recession in the textile industry in 1930–31, established her reputation as a successful regional novelist. Published in 1932, the novel received more than 530 reviews, went into twenty-nine editions in England, sold more than 40,000 hardback copies in the United States and was translated into eight languages. Another local author, Eleanor Gaukroger, a descendant of the popular dialect poet John Hartley, writing under the pseudonym of Jenny Wren, published popular anthologies of short stories rich in local dialect and recording 'accents of a life that under the pressure of modern education and civilisation is slowly, but surely passing away'.[89]

Several local authors, including Phyllis Bentley, whose novel *Inheritance* was serialised on the BBC North Region, reached larger audiences through the new medium of radio during this period. The Revd G. Bramwell Evens commenced his immensely popular BBC *Children's Hour* Romany radio broadcasts while stationed as a Methodist minister at King Cross Methodist Church in Halifax during the period 1929–39. He found the graveyard adjoining his manse a rich habitat for wildlife and was able through binoculars to observe sparrowhawks and peregrines perched on the nearby Wainhouse Tower. However, no local broadcaster achieved greater success through this medium than Wilfred Pickles (1904–78), who made his début as a contributor to BBC *Children's Hour* in 1927. He went on to make broadcasting history in December 1941 as the first national newsreader not only to speak with a pronounced northern accent, but also to sign off his final bulletin of the day with an impromptu flourish in the vernacular, wishing his northern listeners 'good-neet'. His invitation to read the news formed part of the wartime security strategy of Brendan Bracken, Minister of Information, to foil Nazi propagandists, who had become adept at imitating BBC Oxford accents. Pickles's début as a newsreader created a furore at the time. This former Halifax builder featured in every kind of article, from gossip columns to cartoons, where he was invariably depicted with his shirt sleeves rolled up and wearing a muffler and cloth cap. Nevertheless, the experience proved the springboard for his future highly successful career as one of the most popular broadcasters in the history of the medium.[90]

Halifax also produced one of the greatest painters of the inter-war years in Sir Matthew Smith (1879–1959), the son of a Halifax wire manufacturer. His choice of career was facilitated by his family's considerable industrial fortune. After a public-school education at Giggleswick, he worked for a Bradford wool company and then his father's wire making firm in Halifax before training first at the Manchester School of Art and then at the Slade in London. He then moved to France, where he developed his bold use of colour under the influence of Henri Matisse and at the artist's colony at Pont Aven in Brittany. Delicate in health, shy and retiring, he became best known for his landscape, nude and still-life paintings, especially his flowerpieces. He was described by Augustus John as 'the most brilliant and individual figure in modern English painting'. From a markedly less privileged background, Herbert Read, educated at the Crossley Orphanage in Halifax, emerged as a leading art critic and art historian during the inter-war years, with acclaimed publications on *The Meaning of Art* (1931), *Art and Industry* (1934) and *Art and Society* (1936). Thus, culturally, the inter-war years in Halifax provide evidence of vitality, and of continuity as well as change.[91]

'Black Halifax boiled in phosphorus'

Meanwhile, economic, social and cultural change, and local government institutions, began to alter Halifax's built environment. During the inter-war years municipal initiatives directed at slum clearance, road widening and retail development brought changes to the physical appearance of the town centre and spawned new green field housing developments around its western and northern peripheries at Pellon, Ovenden, Mixenden and Boothtown. Cross Fields, one of the most squalid areas of the town, became the first slum housing clearance project in 1926, making way for the Odeon cinema and later a new bus station. Other road widening schemes resulted from the increase in motor traffic during the inter-war years. When the local master woodcarvers, Jacksons of Coley, chose to depict transport scenes through the ages on an exterior beam over the entrance of the reconstructed Royal Oak public house (completed in 1931), they included a carving of a motor vehicle, signifying the arrival of the motor age in Halifax. In 1936, a brochure for a shopping festival and exhibition in Halifax provided further confirmation, proclaiming that 'horses are vanishing from our streets and taking to the meadows and hills' and that 'electric trams, motor-buses and taxis have taken the place of the omnibus, hansom cab and phaeton'. In the same year, a special feature for the motorist in the *Halifax County Borough Directory* commended the Trinity Garage Co. Ltd of Skircoat Road as 'one of the best-equipped and most up-to-date garages in the provinces', with showrooms housing a 'range of approximately 50 new and used cars', a petrol

The broadcaster Wilfred Pickles and his wife Mabel with his parents and his elder brother Alderman Arthur Pickles, Mayor of Halifax 1951–52 and his sister-in-law, the Mayoress. Wilfred Pickles (1904–78), whose popular radio quiz show 'Have a Go' attracted an audience of 26 million listeners around the world at its peak, was born in Conway Street, Hopwood Lane, Halifax. He became an assistant at Mitchell's gentlemen's outfitters in Crown Street, Halifax before becoming an apprentice with his father's building firm. His interest in amateur dramatics led to a distinguished career in broadcasting, the theatre and cinema and he made broadcasting history in December 1941 as the first national newsreader with a distinctive northern accent. (Photograph: J. A. Hargreaves)

filling station, and a suite of lock-up garages available for rent at reasonable rates. Indeed, during the inter-war years a proliferation of petrol filling stations, car showrooms and garages appeared throughout the town.[92]

The evolution of Halifax from a cloth producing centre into a financial services centre was symbolised by the acquisition by the Halifax Permanent Building Society in 1919 of the elegant York Buildings in Commercial Street for their new head office. Built in 1904–05 for Alexander Scott, drapers and milliners, the premises were extensively refurbished between 1919 and 1921. The adjacent Victoria Buildings were acquired and adapted between 1925 and 1927 to provide additional accommodation for the expanding society. They were subsequently retained as the headquarters of the amalgamated Halifax Permanent and Halifax Equitable Building Societies after 1927, releasing the former head office of the Halifax Equitable in Silver Street for use by Martins Bank Limited. The erection of the lofty domed Westminster Bank in 1927 at the northern end of Commercial Street further enhanced Halifax's developing financial services sector. Meanwhile, the Halifax Post Office on Commercial Street was enlarged to provide accommodation for the first local automated telephone exchange, which commenced operations on 18 June 1927. Moreover, in 1929, further land and buildings adjoining the Halifax Building Society head office in Alexandra Street were acquired and a major extension opened in 1931, designed by local architects Clement Williams and Sons to provide extra strong-room accommodation, Alexandra Hall with seating for 700 for the society's annual general meetings, several shops and a café.[93]

Former dilapidated cloth warehouses were also demolished for a new retail and office development at Bull Green as part of a municipal improvement scheme first mooted in 1904 to allow widening of the main arterial route from Halifax to the west. Clearance of the site finally began in 1924, and the development, planned by the Halifax borough engineer A. C. Tipple and featuring a substantial block of buildings, was completed in 1932. They included five ground-floor shops, extensive upper-floor office accommodation, and an attractive terraced and landscaped frontage. During the previous year, another new retail development was completed with the opening on 2 June 1931 of the imposing Prince's Arcade with accommodation for twenty-seven shops at the junction of the recently widened Woolshops and Market Street. Designed by the borough architect and constructed at a cost of

Cross Fields. This photograph, taken in the mid-1920s from the balcony of Halifax Town Hall, shows one of the poorest and most densely populated areas of the town centre, with parallel streets of back-to-back houses dominating the foreground. In the background, with its tower and double-arched entrance, can be seen the new Ebenezer Primitive Methodist Church in St James Road, built in 1922 as a replacement for its predecessor chapel of 1822. The church was connected to a large Sunday School at the rear of the building. Further along the road the Friendly and Trades Club, formerly the Oddfellows' Hall, which was opened in 1840 and demolished in 1963, is clearly visible. Cross Fields was the first slum area in the centre of the town to be cleared in 1926. It later provided the site for the first Halifax Bus Station. (Photograph: J. A. Hargreaves)

£55,000, it aimed to attract shoppers to Halifax from other towns. These municipal retail developments were complemented by the establishment of branches of new chain stores in the town such as Boots at the junction of Corn Market with Old Market and Marks and Spencers and Woolworths on Southgate. Perhaps the most impressive development of this type was the demolition of a huddle of small shops in Old Market and the opening of a stylish new store by Burton's the tailors, with a billiard hall and skating rink on its upper floors. Finally, no fewer than seven public houses were reconstructed in and around the town centre, including the New Talbot, the Bull's Head, the Shay Hotel and the Three Pigeons.[94]

However, despite such obvious evidence of private and municipal redevelopment, little had been done to improve the constricted northern access to the town. Elsewhere the historic Clare Hall had been acquired and demolished, but the scheme to build a new swimming pool on the site was postponed with the outbreak of war in 1939. There was also continuing criticism of the lack of effective town-planning regulations, with recent instances cited where works had been 'placed cheek by jowl with dwellings' and growing concern about atmospheric pollution which had left

Bull Green, Halifax, 1940. Former dilapidated cloth warehouses were demolished for a new retail and office development at Bull Green as part of a municipal improvement scheme first mooted in 1904 to allow widening of the main arterial route from Halifax to the west. Clearance of the site finally began in 1924 and the development, planned by the Halifax borough engineer A. C. Tipple and featuring a substantial block of buildings, was completed in 1932. They included five ground-floor shops, extensive upper-floor office accommodation, and an attractive terraced and landscaped frontage. The project had incurred costs of £32,000 for business compensation and land clearance and £26,000 for building and landscaping. (Photograph: S. Gee)

Bull Green, Halifax. Hx/A. 116.

buildings 'overlaid and swathed in sooty vestments'. J. B. Priestley, visiting the town in 1933, pronounced Halifax 'more interesting than Leeds as a genuine West Riding product', but he noticed that 'factories and rows of houses seem to be sticking up and out at all mad angles'. He concluded that the town was 'a grim, craggy place'. Ted Hughes (1930–98), who was born and grew up in the 1930s at Mytholmroyd, later described neighbouring Halifax disparagingly as 'Black Halifax boiled in phosphorus', while the local historian, T. W. Hanson, commenting on the grand entrance to the White Swan Hotel in Princess Street, observed that 'the stone swan carved in high relief over the entrance is no longer white, for the soot has spread a black velvety texture over the whole front'. Later visitors, Ella Pontefract and Marie Hartley, looking down on Halifax from Beacon Hill on a still winter's day in 1939, were appalled by the extent of the atmospheric pollution:

> you see the town in the deep valley below through a curtain of smoke, black smoke from the chimneys and white from the water-cooling towers mingling into a thick grey haze.

Old Halifax was still present, as well as signs of the new. Another twenty years were to elapse before this problem began to be addressed with discernible results.[95]

Southgate and Princess Street, 1940. One of the most impressive retail improvements during the inter-war years involved the demolition of a huddle of old shops in Old Market and the opening of a stylish new menswear store by Montague Burton Ltd, with a billiard hall and skating rink on its upper floors. The store is visible in the right foreground, occupying numbers 2–4 Princess Street. Further along the street the sign for Pohlmann and Son can be seen projecting from the building. During the inter-war years this pianoforte supplier had also become a radio dealer. The increase in motor traffic is evident with the provision for street parking and the display of AA and RAC recommendation signs at the White Swan Hotel on the left. (Photograph: S. Gee)

SOUTHGATE AND TOWN HALL, HALIFAX. 3

7

Post-War Halifax: from County Borough to Metropolitan Borough, 1946–2019

W HEN HALIFAX CELEBRATED its centenary as a municipal borough in March 1948, no fewer than eighteen Yorkshire mayors, watched by thousands of Halifax people, processed to Halifax Parish Church for a service of thanksgiving. In his address, the Archbishop of York, the Rt Revd Dr Cyril Garbett, reflected upon how municipal government in the past century had sought to deal with 'the terrible legacy of neglect' of the Industrial Revolution by:

> creating a town which was healthy as well as prosperous, in which the slums were gradually abolished, in which schools were built for its children and its youth, in which open spaces and parks offered recreation, in which museums and libraries were established, and in which provision was made for the aged and needy.

On the following day at a specially convened meeting of the council, the Mayor of Halifax, Alderman Charles Holdsworth, a road haulage contractor and property developer, recorded a message of greeting to his mayoral successor in the year 2048, expressing the hope that local government during the next century would 'secure a new lease of life'.[1] Neither the archbishop nor the mayor, however, could have foreseen that in little over a quarter of a century, at midnight on 31 March 1974, Halifax would have ceased to exist as a county borough, superseded by the Metropolitan Borough of Calderdale. The reorganisation of local government in 1974, however, effectively restored to Halifax its pre-industrial role as the centre of administration for its hinterland, since the boundaries of the new metropolitan borough were almost coterminous with those of the vast medieval parish of Halifax. This chapter will examine the impact of economic and social change on Halifax in the period since the Second World War and assess how successfully the Halifax County Borough and Calderdale Metropolitan Borough Councils responded to the challenges of manufacturing decline and an emergent post-industrial economy and increasingly diversified society.

Population

Apart from spurts of growth in the late 1940s, the 1980s and between 1998 and 2001, the population of Halifax and Calderdale, as shown in Table 7.1, continued to decline in the late twentieth and early twenty-first centuries, in contrast to national and regional trends. The first post-war census revealed a slight rise in the population of the county borough from 98,115 in 1931 to 98,404 in 1951, a product of the post-war baby boom and an influx of refugees from the Nazi and Stalinist persecutions in central and eastern Europe. But Halifax had the lowest proportion of residents aged between fifteen and forty-four and the highest proportion of residents aged sixty-five and over of any county borough in the West Riding in 1951, and by 1961 the population of the county borough had declined by 0.23 per cent to 96,120. Moreover, this occurred despite a wave of immigration from the New Commonwealth, mainly of dispossessed Mirpuri migrant workers from Kashmir seeking night-shift employment in local textile mills in the 1950s. Immigrant numbers reached a peak of 3,360 in 1961–62 before the imposition of immigration restrictions by the Macmillan government's Commonwealth Immigrants Act. Thereafter, the pace of net outward migration by indigenous young adults quickened. As a result, between 1961 and 1971 the population of the county borough fell by a further 0.52 per cent to 91,272. By 1981, it had further declined to 87,488. By then, Halifax formed part of the metropolitan borough of Calderdale, which also experienced a decline in population of 1.4 per cent from 192,946 in 1971 to 190,330 by 1981, when the new metropolitan borough had a much higher proportion of elderly residents than other comparable local authorities.[2] However, after decades of decline, the population of both Halifax and Calderdale began to grow after 1981, reaching 87,675 and 191,585 respectively by 1991. This was partly a result of the increasing appeal of Calderdale's countryside to commuters working in large conurbations on both sides of the Pennines. It was also a consequence of a growth in Calderdale's ethnic minority communities, which were concentrated in West Central Halifax in the St John's and Town Wards.[3] Calderdale's ethnic minorities, with their larger than average family sizes, grew from 6,500 in 1981 to 8,743 in 1991, rising from 3.5 per cent to 4.6 per cent of the total population: the majority had been born in the United Kingdom. Although this represented a lower proportion than in the neighbouring districts of Bradford (15.6 per cent), Kirklees (10.7 per cent) and Leeds (5.8 per cent), Calderdale's ethnic minority communities were generally more homogeneous than in some other parts of West Yorkshire, with fewer families in 1991 with Indian (5.9 per cent), Bangladeshi (3.7 per cent) and Afro-Caribbean (3.1 per cent) than Pakistani origins (71.8 per cent).[4]

Population growth was not sustained after 1991, however, and by 2001 the population of Calderdale had fallen slightly by 0.3 per cent, reversing the growth experienced in the 1980s and contrasting with a population growth of 0.8 per cent across West Yorkshire and 2.6 per cent in the neighbouring metropolitan borough of Kirklees. This was mainly due to changing patterns of migration and Calderdale's lack of any higher educational institution resulting in more people, particularly young adults, leaving the district than moving into it. By 2001 although Calderdale's ethnic minority population had increased by one third to 13,000 residents, two thirds of whom described themselves as Asian/Asian British, mostly Pakistani from Kashmir; this comprised a lower percentage of the population than in England or West Yorkshire as a whole. However, whilst Calderdale's population density of 5.76 per hectare in 2016 was the lowest of any local authority in West Yorkshire, identifying Calderdale as one of the smallest districts in England in terms of population, it remained one of the largest in terms of area, with over four-fifths of Calderdale described as rural by the national census of 2011. The local authority population was described, perhaps more recognisably from the perspective of its residents, as 'urban with major conurbations' by the Government Statistical Service in its 2011 Rural Urban Classification for Local Authority Districts in England, because over three-quarters of the population lived in urban areas, including approximately 88,000 in Halifax itself. By 2011, the proportion of adults between the ages of twenty and forty was significantly less than those in the forty to sixty-nine-year-old age groups and the proportion of males to females lower in the seventy-five plus age group, illustrating that a key determinant to higher life expectancy was gender. The total population of Halifax itself grew by 0.67 per cent from 83,440 inhabitants in 2011 to an estimated 91,271 in 2016. In the 2011 Census, Calderdale's largest ethnic group remained White British (86.7 per cent) and its second largest ethnic groups Asian/Asian British (8.3 per cent), of which the majority were Pakistani (6.8 per cent of the total). Demographically, therefore, Halifax and Calderdale were not merely static communities after 1945. The ethnic composition of the population had changed and the age profile was shifting towards the middle-aged and elderly.[5]

The 2011 Census also revealed for the first time since 1851 the diversity of religious beliefs in Calderdale ranging from Christian (60.6 per cent) to Jewish (0.1 per cent) and encompassing Muslim (7.8 per cent); Buddhist (0.3 per cent); Hindu 0.3 per cent; Sikh (0.2 per cent) and those declaring no religion (30.2 per cent). The 2011 Census also recorded, following a change in legislation enacted in July 2013 and coming into force in March 2014, that there were 491 people in registered same sex civil partnerships in Calderdale, amounting to 0.3 per cent of the population. Calderdale MBC Equality and Cohesion team, in partnership with Calderdale Interfaith Council, continues to support inter-faith activity, recognising that 'the faith sector plays an important role in bringing communities together to promote a shared sense of belonging and fostering good community relations'. For example, in 2016, it co-ordinated Holocaust Memorial Day, promoted food festivals to encourage sharing food as a way of bringing communities together, and organised a meeting between Imams and Clergy, the first of its kind in Calderdale.[6]

Table 7.1 Population of Halifax, 1951–2016 and Calderdale, 1971–2017

	Halifax	*Calderdale*
1951	98,404	
1961	96,120	
1971	91,272	192,946
1981	87,488	190,330
1991	87,675	192,900
2001	82,056	192,405
2011	88,134	203,800
2017	91,338	209,500

Sources: Census, 1961, 1971; *Census Digest* (Calderdale MBC, Halifax: 1983); Census 2001 Key Statistics (Calderdale MBC, Halifax: 2003); ONS Census 2011, ONS Census Estimates 2017.

Employment and industry: the decline of manufacturing and the growth of the service sector

Demographic shifts highlighted in census data may be largely explained by reference to the economic experience of Halifax in particular and Calderdale in general. Employment statistics for Calderdale for the period 1951–91, as shown in Table 7.2, reveal a decline in the number of jobs in the manufacturing sector and a growth of jobs in the service sector, particularly after 1971. Whereas manufacturing accounted for 70 per cent and the service industries for 24 per cent of employment in Calderdale in 1951, by 1991 manufacturing employed 38 per cent of the workforce and services 57 per cent.

Within the manufacturing sector the decline of those employed in textiles was most dramatic, falling from almost 36 per cent of the total workforce in 1951 to a mere 5 per cent of the total workforce in 1991. The associated clothing industry saw its workforce fall almost 75 per cent over the same period. Engineering jobs also fell by almost 25 per cent, but less dramatically than textiles. However, the decline of manufacturing was a more protracted process in Calderdale than in other parts of West Yorkshire on account of the area's continuing industrial diversification and its profusion of relatively small industrial units, so that by 1961 some 61 per cent of employees in Calderdale worked in establishments employing under 250, compared with a national average of 42 per cent. Consequently, while manufacturing employment declined steadily from 1951 and rapidly from 1971, it only fell below 50 per cent of total employment in Calderdale for the first time after 1981. Manufacturing therefore remained proportionately stronger in the local economy than in both the regional and national economy. In the mid-1960s 65 per cent of all employees in the area were engaged in manufacturing, compared with 43 per cent regionally and 38 per cent nationally; and by 1993, 34 per cent of employees in

Calderdale worked in manufacturing industries compared with 24 per cent in West Yorkshire and 19 per cent in Great Britain.[7]

The number of job losses especially in manufacturing accelerated between 1966 and 1971, 1976 and 1981 and 1979 and 1983. Economic recession led to the contraction and closure of many of Calderdale's traditional industries. Unemployment in Calderdale reached 11,500 (13 per cent) in 1983, and between 1979 and 1983 applications for benefits from those on low incomes increased by 42 per cent. Moreover, job losses had a disproportionate effect on male workers, so that by 1983 Calderdale had the highest proportion of working women in West Yorkshire (67 per cent).[8] It is true that, between 1983 and 1988 Halifax achieved a marked reduction in unemployment figures from 13 per cent to 7 per cent, better than anywhere else in the north. This was as a result of Ernest Hall's remarkable regeneration of Dean Clough and associated Business in the Community initiatives. The achievement resulted in the removal of Halifax from the government's urban aid list. However, its economy remained fragile and its unemployment figure remained above the national average, rising to 10.5 per cent following the recession of 1990–92.[9]

As manufacturing declined, jobs in the service sector increased. Indeed, from the mid-1980s the service sector became the dominant sector within the local economy. A study of Halifax and the Calder Valley in 1968 concluded that the service sector, with the notable exception of the Halifax Building Society, was considerably below national and regional averages and was devoted predominantly 'to the satisfaction of local needs'. The growth in services was slow in the 1950s and 1960s with an increase of 5 per cent between 1959 and 1966, only half the regional and national increase. However, between 1981 and 1991, employment in the service sector increased by an amount greater than that achieved in the 30 years prior to 1981. The service sector in Calderdale increased its share of employment from 44 per cent in 1981 to 57 per cent in 1991. This was mainly as a result of an increase in the number of women obtaining jobs especially in banking, finance and insurance, hotels, catering, personal services and recreation. Moreover, the number of employees in services continued to increase between 1991 and 1993 despite an overall fall in the number of employees in Calderdale.[10]

The decline of manufacturing in West Yorkshire after 1945 has been blamed on the failure of government economic policies. Professor Arthur Marwick, writing in 1982, maintained that after 1945 there was 'no real recovery' for the woollen industry and 'West Yorkshire was on the way to becoming more a museum than a hive of industry' since it was there:

> that the post-war policies of the Labour Government, aimed at the distribution of industry, were at their most unsuccessful. New industries were excluded, and even established textile firms were encouraged to expand in areas whose need was felt to be greater, for example the North-East.[11]

Table 7.2 Employment in Calderdale, 1951–91

	1951	1961	1971	1981	1991
Agriculture	849	842	586	450	542*
Mining	546	512	87	64	
PRIMARY	**1,395**	**1,354**	**673**	**514**	**542**
Food/drink	5,010	5,124	5,709	7,329	4,279
Chemicals	798	767	557	862	929
Metal manufacturing	793	1,637	995	1,088	*
Engineering	11,495	11,421	10,885	9,200	8,640
Vehicles	1,628	487	677	1,308	1,036
Metal goods	4,184	3,586	3,617	3,055	1,400
Textiles	34,519	30,179	19,142	7,856	3,907
Leather	967	565	422	107	*
Clothing	5,202	4,341	2,999	2,159	1,319
Bricks/pottery	1,551	1,410	1,210	1,449	1,458
Timber/furniture	1,215	1,532	1,673	2,121	2,081
Paper/printing	750	978	1,533	1,250	1,353
Other manufacturing	361	572	732	800	1,393
MANUFACTURING	**68,473**	**62,599**	**50,151**	**38,584**	**28,550**
CONSTRUCTION	**3,556**	**3,723**	**2,680**	**2,420**	**2,599**
Gas/electricity/water	906	1,225	1,033	1,098	532
Transport/communication	3,883	2,892	2,744	2,466	2,648
Distribution	6,865	6,840	4,944	6,808	8,388
Financial services	735	1,093	1,970	4,428	8,572
Professional services	5,037	5,995	8,289	9,441	12,337
Miscellaneous services	3,514	4,358	4,779	4,569	6,103
Public administration	2,637	2,454	3,442	3,337	4,295
SERVICES	**23,577**	**24,857**	**27,201**	**32,147**	**42,875**
TOTAL	**97,001**	**92,533**	**80,705**	**73,665**	**74,566**

* categories with low numbers combined or disregarded
Sources: *Ministry of Labour Census*, 1951, 1961; *Department of Employment Census*, 1971–91; *Calderdale Report*, 1994–95, p. 13.

One major Halifax textile company certainly relocated to the North East during the immediate post-war period. In September 1945 Patons and Baldwins, the Halifax woollen and worsted yarn spinners founded in 1785, which at its peak had employed a workforce of 3,000, announced the closure of its Clark Bridge Mills and its intention to move to a green field site near Darlington in 1947. Moreover, in a later industrial survey undertaken for the Yorkshire and Humberside Economic

Workers at Crossley Carpets holding their redundancy notices, February 1982. Carpets International announced the planned closure of virtually the whole of the Dean Clough complex with the loss of over 400 jobs on 28 January in a bid to turn losses into profits. The *Halifax Courier* described the announcement of the closure as 'one of the biggest disasters in Halifax's long industrial history'. By 1982 Carpets International had only one member of the Crossley family on its eleven-strong board. Jonathan Crossley was vice-chairman of Carpets International and chairman of Carpets International (Northern). The workforce at Dean Clough was reduced to around 300 and there was speculation about what use might be made of the eight large mills and other buildings on the site. (Photograph: *Halifax Courier*)

Planning Council and Board in 1967, many firms commented on the locational disadvantages of Halifax, complaining of unfavourable treatment compared with development areas, where government inducements were provided for industry. There were also difficulties in obtaining conveniently situated land suitable for development and the negative impact of the urban environment on the recruitment of executives. Consequently, during the period 1953–67 more firms transferred production out of the area than into the area. Other explanations of manufacturing decline in textiles have focused upon changes of fashion, the introduction of a range of new synthetic fibres from the 1950s such as nylon and rayon and also on increasing foreign competition, particularly from Asia and the Pacific Rim where labour costs were cheaper. Nevertheless, the 1967 survey confirmed the continuing importance of manufacturing industries and the dominance of textiles in particular in Halifax and the Calder Valley, with woollens and worsteds still the largest component, with carpets the fastest growing element, and with clothing embracing a wide range of garments from overalls and ladies' coats to suits and dresses.[12]

Another outstanding local textile firm, John Holdsworth and Co. Ltd, became a world leader in its field by the 1990s, providing a remarkable example of the successful modernisation of a family business spanning 175 years and six generations.[13] William Holdsworth (1922–69) had served in the RAF as a Spitfire fighter aircraft pilot instructor in the Second World War, married Dina Maria Kuperus in Amsterdam in 1946 and had five children. However, he died at the age of 46 in 1969 and his widow, who had herself shared the leadership of the firm with her husband, contributed to the post-war success of the business. Indeed, Holdsworths doubled their sales and profits between 1946 and 1952 with the post-war demand for moquette for railway carriages, buses and ships and the large orders for navy blue and khaki worsted yarns which were needed after the outbreak of the Korean War in 1950. This enabled a new worsted spinning plant to be installed and soon exports amounted to 10 per cent of turnover. However, in the decade following the collapse of world markets in 1952, the firm became more reliant on the domestic market, and its trading situation deteriorated to such an extent that by 1963 sales had almost halved. The firm had sustained heavy losses as a result of increasing competition from overseas and from new synthetic fibres such as dralon. Nevertheless, the firm managed to survive by stringent cost control, streamlining its workforce, investing in new machinery and specialising in weaving moquette for commercial transport rather than the domestic upholstery

The last workers at the Elizabeth Shed with the final roll of carpet to leave the empty warehouse at Dean Clough in January 1987. For many of the employees it marked the end of more than a generation working for John Crossley and Sons Ltd and Carpets International Ltd. The Elizabeth Shed, opened in Shroggs Road in 1963, had been one of the most recent extensions to the vast Dean Clough complex, where carpet manufacture had taken place since 1803. (Photograph: *Halifax Courier*)

market. Between 1969 and 1979 the company increased its exports as a percentage of turnover from 10 per cent to 35 per cent. The acquisition of new Gusken shuttle-less rapier looms in 1979–80, the introduction of computer-aided design technology, the phased refurbishment of Shaw Lodge Mills, the development of new overseas markets in North America, Australasia, South Africa, the Middle and Far East and the continued exploitation of the European market during the 1980s enabled the firm to become a market leader, increasing its turnover from £3 million in 1979 to over £10 million by 1990. During the subsequent world recession, turnover dropped by 1992 to £7.8 million, but the astute acquisition of the rival Irish business of Max Birr Ltd in December 1991 and the bus and coach division of the neighbouring West Yorkshire firm of Firth Fabrics Ltd, enabled turnover to reach £14.5 million by the end of 1994. Capital reinvestment recommenced through the acquisition of twelve computerised looms with piletronic jacquards, but the strong pound at the end of the decade resulted in fifty redundancies at the family textile firm, which, despite the redundancy programme, remained one of the district's biggest firms with a workforce of around 300.[14]

Other textile firms, however, ultimately fared less well. By investing in new technology, pruning its workforce, paying competitive wage rates and maintaining its reputation for high quality and prompt delivery, John Crossley and Sons remained profitable into the early 1970s. Indeed, in 1961 the new Elizabeth Shed was built on largely reclaimed land at Shroggs Road and was extended in 1968. However, in 1969 Crossleys merged with Carpet Trade Holdings and the Carpet Trades Manufacturing Co. of Kidderminster to form Carpets International, and in 1970, on the retirement of Patrick Crossley, the headquarters of the group moved to Kidderminster. By 1975 when a new carpet printing plant was installed at Elizabeth Shed the number of employees had fallen below 2,000, and by 1977 the workforce numbered 1,600. After the closure of the jute spinning and Duravell departments and the transfer of planning, cutting and dispatching to Northallerton and Wilton weaving to Kidderminster, at least one-third of the vast industrial complex stood idle. In January 1982 the decision was taken to close the entire carpet factory, sending shock waves throughout the local community: the Elizabeth Shed produced its last roll of carpet in 1987. Moreover, Calderdale's other established carpet manufacturing firm, Firth Carpets of Bailiff Bridge, acquired by Readicut after a takeover battle in 1968 and then sold to the American-owned company, Interface Europe, in 1997, finally closed in 2002, with the loss of nearly 300 jobs. Its closure came about as a result of adverse trading conditions, despite its success in weathering periodic recessions in the 1980s and 1990s.[15]

Nevertheless, despite the systematic destruction of their redundant machinery at Dean Clough by Carpets International in order to prevent its acquisition by potential competitors, the carpet industry did not disappear completely from the town. Avena Carpets, started by seven former employees of Crossleys in January 1976 following the closure of the figured Wilton department at Dean Clough, returned to Haley Hill in 1983, after trading initially from Denholme. It quickly established a reputation for weaving fine Brussels Wilton carpets and secured prestigious contracts for carpeting the throne room at Windsor Castle and the guest room of the White House in Washington. By 1988 the firm's workforce had grown to 30. Other firms that were founded by former Crossley employees and executives, including members of the Crossley family, were Hebble Rugs, founded by Jonathan Crossley in May 1982 at Bowling Dyke, which subsequently moved to premises in Lewis Street; Halifax Carpets, established by Charles Crossley at Black Dyke Mills, Queensbury; and Silvarea Textiles Ltd, operating from the new Dean Clough Business Park.[16]

By the mid-1990s, however, the extent of the decline of textiles within the local economy was starkly apparent. Willey and Pearson closed their Scarborough Mills in Haugh Shaw Road in 1994 and the site was subsequently acquired by Tesco for their second Halifax supermarket. By 1998, Joseph Horsfall and Sons Ltd at Clarence Mill was the sole surviving worsted spinning mill in Halifax with an annual turnover of just under one million pounds and a workforce of 25. The firm had survived into the twenty-first century partly on account of its relatively small size, with around 30 employees, allowing virtually instant product flexibility and rapid delivery of its products, together with its hands-on management through five generations of the same family and its cautious approach to investment. However, following the senior director, Brian Butler's sudden death in 2002, both his brother Michael, who was well into his seventies, and his co-director, Richard Brownridge, whose retirements were imminent, reluctantly decided to close Clarence Mills in March 2008, after a century-and-a half in business. By December of the same year Cawthra Brothers Ltd, Commission Weavers of Milton Shed, the last business of its kind in Halifax, who had provided woven fabric for royalty and top international brands was also facing closure. Mervyn and David Cawthra, whose grandfather Wright Cawthra had founded the firm some 90 years before, and whose father Milton had succeeded him in the business, which had provided a living for 40 employees, blamed changes in fashion in the ties business for declining sales. They decided 'to get out while still just making a profit', dismantling a couple of their looms for export to India and working 50 to 60 hours per week until the end. Moreover, John Holdsworth and Company, the world's leading producer of moquette for transport seating also closed in 2008 after having been established at their Shaw Lodge Mills for six generations. They did, however, secure planning permission for the redevelopment of an urban village and also developed a wide range of other activities on their extensive site, including the Artworks Art School and a soccer centre.[17]

Engineering, the second largest manufacturing sector in Halifax in 1945, displayed growth rates below regional and national averages during the period up to 1967. Domestic electrical equipment and small tools expanded substantially, but machine tools, the largest group within the sector, increased its employment only marginally. Moreover, increases were offset by the transfer of production to other areas both within and beyond Calderdale. In 1966, for example, the Halifax Rack and Screw Cutting Co. Ltd moved to a new purpose-built factory in Brighouse and in 1996 the Carrington Wire Division of SG Industries moved from Pellon

Joseph Horsfall and Sons, Clarence Mill, Halifax, 1998. The sole remaining worsted spinning firm in Halifax by 1998 had been founded before 1866, moving to Clarence Mill in Pellon Lane in 1894. Three generations of Horsfalls ran the company until the Butlers who had married into the family took over. When the managing director, Brian Butler, photographed with his cousin Michael Butler, production director, entered the business in the 1950s there were fifty-one spinning firms in the district. The firm's survival has depended upon its flexibility, its ability to meet changing demands and its willingness to supply small orders. In 1998, Brian Butler told the *Halifax Courier*: 'We are a family run firm. Our livelihood depends on Halifax and we have a vested interest in staying in Halifax and employing in Halifax'. When Brian died in harness in 2002, his cousin Michael succeeded him as managing director. (Photograph: *Halifax Courier*)

Lane to a more convenient site at the Lowfield Business Park in Elland, while Churchill Redman transferred production to Blaydon in 1971 and Pegler Hattersley to Doncaster in 1987. Moreover, the increasing application from the mid-1960s of computer-aided design and computer-directed machinery led to a reduction of employment opportunities. There was also an increasing number of amalgamations and closures. The acquisition of Asquiths by Staveley Industries and of Butlers by the Elliott Machine Tool Co. was followed by the closure of Lumbys. Drakes at Ovenden closed in 1968 as a result of the changeover from coal to natural gas. Stirks, which had been taken over by A. Wickman of Coventry, was closed in 1980; Farrar Engineering in 1985; and the Automatic Standard Screw Co. in 1993 following the contraction of its UK market. Moreover, the purchase of Butlers by Marbaix (Holdings) Ltd. of Basingstoke in 1993, who had recently acquired

Asquiths, led to the effective amalgamation of the two firms at the Mile Thorn site, with a combined workforce of 120 in 1997. By January 2000, however, as customers for both home orders and exports, hit by the strong pound, dried up, fifty job losses were announced and the remaining design expertise transferred to a sister operation in Wolverhampton. The once great machine tool companies effectively went out of business, leaving a remnant maintenance and support operation in Calderdale.

Some local engineering firms, however, did achieve remarkable success in exports, becoming world leaders in their fields. James H. Heal and Co. Ltd, manufacturers of textile testing equipment, and Crosrol Ltd, manufacturers of carding machinery, both received the Queen's Award for Export in 1995, Crosrol for the fifth time. James H. Heal displayed a remarkable resilience in marketing its textile technology, operating by 2018 from two adjoining former textile mills, a short distance from Halifax town centre. In a recruitment advertisement in January 2018 for a textile technologist at a salary rising from £28,000 to £33,000 per annum, the firm proclaimed that 'the company had grown ten per cent each year for the previous three years and continued to expand their global customer base with exciting opportunities to expand into new markets'.[18] Crosrol, founded in 1946 by André Varga (1893–1998), the Hungarian commercial director of a Belgian firm of card makers who had settled in England following the Nazi invasion of Belgium in 1940, exported 99 per cent of the machinery it made in 1995. However, in 2001 the firm went suddenly into receivership on account of the strength of sterling and major competitors in Europe, with the loss of 340 jobs, not long after the death of its 105-year-old founder. In 2002 the manufacturing of all new machinery was moved to Shanghai in order to be able to continue to supply quality carding machines at the most economical prices and develop new Asian markets. In Pakistan, the company enjoys an 80 per cent market share and in Bangladesh a 50 to 60 per cent market share, together with important markets in Vietnam, Indonesia and India.[19]

By 1996, another local firm, Crosslee, had become Europe's largest tumble dryer manufacturer, employing a workforce of nearly 600. Formed as a result of a bold and enterprising management buyout after Philips had announced the closure of their Hipperholme factory in 1986, the firm was a successor of the Ajax Machine Tool Co. which had developed the celebrated Ada washing machine in 1944 and had achieved annual sales of 36,000 in the 1950s.

Some specialist manufacturing has continued, such as Reflecting Road Studs, which has remained undaunted by alternative electronically operated approaches to road safety. The inventor of the Catseye, Percy Shaw (1890–1976), was commemorated by both the very first Yorkshire Society county-wide plaque unveiled in his memory on his former home in Boothtown in 1986, and subsequently also by the Halifax Civic Trust, whilst on the Broad Street Plaza an early twenty-first century pub was also named in his honour. His obituary in *The Times* recognised the global significance of Shaw's achievement, recording that his Catseye studs now marked 'traffic lanes on highways all over the world'. Not since the death, exactly 200 years earlier, of John Harrison (1693–1776), whose marine chronometer enabled navigators to compute their longitude at sea within an accuracy of half a degree, had an invention by a Yorkshireman had such a universal impact on travel safety worldwide.[20]

The confectionery industry, the third largest manufacturing component in Halifax in 1945, increased its employment significantly by the mid-1960s, but subsequently contracted as a result of a series of amalgamations and closures. The biscuit manufacturing firm Meredith and Drew, which had moved to a disused foundry in Ovenden from the East End of London following the Blitz, expanded rapidly in Halifax during the 1950s and 1960s before amalgamating with United Biscuits in December 1966. Unfortunately, the cost of modernising the Ovenden site resulted in the decision to close the Halifax KP Foods Plant at Ovenden in 1988, making 1,000 workers redundant. In 1969 the leading local toffee and chocolate manufacturers, Mackintosh's, maker of Rolo and Quality Street, merged with Rowntree of York led by Donald Barron (1921–2015), a Scottish accountant, who had become chairman of Rowntree & Co, maker of KitKat biscuits and Polo mints in 1966, to create Rowntree Mackintosh. The deal, a defensive move on the part of Rowntree, brought together two established confectionery firms, similar in ethos, with a combined 25 per cent share of the UK confectionery market, and

The new administrative headquarters of the Halifax Building Society under construction, June 1972. The building was designed by Professor Sir George Grenfell-Baines of the Building Design Partnership and constructed by John Laing Construction Ltd to replace the former head office in Commercial Street, which had been in use since 1921. Work began on the site of the former Ramsden's Stone Trough Brewery in 1969 and the society moved into the new premises in 1973. (Photograph: Halifax plc)

firepower to invest in brands at home and abroad. Following a major upset in 1973 when a cocoa trader in the company took unauthorised positions that caused losses of some £32 million, Barron was persuaded to stay on and restored the company's fortunes so effectively that by the time he retired from the chair in 1981, group sales had multiplied tenfold under his leadership. However, in 1986 Rowntree Mackintosh closed their Queen's Road factory with the loss of 380 jobs but the subsequent merger of Rowntree Mackintosh with Nestlé UK in 1991, when the firm had 2,500 employees in Halifax, was followed by a major redevelopment of the Albion Mills site, demonstrating a commitment to the continued production of key lines in Halifax.[21] By contrast, the local brewing industry after similar post-war expansion, had completely collapsed by the end of the century. Thomas Ramsden's Stone Trough Brewery, which reached the peak of its prosperity in 1954, was closed in 1967 following its amalgamation with the Leeds-based Joshua Tetley in 1964. In 1968 brewing ceased at Richard Whitaker's Corporation Street Brewery following its merger with Samuel Whitbread, and in 1996 Scottish Newcastle announced the closure of Samuel Webster's Fountain Head Brewery with the loss of 182 jobs, after 160 years of operation in the Wheatley Valley.[22]

As noted, however, the decline of manufacturing was offset by the growing strength of the services sector. The Halifax Building Society entered its centenary year in 1953 with total assets of £177,212,000, of which £136,759,000 represented loans on mortgage. In half a century its total assets had multiplied by more than a hundred-fold and its financial strength was unchallengeable. During the second half of the twentieth century it made a major contribution to the local economy. By

HM Queen Elizabeth II opens the new administrative headquarters of the Halifax Building Society on 13 November 1974. The Queen, making her first visit to the town since 1949, is photographed chatting to the Earl of Halifax, the patron of the Halifax Building Society. Also pictured, from left to right, are the Mayor of Calderdale, the chairman of the Halifax Building Society, Mr Ian Maclean and Mrs Maclean, with some of the thousands of local spectators who witnessed the visit in the background. She was shown the society's first mortgage deed, dated 1853, and the society's computer centre, where a teleprocessing network connects the society's 280 branches directly to the main computer. In the forty years from 1927 to 1967 there had been two relatively minor extensions to the society's Commercial Street headquarters. In the next thirty years the Trinity Road site was developed and additional accommodation provided at Copley and Dean Clough. (Photograph: Halifax plc)

1994, with 3,134 employees, it was by far the largest private employer in Calderdale, ahead of Nestlé UK Ltd with 1,400 and Marshalls plc with 961 employees. In 1967 a new computer centre was built on the site of Trinity Road Baptist Church, and the adjacent premises of the former Stone Trough Brewery were acquired for redevelopment as a new head office, opened in 1974 by HM the Queen. In 1986 John Spalding, chief executive of the Halifax Building Society, reaffirmed the society's commitment to Halifax and Calderdale. He argued that with modern telecommunications there was no reason other than tradition for companies to have their headquarters in London. In 1989 a £25 million computerised data centre was opened at Wakefield Road, Copley, employing 600 staff.

By the early 1990s with building society membership nationally embracing 70 per cent of the population, the potential for future society growth was becoming limited. In November 1994, the Halifax Building Society with 706 branches, assets of £67 billion and profits of £866 million announced its intention to merge with the Leeds Permanent Building Society, with 455 branches, assets of £19.5 billion and profits of £186 million, and subsequently to convert to a public company. The combined assets of the two societies would total £86.5 billion with profits of £1.05 billion and a network of 1,161 branches, some 400 of which overlapped. The merger was approved by 97 per cent of Halifax members and 95 per cent of Leeds members on 22 May 1995 and the conversion by 97 per cent of borrowers and investors of the amalgamated society on 24 February 1997. It was followed by the biggest stock market flotation in history, 7.6 million people sharing no less than £18 billion. The merger and the change of status from a mutual society to that of a public company resulted in certain operations such as financial services and share dealing being headquartered in Leeds, and in 1998 the treasury department moved from Halifax to London. Nevertheless, the new Halifax plc group head office remained at Halifax with information systems and general insurance at Copley. Indeed, the employment base of the Halifax in Calderdale increased to 4,283 in 1998. Moreover, the bonus payments to local investors and employees of the Halifax provided an estimated £25 million windfall for local businesses, with travel agents especially reporting an upturn in holiday bookings.

When news of another proposed Halifax plc merger, this time with the Bank of Scotland, broke on 4 May 2001, one BBC regional journalist gloomily portrayed the proposal as marauding Scottish raiders invading Yorkshire to snatch the jewel of the crown of England's financial institutions. Moreover, despite the proposed appointment of the Halifax's James Crosby as chief executive of the new bank and reassurances to Calderdale employees about job security and a generally favourable verdict from economic commentators and the national media on the potential strengths of an institution combining the corporate banking experience of the Bank of Scotland with the retail banking prowess of the Halifax, there was stunned reaction in Halifax. The *Halifax Courier* ran banner headlines proclaiming the end of the Halifax and claiming betrayal at the prospect of control of the new HBOS moving to Edinburgh. However, the immediate fears were not realised and the creation of the fifth largest UK bank brought continuing benefits to Calderdale,

The approval of the merger between the Halifax and Leeds Permanent Building Societies, 22 May 1995. Roger Boyes, chief executive of the Leeds Permanent Building Society, and Mike Blackburn, chief executive of the Halifax Building Society, shake hands outside the Victoria Theatre, Halifax, following the approval by members of both societies for the merger of the two societies. (Photograph: Halifax plc)

where the retail headquarters of the bank continued to be based. Indeed, by August 2003, when the 150th anniversary of the foundation of the Halifax Permanent Benefit Building Society was celebrated with a spectacular firework display in Halifax, the new bank had 22 million customers, two million of whom had been won since the merger in 2001. With assets of £355 billion, HBOS also had 1,100 branches across the UK and employed over 60,000 people, some 6,000 of them in Calderdale.[23]

The impact of the financial crisis of 2007–08, however, put the global spotlight on Halifax on account of the failure of the amalgamated Halifax Bank of Scotland, with the loss of £54 billion, thereby becoming 'the worst banking collapse in modern history', where the bank 'went from being one of the most trusted, to one from which customers could not wait to remove their money'.[24] As early as August 2007, after the financial collapse of Northern Rock, when Alistair Darling, the Labour Chancellor of the Exchequer, enquired which other financial institutions might be exposed to the turbulent United States market, he was informed that further potential victims included HBOS, despite its reputation hitherto as 'solidly sound'. Although administered from lofty historic offices of the former Bank of

Board members of the Halifax Building Society pose for photographs outside the Old Cock Inn, Halifax, immediately after the conversion of the Halifax Building Society to Halifax plc on 16 July 1997. The Halifax Permanent Building Society had been founded in 1853 following a meeting in the oak room of the hotel in December 1852. (Photograph: Halifax plc)

Scotland situated on The Mound in Edinburgh, the bank had nonetheless retained the trading brand identities of its historic forebears including the former Halifax Building Society and the administration of the Lloyds Banking Group's largest mortgage repository remained in Trinity Road, Halifax, secure in purpose-built premises on the site of the former Ramsden's Brewery. It was 'becoming clear that HBOS was losing money, not through involvement in complicated financial dealings but through bad judgment on commercial loans'.[25] The Prime Minister, Gordon Brown, pinpointed 'the cardinal mistake at HBOS, the one that resulted in the surrender of their independence to Lloyds TSB and then necessitated a wholesale government rescue, was to stake everything on rising prices in the property market'.[26] Indeed, by 2008, as the global banking crisis escalated, HBOS became alarmingly over-exposed, in the view of Alistair Darling, having lent billions of pounds 'on the back of rapidly rising house prices and a property market which seemed to promise limitless returns' at a time when no regulator anywhere in the world had recognised the growing risks facing the banking system. Threatened with collapse, HBOS, therefore, had no option but to agree to a takeover by Lloyds Bank in September 2008, with the government acquiring major share holdings in the Lloyds group of 32 per cent and a 58 per cent stake in HBOS. Indeed, Lord Dennis Stevenson, the chairman of HBOS, acknowledged that the bank's corporate lending unit had 'lent too much' and that 'we made some mistakes and that is the bottom line'. Ultimately, he and all the non-executive directors were dismissed. Subsequently Andy Hornby, the HBOS chief executive, resigned, without taking a redundancy payment, and there were other resignations including former chief executive Sir James Crosby. HBOS was not alone in taking on risks 'it did not understand and failed to make provision for', since 'every single building society that had demutualised in the 1980s either failed or had to be taken over'. Besides the high-profile resignations, thousands of HBOS employees lost their jobs and savings, with more than 28,000 jobs being shed by the middle of 2011. Moreover, during the previous year Lloyds gave HBOS branches a makeover, removing the Halifax name and launching a new advertising campaign focusing on 'traditional banking values'.[27]

The Halifax was not the only corporate financial institution to be based in Halifax during this period. The decision to site the Bradford Pennine Insurance Group headquarters at North Park in Halifax, following the merger of the Bradford and Pennine insurance companies in 1964, was taken because land and property were competitively priced in Halifax and living costs low. Following a series of mergers with Phoenix Assurance in 1971, Sun Alliance in 1984 and Royal Assurance in 1996, the Royal and Sun Alliance employed a workforce of 750 at the Dean Clough Business Park by 1998. In addition, in 1997 the neighbouring Hebble Brook Business Park at Mixenden became the headquarters of three companies within the Provident Financial Group, namely Provident Insurance, Colonnade Insurance Brokers and Hebble Insurance Management Services. Provident Insurance, employing 280 staff in Calderdale in 1998, had commenced trading as Halifax Insurance in a terraced house in Prescott Street in 1966, moving to the redundant Holy Trinity Church in 1987, and acquiring other buildings around Blackwall in 1989 and 1992. Between 1989 and 1994 the number of its policy holders increased from 160,000 to 850,000, and the firm, which had initially focused on motor cycle insurance, became a major specialist provider of motor insurance for female drivers. Acquired by the Bradford-based Provident Financial Group in 1978, it had taken the name of the parent group by agreement with the Halifax Building Society after obtaining a high court injunction against the use of its original trading name by the building society giant when the latter entered the motor insurance business in 1993. Colonnade, originally based in Bradford, expanded rapidly in the 1980s and 1990s. By 1998 it had 320,000 policy holders, 720 employees, a nationwide network of branches and a large telephone call-centre at Mixenden, where Hebble Insurance Management Services, the centralised management service company for the group, accounted for a further 140 employees.[28]

One of the fastest growing corporate finance groups in Halifax in the late 1990s was Gartland, Whalley and Barker. This company which specialised in taking stakes in industrial groups, nurturing them and then floating them off on the stock market, was founded in 1989 by Tony Gartland, former chairman of the FKI Babcock group, which he had built up from a small privately-owned company, but which relocated to the south of England in January 2000. The *Financial Times* described him as a Yorkshire entrepreneurial phenomenon with 'a well-conceived strategy'. By 1998, Gartland, Whalley and Barker employed some twenty-four staff at Belle Vue, Sir Francis Crossley's former residence in Hopwood Lane, renamed by the company Crossley House. In 1996–97 Gartland, Whalley and Barker's profits rose 63 per cent with eight astute new acquisitions in Britain and one in America. By 1998 Gartland's stake in Gartland, Whalley and Barker, was valued at £59.4 million, which with other assets in excess of £5 million made him one of the wealthiest businessmen in Yorkshire, enabling him to play a prominent role in the development of the Calderdale Community Foundation, a locally managed charitable endowment fund, launched in 1993.[29]

The growth of the service sector in Calderdale in the 1980s was also stimulated by the development of tourism, which was accelerated by the devastating impact of the 1979–82 recession on the manufacturing sector. It has been estimated that in 1982 Calderdale venues accounted for around 10 per cent of total tourist activity in West Yorkshire, representing around a quarter of a million visits, three-quarters

Halifax Insurance Co., Holy Trinity Church, Harrison Road, Halifax, 1988. This former Georgian church was designed by Leeds architect, Thomas Johnson, for the Vicar of Halifax, the Revd Dr Henry William Coulthurst in 1798, to provide additional church accommodation as the population of the town expanded westwards. It was declared redundant in 1978, restored with assistance from English Heritage, and re-occupied in 1987 by the Halifax Insurance Co., providing attractive open-plan office accommodation for ninety-five employees. (Photograph: Ian Beesley)

of a million overnight stays and an estimated expenditure of £7.5 million. While the major West Yorkshire attractions with over 100,000 visitors a year, such as the Brontë Parsonage and the Keighley and Worth Valley Railway, were situated outside Calderdale, both Shibden Hall and Bankfield Museum were attracting over 50,000 visitors a year by 1982. The Civic Trust report in 1984 concluded that 'with its combination of unique landscape and largely unspoiled towns and villages steeped in history' and its proximity to major motorway routes and airport connections, Calderdale had environmental assets no less marketable to tourists 'than the products of its formerly bustling factories'. Calderdale, however, with only 2,500 bed spaces, nearly 70 per cent of which were in the self-catering sector, had an acute shortage of quality serviced overnight accommodation and lacked a single major attraction to entice visitors to Calderdale until the opening of the Eureka National Children's Museum in 1992. However, visits to Calderdale Tourist Information Centres showed a steady growth during the 1980s, although the number of visitors to the Tourist Information Centre at the Halifax Piece Hall fluctuated in contrast to the rising spiral of visitors to Hebden Bridge, stimulated by the proximity of Hardcastle Craggs. Nevertheless, by 1998 day-trippers were spending annually an estimated £12 million in Halifax and overnight visitors £3 million.[30]

Retailing remained a vital element within the local economy throughout the second half of the twentieth century. Halifax accounted for over 60 per cent of Calderdale's retail turnover in 1971. Brighouse, the next largest retail centre in Calderdale, accounted for only 13 per cent. This contrast emphasised the continuing role of Halifax as a major retail centre for its periphery. Moreover, the overall retail space in Halifax increased by over 10 per cent between 1988 and 1998, when a survey revealed that half the retail floor space in Calderdale was concentrated in Halifax town centre. However, the development of the retail sector throughout the period was fraught with controversy. Plans for a major new shopping development in Halifax were first mooted in 1951, but over thirty years elapsed before the successful Woolshops centre finally opened in 1983, with provision for thirty-three shops, including premises for Woolworths, Boots, Sainsburys, W. H. Smith and Mothercare.[31] The original scheme had envisaged massive blocks of flats, play areas, a bowling green, health centre, dance hall and parking for 3,750 cars. Even as late as 1977 a large covered Arndale Centre modelled on centres in Bradford and Manchester was being planned. However, members of the Halifax Civic Trust, led by their chairman, the carpet manufacturer Charles Crossley, were concerned at the impact of the scheme on listed buildings in the town centre. They forced the issue to a public inquiry and commissioned a firm of architects to produce plans for an alternative development on a smaller scale. After the inquiry the government rejected the £30 million Arndale Scheme. This was hailed by the *Halifax Courier* as a 'major victory for the conservation movement'. The revised scheme proved so successful that in 1998 approval was given for an expansion of the development, though this dealt the final blow to an imaginative scheme for the redevelopment of Westgate, which had experienced difficulties in attracting a major anchor store. However, the demolition of the extensive former Smith Wire Works permitted a major new retail development including a health club, gym and swimming pool in Charlestown Road completed in 2003, when plans were also finally approved for the development of a long-delayed plaza in Broad Street.[32]

By the 1990s, however, there were growing concerns about the impact of out-of-town shopping centres and supermarkets on town centre shopping. An increasing number of town centre retail outlets were being converted into pubs, clubs, wine bars and charity shops. The number of empty shops in Halifax rose from 7 per cent in 1988 to 11 per cent in 1998, although this was still below the national average of 14 per cent. Moreover, council income from the Piece Hall, where there were also untenanted shops and market stalls, declined sharply from £278,542 in 1993–94 to £140,934 in 1997–98. Consequently, the promotion of Halifax as a retail centre became a major priority in the regeneration of the town and led to the establishment of a Halifax Town Centre Forum and the appointment of a town centre manager in February 1996. This initiative was funded principally by the private sector with the aim of making Halifax Town Centre an attractive, lively and successful shopping venue. A new shopping guide, published in 1998, listed over 300 shops in the town centre, including 33 fashion stores, sixteen jewellers, eleven shoe shops, ten furniture stores, six fishmongers, six bookshops, five florists, four supermarkets, two covered markets and two department stores. Between 1996 and 1999 the number of empty shops in the town centre was reduced to eight. However, while the closure in 1999 of Halifax's struggling co-operative retail store marked the end of an era spanning almost a century, the continuing expansion of Harvey's, Halifax's remaining department store, which celebrated its fiftieth anniversary in 2001, proved to be the major post-war retailing success story in the town. The sole survivor of a chain of stores founded by Edgar Thomas Harvey in Dewsbury in the 1920s, the Halifax store, formerly Waddington's Furriers, was purchased by Ian and Dorothy Harvey in 1951. Following Ian Harvey's untimely death at the age of fifty, the store was developed by their son Roger, who joined the company at the age of twenty, with the support of his wife Sue and daughter Tracy. The store, employing a staff of more than 120 by 2001, expanded into neighbouring premises on Powell Street and Commercial Street, offering a wide range of cosmetic, fashion, gift and household products, together with an in-store restaurant, and remains one of the very few independent department stores to survive in West Yorkshire.[33]

The economic restructuring and regeneration of Halifax and Calderdale in the 1980s owed much to two other inter-related factors. The first was the drive and vision of Ernest Hall, an accomplished concert pianist, industrial entrepreneur and property developer, who transformed Dean Clough from a redundant carpet mill into a major centre for business, education and the arts. Born into a working-class family in Bolton, Hall had developed an early passion for music, but after a promising education at the Royal Manchester College of Music he had embarked upon a successful career in textiles. He came to live in Calderdale and saw the potential of Dean Clough in 1983 for realising his vision, inspired by the Dartington ethic, of 'a practical utopia' by creating a balanced environment in which both commerce and culture could interact and thrive. By 1995, Dean Clough provided accommodation for some 200 companies and organisations employing around 3,000 people, together with an enterprise campus providing training for both college students and company employees, a contemporary art gallery, a language laboratory, the Henry Moore Sculpture Trust Studio, two theatre companies, and the first regional centre of the Royal Society for the Encouragement of the Arts, Manufactures and Commerce. Hall's commitment to the arts both regionally and nationally led to honours, including an OBE in 1986 and a knighthood in 1993 and his appointment as Deputy Lieutenant of West Yorkshire and Chancellor of the University of Huddersfield. The success achieved by Hall at Dean Clough impressed visitors, including the then Prime Minister, Margaret Thatcher, who described it in 1987 'as a showcase of small industrialised units, and an example of what can be achieved through innovation and enterprise'.[34]

The second factor was the influence of Business in the Community, an initiative spearheaded by its president, HRH the Prince of Wales, which selected Calderdale as the pilot for an innovatory partnership scheme in 1986, partly on account of Hall's remarkable success and partly because Calderdale, with unemployment below the national average, failed to qualify for either government or European Community assistance. The scheme was Business in the Community's most ambitious project since its foundation by a small group of businessmen in the wake of the inner-city disturbances of 1981 in Brixton and Toxteth. When HRH the Prince of Wales personally launched the 'demonstration partnership' on 9 December 1986, designed to regenerate the entire 140-square mile metropolitan district of Calderdale, he expressed the hope that it would become the model for other such schemes in other regions suffering from industrial decline. Calderdale was similar in size to the North American town of Lowell, near Boston, Massachusetts, which had provided the inspiration for the project. The partnership received all-party support from Calderdale Metropolitan Borough Council and the enthusiastic backing of Calderdale's newly appointed chief executive, Michael Ellison, a native of the town who had lived as a child in the socially deprived St John's Ward.[35]

Business in the Community's project team under Richard Wade and Paul Greetham began sponsoring co-operative links between the community, its local politicians and businessmen, and generated plans for a variety of new businesses and attractions, including an interactive children's museum, Eureka, funded by grants from central government, the Clore and Vivien Duffield Foundations, business sponsorship and Calderdale Council. Eureka, the first museum of its kind in the UK, which opened in July 1992 on a previously derelict site next to the railway station, rapidly achieved phenomenal success, attracting its millionth visitor in March 1995, well ahead of target and scooping a host of awards for its imaginative approach to active learning and child development. Business in the Community also encouraged the development of industrial, retail, leisure and tourist facilities, improved transport links, and environmental improvement programmes. The support of the Prince of Wales was undoubtedly a key factor in the success of the project. Everywhere he went he extolled the virtues of the Calderdale experiment in speeches to business leaders, city financiers and American architects in Pittsburgh, and he made a series of personal visits to Calderdale to monitor the progress of the partnership.

Halifax and Calderdale therefore successfully made the turbulent transition from a predominantly manufacturing economy to an economy increasingly dependent upon services during the second half of the twentieth century, just as previously Halifax had evolved from economic dependence on subsistence agriculture into a thriving commercial and industrial centre. Moreover, this was achieved without a complete abandonment of Calderdale's manufacturing inheritance. Indeed, the 2001 Census confirmed that manufacturing remained the largest single sector of employment within Calderdale, contrasting sharply with the national average, and that within West Yorkshire, only Kirklees had a higher proportion of its workforce engaged in manufacturing. Carpet and moquette weaving, precision engineering and confectionery production ensured a continuation of economic diversification within the local economy. The remarkable growth of the service sector in Halifax in the last quarter of the twentieth century was facilitated by a telecommunications

The official inauguration of the Calderdale Partnership on 6 February 1987. Calderdale was selected by Business in the Community from a short-list of several northern towns to participate in a pioneer partnership scheme between the private and public sectors. HRH the Prince of Wales travelled to Calderdale to launch the partnership at Dean Clough. The meeting was also attended by the Mayor of Calderdale, local councillors, members of Business in the Community's governing council, participants in similar schemes in the USA, and local business and community leaders. (Photograph: Sir Ernest Hall)

The Eureka Museum for Children, Halifax, was opened in July 1992 by HRH the Prince of Wales. It was funded by the Clore and Vivien Duffield Foundations, business sponsorship, government grants and Calderdale Metropolitan Borough Council. It was designed to teach children about themselves and the world around them, using a hands-on, fun approach to learning and development. By August 1997, two million visitors had explored the innovative new museum, with its 400 or more interactive activities, games and challenges. By 1999, the museum had won eighteen prestigious awards, including the English Tourist Board Visitor Attraction of the Year award in 1993. (Photograph: Eureka)

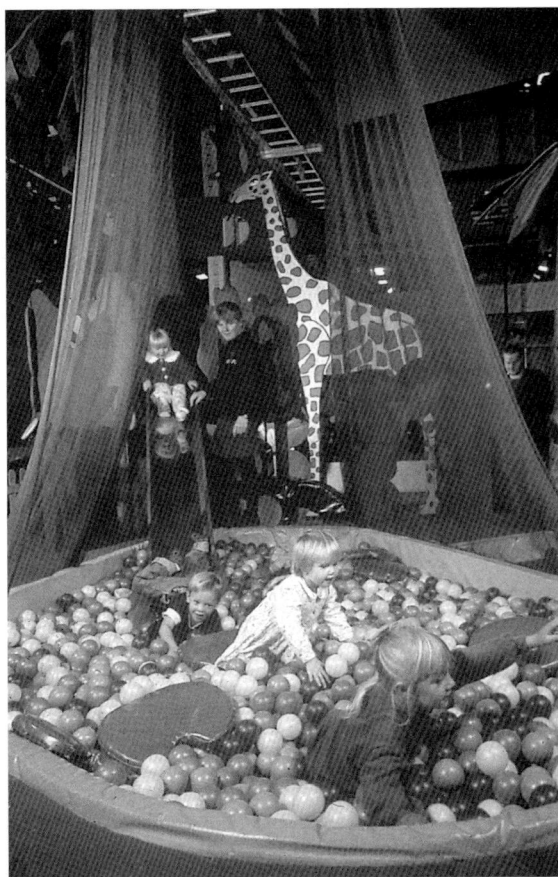

revolution, which finally neutralised some of the constraints which geographical factors had imposed upon Halifax's economic and urban development at the beginning of the twentieth century. Indeed, during the late twentieth century there was also a growing realisation that Halifax's remote and rugged Pennine location, which was proving increasingly attractive to both commuters and tourists, had considerable potential for further economic development. This was accompanied by an increasing recognition that economic restructuring depended not merely on market forces but upon a partnership for renewal between private investment and public authorities. Indeed, Halifax was a pioneer in pursuing this form of partnership, which was itself largely learned in the early Thatcher years from the United States. This unusual combination of factors was to provide the springboard from which Halifax would launch itself with confidence into the twenty-first century.[36]

Local government

The period after 1945 witnessed a considerable increase in the role of central government and the public services. To what extent were the county and metropolitan boroughs of Halifax and Calderdale affected by these changes, and how did their roles within the local community change in the second half of the twentieth century and the early years of the twenty-first century?

As a county borough, Halifax after 1945 still retained considerable local responsibilities for education, health, housing, highways, markets, public transport, fire and civil defence. Moreover, post-war requirements led to the development of responsibilities for town planning and social services, in dedicated departments by 1965 and 1971. Borough architects, town planners and engineers worked in close partnership on an increasing variety of related schemes. These included the design and planning of new housing estates, high-rise flats, offices, shops and schools; a new swimming pool on Huddersfield Road opened in 1966; a new central cleansing and transport depot on Battinson Road in 1968; a new fire station at King Cross opened in 1970; a multi-storey car park on Cow Green opened in 1971; and a multi-million-pound inner relief road opened in 1973. The new social services department established as a result of the Local Authority Social Services Act 1970 aimed to provide a co-ordinated approach to social work, taking over the functions of the welfare services committee and children's committee and some of the functions of the health committee. The growth of the proportion of elderly people within the local community, a rising divorce rate and changing patterns of family life generated an increasing range of problems for the new department in the last three decades of the twentieth century.[37]

However, local authorities like Halifax also lost some of their roles and also their sources of revenue with the creation of nationalised public utility companies for electricity, gas and water between 1949 and 1961. And some duties were transferred to other public authorities like the Halifax Area Hospitals Management Committee in 1948 and the West Yorkshire Police Authority in 1968. Indeed, the scope and resourcing of local administration became a matter of considerable debate during this period, leading to the Redcliffe-Maud inquiry into the financing of local government in 1968 and local government reorganisation in 1974. Redcliffe-Maud's inquiry ranked Halifax the poorest of seventy-nine English local authorities with a rateable value of only £29.60 per head of population, underlining the relatively limited local resources available to fund services. The case for merging Halifax into a larger unit of local government, covering a wider geographical area, was therefore strong. However, after local government reorganisation, Calderdale was the fifth smallest of the thirty-six new metropolitan districts and the smallest metropolitan borough in West Yorkshire. It commanded only 7.6 per cent of the rateable value of the West Yorkshire Metropolitan County although it comprised 17.6 per cent of the county's land area. Indeed, the West Riding County Council, in its observations on the government White Paper which proposed to modify the Redcliffe-Maud proposals by placing the responsibility for the administration of education at district rather than county level, insisted that of the metropolitan districts in West Yorkshire only Leeds and Bradford would have sufficient resources to provide an adequate education service.[38]

Moreover, the abolition of the West Yorkshire Metropolitan County Council in 1986 and the creation of single tier local authorities further depressed Calderdale's financial situation. Calderdale had benefited from the redistributive effect of the provision by the metropolitan county of some services such as road gritting and snow clearing, but now more responsibilities were devolved upon district councils. On the other hand, Conservative government policies in the 1980s and 1990s resulted in the loss by district authorities like Calderdale of some responsibilities because of the sale of council houses, schools opting out of local education authority control, the autonomy of further education colleges, the implementation of care in the community schemes, and the privatisation of some council services: for example, in 1994 Calderdale Council lost its refuse collection contract to an outside contractor. There were also major changes in the way local government was financed, with the changeover in 1990 from rates to the controversial community charge and its subsequent replacement by the council tax in 1993, and the still tighter control of local government spending by central government through charge capping from April 1990, when Calderdale Council was obliged to cut its agreed budget from £132 to £125 million. In spite of these reorganisations and rigorous financial controls, first Halifax and then Calderdale continued to provide a range of services to the community.[39]

Education, in particular, required major resourcing after 1945 to implement the provisions of the 1944 Butler Act, and to accommodate the post-war population bulge and the raising of the school leaving age to fifteen in 1944 and sixteen in 1973. School buildings, which had been neglected in Halifax during the inter-war years, had to be modernised and extended. Although greater progress was made after 1945 than in the preceding period, in some years there were severe constraints on expenditure, as in 1956 when the education budget estimate was cut by £80,000 even though the Ministry of Education identified Halifax as being the fourth most under-staffed education authority in the country. The first of a dozen new primary schools built between 1949 and 1970 was opened in 1949 to serve the new Cousin Lane housing estate at Ovenden. Two new secondary schools were also opened in 1952 on green field sites at Illingworth and Exley, the J. H. Whitley Secondary School and Exley Secondary School. In 1957, the Junior Technical High School, later Highlands, and St Thomas More's Roman Catholic Secondary School were opened at Illingworth, followed by the Holy Trinity Church of England Senior School in 1962.

In 1964 protracted debates began in Halifax about the reorganisation of secondary education. The arguments for selective education, although often couched in meritocratic terms, versus notions of social egalitarianism, reflected deeper social and political divisions within the local community. A 1966 report suggested a three-tier system with transfer between tiers at nine and thirteen. This was approved by the education committee and council by the narrowest of margins, prompting a rash

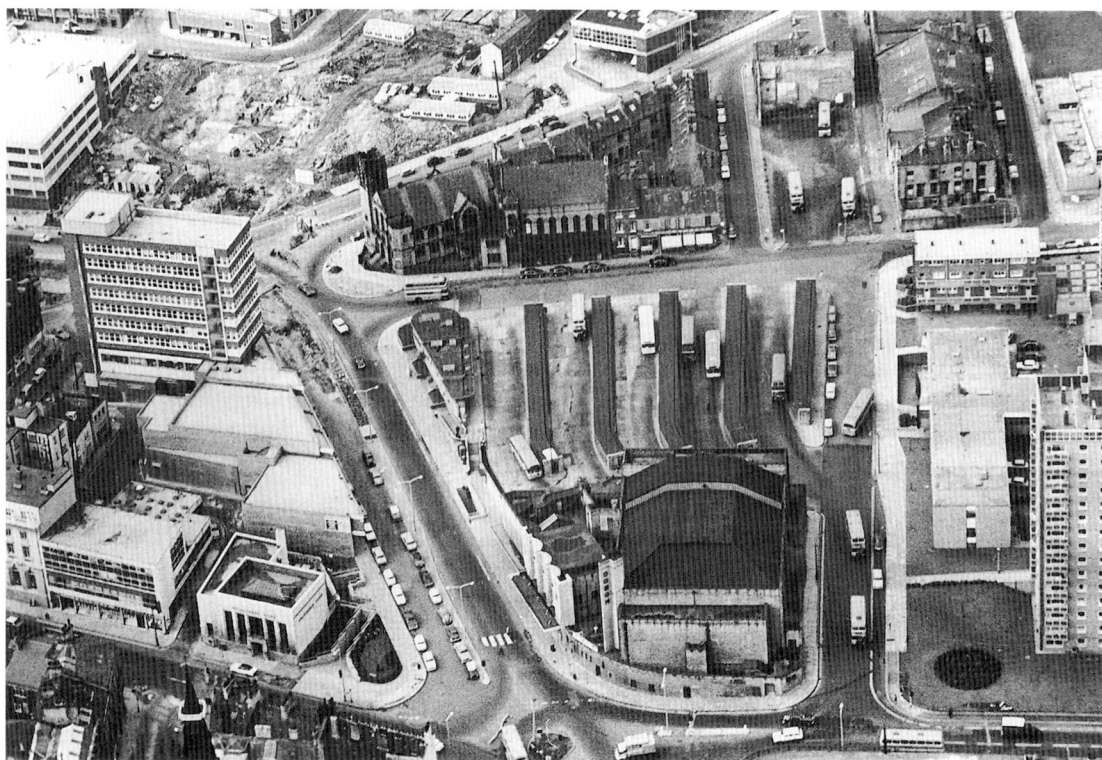

Redevelopment of Cow Green and Broad Street, 1970. This aerial photograph appeared in the *Halifax Courier* with the caption: 'Halifax steadily growing taller'. New high rise flats are visible on the extreme right, while a site for the construction of another tower block is being cleared at the top left of the photograph alongside the new multi-storey car park on Cow Green opened in 1971. Crown House, the first high rise office block to be built in Halifax and the Broad Street retail development, commenced in 1968 at a cost of £250,000, is nearing completion, together with the modification of the adjacent road network. The Broadway supermarket is visible in the left foreground sandwiched between the National Provincial and the Yorkshire banks. The new bus station at Cross Fields occupies a former slum clearance site behind the Odeon cinema. (Photograph: *Halifax Courier*)

speculation from the *Halifax Courier* that the eleven-plus would end in Halifax by 1970. However, the proposed three-tier plan went through a series of revisions, encountering strong opposition from the grammar school lobby, and by 1972 it had failed to secure acceptance by both the council and the Ministry of Education and the issue remained unresolved when Calderdale Metropolitan Borough Council was established in 1974. Calderdale assumed responsibility for schools formerly administered by the West Riding County Council. It inherited a number of successful comprehensive schools such as Calder High School, established in 1953, and Brooksbank School, Elland, established in 1959. However, it also acquired a number of seemingly intractable problems which the county council had been grappling with since 1937, for example the future of the small voluntary-aided grammar schools at Hipperholme and Rastrick. In 1985 Calderdale refused to accommodate Hipperholme Grammar School as a voluntary-aided school, but it became independent, losing its head and two-thirds of its staff who expressed a preference to remain within the state sector. It survived by the astute sale at the top of the market of surplus playing fields and by fundraising efforts which realised over half a million pounds between 1984 and 1998. Rastrick amalgamated with a failing secondary modern in 1984 and was transformed into a highly successful voluntary-controlled comprehensive school, one of several which opted for grant-maintained status in 1993.[40]

In Halifax itself, the Crossley Heath School, an amalgamation of the neighbouring Heath and Crossley and Porter grammar schools, and the North Halifax Grammar School, an amalgamation of the Highlands and Princess Mary high schools in 1985, were consistently placed in the top 150 secondary schools in national examination league tables, and Ofsted reports recognised the quality of educational provision at both schools. However, there was growing concern about the problems faced by the remaining non-selective former secondary modern schools in Halifax, such as Halifax High School, the successor of the Clare Hall and Haugh Shaw secondary schools, where 578 of the 700 pupils on roll in 1995 came from homes where English was not the first language and where many had reading ages below

Burdock Way, 1973. The increase in road traffic created growing pressure after 1945 for schemes to relieve town-centre congestion. In 1967 the Ministry of Transport approved the construction of a ring road around the town centre, and in 1970 confirmation of a government grant for 75 per cent of the cost of the project was received. The road network incorporating a massive concrete flyover was completed within two years at a cost of £4.5 million and opened in April 1973. It was named after Alderman John Burdock, a long-serving member of the Halifax County Borough Council. (Photograph: *Halifax Courier*)

the national average. Moreover, at the Ridings School, another school with a large number of children with special learning needs, which came into being as a result of a merger of the Holmfield and Ovenden secondary schools, there was a major crisis in 1996 following the breakdown of discipline at the school.[41] The crisis was defused when the local education authority approached Peter Clark, head of the neighbouring grant maintained school at Rastrick, to manage the Ridings School with Anna White, deputy head of Todmorden High School, as associate head. Their competent leadership rescued the school from direct intervention by the Department for Education, Clark returning to Rastrick with a CBE, a national celebrity, and White securing permanent appointment to the headship in 1998. The media, whose coverage of the problem became the subject itself of controversy, dubbed the Ridings the worst school in Britain and the problems of the school became a focus for the national debates surrounding education prior to the 1997 general election. A subsequent inspection criticised the leadership of the local education authority's senior management team and the Director of Education, Ian Jennings, ultimately took early retirement in September 1998. Under the leadership of his successor, Carol White, a former history teacher and adviser, Calderdale schools topped the West Yorkshire GCSE examination league tables in 2002; controversial plans for a new secondary school on the site of the former barracks at Wellesley Park won council approval and Calderdale Council achieved national recognition as a beacon of excellence in secondary education, earning Carol White promotion to deputy chief executive of the authority in 2003. A growing concern within Calderdale was the limited retention of students in post-sixteen education and the loss of students to neighbouring authorities, especially Greenhead and Huddersfield New Colleges in Kirklees and to a lesser extent to Rochdale and Burnley. Indeed, Todmorden High School opted to close its sixth form in 2018, because of the problem of recruiting sufficient students to ensure viability. Meanwhile Trinity Academy, supported by Steve Evans, Head of Rastrick High School, backed a proposal for a new sixth form college in Northgate, Halifax 'for all 16–19 learners in Calderdale seeking to pursue both academic and vocational qualifications from September 2019'.[42]

Academies, state-funded schools directly funded by the Department of Education, remain independent of local authority control as self-governing non-profit charitable trusts, but may receive additional support from personal or corporate sponsors. Developed on the recommendations of his education advisor Andrew Adonis and established by Tony Blair's Labour Government through the Learning and Skills Act of 2000, which amended a section of the Education Act of 1966 relating to City Technology Colleges, their aim, according to Education minister, David Blunkett, was 'to improve pupil performances and break the cycle of low expectations'. Their name was changed to Academies by an amendment to the Education Act of 2002 and they were supported by the Conservatives from their inception, who in coalition with the Liberal Democrats secured the Academies Act of 2010, but they were opposed by some trade unionists and parents. By September 2012, nationally, most secondary schools and over 25 per cent of primary schools had become academies. A School Census in January 2017 revealed a total of one all-through, 21 primary and eight secondary academies, totalling 30 academies in Calderdale. Academies are not obliged to follow the National Curriculum, but must ensure that their curriculum is broad and balanced and includes the core subjects of mathematics and English. They remain subject to inspection by Ofsted.[43]

By 1993, a century after its foundation as the Halifax Technical School, Calderdale College was operating independently of local authority control under the supervision of the Department of Education. The Second World War had interrupted local education authority plans to extend the College, but following a bequest from former Mayor of Halifax Percival Whitley, a new building was finally opened on Francis Street in 1957 by Halifax born Sir John Wolfenden (1906-1985), notable for his Chairmanship of the Wolfenden Report of 1957. One of Whitley's achievements had been to establish links between Halifax and the city of Aachen after a group of students from the college had travelled to Germany to build a hostel for families returning to the war-ravaged town in 1949. This proved the springboard for the launch of a growing series of cultural exchanges between the two centres in the 1950s. During the 1950s and 1960s most of the college's students were part-time or day-release students, but during the 1970s increasing numbers of students enrolled on full-time courses. In the 1980s many enrolled on vocational training relevant to careers in the new service industries such as tourism and leisure, hospitality and catering, and business administration, and the college worked closely with the Manpower Services Commission, the Training and Enterprise Councils, and agencies of the European Community to develop retraining programmes as the local economy was restructured. By 1998 with a budget of over £12 million, a staff of over 360 and more than 7,500 students, including more than 25 per cent of young people in post-16 education in Calderdale, Calderdale College also had links with over 240 companies and organisations throughout the area. Moreover in 2003 the campus was redeveloped, with support from the European Union urban regeneration project, to provide a new state-of-the-art regional centre of excellence for training in building conservation and architectural restoration skills. Whilst Calderdale remained the only West Yorkshire metropolitan district without a single institution of higher education within its boundaries by the end of the twentieth century, many students from Calderdale pursued undergraduate and post-graduate courses at the neighbouring University of Huddersfield. In addition, Leeds Becket University established a Business Centre in Halifax, supporting business success in Calderdale in temporary accommodation at Dean Clough, seeking to drive economic growth across Calderdale, to be based permanently in a former warehouse on Horton Street. Calderdale Council Leader, Tim Swift, welcoming the new initiative, referred to Calderdale's strong entrepreneurial tradition with over 6,800 small businesses already based in Calderdale.[44]

Advances in medicine and a reorganisation of health service provision resulted in a changing role for the local authority in the post-war improvement of public health. The availability of sulphonamide drugs, antibiotics and mass immunisation programmes through the National Health Service after 1948 gradually reduced high mortality rates from infectious diseases. Although there were 53 deaths from tuberculosis in Halifax in 1947 and 63 beds maintained at Northowram Hospital in 1970 for cases of tuberculosis and other infectious diseases and chest conditions, the number of deaths from infectious diseases and bronchitis was declining after 1945. G. C. F. Roe, Halifax's Medical Officer of Health, who had responsibility for monitoring public health within the county borough, expressed alarm at the harmful effects of atmospheric pollution in 1948: 'Clean air does not exist. Who knows how much damage results to the human body from smoke and chemicals emitted into the air we inhale'.[45] Environmental and socio-economic factors contributed to a rise in the number of deaths from cancer and coronary heart disease and Halifax had the highest death rate of all the West Riding county boroughs in the period 1961–65. Calderdale's mortality rate from heart disease though declining during the period 1974–87 was still higher than both the regional and national average, and the problem remained particularly acute amongst lower socio-economic groups in Mixenden, St John's, Todmorden and Ryburn Wards, where the exceptionally high incidence of the disease was related to poor diet, smoking, alcohol and lack of exercise. Moreover, while the perinatal mortality rate in Calderdale was more than halved between 1974 and 1987, the infant mortality rate in Calderdale remained slightly above the regional average.[46]

The new Laura Mitchell Clinic, catering for a wide range of local health services including family planning, opened in October 1968 and the Frank Swire Health Centre in May 1970. After 1948 the Halifax Area Hospitals Management Committee assumed responsibility for the management of both the Halifax General Hospital, formerly administered by the local authority, and the Royal Halifax Infirmary, a former voluntary hospital, as parts of the National Health Service. An ageing population required new initiatives in the care of the elderly, and a new geriatric unit with provision for 256 patients was opened at Northowram in September 1970. New psychiatric and maternity units were opened at Halifax General Hospital in April and June 1971. The need for a new hospital was under consideration as early as 1968 and after intensive campaigning and a succession of management reorganisations between 1974 and 1997 the Calderdale and Kirklees Health Authority finally obtained government approval for the commencement of work in 1998 on a new hospital on the site of the Halifax General Hospital, opened in 2001. Following the incorporation of the Royal Halifax Infirmary into the National Health Service in 1948, the voluntary tradition was kept alive when Halifax became the first town to form a League of Friends of Halifax Hospitals whose stated object was to continue 'that spirit of voluntary help and service in sympathetic assistance and comfort for patients and nurses in Halifax hospitals which was characteristic of Halifax people prior to the passing of the National Health Act, 1946'.[47] There was also strong support for the development of a hospice at Elland, and appeals for a body scanner for the Royal Halifax Infirmary in 1988–89 and for a cancer treatment unit at the new Calderdale Royal Hospital in 2000 raised respectively £500,000 and £800,000 following highly successful campaigns in the *Halifax Courier*.[48]

Calderdale Royal Hospital, 2003. The need for a new hospital to replace the Royal Halifax Infirmary on Free School Lane, the Halifax General Hospital on Dryclough Lane and Northowram Hospital had been under consideration as early as 1968. After intensive campaigning and a succession of management reorganisations between 1974 and 1997 the Calderdale and Kirklees Health Authority finally obtained government approval for the commencement of work in 1998 on a new hospital on the site of the Halifax General Hospital. The £78 million hospital, designed to complement the original buildings of the Halifax General Hospital, opened in 2001. (Photograph: *Halifax Courier*)

The role of local government in the provision of housing which had developed during the inter-war years underwent further changes during the second half of the twentieth century. In 1954 Halifax had the highest proportion of back-to-back houses in the Calder Valley, but by 1966 the Halifax County Borough had the lowest proportion of houses without a fixed bath and water closet in the Calder Valley and the lowest proportion without hot water apart from Brighouse. By 1970 slum clearance was continuing at a rate of 700 to 800 houses a year. By 1972 over 6,000 council houses had been built since 1945 on large new estates encompassing the north-east of the town at Mixenden, Illingworth and Ovenden. However, 26 per cent of Calderdale's housing stock was sold between 1971 and 1991, and only 245 new council houses were built between 1980 and 1990. By 1992 waiting lists for council houses were the highest on record, but by 1995 Calderdale Housing Department was responsible for only 13,700 homes and by 2001, after the council's remaining housing stocks had been transferred to Pennine Housing, the proportion of social housing in Calderdale was significantly below the English average. The role of the local authority in the provision of housing had therefore changed dramatically. Between 1990 and 1995, 524 dwellings were under construction by housing associations, 989 by private builders and none by the local authority, which recognised that housing associations had now taken on the role of being the main providers of new social housing.

However, in 1997 there were some 200 empty council houses in North Halifax, mostly concentrated on estates with a poor reputation and high investment needs. They displayed an array of intractable problems poignantly captured in the photographs and prose of Nick Danziger, which were published in 1996. They included drug abuse, graffiti, vandalism and violence, with tension on one estate 'more like Sicily than Yorkshire'. In 1999, the council's economic and community development sub-committee undertook responsibility for co-ordinating a major project of social and environmental improvement on the troubled estates of Mixenden, Illingworth and Ovenden. Significantly, the project was funded by resources provided by a variety of agencies acting in partnership, including more

Cripplegate House, Shibden Park. The late-medieval, timber-framed house, which stood originally in Cripplegate, between King Street and Lower Kirkgate, was rescued from destruction by the antiquary John Lister, who purchased the structure from the railway authorities in the early 1870s. It was later restored and re-erected in the grounds of Shibden Hall, which were officially opened to the public by the Prince of Wales in October 1926. However, following serious neglect, which had aroused considerable controversy, it was finally demolished in 1971. (Photograph: H. Armitage)

Timbered House, Shibden Park, Halifax.

Open-air market, Halifax Piece Hall, 1980. The former Manufacturers' Piece Hall was acquired by Halifax Corporation in 1868 for use as a wholesale fish, fruit and vegetable market and opened in 1871. In the 1890s, sheds and lean-to buildings were erected in the courtyard, remaining there for eighty years until the Halifax Council finally resolved in 1973 to apply for funding to restore the building, which had been scheduled as an ancient monument in 1928. The building was re-opened in 1976 with an open-air market, textile museum, art gallery, antique and craft shops and other retail outlets. In 1976, Calderdale MBC resolved to promote the Piece Hall as 'a centre of tourism, culture and entertainment'. (Photograph: J. G. Washington)

than £4 million from the government's regeneration budget, £2.7 million from Calderdale Council, £1.1 million from the employment service and the rest from businesses, Calderdale College and the Calderdale and Kirklees Training and Enterprise Council. This emphasises the changing role of local government from provider to facilitator.[49]

Alderman Charles Holdsworth, in his address at Halifax's centenary celebrations in 1948, suggested that Halifax, having spent a century securing material improvements such as 'drains, sewers, public health, highways and parks', it was now time for the local authority to concern itself more 'with the cultural aspects of life'. During the following half-century, however, the role of the local authority in this sphere was severely constrained by limited resources. The appointment of Frank Atkinson as director of museums in Halifax in 1951 proved an inspired choice, and when the Shibden Hall Folk Museum was opened by the Duke of Devonshire in 1953 it was the only open air folk museum in England. But the demolition in 1971 of the timbered house, which had been painstakingly moved in the early 1870s by John Lister from the centre of Halifax to the grounds of Shibden Hall, revealed a reluctance to realise the full potential of Lister's and Atkinson's vision.[50]

However, recognition of the potential of Halifax Piece Hall in 1973 proved a major turning point. The future of the Piece Hall, then in use as a wholesale fruit and vegetable market, hung in the balance following the recommendation of the development committee not to submit an application for a grant for its restoration under the 'Operation Eyesore' scheme. It was saved not by the casting vote of the mayor as often asserted but by the development committee chairman Councillor Keith Ambler, a fancy yarn manufacturer and Conservative councillor for Northowram, who spoke passionately against the recommendation of the development committee he had chaired. He was supported by the vice-chairman, Hugh Lawler, a master baker and Labour councillor for Lee Mount. After a lively debate in which one councillor had argued that the Piece Hall 'should be pulled down' and another had suggested that 'fruit could disappear from Halifax if the wholesalers were to move', they received the backing of council by 29 votes to 12, with support from representatives of all three parties. Ambler had argued that 'a complete facelift and other use of the valuable Piece Hall would be far more beneficial to the town and rate-payers than its present use which had been under review since 1923'. He concluded: 'We have a unique building steeped in history and very much part of the town's past. It could well be part of the town's future, too'.[51] The restored Piece Hall was re-opened in 1976, with a new market and a variety of smaller retail outlets. In 1985 Calderdale Industrial Museum was opened in an adjacent former engineering works, winning the best industrial museum award in the following year, but financial constraints forced it to close to the public in 1998.

Other cultural projects included municipal provision for music and the performing arts and new leisure and library facilities. In 1960 Halifax Council purchased the Victoria Hall for use as a civic theatre, and Gordon Brooksby (1923–96), under the auspices of the Halifax Arts Council and later Calderdale Leisure Services, arranged an ambitious programme of over 100 visits by international symphony orchestras between 1972 and 1996. However, an attempt to provide a permanent base in Halifax for the Northern Ballet Theatre at Spring Hall, which had been presented to the town for the use of local people by Patons and Baldwins in 1948, proved more controversial. Though Christopher Gable received critical acclaim for a series of productions developed there, notably *Romeo and Juliet* and *Swan Lake*, the company left Halifax in 1996 to move into purpose-built accommodation in Leeds. The former army barracks which were also acquired by the council and renamed Wellesley Park in 1963 were used as a base for musical and physical education activities for schoolchildren, until the closure of the barracks under plans for the development of a new secondary school resulted in these activities becoming privatised. The creation of the metropolitan district of Calderdale facilitated the development of two major cultural and recreational amenities in the early 1980s. The new North Bridge Leisure Centre, opened in 1982, provided facilities for a wide range of sports and in 1988 hosted a major Council of Europe Conference on 'heritage and successful town regeneration'. Finally, after almost four decades of campaigning, the new Calderdale Central Library, with some of the finest archive storage facilities in Europe, opened in 1983 on a site adjacent to imposing new civic buildings in Northgate. The declared intention for its relocation in 2017 was initially to allow space for retail development, which never materialised and it is currently under consideration as a base for a sixth form college to help stem the seepage of post-16 students to other authorities, and also to introduce a younger age range of retail customers to the central area.[52]

The development of Calderdale Metropolitan Borough's tourist strategy, another new role for the local authority, was partly in response to the re-opening of the Piece Hall in 1976 and a growth of interest in the town's unique built environment following the removal of industrial grime from many local buildings in the early 1970s. It was also stimulated by a growing appreciation of the recreational potential of Calderdale's natural environment following the restoration of the Rochdale Canal and the designation in 1978 of the Calderdale Way, a fifty-mile public footpath around Calderdale's rural periphery, the first public recreational footpath route of its kind to be developed in England. In its 'Tourism Policy for Calderdale', published in February 1980, Calderdale Council saw the encouragement of tourism as a means of 'fostering civic pride, generating commercial confidence and helping to create a new image of Calderdale as a pleasant and interesting place to live'. An annual Calderdale Walking Festival, introduced in 1997, quickly proved its popularity with visitors, attracting 1,600 participants in 1998, when Calderdale Council's Tourism Unit received over 13,000 requests for its accommodation brochure.[53]

There had been strong all-party support for the Calderdale Inheritance Project, which had commenced in 1983. It had a ten-year programme of economic, social and environmental improvement, focusing upon the promotion of the town's heritage. Labour councillors, however, were keen to re-assert housing and social welfare priorities, and in 1989 the Inheritance programme was transformed into the 'Fair Shares Inheritance and Community Development Project'. Subsequently, political differences diminished as private sector investment in the project increased year by year, especially after the half-way stage had been reached in 1988. By 1990, other investment in the project amounted cumulatively to some fourteen times the Council's expenditure. The realisation that urban regeneration and cultural renaissance could be achieved through partnership between local government and the private sector reassured councillors concerned about shrinking public financial resources, particularly following the advent of charge-capping in 1990.[54]

The second half of the twentieth century had therefore witnessed major changes in local government. The County Borough of Halifax had been superseded by a larger administrative unit, the Metropolitan Borough of Calderdale, though the new authority remained relatively small, generating recurring concerns about its viability. Moreover, during the period local government lost some roles in the provision of public services. On the other hand, the development of the notion of partnership between the local authority, central government and the private sector offered new opportunities for the creative involvement of local government in economic, social and environmental improvement.

Local politics

Both nationally and locally in the quarter of a century which followed the end of the Second World War there developed a broad political consensus which recognised the need for improved public services. No party had overall control of Halifax County Borough Council during the period from 1945 to 1969, when a landslide victory gave the Conservatives an overall majority for the first time for half a century. Moreover, despite a swing to Labour in 1971, which enabled Labour to take five seats from the Conservatives and three from the Liberals, the Conservatives still maintained control with a majority of six. In 1972, after Labour gained another eight seats, Labour and the Conservatives both held twenty-six seats and the council became hung, with the Liberals holding the balance with seven seats.

The new metropolitan borough of Calderdale had only fifty-one elected members until the number was increased to 54 after the rationalisation of ward boundaries in 1979, whereas there had been no fewer than 215 elected representatives serving on the predecessor authorities. The first elections for the new Calderdale Council in 1973 gave Labour control but with an overall majority of only two. The *Halifax Courier* observed that the 'closeness of the vote in Calderdale repeats the unclear succession of power in Halifax which for years has given neither of the biggest parties a sizeable majority'. The turnout, which was regarded as 'the single biggest problem facing the new council', was far higher outside the former Halifax County Borough than in the borough where electors were not used to casting votes in both county and district elections and where the periphery appeared determined to assert itself in the first elections to the new authority.[55]

A resounding Conservative win in 1975 swept the ruling Labour group out of power, with the Conservatives gaining eleven seats from their Labour opponents and returning five of their own candidates, giving them a total of twenty-eight seats, whereas Labour seats on the council were reduced from twenty-seven to eighteen and the Liberal representation remained unchanged at five. By 1979, however, the number of Conservative seats had fallen to twenty-three, only one more than Labour and the Liberal representation had increased to nine, once more giving no single party overall control. For a decade parties took turns in chairing committees. For example, in 1985–86 the Conservatives and Liberals each took chairs of committees for six months. Indeed, at one time, chairmanship of council and its committees passed from party to party on a six-weekly basis, scarcely a formula, critics observed, for decisive political action.[56]

A by-election in April 1989 gave the Labour group a majority using the mayor's casting vote, and Labour retained control until the municipal elections in May 1992, when the council again became hung. During the following three years there were no fewer than fourteen different political leaders. In the elections of May 1995, however, six Conservative seats were lost to Labour, including the Conservative strongholds of Ryburn, Warley, Hipperholme and Lightcliffe. Labour regained political control, and under the leadership of Councillor Pam Warhurst

The last Mayor of the County Borough of Halifax, Raymond Talbot, photographed with newly-elected members of Calderdale Council in May 1973. They served for twelve months as a shadow authority before officially taking charge of local government. (Photograph: *Halifax Courier*)

began to implement a distinctly New Labour vision of social justice for all the people of Calderdale. This involved developing partnerships with key stakeholders including the private sector to enhance the value of council services, and promoting sustainable development to ensure better provision for the future within the constraints of government policies.[57]

Despite the boldness of the vision and the energy of Warhurst in forging ahead with its implementation in difficult circumstances, the party suffered a rebuff by the electorate. Subsequent elections focused on educational issues: problems at the Ridings School, the threatened closure of the Queen's Road Junior and Infant School and the music and physical education centre. Moreover, the dismissal of Michael Ellison, the authority's widely respected chief executive, for reasons which were never fully explained had also provoked controversy. Labour's share of the vote, which had been 48 per cent in the 1996 local elections and 50 per cent in the 1997 general election plummeted to 29 per cent in the 1998 local elections on a low turnout. The main beneficiaries were the Conservatives who increased their share of the vote from 29 per cent in the 1996 elections to 42 per cent in the 1998 elections, though the Liberal Democrats also increased their share from 22 per cent in 1996 to 26 per cent in 1998.

An editorial in the *Halifax Courier*, commenting on the results of the 1998 local elections, which deprived Labour of its majority and made it dependent on the casting vote of the Labour mayor, concluded that:

> The diverse economic, social and political nature of our district means that it was never destined to become the fiefdom of any one party. Calderdale is neither a leafy Tory suburb nor urban Labour stronghold. It is both of those things and much more besides, with a fairly strong tradition of Liberalism thrown in for good measure.[58]

Electoral wards, metropolitan borough of Calderdale, 1979–2004.

As a result of the 1999 local elections Labour lost six seats to the Conservatives and one to the Liberal Democrats, but increased its share of the vote to 35 per cent despite another low turnout. Although losing overall control of the council, Labour remained the largest political group with twenty seats, followed by the Conservatives with nineteen seats, and the Liberal Democrats holding the balance with fourteen seats. The legacy of Labour control included an innovatory system of Cabinet government: a representative group of seven councillors was responsible for major decisions, scrutinised by council committees and implemented by streamlined directorates with redesignated responsibilities for schools and children's services, community services, regeneration and development, central services and social care. However, in 2000 on a turnout of less than a quarter of the total electorate Labour lost half of their twenty seats, including that of their leader Michael Higgins, when their share of the vote dropped to 28.5 per cent, enabling the Conservatives, who had been highly critical of recent above inflation council tax rises, to regain overall control for the first time in twenty-one years with a 44 per cent share of the vote. But Conservative control of the council under the leadership of John Ford proved short lived, when, in the 2002 local elections, with a higher turnout of the electorate, the Conservatives lost three seats to Labour, including that of their deputy leader, Stephen Baines. However, they remained the largest political group with twenty-five seats, followed by the Liberal Democrats with thirteen, Labour with thirteen and a solitary Independent.

Then in 2003 the political complexion of Calderdale changed dramatically with the election of Adrian Marsden, the first British National Party candidate to be elected to a council east of the Pennines, at a by-election in the Mixenden ward in January. Later, in May 2003 the BNP achieved further successes with the election of Richard Mulhall at Illingworth, entitling the party to official group status on the council with an office at Halifax Town Hall. The BNP also came second in four other wards, hot on the heels of Labour's Linda Riordan in Ovenden and the Conservative veteran Bill Carpenter in Northowram and Shelf, and pushing the Labour leader Bob Metcalfe, who had represented the ward since 1979, into third place at Mixenden. Moreover, in the eight seats in which they fielded candidates they captured almost 6,000 votes, 11.8 per cent of the total votes cast. Their electoral success, which one seasoned *Halifax Courier* reporter suggested had opened up 'a jagged new faultline … across Calderdale's political landscape', could no longer be dismissed as an aberration. They had clearly engaged with significant sections of the electorate on local issues, particularly in the areas of greatest social deprivation, though, as the Conservative leader John Ford observed, they had also 'got a lot of support by campaigning on the issue of asylum seekers' playing 'on people's fears time and again' and that had 'a major influence' on how many of their supporters had voted. On a higher electoral turnout of 34.4 per cent in 2003, 1.8 per cent higher than in 2002, the Conservatives had obtained 25 seats with a 30.7 percentage share of the vote, Labour 10 seats with 27.7 per cent and the Liberal Democrats 16 seats with 27.7 per cent, leaving no party with overall control. Moreover, with a by-election pending the tragic death of the Liberal Democrat Stephen Pearson, who had fought a hard campaign to stem the advance of the BNP in Mixenden and then succumbed to cancer within three months of the election, and the prospect of every council seat up for re-election in 2004 following a reduction of the total number of wards from 54 to 51 with the redrawing of ward boundaries, municipal politics entered a greater state of flux in Calderdale than had been experienced since 1974. Attributing the success of the BNP to disillusionment with the performance of the mainstream parties, the *Halifax Courier* reflected in its editorial: 'Somehow, the newly shaped Calderdale Council, even if it is, as usual, a hung authority, has to develop the vision necessary to recapture the respect of the electorate'. Eventually the influence of the BNP diminished and by 2018 of the 51 Calderdale Councillors representing seventeen wards in Calderdale, twenty were women and two represented ethnic minorities, namely Faisal Shoukat, who also served as a member of the cabinet, and Ferman Ali, who also served as Mayor of Calderdale in 2017–18, both representing Park Ward. The state of the parties after the 2018 election was Labour 24 (+1) Conservative 20 (-1) Liberal Democrats 6 (+1) and Independents 1. The most sensational result was that Labour's Colin Hutchinson, a retired doctor, took Skircoat for Labour for the first time in Calderdale's forty-four year history, ousting senior Conservative Andrew

Tagg by just fifty-four votes in the closest contest of the day. Another close-run contest with just 149 votes in it saw Steven Leigh gain Ryburn for the Conservatives from the former Conservative Councillor Rob Holden who had switched from the party to stand as an Independent. However, Colin Raistrick retained his Independent seat in Hipperholme and Lightcliffe with a 217 majority, whilst Conservative Will Smith-Moorhouse lost Luddenen Foot to Scott Patient by 558 votes and the Liberal Democrats gained Warley from Labour. Overall support for the two largest parties Labour and Conservative largely held up at the expense of Liberal Democrat, UKIP and Green party votes, with Calderdale Council remaining in no overall control and Labour having gained one net seat as the largest party continuing to run the council on a minority basis until the election of May 2019, when Labour gained 4 councillors and took control of the council with an overall majority of 5 seats.[59]

Although Halifax remained the centre of administration for the new metropolitan district of Calderdale, Halifax councillors were in a minority on Calderdale Council after 1973 and leadership roles were often filled by councillors from other parts of the district. Indeed, the first leader of Calderdale Council was Harry Wilson, a retired headteacher and former Labour Leader of Todmorden Council and Mayor of Todmorden, who had served on the former Todmorden Council since 1947. John Bradley, a former further education lecturer, who served as leader of the Conservatives on Calderdale Council from 1974 until 1991 and leader of the Council from 1976 to 1979, was a member of the former Queensbury and Shelf Urban District Council and chairman in 1973–74. Prominent Liberals, notably David Fox, David Shutt, Stephen Pearson and Margaret Riley, had their power bases in Elland, Greetland and Stainland. Some long-serving councillors served on both the Halifax and the Calderdale councils, for example, John Ford and Eric Whitehead, Conservative councillors for Skircoat, and Joe Tolan, Labour councillor for Ovenden. Among the newer members were the first two representatives of the Asian community, Mohammed Najib, elected for Labour at a by-election in 1986, and Shakar Saghir, the successful Conservative candidate for the St John's Ward at the 1998 election, which ended the 46-year political career of Liberal Democrat, Albert Berry, Labour mayor of Halifax in 1970 and of Calderdale in 1988.

Calderdale Council included a much higher proportion of women members in 1998 than had Halifax in 1945. In 1945 Jennie Latham and Miriam Lightowler were the only female Halifax councillors, and when the veteran Mrs Lightowler retired in 1952, there were only four other women councillors. However, by 1998 a third of the members of Calderdale Council were women and by 2018, nearly half of Calderdale councillors were female. Women had served as the leaders of all three main parties, including Ann McAllister for the Conservatives, Janet Battye for the Liberal Democrats and Pam Warhurst for Labour. Pam Warhurst, a former animal rights activist, also served as the first woman leader of the council from 1995 to 1999, when she left the council to become the first woman chairman of the Calderdale Healthcare NHS Trust and vice-chairman of the new Countryside Agency established to implement the Labour Government's right to roam policy.

Lord Shutt of Greetland. David Shutt was born at Farsley, the son of a builder, and left school at the age of sixteen to train as an accountant, joining a Halifax firm of accountants in 1969. He was elected to Calderdale Council in Greetland and Stainland in 1973, stood down in 1990 and was re-elected in 1995 and 1999. He became the first Liberal Mayor of Calderdale and the council's youngest in 1982. A member of the Society of Friends, he regarded political service as a 'high calling' and was awarded a life peerage in May 2000. However, he resolved to retain his seat on Calderdale Council until his retirement in May 2003, advising the Boundary Committee for England on boundary changes for Calderdale for implementation in 2004, which proposed a reduction in the number of wards from 54 to 51. Reflecting on the changes which he had witnessed in local government during his involvement in local politics from 1973 to 2003, he observed: 'Instead of providing services, the council now enables others to do much of the work and is involved in more than 100 partnerships' (Photograph: *Halifax Courier*)

During the period from 1945 to 1998 the occupational composition of the council had also changed. In 1945 there was only a handful of representatives from the professions on Halifax Council, including a solitary architect, chemist and a former schoolmaster, but a stronger representation of manufacturers, quarry owners, engineers, retailers and tradesmen. In 1998, the professions were more strongly represented on the Calderdale Council, especially lecturers, teachers, educational administrators and social workers. A number of councillors also had industrial and commercial backgrounds, several in engineering though none in textiles (with the exception of a solitary self-employed tailoress) and there were relatively fewer representatives from the retail sector. However, by 2018, there were two married couples, including the Labour Leader of the Council Tim Swift and his wife Megan, and Deputy Labour Leader and Regeneration and Economic spokesman, Barry Collins and his wife Anne. However, despite these leadership roles, Councillor Collins in one of his annual reports emphasised that the 'ward councillor's most important job' remained to 'try to ensure that the council itself operates effectively in the service areas of most importance to local residents and their communities'. Local politicians by the twenty-first century had become, by occupation at least, less representative of dominant local economic interests. Indeed, many now considered themselves full-time politicians and this was reflected in the increases in allowances for councillors, which more than doubled between 1990 and 1998 from £100,000 to £198,000 and then almost doubled again to £403,380 by 2002. David Shutt, an accountant by profession, was a highly committed, long-serving Calderdale councillor from 1973 to 2003, with a keen interest in local government, which he regarded as a 'high calling'. Shutt resolved to continue to sit on Calderdale Council after having been awarded a life peerage as Baron Shutt of Greetland in May 2000, retiring from the Council in May 2003 after having advised the Boundary Committee for England on the revision of the electoral boundaries of Calderdale. He served successively as Liberal Democrat Deputy Chief Whip and Chief Whip in the House of Lords, becoming Government Chief Whip, after the formation of the coalition by David Cameron and Nick Clegg from May 2010 until May 2012. A distinguished parliamentarian he became the first Calderdale politician to serve as Captain of the Yeomen of the Guard between May 2010 and May 2017 and was also appointed to the Privy Council, continuing to raise matters relating to Calderdale, such as pressing for a commitment about the upgrade and electrification of the trans-Pennine rail route in January 2018.[60]

The economic and social complexity of Halifax in the late twentieth and early twenty-first centuries was reflected in the electoral politics of the Halifax parliamentary constituency, where an oscillation in allegiances made Halifax a marginal constituency for much of the period. In the 1950 general election the Halifax Conservative and Liberal Associations failed to agree on a joint anti-socialist candidate, and Dryden Brook was re-elected for Labour with a majority of 8,344. However, the Liberals decided not to contest the next general election, and so when Clement Attlee went to the country to strengthen his narrow House of Commons majority in October 1951 Brook's majority was slashed to 763. Moreover, at the 1955 election when Maurice Macmillan was returned for the Conservatives with a majority of 1,535, again no Liberal stood. The son of the future Conservative Prime Minister, Macmillan conquered a serious alcohol problem during the late 1950s. He held the seat in 1959 with an increased majority of 2,515, when he defeated Peter Shore, the future Labour minister, again without Liberal opposition. However, Macmillan lost the 1964 election to Dr Shirley Summerskill, the daughter of Baroness Edith Summerskill, a former Labour minister and party chairman, who obtained a majority of 1,058. Labour clearly benefited from the entry of a Liberal into the contest, which split the Conservative vote. Macmillan later renewed his association with Halifax by taking the title of Viscount Ovenden, when his father was created Earl of Stockton in 1984.[61] Shirley Summerskill, one of only five new women elected to the House of Commons in 1964, increased her majority to 5,702 in 1966, a margin which exceeded the number of votes obtained by the Liberal candidate in that election. However, in 1970, when Heath's Conservative government was swept into office, the Conservative candidate, G. A. Turner, obtained an increased share of the vote, and Summerskill's majority was reduced to 198. The situation was reversed after the confrontation between Heath and the miners and the three-day week in February 1974, when Summerskill was re-elected with a majority of 3,003. She then increased her majority to 4,178 in the election of October 1974, at the end of the shortest parliament of the twentieth century. For the first time at this election, immigration became an issue, when R. S. Pearson stood as a Powellite, obtaining 919 votes. At the 1979 election, following the defeat of Callaghan's Labour government on a vote of confidence, Shirley Summerskill was returned with a reduced majority of 1,234 over local Conservative councillor, John Ford, with a National Front candidate trailing the Liberal candidate in fourth place, and obtaining a mere 0.9 per cent of the votes.

In June 1983 with a commanding lead in the opinion polls following the Falklands conflict, Margaret Thatcher called a snap election, and Roy Galley, a local councillor, was returned for Halifax for the Conservatives with a majority of 1,869. However, he failed to retain the seat in 1987, losing to another local councillor, Alice Mahon, a lecturer in trade union studies and former nursing auxiliary, who obtained a majority for Labour of 1,212. Although Alice Mahon held on to her seat in 1992, with a swing of 0.6 per cent from Labour to the Conservatives, her majority was cut to 478 and the seat became the most marginal Labour seat in Yorkshire. However, in 1997, with a swing of 10.7 per cent to Labour, she increased her majority to 11,212, the largest majority obtained by any Halifax Member of Parliament since 1931. In 2001 she retained her seat despite a swing of 3.5 per cent from Labour to the Conservatives and the reduction of her majority by almost 50 per cent. With a reputation for her hardline, feminist, left-wing views, she developed a strong interest in health and welfare issues and proved no less outspoken in opposing Labour policies with which she disagreed than she had been in attacking those of the Thatcher and Major governments. In a dispute over female quotas in the Shadow Cabinet elections in 1993, for example, she had claimed that 'some of the men in the Parliamentary Labour Party would be more at home in Jurassic Park'. She was one of the most persistent Labour back bench opponents of the international conflicts in Afghanistan, Kosovo, the Gulf and Iraq and of the creation of foundation hospitals. Indeed, she refused to accept the party whip on no fewer than fifty-five occasions between 1992 and 1997 and voted against the Blair government on twenty-five occasions in all the major revolts between 1997 and 2001, forfeiting her brief tenure of office as parliamentary private secretary to the culture secretary, Chris Smith, after voting against 'punitive and cruel' lone parent benefit cuts in 1997. In 2002 she announced her intention to retire at the next general election after fifteen years service as Halifax's Member of Parliament.

Table 7.3 Parliamentary election results in the Halifax constituency, 1950–2019

Election	Turnout (%)	Candidate	Party	Votes	share (%)
1950	85.1	D. Brook	Lab	28,800	47.6
		C. H. Lucas	Cons	20,456	33.9
		A. Pickles	Lib	9,573	15.9
		R. H. Blackburn	Ind	1,551	2.6
1951	84.2	D. Brook	Lab	30,433	50.6
		C. H. Lucas	Cons	29,670	49.4
1955	80.2	M. V. Macmillan	Cons	28,306	51.4
		D. Brook	Lab	26,771	48.6
1959	83.3	M. V. Macmillan	Cons	29,212	52.2
		P. D. Shore	Lab	26,697	47.8
1964	82.1	S. Summerskill	Lab	23,143	43.7
		M. V. Macmillan	Cons	22,085	41.8
		J. F. Crossley	Lib	7,664	14.5
1966	80.4	S. Summerskill	Lab	25,391	50.3
		G. A. Turner	Cons	19,687	39.0
		D. A. Carlin	Lib	5,423	10.7
1970	73.5	S. Summerskill	Lab	24,026	49.4
		G. A. Turner	Cons	23,828	48.9
		A. J. W. Graham	Ind	847	1.7
1974 (Feb.)	81.2	S. Summerskill	Lab	20,970	40.9
		S. R. Lyons	Cons	17,967	35.1
		A. Clegg	Lib	12,300	24.0
1974 (Oct.)	74.6	S. Summerskill	Lab	20,976	44.3
		S. R. Lyons	Cons	16,798	35.5
		A. Clegg	Lib	8,693	18.3
		R. S. Pearson	Ind	919	1.9
1979	76.7	S. Summerskill	Lab	21,416	43.8
		J. Ford	Cons	20,182	41.3
		A. Clegg	Lib	6,853	14.0
		B. Wadsworth	Nat Fr	455	0.9
1983	75.1	R. Galley	Cons	22,321	40.9
		S. Summerskill	Lab	20,452	37.4
		F. Cockroft	SDP	11,868	21.7
1987	77.7	A. Mahon	Lab	25,115	43.4
		R. Galley	Cons	23,529	41.3
		L. Cockroft	Alliance	8,758	15.3
1992	78.7	A. Mahon	Lab	25,115	43.5
		T. R. Martin	Cons	24,637	42.6
		I. R. Howell	Lib Dem	7,364	12.8

		R. Pearson	Nat	649	1.1
1997	70.5	*A. Mahon*	Lab	27,465	54.3
		R. Light	Cons	16,253	32.2
		E. Waller	Lib Dem	6,059	12.0
		C. Whitaker	UKIP	779	1.5
2001	57.8	*A. Mahon*	Lab	19,800	49.0
		J. Walsh	Cons	13,671	33.8
		J. Durkin	Lib Dem	5,878	14.5
		H. Martinek	UKIP	1,041	2.5
2005	61.1	*L. Riordan*	Lab Co-op	16,579	41.8
		K. Hopkins	Cons	13,162	33.2
		M. Taylor	Lib Dem	7,100	17.9
		G. Wallace	BNP	2,627	6.6
		T. Holmes	Nat Front	191	0.5
2010	61.9	*L. Riordan*	Lab Co-op	16,278	37.4
		P. Allott	Cons	14,806	34.0
		E. Wilson	Lib Dem	8,335	19.0
		T. Bates	BNP	2,760	6.0
		D. Park	Ind	722	3.0
		J. Sangha	UKIP	654	1.5
2015	62.1	*H. Lynch*	Lab	17,506	40.0
		P. Allott	Cons	17,078	39.0
		L. Phillips	UKIP	5,621	12.8
		M. Ilyas	Lib Dem	1,629	3.7
		G. Scott	Green	1,142	2.6
		A. Javad	Respect	465	1.1
		T. Bendrien	Christian	324	0.7
2017	67.9	*H. Lynch*	Lab	25,507	52.8
		C. Pearson	Cons	20,131	41.7
		M. Weedon	UKIP	1,568	3.2
		J. Baker	Lib Dem	1,070	2.2
2019	64.61	*H. Lynch*	Lab	21,496	46.27
		K. Ali	Cons	18,927	40.74
		S. Wood	Brexit	2,813	6.05
		J. Baker	Lib Dem	2,276	4.90
		B. Jessop	Green	946	2.04

Sources: F. W. S. Craig, *British Parliamentary Election Results, 1950–73* (Parliamentary Research Services: 1983), *British Parliamentary Election Results, 1974–83* (Parliamentary Research Services: 1984); F. W. S. Craig (ed.), *Britain Votes* 4 (Parliamentary Research Services: 1988); C. Rallings and M. Thrasher, *Britain Votes* 5 (Parliamentary Research Services: 1993); R. Waller and B. Criddle, *The Almanac of British Politics* (Routledge, London: 2002), BBC Election Results, 2005–19 (bbc. co.uk/news/election).

Her successor, Linda Riordan, standing as a Labour Co-operative candidate, polled seven per cent fewer votes in 2005, but was nonetheless returned with 41.8 per cent of the votes. Conservative candidate Kris Hopkins polled 13,162 votes, amounting to one third of votes cast, a slightly reduced Conservative share of the votes since the Liberal Democrat candidate Michael Taylor obtained an increased share of 17.9 per cent, leaving BNP and National Front candidates trailing with 6.6 per cent and 0.5 per cent respectively, giving Labour a majority of 3,417 on a slightly increased turnout. Riordan retained the seat for Labour in 2010, with a 4.4 per cent decrease in her share of the vote, whilst Philip Allott and Elizabeth Wilson slightly increased the Conservative and Liberal Democrat shares, with a declining BNP vote

Alice Mahon MP voicing her opposition to the war in Iraq at a meeting at the Houses of Parliament in 2003. In December 2002 the veteran peace campaigner announced her decision not to contest the Halifax seat, which she had held since 1987, at the next general election. Born in Halifax into a socialist family, the family had moved to Shelf on the outbreak of the Second World War. After leaving school to work in various factories, offices and shops she became a keen trade unionist and while employed for eight years as a nursing auxiliary at Northowram Hospital, she became a shop steward for NUPE. When she was elected to Calderdale Council in 1982, she gave up her job to undertake further education and after graduating became a trade union lecturer at Bradford. In 1987 she was elected MP for Halifax and held her seat in 1992 when it became the most marginal Labour seat in Yorkshire. However in 1997, she obtained the largest majority obtained by any Halifax MP since 1931. A hard-working constituency MP, she gained a reputation for her controversial left-wing views, but proved no less outspoken in opposing Labour policies with which she disagreed than she had been in attacking those of the Thatcher and Major governments. (Photograph: Alice Mahon, MP)

and on a slightly increased turnout. There were two other candidates, however, Jay Sangha for UKIP, who polled 1.5 per cent and an Independent candidate, Diane Park, who took 722 votes. In the 2015 General Election, the Conservative campaign was launched by David Cameron from Dean Clough in Halifax, proclaiming his commitment 'to deliver more jobs, lower taxes, build homes, and give people dignity and security during retirement'. For the young, new apprenticeships would be created and 100,000 new starter homes would be built. He also promised a referendum on Britain's place in Europe. Halifax was considered to be a key marginal seat for the Conservatives to win if they were to secure a parliamentary majority. During his visit, the Prime Minister met with staff at the Halifax-based insurers Covea, congratulating the firm for expanding its work force by more than twenty per cent during the previous year. However, Holly Lynch, the Labour candidate selected following the retirement of Linda Riordan, like her predecessor a native of Halifax, won Halifax by just 428 votes, becoming one of the youngest candidates ever returned for the Halifax seat. She increased the Labour share of the vote by 2.6 per cent, campaigning on issues which included policing, education and reconfiguration of the hospital trust. The Liberal Democrat candidate, Mohammed Ilyas, obtained a reduced Liberal share of 3.7 per cent of the votes, fewer than Liz Phillips (UKIP) who polled 5,621, and only just ahead of Gary Scott (Green) who polled 2.6 per cent of the votes. From 2014 Calderdale had faced having its accident and emergency departments downgraded, but Huddersfield, given the age of its hospital buildings, appeared more vulnerable to closure. Nevertheless, the degree of uncertainty was exploited by the Labour candidate, whose campaign also highlighted transport issues urging electrification of rail links to Leeds and Manchester and relieving commuter crush by addressing rail capacity issues.

During the period 1945–2015 Labour had succeeded in winning Halifax in most elections, losing only in disastrous years like 1955, 1959 and 1983, but until 1997 the contests were invariably close-run, especially when fought by three or more candidates. Moreover, during a period when relatively few constituencies were represented by women, Halifax was represented by women MPs for nearly two-thirds of the seventy-two years from 1945 to 2017, assisted by Labour all-female short lists.[62] In 2016 the political landscape in Calderdale and Halifax, as elsewhere, was transformed by the result of the referendum on membership of the European Union, with 58,975 (55.7 per cent) voting to leave the European Union; 46,950 (44.3 per cent) voting to remain, from a turnout of 70.7 per cent across Calderdale. Indeed, all but three of Yorkshire's local authorities backed leaving the Community. In the 2017 General Election launched by Theresa May, Linda Riordan's successor in Halifax, Holly Lynch, defended a 1 per cent majority to hold the seat for Labour, campaigning for better protection for emergency service workers and opposing court closures, gaining 52.7 per cent of the vote, an increase of 12.7 per cent. Her Conservative opponent, Chris Pearson, a Greetland and Stainland councillor and local businessman providing specialist services to young people and adults with learning and physical disabilities, polled 20,131 votes, also representing a gain of 2.7 per cent since 2015. However, despite the Brexit referendum outcome, Mark

Weedon (UKIP) polled 1,568 votes, a loss of 9.6 per cent, whilst James Baker (Lib) polled 1,070, a loss of 1.5 per cent since 2015. A *Halifax Courier* analysis in 2017 of the performance of Calderdale's two MPs, in terms of their contributions to parliamentary debates and questions, together with their voting record, revealed that both Holly Lynch and Craig Whittaker (Con, Calder Valley) were outperforming most of their regional contemporaries over a twelve-month scrutiny. Lynch, shadow minister for flooding, spoke in 29 debates, received answers to 71 written questions and voted in 88 per cent of votes, whilst Whittaker, a government assistant whip (which limited his opportunities for speaking in debates), spoke in twelve debates, received answers to 31 written questions and voted in 94 per cent of votes.[63]

Two years later in Halifax, unlike some neighbouring West Yorkshire constituencies which fell to the Conservatives, such as Colne Valley, Keighley, Wakefield and Dewsbury, Holly Lynch was re-elected in December 2019 for the third time in succession, to represent Halifax at Westminster. However, her majority was reduced by a half by the intervention of the Brexit Party's candidate, Sarah Woods, who may also have denied victory to the Conservative, Kashif Ali, an Oldham barrister, by possibly dividing the Brexit vote as well as taking votes from Labour. Holly Lynch, speaking after her result was announced, attributed the extent of the Labour Party's defeat, nationally and the Conservative landslide win, to a combination of unpopular leadership of the party and unrealistic policies. In the adjacent constituency of Calder Valley, Conservative Craig Whittaker defended his seat with an increased majority, whilst the Liberal Democrats suffered disappointing results in both Calderdale constituencies. Indeed, the Liberal Democrat candidate in the Calder Valley was challenged by a Liberal, claiming to represent 'real Liberalism', but who came bottom of the poll, with 725 votes, whilst in Halifax that unenviable position was occupied by the Green Party representative, who polled 946 votes, according to the *Halifax Courier* of 19 December 2019. Boris Johnson undeniably achieved the most convincing General Election victory by the Conservatives since 1987, with an overall majority of 80 seats, through his determination to honour the result of the 2016 United Kingdom European Union membership referendum. The Labour Party lost 59 seats, many from across the North and Midlands and some of which had been held by Labour for generations; from Blyth Valley, which was the first seat to declare its result in 2019, to Bolsover which had returned Dennis Skinner since 1970, but whose defeat in 2019 denied him the opportunity of becoming father of the House of Commons. The Halifax result, therefore, ran counter to both the regional and national trends.

Religious, social and cultural life

It would be a mistake to assume that life in Halifax was determined solely by politics and public authorities. While these might facilitate or mould social behaviour, much also depended on the personal energies and inclinations of local people. For example, during the second half of the twentieth century there was increasing evidence of the decline of religious observance and the growing secularisation of leisure. The first poll taken at a public meeting in the Victoria Hall in January 1947 produced a resounding victory for the Halifax Citizen's Sunday Defence Committee: 1,039 votes to 673 against the opening of cinemas on Sundays. However, in February 1947, a poll of electors, 25.1 per cent of whom recorded their votes, reversed the decision by 9,935 votes to 8,458, a majority of 1,477. Total attendances at the first Sunday cinema performances in March reached 7,000. Moreover, the second half of the twentieth century witnessed the closure of a considerable number of churches and chapels of all denominations, including the Anglican churches of Holy Trinity, St James's and St Mary's; the Methodist churches of Wesley Broad Street, Brunswick, Hanover Street, Rhodes Street and St John's in Prescott Street; Range Bank, Square, Stannary and Sion Congregational Churches; Trinity Road Baptist Church; Clare Road Quaker Meeting House; and Northgate End Unitarian Church. Attendance and membership at many other places of worship was also declining. Between 1959 and 1983, for example, Halifax Methodist circuit membership declined rapidly from 2,896 to 1,574. Though the rate of decline subsequently slowed down there had been a further reduction to 1,132 by 1998. The number of ministers had also been reduced from twelve to six during the period 1959 to 1998.[64] In 2010, 31 Methodist Circuits throughout Calderdale were united to form the new Calderdale Circuit. Methodist involvement was continued in many areas, including in the award winning inter-denominational New Ebenezer Food and Support Drop In Centre where in 2012 volunteers gave out a record number of 392 food parcels over Christmas and New Year and on Christmas Day provided turkey dinners for 51 people and 22 volunteers. Another inter-denominational project initiated in Halifax in 2005 by Paul and Jean Blakey from the King's Church, based at a fair-trade café which Churches Together were operating in partnership with Halifax YMCA, and supported by the local police, also made a huge impact on casualties of the night-time revelry in Halifax town centre. Indeed, the concept of Street Angels was soon replicated nationally and acclaimed by church leaders of all denominations, including the Revd Ruth Gee, a former Methodist minister in Halifax and President of the Methodist Conference in 2013–14, who observed that street pastors were 'a visible expression of the love of Jesus, offered by volunteers who are transforming the night-time economy' through a 'vision that was born in Halifax'. However, by 2018 nine further churches at Ebenezer Bailiffe Bridge, Lindwell, Luddenden, Lumbutts, Mytholmroyd, Old Town, Southowram, Walsden and West End Queensbury had closed. The number of ministers had also been reduced to six circuit ministers and three assistants, but there were 26 active fully accredited Local Preachers. The West Yorkshire District of the Methodist Church had also merged with the Leeds District in 2017 to form the new Yorkshire West District with twelve circuits, chaired by the Revd Dr Roger Walton, the former Chair of the West Yorkshire District and a former President of the Methodist Conference.[65]

As a consequence of the inner relief road development, however, there were also new churches built in the centre of the town for the congregations of Salem Methodist, Elim Pentecostal and the Salvation Army, and others were built to serve new community needs in other parts of the town such as the Anglican Church of the Holy Nativity at Mixenden, the Roman Catholic Churches of St Malachy's and St Alban's, and the Methodist churches of St Andrew's and Highgate. Although ministering within an incredibly small parish with a tiny resident population reduced considerably by ecclesiastical subdivision and demographic change, the Vicar of Halifax retained the patronage of no fewer than twenty-six benefices in Calderdale. An energetic incumbent like Eric Treacy, who served as Vicar and Archdeacon of Halifax from 1950 to 1961, and was adept at using the media, was still able to exercise considerable influence within the local community to such an extent that he was dubbed 'the ecclesiastical mayor of Halifax'. The Revd Canon Hilary Barber, who moved to Halifax in 2007 after twelve years in the Manchester diocese, also had a similarly dynamic impact at Halifax Parish Church and within the community during its transformation into a new urban

Yorkshire Day Celebrations at Halifax, 1 August 2003. Guests, including civic dignitaries from across the county, photographed outside the retail headquarters of HBOS, which celebrated its 150th anniversary in 2003 with a spectacular firework display later in the month. Also involved in the celebrations were the Duke of Wellington's Regiment (West Riding), which celebrated its tercentenary in 2002. Bandsmen from the regiment led the civic procession from Halifax Town Hall to Halifax Parish Church for a service of thanksgiving and performed at a concert in the evening at the Halifax Piece Hall, where earlier in the day members of the regiment had re-enacted the traditional 'havercake' recruiting ceremony, distributing oatcake among the large crowds. Pictured with the Mayor of Calderdale, Councillor Mrs Geraldine Carter and her Consort, Mr Brian Carter (from the centre right of the front row) are guest speaker Harry Gration of BBC *Look North*, the Revd Canon Peter Calvert, Acting Archdeacon of Halifax, the Revd Wendy Wilby, the first female Vicar of Halifax, Brigadier Andrew Meek of the Duke of Wellington's Regiment, Councillor Ann McAllister, the Deputy Mayor of Calderdale, Councillor John Ford, Leader of Calderdale Council and Mr Paul Sheehan, Chief Executive of Calderdale MBC. (Photograph: Simon Ryder)

Muslim procession, July 1996 to mark the anniversary of the birth of the prophet Muhammad. Hundreds of Sunni Muslim men and boys after joining together for prayers at the Madni Mosque walked through West Central Halifax, carrying banners, as part of the Eid Milad Un Nabi festival. The procession was led by Abdul Sattar Khan Niazi, a member of the Pakistan Senate and a former religious leader. The recording artist, Mohammed Rafiq Chishiti, from Lahore, Pakistan, also took part in the celebrations. (Photograph: *Halifax Courier*)

Halifax Minster. He developed the Minster's long tradition of music making, including the establishment of an Organ Academy, the acquisition of a Snetzler organ and an expanded concert programme, as well as supporting business and tourism initiatives focused upon Halifax, with a commitment to helping Halifax 'to punch above its weight' in competition with other northern towns on the M62 corridor. He also took inspiration from the church's historic medieval links with Cluny, placing an emphasis on the Benedictine encouragement of daily worship, education, culture and hospitality, together with civic engagement. He also believed in strengthening regional links with the first new Anglican diocese since 1929, the Anglican Diocese of Leeds created in 2014, and with the Duke of Wellington Regiment and Association, subsequently subsumed in the Yorkshire Regiment; national connections with the Greater Churches and Urban Minster networks and international associations with Halifax's twin town of Aachen and with the Minster's mission partner, the Cathedral Church of St Peter, Kowak, in the Diocese of Rorya in Tanzania.[66]

Mary Morris conducted a detailed independent survey into voluntary organisations in the County Borough of Halifax in 1962 and reported that there were some seventy-one churches and places of worship in the town including fourteen Church of England, two Baptist, seven Congregational, four Methodist circuits embracing thirty-three churches (not all of which were within the county borough), three Pentecostal, four Roman Catholic and eight other denominations. She concluded that while congregations were considerably smaller than fifty years ago, worshippers were more likely to attend 'from real conviction'. She also revealed that many of the 193 voluntary organisations in her survey 'were founded by active members of religious bodies and are still dependent on such people for their voluntary workers'. Furthermore, although some churches were experiencing a decline in attendance and membership in the late twentieth century, others were growing, especially the evangelical churches such as St George's at Lee Mount, All Saints' in Dudwell Lane, Christ Church at Pellon, and the Calderdale Community Church, which bought the redundant Park Road Baths for conversion into a 400-seat worship and community centre in 1997, re-named the King's Centre.

There were also other examples of imaginative attempts by the churches to serve the needs of their local communities. For example, youth clubs were operated by local Methodist churches at Boothtown, King Cross and St Andrew's in partnership with the local authority. Similarly, the Bembridge Community Centre was developed at Park United Reform Church; a Christian Contact Centre, financed initially by contributions from thirty-eight churches of different denominations, operated from empty shops in the town centre during the summers of 1996 and 1997; and an Afro-Caribbean Community Centre linked with the New Testament Church of God in Akeds Road was opened.

The earliest ecumenical move in the former Diocese of Wakefield during this period came in 1969. With the support of Bishop Eric Treacy, Hipperholme Methodist deaconess Sister Alice N. Hodlin (1921–2003), who served in Halifax from 1967–77, worked with the Vicar of Copley, Brian Cole, and the Methodist minister Ian Lewis, in Copley itself and at Halifax General Hospital, funded partly by the diocese in a missional collaboration which lasted over five or six years.[67]

Moreover, in September 2003 Hipperholme Methodist Church entered into a Local Ecumenical Partnership with Lightcliffe United Reformed Church, forming the new Christ Church congregation twelve years after Crowtrees Methodist Church and St Matthew's Church at Rastrick had embarked upon a similar partnership. Not only were there greater signs of co-operation between Christians of different denominations, but also between Christians and Muslims, especially following increasing international tension in the Middle East and the terrorist attacks on New York and Washington on 11 September 2001. Joint prayers had been offered by Christians and Muslims during the First Gulf War, and a Christian–Muslim dialogue was initiated in 1995 'to break down barriers and bring a clearer understanding between the two faiths'. For during the late twentieth century, Halifax had become a multi-cultural society, symbolised by the opening of the new purpose-built Central Jamia Mosque Madni in Gibbet Street between 1982 and 1984, in the heart of the West Hill Park suburb, which had been developed by the Crossleys, Victorian Nonconformist manufacturers in the mid-nineteenth century. The mosque, blending in well with its surroundings, with ashlar facing patterned with arches, and surmounted with a dome and three minarets of varying heights includes an education centre.[68] However, the 2001 Census, which provided statistics about religious adherence in England and Wales for the first time since 1852, revealed that despite evidence of a decline in religious observance in the second half of the twentieth century, a mere 16.4 per cent of the population of Calderdale professed no religious adherence. Indeed, the vast majority indicated their continuing identification with some form of religious expression with no fewer than 69.6 per cent describing themselves as Christian; 5.3 per cent as Muslim; 0.2 per cent as Buddhist and Hindu; 0.1 per cent as Jewish and Sikh and 0.2 per cent as other religions.[69]

There were, however, alternative forms of cultural expression in Halifax during this period. The immediate post-war years saw an increase in spectators at sports fixtures at Thrum Hall and the Shay, at least until the advent of television and the growth of supermarket shopping in the late 1950s. In 1949 Halifax reached the Rugby League Cup Final from the lowest league position ever recorded by a finalist, but also became the first team not to score in the final. Four years later they reached Wembley again, and when the match against Warrington went to a replay at Odsal Stadium it attracted record crowds of 102,575 who witnessed Halifax lose after a try by wing Arthur Daniels was disallowed in the closing minutes. The club also reached Wembley in 1956, losing to St Helen's, but finished runners-up to Warrington in the League. The 1960 season saw Halifax heading the League table by December, but they did not achieve similar success again for over a quarter of a century. In 1986, with the backing of the club president David Brook, the Halifax-born chairman of Modern Maintenance Products, and the coaching skills of Chris Anderson, they won the League championship and in 1987 the Rugby League Challenge Cup, returning home to an enthusiastic public reception from 70,000 fans, lining the streets of the town. In 1988 Halifax reached the Challenge Cup Final again when, after a scoreless semi-final against Hull, Tony Anderson broke the deadlock in the replay, but at Wembley Halifax lost to a confident Wigan embarking on the first of a succession of eight final victories. In 1996, the club entered the new Super League as Halifax Blue Sox and played their final game at Thrum Hall on 21 March 1998 before moving to the Shay to share the stadium with Halifax Town AFC. Although Halifax finished in the top three clubs in the 1998 season by the end of 2003 season, having ditched the designation Blue Sox for their more traditional playing name of Fax, reached their nadir after a record run of Super League defeats. Ironically, it was the Australian coach Tony Anderson who had shared as a player in the triumphs of the late 1980s who presided over the club's relegation to National League One, after a major financial crisis had obliged the club to part with some of its most seasoned players. The establishment of the Calderdale Community Stadium Ltd jointly by Halifax Rugby League Football Club and Halifax Town and their supporters in 1987 after the Halifax Stadium Development Company had crashed with debts approaching £100,000 promised to relieve some of the financial uncertainty for both clubs. With the prospect of sponsorship for the club's community programme by Halifax Home Insurance, Anderson vowed that he would forge a Fax team capable of regaining Super League status by 2005.[70]

As mentioned in the previous chapter, a speedway track was constructed in 1949 in one of many attempts to achieve financial solvency. The track's total length was 402 yards and nearly 3,000 cubic yards of earth was moved to accommodate it. The Halifax Dukes, a name chosen to honour the Duke of Wellington Regiment garrisoned in the town, held their first meeting on 6 April 1949, with Yarmouth Bloaters. However, low speedway gate receipts necessitated its closure in 1952, though it resumed in 1966, eventually transferring to Odsal Stadium in 1986 after a financial dispute with the football club and following the tragic death of its young super-star Kenny Carter (1961–86). Indeed, it achieved more enduring success than a one-off meeting of midget car racing watched in November 1951 by 15,000 spectators, three times higher than the average speedway gate, which despite pulling in the crowds was nevertheless not repeated. Halifax Town proved capable of attracting a record attendance of 36,885 spectators at the Shay for the match between Halifax Town and Tottenham Hotspur in the fifth round of the FA Cup on 14 February 1953, despite recurring financial difficulties. However, the promotion of ice skating by Halifax Town secretary, Norman Howe, taking advantage of the 'big freeze' of 1963, proved a short-term bonus to the club. Similarly, on 29 December 1966 England international Jack Charlton opened a golf driving range at the Shay, which apparently resulted in some 200 lost balls each week before its closure in December 1967. Underlying problems, however, remained and with Halifax Town apparently on the verge of bankruptcy in December 1986, the Labour controlled Calderdale Council under the leadership of David Helliwell, controversially incurred criticism for promoting 'soccer on the rates', after putting forward a rescue package that included buying back the Shay's lease and selling shares in the club to a consortium headed by local businessman Jim Brown. Subsequently, Halifax Town was largely operated by Calderdale Council from 1987–91 to prevent the club's closure. Helliwell argued that he was simply seeking to ensure that football clubs were 'more the servants of the local community and less the hobby of members of the business community'. By the 1990s, Halifax had returned to private hands, but was relegated to the Vauxhall Conference in 1993. Jim Brown, however, became chair from August 1998 to October 2000 and was instrumental in instigating further work on the ground's terracing that enabled the club to achieve league status in 1998, attracting a crowd of 6,357 to their final match of the season at the Shay. Halifax Town AFC owed its promotion to the Football League in 1997–98 to the astute management of George Mulhall and the goal scoring ability of Geoff Horsfield who went on to be a Premiership player. Halifax Town AFC played 90 full seasons over 97 years before liquidation and 100 years of representative Association Football was celebrated in Halifax in 2011. Moreover, Halifax Town gained three promotions under manager Neil Aspin which took the club back to the National League. But Halifax Town's promotion proved short lived and after narrowly avoiding relegation in 2001, with a point from a goal-less draw against third division champions Brighton in the penultimate match of the season, they again suffered relegation to the Nationwide Football Conference in 2002. In the following season Halifax lost ten consecutive Conference matches and brought in a psychic to 'untangle energy lines' considered to be hampering team performance. For the 2008–09 season as FC Halifax and playing in the Unibond First Division North, the new club finished the season in the top half of the League and in the following season were unbeaten in their last seventeen league matches, rising to the top of the League Table, a position they held in the following season when Jamie Vardy became the first player to score hat-tricks in successive matches since Clem Smith during the war season of 1945–46. However, by the end of 2017

Community Relations Partnership Cup match at the Shay in May 1996 between Queen's Road Football Club and the Halifax Police. The police won the match, which was organised by community PC Lisa White, by 6 goals to 4. The event was designed to forge links between the police and the local Asian community and subsequently became an annual sporting fixture. In 1998 the match, which was again won by the police, was followed by a presentation of medals by the Deputy Mayor of Calderdale, Councillor Leslie Smith, at a reception hosted by Superintendent Jawaid Akhtar, the first Asian divisional commander of the Halifax Police. Halifax avoided the more serious racial disturbances which erupted in neighbouring Bradford in 1995 and 1998. When confrontations occurred between Asian youths and the police in Halifax in November 1998, they were quickly defused with the assistance of community leaders. (Photograph: *Halifax Courier*)

Phil Bull at a race meeting at Haydock Park on 5 September 1981, sporting a Savile Row tailored suit and his favourite red and white straw hat with his trademark cigar protruding over his white beard. The Timeform Gold Cup is run at Doncaster as the Vertem Futurity Trophy (Photograph: June Paxton White).

they had slipped into the lower half of the League Table with a winless run of twelve games, attracting an attendance of 1,618.[71]

However, amateur soccer achieved growing popularity in Halifax in the second half of the twentieth century. When the Halifax and District Association Football League, which had started with eight clubs in 1898, celebrated its centenary in 1998, it had fifty-eight teams playing in five divisions. Moreover, amateur cricket also continued to thrive at no fewer than forty-four club venues in Calderdale in 2003, mainly, though not exclusively hosting fixtures in the Halifax League. Sport was not only a major leisure pursuit for many of the town's residents, it was also central to the town's identity. Thousands lined the route of the Tour de France through Calderdale in July 2014, including its longest section of continuous ascent through Cragg Vale, as twenty-two teams of cyclists with their yellow bikes generated a carnival atmosphere along the challenging scenic route, festooned with thousands of metres of yellow bunting. They later welcomed the announcement that the Halifax Piece Hall had been selected as the starting point for the final day of the 2018 event. Besides cycling, the Calderdale countryside provided an arduous environment for fell running at a variety of levels. For example, staff from Lloyds Banking Group including runners from Halifax Harriers and Stainland Lions travelled to London to compete in the annual Inter Financial Services Cross Country race in 2015. The men's team performed well amidst stiff competition, whilst the ladies team came away from Richmond Park with prizes for achieving second place overall. Students from the North Halifax Taekwondo Club, based at Threeways Sports Centre, Nursery Lane, Ovenden, came away from the British Federation's championships with a bumper haul of nineteen medals. Meanwhile at the other end of the age spectrum, for those more comfortable exercising on level services, a wide network of bowlers competed in the Halifax Bowling Club Henselite Indoor League under such a galaxy of playing names as Avengers, Eskimos, Phoenix, Rockets and Spartans. Indeed, Calderdale was chosen by Sport England as one of twelve pilot areas to work on a new approach to encouraging more active communities, after a survey classed 32 per cent of residents as rarely active.[72]

Halifax, nonetheless, also produced some larger-than-life sports personalities during the second half of the twentieth century, including one of the most colourful figures of the English turf, Phil Bull (1910–89), the son of a Hemsworth miner. Bull was a Leeds University mathematics graduate and trained schoolteacher, who became better known as a professional gambler, racehorse owner and publisher. He made Halifax, somewhat incongruously, the headquarters of his Timeform Organisation, which from 1948 published by his own publishing company Portaway Press, a series of definitive directories of performance ratings for every British racehorse and ultimately internationally. Indeed, it was said of Bull that 'there is no more familiar figure on English racecourses than the stocky, bearded Phil Bull', and Timeform ratings, subsequently owned by online betting exchange Betfair, became adopted as British horse racing's unofficial but authoritative measure of

Cricket match between Blackley and Lightcliffe, 2015. Many long established local cricket clubs continued to thrive, playing in organised leagues and cup competitions and improving their grounds and social facilities. (Photograph: G. Sutcliffe)

racehorse performance. Bull founded the Hollins Stud in Halifax with four mares and there he bred Romulus, winner of the Greenham Stakes, the Sussex Stakes, the Queen Elizabeth II Stakes and the Prix du Moulin and also Eudaemon, winner of the Gimcrack Stakes and the Champagne Stakes. He rarely owned more than one horse at a time and the stud declined during the 1970s and 1980s, but he was briefly chairman of the Horse Racing Advisory Council in 1980 and established the Timeform Gold Cup, a mile race for two-year-olds in 1961.

Equally well-known in the world of British wrestling was former Halifax coal-miner, rugby player and Coldstream Guardsman, Shirley Crabtree (1930–97), whose antics in the ring as Big Daddy and other assumed personas including the Battling Guardsman, The Blond Adonis and Mr Universe, contributed to televised professional wrestling becoming a cult spectator sport in the 1970s. Wrestling was popularised by ITV's *World of Sport*, which amongst its fan base encompassing both youngsters and their grannies also reputedly numbered the Prime Minister, Margaret Thatcher and H.M. The Queen. However he retired from wrestling following an opponent's fatality from which he was exonerated in 1988, when the sport had passed the peak of its popularity.[73]

A native of Halifax, the international soccer referee Arthur Ellis (1914–99) refereed the 1952 F.A. Cup Final, in the World Cups of 1950, 1954 and 1958, and over forty international matches. Stern but cheerful, he 'elevated soccer-refereeing into an art form'. Following his retirement, he enforced the rules in the BBC's *It's a Knockout* for eighteen years and for many years chaired the Pools Panel.[74] Adopted by Halifax couple, Ralph and Dorothy Moore, and educated at Crossley and Porter School, Halifax, Brian Moore (b. 1962) became the pugnacious England Rugby Union hooker and uncompromising pundit of the game.[75]

Thousands gathered for a Blues, Folk, Jazz and Pop Festival held at Krumlin, Barkisland, in mid-August 1970, featuring big names including Elton John. However, torrential rain and gale force winds turned the site into a quagmire and the exposed, high altitude, led to many requiring hospital treatment for exposure and to the bankruptcy of the festival's two organisers. (Photograph: *Halifax Courier*)

The Halifax and District Amateur Cricket Association Collinson Cup, The Halifax Cricket League Parish Cup and Crossley Shield finals remained highlights in the Calderdale cricketing year, attracting a variety of high profile sponsors including Ace Cricket Bats, Briggs Priestley Limited, Engravers and Signmakers, Jack Lees Sports and Trinity Insurance, enabling at modest admission charges adults, children and old age pensioners by programme. During this period there was also increasing evidence of ethnic and gender diversity in cricket in Halifax and Calderdale. For example the Kashmir Foundation competed against Walsden in the Collinson Cup Final in 1999, and Queen's Road Muslims reached the Collinson Cup Final in successive seasons in 2002 and 2003, and their opponents, West End, fielded a team including a mixture of white and ethnic minority players.[76] Moreover, it was whilst captaining the England Ladies team at the former Mackintosh cricket ground in Halifax in 1978 that Rachel Heyhoe Flint (1939–2017), the legendary pioneer of women's cricket, who was the first female cricketer to hit a six in a Test match and was dubbed the 'W. G. Grace' of women's cricket, learned of her dismissal as England's captain.[77]

Halifax was a town, like all others, with plural cultural activities in the second half of the twentieth century, many of which operated under considerable difficulties. The problems of the Halifax Choral Society of rising costs, lack of male recruits, and the lure of professionalism were highlighted in a report in the *Yorkshire Post* in 1949. Moreover, many of the problems had not eased significantly by 1991, when it cost the society nearly £15,000 to stage their annual performance of the *Messiah* at the Halifax Civic Theatre. The concert made a loss of £6,800, despite performing to a full house. Nevertheless, under the leadership of John Pryce-Jones, the society received a growing number of invitations to sing in nationally prestigious venues and premiered Mozart's arrangement of Handel's *Judas Maccabaeus* in Halifax in June 2002, which had been discovered in the local archives by a music student. During its bicentenary season in 2017–18 it performed a specially composed new oratorio, *Holy Face*, by Professor Philip Wilby, husband of the first woman Vicar of Halifax, the Revd Wendy Wilby. The oratorio, with a large augmented choir and orchestra, is based on a mistaken legendary tradition encapsulated in the Victorian municipal borough coat of arms, associating an impression of the face of John the Baptist with the town's origins. During this season, the Choral Society also released a recording in collaboration with the world famous Black Dyke Band and the Black Dyke Band enhanced the annual Carols and Brass Concert which played to a full house. The Choral Society celebrated its bicentennial annual performance of Handel's *Messiah* in December 2018 and also of Haydn's *Creation*, which was first performed at the society's opening concert in 1818. The Victoria Theatre besides hosting Halifax Choral Society performances, offered a wide range of cultural experiences ranging from internationally acclaimed ballet, opera and theatre to its popular Christmas pantomimes and other forms of family entertainment. The Northern Broadsides based at the Viaduct Theatre at Dean Clough and with its distinctive vernacular touring company continued to offer acclaimed performances of Shakespearean classics, developed with panache by actor-director, Barrie Rutter

OBE until his departure in 2017, achieving regional and national distinction; whilst Square Chapel Centre for the Arts also offered a varied programme of innovatory productions in its expanded facilities designed by Evans Vettori in 2016–17.[78]

Moreover, even the new popular culture experienced challenges. The Plebeian Jazz Club founded in April 1961 by four former students of Clare Hall School attracted such a large cult following that it was soon evicted from the third floor of Martins Mill and had to seek alternative accommodation in the Upper George Yard. Broadening its appeal from jazz to rock music and rhythm and blues, the Plebs attracted such star names as Rod Stewart, Joe Cocker, Ginger Baker and Jack Bruce and within a year boasted some 700 members. In February 1962, the *Halifax Courier* reported sell-out concerts for a rock concert at the Odeon cinema. Sadly, the 3,000 fans who attended the two performances were disappointed when laryngitis obliged top-of-the-bill crooner Billy Fury to cut his act. Furthermore, a Halifax Pop and Blues Festival held at Thrum Hall to raise much needed funds for Halifax Rugby League Club in April 1970 left the club with a deficit of £11,000 after only 2,750 turned up on a freezing cold night. Then in August of the same year thousands of rock fans experienced the worst weather to ever hit a British rock festival devastating the festival site, which was completely rained out by the Sunday.

However, during the 1970s and 1980s the legendary barrelhouse blues pianist and former boxer, William Thomas 'Champion Jack' Dupree, born into poverty in New Orleans 1909 and orphaned by the Ku Klux Klan soon after, settled in Ovenden, Halifax, where he raised a family and played his unique blues music up and down the Calder Valley and beyond. His connection with Halifax was celebrated in a concert at Dean Clough in February 2003, and commemorated by the commissioning of a bronze memorial by local artist Ian Judd.[79] Although amateur drama flourished following the opening by the Halifax Thespians of the Halifax Playhouse in a redundant Methodist chapel in 1949, and the establishment of an Actors Workshop by Mike and Lottie Ward in 1985 to nurture young talent, the lure of television and an increasingly home-centred culture resulted in a decline of support for the performing arts and even the cinema. Many homes acquired television sets for the coronation of Queen Elizabeth II in 1953: the number of television licences in the Halifax postal area had reached 15,113 in 1955. The Grand Theatre finally closed in 1956, and the Palace Theatre was demolished in 1959 while the Odeon, Gaumont (re-named the Astra in 1973), and Regal (re-named the ABC in 1976) cinemas closed in 1975, 1982, and 2002, leaving Halifax without a single cinema. Mary Morris reported in 1962 that some of the town's cultural societies were experiencing difficulties, and in 1964 the epitome of local cultural societies, the Halifax Literary and Philosophical Society, was finally dissolved. But Halifax was still considered 'a bookish town with probably more established writers than any other Yorkshire town'. The novelist Phyllis Bentley's autobiography was published in 1961 and other celebrities with local roots of birth or residence followed her into print, including the controversial judge James Pickles and the journalist Sir Bernard Ingham. Maurice Procter, a Halifax police constable, achieved success on both sides of the Atlantic as a thriller writer; likewise, John Marsh, as a writer of biography

Halifax in 1951. This painting of Halifax viewed from Beacon Hill by Charles Cundall, RA, on a relatively clear day, shows a profusion of mill chimneys still dominating a congested built environment. Vegetation on the lower slopes of Beacon Hill in the foreground remains sparse and the atmosphere clouded by the emissions from the cooling towers and chimneys right of centre. (Photograph: Halifax plc)

and romantic fiction, under a variety of pseudonyms, Glyn Hughes as a novelist and poet, and Juliet Barker for her acclaimed biographies of the Brontës and William Wordsworth, literary subjects with historical connections with Calderdale. In the field of science, prominent scientists from Calderdale with international reputations include nuclear physicist Sir John Cockcroft (1897–1967); inorganic chemist Sir Geoffrey Wilkinson (1921–96) and biochemist Oliver Smithies (1925–2017). All three were outstanding Nobel Prize winners in their respective fields. Finally, two major historians of the post-war era, G. N. Clark (1890–1979) and E. P. Thompson (1924–93), were influenced by their associations with Halifax, the former by birth and the latter by residence. The son of a Halifax draper and councillor, G. N. Clark succeeded G. M. Trevelyan as Regius Professor of Modern History at Cambridge in 1943, edited the prestigious Oxford History of England and the New Cambridge Modern History, was knighted in 1953 and served as President of the British Academy from 1954 to 1958. E. P. Thompson's classic *The Making of the English Working Class*, published in 1963 while the author, an extra-mural lecturer at the University of Leeds, was resident in Halifax, has been hailed as 'probably the most imaginative post-war work of English social history' and, interestingly, as

The sprawling railway goods yard extending northwards beyond North Bridge, the twin cooling towers dominating the eastern periphery of the town centre and the remaining factory chimneys in this photograph of Halifax illustrate the industrial character of the town centre as late as 1967. (Photograph: G. Whippey)

essentially a study of 'the Halifax working class ... a tribute to the small manufacturing communities of the Calder Valley whose spirit is the heart and meaning of the book'.[80]

'A town full of character and hidden beauty'

Halifax since 1945 has experienced demographic changes, economic restructuring, a transformation in local government, and has shared in cultural transformations affecting the rest of Britain. How have these forces affected Halifax's built environment? Halifax unlike Manchester and Sheffield escaped relatively unscathed from the Luftwaffe in the Second World War, but its congested townscape was ripe for renewal after 1945. The town also continued to suffer severely from the effects of industrial pollution. Photographs of the town through the haze of smoke from Beacon Hill in the 1940s and 1950s were often censoriously captioned 'The Devil's cauldron'. Hundreds of saplings planted by Charles Holdsworth to mark his mayoralty in 1948 succumbed to industrial pollution. It was not until the clean air legislation of 1956 began to be implemented locally that vegetation started to return to Beacon Hill. John Priestley in his reflections on growing up in Halifax during the Fifties and Sixties recalled not being able to see more than a couple of yards in the dense fogs and having 'to feel my way 'running my hand along a wall'.

He also recalled during the 1960s the pervasive smells emanating from Ramsden's brewery which used to waft over the town centre mingling with those from the abattoir and the gas works where the process involved the burning of coke and the appalling stench from Mitchell's bone glue works at Southowram above the town. Eventually when some of the worst offenders were taken to court a defence lawyer from London boldly submitted that 'Halifax is a town full of smells' but he lost his case. The Halifax-born artist Sir Matthew Smith, though he had once thought Halifax 'the ugliest place on earth', was beginning to change his mind about the town in 1958 when he commended it in correspondence to a friend as 'enchanting as ever'. In an earlier letter to Alden Brooks in February 1954 he had recognised its potential when he had written:

> Halifax seems a wonderful place, wonderful scenery all round and the town itself solidly built of stone, not a brick to be seen, this seemed to give it a great character, and at night very Van Gogh like I saw the biggest half moon perched just above a rugged outline of houses and street that I have ever seen.[81]

Although the architectural historian Nikolaus Pevsner found the situation of the town spectacular in the 1950s, he deplored the ubiquitous slum housing, the evident lack of planning in the post-war townscape and the impact on the natural environment of pollution from the multitude of mills of various sizes 'encroaching on its boundaries on all sides'. The recently created open spaces which he observed within the town centre owed more, he opined, to 'traffic than to aesthetic considerations'. The site of the town hall was too congested, and 'as for building in the town centre there is nothing of a high order' except for the Piece Hall which he regarded as 'the most noteworthy architectural monument of Halifax'.[82] In 1966 an official report concluded that in comparison with other parts of the Calder Valley,

Photograph of the Mayor of Calderdale Councillor Ferman Ali at the re-opening of Halifax Piece Hall. (Photograph: Halifax Piece Hall Trust)

Woolshops showing the medieval half-timbered house, on the far right, the oldest house in the town centre and the new bronze Duke of Wellington's Regiment Memorial on the left. In the distance is Old Market and a glimpse of the Union Cross Hotel. (Photograph: G. Sutcliffe).

Halifax had a larger share of derelict land 'so damaged by industrial, or other development that it is an eyesore'.[83]

In 1970 Dr Arthur Raistrick warned of the danger of replacing mill chimneys and terraced housing by high-rise office blocks leaving 'nothing to distinguish Sheffield from Halifax or Bradford unless one can catch a glimpse through some concrete canyon of a fragment of the friendly hills'.[84]

However, John Minnis, referring to a revealing aerial photograph of Halifax taken on 23 March 1973 commented that it illustrated how an entirely new townscape 'began to grow up, doing away with the close-knit urban fabric and replacing it with something much more open, fragmented by wide roads with few crossing places and interspersed with large buildings set away from them but having little relation to one another or to the earlier industrial town'. Specifically, he noted, as had Pevsner before him, that Barry's magnificent Halifax Town Hall

(1859–62) with its elegant tower had 'lost its place in the architectural hierarchy of Halifax, being dwarfed by numerous residential tower blocks'. He observed how 'the width of the new roads and the space taken up by their junctions and roundabouts had introduced an entirely new element into the morphology of the town'. Conceding nevertheless, that 'the town centre of Halifax remained relatively intact, with through traffic diverted to the edge' he pondered whether 'the scale of the destruction on the periphery' was a price worth paying for the intrusive features which remained.[85] Moreover, by 1973 some £560,000 had been allocated to Halifax through grant-aided 'Operation Eyesore' schemes to make it 'one of the most clean-up-conscious towns in Britain'. Indeed, the increasing use of electricity for motive power, the impact of clean air legislation, stone-cleaning and new pedestrianisation schemes soon began to change the way in which the town was perceived by visitors. Ian Nairn in a television documentary in 1975 found Halifax more expressive and architecturally interesting than neighbouring Huddersfield, and he concluded that Halifax viewed from Beacon Hill occupied 'one of the most dramatic town sites anywhere in Britain'.[86]

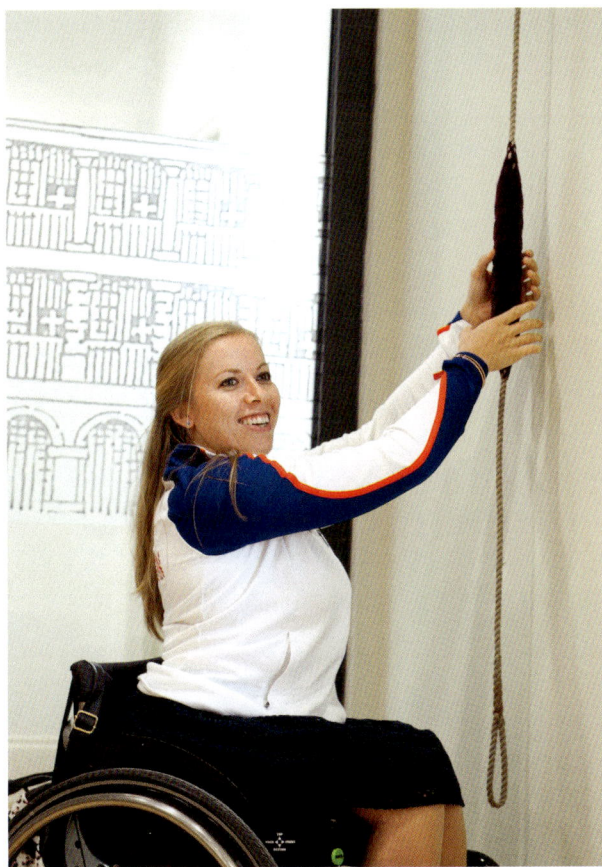

Hannah Cockroft, the record-breaking Paralympic Halifax wheelchair racer specialising in sprint distances was the popular public choice to toll the Piece Hall Bell following the official re-opening of the re-configured cloth hall in 2017. Competing for Britain at the 2012 Summer Paralympics she won two gold medals and three further gold medals at Rio. Her father, a welder, built her first racing chair. In honour of her achievements at London 2012 Royal Mail issued two postage stamps featuring her and painted two post boxes gold in Halifax and her home village of Mount Tabor. After a return to winning form in 2019, Hannah won her eleventh world title by securing a gold medal at the World Para Athletics Championships at Dubai. (Photograph: Halifax Piece Hall Trust)

Sir John Betjeman discerned the town's future potential when he wrote in 1979:

Halifax is full of character and hidden beauty. The Piece Hall is symbolic of its hidden and great worth. The skyline of Halifax, its churches, chapels, mills and warehouses, is something never to be forgotten, and gives Halifax its identity.[87]

Pevsner's criticism in 1959 that there had been few notable twentieth-century contributions to the townscape was subsequently remedied by the new headquarters of the Halifax Building Society and the spectacular flyover spanning North Bridge and the new headquarters of the Halifax Building Society. Nairn viewed the latter as the twentieth-century equivalent of the Piece Hall, the 'grand gesture' of the eighteenth century. Civic Trust reports on Halifax in 1984 and Calderdale in 1986, while critical of the continuing evidence of industrial dereliction, extolled the town's outstanding architectural merit. By 1984 there were no fewer than fourteen conservation areas in Calderdale including most of Halifax Town Centre. The momentum to celebrate Halifax's rich architectural and historical heritage whilst adapting it to contemporary requirements gathered pace in the early twenty-first century with the relandscaping and refurbishment of Halifax Piece Hall, Square Chapel, and the creation of a new library and archives on the adjacent restored

Sir Ernest Hall, wearing the robes of Chancellor of the University of Huddersfield, whose drive and vision transformed the former centre of the Crossley carpet empire at Dean Clough into a major centre for business, education and the arts. Sir Ernest's son, Jeremy Hall, who continued to realise his father's vision, revealed in an interview to BBC *Look North* in January 2020 that currently no fewer than 150 businesses were operating from the Dean Clough site. (Photograph: Helen J. Bray)

Square spire site. Major improvements were also undertaken to improve the southern access to the town and the Calderdale Royal Hospital, and rail links were enhanced with a regular main line services by Grand Central to London, though there were continuing concerns about congestion on regional services at peak times and pressure for electrification of the service to Leeds. Moreover, Halifax's hinterland and Calderdale as a whole contained the greatest density of pre-industrial vernacular architecture in northern England with no fewer than 3,655 listed buildings in 1988, the highest ratio of listed buildings to population in West Yorkshire. It also contained a range of opportunities for exploration of its increasingly accessible, surrounding countryside and rural heritage by cycling, hiking and waterway. In 1989 Glasgow University placed Halifax second only to Exeter and above York, Wakefield and Huddersfield in a national survey of the quality of life in medium-sized towns based upon such criteria as cost of living, cost of housing, access to scenic countryside and sports facilities. By then, it was clear that local residents had recovered their self-esteem.[88]

The unique built environment of Halifax reveals its fascinating urban history. As the seminal Civic Trust report of 1984 recognised, in the surviving, built environment of Halifax are 'several towns overlayed'. Major features of the late medieval and early modern town have survived, including one of the finest medieval parish churches, now Halifax Minster in West Yorkshire. The line of the medieval track to the town, from Wakefield into Woolshops, passes the rare inner urban survival of a restored seventeenth-century half-timbered house, one of only three dozen buildings with exposed external timber-framed walls to have survived in the metropolitan county of West Yorkshire, and the sole surviving fully intact domestic structure from this era. Also evident are outstanding features of the Georgian market town with its fine town houses, neo-classical Square Chapel and Holy Trinity Church and vestiges of Denis Chantrell's façade of Sion Chapel Wade Street, incorporated with the town's only surviving external Victorian archway into the redeveloped late-twentieth-century bus station. The magnificent manufacturers' Piece Hall is recognised as 'one of the most remarkable buildings of its kind in the whole of Europe'. Indeed, as the sole cloth hall in Yorkshire to survive in its entirety it has been declared Yorkshire's most significant secular building by no less an authority than the architectural historian, Colum Giles.[89] And then there are the markets, mills and warehouses of the Victorian industrial town, with many of the technological achievements of this era reflected in the re-opened Calderdale Industrial Museum. 'With one of the most consistently homogeneous town centres in the United Kingdom', Halifax has also been recently authoritatively pronounced 'perhaps the best Victorian town centre in England'.[90] Halifax indeed boasts one of the finest provincial town halls in England, designed by the boldly innovative architect of the Houses of Parliament, Sir Charles Barry, and nearby are no fewer than three pioneering model industrial communities at Akroydon, Copley and West Hill Park. The town is overlooked by Sir George Gilbert Scott's soaring Gothic masterpiece of All Souls' Church at Haley Hill, which Scott considered his finest church building. Finally, the rich historical

Halifax in 1995. Mill chimneys no longer dominate the Halifax townscape in this 1995 view of Halifax from Beacon Hill, with the solitary exception of J. E. Wainhouse's tower on the distant skyline, which was conceived as a chimney for a dyeworks but then embellished and transformed into a Victorian folly of monumental proportions. The Halifax townscape is now dominated by the administrative headquarters of Halifax plc in the centre of the photograph. However, evidence of the town's medieval inheritance is also visible in the still smoke-encrusted, towered form of the Halifax Parish Church in the foreground. Beyond to the left, the red-bricked, gabled Square Chapel and the magnificent rectangular Manufacturers' Piece Hall, extending horizontally across the centre of the photograph, testify to the town's rich Georgian heritage. And finally, the soaring, crotcheted spire of the later Square Congregational Church provides a glimpse of the delights of the town's Victorian legacy. (Photograph: Halifax plc)

tapestry is completed by a twentieth-century financial quarter, with the diamond-shaped fortress of the only retail headquarters of a major UK financial institution outside London, and an array of banks, building societies and insurance companies extending along Commercial Street and around Blackwall and Ward's End. There is also the largest privately financed mill regeneration scheme in Europe at Dean Clough, triumphantly rescued by Sir Ernest Hall, operating from one of the most creatively productive and resilient ravines in the world for over two centuries and the exposed steel, stone and glass structure of the first interactive children's museum in the United Kingdom, financed by the Vivien Duffield Trust, close to Butterworth's restored Victorian railway station; Hawkshaw's Gothic south-facing portal 'powerful and menacing' of his tunnel through Beacon Hill and the rare surviving coal drops close to the station forming part of the townscape vista for railway passengers emerging from the tunnel.[91]

The vested interests of market traders and town centre retailers in the post-war years and the timely development of a strong conservationist lobby in Halifax from the 1970s succeeded in preventing the wholesale redevelopment of the town along the lines experienced by other neighbouring West Yorkshire towns and cities. So, Halifax retained its Piece Hall and Victorian Borough Markets, unlike neighbouring Huddersfield where the eighteenth-century Cloth Hall was demolished to make way for a cinema in 1935 and the Victorian Market Hall was swept away in an ill-conceived redevelopment scheme in 1970, and unlike Bradford where the Swan Arcade and Kirkgate Market fell victim to an orgy of destruction between 1955 and 1965. Moreover, the curtailment of atmospheric pollution after 1956 and the removal of the accretions of industrial grime from town centre buildings have revealed both the spectacular beauty of Halifax's urban location and the splendour of its built environment. Imaginative new uses have been found for some of the town's redundant churches, chapels, mills and warehouses and the magnificent manufacturers' Piece Hall, but Halifax lacks the spectacular water features of neighbouring Bradford. The Hebble Brook, which might be made more accessible between Dean Clough and the Minster as a green corridor, remains largely concealed despite the disappearance of the massive cooling towers which originally proved so stubbornly resistant to demolition.

Halifax's built environment remains, therefore, perhaps the most completely surviving testimony to the changing political, economic, social and cultural history of a northern urban community throughout recorded history from the medieval era to the twenty-first century. Moreover, the geographical factors which inhibited Halifax's continuing industrial development at the beginning of the twentieth century, most notably problems of accessibility and a shortage of undeveloped flat land for large-scale industrial development, proved to be of less significance to the town's economic vitality in the telecommunications age of the present day where the town's spectacular enclosed setting is widely considered to enhance not only Halifax's scenic urban location but also both the sense of community and individuality which have been the town's twin strengths throughout its fascinating history.[92]

Notes

Chapter 1: Introduction: geography and environment

1 P. Bentley, 'The romance of Halifax' in J. J. Mulroy, ed., *The Story of the Town that Bred Us* (J. J. Mulroy, Halifax: 1948), p. 9.

2 J. Ogden, 'The shaping of Calderdale' in *The Calderdale Way* (Calderdale Way Association, Calderdale: 1978), pp. 9–11.

3 A. Briggs, *Iron Bridge to Crystal Palace: Impact and Images of the Industrial Revolution* (Thames and Hudson, London: 1979), p. 64.

4 D. James, *Bradford* (Ryburn, Halifax: 1990), p. 18; G. Firth, *A History of Bradford* (Phillimore, Chichester: 1997), p. 48.

5 J. B. Priestley, *English Journey* (Folio Society reprint, London: 1997), p. 162.

6 For a development of this theme see A. Dingsdale, 'Yorkshire mill town: a study of the spatial patterns and processes of urban industrial growth and the evolution of the spatial structure of Halifax, 1801–1901', unpublished Ph.D. thesis, University of Leeds, 1974.

7 J. A. Hargreaves, 'Percy Shaw (1890–1976)', *Oxford Dictionary of National Biography* (Oxford University Press, Oxford: 2004) [hereinafter *ODNB*].

8 For Ted Hughes's Calder Valley connections see G. Hughes, *Ted and I: A Brother's Memoir* (The Robson Press, London: 2012) and for Sally Wainwright, *Yorkshire Post*, 13 June 2011; *Halifax Courier*, 25 September 2013 and the *Guardian*, 6 February 2016.

9 J. A. Hargreaves, 'Wilfred Pickles (1904–1978)', *ODNB*; R. Danes, *Who's the Daddy? The Life and Times of Shirley Crabtree* (Pitch Publishing, Durrington: 2013); and obituary of John Noakes, *Independent*, 29 May 2017.

10 G. Moorhouse, *Britain in the Sixties: The Other England* (Penguin Books, London: 1964), p. 148.

11 J. A. Jowitt, ed., *Model Industrial Communities in mid-nineteenth century Yorkshire* (University of Bradford, Bradford: 1986), pp. 73–88.

12 Published Home Office figures and data collected by the St Augustine's Centre in Halifax show that in March 2016 there were some 278 asylum seekers being supported in Calderdale while awaiting a decision on their claim (http://www.migrationyorkshire.org.uk); K. Comer, 'Health Needs Assessment of Refugees and Asylum Seekers in Calderdale' (Calderdale MBC, Halifax: 2016).

Chapter 2: A Pennine backwater: Halifax before 1500

1 This tripartite classification of prehistory into Stone Age, Bronze and Iron Age was originally devised by Christian Thompson (1788–1865), but subsequently refined with further sub-divisions. The Stone Age, for example, has been sub-divided into the Palaeolithic (Old Stone Age), the Mesolithic (Middle Stone Age) and the Neolithic (New Stone Age), with further sub-divisions of the Palaeolithic

into Lower, Middle and Upper. Dating is inevitably approximate – for further elucidation see S. Friar, *The Local History Companion* (Sutton Publishing, Stroud: 2001), p. 416.

2 D. Hey, *A History of Yorkshire: 'County of Broad Acres'* (2nd edition, Carnegie Publishing, Lancaster: 2011) [hereinafter *Yorkshire*], pp. 7–32; C. Waddington, 'Mesolithic re-colonisation of Britain following the drowning of North Sea landscapes' in N. Ashton and C. R. E. Harris, eds, *No Stone Unturned: Papers in Honour of Roger Jacobi*, Lithic Studies Society Occasional Paper 9 (Oxbow, Oxford: 2015) [hereinafter *No Stone Unturned*].

3 G. G. Watson, *Early Man in the Halifax District* (Halifax Scientific Society, Halifax: 1952); T. G. Manby, S. A. Moorhouse and P. Ottaway, eds, *The Archaeology of Yorkshire: An assessment at the beginning of the 21st century* (Yorkshire Archaeological Society (YAS), Leeds: 2003) [hereinafter *Archaeology of Yorkshire*], p. 31; Hey, *Yorkshire*, pp. 7–32.

4 T. G. Manby, 'The Late Upper Palaeolithic and Mesolithic Periods in Yorkshire' in Manby, Moorhouse and Ottaway, eds, *Archaeology of Yorkshire*, p. 31; Hey, *Yorkshire*, pp. 3, 8; F. Jolley, 'Antiquarian Flint Collections and their role in the study of Calderdale's prehistory in the twenty-first century', *Transactions of the Halifax Antiquarian Society* [hereinafter *THAS*] 18 (2010), pp. 129–41.

5 K. Boughey, 'Mesolithic sites in Keighley and Oxenhope Moors: the local lithic collection of Stuart W. Feather', *Yorkshire Archaeological Journal* [hereinafter *YAJ*] 81 (2009), pp. 1–46; B. Howcroft, 'Widdop and Gorple Reservoirs: sites and finds', YAS *Prehistoric Research Section Bulletin* [hereinafter *PRSB*] 44 (2007), pp. 48–58; idem, 'Recent arrowhead find at Baitings Reservoir, Calderdale', YAS *PRSB* 48 (2011), p. 70; idem, 'Prehistoric sites on Wadsworth and Midgley Moors, Calderdale', YAS *PRSB* 48 (2011), pp. 88–98; idem, 'The Dennis Wilford Beasley Lithics Assemblage; assessment and report',

Prehistoric Yorkshire [hereinafter *PY*] 51 (2014), pp. 20–26; idem, 'Prehistoric Barkisland: an archaeological report and survey of multi-period sites in the upper reaches of the Ryburn Valley', *PY* 52 (2015), pp. 43–55; F. Jolley, 'A group of arrowheads from the Pennines in the collections of Brian Howcroft', YAS *PRSB* 45 (2008), pp. 59–62; P. M. Rawson, 'An analysis of the flint collection of E. V. and H. Darby', B.A. dissertation, University of Nottingham, 1993.

6 M. L. Faull and S. A. Moorhouse, *West Yorkshire: An Archaeological Survey to AD 1500* (4 vols, West Yorkshire Metropolitan County Council, Wakefield: 1981), 1, pp. 82–88 [hereinafter *West Yorkshire: An Archaeological Survey*]; J. A. Gilks, 'The mesolithic in and around Halifax', *THAS* (1991), pp. 1–25.

7 T. G. Manby, 'Typology, materials and distribution of flint and stone axes in Yorkshire' in T. H. McK. Clough and W. A. Cummins, eds, *Stone Axe Studies*, Council of British Archaeology [hereinafter CBA] Research Report 23 (Oxbow Books, Oxford: 1979), p. 72; F. Jolley, 'A polished flint axe from Beaumont Park, Huddersfield', *The Archaeological Forum Journal*, CBA Yorkshire, n.s. 2 (2013), p. 136.

8 H. Ling Roth, *The Yorkshire Coiners, 1767–83 and notes on Old and Prehistoric Halifax* (F. King and Sons Ltd, Halifax: 1906); K. Boughey and P. Bray, 'The Saltonstall Early Bronze Age Axe', *PY* 53 (2016), pp. 99–103.

9 Hey, *Yorkshire*, p. 7; J. A. Gilks, 'An early bronze age flat axe from Norland town, near Halifax', *THAS* 1 (1993), pp. 12–14; C. Burgess, *Bronze Age Metalwork in Northern England* (Oriel Press, Newcastle-upon-Tyne: 1968), pp. 7–28.

10 F. Jolley, 'An early Bronze Age axe from Lower Saltonstall, near Halifax, and its significance for the Prehistory of Calderdale', *THAS* 26 (2018).

11 R. A. Varley, 'Bronze Axes from Calderdale', *YAJ* 49 (1977), pp. 51–58; B. Jennings, *Pennine Valley* (Smith Settle, Otley: 1992), pp. 5, 16–17; Faull and Moorhouse, *West Yorkshire: An*

Archaeological Survey 1, pp. 90–91, 93, 107–09, 118; 4, Maps 5, 6; Gilks, *THAS* 1 (1993), pp. 12–14; N. Lunn, 'Bronze age man in the Pennines', *Huddersfield and District Archaeological Society Bulletin* 18 (1966). I am grateful to Jenny Marriott of the West Yorkshire Archaeological Service for information on the dating of the prehistoric finds.

12 Gilks, *THAS* (1991); A. Myers, 'A flint for all seasons? The organisation of settlement and technology on the Earlier Mesolithic of northern England' in Ashton and Harris, eds, *No Stone Unturned*, pp. 167–89; P. R. Preston, 'Lithics to Landscapes: Hunter Gatherer tool use, resource exploitation and mobility during the Mesolithic of the Central Pennines, unpublished DPhil thesis, University of Oxford, 2011; Waddington in Ashton and Harris, eds, *No Stone Unturned*, pp. 221–32; www.mustfarm.com/ bronzeagesettlement; *Daily Telegraph*, 12 January 2016.

13 D. Shepherd and F. Jolley, 'An interim account of rock markings in the South Pennines', YAS *PRSB* 45 (2008), pp. 54–59; *idem*, 'Marked Rocks of the South Pennines', YAS *PRSB* 48 (2011), pp. 56–64; *idem*, 'A Bronze Age Field Boundary in the South Pennines', *PY* 53 (2016), pp. 106–09; D. Shepherd, 'Prehistoric Standing Stones in the South Pennines', *THAS* 17 (2009), pp. 15–27.

14 F. and E. Elgee, *The Archaeology of Yorkshire* (S. R. Publishers, Wakefield: 1971); A. Raistrick, 'The Bronze Age in West Yorkshire', *YAJ* 29 (1929), pp. 354–65; Watson, *Early Man in the Halifax District* and T. G. Manby, 'The Bronze Age in West Yorkshire' in T. G. Manby and P. Turnbull, eds, *Archaeology in the Pennines: Studies in honour of Arthur Raistrick*, British Archaeological Report [hereinafter BAR], British Series 158 (Oxford: 1986).

15 F. Pryor, 'When Francis dug the Fens', *Current Archaeology* March (2015), p. 29.

16 Hey, *Yorkshire*, pp. 23–28; F. Pryor, *Making of the British Landscape* (Allen Lane, London: 2010), pp. 142–64; B. Cunliffe, *Iron Age Communities in Britain: An account of England, Scotland and Wales from the seventh century BC until the Roman conquest* (Routledge and Kegan Paul, London: 1975), p. 54.

17 P. Ottaway, *Roman Yorkshire: People, Culture and Landscape* (Blackthorn Press, Pickering: 2013), p. 37.

18 Pryor, *Making of the British Landscape*, p. 764; Hey, *Yorkshire*, pp. 30–32; I. A. Richmond, *Roman Britain* (2nd edition, Penguin Books, London: 1963), p. 16; Cunliffe, *Iron Age Communities in Britain*, pp. 54, 110–12, 205.

19 Cunliffe, *Iron Age Communities in Britain*, p. 205; Hey, *Yorkshire*, pp. 32–33, 36; Ottaway *Roman Yorkshire*, p. 46.

20 P. Salway, *Roman Britain* (Oxford University Press, Oxford: 1984), p. 3; N. Redhead, 'The Historical Context' in J. Walker, ed., *Castleshaw: The Archaeology of a Roman Fortlet* (Greater Manchester Archaeological Unit: 1989), p. 13.

21 Hey, *Yorkshire*, pp. 40–41; Redhead in Walker, ed., *Castleshaw*, p. 14; R. M. T. Hill and C. N. L. Brooke, 'From 627 until the Early Thirteenth Century' in G. E. Aylmer and R. Cant, *A History of York Minster* (Oxford University Press, Oxford: 1977), pp. 1–43 at pp. 1–3.

22 J. A. Gilks, 'The Roman tilery at Grimescar, Fixby, in the Ancient Parish of Halifax: Discovery and Excavations, 1956–57 and 1964', *THAS* n.s. 25 (2017), pp. 33–40.

23 J. Watson, *The History and Antiquities of the Parish of Halifax* (T. Lowndes, London: 1775), p. 32; H. P. Kendall, 'Roman evidences in the parish of Halifax', *THAS* n.s. 2 (1994), pp. 15–27; D. Haigh, '"At Gretland in the toppe of an hill"; four hundred years of the Greetland Roman altar, 1597–1997', *THAS* n.s. 5 (1997), p. 162.

24 Faull and Moorhouse, *West Yorkshire Archaeological Survey* 1, pp. 124, 126–27, 132, 154–67; Watson, *The History and Antiquities of the Parish of Halifax*, p. 32; H. P. Kendall, 'Roman evidences in the parish of Halifax', *THAS* (1912), p. 79; D. Haigh, 'Blue Ball and Baitings, Soyland: a tall story explained', *THAS* 2

(1994), pp. 15–27; Haigh, *THAS* (1997), pp. 13–35.

25 B. Hobson, G. Clay and G. Brown, *The Romans in Huddersfield – A New Assessment*, Huddersfield and District Archaeological Society (Archaeo Press, Huddersfield: 2015), pp. 1–6, 29.

26 Hey, *Yorkshire*, p. 47; Faull and Moorhouse, *West Yorkshire Archaeological Survey* 1, pp. 179, 182, 187; P. Stafford, *Unification and Conquest: A Political and Social History of England in the Tenth and Eleventh Centuries* (Edward Arnold, London: 1989), pp. 25–29; M. Townend, *Viking Age Yorkshire* (Blackthorn Press, Pickering: 2014), pp. 113–14.

27 Hey, *Yorkshire*, pp. 49, 53–54; J. A. Hargreaves, 'The Minster Church of St John the Baptist, Halifax, West Yorkshire: the medieval foundations' in C. Donovan, ed., *A Fresh Approach: Essays presented to Colin Platt in Celebration of his Eightieth Birthday* (Trouser Press Publishing, Ash Vale: 2014), p. 26; P. Hunter Blair, *Anglo-Saxon England* (Folio Society, London: 1997), pp. 39, 45; H. P. R. Finberg, *The Formation of England 550–1042* (Paladin/Hart-Davis, MacGibbon, London: 1974), p. 25.

28 Hey, *Yorkshire*, pp. 54–56; J. A. Heginbottom, 'Early Christian Sites in Calderdale', *THAS* (1989); J. F. Webb, ed., *Lives of the Saints* (Penguin, London: 1965), pp. 131–206. I am grateful to Professor Richard Morris of the University of Huddersfield for discussing with me the Exley evidence.

29 A. Williams and G. H. Martin, eds, *Domesday Book: A Complete Translation* (Penguin Books, London: 2002), p. 788; T. W. Hanson, *The Story of Old Halifax* (F. King and Sons, Halifax: 1920), p. 111; H. P. Kendall, 'Domesday Book and after', *THAS* (1935), pp. 29–31; A. H. Smith, 'Place names of the ancient parish of Halifax', *THAS* (1936), pp. 219, 229–30.

30 Faull and Moorhouse, *West Yorkshire Archaeological Survey* 1, pp. 216–18; Hargreaves in Donovan, ed., *A Fresh Approach*, p. 26.

31 A. H. Smith, *The Place Names of the West Riding of Yorkshire*, III (Cambridge University Press, Cambridge: 1961), pp. 104–06; Faull and Moorhouse, *West Yorkshire Archaeological Survey* 1, pp. 175, 177, 204–07; Jennings, *Pennine Valley*, pp. 16–17; *Halifax Guardian*, 19 August 1848. I am grateful to Dr George Redmonds for discussing with me this place-name evidence.

32 Hanson, *Old Halifax*, p. 111; Kendall, *THAS* (1935), pp. 29–31; Smith, *THAS* (1936), pp. 219, 229–30.

33 J. Lister and J. H. Ogden, eds, *Poll Tax (Lay Subsidy) 1379* (Halifax Antiquarian Society, Halifax: 1906), p. 48; M. Wood, *Domesday: A Search for the Roots of England* (BBC Publications, London: 1986), p. 18.

34 D. Carpenter, *The Struggle for Mastery: Britain 1066–1284* (Allen Lane, London: 2003), pp. 76–77; Stafford, *Unification and Conquest*, p. 106; M. L. Faull and M. Stinson, eds, *Domesday Book: Yorkshire* (Phillimore, Chichester: 1986), pp. 299, c, d, IY15; Hanson, *Old Halifax*, p. 21; Jennings, *Pennine Valley*, pp. 13–14; W. E. Wightman, 'The significance of "waste" in the Yorkshire Domesday', *Northern History* X (1975), p. 67; D. R. Roffe, 'Domesday Book and northern society: a reassessment', *English Historical Review* CV (1990), pp. 310–36 and 'The Yorkshire summary: a Domesday satellite', *Northern History* XXVII (1991), pp. 242–60; D. M. Palliser, 'Domesday Book and the "harrying of the north"', *Northern History* XXIX (1993), pp. 1–23; B. Jennings, 'The study of local history in the Pennines: the comparative dimension', *THAS* 3 (1995), pp. 13–30.

35 Jennings, *Pennine Valley*, pp. 28–38; Jennings, *THAS* 3 (1995), pp. 13–30; N. Smith, *Patterns in the Landscape: Evaluating Characterisation of the Historic Landscape in the South Pennines*, BAR British Series 604 (Archaeopress, Oxford: 2014), pp. 123–26; O. Rackham, *Trees and Woodland in the British Landscape* (second edition, J. M. Dent, London: 1981), pp. 50–51.

36 Jennings, *Pennine Valley*, pp. 40–41; P. F. Ryder, *Medieval Churches of West Yorkshire* (West Yorkshire Archaeological

Service, Wakefield: 1993), p. 155. I am grateful to Peter Ryder for discussing his interpretation of the tombstone evidence with me.

37 See Table 2.1; Jennings, *Pennine Valley*, pp. 41–42.

38 J. Lister, 'The Making of Halifax' in Ling Roth, ed., *Yorkshire Coiners*, pp. 130–31, 136; Jennings, *Pennine Valley*, p. 37; M. Habberjam, M. O'Regan and B. Hale, eds, *Court Rolls of the Manor of Wakefield, 1350–52* (YAS, Leeds: 1987), vol. VI, pp. xii–xiii; D. Hey, *Yorkshire from AD 1000* (Longman, London: 1986), p. 89; C. Spencer, 'Halifax Tithes', *THAS* (1986), p. 15; H. Poole, *Lewes Priory* (Lewes Priory Trust, Lewes: 2000), p. 19; B. Atack, I. Bailey, J. Page and C. Ray 'The people of the parish of Halifax: 1539 to 1670' in N. Smith, ed., *History in the South Pennines: The Legacy of Alan Petford* (Hebden Bridge Local History Society, Hebden Bridge: 2017), p. 33.

39 H. M. Jewell, ed., *Court Rolls of the Manor of Wakefield, 1348–50* (YAS, Leeds: 1987), vol. II, pp. xii–xiii; C. M. Fraser, 'Introduction' in Habberjam, O'Regan and Hale, eds, *Court Rolls of the Manor of Wakefield, 1350–52*, pp. xii–xvi.

40 Lister in Ling Roth, ed., *Yorkshire Coiners*, pp. 130–31, 135–38, 143–44; Jennings, *Pennine Valley*, p. 37; Jewell, ed., *Court Rolls of the Manor of Wakefield, 1348–1350*, pp. xviii–xxi, 136, 260; Habberjam, O'Regan and Hale, eds, *Court Rolls of the Manor of Wakefield, 1350–52*, pp. xii–xiii, xv–xvi, xxii; Hey, *Yorkshire from AD 1000*, p. 89.

41 Lister in Ling Roth, ed., *Yorkshire Coiners*, pp. 135, 138, 143–44; Hanson, *Old Halifax*, pp. 57, 66; Hey, *Yorkshire*, pp. 109–10.

42 J. A. Gilks, 'Yorkshire Archaeological Register', *YAJ* 43 (1971), pp. 196–97; 44 (1972), p. 223; 45 (1973), p. 204; 46 (1974), p. 147; C. Giles, *Rural Houses of West Yorkshire 1400–1830* (HMSO, London: 1986), pp. 26–36; C. Platt, *Medieval England* (Routledge and Kegan Paul, London: 1978), pp. 202–03.

43 T. W. Hanson, 'Halifax Parish Church, Norman Era', *THAS* (1953), p. 24;

J. Lister, 'Priors of Lewes, Lords of Halifax Manor', *THAS* (1922); E. Mason, *William II Rufus, the Red King* (Tempus, Stroud: 2005), p. 59. Hargreaves in Donovan, ed., *A Fresh Approach*, pp. 23–34.

44 D. C. Douglas, *William the Conqueror* (Methuen, London: 1964), pp. 99–101, 203, 232, 269, 272, 328; D. Bates, *William the Conqueror* (Tempus, Stroud: 1989, revised 2004), pp. 79, 81, 134, 170, 183; W. Farrer and C. T. Clay, eds, *Early Yorkshire Charters*, vol. viii (Cambridge University Press, Cambridge: [1949] 2013), pp. 1–47, 59–62; Hanson, *THAS* (1953), p. 21.

45 F. Barlow, *The English Church 1066–1154* (Longman, London: 1979), p. 7.

46 Poole, *Lewes Priory*, p. 6; G. Mayhew, *The Monks of St Pancras. Lewes Priory, England's Premier Cluniac Monastery and its Dependencies 1076–1537* [hereinafter *Monks of St Pancras*] (Lewes History Press, Lewes: 2014), pp. 18–19.

47 C. Waters, *Gundrada de Warenne* (Exeter: 1884); Clay, ed., *Early Yorkshire Charters*, vol. viii, pp. 40–46; Douglas, *William the Conqueror*, p. 267.

48 Hanson, *Old Halifax*, p. 32.

49 Foundation charter of Lewes Priory, L. F. Salzman, ed., *The Chartulary of the Priory of St Pancras of Lewes* (Sussex Record Society, Sussex: 1932), vol. 38, p. 3 cited in R. H. C. Davies, *A History of Medieval Europe* (Longmans, London: 1957), p. 263; C. Platt, *The Parish Churches of Medieval England* (Chancellor Press, London: 1981, second edition 1995), p. 32; C. Platt, *The Abbeys and Priories of Medieval England* (Chancellor Press, second edition, London: 1995), pp. 8–11, 24, 38.

50 R. W. Southern, *The Making of the Middle Ages* (Hutchinson, London: 1953), pp. 163–65.

51 Cited in Lister, *THAS* (1922).

52 C. Platt, *Medieval Britain from the Air* (George Philip, London: 1984), p. 39; Platt, *Abbeys and Priories*, p. 68.

53 Mayhew, *Monks of Saint Pancras*, p. 324.

54 Lister, *THAS* (1922), p. 13; Hargreaves in Donovan, ed., *A Fresh Approach*, pp. 28–29.

55 C. N. L. Brooke, *From Alfred to Henry III, 871–1272* (T. Nelson, Edinburgh: 1961), p. 143.

56 Mayhew, *Monks of St Pancras*, p. 81.

57 Poole, *Lewes Priory*, p. 7; Hargreaves in Donovan, ed., *A Fresh Approach*, p. 29.

58 R. Bretton, 'Halifax Parish Church', *THAS* (1967), p. 74; Hanson, *THAS* (1953), p. 28; Lister, 'Halifax Parish Church: An Early Chapter of its History', *THAS* (1905), pp. 164–65; Lister, *THAS* (1922); Mayhew, *Monks of St Pancras*, pp. 281, 283–87.

59 Barlow, *English Church 1066–1154*, pp. 181, 233.

60 Hanson, *Old Halifax*, pp. 34–35; Lister, *THAS* (1905), pp. 164–65 and (1922).

61 Jennings, *Pennine Valley*, pp. 18–19, 55; Spencer, *THAS* (1986), pp. 11–13.

62 J. A. Gilks, 'Yorkshire Archaeological Register', *YAJ* 43 (1971), pp. 196–97; 44 (1972), p. 223; 45 (1973), p. 204; 46 (1974), p. 147; Platt, *Medieval England*, pp. 202–03; Habberjam, O'Regan and Hale, eds, *Wakefield Court Rolls 1350–52*, VI, pp. xix–xx, 92.

63 Mayhew, *Monks of St Pancras*, p. 211; West Yorkshire Archive Service (WYAS), Calderdale HAS/B:21/33, MS Notes of F. A. Leyland junior relating to Halifax Parish Church and the *Halifax Guardian*, 13 June 1874.

64 Mayhew, *Monks of St Pancras*, p. 211.

65 G. Harriss, *Shaping the Nation. England 1360–1461* (Oxford University Press, Oxford: 2005), p. 277.

66 Giles, *Rural Houses of West Yorkshire*, pp. 107–12; J. W. Houseman, 'Notes and comments on the Halifax churchwardens' accounts, 1620–1714', *THAS* (1925); Hanson, *Old Halifax*, pp. 129–33; E. W. Crossley, *The Monumental and Other Inscriptions in Halifax Parish Church* (John Whitehead and Son, Leeds: 1909), p. 146; P. J. P. Goldberg, *Women, Work, And Life Cycle in A Medieval Economy: Women in York and Yorkshire c. 1300–1520* (Clarendon Press, Oxford: 1992), pp. 75–76.

67 Faull and Moorhouse, *West Yorkshire Archaeological Survey* 3, pp. 781–82, 786, 810; J. A. Gilks, 'Boothtown Hall: a fifteenth-century house in the parish of Halifax', *YAJ* 46 (1974), pp. 80–81; J. A. Heginbottom, 'Fences and fields: the evolution of the Calderdale rural landscape from prehistoric times to the present day', *THAS* 1 (1993), p. 31; Jewell, ed., *Court Rolls of the Manor of Wakefield, 1348–50*, p. xxi.

68 Jennings, *Pennine Valley*, p. 42; M. J. Ellis, 'A study in the manorial history of Halifax parish in the sixteenth and early seventeenth centuries', II, *YAJ* XL (1961), p. 431; Lister in Ling Roth, ed., *Yorkshire Coiners*, pp. 143, 149–51.

69 Faull and Moorhouse, *West Yorkshire Archaeological Survey* 1, pp. 241, 385–86, 399–400, 726–27, 746; M. J. Ellis, 'A study in the manorial history of Halifax parish in the sixteenth and early seventeenth centuries', I, *YAJ* xl (1960), pp. 250–64; Lister in Ling Roth, ed., *Yorkshire Coiners*, pp. 126–30; J. H. Patchett. 'The development of the area to the west of Halifax Parish Church, c. 1540–c. 1965', *THAS* n.s. 13 (2005), pp. 13–33.

70 A. Jones, *A Thousand Years of the English Parish* (Windrush Press, Moreton-in-Marsh: 2000), pp. 21–22, 89.

71 Smith, *Patterns in the Landscape*, pp. 15–16, 139–40.

72 Mayhew, *Monks of St Pancras*, pp. 9–10, 30–31, 38–39, 210–12, 238, 283–87, 301; YAS, Leeds, DD12/II/H/16; WYAS, Calderdale, HAS/B: 21/33 and *Halifax Guardian*, 13 June 1874.

73 M. E. Francois, 'The social and economic development of Halifax, 1558–1640', *Proceedings of the Leeds Philosophical and Literary Society* (*PLPLS*) 11 (1966), p. 220; Faull and Moorhouse, *West Yorkshire Archaeological Survey* 1, p. 216; Hey, *Yorkshire*, p. 59; A. Goodwin, 'How the ancient parish of Halifax was divided', *THAS* (1961), pp. 23–36; A. Betteridge, 'Halifax before the Industrial Revolution', I, *THAS* (1978), pp. 17–41.

74 Mayhew, *Monks of St. Pancras*, p. 279; A. Murphy, 'The Medieval Glazing of St Mary's Church, Elland', *THAS* n.s. 24 (2017), pp. 15–31.

75 Mayhew, *Monks of St. Pancras*, p. 281; WYAS, Calderdale SH6/C&M/9; Lister,

THAS (1922), pp. 49–50; J. N. Miner, *The Grammar Schools of Medieval England: A. F. Leach in Historiographical Perspective* (McGill-Queen's University Press, Montreal: 1990), p. 48; Ling Roth, ed., *Yorkshire Coiners.*

76 Faull and Moorhouse, *West Yorkshire Archaeological Survey* 3, pp. 626–27, 631, 652; S. Moorhouse, 'Documentary evidence for the landscape of the manor of Wakefield during the Middle Ages', *Landscape History* 1 (1979).

77 Atack, Bailey, Page and Ray in Smith, ed., *History in the South Pennines*, p. 33; J. Barker, *England, Arise: The People, the King and the Great Revolt of 1381* (Little,

Brown, London: 2014), pp. 366–71; Jewell, ed., *Court Rolls of the Manor of Wakefield, 1348–50*, pp. xviii–xix.

78 Francois, *PLPLS* (1966), p. 220; Gilks, *YAJ* 43 (1971), pp. 196–97; 44 (1972), p. 223; 45 (1973), p. 204; 46 (1974), p. 147; Heginbottom, *THAS* (1993), pp. 18–21; Lister in Ling Roth, ed., *Yorkshire Coiners*, pp. 142–44, 182–83; Hanson, *Old Halifax*, pp. 76–78; Ryder, *Medieval Churches of West Yorkshire*, pp. 36, 52, 56, 63, 75–77, 155.

79 G. Sheeran, *Medieval Yorkshire Towns* (Edinburgh University Press, Edinburgh: 1998), pp. 22, 25.

Chapter 3: 'The inhabitants do altogether live by cloth making': Halifax and its hinterland, 1500–1750

1 M. E. Francois, 'The social and economic development of Halifax, 1558–1640', *PLPLS* 11 (1966), pp. 225–26; W. Camden, *Britannia* (George Bishop, London: 1586), p. 692; H. Holroyde, 'Protestantism and Dissent in the parish of Halifax, 1509–1640', *THAS* (1988), p. 20; A. Betteridge, 'Halifax before the Industrial Revolution', I, *THAS* (1978), pp. 31–32, 38; J. A. Hargreaves, 'Religion and Society in the Parish of Halifax *c.* 1740–1914', unpublished Ph.D. thesis, Huddersfield Polytechnic, 1991, p. 27; J. Smail, *The Origins of Middle-Class Culture* (Cornell University Press, Ithaca and London: 1994), p. 35; B. Atack, I. Bailey, J. Page and C. Ray, 'The people of the parish of Halifax, 1539 to 1670: Parish registers and the reconstruction of the population' in N. Smith, ed., *History in the South Pennines: The Legacy of Alan Petford* (Hebden Bridge Local History Society, Hebden Bridge: 2017), pp. 40–41, 47, 61, 64–66.

2 Camden, *Britannia*, p. 692; D. Defoe, *A Tour Through the Whole Island of Britain* (Yale University Press, New Haven and London: 1991), p. 258.

3 P. Clark and D. Souden, *Migration and Society in Early Modern England* (Hutchinson, London: 1987), p. 236; Atack, Bailey, Page and Ray in Smith,

ed., *History in the South Pennines*, pp. 33, 64–66; N. Smith, *Patterns in the Landscape: Evaluating Characterisation of the Historic Landscape in the South Pennines*, BAR British Series 604 (Archaeopress, Oxford: 2014), pp. 63–65.

4 D. Hey, *Yorkshire from AD 1000* (Longman, London: 1986), pp. 7, 96.

5 F. Pryor, *The Making of the British Landscape* (Allen Lane, London: 2010), p. 533; W. Camden, *Britannia*, From Weaver to Web, online Visual Archive of Calderdale History; H. Heaton, *The Yorkshire Woollen and Worsted Industries* (Oxford University Press, Oxford: 1965), pp. 54–55, 68–72; C. Dyer, *Making a Living in the Middle Ages. The People of Britain 850–1520,* (Yale University Press, London: 2002), pp. 308–09; Atack, Bailey, Page and Ray, in Smith, ed., *History in the South Pennines*, pp. 33–66; N. Smith, *Patterns in the Landscape*, pp. 139–40.

6 D. M. Palliser, *The Age of Elizabeth* (Longman, London: 1992), p. 289; R. N. Thornes, *West Yorkshire: 'A Noble Scene of Industry'* (West Yorkshire Metropolitan County Council, Wakefield: 1981), pp. 7–12.

7 J. Thirsk, 'Industries in the countryside' in F. J. Fisher (ed.), *Essays in the Economic and Social History of Tudor England in honour of R. H. Tawney* (Cambridge

University Press, Cambridge: 1961),
pp. 70–88; B. Jennings, 'The study of local
history in the Pennines: the comparative
dimension', *THAS* 3 (1995), pp. 22–28;
Heaton, *Yorkshire Woollen and Worsted
Industries*, p. 77.

8 B. Jennings, *Pennine Valley* (Smith Settle,
Otley: 1992), p. 43; T. W. Hanson, *The
Story of Old Halifax* (F. King, Halifax:
1920), pp. 84–86; C. Giles, *Rural Houses
of West Yorkshire, 1400–1830* (HMSO,
London: 1986), pp. 26–47; Heaton,
Yorkshire Woollen and Worsted Industries,
p. 76.

9 Hey, *Yorkshire*, p. 96; G. Parker,
Cambridge Illustrated History of Warfare
(Cambridge University Press, Cambridge:
1995), pp. 151–52; Francois, *PLPLS* (1966),
p. 217; Hanson, *Old Halifax*, p. 112;
Heaton, *Yorkshire Woollen and Worsted
Industries*, pp. 19, 81–84.

10 2 and 3 Philip and Mary c. 13, 1555.

11 Hey, *Yorkshire*, p. 110; Heaton, *Yorkshire
Woollen and Worsted Industries*, p. 94;
Hanson, *Old Halifax*, pp. 112–13, 184–85;
Palliser, *Age of Elizabeth*, pp. 205, 267,
289–90; J. Addy, *The Textile Revolution*
(Longman, London: 1976), pp. 67–68.

12 Heaton, *Yorkshire Woollen and Worsted
Industries*, pp. 268–71; Hanson, *Old
Halifax*, pp. 179–83; Smail, *Origins of
Middle-Class Culture*, p. 75.

13 R. Bennett, 'Enforcing the law in
revolutionary England: Yorkshire,
c. 1640–*c.* 1660', Ph.D. thesis, University of
London, 1987, https://kclpure.kcl.ac.uk/
portal, pp. 59–60, Figure 3.2.

14 Defoe, *Tour*, pp. 257, 259.

15 Francois, *PLPLS* (1966), pp. 252–55;
H. P. Kendall, 'Gleanings from local
Elizabethan wills', *THAS* (1915), pp. 119,
126, 128; J. A. Heginbottom, 'Fences and
fields: the evolution of the Calderdale rural
landscape from prehistoric times to the
present day', *THAS*, 1 (1993), p. 15.

16 M. J. Ellis, 'A study in the manorial
history of Halifax parish in the sixteenth
and early seventeenth centuries', II, *YAJ*
xl (1961), pp. 420–22; Thornes, *West
Yorkshire*, pp. 34–36; Betteridge, *THAS*
(1978), p. 27; Hanson, *Old Halifax*, p. 185;
C. M. Fraser, ed., *The Court Rolls of the*

Manor of Wakefield for 1608–09 (YAS,
Leeds: 1996), pp. 118, 175.

17 Giles, *Rural Houses of West Yorkshire*,
pp. 107–12; C. Platt, *The Great Rebuildings
of Tudor and Stuart England* (UCL
Press, London: 1994); T. W. Hanson,
'Halifax builders in Oxford', *THAS* (1928)
pp. 253–317; J. W. Houseman, 'Notes and
comments on the Halifax churchwardens'
accounts, 1620–1714' *THAS* (1925);
Hanson, *Old Halifax*, pp. 129–33.

18 J. A. Heginbottom, 'Halifax is made of
wax', *THAS* (1990) 2; H. Ling Roth, *The
Yorkshire Coiners, 1767–83 and notes
on Old and Prehistoric Halifax* (F. King
and Sons Ltd, Halifax: 1906), p. 239;
J. C. Bateman, 'Precursors of the Local
Heavy Ceramic Manufacturing Industry:
Pot Making From the 1640s to 1986',
THAS n.s. 25 (2017), p. 43.

19 J. A. Heginbottom, 'Iron and wool:
ironworking and the woollen textile
industry in Calderdale from the Middle
Ages to the Industrial Revolution', *THAS*
5 (1997), pp. 54–65; Thornes, *West
Yorkshire*, pp. 28–31; Kendall, *THAS*
(1915), pp. 118–19; Smail, *Origins of
Middle-Class Culture*, p. 95.

20 West Yorkshire Archive Service, Leeds
District Archives, Lease of greater and
lesser Blackwell Hall, Halifax by John
Waterhouse of Shibden and his heir
Robert Waterhouse to Robert Waterhouse
of Halifax, 7 Jan 1562, TN/HX/A55;
G. Sheeran, *Medieval Yorkshire Towns*
(Edinburgh University Press, Edinburgh:
1998), p. 114; British Museum, Letter of
James Ryder to Lord Burghley, 3 January
1589, Lansdowne MSS, v. 119, f. 118.
I am grateful to Dr Alan Betteridge
for supplying me with copies of these
documents.

21 S. Hughes, 'Church and Society in the
Seventeenth Century Parish of Halifax',
unpublished dissertation, St John's
College, York, 1974, pp. 12–13.

22 C. Morris, ed., *The Illustrated Journeys of
Celia Fiennes, 1685–c. 1712* (Alan Sutton,
Stroud: 1995), p. 182; Defoe, *Tour*, p. 261.

23 Hey, *Yorkshire*, p. 183.

24 Defoe, *Tour*, p. 259.

25 Thornes, *West Yorkshire*, pp. 42–45;

W. B. Crump, 'Halifax visitors' book', I, *THAS* (1937), pp. 35, 41; J. H. Priestley, 'The Rochdale to Halifax and Elland turnpike', *THAS* (1952), pp. 95–114; (1953), pp. 31–53; E. Pawson, *Transport and Economy: The Turnpike Roads of Eighteenth-Century Britain* (Academic Press, London: 1977), p. 344.

26 Distraint of knighthood refers to the practice whereby English kings in an attempt to increase the number of knights who could be required to perform military service and other duties or pay a fine, which became used as a money-raising device by monarchs until it was condemned as an abuse of power by Charles I. Hearth Tax was levied from 1662 at two shillings per hearth, except by those exempted on grounds of poverty and repealed at the Glorious Revolution as an infringement of liberty, since it allowed the searching of taxpayers' homes, J. Gardiner and N. Wenborn, eds, *The History Today Companion to British History* (Collins and Brown Ltd, London: 1995), pp. 239, 373.

27 Francois, *PLPLS* (1966), pp. 217–38, 246; Smail, *Origins of Middle-Class Culture*, pp. 29–30; Holroyde, *THAS* (1988), pp. 23–24; 'Halifax landowners in 1630–32', *Halifax Guardian Almanack* (1902); W. and S. Sheils, 'Textiles and reform: Halifax and its hinterland' in P. Collinson and J. Craig (eds), *The Reformation in English Towns, 1500–1640* (Macmillan, London: 1998), p. 133 Hanson, *Old Halifax*, pp. 94–102, A. F. Upton, *Sir Arthur Ingram* (Oxford University Press: 1961), pp. 45–51; Bennett, Ph.D. thesis, pp. 60–64.

28 Betteridge, *THAS* (1978), pp. 22, 27. Copyhold was a form of medieval manorial land tenure which evolved out of serfdom and became the dominant form of land tenure in nineteenth century England, Gardiner and Wenborn, eds, *History Today Companion*, pp. 198–99.

29 Betteridge, *THAS* (1978), pp. 27–28; Smail, *Origins of Middle-Class Culture*, pp. 94–95.

30 Smail, *Origins of Middle-Class Culture*, pp. 21, 26–27, 93–95. For scrivener see Gardiner and Wenborn, eds, *History Today Companion*, p. 681.

31 Betteridge, *THAS* (1978), pp. 19, 22, 25–28; A. Betteridge, 'Halifax before the Industrial Revolution', II, *THAS* (1979), pp. 89–90; Smail, *Origins of Middle-Class Culture*, pp. 25, 37; Holroyde, *THAS* (1988), p. 30; A. L. Beier, *Masterless Men* (Methuen, London: 1985), p. 45; YAS, Wakefield Court Rolls, 15 October 1537, MD 225/1/263A/5/80B; Defoe, *Tour*, p. 256.

32 Francois, *PLPLS* (1966), pp. 243, 247; Thornes, *West Yorkshire*, p. 51; West Yorkshire Archive Service, Calderdale District Archives, Letter from John Waite to Nicholas Denman, Mayor of Hull, 24 August 1645, MISC: 331/1; Smail, *Origins of Middle-Class Culture*, p. 24.

33 Smail, *Origins of Middle-Class Culture*, pp. 24, 37–38, 82–84, 95–101.

34 P. N. Farrar, 'John Waite and the plague of 1645', *THAS* (1978); Betteridge, *THAS* (1978), pp. 31–32; T. Wright, *The Antiquities of Halifax* (Scholar's Choice, Leeds: [1738] 2015), p. 15.

35 Sheils, in Collinson and Craig, eds, *The Reformation in English Towns*, pp. 140, 143.

36 Hanson, *Old Halifax*, pp. 89–94; see transcript WYAS, Calderdale, SH6/C&M/9 and J. Lister, 'Priors of Lewes, Lords of Halifax Manor', *THAS* (1922) pp. 49–50.

37 J. Youings, *The Dissolution of the Monasteries* (George Allen and Unwin Ltd, London: 1971), p. 65.

38 Mayhew, *Monks of St. Pancras*, p. 301.

39 Hanson, *Old Halifax*, pp. 89–94; see transcript WYAS, Calderdale, SH6/C&M/9 and J. Lister, 'Priors of Lewes, Lords of Halifax Manor', *THAS* (1922) pp. 49–50, 301.

40 C. Haigh, *English Reformations: Religion Politics and Society under the Tudors* (Oxford University Press, Oxford: 1993), p. 201; A. G. Dickens, *Lollards and Protestants in the Diocese of York* (Oxford University Press, Oxford: 1959), pp. 149, 172; Holroyde, *THAS* (1988), p. 20.

41 E. Duffy, *The Stripping of the Altars, Traditional Religion in England 1400–1580* (Yale University Press, New Haven

and London: 1992), p. 479; J. Youings, *Sixteenth Century England* (Allen Lane, London: 1984); Holroyde, *THAS* (1988), p. 26; Dickens, *Lollards and Protestants*, pp. 198, 217; Sheils in Collinson and Craig, eds, *Reformation in English Towns*, pp. 138–39.

42 Dickens, *Lollards and Protestants*, p. 181; Holroyde, *THAS* (1988), p. 26; Sheils in Collinson and Craig, eds, *Reformation in English Towns*, pp. 140, 142–43.

43 Dickens, *Lollards and Protestants*, pp. 225–26; J. M. Turner and J. A. Hargreaves, *Thunderclaps from Heaven* (Calderdale Metropolitan Borough Council, Halifax: 1984), pp. 8–9; Haigh, *English Reformations*, p. 219.

44 R. Whiting, *The Blind Devotion of the People* (Cambridge University Press, Cambridge: 1989), p. 266; Turner and Hargreaves, *Thunderclaps from Heaven*, p. 9.

45 C. Hill, *Society and Puritanism in Pre-Revolutionary England* (Secker and Warburg, London: 1964), pp. 137–38; J. H. Turner, *Halifax Books and Authors* (Idle: 1906), pp. 46–47; Holroyde, *THAS* (1988), pp. 29–32.

46 J. Addy, 'The uncontrollable and ungovernable parish of Halifax in the seventeenth century', *THAS* 1 (1993), p. 37; C. T. Clay, 'The protestation of 1641 – Halifax signatories', *THAS* (1919), pp. 105–15.

47 T. Royle, *Civil War. The Wars of the Three Kingdoms 1638–1660* (Abacus, London: 2005), pp. 260–65.

48 Atack, Bailey, Page and Ray in Smith, ed., *History in the South Pennines*, pp. 63–64.

49 Jennings, *Pennine Valley*, pp. 70–72; H. P. Kendall, 'The Civil War in Halifax parish, 1639–50', *THAS* (1909–11); Atack, Bailey, Page and Ray in Smith, ed., *History in the South Pennines*, p. 64; A. J. Hopper, '"The Readiness of the People": The Formation and Emergence of the Army of the Fairfaxes, 1642–43 (Borthwick Institute of Historical Research, York: 1997), pp. 2, 4, 12; Smail, *Origins of Middle-Class Culture*, p. 31; Hanson, *Old Halifax*, pp. 137–63.

50 Houseman, *THAS* (1925), pp. 137–67.

51 C. M. Fraser, ed., *The Court Rolls of the Manor of Wakefield from September 1687 to September 1688* (YAS, Leeds: 2002), pp. vii–viii; G. N. Clark, *The Later Stuarts 1660–1714* (Oxford University Press, Oxford: 1955), pp. 102, 106, 116, 121, 131, 181–82; M. Kishlansky, *A Monarchy Transformed Britain 1603–1714* (Allen Lane, London: 1996), pp. 269, 275.

52 E. Vallance, *The Glorious Revolution: 1688 Britain's Fight for Liberty* (Little Brown, London: 2006), pp. 192–93; Houseman, *THAS* (1925); J. Oates, 'Halifax and the Jacobite Rebellion of 1745', *THAS* 9 (2001), p. 102; Turner, *Halifax Books and Authors*, pp. 11–17; G. V. Bennett, 'John Tillotson: portrait of a liberal' in G. Powell, ed., *To the Church of England* (Churchman Publishing, Worthing: 1988), pp. 75–86; W. J. Sheils, 'Oliver Heywood and his Congregation' in W. J. Sheils and D. Wood, eds, *Voluntary Religion* (Basil Blackwell, London: 1986).

53 Oates, *THAS* 9 (2001), p. 101.

54 J. Crabtree, *Concise History of the Parish and Vicarage of Halifax* (Hartley and Walker, Halifax: 1836), pp. 145–46; C. E. Whiting, ed., 'Two Yorkshire Diaries', YAS Record Series, vol. cxvii (York: 1952), p. 109.

55 A. Jessop, *Three Yorkshire Diaries* (Smith Settle, Otley: 1990), pp. 95–135.

56 Oates, *THAS* 9 (2001), pp. 100–05.

57 J. A. Hargreaves, 'Methodist growth and secession in the parish of Halifax, 1740–1851', *THAS* 7 (1999), pp. 51–52; C. Stell, 'Calderdale Chapels', *THAS* (1984), pp.16–22; E. V. Chapman, *John Wesley and Co* (Halifax: 1952), pp. 5–13.

58 S. A. and M. J. Raymond, *The Yorkshire Poll Book, 1741* (Raymonds, Exeter: 1997); J. F. Quinn, 'Yorkshiremen go to the polls: county contests in the early eighteenth century', *Northern History* XXI (1985), pp. 137–74; Smail, *Origins of Middle-Class Culture*, pp. 160–61.

59 'The Diary of Arthur Jessop' in E. Beardsell, *Three Huddersfield Diaries* (Toll house Reprints, Holmfirth: 1990), p. 109; Oates, *THAS* 9 (2001), pp. 100–06.

60 Betteridge, *THAS* (1978), pp. 18–19; M. J. Ellis, 'A study in the manorial

history of Halifax parish in the sixteenth and early seventeenth centuries', I, *YAJ* xl (1960), pp. 252–54; Bennett, Ph.D. thesis, p. 69.

61 Betteridge, *THAS* (1978), pp. 19–26.

62 Hughes, dissertation, p. 18; Farrar, *THAS* (1978).

63 Dickens, *Lollards and Protestants*, p. 2, n. 3; J. Lister, 'Halifax in the time of Queen Elizabeth', *THAS* (1921), p. 55; Betteridge, *THAS* (1978), p. 19.

64 Addy, *THAS* (1993); Holroyde, *THAS* (1988), p. 20; Hanson, *Old Halifax*, p. 134; Bennett, Ph.D. thesis.

65 J. Barlow, *An Exposition of the Second Epistle of the Apostle Paul to Timothy* (John Bellamie, London: 1625).

66 Sheils in Collinson and Craig, eds, *Reformation in English Towns*, p. 142. H. Caffrey, *Almshouses in the West Riding of Yorkshire 1600–1900* (Heritage Marketing and Publications Ltd, King's Lynn: 2006), pp. 79–81.

67 P. W. Robinson, 'John Aked, joiner and raff merchant (1751–1810)', *THAS*, n.s. 25 (2017), pp. 65–68.

68 Betteridge, *THAS* (1979), pp. 82–88; Caffrey, *Almshouses in the West Riding of Yorkshire*, pp. 79–82.

69 Holroyde, *THAS* (1988), pp. 19–20; A. Thirlwell, *Folio Anthology of Autobiography* (Folio Society, London: 1994), p. 40; J. T. Hughes, 'Laurence Sterne (1713–1768) and Hipperholme Grammar School, Halifax', *THAS* 9 (2001) pp. 53–62; I. Campbell Ross, *Laurence Sterne: A Life* (Oxford University Press, Oxford: 2001), pp. 29, 33, 44; Francois, *PLPLS* (1966), pp. 275–77; Sheils in Collinson and Craig, eds, *Reformation in English Towns*, p. 142; A. J. Petford, 'Matthew Broadley's benefactions of 1648 and the origins of the grammar school at Hipperholme', *THAS* 6 (1998), pp. 30–35; J. T. Hughes, 'Henry Power (1626–1668) of New Hall, Elland and experiments on barometric pressure', *THAS* 10 (2002), pp. 14–26.

70 Betteridge, *THAS* (1978), p. 31; (1979), p. 83; M. W. Garside, 'Halifax schools prior to 1700', *THAS* (1924); Caffrey, *Almshouses in the West Riding of Yorkshire*, pp. 79–82; J. A. Hargreaves, 'Nathaniel Waterhouse', *ODNB*.

71 Betteridge, *THAS* (1978), pp. 30–31; (1979), p. 98; Kendall, *THAS* (1915), p. 145; J. T. Hughes, 'Sir Thomas Browne, Shibden Dale, and the writing of Religio Medici', *Yorkshire History Quarterly* 5 (2000), pp. 89–94; K. Wrightson, *English Society, 1580–1680* (Routledge, London: 1982), pp. 198–99. I am grateful to Dr K. Wrightson for this reference.

72 P. Borsay, *The English Urban Renaissance* (Clarendon Press, Oxford: 1989), p. 285.

73 Sheils in Collinson and Craig, eds, *Reformation in English Towns*, p. 142.

74 Addy, *THAS* (1993), pp. 37–38, 40.

75 Betteridge, *THAS* (1978), p. 29; Holroyde, *THAS* (1988), p. 20; J. Addy, *Sin and Society in the Seventeenth Century* (Routledge, London: 1989), pp. 116, 157–58; *THAS* (1993).

76 M. W. Garside, 'The social history of Halifax in the seventeenth century', *THAS* (1923), p. 74.

77 Betteridge, *THAS* (1978), p. 33; Lister, *THAS* (1921), p. 38; Garside, *THAS* (1923), pp. 79–81; Keith Thomas, *Religion and the Decline of Magic* (Weidenfeld and Nicolson, London: 1971), p. 592.

78 Addy, *THAS* (1993), pp. 38–39; Garside, *THAS* (1923), pp. 68–69; Borsay, *English Urban Renaissance*, p. 366; Smail, *Origins of Middle-Class Culture*, pp. 185–86; WYAS, CDA, Horse racing agreement, MISC: 325.

79 Smail, *Origins of Middle-Class Culture*, pp. 35–37; *Encyclopaedia Britannica*, vol. 18, 1979, p. 1037; D. Baker, '1766 and All That': William Herschel and the Snetzler Organ of Halifax Minster', *THAS* (forthcoming).

80 Crump, *THAS* (1937), pp. 26–28; Bennett, Ph.D. thesis, pp. 59–60; Ellis, *YAJ* (1961), p. 422; Francois, *PLPLS* (1966) pp. 217–24.

81 W. B. Crump, 'Ancient highways of the parish of Halifax', V, *THAS* (1926); P. Ryder, *Medieval Churches of West Yorkshire* (West Yorkshire Archaeology Service, Wakefield: 1993), p. 155.

82 Mayhew, *Monks of St Pancras*, pp. 281, 283.

83 Hanson, *Old Halifax*, pp. 177–78;

J. Lister, 'The genesis of the Halifax Manufacturers' Hall' in Ling Roth, *Yorkshire Coiners*, pp. 207; Betteridge, *THAS* (1979), pp. 85–86; T. W. Hanson, *Halifax Street Lore* (William Paterson Ltd, Halifax: 1932), pp. 14–15; P. Thornborrow, 'Timber-framed buildings in West Yorkshire: an overview', *Archaeology and Archives in West Yorkshire*, West Yorkshire Archaeology Service, 16 (2003), pp. 5–6; Sheeran, *Medieval Yorkshire Towns*, p. 144; C. Giles, *The Building of Halifax: A history and celebration* (CMBC/English Heritage, Halifax: 2010), p. 11; Hargreaves, Ph.D. thesis, p. 122.

84 M. W. Garside, 'The Halifax Piece Hall', *THAS* (1921), pp. 169–73.

85 A. McInnes, *The English Town, 1660–1760* (Historical Association, London: 1980), pp. 5–6; Francois, *PLPLS* (1966), pp. 217–24; Ellis, *YAJ* (1961), p. 425.

86 Garside, *THAS* (1921), pp. 169–73.

87 Heginbottom, *THAS* (1990), pp. 2, 16; Betteridge, *THAS* (1979), p. 98; Wright, *Antiquities of Halifax*, pp. 14–15.

Chapter 4: 'An astonishing trading town': Halifax in the age of industrial expansion, 1750–1850

1 *Bailey's Northern Directory* (Warrington: 1781), pp. 200–03; S. L. Ollard and P. C. Walker, eds, *Archbishop Herring's Visitation Returns, 1743* (YAS, Leeds: 1928–29); University of York, Borthwick Institute of Historical Research. Archbishop Drummond's Visitation Returns, 1764; Census Returns, 1801–51.

2 J. J. Cartwright, ed., *The Travels through England of Dr Richard Pococke* (Camden Society, London: 1888), p. 50. Serges were originally fabrics with a worsted warp and woollen weft, though the term later came to be used for worsted warp and worsted weft cloth.

3 J. Watson, *History and Antiquities of the Parish of Halifax* (T. Lowndes, London: 1775), pp. 8, 69–70.

4 T. Pennant, *Tour in Scotland*, 1770, cited in H. Heaton, *The Yorkshire Woollen and Worsted Industries* (Oxford University Press, Oxford: 1965), p. 271.

5 T. Twining, *Recreations and Studies of a country clergyman of the eighteenth century* (London: 1882), pp. 98–99.

6 C. Dibdin, *The musical tour of Mr Dibdin* (Sheffield: 1788), pp. 276 and 279.

7 E. Sigsworth, *Black Dyke Mills* (Liverpool University Press, Liverpool: 1958), pp. 18–25; J. Simpson, *The Journal of Dr John Simpson of Bradford* (Local Studies Department, City of Bradford Metropolitan Council, Bradford: 1981), p. 41; J. Pigot, *National Commercial Directory* (J. Pigot and Company, London and Manchester: 1834), p. 227.

8 Table 4.2; D. T. Jenkins, 'The cotton industry in Yorkshire, 1780–1900', *Textile History* 10 (1979), pp. 78–82; T. W. Hanson, *The Story of Old Halifax* (F. King and Sons, Halifax: 1920), pp. 239–40; G. Ingle, *Yorkshire Cotton* (Carnegie Publishing, Preston: 1997), pp. 130–60.

9 H. Holroyde, 'Power technology in the Halifax textile industry, 1770–1850', *THAS* (1980).

10 H. Holroyde, 'Textile mills, masters and men in the Halifax district, 1770–1851', *THAS* (1979); N. Rycroft et al., '1851 census returns for Halifax and Skircoat townships', I, *THAS* (1979), p. 118.

11 C. Aspin, ed., *The Yorkshire Textile Districts in 1849* (Helmshore Local History Society, Helmshore: 1974), p. 13.

12 D. Koch, *Ralph Waldo Emerson in Europe: Class, Race and Revolution in the Making of an American Thinker* (I. B. Tauris, London and New York: 2012), pp. 92–93.

13 J. Crabtree, *Concise History of the Parish and Vicarage of Halifax* (Hartley and Walker, Halifax: 1836), pp. 296, 312; W. White, *Directory of the Clothing Districts of the West Riding of Yorkshire* (David and Charles reprint, Newton Abbot: 1969), p. 546.

14 R. N. Thornes, *West Yorkshire: 'A Noble Scene of Industry'* (West Yorkshire Metropolitan County Council, Wakefield:

1981), pp. 42–44; D. Taylor, 'Annals of the parish of Halifax', *THAS* (1972), p. 116.

15 Thornes, *West Yorkshire*, pp. 44–46; Sigsworth, *Black Dyke Mills*, p. 25.

16 H. W. Harwood, *Centenary Story* (Halifax: 1948), p. 19.

17 H. P. Kendall, 'Halifax hunts and huntsmen', *THAS* (1928), pp. 63–65; Hanson, *Old Halifax*, p. 199; J. Meynell, *Halifax Town: The Complete Record* (DB Publishing, Westcliff-on-Sea: 1999), pp. 171–73; *Halifax Journal*, 18 April 1807.

18 J. Barker, *Wordsworth A Life* (Viking, London: 2000), p. 87; J. Barker, *William Wordsworth: A Life in Letters* (Penguin Books, London: 2007), pp. 45, 68; R. Gittings and J. Manton, *Dorothy Wordsworth*, (Oxford University Press, Oxford: 1988), pp. 3–4, 7, 10–11, 13, 15.

19 A. G. Hill, ed., *The Letters of Dorothy Wordsworth* (Oxford University Press, Oxford: 1981), pp. 141–42.

20 J. Liddington, *Family Fortune: Land, gender and authority* (Rivers Oram Press, London: 1997); D. M. Lang, 'Georgia in 1840: the Lister diaries', *THAS* (1989). I am grateful to Jill Liddington and Helena Whitbread for sharing with me their research on Anne Lister.

21 Twining, *Recreations and Studies*, pp. 98–99.

22 J. S. Curl, *Georgian Architecture in the British Isles 1714–1830* (second edition, English Heritage, Swindon: 2011), p. 271.

23 Simpson, *Journal*, p. 41.

24 P. W. Robinson, 'Lilly Lane baths and Albion mill', *THAS* (1991).

25 R. Bretton, 'Colonel Edward Akroyd', *THAS* (1948), pp. 67, 69; E. Webster, 'Edward Akroyd', *THAS* (1987), pp. 19–20, 36; E. Webster, *Dean Clough and the Crossley Inheritance* (E. Webster, Halifax: 1988), pp. 4–9.

26 *Walker's Directory of the Parish of Halifax* (Halifax, 1845; Ryburn Archive Edition, Ryburn publishing, Halifax: 1991), pp. 62–93; Pohlmann and Sons Piano Manufacturers WYAS, Calderdale WYC118.

27 J. Smail, *The Origins of Middle-Class Culture* (Cornell University Press, Ithaca and London: 1994), pp. 21, 26–27,

93–95; Dibdin, *Musical Tour*, pp. 196, 205; A. B. Granville, *Spas of England*, 1 (Adams and Dart reprint, Bath: 1971), pp. 400–01.

28 A. Porritt, 'Eighteenth and nineteenth century clubs and societies in Halifax', *THAS* (1964); *idem*, 'The old Halifax theatre, 1789–1904', *THAS* (1956); Smail, *Origins of Middle-Class Culture*, p. 183; R. Cowgill, '"The most musical spot for its size in the kingdom": music in Georgian Halifax', *Early Music* 28:4 (November 2000), pp. 557–75; K. Taylor, 'Theatre in Halifax *c.* 1750–1840', *THAS* 10 (2002), pp. 58–67.

29 W. B. Crump, 'Halifax visitors' book', II, *THAS* (1938), pp. 93, 110–11; D. Bridge, 'William Milner: printer and bookseller', *THAS* (1969); D. Taylor, *THAS* (1972), pp. 114, 117; E. Webster, 'The Halifax Guardian and Halifax Courier: newspaper rivals in the nineteenth century', *THAS* 4 (1996), pp. 58–67.

30 Smail, *Origins of Middle-Class Culture*, pp. 101–02.

31 A. Betteridge, 'Halifax before the Industrial Revolution', I, *THAS* (1978), pp. 27–28; II, *THAS* (1979), p. 101.

32 P. Hudson, 'Proto-industrialisation: the case of the West Riding wool textile industry in the eighteenth and early nineteenth centuries', *History Workshop Journal* 12 (1981), pp. 12, 51, 61; Crabtree, *Concise History*, pp. 307, 309; N. Rycroft et al., *THAS* (1979), pp. 112, 122.

33 J. T. Ward, *The Factory Movement, 1830–55* (Macmillan, London: 1962), pp. 35, 107; Aspin, ed., *Yorkshire Textile Districts*, pp. 14–16; J. A. Hargreaves and E. A. H. Haigh, eds, *Slavery in Yorkshire: Richard Oastler and the campaign against child labour in the Industrial Revolution* (University of Huddersfield Press, Huddersfield: 2012).

34 E. Webster, 'Cornelius Ashworth of Waltroyd', *THAS* (1985).

35 J. G. Washington, 'The origins and development of the Royal Halifax Infirmary, 1807–1995', *THAS* 4 (1996), pp. 66–72.

36 G. R. Dalby, 'Halifax town trustees', *THAS* (1957); J. Smith, *Second Report*

of the Commissioners for enquiring into the state of the large towns and populous districts (London: 1845), pp. 158–60.

37 J. Ginswick, ed., *Labour and the Poor in England and Wales 1849–51* (Frank Cass, Sheffield: 1983), vol. 1, p. 173.

38 J. Styles, '"Our traitorous money makers": the Yorkshire coiners and the law, 1760–83' in J. Brewer and J. Styles, eds, *An Ungovernable People* (Hutchinson, London: 1980), pp. 207, 214; J. Marsh, *Clip a Bright Guinea* (Robert Hale, London: 1971), pp. 162–63.

39 J. A. Hargreaves, 'Religion and society in the parish of Halifax, *c.* 1740–1914', unpublished Ph.D. thesis, Huddersfield Polytechnic, 1991, p. 243; Marsh, *Clip a Bright Guinea*, pp. 172–76; Smail, *Origins of Middle-Class Culture*, p. 194.

40 G. S. Phillips, *Walks Around Huddersfield* (Bond and Hardy, Huddersfield: 1848), pp. 51–52.

41 D. G. Wright, 'The West Riding textile districts in the mid-nineteenth century' in J. A. Jowitt, ed., *Model Industrial Communities in mid-nineteenth century Yorkshire* (University of Bradford, Bradford: 1986), pp. 5, 8, 12, 73.

42 J. A. Hargreaves, 'The Georgian and early Victorian church in the parish of Halifax, 1740–1851', *THAS* (1991), pp. 44–82; J. M. Turner and J. A. Hargreaves, *Thunderclaps from Heaven: Calderdale's Heritage of Nonconformity* (Metropolitan Borough of Calderdale, Halifax: 1984), pp. 11–12.

43 Hargreaves, Ph.D. thesis, pp. 88–91, 96–97.

44 J. A. Hargreaves, 'Methodist growth and secession in the parish of Halifax, 1740–1851', *THAS* 7 (1999), pp. 51–59; J. A. Hargreaves, 'John Wesley and West Yorkshire', *Down Your Way: Yorkshire's County Magazine* 67 (2003), pp. 57–59.

45 J. A. Hargreaves, 'Alexander Kilham (1762–1798)' in T. Larsen, ed., *Biographical Dictionary of Evangelicals* (Inter-Varsity Press, Leicester: 2003), pp. 342–43.

46 J. A. Hargreaves, 'The revival of Old Dissent: Baptists and Independents in the parish of Halifax, 1743–1851', *THAS* 9 (2001), pp. 88–95.

47 Hargreaves, Ph.D. thesis, pp. 98–114; J. A. Hargreaves, 'Catholic communities in Calderdale in the eighteenth and nineteenth centuries', *THAS* 3 (1995), pp. 57–70.

48 Hargreaves, Ph.D. thesis, pp. 154–76, 227–40; Koch, *Ralph Waldo Emerson in Europe*, pp. 92–93.

49 Hargreaves, *THAS* (1991), pp. 44–82.

50 J. A. Hargreaves, 'Methodist attitudes to education and youth: Halifax, 1800–2000' in D. W. Bebbington and T. Larsen, eds, *Modern Christianity and Cultural Aspirations* (Sheffield Academic Press/ Continuum, London: 2003), pp. 198–219; Hargreaves, Ph.D. thesis, p. 199.

51 Hargreaves, Ph.D. thesis, pp. 176–200; Crump, *THAS* (1938), pp. 98–99; Cowgill, *Early Music* (2000), p. 562; J. Golland, 'A dramatic discovery or a manly enterprise', *Local History Magazine* 42 (1994).

52 Smail, *Origins of Middle-Class Culture*, pp. 138–39, 160–62; 182 and 218; E. A. Smith, 'The Yorkshire elections of 1806 and 1807: a study in electoral management', *Northern History* II (1967), pp. 62–90.

53 E. Webster, 'Parliamentary elections in the parish of Halifax 1806–1837', *THAS* 1 (1993), pp. 43–45; E. Royle and J. Walvin, eds, Ellen Gibson Wilson, *The Great Yorkshire Election of 1807: Mass Politics in England before the Age of Reform* (Carnegie Publishing, Lancaster: 2015), pp. 128, 130; J. Belchem, *'Orator' Hunt: Henry Hunt and English Working-Class Radicalism* (Clarendon Press, Oxford: 1985), p. 127.

54 J. A. Hargreaves, 'Methodism and Luddism in Yorkshire, 1812–1813', *Northern History* XXVI (1990), pp. 160–85; *idem*, '"Evangelical piety and Gallic flippancy": religion and popular protest in the parish of Halifax in the age of revolution, 1775–1848' in K. Dockray and K. Laybourn, eds, *The Representation and Reality of War: The British Experience: Essays in Honour of David Wright* (Sutton Publishing, Stroud: 1999); *idem*, *Factory Kings and Slaves: South Pennine Social Movements, 1780–1840* (Pennine Heritage, Hebden Bridge: 1982), pp. 4–5.

55 *Morning Post*, 2 October 1819.

56 Webster, *THAS* (1993), pp. 44, 46–47; J. A. Jowitt, 'Parliamentary politics in Halifax, 1832–47', *Northern History* XII (1976), pp. 172–201.

57 J. A. Hargreaves, 'Methodism and electoral politics in Halifax, 1832–1848', *Northern History* XXXV (1999), pp. 139–60.

58 J. A. Jowitt, 'From Whiggery to Liberalism: Sir Charles Wood and Halifax, 1832–65', *THAS* 2 (1994).

59 Liddington, *Family Fortune*, pp. 139–41.

60 M. Chase, *Chartism: A New History* (Manchester University Press, Manchester: 2007), pp. 217–18; F. C. Mather, *Public Order in the Age of the Chartists* (Manchester University Press, Manchester: 1959), pp. 174–75, 116–17; D. and E. P. Thompson, 'The Dignity of Chartism: Halifax as a Chartist Centre' in S. Roberts, ed., *The Dignity of Chartism: Essays by Dorothy Thompson* (Verso, London: 2015), pp. 73–124; J. A. Hargreaves, *Benjamin Rushton. Handloom Weaver and Chartist* (Friends of Lister Lane Cemetery, Screeve, Halifax: 2006), pp. 1–40; J. A. Hargreaves, 'Guns and Roses: Benjamin Wilson (1824–97) of Salterhebble, Chartist and Horticulturist' in J. Billingsley, ed., *Aspects of Calderdale: Discovering Local History* (Wharncliffe Books, Barnsley: 2002), pp. 77–88; J. A. Hargreaves, 'Benjamin Rushton' and 'Benjamin Wilson' in *ODNB* and M. Taylor, *Ernest Jones, Chartism and the Romance of Politics 1819–69* (Oxford University Press, Oxford: 2003), pp. 1–136.

61 B. Jennings, *Pennine Independency* (Pennine Heritage, Hebden Bridge: 1982), pp. 14–16; Betteridge, I and II, *THAS* (1978 and 1979); J. W. Houseman, 'The development of local government in the parish of Halifax, 1760–1848', *THAS* (1929); Dalby, *THAS* (1957); White, *Clothing Districts of the West Riding, 1853*, pp. 547–48.

62 Jennings, *Pennine Independency*, p. 14; Houseman, *THAS* (1929), p. 121.

63 Betteridge, *THAS* (1978), pp. 18–34.

64 Jennings, *Pennine Independency*, pp. 14–16; Betteridge, *THAS* (1979), pp. 88–95; C. Spencer, 'Township workhouses', *THAS* (1983), pp. 42–47.

65 Dalby, *THAS* (1957); Houseman, *THAS* (1929), pp. 173–79.

66 Hargreaves, Ph.D. thesis, p. 239; Hargreaves in Billingsley, ed., *Aspects of Calderdale*, pp. 77–88; Taylor, *Ernest Jones, Chartism*, pp. 102–04.

67 *Commercial Directory for 1819–20*, (Huddersfield Local History Library, Manchester: 1819), pp. 140–41.

68 *Yorkshire Directory 1822–23*, privately bound (Huddersfield Local History Library: 1823), pp. 609–15.

69 Pigot, *National Commercial Directory*, p. 227–28.

70 P. J. Corfield, *The Impact of English Towns, 1700–1800* (Oxford University Press, Oxford: 1982), p. 23; A. Betteridge and D. Bridge, eds, *Maps and Views of Old Halifax* (Ryburn, Halifax: 1991).

71 R. Bretton, 'The Square and the Piece Hall, Halifax', *THAS* (1961), pp. 67–72; J. A. Heginbottom, 'Halifax is built of wax', *THAS* (1990), pp. 1–28.

72 D. Cruickshank, *A Guide to the Georgian Buildings of Britain and Ireland* (Weidenfeld and Nicolson, London: 1985), pp. 132–33, 213.

73 The Halifax Piece Hall Management Committee Book, 1778–1868, WYAS, CDA, WYC: 1682, p. 9.

74 W. White, *Historical Gazetteer and Directory* (Sheffield: 1837), p. 399.

75 P. Smithies, *The Architecture of the Halifax Piece Hall, 1775–79* (C. P. Smithies, Halifax: 1988), p. 19.

76 M. W. Garside, 'The Halifax Piece Hall', *THAS* (1921), p. 180; see also F. A. Leyland, *Halifax Courier*, 9 April 1887 and Smithies, *Architecture of the Halifax Piece Hall*, p. 17.

77 Curl, *Georgian Architecture*, pp. 263–65; C. Giles, *The Building of Halifax: A history and celebration* (CMBC/English Heritage, Halifax: 2010), p. 16; R. Harman and N. Pevsner, *The Buildings of England, Yorkshire West Riding: Sheffield and the South* (Yale University Press, New Haven and London: 2017) [hereinafter *Yorkshire West Riding*] p. 275.

78 R. A. Innes, FMA, Director of Calderdale Museum's Service, *The Halifax Piece Hall* (Calderdale Museum's Service: Halifax,

1974); Smithies, *Architecture of the Halifax Piece Hall*, pp. 19–20.

79 Smithies, *Architecture of the Halifax Piece Hall*, pp. 21–23.

80 Ivan Hall, *John Carr of York Architect (1723–1807): A Pictorial Survey* (Ricaro Books, Horbury: 2013), p. 62; H. M. Colvin, *A Biographical Dictionary of English Architects. 1660–1840* (John Murray, London: 1954), pp. 122–25.

81 *Leeds Intelligencer*, 3 January 1775 and S. Gee, *Who designed the Halifax Piece Hall?* (S. Gee, Halifax: 2017), p. 8; P. W. Robinson, 'John Aked, joiner and raff merchant (1751–1810), *THAS* n.s. 25 (2017), pp. 64–88.

82 Smithies, *Architecture of the Piece Hall*, pp. 19–20; Giles, *Building of Halifax*, p. 16.

83 Harman and Pevsner, *Yorkshire West Riding: Sheffield and the South*, pp. 271–72; C. Stell, 'Calderdale Chapels', *THAS* (1984); C. Wakeling, *Chapels of England. Buildings of Protestant Nonconformity* (Historic England, Swindon: 2017), pp. 56–58; C. Webster, 'Chantrell in Halifax: Classicism and the Sloane Legacy', *The Georgian Group Journal* xxii (2014), pp. 167–82.

84 Watson, *History and Antiquities of the Parish of Halifax*, p. 201; H. Ling Roth, *The Yorkshire Coiners, 1767–1783* (S. R. Publishers reprint, Wakefield: 1971), p. 112; Cruickshank, *Georgian Buildings of Britain and Ireland*, pp. 132–33, 213; K. Grady, *The Georgian Public Buildings of Leeds and the West Riding* (Thoresby Society, Leeds: 1989), pp. 156–58.

85 Hanson, *Old Halifax*, pp. 260–61.

Chapter 5: 'Town of a hundred trades': Victorian and Edwardian Halifax, 1851–1914

1 Census of England and Wales, 1871; S. J. D. Green, *Religion in the Age of Decline* (Cambridge University Press, Cambridge: 1996), pp. 54–55.

2 Census of England and Wales, 1901.

3 Anon, *The Restoration of Halifax Parish Church* (Halifax: 1877), p. 21, cited in Green, *Religion in the Age of Decline*, p. 26; Asa Briggs, *Victorian Cities* (Odhams Press, London: 1963), p. 149.

4 T. Baines, *Yorkshire Past and Present*, 2 (London: 1875), pp. 403–04; G. P. Wadsworth, ed., *Halifax: A Commercial and Industrial Centre* (Sells, London: 1915), p. 30.

5 A. Dingsdale, 'Yorkshire mill town: a study of the spatial patterns and processes of urban industrial growth and the evolution of the spatial structure of Halifax, 1801–1901', unpublished Ph.D. thesis, University of Leeds, 1961, p. 33; Green, *Religion in the Age of Decline*, p. 39; A. Miller, 'What were the factors that enabled John Crossley and Sons Ltd to become the largest manufacturer of carpets in the world between 1840 and 1914?' unpub. dissertation, University of Durham, 1995, pp. 14, 44; J. A. Jowitt, 'Parliamentary politics in Halifax, 1832–47', *Northern History* XII (1976), pp. 172, 199; Baines, *Yorkshire Past and Present*, 2, p. 415; E. Webster, *Textiles and Tools* (Halifax: n.d.), p. 36; *Halifax Courier*, 7 January 1854.

6 *Halifax Guardian*, 21 August 1897.

7 E. Webster, *Halifax the Town We Live In* (E. Webster, Halifax: 1965), p. 32; *The Times*, 24 August 1897.

8 H. W. Harwood, *Centenary Story* (Halifax Courier, Halifax: 1948), pp. 39–40; J. M. Brendan in J. J. Mulroy, ed., *The Story of the Town that Bred Us* (J. J. Mulroy, Halifax: 1948), pp. 38–39, 56–59, 91–92, 96–99; E. Webster, *From rule of thumb to CNC: Two hundred years of engineering and machine tools in Calderdale* (E. Webster, Halifax: 1997), p. 44; Anon, *Butler, 1868–1968* (Halifax: 1968); J. A. Hargreaves, *Halifax in Old Picture Postcards* (European Library, Zaltbommel: 1989), p. 52.

9 Harwood, *Centenary Story*, p. 39; D. Jeremy, 'John Mackintosh, Halifax Methodist and toffee manufacturer, 1868–1920: a typical Victorian entrepreneur?', *THAS* 5 (1997), pp. 116–31.

10 Wadsworth, *Halifax: A Commercial and*

Industrial Centre, p. 18; Hargreaves, *Halifax in Old Picture Postcards*, pp. 12–13.

11 E. Webster, *Under the Clock* (Calderdale Amenities and Recreation Department, Halifax: 1985); Hargreaves, *Halifax in Old Picture Postcards*, pp. 33–35; M. Blatchford, *The History of the Halifax Industrial Society* (Halifax: 1901), pp. 21, 54, 210–16.

12 Wadsworth, *Halifax: A Commercial and Industrial Centre*, pp. 92–94, 107; W. C. E. Hartley, *Banking in Yorkshire* (Dalesman, Clapham: 1975), pp. 120–22; H. B. Sellers, *Memoranda from a note book on the Yorkshire Penny Bank* (Leeds: 1899), pp. 3–40; E. M. Wavell, *Growth of our Borough* (Halifax Guardian, Halifax: 1898), pp. 13–14.

13 M. H. Yeadell, 'Building societies in the West Riding of Yorkshire and their contribution to housing provision in the nineteenth century' in M. Doughty, ed., *Building the Industrial City* (Leicester University Press, Leicester: 1986), pp. 59–60, 72, 76–78, 96–99; E. Webster, 'Nineteenth century housing in Halifax and the growth of the town', *THAS* (1986), pp. 80–82; O. R. Hobson, *A Hundred Years of the Halifax* (Batsford, London: 1953), pp. 60, 62, 78–79, 90; R. Rodger, *Housing in Urban Britain, 1780–1914* (Macmillan, London: 1989), pp. 23–24; M. J. Daunton, *House and Home in the Victorian City* (Edward Arnold, London: 1983), pp. 97–98; P. Pugh, *The Strength to Change* (Penguin, London: 1998), pp. 46–48.

14 J. Simmons, *The Victorian Railway* (Thames and Hudson, London: 1995), p. 22.

15 J. Minnis with S. Hickman, *The Railway Goods Shed and Warehouses in England* (Historic England, Swindon: 2016), pp. 105, 111.

16 Harwood, *Centenary Story*, pp. 19–22; G. Sheeran, *Railway Buildings of West Yorkshire, 1812–1920* (Ryburn, Keele University Press, Keele: 1994), p. 17; R. Harman and N. Pevsner, *The Buildings of England, Yorkshire West Riding: Sheffield and the South* (Yale University Press, London and New York: 2017), p. 278); *Halifax Courier*, 17 March 1998.

17 Wadsworth, *Halifax: A Commercial and Industrial Centre*, pp. 19–22, 27.

18 Wavell, *Growth of our Borough*, pp. 7, 9; H. B. Priestley, *Halifax in the Tramway Era* (Turntable Publications, Sheffield: 1977); J. R. Moore, 'Halifax Corporation Tramways', I, *THAS* (1974).

19 Dingsdale, DPhil thesis, pp. 340–49, 373–74.

20 J. Ginswick, ed., *Labour and the Poor in England and Wales 1849–51* (Frank Cass, Sheffield: 1983), vol. 1, p. 173.

21 Hargreaves, *Halifax in Old Picture Postcards*, pp. 9, 85.

22 F. Pigou, *Phases of My Life* (London: 1898), pp. 83–86.

23 G. Sheeran, *Brass Castles* (Ryburn, Halifax: 1993), pp. 8, 13; J. Wild, 'Some local people of note', *THAS* (1976), pp. 29–30; Green, *Religion in the Age of Decline*, pp. 102, 142, 144.

24 Webster, *THAS* (1986), pp. 83–86; Sheeran, *Brass Castles*, pp. 83, 106.

25 A. A. Thomson, ed., *By Faith and Work* (Hutchinson, London: 1966), pp. 28–29; Jeremy, *THAS* 5 (1997), p. 125; N. Watson, *Holdsworths of Halifax* (unpublished typescript), p. 25.

26 W. White, *Directory of Leeds and the Clothing Districts of Yorkshire* (David and Charles reprint, Newton Abbot: 1969); F. Smith, *Directory of Halifax* (Halifax: 1874); J. N. Bartlett, *Carpeting the Millions* (John Donald, Edinburgh: 1978), pp. 142–43; Webster, *THAS* (1986), pp. 83–86.

27 J. H. Waddington, *Essays and Addresses* (Halifax: 1939), p. 56.

28 Census of England, 1881; Green, *Religion in the Age of Decline*, pp. 61–62.

29 N. Rycroft et al., '1851 census returns for Halifax and Skircoat townships', I, *THAS* (1979), pp. 113–14.

30 Green, *Religion in the Age of Decline*, pp. 46–49; Webster, *From Rule of Thumb to CNC*, p. 49; Daunton, *House and Home in the Victorian City*, p. 81.

31 Green, *Religion in the Age of Decline*, pp. 80–84; Webster, *THAS* (1986), pp. 85–86; Sheeran, *Brass Castles*, p. 11; W. Pickles, *Have Another Go* (David and Charles, Newton Abbot: 1978), p. 15.

32 K. Tiller, 'Late Chartism: Halifax 1847–58' in J. Epstein and D. Thompson, eds, *The Chartist Experience* (Macmillan, London: 1982), p. 318; E. Royle, *Chartism* (Longman, London: 1996), p. 127.

33 Tiller in Epstein and Thompson, *The Chartist Experience*, pp. 311–44; J. A. Hargreaves, '"Hear, O our God! For We are Despised"; The Faith and Politics of a Marginalised Methodist Preacher and Radical Agitator, Benjamin Rushton of Halifax (1785–1853)' in A. Alyal, S. Anderson and R. Mitchell, *Victorian Cultures of Liminality: Borders and Margins* (Cambridge Scholars Publishing, Newcastle-upon-Tyne: 2018), pp. 167–87; E. Evans, *The Forging of the Modern State: Early Industrial Britain 1783–1870* (Longman, London and New York: 1996), p. 224.

34 J. A. Jowitt, 'From Whiggery to Liberalism: Sir Charles Wood and Halifax, 1832–65', *THAS* 2 (1994), pp. 43–54; A. Porritt, 'The Rt Hon. Sir James Stansfeld', *THAS* (1971), pp. 87–100.

35 B. Wilson, 'The Struggles of an Old Chartist' in D. Vincent, *Testaments of Radicalism* (Europa, London: 1977), pp. 211–42; Tiller in Epstein and Thompson, *The Chartist Experience*, pp. 318–44.

36 J. A. Hargreaves, K. Laybourn and R. Toye, *Liberal Reform and Industrial Relations: J. H. Whitley (1866–1935), Halifax Radical and Speaker of the House of Commons* (Routledge, London and New York: 2018), p. 3.

37 P. A. Dawson, 'The Halifax Independent Labour Movement: Labour and Liberalism 1890–1914' in K. Laybourn and D. James, eds, *The Rising Sun of Socialism* (West Yorkshire Archive Service, Wakefield: 1991), pp. 45–74; K. Laybourn and J. Reynolds, *Liberalism and the Rise of Labour, 1890–1918* (Croom Helm, London: 1984), pp. 21, 24–25, 35, 42, 44, 51–52, 58–59, 62, 65, 69, 79, 93, 106, 109, 116–18, 120, 130–33, 149, 167.

38 *Halifax Courier*, 24 February 1998; Webster, *From Rule of Thumb to CNC*, p. 89; J. Liddington, *Rebel Girls their fight for the vote* (Virago, London: 2006),

pp. 89–90; J. Liddington, *Vanishing for the Vote: Suffrage, Citizenship and the Battle for the Census* (Manchester University Press, Manchester: 2014), pp. 116, 355–56.

39 Wavell, *Growth of our Borough*, pp. 4–6; J. A. Hargreaves, 'Religion and Society in the Parish of Halifax, c. 1740–1914', unpublished Ph.D. thesis, Huddersfield Polytechnic, 1991, pp. 238–40.

40 Wavell, *Growth of our Borough*, pp. 8, 10–11.

41 Daunton, *House and Home in the Victorian City*, pp. 256–60; E. Webster, 'William Ranger's reports on the sanitary condition of Halifax, 1850–51', *THAS* 6 (1998), p. 77.

42 Harwood, *Centenary Story*, pp. 15–17; H. W. Harwood, 'The making of our municipality' in Mulroy, ed., *The Story of the Town that Bred Us*, pp. 16–35; Daunton, *House and Home in the Victorian City*, pp. 256–60; Wavell, *Growth of our Borough*, pp. 10–11.

43 M. Girouard, *The English Town* (Yale University Press, Yale: 1990), pp. 209–10; R. de Z. Hall, *Halifax Town Hall* (County Borough of Halifax, Halifax: 1963), pp. 26–48, 73; D. Cannadine, *Victorious Century: The United Kingdom, 1800–1906* (Allen Lane, London: 2017) p. 329; J. A. Hargreaves, 'Out and About in Halifax 1863–2013', *The Historian* 116 (2012), pp. 31–35.

44 E. Webster, 'Halifax Schools, 1870–1970', *THAS* (1972), pp. 10–36; Harwood, *Centenary Story*, pp. 23–26; W. A. Davies, 'Local educational history' in Mulroy, ed., *The Story of the Town that Bred Us*, pp. 81–84.

45 Hargreaves, *Halifax in Old Picture Postcards*, pp. 21, 22, 55, 80, 84, 96; S. Graham, '"Dare to be wise": what does the architecture of early public libraries reveal about the ideas and ideals of the time?' in N. Smith, ed., *History in the South Pennines: The Legacy of Alan Petford* (Hebden Bridge Local History Society, Hebden Bridge: 2017), p. 139.

46 J. G. Washington, 'Poverty, health and social welfare: the history of the Halifax Union Workhouse and St John's Hospital, 1834–1972', *THAS* 5 (1997), 89–94; Harwood, *Centenary Story*, pp. 27–29.

47 Wadsworth, *Halifax: A Commercial and Industrial Centre*, pp. 65–66; Wavell, *Growth of our Borough*, pp. 12–13, 16.

48 J. G. Washington, 'The origins and development of the Royal Halifax Infirmary, 1807–1995', *THAS* 4 (1996), 68–85; J. A. Jowitt, ed., *Model Industrial Communities in mid-nineteenth century Yorkshire* (University of Bradford, Bradford: 1986).

49 K. Laybourn, *The Evolution of British Social Policy and the Welfare State* (Keele University Press, Keele: 1995), pp. 153–57; K. Laybourn, ed., *Social Conditions, Status and Community 1860–c. 1920* (Sutton Publishing, Stroud: 1997), pp. 9–26; G. Sutcliffe, 'The Mayor's "Bounty Baby" Scheme of 1908 and Infant Welfare in Edwardian Halifax', *THAS* n.s. 23 (2015).

50 Cannadine, *Victorious Century*, pp. 328–29. Hargreaves, Ph.D. thesis, pp. 88–92, 191–92; Green, *Religion in the Age of Decline*, p. 91.

51 J. A. Hargreaves, 'The Church of England in Late-Victorian Halifax, 1852–1914', *THAS* (1992), pp. 27–28; *idem*, 'High-Victorian expansion and Edwardian decline: Baptists and Congregationalists in Halifax and its hinterland, 1852–1914', *THAS* 10 (2002), p. 106.

52 Hargreaves, Ph.D. thesis, pp. 406–09; Hargreaves, *THAS* 10 (2002), pp. 96–125.

53 J. K. Walton, *Fish and Chips and the British Working Class 1870–1940* (Leicester University Press, Leicester: 1992), pp. 26–27; L. Morgan, 'The diary of Henry William Pohlmann (1853–1891)', *THAS* 11 (2003), p. 135; A. E. Dingle, *The Campaign for Prohibition in Victorian England: The United Kingdom Alliance, 1872–95* (UK Alliance, London: 1980).

54 A. Hardcastle, *The Thrum Hall Story: A History of Halifax R.L.F.C.* (Andrew Hardcastle, Halifax: 1986), pp. 48–49; A. Hardcastle, *Halifax Rugby League: The First 100 Years* (Tempus, Stroud: 1999), pp. 26–29.

55 J. Meynell, *Halifax Town: The Complete Record* (DB Publishing, Westcliff-on-Sea: 1999), pp. 10–11; *Halifax Courier*, 20 April 1911.

56 E. Webster, 'Leisure and pleasure in nineteenth century Halifax', *THAS* (1989); D. Hirst, *Halifax Bradley Hall Golf Club: A Century of Golf 1907–2007* (Bradley Hall Golf Club, Halifax: 2007), pp. 11, 16, 18.

57 Webster, *THAS* (1989); J. Black, *The English Press, 1621–1861* (Sutton Publishing, Stroud: 2001), p. 193; A. Whelan, 'John Hartley, "The Yorkshire Burns"' in J. Billingsley, ed., *Aspects of Calderdale* (Wharncliffe Books, Barnsley: 2002), pp. 125–36; R. Dimbleby, *A Yorkshire Dialect Treasure Trove: Discovering John Hartley's Clock Almanacks, 1867–1916* (Rodney Dimbleby, Brighouse: 2014).

58 R. Taylor, A. Kafel and R. Smith, *Crossley Heath School* (Tempus Publishing Ltd, Stroud: 2007), p. 36.

59 C. Binfield, *So Down to Prayers: Studies in English Nonconformity, 1780–1920* (Dent, London: 1977) p. 147; T. Hunt, *Building Jerusalem. The Rise and Fall of the Victorian City* (Weidenfeld and Nicholson, London: 2004), p. 180; Cannadine, *Victorious Century*, p. 329; Hargreaves, *The Historian* 116 (2012), p. 31; *White's Directory of Leeds, Bradford, Huddersfield, Halifax, Wakefield and Dewsbury* (Sheffield: 1866), pp. 684–771; C. Giles, *The Building of Halifax: A history and celebration* (CMBC/English Heritage, Halifax: 2010), pp. 36–37.

60 Hunt, *Building Jerusalem*, p. 52

61 Sheeran, *Railway Buildings of West Yorkshire*, pp. 16–17.

62 D. Taylor, 'Annals of the Parish of Halifax', *THAS* (1972), p. 122; Morgan, *THAS* (2003), p. 133.

63 *Yorkshire Weekly Post*, 16 June 1910.

64 J. S. Fletcher, *A Picturesque History of Yorkshire* (J. M. Dent, London: 1900), p. 50; Blatchford, *The History of Halifax Industrial Society*, p. 10.

65 Wadsworth, *Halifax: A Commercial and Industrial Centre*, p. 35.

1 K. Laybourn, *Britain on the Breadline* (Sutton Publishing, Stroud: 1998); J. Stevenson and C. Cook, *Britain in the Depression* (Longman, London: 1994).

2 Letter to Samuel Walker's sister from Corporal W. Sim, Signals, 5th Army Corps, British expeditionary Force, 1 May 1915 and newspaper cuttings May 1915.

3 A. Clare, ed., *For King and Country: Calderdale's First World War Centenary 2014–18* (Bankfield Museum, CMBC, Halifax: 2014).

4 D. Millichope, *Halifax in the Great War* (Pen and Sword Military, Barnsley: 2015), pp. 21–26, 151–53, 274–79; P. Thomas, *Seeing it Through: Halifax and Calderdale during World War II* (P. Thomas, Hebden Bridge: 2005), pp. 7–8, 15–22; J. J. Mulroy, ed., *The Story of the Town that Bred Us* (J. J. Mulroy, Halifax: 1948), pp. 117–18; Clare, ed., *For King and Country*, p. 36.

5 T. R. Hornshaw, 'Calderdale and the wars of the twentieth century, 1899–1945', *THAS* 6 (1998), pp. 117–31; Mulroy, ed., *The Story of the Town that Bred Us*, pp. 71–74, 119; D. Albon, *Copley and District, 1935–50* (Halifax: n.d.), p. 34; *Calderdale at War* (Calderdale Museums Service, Halifax: 1982), pp. 2, 13; Thomas, *Seeing it Through*, pp. 7–8.

6 Hornshaw, *THAS* 6 (1998), p. 131.

7 Census, 1921, 1931; J. Reynolds and K. Laybourn, *Labour Heartland* (Bradford University Press, Bradford: 1987), pp. 5–10.

8 Reynolds and Laybourn, *Labour Heartland*, p. 10; J. H. Waddington, *Essays and Addresses* (Halifax: 1939), p. 26.

9 Alderman J. Radcliffe, speech on election as mayor, 9 November 1938, Calderdale Central Library, Horsfall Turner Collection.

10 Reynolds and Laybourn, *Labour Heartland*, Table 1.6, p. 23.

11 N. Watson, *Holdsworths of Halifax* (unpublished typescript), pp. 38–40; P. Bentley, *O Dreams, O Destinations* (Gollancz, London: 1962), p. 109; E. Webster, *Dean Clough* (Dean Clough Publications, Halifax: 1988), p. 21.

12 60th Annual Report Halifax Chamber of Commerce, 1921, pp. 8–9; Bentley, *O Dreams, O Destinations*, pp. 156–57; Watson, *Holdsworths*, p. 40.

13 S. Constantine, *Social Conditions in Britain, 1918–1939* (Methuen, London: 1983), pp. 42–43; Watson, *Holdsworths*, p. 43.

14 *Annual Report Halifax Chamber of Commerce* (Halifax: 1925), p. 2; (1928), p. 8.

15 J. A. Hargreaves, 'J. H. Whitley (1866–1935) A Speaker shaped by his Halifax roots' in J. A. Hargreaves, K. Laybourn and R. Toye, eds, *Liberal Reform and Industrial Relations: J. H. Whitley (1866–1935), Halifax Radical and Speaker of the House of Commons* (Routledge, London and New York: 2018), p. 20.

16 K. Laybourn, *The General Strike Day by Day* (Sutton Publishing, Stroud: 1996), p. 151; Bentley, *O Dreams, O Destinations*, pp. 134–37; Watson, *Holdsworths*, p. 43; Webster, *Dean Clough*, pp. 17, 22; *Halifax Chamber of Commerce Journal*, June 1926, vol. vi, no. 67; Mulroy, ed., *Story of the Town that Bred Us*, p. 118.

17 Reynolds and Laybourn, *Labour Heartland*, p. 100.

18 Watson, *Holdsworths*, p. 43; Webster, *Dean Clough*, p. 22.

19 Constantine, *Social Conditions*, p. 43.

20 Watson, *Holdsworths*, p. 47.

21 Webster, *Dean Clough*, p. 25; Reynolds and Laybourn, *Labour Heartland*, p. 12; *Kelly's Directory of the Textile Industries* (London: 1928), p. 565.

22 Watson, *Holdsworths*, p. 50.

23 Census, 1921 and 1931; Reynolds and Laybourn, *Labour Heartland*, p. 12.

24 Watson, *Holdsworths*, pp. 53–54.

25 Reynolds and Laybourn, *Labour Heartland*, p. 11; P. Bryan, *Wool, War and Westminster* (Tom Donovan, London: 1993), p. 29; Watson, *Holdsworths*, p. 45; *Kelly's Directory*, p. 565.

26 Reynolds and Laybourn, *Labour Heartland*, p. 11.

27 Census, 1921 and 1931; Reynolds and Laybourn, *Labour Heartland*, p. 12.

28 *Commercial Year Book of the Halifax*

Chamber of Commerce (London: 1918), p. 47.

29 G. P. Wadsworth in *Halifax Publicity Week, October 10–17, 1931* (Halifax Chamber of Trade, Halifax: 1931), p. 9; P. Saunders, 'Halifax: Town of Industries and Hills', *Trade and Engineering* (October, 1936); S. Constantine, *Unemployment in Britain Between the Wars* (Longman, London: 1980), p. 19; G. Hughes, *Ted and I: A Brother's Memoir* (The Robson Press, London: 2012), pp. 3–4, 63.

30 E. Webster, *From Rule of Thumb to CNC: Two hundred years of engineering and machine tools in Calderdale* (E. Webster, Halifax: 1997), pp. 25, 30, 36, 55, 70, 74–75; *Butler, 1868–1968* (Butler Machine Tool Co., Halifax: 1968), pp. 5–6; *With the World at War We Were not Idle* (G. H. Gledhill and Sons, Halifax: n.d.), p. 4; S. Glynn and A. Booth, *Modern Britain* (Routledge, London: 1996), p. 69.

31 *Annual Report Halifax Chamber of Commerce*, 1921, p. 9; 1925, p. 2.

32 Webster, *From Rule of Thumb to CNC*, pp. 36, 76.

33 *Annual Report Halifax Chamber of Commerce*, 1928, p. 8; Webster, *From Rule of Thumb to CNC*, pp. 53, 66–67, 85, 87; Census, 1921; 1931.

34 Webster, *From Rule of Thumb to CNC*, pp. 70, 77, 81–82, 92, 96.

35 Webster, *From Rule of Thumb to CNC*, pp. 70, 82, 94, 97; *With the World at War, We Were Not Idle*, pp. 5, 8, 10, 13.

36 Webster, *From Rule of Thumb to CNC*, p. 55.

37 G. W. Crutchley, *John Mackintosh* (Hodder and Stoughton, London: 1921), p. 114.

38 *Ibid.*, pp. 63–64, 113–17; A. A. Thomson, *By Faith and Work* (Hutchinson, London: 1966), pp. 50–51, 62, 66, 91, 93f.

39 Glynn and Booth, *Modern Britain*, pp. 65, 81–82; Census, 1921, 1931; O. Hobson, *A Hundred Years of the Halifax* (Batsford, London: 1953), p. 77; Bryan, *Wool, War and Westminster*, p. 157.

40 M. Hartley and J. Ingleby, *Life and Tradition in West Yorkshire* (Smith Settle, Otley: 1990), pp. 65, 139; *Halifax County Borough Directory, 1936* (Cade Publications reprint, Halifax: 1998), p. 403.

41 J. A. Hargreaves, '"The Catseye Man": Percy Shaw of Halifax, road stud manufacturer, 1890–1976', *THAS* 4 (1996), pp. 126–34.

42 Hobson, *Halifax*, pp. 87–89; Thomson, *By Faith and Work*, p. 76.

43 Hobson, *Halifax*, pp. 82–83, 106–14; R. K. Bacon, *The Life of Sir Enoch Hill* (London: 1934).

44 Hobson, *Halifax*, p. 93.

45 Hobson, *Halifax*, pp. 95–96.

46 Hobson, *Halifax*, pp. 73, 82, 117–18, 121.

47 *Halifax Chamber of Trade, Shopping Festival and Exhibition* (Halifax Chamber of Trade, Halifax: 1936), p. 3.

48 Waddington, *Essays and Addresses*, pp. 11–12.

49 W. Pickles, *Sometime Never* (Werner Laurie, London: 1951), p. 89.

50 Census, 1921, 1931.

51 Census, 1921, 1931; Hobson, *Halifax*, p. 75; *Halifax Equitable Benefit Building Society Jubilee* (Halifax Equitable Building Society, Halifax: 1921), p. 144.

52 Webster, *Rule of Thumb to CNC*, p. 89.

53 J. Stevenson, *British Society, 1914–45* (Penguin, London: 1984), p. 307; B. Keith-Lucas, *English Local Government in the Nineteenth and Twentieth Centuries* (Historical Association, London: 1977), pp. 26–29; B. J. Barber and M. W. Beresford, *The West Riding County Council, 1889–1974* (West Yorkshire Metropolitan County Council, Wakefield: 1979), pp. 84–85; *Halifax Official Handbook* (Halifax Corporation, Halifax: 1939), pp. 18–24.

54 Barber and Beresford, *West Riding County Council, 1889–1974*, pp. 242–46; Keith-Lucas, *English Local Government*, pp. 31–32; Halifax Extension Bill, 1935, Calderdale Central Library, L3117.

55 *Local Government Journal and Officials' Gazette* (April 1935), p. 109; *Halifax Official Handbook*, pp. 18–21; *Halifax County Borough Directory*, p. lxxii; H. B. Priestley, *Halifax in the Tramway Era* (Turntable Publications, Sheffield: 1977), p. 4; Mulroy, ed., *Story of the Town that Bred Us*, p. 33; D. Bell, *Hebble*

Remembered (Becknell Books, King's Lynn: 1983).

56 *Annual Report Halifax Chamber of Commerce*, 1925, pp. 21–22; Waddington, *Essays and Addresses*, p. 12; *Halifax County Borough Directory*, p. xl; *Local Government Journal and Officials' Gazette* (April 1935), pp. 107–11.

57 Hartley and Ingleby, *Life and Tradition in West Yorkshire*, p. 35; Webster, *Dean Clough*, p. 22.

58 K. Laybourn, *The Evolution of British Social Policy and the Welfare State* (Keele University Press, Keele: 1995), pp. 122–26; E. Webster, 'Halifax Schools, 1870–1970', *THAS* (1972), pp. 37–46; *Halifax Official Handbook*, pp. 23–24; Bentley, *O Dreams, O Destinations*, p. 87; Bryan, *Wool, War and Westminster*, pp. 29–30; J. A. Hargreaves, 'Dr Dorothy Hincksman Farrar (1899–1987)' in J. A. Vickers, ed., *A Dictionary of Methodism in Britain and Ireland* (Epworth Press, Peterborough: 2000), p. 117.

59 Webster, *THAS* (1972), p. 40; Bentley, *O Dreams, O Destinations*, p. 115; *Halifax Official Handbook*, p. 23.

60 *Halifax County Borough Directory*, p. lv; Bentley, *O Dreams, O Destinations*, p. 114; J. Cockcroft, *Not a Proper Doctor* (Pennine Heritage, Hebden Bridge: n.d.), p. 38.

61 J. G. Washington, 'The origins and development of the Royal Halifax Infirmary', *THAS* 4 (1996), pp. 78–81; R. Chew, *100 Years of Caring. A History of the Royal Halifax Infirmary* (Calderdale and Kirklees Health Authority, Halifax: 1996), pp. 11–14; J. A. Hargreaves, *Sowerby Bridge in Old Photographs* (Smith Settle, Otley: 1994), p. 175.

62 *Halifax Official Handbook*, pp. 11–16, 23; *Halifax County Borough Directory*, p. li.

63 Reynolds and Laybourn, *Labour Heartland*, p. 27, 29; Laybourn, *Britain on the Breadline*, Table 3.3, p. 86; Halifax Housing Committee, Housing Statistics, August 1929; *Halifax Official Handbook*, 1939, p. 11; 1947, p. 40; *Daily News and Westminster Gazette*, 4 March 1930.

64 Thomson, *By Faith and Work*, p. 42; J. Wild, 'Some local people of note', II, *THAS* (1977), p. 64; Webster, *From Rule of Thumb to CNC*, p. 89; R. Rooney, B. Lewis and R. Schuhle, *Home is Where the Heart is* (Yorkshire Arts Circus: 1989), p. 36.

65 Reynolds and Laybourn, *Labour Heartland*, pp. 47–50, 141, 144–47; *Halifax Courier and Guardian Historical Almanack*, 1925–1939.

66 D. Beddoe, *Discovering Women's History* (Longman, London: 1998), p. 176; 'Women civic leaders', *Halifax Courier Yearbook*, 1965; Bentley, *O Dreams, O Destinations*, p. 114; Mulroy, ed., *The Story of the Town that Bred Us*, p. 118; *Halifax Courier*, 4 August 1998; J. G. Washington, 'The history of the Halifax General Hospital, 1897–1987', *THAS* 6 (1998), pp. 105, 107.

67 K. Laybourn and J. Reynolds, *Liberalism and the rise of Labour* (Croom Helm, London: 1984), pp. 183–85, 191–92, 196–98; Reynolds and Laybourn, *Labour Heartland*, p. 37.

68 Wild, *THAS* (1977), pp. 75–76; J. A. Hargreaves, 'J. H. Whitley (1866–1935): a Speaker shaped by his Halifax roots' and K. Laybourn, 'J. H. Whitley and Halifax politics between 1890 and 1906: the politics of social reform' and R. Toye, 'J. H. Whitley as Speaker of the House of Commons, 1921–28' in Hargreaves, Laybourn and Toye, eds, *Liberal Reform and Industrial Relations*, pp. 7–27, 67–85, 103–12.

69 Hargreaves, Laybourn and Toye, eds, *Liberal Reform and Industrial Relations*, pp. 1–29, 67–85.

70 Reynolds and Laybourn, *Labour Heartland*, p. 85; *Halifax Courier*, 28 July 1998.

71 Reynolds and Laybourn, *Labour Heartland*, pp. 98, 123; F. W. S. Craig, *British Parliamentary Election Results, 1918–1949* (Postal Reference Publications, Glasgow: 1969), p. 140.

72 *Yorkshire Post, The Daily Telegraph*, 28 June 1945. I am grateful to Sophie Clapp, Archivist, Churchill Archives Centre, Churchill College, Cambridge, for providing me with details of the visit.

73 Reynolds and Laybourn, *Labour Heartland*, pp. 118, 139; *Halifax Courier*, 1 August 1997.

74 Bentley, *O Dreams, O Destinations*, pp. 116, 205–06, 208; Reynolds and Laybourn, *Labour Heartland*, pp. 141, 144–47.

75 *Halifax Courier*, 19 May 1998.

76 Crutchley, *John Mackintosh*, pp. 210–11.

77 J. A. Hargreaves, 'Religion and society in the parish of Halifax, c. 1740–1914', unpublished Ph.D. thesis, Huddersfield Polytechnic, 1991, p. 410; *Methodist Times*, 11 July 1929.

78 Waddington, *Essays and Addresses*, pp. 33–34.

79 T. Hughes, *Remains of Elmet* (Faber, London: 1979), p. 8.

80 D. Hirst, *Halifax Bradley Hall Golf Club: A Century of Golf 1907–2007* (Halifax Bradley Hall Golf Club, Halifax: 2007), p. 19; S. J. D. Green, *Religion in the Age of Decline* (Cambridge University Press, Cambridge: 1996), pp. 372–90; *Halifax Courier*, 22 September 1998.

81 Watson, *Holdsworths*, pp. 40–43, 55; A. Hardcastle, *The Thrum Hall Story: A History of Halifax R.L.F.C.* (Andrew Hardcastle, Halifax: 1986), p. 82; Hobson, *Halifax*, pp. 110–11; J. K. Walton, '"The Queen of the Beaches" Ostend and the British, from the 1890s', *History Today* (August 2001), pp. 21–22; J. Hudson, *Wakes Week* (Alan Sutton, Stroud: 1992).

82 J. A. Hargreaves, *Halifax in Old Picture Postcards* (European Library, Zaltbommel: 1989), pp. 11, 72, 137; Bentley, *O Dreams, O Destinations*, pp. 111–12; M. Musson, V. Brearley and P. Webb, in *Sport in Past Times: Sport and Leisure in Calderdale 1920–80* (Age Concern, Halifax: n.d.), pp. 9–10 and 20.

83 Hardcastle, *Thrum Hall Story*, pp. 49, 64–88; Hargreaves, *Halifax in Old Picture Postcards*, p. 123.

84 T. Warren, *Halifax Speedway 1928–51: An illustrated History* (Ovenden Printing Company, Halifax: 1951), pp. 1–34; *Halifax Courier*, 17 November 2017.

85 W. Pickles, *Have Another Go* (David and Charles, Newton Abbot: 1978), pp. 25–26; J. A. Hargreaves, 'Wilfred Pickles', *ODNB*; Bentley, *O Dreams, O Destinations*, pp. 112–13; Hardcastle, *Thrum Hall Story*, p. 74.

86 T. Earnshaw, *A Tribute to Eric Portman* (Reel Solutions, Halifax: 2012); Norman Hudis, *Dinner with Ribbentrop*, a semi-autobiographical and semi-fictional portrait of the meeting, dating from the early 1970s.

87 *Halifax County Borough Directory*, p. 420; Mulroy, ed., *Story of the Town that Bred Us*, p. 61; D. Baker, 'Glee Unions in Halifax and District from the Eighteenth to the Twentieth Centuries', *THAS* n.s. 24 (2016), pp. 46–69.

88 Mulroy, ed., *Story of the Town that Bred Us*, p. 61; J. B. Priestley, *English Journey* (Folio Society reprint, London: 1997), p. 162; *Halifax Courier*, 21 September 1998; *Halifax Choral Society*, Halifax, 1992; R. A. Edwards, *And the Glory* (W. S. Maney and Son, Leeds: 1986), pp. 48, 113.

89 Bentley, *O Dreams, O Destinations*, pp. 137, 147, 173; L. Schroeder, foreword, J. Wren, *Yorkshire Hill-Folk* (Halifax Courier, Halifax: 1928); Waddington, *Essays and Addresses*, p. 46.

90 Bentley, *O Dreams, O Destinations*, p. 173; D. Russell, 'Serving the West Riding: the work and career of Phyllis Bentley (1894–1977)', *THAS* (2017), pp. 125–48. E. Evens, *Through the Years with Romany* (University of London Press, London: 1946), pp. 118–28; J. A. Hargreaves, 'George Bramwell Evens (1884–1943)', *ODNB*; Pickles, *Have Another Go*, pp. 56–62, 120; M. Pickles, *Married to Wilfred* (Odhams Press, London: 1956), pp. 58–60, 99–107; J. A. Hargreaves, 'G. Bramwell Evens' and 'W. Pickles', *ODNB*.

91 *Halifax Courier*, 13 July 1990; I. Chilvers, H. Osborne and D. Farr, *The Oxford Dictionary of Art* (Oxford University Press, Oxford: 1988), pp. 411, 466.

92 D. Cant, 'Jackson of Coley (1867–1931), master woodcarver', *THAS* 2 (1994), pp. 95, 100; *Halifax Chamber of Trade, Shopping Festival and Exhibition*, p. 35; *Halifax County Borough Directory*, pp. 479–80.

93 Hobson, *Halifax*, pp. 90–91, 102.

94 *Halifax Courier*, 18 August 1998; *Halifax Official Handbook*, 1947, pp. 18–19; A. Betteridge, D. Bridge

and P. H. Thornborrow, *Calderdale Architecture and History* (Ryburn, Halifax: 1988), pl. 105; S. Gee, *Around Halifax* (Chalford Publishing Company, Stroud: 1996), pp. 13, 21.

95 Mulroy, ed., *Story of the Town that Bred Us*, p. 61; *Halifax Shopping Week*, pp. 97, 107; Priestley, *English Journey*, p. 162; Hughes, *Remains of Elmet*, p. 124; E. Pontefract and M. Hartley, *Yorkshire Tour* (J. M. Dent, London: 1939), p. 117.

Chapter 7: Post-War Halifax: from County Borough to Metropolitan Borough, 1946–2019

1 *Halifax Courier*, 22 March 1948.

2 *Census, Yorkshire West Riding* (HMSO, London: 1963 and 1973); *Census Digest, Calderdale MBC* (Halifax: 1983 and 1993); *Report on Census Key Statistics for 2001 for Calderdale MBC* (Halifax: 2003); Yorkshire and Humberside Economic Planning Council and Board, *Halifax and the Calder Valley* (HMSO, London: 1968), pp. 15–18.

3 *Halifax Courier*, 9 January 1988; *Calderdale Trends*, Autumn 1990 and Summer 1993; *Census Digest, Calderdale MBC* (Halifax: 1983 and 1993).

4 *Calderdale Report*, 1982–83, p. 7; *Calderdale Trends*, Winter 1990 and 1993.

5 *Report on Census Key Statistics for 2001 for Calderdale MBC* (Halifax: 2003); Office of National Statistics, Census, 2011; National Statistics (ONS), 2016, Mid-Year Population Estimates taken from Local Government Information; Government Statistical Service, Rural Urban Classification for Local Authority Districts in England, 2011; R. Harman and N. Pevsner, *The Buildings of England, Yorkshire West Riding: Sheffield and the South* (Yale University Press, London and New York: 2017), p. 267, the figure of 88,000 for 2011 is an approximation.

6 Calderdale MBC, *Everyone Different Everyone Matters Progress Report* 2017.

7 *Calderdale Report*, 1995–96; *Halifax and Calder Valley: An Area Study*, pp. 12, 33.

8 *Calderdale Report*, 1982–83, p. 7.

9 *Calderdale Report*, 1990–91, p. 2; 1991–92, p. 5; 1992–93, p. 9; 1995–96, p. 10; *Halifax Courier*, 9 October 1990, 1 February 1991.

10 *Calderdale Report*, 1994–95, p. 12.

11 A. Marwick, *British Society since 1945* (Penguin, London: 1982), pp. 29–30.

12 *Halifax and the Calder Valley*, pp. 12, 126, 128.

13 *Halifax Courier*, 30 December 1994.

14 N. Watson, *Holdsworths of Halifax* (unpublished typescript), chapters 4–7; *Halifax Courier*, 27 September 2000.

15 E. Webster, *Dean Clough* (Dean Clough Publications, Halifax: 1988), pp. 28–29, 32–33; *Halifax Courier*, 3 March 1999, 12 December 2001.

16 Webster, *Dean Clough*, p. 33; *Halifax Courier*, 20 September 1986, 19 February 1988.

17 W. L. Horsfall, 'Joseph Horsfall, Worsted Spinners, the final years, 1938–2008', *THAS* 19 (2011), pp. 153–65; www.britishwool.org.uk; *Halifax Courier*, 23 February 2006, 27 March 2009, 16 August 2013.

18 www.indeed.co.uk/textile jobs in Calderdale, 18 January 2018.

19 *Halifax Courier*, 14 February 2001; *Textile Magazine*, 3 September 2012.

20 E. Webster, *From Rule of Thumb to CNC: Two hundred years of engineering and machine tools in Calderdale* (E. Webster, Halifax: 1997), pp. 11, 13–15, 17, 26, 36–37, 39, 47–53, 73, 77, 80, 83, 92, 97–98, 100, 103–04, 109; *Halifax and Calder Valley*, pp. 12–13; *Halifax Courier*, 30 December 1994, 9 October 1995, 4 December 1995, 22 September 1998, 5 December 1998, 27 September 2000, 15 February 2001; *Calderdale News*, 4 January 1996; J. A. Hargreaves, 'Percy Shaw, 1890–1976', *ODNB* and J. A. Hargreaves, '"The Catseye Man": Percy Shaw of Halifax, road stud manufacturer, 1890–1976', *THAS* (1996), pp. 126–34; *The Times*, 3 September 1976.

21 *Halifax Courier*, 16 October 1986, 11 April 1991; *Daily Telegraph*, 13 January 2016.

22 P. W. Robinson, 'Stone Trough Brewery', *THAS* (1989), p. 18.

23 O. Hobson, *A Hundred Years of the Halifax* (Batsford, London: 1953), p. 144;

Calderdale Trends, Autumn 1994; *Halifax Courier*, 9 December 1986; P. Pugh, *The Strength to Change* (Penguin, London: 1968), pp. 9, 84, 100, 102, 182; Len Tingle, BBC Radio Leeds, 4 May 2001; *Halifax Courier*, 4 May 2001, 9 May 2001, 30 July 2003.

24 R. Perman, *Hubris: How HBOS Wrecked the Best Bank in Britain* (Birlinn Ltd, Edinburgh: 2013), p. xx.

25 A. Darling, *Back from the Brink, 1000 Days at Number 11* (Atlantic Books, London: 2012), p. 47.

26 G. Brown, *Beyond the Crash: Overcoming the First Crisis of Globalisation* (Simon and Schuster, London: 2010), p. 98.

27 A. Darling, 'Foreword' in Perman, *Hubris*, pp. xi–xv; Darling, *Back from the Brink*, p. 172; Brown, *Beyond the Crash*, pp. 65–66, 99.

28 *Halifax Courier*, 20 October 1983. I am grateful to Karen Hales of Royal Sun Alliance and Chris Johnstone of Provident Insurance and Colonnade Insurance Brokers, for supplying me with this information.

29 *The Sunday Times*, 6 April 1997, 19 April 1998; *Calderdale Community Foundation Annual Report*, 1993; *Halifax Courier*, 28 December 2000. I am grateful to Jane Gaze for providing me with information about Gartland, Whalley and Barker.

30 *Halifax in Calderdale: A Strategy of Prosperity* (Civic Trust: 1984), pp. 8–13, 65–66; *Calderdale Tourism Impact Study* (Ecotec, Birmingham: 1990), p. 20; *Halifax Courier*, 14 July 1998.

31 *Calderdale the Challenge* (Civic Trust, London: 1986), pp. 19–20; *Halifax Courier*, 14 July 1998.

32 *Halifax Courier*, 6 October 1993, 2 December 1993, 14 July 1998, 16 February 2002; *Halifax Civic Trust Report*, 1995.

33 *Halifax Courier*, 11 November 1998, 28 January 1999, 31 March 2001; *Halifax Shopping Guide* (Halifax Town Centre Forum: 1998).

34 *Halifax Courier*, 7 April 1987.

35 *Halifax Courier*, 9 December 1986.

36 *Calderdale Report*, 1986–87, p. 7; M. Middleton, *Cities in Transition* (Michael Joseph, London: 1991), p. 205;

A. Holden, *Charles* (Weidenfield and Nicolson, London: 1988), pp. 145–55; J. Dimbleby, *The Prince of Wales: A Biography* (Little, Brown, London: 1994), pp. 367–68; *Vision in Calderdale* (Calderdale Partnership, Halifax: 1989); *Report on Census Key Statistics for 2001 for Calderdale MBC* (Halifax: 2003).

37 *Halifax Official Guide* (Halifax County Borough, Halifax: 1972).

38 C. B. Phillips and J. H. Smith, *Lancashire and Cheshire from AD 1540* (Longman, London: 1994), Table 5.15, p. 371; *Halifax in Calderdale*, p. 8; B. J. Barber and M. W. Beresford, *The West Riding County Council, 1889–1974* (West Yorkshire Metropolitan County Council, Wakefield: 1978), pp. 253–54.

39 *Calderdale Report*, 1989–90, p. 2; 1990–91, p. 2; 1991–92, p. 2; 1993–94, p. 7.

40 E. Webster, 'Halifax Schools, 1870–1970', *THAS* (1972), pp. 46–49; *Calderdale News*, 19 March 1998; C. C. Robinson, ed., *Birth and Rebirth* (Hipperholme Grammar School, Halifax: 1997), pp. 12–14; P. Clark, *Back from the Brink* (Metro, London: 1998), p. 3–5. I am grateful to Mr C. C. Robinson for information about Hipperholme Grammar School.

41 *The Sunday Times*, 25 October 1998, p. 44; *Halifax Courier*, 9 October 1995.

42 Clark, *Back from the Brink*; *Calderdale Report*, 1996–97, pp. 29–30; *Halifax Courier*, 1 April 2003, 3 May 2003.; *Todmorden News*, 7 April 2017; *Huddersfield Examiner*, 24 September 2017.

43 Calderdale School Census, January 2017, www.calderdale.gov.uk

44 *Calderdale College. A Century of Achievement*, Halifax, 1993; D. Harpwood, *Golden Years of Halifax* (True North Books, Halifax: 1998), pp. 35–39; *Halifax Courier*, 7 May 1988, 25 November 2002, 22 August 2003. www.leedsbeckett.ac.uk.

45 *Halifax Courier*, 15 July 1998.

46 *Halifax Courier*, 9 December 1989.

47 *Annual Report of League*, 1958; *Halifax Courier*, 6 July 1988.

48 *Halifax and the Calder Valley*, pp. 71, 73, 77; *Halifax Guide*, 1972, p. 65; *Halifax Courier*, 15 June 1989, 18 January 2002.

49 *Halifax and Calder Valley*, p. 143;

Yorkshire Life, March 1970; *Calderdale Trends*, Spring 1992; *Halifax Official Guide*, 1972, p. 55; *Calderdale; What Future?* Halifax, 1972, p. 6; *Calderdale Report*, 1995, p. 55–56; 1997, p. 51; N. Danziger, *Danziger's Britain: A Journey to the Edge* (Harper Collins, London: 1996), p. 56; *Halifax Courier*, 18 January 1999; *Report on Census Key Statistics for 2001 for Calderdale MBC* (Halifax: 2003).

50 *Halifax Courier*, 22 March 1948; P. Brears and S. Davies, *Treasures for the People* (Yorkshire and Humberside Museums Council: 1989), pp. 60–61, 77–78.

51 *Halifax Courier*, 4 January 1973; *Halifax Courier*, 26 October 1998; *Halifax Official Guide*, 1972.

52 *Halifax Courier*, 26 October 1998; *Halifax Official Guide*, 1972. I am grateful to Mrs Betty Brooksby for information about concerts at the Victoria Theatre.

53 *Calderdale Tourism Impact Study*, p. 5; *Halifax Courier*, 23 January 1999.

54 Middleton, *Cities in Transition*, p. 207; A. Machin, *Making Sense of Tourism, 1: The Beckoning Horizon* (Westwood Start, Halifax: 2016), pp. 10–11.

55 *Halifax Courier*, 10 May 1970, 14 May 1971, 5 May 1972, 11 May 1973.

56 *Halifax Courier*, 6 May 1976, 5 May 1978, 3 May 1979; Middleton, *Cities in Transition*, p. 207.

57 *Calderdale Report*, 1992–93, p. 3; Middleton, *Cities in Transition*, p. 207; *Halifax Courier*, 1 June 1995.

58 *Halifax Courier*, 8 May 1998.

59 *Halifax Courier*, 7 May 1999, 5 May 2000, 3 May 2002, 2 May 2003, 4 May 2008. There were no council elections in 2001.

60 *Halifax Courier and Guardian Historical Almanack*, 1945, pp. 25–29; *Halifax Courier*, 12 November 1998, 16 May 2000, 18 April 2003, 9 August 2003; *London Gazette*, 31 December 1992 and 17 May 2000; Calderdale Councillors, 2010–11, 2015–16, 2017–18.

61 *Halifax Courier and Guardian Historical Almanack*, 1951; R. Davenport-Hines, *The Macmillans* (Heinemann, London: 1992), p. 242.

62 R. Waller and B. Criddle, *The Almanac of British Politics* (Routledge, London: 2002), p. 414.

63 *Halifax Courier*, 19 January 2018.

64 *Halifax Courier and Guardian Historical Almanack*, 1947; *Epworth Review*, January 1985, p. 5; *Halifax Circuit Directory*, 1998.

65 P. Blakey, *Street Angels* (Christian Nightlife Initiatives Network, second edition: 2014), pp. i–iv, 3–9, 149; Calderdale Methodist Circuit, *Preaching Plan*, December 2017–February 2018; Methodist Church West Yorkshire District, *Directory 2011–12*, pp. 19–21; Methodist Church Yorkshire West District, *Directory 2017–18*, pp. 32–33.

66 J. Peart-Binns, *Eric Treacy* (Ian Allan, London: 1980), p. 141; www.halifaxminster.org.uk.

67 K. Taylor, *Wakefield Diocese: Celebrating 125 Years* (Canterbury Press, Norwich: 2012), p. 169, though her name was recorded inaccurately as Hodgkin see E. D. Graham, *Ministering Sisters: A Directory of the Members of the Wesley Deaconess Order 1890–1988 and Their Appointments* (Wesley Historical Society, Evesham: 2014), p. 210.

68 Harman and Pevsner, *Yorkshire West Riding*, p. 293.

69 M. Morris, *Social Enterprise: A study of the activities of voluntary societies and voluntary workers in an industrial town* (National Council of Social Service, London: 1962), pp. 13, 107–08; *Changes*, November 1998, Calderdale Community Church, Halifax, pp. 3–4; J. M. Turner, *Modern Methodism in England, 1932–98* (Epworth, Peterborough: 1998), p. 76; *Halifax Courier*, 16 April 1997, 12 November 1997; *Halifax Courier*, 30 October 1995. I am grateful to Mrs Dorothy Moore for information about the Christian Contact Centre and to Calderdale Central Library for access to the Census 2001 data on the Neighbourhood Statistics website (http://www.neighbourhood.statistics.gov.uk/).

70 A. Hardcastle, *The Thrum Hall Story: A History of Halifax R.L.F.C.* (Andrew Hardcastle, Halifax: 1986), pp. 89, 91, 99–100, 105, 126–28; *Halifax Courier*, 4 May 1987, 17 October 1998, 25 October

70 2000, 11 February 2003, 17 June 2003, 3 October 2003.

71 J. Meynell, *Halifax Town: A Complete Record* (DB Publishing, Westcliffe-on-Sea, 1999), pp. 179–81, 558, 576–93; *Halifax Courier*, 8 December 2017; D. Russell, *Football and the English: A Social History of Association Football in England, 1863–1995* (Carnegie Publishing, Lancaster: 1997), pp. 222–23.

72 *Halifax Courier*, 4 December, 8 December, 2015.

73 S. Rowlands, *Phil Bull Twenty-Five Years On*, Timeform 2014; Obituary, Shirley Crabtree, *The Independent*, 3 December 1957.

74 A. Ellis, *Refereeing Around the World* (Hutchinson, London: 1954); Obituary *The Independent*, 7 June 1999.

75 B. Moore and S. Jones, *The Autobiography* (Corgi, London: 1996); B. Moore, *Beware of the Dog: Rugby's Hard Man Reveals All* (Simon and Schuster, London: 2010).

76 P. Davies, *Matchday Programmes in Calderdale and Kirklees* (The Cricket Heritage of Calderdale and Kirklees: Huddersfield: n.d.), pp. 15, 16, 17, 25, 28, 31, 38.

77 *Halifax Official Guide*, 1972, pp. 98–99; *Halifax Courier*, 28 October 1998, 24 May 1999, 4 May 2001; P. Davies, *Home Soil: Exploring and Celebrating the Cricket Grounds of Calderdale* (Church in the Market Place Publications, Buxton: 2003); *The Independent*, 18 January 2017.

78 Harman and Pevsner, *Yorkshire West Riding*, p. 271.

79 R. A. Edwards, *And the Glory* (W. S. Maney and Son, Leeds: 1986), p. 113; *Yorkshire Post*, 19 January 1999; *Halifax Courier*, 29 February 1992, 31 January 2003; J. S. Wharton, *Plebs The Halifax Jazz Club 1961–1968* (Sephton Enterprise Publications: 2001); Hardcastle, *Thrum Hall Story*, p. 112; J. A. Hargreaves, 'William Thomas Dupree', *ODNB*.

80 *Yorkshire Life*, March 1970; E. Royle, 'Historians and the Making of the English Working Class, 1963–1988', *THAS* (1989), p. 81; J. A. Hargreaves, 'Planting the liberty tree', *THAS* (1988), pp. xviii–xx; J. Harber, 'Edward Thompson (1924–93)', *THAS* 2 (1994), pp. 125–28 and editorial comment pp. 7–9.

81 M. Yorke, *Matthew Smith His Life and Reputation* (Faber and Faber, London: 1997), p. 1.

82 N. Pevsner, *Yorkshire, the West Riding* (Penguin, London: 1959), p. 229.

83 *Halifax and the Calder Valley*, p. 137.

84 A. Raistrick, *The Making of the English Landscape: West Riding of Yorkshire* (Hodder and Stoughton, London: 1970), p. 167.

85 J. Minnis, *England's Motoring Heritage from the Air* (English Heritage, Swindon: 2014), pp. 258–59.

86 *Halifax Courier*, 4 January 1973; *Nairn's Journeys*, BBC Television (Manchester: 1975).

87 *Halifax in Calderdale: A Strategy for Prosperity* (Civic Trust, London: 1984), p. 1.

88 Pevsner, *Yorkshire, the West Riding*, pp. 229, 231; *Halifax in Calderdale* (1984), pp. 11–13; *Context*, Association of Conservation Officers, 18 (Spring 1988), p. 6; *Quality of Life in Britain's Intermediate Cities* (Glasgow: 1989).

89 C. Giles, *The Building of Halifax: A history and celebration* (CMBC/English Heritage, Halifax: 2010), p. 16.

90 Harman and Pevsner, *Yorkshire the West Riding*, p. 278.

91 Simmons, *Victorian Railway*, p. 22.

92 Halifax Civic Trust Report; E. A. H. Haigh, ed., *Huddersfield: A most handsome town* (Kirklees Leisure Services, Huddersfield: 1992), pp. 330, 353; G. Firth, *A History of Bradford* (Phillimore, Chichester: 1997), pp. 134–35.

Index

Numerals in **bold** indicate illustrations

Abbreviation: **tab** = table

Defoe, Daniel (*continued*)
on religious dissent 81
on rural industry 2
on worsted shalloon production 58
Deira, kingdom of 23
Dewsbury Minster Church 26
Dibden, Charles
impressions of Halifax (1788) 122, 142
on Piece Hall activity 107
Dickens, A. G.
on heresy under Mary I 73
on public order in mid-Tudor Yorkshire 88
Dickens, Charles
on condition of Halifax (1858) 227
Dighton, William 130
diseases, plagues and epidemics *see also* Black
Death
(1361–2), (1369) and (1375) 33
(1550–1750) affect on population numbers 53
(1587) typhus 70
(1645) 70, 77
(1750–1850) 129, 130, 134
(1780s) smallpox 129
(1800–1900) associated with housing 130
(1914–45) 259
(1946–2019) 310, 315–16
dissent and nonconformity 79, 81–2, 136, 138,
139, 160, 217, 218
Dodsworth, Roger 45
on Fixby Roman site 19
on windows in Halifax Parish Church 45
on windows in Parish Church 19
Domesday Book (1086)
extent of farming and woodland 29, 30
and the harrying of the north 28–9
interpretation of the omission of Halifax
25–6, 34
and survey of Yorkshire 26
Drayton, Thomas de, Vicar of Wakefield
and Black Death 32
Dugdale, Richard Swarbrick 226
Duke of Wellington's Regiment **232**
and Halifax Minster Church 337
memorial in Woolshops xix, **350**
World War One casualties 230
in World War Two 234–5
Duncombe, Henry 145
Dupree, William Thomas 'Champion Jack'
346
Dyson, Sir George 279–80
Dyson, Stanley Gilbert 233

Early man in Halifax (Watson) 9
Ebenezer Primitive Methodist Church, St
James Road 168, *283*, **312**
Food and Support Drop In Centre 335
Ecclesiastical history of the English people
(Bede) 22
Edgar Atheling, King 28
education
seventeenth and eighteenth century 91–2
nineteenth century 141, 210–13
(1914–45) 252, 256–9
(1946–2019) 310–11, 311–15
eleven-plus examination 312
Grammar School near Parish Church 47,
101
Halifax School Board 205, 210–13
Heath Grammar School 75, 91, 92, **94**, 212,
257, 258
Hipperholme Grammar School 92, 203,
233, 312–13
Education Act, Elementary (Forster) (1870)
205, 213, 254
Education Act (Balfour) (1902) 201, 212, 252
Education Act (Butler) (1944) 311
Edward, Prince of Wales (later Edward VII)
209, 212
Edward, Prince of Wales (later Edward VIII
and Duke of Windsor) 240, 260
Edwards booksellers and binders, Old Market
123, 128
Edwards, Sir Henry 117, 150, 152, **152**, 196,
197, 226
Edwin, King of Northumbria 23, 25
Electric Cinema, Ward's End 223
Elim Pentecostal Church, Hall Street 335
Elizabeth II, Queen **299**
Elland 170
market charter 31
Elland chapelry 46
Ellis, Arthur 344
Ellison, Michael 307, 323
Elmet, kingdom of 23
Emerson, Ralph Waldo
visit to Halifax (1848) 110, 139
employment and unemployment 240, 241,
252, 267, 289–309, **291 (tab)**, 300, 301, 303
enclosure of land 59
engineering and machine tool industry 177,
242–4
decline 295, 296–7
English language development 24

Upper Shibden Hall 95
Vallance, Edward
  on Glorious Revolution 80

Vardy, Jamie 341
Venutius, King of Brigantes 18
Victoria Buildings, Commercial Street 282
Victoria Hall xvii, 223, 279, 320
Victoria reservoir 206
Vikings 22–8
Vue Cinema, Broad Street xvii

Waddington, Joseph Harold
  on changes to retailing 249, 255
  on church attendances 272
  on family sizes in inter-war years 237
  on Victorian and Edwardian changes
    192–3
Wainhouse, John Edward 226
Wainhouse Tower 226, **226**
Wainwright, Sally xvii, 6
Waite, Revd John 88
Wakefield Court Rolls *see also* Halifax
  Manorial Court (Moot Hall), Nelson
  Street
  Black Death interpolations 31, 32
  fulling in thirteenth century 41
  in reign of James II 80
  roof repairs to Halifax Church (1352) 40
  textile occupational names 30
Wakefield Diocese 218
Wakefield Gate (Magna via) 47, **48**
Wakefield, Manor of 25, 157 *see also* Halifax-
  cum-Heptonstall sub-manor
  and decline in land value following the
    harrying of the north 29
  lay subsidy returns (1334) (1379) 28, 30,
    32 (tab), 33
  and reduced power in seventeenth and
    eighteenth centuries 84
Wakefield Manorial Court *see also* Halifax
  Manorial Court (Moot Hall), Nelson
  Street
  business of 84–5
  circuit nature of 42
Wakeling, Christopher
  on Square Chapel 167–8
Walker, Samuel 231
Walker, Saville 233
Wallace, William 216, **217**
Wallington/Wilburton Complex (bronze age
  phase) 13

Walsden
  name origin 26
Walshaw Dean reservoir 206
Walter, Hubert, Rector of Halifax Church 39
Walton, Revd Roger 335
Warburton, John 101
Warenne, de, Earls of
  arms of
    colours of 40, 42
    at St Thomas à Becket Church
      Heptonstall 40, 44
  granting of advowson for sub-manor of
    Halifax-cum-Heptonstall and Halifax
    Church 34, 36–7, 42
  and granting of charter for Manor of
    Wakefield from Crown 34
  and Halifax Church appointments 39, 44
Warenne, William de, 1st Earl of Surrey
  (1036–88) 34–5
Warenne, William de, 2nd Earl of Surrey
  (1071–1138) 34–5
Warenne, William de, 3rd Earl of Surrey
  (1118–48) 36, 42
Warhurst, Pam 322–3, 326
Warley 66
  and Black Death 32–3
Warley Road School 212
  swimming baths 211
water power 107, 109, 173
water supplies and sanitation
  nineteenth century 205, 206
  twentieth century 253, 259, 260
  Acts of Parliament pertaining (1760s and
    1823) 159
  Corn Market 134, **134**
  manorial regulation 84–5
  Ranger sanitation reports (1850–1) 134, 159,
    186, 206
  reservoirs 206
Waterhouse Charitable Trust 94, 129
Waterhouse, Dorothy 81
Waterhouse family of Shibden Hall 62, 64,
  65, 84
Waterhouse, John, of Shibden (d.1540) 49,
  51, 88
Waterhouse, Nathaniel 81, 90, 94, 96, 101
Waterhouse Trust 90
Watroyd, Wheatley **131**
Watson, Andrew 224–5
Watson, Revd John 19, 27, 45
  on fabric of Halifax Parish Church 45
  on fulling mills 107

About the author

John A. Hargreaves has lived in Calderdale for almost five decades, during which period he has been a member of the Halifax Antiquarian Society, serving as secretary, vice-president, president and editor of 28 volumes of the society's annual *Transactions*. He is also a life member of the Halifax Civic Trust and currently has served for many years as chairman. He was born in Burnley and educated at Heasandford Junior and Infant School and Burnley Grammar School. He subsequently obtained an honours degree in history and a PGCE at the University of Southampton. He has taught and lectured extensively in secondary, higher and adult education, on both sides of the Pennines, but mainly in West Yorkshire, where he met and married his wife, Susan, in Marsden. They subsequently moved to Halifax, where all four of their children were born, and have lived in Calderdale since 1972. He obtained an M.A. with distinction and a Ph.D. at the University of Huddersfield for his research on Calderdale religious and social history, and has been a Visiting Research Fellow at the university for many years. He has been the recipient of three Yorkshire History Prize awards and also became more

recently an Associate of the Leeds Centre for Victorian Studies. His many publications include a full-length history of Halifax, now entering its third edition in 2020, pictorial histories on Halifax and Sowerby Bridge, and almost fifty articles for the *Oxford Dictionary of National Biography*, many relating to Calderdale subjects including one on Percy Shaw, the Halifax inventor, who was selected for a special preview edition illustrating the range and style of the volume published by Oxford University Press in 2003–4. He has also co-edited for Routledge a collection of studies on J. H. Whitley, whose biography he is now writing. For recreation he enjoys music, fell walking, swimming and spending time with his wife and family.